THIRD EDITION

College Learning And Study Skills

Debbie Guice Longman
Southeastern Louisiana University

Rhonda Holt Atkinson
Louisiana State University

WEST PUBLISHING COMPANY

MINNEAPOLIS/ST. PAUL   NEW YORK   LOS ANGELES   SAN FRANCISCO

Cartoons: Richard Longman
Copyediting: Marilyn Taylor
Composition and Film: Carlisle Communications
Cover and Interior Design: Peter Thiel
Cover Image: © David Jeffrey, Image Bank
Index: Cindy Dolan
Production, Prepress, Printing and Binding by West Publishing Company

WEST'S COMMITMENT TO THE ENVIRONMENT

In 1906, West Publishing Company began recycling materials left over from the production of books. This began a tradition of efficient and responsible use of resources. Today, up to 95 percent of our legal books and 70 percent of our college and school texts are printed on recycled, acid-free stock. West also recycles nearly 22 million pounds of scrap paper annually—the equivalent of 181,717 trees. Since the 1960s, West has devised ways to capture and recycle waste inks, solvents, oils, and vapors created in the printing process. We also recycle plastics of all kinds, wood, glass, corrugated cardboard, and batteries, and have eliminated the use of styrofoam book packaging. We at West are proud of the longevity and the scope of our commitment to the environment.

Library of Congress Cataloging–in–Publication Data

Longman, Debbie Guice.
    College learning and study skills / Debbie Guice Longman, Rhonda Holt Atkinson. —3rd ed.
       p.   cm.
    Includes index.
    ISBN 0-314-01231-1 (soft)
    1. Study, Method of.   2. College student orientation—United States.   I. Atkinson, Rhonda Holt.   II. Title.
LB2395.L58   1992
378.1'702812—dc20   92-30204
   CIP

To Alden J. Moe and Ray R. Buss for your friendship and support.

Contents

Chapter 6   THINKING CRITICALLY: ANALYSIS, SYNTHESIS AND EVALUATION   230

Chapter 7   TESTS: PREPARING FOR AND TAKING THEM   280

Chapter 8

USING GRAPHICS IN TEXT 326

Preface

We wrote the first edition of *College Learning and Study Skills* to help students succeed and prosper in college. Specifically, we intended to help students develop strategies for time management, study skills, test taking, using their libraries, and writing research papers. In addition, we sought to accomplish four objectives: to provide information in a context suitable for post-secondary developmental learners; to help post-secondary developmental students become more active learners; to explain the mental processes involved in learning; and to incorporate recent theories and research into reading and study skill instruction at the post-secondary level.

We have been pleased by the response to the book. Instructors and students with whom we have spoken have felt, as we have, that the first edition of *CLASS* met these objectives. An additional survey of users of *CLASS* from around the country generally agreed. We realized, however, that revisions were needed to meet the changing needs of the students for whom the book was written.

CLASS (2E), revised using comments from users and reviewers, was enormously successful. Our goal for the third edition of *CLASS* is for it to also fulfill the needs of its users. In an effort to meet that goal, we have once again relied on information from the people who use the text—both instructors and students.

Many of the best features of CLASS (2E) remain in this text—for example, the Write to Learn and Group Learning Activity exercises remain; so does much of the information. Nonetheless, this edition of *CLASS* contains several new features. First, each chapter of *CLASS* (3E) continues to be refined; for example, the library chapter now contains information on computerized library searches. Approximately 75% of the exercises are new. Second, the text now contains a chapter on critical thinking. To include this new information, we specifically over-hauled the chapters on memory, listening and notetaking, and reading. Third, the vocabulary development activities are now much more than simple exercises which precede and come after a chapter. Vocabulary development in *CLASS* (3E) follows each chapter and contains two features: (1) information about vocabulary associated with the topic discussed in the chapter and (2) activities to promote internalization of vocabulary concepts. Next, four new sample chapters provide reading experiences in content areas, and several new essays promote reading in other print forms.

A newly revised instructor's manual and computer program accompany this text. The computer disk, now easier for instructors and students to use, includes the following five programs: HIGH-LITE (indicating the importance of previewing and background knowledge); TESTER (reinforcing test-taking strategies); SCANNER (providing realistic practice in varying reading speed); ANALOGY (extending practice of complex word relationships); and HANGMAN (providing practice in determining the meanings of new words, using the context, and deriving meaning through structural analysis).

Although *CLASS* is designed for use in a post-secondary study skills course, it also can serve as the principal text for an advanced reading course or as a resource for English classes or learning assistance centers. It also may be used by the student independently.

The completion of any major project requires the assistance of many people. We wish first to thank our families who support and assist us in so many ways.

In addition, we wish to acknowledge the support of our colleagues at both SLU and LSU. To Alana Allen, we owe a debt of great magnitude—her work with permissions was inspired (perhaps by the desperation on our faces). Our heartfelt thanks goes to Clark Baxter and Joe Terry, whose support and encouragement never falter. In addition to our gratitude, Stacy Lenzen has earned our respect and friendship. Our hope is that her expected child grows to be as intelligent, courteous, and competent as she is. Finally, we acknowledge and thank our reviewers whose efforts made this manuscript the book it is:

Mary Biasotti	Dutchess Community College
Kathleen Brennan-Sortino	Dutchess Community College
Jeanne Chaltain	Dutchess Community College
Sharon K. Conley	Colorado State University
Carolyn G. Curtis	Mattatuck Community College
Larry Flescher	Milwaukee Area Technical College
Cecily Frazier	Dutchess Community College
Darrell H. Garber	Louisiana Technical University
William E. Hysell	Mohawk Valley Community College
Barbara V. LaRosa	University of Hartford
Nancy Lebran	Dutchess Community College
Virda K. Lester	Tuskegee University
Elisabeth Longbotham	McMurry College
Jack Longbotham	Hardin-Simmons University

Barbara Lyman	Southwest Texas State University
Donna Mealey	Louisiana State University
Bonnie Mercer	Rochester Community College
Elizabeth Miller	Kalamazoo Valley Community College
Nancy F. Mills	University of Hartford
Jo-Ann Mullen	University of Northern Colorado
Lucia Perillo	Saint Martin's College
Margaret Rauch	St. Cloud State University
Melinda Steele	Texas Tech University
Connie Stelly	Louisiana State University
Judy K. Stocks	Texas Tech University
Cindy Thompson	Northeast Louisiana University
Miriam Welker	Eastern New Mexico University
Donna Wood	State Technical Institute at Memphis

1 Winning the Game of Higher Education

OBJECTIVES

By the end of this chapter you will be able to do the following:

1. Set goals for academic success.

2. Identify the principle players at your institution: administrative units, faculty, and others.

3. Recognize the value of campus diversity.

4. Identify your learning strengths and weaknesses.

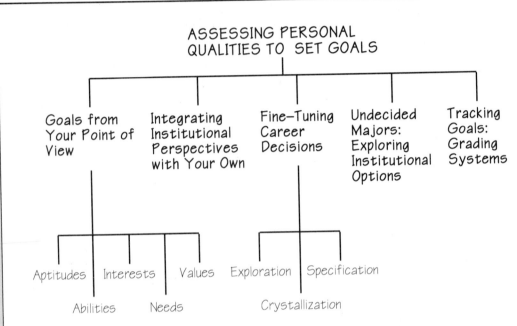

ASSESSING PERSONAL QUALITIES TO SET GOALS

- Goals from Your Point of View
  - Aptitudes
  - Abilities
  - Interests
  - Needs
  - Values
- Integrating Institutional Perspectives with Your Own
- Fine–Tuning Career Decisions
  - Exploration
  - Crystallization
  - Specification
- Undecided Majors: Exploring Institutional Options
- Tracking Goals: Grading Systems

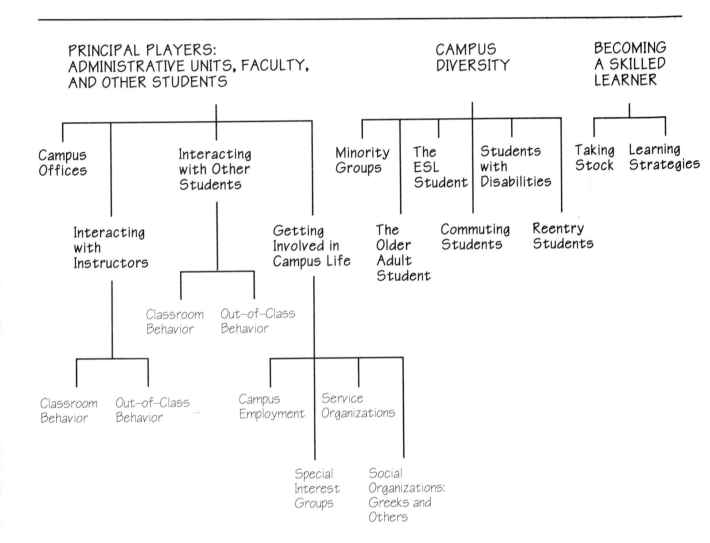

TERMS

abilities
aptitudes
aptitude tests
college catalog
credit hours
crystallization
curricula
ESL students
exploration
fantasy
free elective
grade point average
    (GPA)
interests
interest inventory
intramural sports
needs
quality points
realistic
specification
tentative
values

"Winning isn't everything; it's the only thing."
—VINCE LOMBARDI
Football coach

Winning the game of higher education is like winning any other game. It consists of the same basic process. First, you decide if you really want to play. If you do, you gear your attitudes and habits to learning, then learn the rules of the game. Next, you get into the game and become an active participant. Third, you learn about the other players—administrative units, faculty, and other students. Finally, you develop specific strategies to improve your playing skills. That's what this book is about. Whether you are a new, upper-class, transfer, or reentry student, if you play the game well, you win. If you don't, you're on the bench. Your success or failure depends on you.

ASSESSING PERSONAL QUALITIES TO SET GOALS

Have you ever felt forced to do something "for your own good" that you really didn't want to do? Maybe you had to be in the school play or read aloud. Maybe you had to take a job you didn't like. How successful were you? How did you feel about it? When put in this position, most people do not succeed. They fail because the goal is not their own.

On the other hand, fulfilling another person's desires can help you be successful. Making good grades may not be your goal, but it may be one your family, your boss, or others have set for you. Your goal may be to please those people, not to make good grades. The results are the same, although the two goals are not.

"Whaddaya mean it's not like bowling? Don't we get a few practice frames?"

The key to winning the game of higher education is building your own desire to succeed. To do so, you examine why you are in school. If you are taking courses for any reason other than your desire for learning, your chances of success are lessened. Your chances of success improve if you find a way to make learning your goal.

Goal-setting is essential to achieving success, but some people fail to set goals because they simply don't know how. When it comes to making decisions that will affect the rest of their lives, many feel overwhelmed. Some even allow others to decide for them because it's easier. Many students seem to make decisions about their life goals in ways characterized by the people in Table 1.1. Of those people, only Vera "Sis" Tematic has the right idea about decision-making. Unlike the other characters, she reaches her decisions by following a set plan. Having a set plan like Vera "Sis" Tematic is both efficient and effective. You avoid such pitfalls as procrastination, impulsiveness, and lack of information. Eliminating such errors is essential in learning to make good decisions and setting appropriate and realistic goals.

WRITE TO LEARN

Using Table 1.1, decide which decision-making role (e.g. Willy Nilly, Mia Fraid) best describes you. On a separate sheet of paper, discuss whether this role changes when you make decisions about work, school, and family. If so, how does it change and why?

To set academic goals, think about your life's ambitions. Do you want to graduate with a degree? Do you want to get a better job? Do you want to make more money? Do you want to find a career you enjoy? Do you want to learn skills for a career change? You must determine how much time and effort you must spend studying to achieve what you want to do in life.

GOALS FROM YOUR POINT OF VIEW

Identifying your goals is easier said than done. It requires close examination of the factors that contribute to your point of view—your **aptitudes, abilities, interests, needs,** and **values** (See Figure 1.1). It also requires you assess your point of view from your institution's perspective.

Aptitudes

Aptitudes reflect what you could do—your potential. They are natural or inborn traits that precede ability. These traits may be visible or hidden. Visible traits are ones you already recognize and have developed. Hidden traits are parts of your personality you have not yet explored. For example, you may have an aptitude for music. If you

---

TABLE 1.1   Decision-Making Roles

Hasty Harry. Makes a decision immediately, no matter what. He wants to eliminate the discomfort of ambiguity as soon as possible.

Last-Minute Louie. Always waits until the very last possible second before deciding on anything.

Henrietta Hardhead. Makes a firm decision and refuses to consider any other alternative.

Mia Fraid. Delays any decision for fear of being wrong or appearing foolish.

Wilbur the Wonder Wimp. Avoids deciding because he lacks confidence in his ability to live with the consequences of the decision.

Rebecca the Rebel. Always decides to do exactly the opposite of everyone else, just for the sake of being different.

Ebenezer Appeaser. Always tries to mediate and compromise, to appease and please others by making a decision that makes everyone else happy.

St. Peter Perfectus. Spends an inordinate amount of time deliberating, analyzing, and checking out all sides of the issue in an attempt to make the "perfect" decision.

Lotta Feeling. Always makes impulsive decisions based on emotion, with little thought as to consequences.

Mr. N. Tuition. Plays his hunches and trusts his inner sense of what feels right.

Vera "Sis" Tematic. Chooses carefully and thoughtfully after considering all of the options and the pros and cons of each.

Ida Neaux. Avoids making decisions because of a lack of information.

Freddy the Fence. Has trouble deciding because he swings back and forth from one side of the issue to the other.

Grass-Is-Greener Gertie. Makes a decision and then immediately regrets it, doubts it, worries about the consequences, and wishes she had chosen a different alternative.

Rudy Roulette. Always leaves the decision up to chance or fate.

Willy Nilly. Always lets other people (peers, parents, other authority figures) make the decision.

Sister Mary Alofta, Nun of the Above. Lets the Good Lord decide.

Olive the Above. Has no clear-cut pattern of decision-making, but rather displays some of the characteristics of all the roles.

SOURCE: Reprinted with permission of the American Association for Counseling and Development. Donald, M., and Carlisle, J. (1983). "The Diverse Decision Makers: Helping Students with Career Decisions." *Vocational Guidance Quarterly*.

grew up in a home where you took music lessons or went to concerts, then your aptitude for music is more likely to be developed. If you grew up in a home where music interest was not fostered, then your aptitude for music may be hidden.

One way to learn more about your hidden aptitudes is to take **aptitude tests.** General aptitude tests estimate such abilities as verbal skills, numerical skills, spatial skills, motor coordination, and manual dexterity. More specialized aptitudes, such as music and art, are not evaluated by general aptitude tests.

FIGURE 1.1   Personal Factors in Decision Making

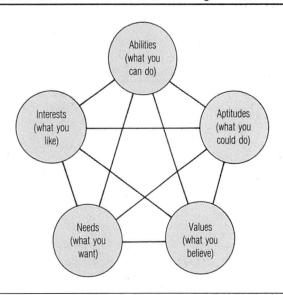

The counseling or placement center at your college probably administers aptitude tests to aid in setting goals and making career choices. Discovering your aptitudes is important in the goal-setting process because being aware of your visible and hidden traits helps you identify areas of interest and clarify career directions.

Abilities

Abilities are what you can do—your capabilities. They are the results of aptitude combined with experience. Abilities are not constant. They increase with practice and decrease with disuse.

Unlike aptitude, which is estimated, ability is measured by performance in two ways: formal tests and informal assessment. Formal tests generally do not measure specific skill areas. Instead, they measure generalized areas, such as intelligence and achievement. Because they measure broad skills, they do not identify specific strengths and weaknesses. Thus, informal assessment is often a better means of measuring ability. You can make an informal self-assessment by looking at those areas in which you excel, examining your past performances, and recalling comments others have made about your skills.

Such assessments may be misleading, however. First, time is a necessary consideration. In other words, suppose you and a friend each work a set of math problems equally well. However, you finish in one hour while your friend takes all day. Your ability in math, then, is probably greater than your friend's. In addition, ability differs in quality or kind. For example, math ability could mean solving complex equations or simply balancing a checkbook.

How do assessments of ability affect your academic goals? They help you identify your subject-area strengths and weaknesses. Knowing these helps you better determine those courses you're ready for and those in which you may need tutoring or other assistance. In addition, knowledge of your abilities helps you plan time and energy commitments needed for academic success.

Interests

Your interests are what you like. How interests develop has never been completely understood. Your experiences with situations and people create some of your interests. The sources of other interests may not be as easily identified.

Interests can and do change. The things that interested you as a child may not interest you now. The things that interest you now may not interest you in the future. Changes in your life cause changes in your interests. College life, for example, contributes to changes in your interests as you are exposed to new ideas and experiences.

Prior to college, your academic experiences and interests were limited to courses available at your high school (English, math, some science and social science subjects). Part- and full-time employment also may have shaped your interests. Postsecondary education now opens realms of information that were previously unavailable to you—for example, anthropology, philosophy, music history, Japanese, and robotics. Your first reaction to such courses might be disinterest. However, what you perceive as disinterest may actually be unfamiliarity. In contrast, you may find courses that you thought would be interesting, are not. You may find such changes in interest frustrating in that you may question your major, your values, and even your reason for being in college. Remember that such changes in interest should be an expected part of the postsecondary education process. Postsecondary education provides you with opportunities to rethink and redefine your interests—and yourself—in the process.

Changing interests do, and should, affect your choice of major and career. While it would be nice if these changes occurred in your first semester or two, often they do not. You may find yourself interested in another major in your junior or senior year. Several options should be considered. First, can you pursue this interest as a variation of your current major? If so, completing your current degree program with additional electives may suffice. Obtaining advanced degrees or certifications after you complete your undergraduate degree might also help you meet your goal. You may find, however, that only an entirely different course of study will meet your needs. For example, you may pursue a degree in business and later find your interests are in medicine. This change may cause you a loss of applicable credits and require additional time. While you may wonder if this extra time and effort is worth it, you should consider that time you will spend in your career will be far longer than the additional time you will spend in school.

You determine your interests in several ways. Some of your current interests are topics you like or activities you enjoy. You discover these by looking at past experiences and preferences. Other, new interests are identified by trying out new activities and by talking to others. You also might identify new interests by taking a standardized **interest inventory.** Interest inventories identify your preferences by assessing broad areas of interest or by comparing your responses with those of people in various occupations. Your college counseling center or placement office probably gives vocational interest tests. Once you take an interest inventory, you will be better prepared to determine the majors you may wish to investigate.

High scores in specific areas of an interest inventory should not be the sole factor in academic decision-making. Sometimes an area of interest indicates a hobby, or avocational interest. For example, suppose your score indicates a high interest in art. You may not paint well enough to major in art, but you can enjoy painting as a hobby or you might choose to be an art historian.

Needs

A. H. Maslow (1954) developed a hierarchy of needs (Figure 1.2). He theorized that your lowest needs are concerned with physical well-being and safety. Unless these basic needs are met, higher-level needs are never realized. Your need for affection concerns interpersonal relationships with others. Self-esteem and independence needs involve your feelings of worth and ability. Your concern for the opinions and approval of others influences your status and approval needs. Self-actualization, the highest level, occurs when you are motivated to be your best for yourself.

Although these needs develop from lowest to highest levels, once developed, they interact. Thus, your needs exist at many levels. They direct and motivate your actions in setting academic goals. No one level or factor determines what your goals should be. The needs that are important to you and your choice of an academic major are unique to you. Thus, the ranking Maslow theorized differs for each person.

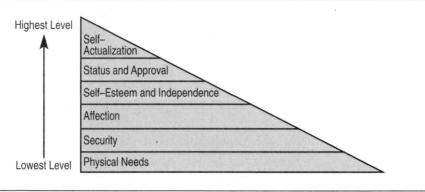

FIGURE 1.2   Maslow's Hierarchy of Needs

Values

Values are the result of your experiences. You derived some of your values from your family and friends. Your thoughts and reactions to situations and people formed other values. Events and people you learned about through television, literature, and other media also shaped them.

Just as new courses shape your interests, new ideas shape your values. High school instructors generally hold the same principles and values as the communities in which they teach. Postsecondary faculty represent a greater diversity of geographical regions, ideas, interests, and, therefore, values. In fact, you may feel as though you have stepped into a wind tunnel of contradictory viewpoints and cultures: animal rights, pro-choice, anti-abortion, liberal, conservative, atheist, Christian, Muslim, vegetarian, politically correct, pacifist, pro-union, and so on. Exposure to these perspectives is part of the postsecondary educational process. Indeed, many college instructors see their role as being academically free to pursue intellectual inquiry and research, ask or stimulate the asking of questions, and/or raise controversial issues. As you encounter more and different views, your ability to listen, read, and think critically about information grows. The opinions, attitudes, and influences of others will have less and less impact as you learn to analyze information and judge for yourself. As a result, professors who require you to choose a position and defend it are generally less interested in your opinion than in your ability to logically support your argument in written or oral form. Helping you define your personal values in this way is also a role of the college instructor.

Why are values important? Values help you rank your needs. Because needs are different for every person and values are derived from needs, values differ. Because values vary, you must examine your needs in terms of what you value most. Your academic goals

affect study and time commitments, course selection, career orientation, and personal and professional associations. Pursuing what you
value in life is essential in achieving life satisfaction.

WRITE TO LEARN

On a separate sheet of paper, respond to the following: What is your major? How do your interests and values support that choice? How have your postsecondary experiences affected your interests, values, and choice of major?

EXERCISE 1.1   For each level of Maslow's hierarchy below, order the career-planning factors in terms of what you value from most important to least important.

SELF-ACTUALIZATION
_____ Challenge
_____ Responsibility
_____ Accomplishment
_____ Knowledge
_____ Fulfillment
_____ Philanthropy
_____ Creativity

STATUS AND APPROVAL
_____ Opportunity for advancement
_____ High position
_____ Competition
_____ Power
_____ Prestige
_____ Recognition

SELF-ESTEEM AND INDEPENDENCE
_____ Freedom
_____ Travel
_____ Adventure
_____ Decision-making authority
_____ Responsibility
_____ Independent work
_____ Creativity
_____ Variety

AFFECTION
_____ Close working relationships with others
_____ Helping others

SECURITY
_____ Job security
_____ Stress
_____ Retirement benefits
_____ Insurance

PHYSICAL NEEDS
_____ Number of hours worked per week
_____ Work environment
_____ Physically demanding
_____ Financial reward

EXERCISE 1.2 The resources listed below help you develop new interests and fine-tune your current ones. Follow the directions in order to maximize your use of each resource.

1. Go to your college bookstore and browse through the textbook sections. Look at texts in your current areas of interest and those that represent new topics for you. What catches your attention? What interests you most? List your top five choices below.

_____

_____

_____

_____

_____

2. Go to your college bookstore or to a commercial bookstore and browse through the tradebook (non-textbook) sections. Look at books in your current areas of interest and those that represent new topics for you. What catches your attention? What interests you most? List your top five choices below.

_____

_____

_____

_____

_____

3. Browse through the course descriptions in your college catalog. Look at courses in your current areas of interest and those that represent new topics for you. Assume that you have all the time, money, and prerequisite knowledge to take

anything you wish. What interests you most? What do you want to know more about? List your top five choices below.

_____

_____

_____

_____

_____

4. Examine the book and course titles you chose. What influenced your choices? What relationship, if any, exists among your choices? Which topics, if any, surprised you? What influence, if any, will this have on your choice of major and career?

_____

_____

_____

_____

_____

EXERCISE 1.3   Read pp. 483–488 (Sample pp. 67–72) on cultural rules in Sample Chapter 1, "Culture: The Ideas and Products People Adopt and Create." Give an example from your postsecondary experience of each of the following: *value, norm, folkway, more, taboo,* and *law.* Do not use any examples included in the sample chapter reading.

1. value _____

_____

2. norm _____

_____

3. folkway _____

_____

4. more _____

_____

5. taboo _____

_____

6. law _____

_____

INTEGRATING INSTITUTIONAL PERSPECTIVES WITH YOUR OWN

The key is not "the will to win"... everybody has that. It is the will to prepare to win that is important.

—BOBBY KNIGHT
Basketball coach

What do you expect from your college? What does your college expect from you? In order to win the game of higher education, you must be, in the words of Bobby Knight, prepared to win. Preparation means that you know what you expect to gain from your college career. It means that you know what your institution expects for you to remain in the game.

Your expectations depend on the goals you've set. You might want a two-year degree or a four-year degree. You might want to go to graduate school. You might not want a degree, but you may want specific course work, certification, or technical knowledge to enhance your career search or status. You might even choose to take courses for fun or personal enrichment.

Your institution's goal is to take raw material (in this case, you) and, through education, turn it into a finished product (again, you). Depending on the institution, that could mean a two-year degree, four-year degree, preparation for graduate work, certification, technical expertise, or personal satisfaction. Most institutions have a variety of programs to meet your individual needs. Once an institution admits you, it expects you will stay until you complete your goals. The institution provides facilities, faculty, and courses to help you reach your goals. It offers counselors and other staff to answer your questions and provide the direction you need. It maintains academic and professional standards so that the education you receive—and the goals you meet—will be of top quality. Finally, the institution expects that you will progress toward your goals in a timely fashion and maintain a minimum grade point average as you go.

Your **college catalog** helps you integrate your institution's perspectives with your own. Revised each year, your catalog is your contract with your institution. It contains the information you need to play the higher education game. For example, you might change your major. Your catalog tells you if your institution offers a degree in your new area of interest. Maybe you want to take a specific course. Your catalog provides you with information about the availability of such a course at your institution and whether or not it will apply to your chosen curriculum. It tells you what to take if you've selected a major. It helps you make wise—and applicable—choices if you're undecided about your major. The institution's grading system ensures that you remain on track to achieve your goals. Academic standing (freshman, sophomore, junior, senior) tells you—and the institution—how you're doing in meeting your goals.

A catalog is not something you commit to memory. You do, however, need to be familiar with it so that you can be prepared for any eventuality—from charges of academic misconduct to course selection and from applying for a scholarship or loan to getting involved in student organizations. Table 1.2 identifies and describes major components of a catalog.

FINE-TUNING CAREER DECISIONS

The best careers advice to give to the young is "Find out what you like doing best and get someone to pay you for doing it."

—KATHERINE WHITEHORN
British journalist

Find out what you don't do well, and don't do it.

—ALF
Television character

If you've followed the advice of Whitehorn or ALF, you probably know something about what you do or do not want to study in college and do in life. As you made your choice, you probably passed through the first few stages of career development (See Figure 1.3). According to Ginzberg, Ginsburg, Axelrad, and Herma (1951), the first stage was probably one of **fantasy.** The sky was the limit, and anything was possible from being author to president, astronaut to rock star.

Then you began to assess your strengths and weaknesses—those things you liked doing best and those that you didn't do well. You entered a **tentative** stage in which you realized that some career options were more appropriate than others.

If you have selected a major, you are probably somewhere in the third—the **realistic**—stage of career development. This stage consists of three parts: **exploration, crystallization,** and **specification.** Choosing a major, then, is not the end of your career decision-making but more often the beginning. Fine-tuning your choice characterizes the realistic stage of career decision-making and continues throughout your college career.

Exploration

In exploration, you evaluate yourself and your career options. Aptitudes, abilities, interests, needs, and values shape your choice. Your

TABLE 1.2 College Catalog Components

ACADEMIC CALENDAR	Lists important dates in the academic year, including registration, first and last days to drop classes, midterm and final exam periods, and holidays and vacations.
STUDENT SERVICES	Identifies nonacademic activities and services available to students, including campus organizations, Dean of Students' Office, housing and food service information, and health services.
ADMISSIONS INFORMATION	Explains criteria for admission to the institution, regulations for the transfer of credits, and availability of special programs.
TUITION AND FEES	Lists in-state and out-of-state costs, including tuition, room and board, fee schedules, student health fees, parking fees, and lab fees. May also identify financial aid opportunities (scholarships, grants, loans, campus jobs).
ACADEMIC POLICIES AND REGULATIONS	Describes certification requirements, academic standards, and registration regulations.
ACADEMIC CLASSIFICATION	Describes how the number of completed credit-hours translates into freshman, sophomore, junior, or senior status. Credit-hour value is approximately equal to the number of hours per week of in-class instruction (lab, studio, or performance courses often involve more hours of in-class instruction than are reflected in credit-hour value). Course-load requirements describe the maximum and minimum hours required to be at full-time status.
ACADEMIC STANDARDS	Discusses the rules governing student conduct, including disciplinary sanctions, academic disciplinary actions, and appeal procedures. These rules apply in cases of academic dishonesty (cheating or plagiarism) or other institutional infractions.
COLLEGE DEGREE REQUIREMENTS	Identifies the specific and elective courses necessary for completion of a degree. These are often divided by semester/quarter or academic year.
COURSE DESCRIPTIONS	Summarizes the content of each course, which is usually identified by a number and title.

FIGURE 1.3   Flowchart of Career Development

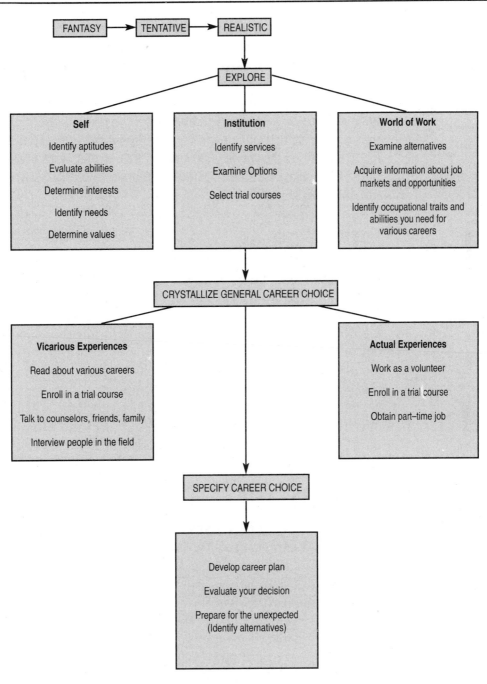

institution's services, educational options, and courses of study also play a role. Finally, you consider the world of work, including alternatives, employment markets, and occupational requirements.

For example, you may find yourself interested in the field of medicine. Your options include hospital administration, physician, medical technician, nurse, physical therapist, and pharmacist, among others. Personal exploration may lead you to eliminate hospital administration (you want to work directly with patients) or physican (you don't want to spend that many years in school). You may find that your institution does not offer courses leading to degrees in physical therapy or pharmacy. Employment projections indicate that people skilled in nursing and medical technology will be in high demand for the next ten years.

Crystallization

Crystallization occurs when you have a general idea of what you want to do. Once you've narrowed your choices, you need to learn about each one. This helps you make an informed decision.

You acquire career information vicariously or directly. Vicarious learning takes place when you learn through the experiences of others. Introductory courses, written information, and discussions with faculty and professionals in the field give you insights about the career you're considering. Direct learning occurs through personal experience. Lab courses, practicums, and internships often give you the opportunity to "try on" a career for a short time. Volunteer work and part-time employment in the field also provide experiences for direct learning.

Specification

After you have pinpointed a career, you should develop a plan for making that career a reality. To do this, you identify the educational requirements and practical experience you need. Next, you establish a timeline for completing any needed coursework. Many courses include "hands-on" experience as part of the content. These courses give you a realistic look at the career you're considering. You then seek volunteer or part-time employment. Job opportunities are found through a network of family, friends, and business contacts, the same people who helped you determine your interests.

The career decision you have struggled to make needs periodic evaluation. You should determine if the job you want meets your needs and interests. In addition, periodic evaluation of the job market allows you to recognize trends in your chosen field. Even after you are working in your chosen field, periodic assessment is necessary. Careful consideration of salary, job security, working conditions, advancement opportunities, and other factors is important.

Frequent assessment also prepares you for the unexpected. The poet Robert Burns once wrote, "The best laid schemes o' mice and men/Gang aft a-gley [(often) go astray]." This is true of the best-laid career plans. Since the unexpected can happen anytime, anywhere, you must be prepared. Such surprises can be good or bad for your career. For example, suppose you prepare for a career teaching English. Upon graduation, you find there are no teaching positions available (bad surprise). However, you discover a job in publishing that lets you use your knowledge of English at a better salary (good surprise). The key to adapting to surprises, both good and bad, is flexibility. Survival of the fittest and evolution are scientific theories that hold that through change life continues. Being open to new ideas, then, is your means of surviving career changes.

UNDECIDED MAJORS: EXPLORING INSTITUTIONAL OPTIONS

If you have not decided on a major, you may fear that your indecision will be costly in terms of time (and money). This does not have to be the case. In most **curricula,** the first year consists of general course work. Even in more specialized curricula, if you carefully select your courses, you can avoid wasting time. Thus, through careful scheduling you can maintain academic progress while keeping all your options open.

For example, consider Fred. Fred is undecided whether to major in business administration, chemical engineering, or criminal justice. Using the curriculum guides suggested in Table 1.3, Fred plans to take English 101, Math 121, Chemistry 101, Speech 161, and Geography 100. All of the courses Fred selected apply to any of the three majors he is considering.

TABLE 1.3   Curriculum Guides

Business Administration	Chemical Engineering	Criminal Justice
Business 101	Chem. 101; 102; 121	Geog. 100 or Hist. 103
English 101; 102	English 101; 102	Crim. Justice 107
Math 121; 122	Math 155; 156***	Math 115 or 121
Science Electives*	Physics 121	Science Electives*
Speech 161 or 162	General Electives**	English 101; 102
General Electives**	Engineering 104	Speech 161

*Choose from Biology, Physics, Botany, Zoology, Chemistry
**Choose from Art, Foreign Language, Geography, History, Music, Speech
***Prerequisite courses are Math 121, 122

All three curricula require English 101.Business administration and criminal justice require Math 121. It is also the prerequisite math course needed in engineering. Engineering requires chemistry, whereas the other two accept any science course. Both business and criminal justice require Speech 161. It is an elective in engineering. Geography is required for criminal justice. It is a general elective in the other two.

One way you make more informed choices about a major is to take trial courses. Such introductory courses provide an overview of the subject area. They consist of general information about many related topics. These courses, if in a general field of study, can often be used as **free elective** credits. If more specialized, they can be considered as an investment in your career choice.

Again consider Fred. Fred can find out more about his chosen fields by taking trial courses. Taking Business 101, Engineering 104, or Criminal Justice 107 would help Fred learn about each career. However, if Fred takes too long or takes too many trial courses, he will hinder his academic progress. Thus, he needs to take these courses within the first year.

Many undecided students delay making career decisions because they mistakenly think that their majors must exactly match the career they desire. That's true for some careers. If you want to be a druggist, you must major in pharmacy. If you want to be a librarian, you need to major in library science. If you want to be a chemist, you need to major in chemistry. On the other hand, some jobs do not require specific majors. You can major in English or business and still be a lawyer, a journalist, or a secretary. Your career decision then, although important, is not a decision that cannot be changed.

Every day, someone makes a career move—to a different job, to a related career, or to an entirely different field. Changing majors may ultimately result in your spending an additional semester or two in school. In comparison to the twenty to forty years you will spend in the work force, this time becomes a very brief investment in your future.

If you have not declared your major, you need to learn more about your goals and explore various career options. When you use your time learning about yourself, taking advantage of campus resources, and finalizing a career decision, your time is well spent.

EXCERPT 1.1   MAJORS JUST DON'T MATTER THAT MUCH   BY WILLIAM RASPBERRY

- Soon to every fledgling student comes the moment to decide. But since Angela's a freshman, my advice is: Let it ride.

WASHINGTON—With apologies to James Russell Lowell, that is pretty much my counsel to my daughter, who is about to begin her first year in college. Soon enough, she'll have to face the sophomore necessity of choosing a major—whether or not she's decided on a career. In the meantime, I tell her, don't worry about it.

A part of the reason for my advice is the memory of my own struggle to decide on a major. I eventually had four of them, none of them related to what was to become my career.

But the more important reason is my conclusion, regularly reinforced, that majors just don't matter that much.

The latest reinforcement is from John Willson, a history professor at Michigan's Hillsdale College, who, having heard once too often the question "But what do I do with a history major?" has decided to do what he can to put his students at ease.

"Every sophomore has a majoring frenzy," he wrote in a campus publication. "It is typical for sophomores to say, 'I want to be an anchorman. Therefore I will major in journalism. Where do I sign up?' They act like they have had a blow to the solar plexus when I say, a) Hillsdale has no major in journalism, and b) if we did, it would no more make you an anchorman than a major in English makes you an Englishman."

But rather than simply repeating what professionals already know, or urging colleges to dispense with the requirement for declaring a major, Willson has reduced his advice to a set of rules and principles.

The first, which college students often find incredible, is that aside from such vocational courses as engineering or computer science, any relationship between majors and careers is largely incidental. Physics majors are hardly more likely to become physicists than business majors to become entrepreneurs. The rule that derives from this principle:

If you wanted your major to be practical, you should have gone to the General Motors Institute.

The second principle is that students (and colleges) should delay the necessity of choosing for as long as practicable. "Most students (and even more parents) have rather vague notions of what the subject of any given subject is. . . . Talk with your parents, but don't let parents, teachers, media experts, television evangelists or fraternity brothers pressure you into a majoring frenzy before you know what the major is all about." In short:

All things being equal, it is best to know what you are talking about, which may even prevent majoring frenzies.

The third is a quote from the Rev. James T. Burtchaell (writing in "Notre Dame" magazine): "Pick your major on the pleasure principle, for what you most enjoy studying will dreaw your mind in the liveliest way to being educated."

The rule: People do not get educated by hitting themselves over the head with hammers.

It's good advice, and not only for students at small liberal-arts colleges. A few years ago, the University of Virginia published a booklet, "Life after Liberal Arts," based on a survey of 2,000 alumni of its college of arts and sciences.

The finding: 91 percent of the respondents not only believe that liberal arts prepared them for fulfilling careers but would not hesitate to recommend liberal-arts majors to students considering those same careers.

Those who responded to the survey included a biology major who later earned a master's of business administration and became president of a bank, a psychology major who was a well-paid executive, and English majors who careers embraced television sales, editorial production, systems analysis and law.

The "winning combination" derived from the Virginia survey: a liberal-arts foundation, complemented with career-related experience and personal initiative. Colleges aren't assembly lines that, after four years, automatically deposit students into lucrative careers. What is far likelier is a series of false starts followed by the discovery of a satisfying career. In the Virginia survey, for example, only 16 percent, reported being happy with their first jobs.

Willson's advice, the results of the University of virginia survey, and my advice to Angela come down to the same thing: Major in getting an education.

SOURCE: Reprinted by permission of Washington Post © 1990.

WRITE TO LEARN

Read the essay by William Raspberry. On a separate sheet of paper, respond to the following: What three principles does he give for declaring a major? What is your opinion concerning the validity of these principles? Would you follow them? Why or why not? Explain the meaning of the phrase "Major in getting an education." Do you agree? Why or why not?

EXERCISE 1.4   Below are curricula guides for the freshman year (fall and spring semesters). Unless otherwise stated, assume that all courses are three-hour credit courses. and that specific subject area courses must be taken in sequence (e.g., English 101 before 102). Use the curricula to answer the questions that follow.

PRE-MED
English 101, 102
Chemistry 100, 110
Chemistry lab 105, 115 (1 credit hour)
Zoology 101, 102 or Biology 101, 102
3 hours of any foreign language
Any 100-level history course
Math 121, 122

ELEMENTARY EDUCATION
English 101, 102
Biology 101, 102 or Zoology 101, 102 or
   Botany 101, 102
History 101, 103
Math 109, 110, or any higher-level
   course
Education 101
Speech 100
Psychology 105

MUSIC
English 101, 102
Approved science electives*
Music Theory 170
Approved math electives**
   (6 credit hours)
Music History 101, 110
Approved general electives***
   (6 credit hours)

HOME ECONOMICS
English 101, 102
Chemistry 100, 110
Chemistry lab 105, 115 (1 credit hour)
Home Economics 101, 102
Math 114, 115 or Math 121, 122
Speech 100
Psychology 105

COMPUTER SCIENCE
English 101, 102
Approved science electives*
  (6 credit hours)
Math 121, 122
Approved general electives***
  (6 credit hours)
6 hours of any foreign language

BUSINESS (Pre-Law Option)
English 101, 102
Approved science electives*
  (6 credit hours)
Math 121, 122
Approved general electives***
  (6 credit hours)
Speech 101
History 101, 103

*Approved science electives: Choose from Biology 101, 102; Botany 101, 102; Zoology 101, 102; Chemistry 100, 110; Geology 105, 110; Astronomy 111, 112
**Approved math electives: Choose from Math 109, 110, 121, 122, 155, 157
***Approved general electives: Choose any art, foreign language, music, psychology, sociology, history, geography.

1. You want to major in music or computer science. You have a job and will only be taking nine hours this semester. What schedule would give you course work that will apply toward either major?

   _____

   _____

   _____

2. You are a transfer student with credits in English 101 and 102, Math 121, and Speech 101. You want to take fifteen to sixteen hours this semester. You want a pre-law or a pre-med degree. What should you take?

   _____

   _____

   _____

3. You plan to major in home economics, elementary education, or music. You want to take twelve hours. What could you take that would apply to all three programs?

   _____

   _____

   _____

4. You are completely undecided about a major. Which of these freshman-level courses could apply to any of the curricula?

   _____

   _____

   _____

5. Which of the courses apply only to the curriculum in which they are found?

_____

_____

_____

TRACKING GOALS: GRADING SYSTEMS

Your goals are the eventual destination you wish to reach, and grades

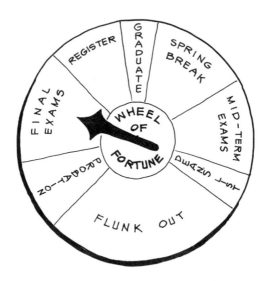

form the compass by which you direct and redirect your efforts.

Traditional grading systems consist of the letter grades *A*, *B*, *C*, *D*, and *F*. Other marks include *NC* (no credit), *P* (pass), *W* (withdraw), *W-grade* (withdraw with a grade), and *I* (incomplete). *P*, *W*, *I*, and *NC* grades are not used to compute your **grade point average (GPA).** Policies concerning *W-grades* vary. Some institutions use the grade in computing GPA while others do not. Check your institution's regulations to be sure. Computation of the GPA is a ratio of **quality points** earned to semester hours attempted. Quality points usually are based on the following four-point scale: $A = 4$; $B = 3$; $C = 2$; $D = 1$; $F = 0$. Because your courses vary in **credit hours,** you cannot always

"Tell your parents you had a cumulative grade of 3.5 this semester."

assume that the average of an *A*, a *B*, and a *C* equals a 3.0 GPA. See Table 1.4 for an example of GPA computation.

Although learning for learning's sake is applauded, the fact remains that grades are used to measure learning. You need to heed your department's and institution's goals for success, as well as your own.

TABLE 1.4   GPA Computation

Course	Grade	Credit Hours		Point Equivalent		Total Quality Points
English 101	C	3	×	(C =) 2	=	6
Math 104	D	4	×	(D =) 1	=	4
Speech 100	B	3	×	(B =) 3	=	9
Physical Education 106	A	1	×	(A =) 4	=	4
Biology 101	W	3				—
Totals		11				23

Quality Points/Semester Hours Attempted =
23/11 = 2.09 GPA

PRINCIPAL PLAYERS: ADMINISTRATIVE UNITS, FACULTY, AND OTHER STUDENTS

You play the game of higher education with the administration, faculty, and other students. Unlike a high school or job setting, you have more choices in determining those with whom you come in contact.

EXERCISE 1.5   Compute the grade point average for the following:

1.   GPA = _____

Course	Grade	Credit Hours	Point Equivalent	Total Quality Points
English 210	A	3	_____	_____
Math 103	F	5	_____	_____
Speech 102	B	3	_____	_____
History 104	C	3	_____	_____
Art 100	W	4	_____	_____
TOTALS				

2.   GPA = _____

Course	Grade	Credit Hours	Point Equivalent	Total Quality Points
English 001	NC	3	_____	_____
Math 006	P	5	_____	_____
Physical Education 107	D	1	_____	_____
Word Processing 101	A	1	_____	_____
TOTALS				

3.   GPA = _____

Course	Grade	Credit Hours	Point Equivalent	Total Quality Points
English 102	C	3	_____	_____
Math 200	D	3	_____	_____
Music 101	B	3	_____	_____
Nursing 100	A	3	_____	_____
Geography 102	W	3	_____	_____
TOTALS				

Your interactions with administrators, faculty, and peers play a role in determining your success in achieving your academic goals.

CAMPUS OFFICES

Although each institution of higher learning has its own campus with its own atmosphere and buildings, all share some common offices and services. Knowing where each is located and what it can do for you provides you with shortcuts to winning the game.

Each staff and faculty department is essential to the institution; however, some departments function "behind the scenes." These departments pertain more to institutional management. The departments described in Table 1.5, on the other hand, are "in front of the camera" and are essential to your academic progress and success.

4. GPA = _____

Course	Grade	Credit Hours	Point Equivalent	Total Quality Points
English 101	D	3	_____	_____
Math 109	C	3	_____	_____
Geology 107	F	3	_____	_____
Physical Education 107	B	1	_____	_____
ROTC 101	A	2	_____	_____
TOTALS				

5. GPA = _____

Course	Grade	Credit Hours	Point Equivalent	Total Quality Points
English 106	F	3	_____	_____
Math 104	D	4	_____	_____
Music 105	B	2	_____	_____
Physical Education 106	A	1	_____	_____
Botany 101	C	4	_____	_____
TOTALS				

List the courses in which you are now enrolled and predict what grade you will receive in each.

6. GPA = _____

Course	Grade	Credit Hours	Point Equivalent	Total Quality Points
Totals				

EXERCISE 1.6 Go to any and all of these offices located on your campus and obtain the following information and items. Your instructor will identify the item you are to find at each office.

1. Admissions Office

   Location: _____

   Office Hours: _____

   Contact Person: _____

   Item Sought: _____

2. Business Office

   Location: _____

Office Hours: _____

Contact Person: _____

Item Sought: _____

3. Career Guidance and Placement Office

Location: _____

Office Hours: _____

Contact Person: _____

Item Sought: _____

4. Correspondence and Extension Division

Location: _____

Office Hours: _____

Contact Person: _____

Item Sought: _____

5. Dean's Office

Location: _____

Office Hours: _____

Contact Person: _____

Item Sought: _____

6. Financial Aid Office

Location: _____

Office Hours: _____

Contact Person: _____

Item Sought: _____

7. Campus Library

Location: _____

Office Hours: _____

Contact Person: _____

Item Sought: _____

8. Student Health Services

Location: _____

Office Hours: _____

Contact Person: _____

Item Sought: _____

TABLE 1.5	Campus Offices and Services
REGISTRAR'S OFFICE	Also called Office of Records and Registration. Tracks courses you take and grades you receive. Evaluates advanced, transfer, or correspondence work. Provides transcripts. May have the responsibility to determine if you meet graduation requirements.
BUSINESS OFFICE	Also called Office of the Treasurer or the Bursar's Office. Records student financial transactions, such as tuition, fees, fines, or other payments.
CAREER GUIDANCE AND PLACEMENT OFFICE	Administers interest, educational, and aptitude tests to assist you in career decision-making. Provides job placement information. May maintain placement files of transcripts and letters of reference that can be sent to prospective employers at your request.
CORRESPONDENCE AND EXTENSION DIVISION	Administers off-campus and independent study courses that are taken by mail.
FINANCIAL AID OFFICE	Also called Student Aid and Scholarship Office. Provides assistance in locating and distributing supplemental funds such as grants, loans, scholarships, and on-campus employment. Your need for financial assistance is often based on responses you provide in a written application.
LIBRARY	Contains text materials for reference and recreation, including books, magazines, newspapers, journals, reference books, microfilms, and computerized documents. May also contain a listening room, teacher education materials, and photocopying facilities. Workshops or classes may be available to familiarize you with library services and holdings.
STUDENT HEALTH SERVICES	Provides medical assistance for students who become physically ill or injured or who have chronic health problems. May also offer mental health counseling. Services are usually free for full-time students and at a small cost for part-time students. Lab work, physical therapy, pharmaceutical drugs, emergency care, and workshops on health-related topics may also be available.

INTERACTING WITH INSTRUCTORS

A popular urban legend (Brunvand, 1989) tells of an instructor whose students changed his behavior. Whenever he walked to the left side of the room, they seemed to lose interest in what he said. They yawned, wrote notes, whispered, and paid little or no attention. When he moved to the right, they sat up straight. They made a point to listen carefully, take notes, and ask questions. The instructor soon began to lecture only from the right side of the class.

Like the students in the story, you, too, can influence the behavior of your instructors. Instructors try to be fair and impartial, but they are people, too. Think about the people you've met in your life. Some had qualities that made you want to know them better. Others had characteristics that made you happy to see them leave. Instructors feel the same way about students. Each semester, they meet a new group of people. They react to and with each one. Your behavior determines if their reactions to you are positive or negative. You control whether or not you are a student worth knowing better.

Classroom Behavior

To obtain and maintain an instructor's goodwill, you must be polite and respectful. Arriving on time, dressed appropriately, makes a good first impression. Your prompt and consistent attendance proves your diligence and commitment to the course. The quality of your work also shows your regard for the instructor and the course. Your work is, after all, an extension of you. Only work of the highest quality in content, form, and appearance should be submitted to an instructor.

Sitting near the front of the room in about the same seat for each class gives the instructor a visual fix on you. Although the instructor may not keep attendance records, he or she will subconsciously look for you and know you are there. Sitting near the front of the room also helps you maintain eye contact with the instructor.

Your apparent interest in the lecture is enhanced when your body language also shows your interest. Facial expressions and movements (smiling, nodding your head, raising your eyebrows) and body language (sitting straight, facing the instructor, arms uncrossed) indicate your openness and desire to learn.

The opposite of this is also true. Nonverbal responses of skepticism or boredom are clear in body language and facial expressions (yawning, reading the newspaper, sighing, looking out the window, rolling your eyes). Body language is especially important when you read your instructor's comments on returned assignments in class. Constructive criticism is part of the learning process and should be a

SOURCE: Reprinted by permission of Glen Dines and *Phi Delta Kappan.*

learning experience. An instructor's critical comments are not a personal attack. Your body language should reflect your ability to accept those comments in the spirit in which they are given.

Some students fear speaking in class. Often they are afraid that their questions will sound "dumb" to either the instructor or other students. Sometimes the class is a large one with several hundred students. Maybe past experiences led to embarrassing results. Generally, however, if something in the lecture confused you, it confused others, too. Many times they are waiting for someone else to make the first move. That person needs to be you. All you have to fear is fear itself, to paraphrase President Franklin Roosevelt.

Speaking in class is less stressful if you know how to phrase your questions or comments. Questions and comments must be relevant and respectful. Nothing frustrates an instructor more than rude questions; long, unrelated stories; or questions whose answers were just discussed. Preceding your questions with what you do understand helps the instructor clarify what confuses you. By briefly stating what you think was just said, you aid the instructor in finding gaps in your knowledge. Another way to help an instructor help you is to be exact about the information you need.

Active participation in class discussions proves your interest. If you ask questions or make comments about the lecture topic, you signal your desire for understanding. However, if you feel you simply cannot ask a question in class, then see your instructor before or after class or make an appointment.

Out-of-Class Behavior

Getting to know an instructor personally involves special effort. Smiling and saying hello when you see an instructor outside of class is a friendly opening gesture. Positive, sincere feedback about lecture topics, the instructor's lecture style, and so on often opens lines of communication. Visiting an instructor's office often and for long time periods also affects how an instructor feels about you—but, unfortunately, the effect is negative. Instructors have office hours so students who have valid problems can contact them. They also use that time to grade papers, complete paperwork, and conduct research. Thus, many instructors resent students who—without reason—constantly visit them.

This does not mean that instructors do not like to talk to you and other students. They do. Talking to you helps them understand your problems and learning needs. It gives them an opportunity to interest you in their content areas.

There are several good reasons to visit an instructor's office. Questions about course content or test items should be asked politely and intelligently. Previous suggestions for asking questions in class also apply here. Appealing a poor grade is another reason for seeing an instructor. Having some viable options to present strengthens your appeal. Indicate that you are willing to write a research paper, do extra reading, take a makeup exam, or work extra problems. That you have thought of these options proves you realize your grade is your responsibility. Whether or not you are allowed to make up work is at the discretion of the instructor. If your instructor refuses to allow you this concession, you need to smile, say "Thank you," and take the grade you've earned. Another legitimate reason for seeing an instructor is to ask for an incomplete grade. Usually students who have valid reasons and the proper attitude have few problems with getting extra time to complete work.

If you discuss your grade with an instructor and feel you have been unfairly treated, you have the right to an appeal. This appeal involves, first, meeting with the professor and attempting to resolve your problem. During the second step of the appeal process, you write a letter to the head of the department in which the course was taught asking for a meeting with that person and your instructor. If

"Never be late, never call your instructor at home after midnight, and, whatever you do, never let 'em see you sweat."

you are not satisfied with the results of this hearing, you may appeal to the dean of the department in which the course was taught. If you are firmly convinced that you are in the right, your final appeal is made to the head of academic affairs at your institution.

There are three "nevers" in getting along with instructors: never miss class, never be inattentive or impolite, and, if you miss class, never say, "I missed class today. Did we do anything important?" Instructors never feel they are teaching unimportant information.

It is possible to win grades and influence instructors. You can do it by remembering the Golden Rule and treating them as you want them to treat you.

INTERACTING WITH OTHER STUDENTS

Just as your behavior toward your instructors affects their perception of you, your behavior also affects the way you are viewed by other students. Because suggestions for interacting with instructors are based on common sense, they also apply in interacting with class-mates.

Classroom Behavior

The first impression you make on your classmates sets the tone for your interactions with them. Probably the first thing they will notice is your appearance. Although how you dress shouldn't matter, it does. It's true that you can wear almost anything in today's class-rooms. However, clothes sometimes form barriers between you and others. Overly expensive or outlandish costumes can alienate or intimidate. Your best bet is clothing that reflects your style and personality but does not draw too much attention to you.

The first day of class is often as unsettling as the first day in a new school or on a new job. You may be eager to meet others but hesitant about taking the first step. One initiative may be taken at any time during the term. It involves smiling and saying hello. Finding out the names of people who sit around you is a second step. To start conversation, you might ask other students if this is their first class, where they're from, or what courses they are taking. In addition to making new friends, knowing the people who sit around you and exchanging phone numbers with them is good insurance for absences. You'll know whom to contact for assignments or notes.

The way you treat your classmates directly corresponds to how they will treat you. Several things can almost guarantee that you will be someone others won't want to know. First, consistent late arrivals or noisiness during lectures distracts people around you. Second, telling numerous personal stories bores everyone. In addition, monopolizing class discussions or asking frequent irrelevant questions annoys others who also wish to contribute. Third, if you show disapproval or voice sarcasm when others make comments, you'll alienate everyone. Your body language often speaks for you, too. What it says may surprise you. The way you sit, move your eyes, or place your arms can signal your disinterest or disapproval.

In every classroom, you are in one of two situations. You either do or do not know about the topic under discussion. If you know, you can make friends by finding classmates who do not know about the topic and helping them learn. Offering help without judging or boasting can be tricky, but it is essential to interaction with others. If you do not know the topic, you need to find someone who does and who is willing to help you. Asking for help gives classmates chances to feel knowledgeable and needed. Sometimes asking for help is just as hard as giving it. You may fear wasting other students' time or making a poor impression. A couple of ways to overcome this fear are to form a study group or ask several students to join you for coffee to discuss class material.

Out-of-Class Behavior

All work and no play can be almost as bad as all play and no work. Getting your degree should be your main goal. Your college classes should, and do, occupy much of your time, but you also need to develop friendships and get involved in other activities. Involvement in extracurricular groups fosters interpersonal skills and leads to the development of leadership skills. Students who are active in an extracurricular or community group or who have other interests tend to

"Thank you for sharing the story your father told last night, but now I think it best that we return to the lesson."

SOURCE: Val Cheatham.

remain in school longer than those who have no such ties. This is because they are no longer simply going to college; they are part of college life.

Many students think that the only place to meet people on campus is the student union or student center. However, many other groups provide opportunities for interacting with other students. First, students may join an **intramural sports** group, which organizes athletic events and services for students who are not part of a school-sponsored athletic team. These activities focus on competition that encourages sportsmanship, leadership, health, and fun. Second, students interested in the same subject often form a club through the student affairs office. This helps them develop friendships with others. Third, students might join other clubs on campus that involve individuals with similar interests or hobbies. Membership often depends on grade point average or other criteria. Fourth, students may seek membership in social sororities or fraternities. Dues finance the activities of such groups. Admittance is often based on grade point averages, and these groups are joined by invitation only. Sororities or fraternities also participate in charity events, such as blood drives and telethons. Finally, leisure or other noncredit courses also provide opportunities for you to meet others.

GETTING INVOLVED IN CAMPUS LIFE

One of the goals of your institution is retention. That means your institution wants you to stay in school until you complete your degree or other educational goal. What motivates a person to remain in school? Courses, curricula, and faculty all play a role in whether or not a student stays enrolled. However, research indicates that the key to retention is how involved a student is in the institution. The student who feels a part of the campus is more likely to stay than the student who merely attends classes on the campus. In addition, job recruiters and employers often seek candidates who are well-rounded with a variety of interests. They want to see students who can handle a diversity of activities while remaining academically successful.

What group should you join? Again, your needs, values, and interests determine which groups suit you best. In general, it really doesn't matter which group you choose, as long as you become involved in campus life.

Campus Employment

Campus employment is one of the most lucrative ways for students to get involved in campus life. While student wages are often minimal, employment offers many other benefits. First, campus employers understand that a student's real job is school. Such employers are willing to let you work around class schedules and often rearrange work hours to accommodate special projects or tests. Campus employment often offers you the opportunity to work within your field of study in such positions as a lab assistant, office worker, tutor, and so on. Even if your campus job is not in your area of interest, it may provide you with experiences relevant to your career or lead you to an entirely new field of interest. Finally, campus employment gives you additional opportunities to meet and know students, faculty, and staff.

Special Interest Groups

Special interest groups are based on the notion that "birds of a feather flock together." Interest groups develop around a variety of topics from academic interests (for example, Accounting Society, Philosophy Club, College Choir, Pre-Law Association, band) to those which are simply for fun (Frisbee Club, Chess Club, intramural sports, Science Fiction Association, computer user groups). Groups may reflect political affiliation (College Republicans), sexual orientation (Gay and Lesbian Alliance), ethnic membership (Arab Students' Association), or religious belief (Inter-Varsity Christian Fellowship). Such groups may be formal or informal. Some are honorary and base membership on academic criteria. Joining these groups gives you opportunities to meet others with similar interests or to develop new interests.

Service Organizations

Service organizations provide various opportunities to work for the common good of your institution or community. These groups include any organization in which you volunteer your time for the benefit of others. Student government associations and residence hall associations represent students in a variety of ways. They organize to further the desires and needs of students they represent. The students who staff campus newspapers and yearbook offices often volunteer to gain experience in journalism and production. Many interest groups have a service organization that provides tutoring, advice, and support to its members. Finally, some organizations (for example, Gamma Beta Phi) provide more traditional forms of service (Big Buddy programs, literacy tutors, drives for food or blood banks).

Why should a busy student devote time to service projects? First, some people believe additional education confers additional responsibility as a citizen. Second, service provides valuable experience in working on committees and projects to accomplish specific goals and tasks. Third, experience with such projects may result in leadership positions in which you can develop additional skills.

Social Organizations: Greeks and Others

Some groups form for strictly social reasons. Like many other campus groups, their purpose is to connect you to other people within the institution. Greek groups have national affiliations and a long tradition. Some students join because their parents, grandparents, or siblings were members. Thus, the networks within such groups are often far-ranging and well-connected. While Greeks are often known for their ability to party, many also focus on academic standards and community service.

A group need not be affiliated with Greeks to be social in nature. Married student groups, members of a particular class or program, or residents of a particular dorm can meet just for fun. While fun is the immediate goal, the long-range effect is friendship and greater assimilation into the institution.

EXERCISE 1.7   Read "How Social Supports Help" on pages 567–568 (77-78) Sample Chapter 4, "Managing Stress." Complete the feature analysis chart below by putting a mark in each box where the social network would fulfill a specific function.

Social Network	Esteem	Status	Social Companionship	Information	Material Support
CAMPUS EMPLOYMENT					
INTEREST GROUPS					
SERVICE ORGANIZATIONS					
SOCIAL ORGANIZATIONS					
FAMILY					

CAMPUS DIVERSITY

Since the late 1960s, postsecondary education has changed. Before then, typical students came from college preparatory schools and had similar economic and/or social backgrounds.

Today, diversity characterizes the typical postsecondary campus. Students come from a variety of academic backgrounds. Age, ethnic identity, and socioeconomic levels vary. Students with learning and other disabilities all find a place on the college campus. International students from a variety of countries and U.S. students from a variety of states may attend the same institution. Students from rural communities and those from metropolitan areas share classrooms and ideas.

Some groups need additional help during their entry into the confusing realm of higher education. Special programs provide chances for personal enrichment and improvement of learning skills. The campus learning center provides academic assistance, tutoring, and a variety of self-help materials.

WRITE TO LEARN

Read pp. 494–497 (Sample Chapter pp. 78–81) on cultural variation in Sample Chapter 1, "Culture: The Ideas and Products People Adopt and Create." On a separate sheet of paper, respond to the following questions: What cultural universals have you noticed at your institution? What cultural changes have occurred? Provide an example based on your experiences at your institution for one of the following: *discovery, diffusion, acculturation, cultural lag.* How do other cultures impact your life and academic pursuits?

WRITE TO LEARN

On a separate sheet of paper, create a chart that identifies which special programs exist on your campus and what service(s) they offer.

MINORITY GROUPS

Minority groups are groups of people who, because of their perceived physical and cultural differences from the dominant group, tend to be treated unequally (Knox, 1990). Minority groups may be defined by race, ethnicity, religion, sex, and age characteristics.

What is college life like if you are a member of a minority group? You may experience some form of prejudice—a learned tendency to think negatively about a group of people—directed toward you. The social outlets available to other students may seem more limited to you. As a result, you may feel isolated and uncomfortable. Involvement, then, is critical for you. Student groups (for example, Society of Women Engineers, Black History Association, Returning Adult Coalition) provide opportunities to network and retain contacts within your minority group.

Membership in other campus groups and associations (for example, music groups, athletics, study groups, dorm groups, professional organizations) provide you with opportunities to become more involved in the campus community, learn more about other cultures, and create new relationships of support. These involvements will help you down the road, when you enter the majority-dominated workforce.

You may also face differences in the academic arena. You may have been actively recruited prior to enrollment only to feel virtually alone once you arrive on campus. Such changes in institutional attitude sometimes result in your having increased feelings of isolation. In addition, faculty may expect more—or, perhaps, less—of you if you are a minority student. Both attitudes present problems in achievement. As a result, you may feel threatened or insulted. Again, your campus connections and networks may be able to help you resolve such problems. You can also confer with minority faculty members and alumni or departmental counselors and administrators. In addition, you should seek the supports available to all students—library services, career planning and placement, counselors, tutors, campus employment, and so on. These, too, provide insights into academia and assist you in becoming more involved in campus life.

THE RETURNING ADULT STUDENT

If you are an older adult student, you possess some advantages over more traditional students. College attendance is your goal, not that of your parents, teachers, or peers. Your life experiences provide a greater background for learning new information. You are sometimes more motivated than younger students. Your maturity and commitment provide you with the will needed to face the problems of an older adult student.

The first problem many adult students face is the redtape that holds together higher education. Particularly trying is registration, a confusing process for anyone. Adults often think that younger students are more experienced and knowledgeable about registration. If registration is computerized, you may feel even more a victim of time. However, no one is ever totally prepared for registration no matter how it's done. If the registration schedule conflicts with your work or household commitments, you may be able to negotiate night registration or registration by mail. If you are a returning student, you have successfully navigated the registration channels at least once already. If you still feel confused about the process, have an experienced friend walk through it with you.

Another problem for returning adult students is transferring credits from other institutions. This procedure is handled by the admissions office. Most problems can be avoided by having transcripts sent to the school you are currently attending as soon as possible. This gives the institution time to evaluate your academic work and make decisions before you register.

As an older adult student, you feel the same pressure to perform that other college students feel. In addition, you face the stress of being in a new situation. Employers, friends, or family may add to this stress by not fully supporting your educational goals. You also may feel the stress of trying to balance academic, work, and personal commitments.

Time probably seems your enemy—an opponent that beats you by moving faster than you can. You combat this problem by being more organized. Like the straw that broke the camel's back, going to school is an overwhelming burden to people who cannot eliminate—without guilt—nonessential responsibilities. Asking friends and family for help involves them in your education. Time is your most valuable resource. You must evaluate each minute you spend. You need to become a careful consumer of it.

A course or workshop in stress management may help you cope with returning to school. Another way to decrease stress is to take a reduced course load during your first term. This enables you to become accustomed to academic demands and the concessions and responsibilities they involve. Involvement in extracurricular activities is another way to adjust to higher education. These activities provide new friends and interests. Your interactions with them give you a recreational outlet. It also breaks barriers between you and traditional students and builds ties between you and other nontraditional students.

Your institution probably offers services designed to meet your particular needs. A day-care center, financial aid, counseling services, and so on, may be available to assist you. In addition, most institutions offer educational courses designed to improve academic skills. You need to find out how to locate these services and courses—either through the catalog, from instructors, or from administrative personnel. You need not be afraid or embarrassed to use them.

Working, being part of a family, and going to school are difficult in and of themselves. Doing all three is, at best, a juggling act.

THE ESL STUDENT

You, as one of many **ESL** (English as a second language) **students,** face a unique situation. You are not only learning new subjects, but you also may be learning a new culture and language.

Like other nontraditional students, improving your study skills is important. Some special learning suggestions may aid your understanding. First, preview your text before class to help you predict the information the lecture will contain. This allows you to avoid misunderstanding the instructor. Second, watch successful American classmates and copy what they do. Your classmates can provide you with a model for notetaking and interacting with instructors and other students. Watching other students helps you identify the behaviors

American students consider appropriate. Third, study with a native student to practice your English and acquire information. Fourth, many institutions provide special classes and workshops to aid you in perfecting your learning skills. Designed expressly for ESL students, they give you a chance to discuss problems and interact with others who are also new to American culture. These programs are well worth your time and investigation.

Overcoming cultural and language differences involves an open mind and varied experiences. Being here is a novelty for you. Meeting you is a novelty for most Americans. The most valuable way for you and natives to learn from one another is for you to become involved with an American family. Your institution's international office or a local church probably keeps lists of families who will invite you into their homes and their lives. Listening to American radio and television and going to movies are also ways of learning about American customs and language. Visiting shopping centers, museums, and restaurants can increase your knowledge of life and language in the United States. Reading newspapers, magazines, and books is also valuable.

One problem for many ESL students that the English they learned in their native countries is British English. Americans and Britons speak different forms of the English language. Although the grammatical structures are the same, there is a variation in vowel sounds. In addition, the rhythm, speed, and slang of American English with its regional differences may be new for you. Your understanding of the language will improve as you hear more of it.

COMMUTING STUDENTS

If you are a commuting student, you may not think of yourself as a nontraditional student. However, if you commute to an institution where the majority of students reside on campus, you face unique problems. Often you may find that courses are available only at inconvenient times. In addition, schedule conflicts may cause you to miss speeches, study sessions, research opportunities, and other learning experiences that enrich academic life. Next, as a commuting student, you are part of a group often called "suitcase" students. With no dorm room or office to serve as a base, you often find that the materials you need are at home, in your car, or at your job. Finally, traveling back and forth limits your contact with others. This often leads to a feeling of alienation and a lack of true assimilation into the institution.

Each of these problems requires creative coping. Solving scheduling problems, for example, involves effective time management. Often each minute you stay on campus needs to be stretched to two.

Urban campus . . . Rural parking

You can stretch time through careful organization and planning. Having the library run a computer search while you attend a study session is an example of such planning. Another way to cope is to find and use alternative resources. Your neighborhood library or videotaped lectures provide reasonable options to supplement what you miss on campus. Using the time you spend commuting to your advantage is another way you can manage more effectively. Listening to tapes, memorizing and rehearsing information, or discussing information with others in your car pool, for example, help you learn while you travel.

To avoid misplacing important materials, you need to be organized and prepared. You become a suitcase student in fact as well as name. To do so, you use a backpack or a briefcase to hold all the books and papers you use each day. By organizing your pack or case each night, you know you're ready for the next day.

Last, you avoid feeling separated from others on campus by consciously attempting to make yourself a part of the school. Reading the campus newspaper, talking with others before and after class, and exchanging phone numbers with classmates decreases your feelings of alienation.

STUDENTS WITH DISABILITIES

If you are disabled in any way, you know that you encounter challenges usually not faced or even considered by others. You may have a chronic (that is, physical or learning disability) or temporary (due to an illness, accident, or surgery) disability. Whatever the case, federal law protects your rights as a student and mandates that appropriate and reasonable accommodations be made for you. It is your responsibility to determine what services you need for academic success and ensure that you receive them.

To locate services, you first contact the admissions office. Its staff should be aware of the services that your institution offers and where to find them. In addition, your college catalog probably lists and describes these services in detail. The academic and student affairs departments, as well as your dean's office, should also provide you with information and assistance.

REENTRY STUDENTS

If you are a reentry student, you are someone who previously entered the institution, left it, and is now returning. The key to your success often lies in the reasons for your previous withdrawal from academic life. You may have run out of money and left school to work until you were once again solvent. Personal problems may have caused you to withdraw. Maybe you weren't ready for college when you first began. Maybe you lacked the academic goals and desire required for success, and you flunked out. Identifying your reason(s) for "stopping out" is critical in helping you avoid old habits and the same mistakes.

If you previously lacked financial resources, you now have a better idea of what it costs—both in time and effort—to stay in school. If you have not already done so, talk to staff members of the financial aid department. They can help you apply for grants and loans. They also place students in work-study jobs and sometimes maintain lists of off-campus employment opportunities. Second, examine your college catalog for scholarships and requirements for application. Many of these specify degree programs, academic classification, and other criteria required for selection. You may be the person who fits the bill. Finally, look for creative ways to cut expenses and make money. Perhaps a faculty or staff member could use a baby-sitter or chauffeur for their children. Maybe they need a responsible person to house-sit while they're on sabbatical leave. Such services could be exchanged for a salary or for room and board.

The types of personal problems which contributed to your previous withdrawal from school span a great range from caring for family members to succumbing to peer pressure. Whatever the cause, determine if the problem is truly resolved, both in your mind and the minds of others. If the problem is not resolved, you must be prepared to handle it, if and when it resurfaces. This may involve examining alternatives personally or with those affected by the problem. You also may need to seek professional counseling or other objective viewpoints to assist you in coping.

Some reentry students are serious-minded and determined, whereas others seem to fall into the same habits that caused their earlier failures. If you now believe that you are ready for learning and to make commitments for success, you must be especially wary. Examine your previous course loads and content; evaluate how you spent your time. Prepare to readjust. Take advantage of the learning assistance services, workshops, and tutorial programs that are available on your campus. Time management and study strategies will be especially relevant for you this second time around.

BECOMING A SKILLED LEARNER

Abraham Lincoln is reported to have said, "You can fool all of the people some of the time, and some of the people all of the time, but you can't fool all the people all the time." In terms of the game of learning, "You can learn all of the information some of the time, and some of the information all of the time, but you can't learn all the information all the time." Only a perfect learner could "learn all the information all the time." So what is a perfect learner?

The perfect learner possesses all the traits of skilled learners. If you are a skilled learner, you know yourself. You know your strengths and weaknesses. More importantly, you know you know. This helps you set learning goals and make plans for meeting them. You look at your choices and choose the best one. You focus your attention on the task at hand. Yet, you remain open to change and new ideas. You manage time and stress effectively. You are an active participant who finds personal meaning in learning.

TAKING STOCK

Who is a perfect learner? No one. No student possesses all the qualities required to learn everything. Instead, the traits that comprise your learning personality vary. Some of these traits are your learning assets. These skills come easily to you. Other learning traits are your deficits. These require more effort on your part. The Learning Questionnaire in Figure 1.4 helps you identify your learning assets and deficits. It aids you in taking stock of where you are as a learner.

This inventory helps you become the best learner you (or anyone) can be. The inventory begins an active, continuing process—the evaluation of your learning assets and deficits. To get an honest idea of your learning personality, you need to invest time and effort in finding your strengths and weaknesses. Once you identify a topic as a strength, your goal is to refine it. When you identify a topic as a weakness, your goal is to improve it.

FIGURE 1.4   Learning Questionnaire

For each question below, circle your response.

1. Do you know how to set learning goals based on your aptitudes, abilities, interests, needs, and values?   Y   N
2. Do you know how to make a class schedule?   Y   N
3. Are you satisfied with your reading ability and speed?   Y   N
4. Do you look over a chapter before reading it?   Y   N
5. Do you know how to use mnemonics to increase your memory?   Y   N
6. Do you construct a note taking outline before lectures?   Y   N
7. Do you know how to use your library's organizational system?   Y   N
8. Do you know the parts and processes involved in a research paper?   Y   N
9. Do you know how to take notes from text graphics?   Y   N
10. Do you know how information is first registered in the brain and then transferred to short-term memory?   Y   N
11. Do you think you are a good test-taker?   Y   N
12. Do you know the difference between a subjective and an objective exam?   Y   N
13. Do you know how to transfer selected information from working memory to long-term memory?   Y   N
14. Do you know step-by-step procedures for examining diagrams, tables, flowcharts, and timelines?   Y   N
15. Do you know how to select and narrow a research topic?   Y   N
16. Do you make and use a working bibliography to research a topic?   Y   N
17. Do you identify a lecture's main idea?   Y   N
18. Do you ask questions about what the text will contain before reading?   Y   N
19. Do you judge the validity of what you read?   Y   N
20. Do you know how to avoid procrastination?   Y   N
21. Do you know how to discuss an academic problem with an instructor?   Y   N
22. Do you know where to find offices of campus assistance (financial aid, dean's office, registrar's office)?   Y   N
23. Do you know the times of day when you study best?   Y   N
24. Do you relate what you already know about a topic to new information about that topic?   Y   N
25. Do you vary your reading speed with different materials?   Y   N
26. Do you know how instructors emphasize important information?   Y   N
27. Are you satisfied with the notes you take during a lecture?   Y   N
28. Do you judge the relevancy of a reference to your research topic?   Y   N
29. Do you know how to find information in your library, conduct interviews, relate personal experiences, and draw conclusions about a research topic?   Y   N
30. Do you know step-by-step procedures for examining bar graphs, circle graphs, and line graphs?   Y   N
31. Do you possess various ways to practice, organize, and associate information for easier recall?   Y   N
32. Do you possess different strategies for studying for and taking different types of exams?   Y   N
33. Do you review exams after they are returned to you?   Y   N
34. Do you know what causes you to forget important information?   Y   N
35. Do you know step-by-step procedures for examining general reference and special-purpose maps?   Y   N
36. Do you evaluate references in terms of origin, recency, objectivity, bias, and author's qualifications?   Y   N

FIGURE 1.4   *Continued*

37. Do you know how to note direct quotes and summarize or paraphrase research information?   Y   N

38. Do you know how to manage test anxiety?   Y   N

39. Do you review your notes several times a week?

40. Do you know how to read for stated and unstated meanings?   Y   N

41. Do you know how to define an unknown word by examining the words that surround it?   Y   N

42. Do you avoid starting new tasks before old tasks are completed?   Y   N

43. Do you recognize the value of a diverse campus?   Y   N

44. Do you participate in social, academic, and service organizations on your campus?   Y   N

45. Do you use time management to accomplish your goals?   Y   N

46. Do you know how text structure organizes information in textbooks?   Y   N

47. When you fail to understand, do you possess plans to recognize this failure and correct it?   Y   N

48. Do you know how to find and use general and specialized content references in your library?   Y   N

49. Do you know how to synthesize or condense information from various sources?   Y   N

50. Do you know why authors include various graphics in textbooks?   Y   N

Interpreting Your Results

If you answered "No" to questions 1, 21, 22, 43, and 44, you need to become more familiar with your institution, the services it offers, and your goals for being in school. If you answered "Yes" to these questions, this topic is one of your learning strengths.
Total "yes" responses for **Campus Orientation** *questions:* _____

If you answered "No" to questions 2, 20, 23, 42, and 45, you need to improve your time management skills (see Chapter 2). If you answered "Yes" to these questions, this topic is one of your learning strengths.
Total "yes" Responses for **Time Management** *questions* _____

If you answered "No" to questions 3, 4, 18, 19, 24, 25, 40, 41, 46, and 47, you need to recognize sources that affect learning from texts (see Chapter 4). If you answered "Yes" to these questions, this topic is one of your learning strengths.
Total "yes" Responses for **Processing Texts** *questions:* _____
Divide by 2: _____

If you answered "No" to questions 9, 14, 30, 35, and 50, you need to review techniques for getting information from text graphics and lecture media (see Chapter 8). If you answered "Yes" to these questions, this topic is one of your learning strengths.
Total "yes" Responses for **Graphics** *questions:* _____

If you answered "No" to questions 5, 6, 17, 26, 27, and 39, you need to recognize sources that affect learning from lectures (see Chapter 3). If you answered "Yes" to these questions, this topic is one of your learning strengths.
Total "yes" Responses for **Learning from Lectures** *questions:* _____

FIGURE 1.4   *Continued*

If you answered "No" to questions 5, 10, 13, 31 and 34, you need to improve your skills in recalling information (see Chapter 5). If you answered "Yes" to these questions, this topic is one of your learning strengths.
Total "Yes" Responses for **Recalling Information** *questions:* _____

If you answered "No" to questions 11, 12, 32, 33, 38, you need to learn test-taking strategies (see Chapter 7). If you answered "Yes" to these questions, this topic is one of your learning strengths.
Total "yes" responses for **Test-taking** *questions:* _____

If you answered "No" to questions 7, 8, 15, 16, 28, 29, 36, 37, 48, and 49, you need to know how to locate information in libraries and write a research paper (see Chapters 9 and 10). If you answered "Yes" to these questions, this topic is one of your learning strengths.
Total "yes" responses for **Library and Research** *questions:* _____
Divide by 2: _____

Summary of Results
On the lines below, enter the totals from the interpretation of results. Then, calculate percentages by multiplying that number by 20. When totals were divided by 2, use the resulting quotient for multiplication.

Title	Total		Percentage
Campus Orientation	_____	× 20 =	_____
Time Management	_____	× 20 =	_____
Processing Texts	_____	× 20 =	_____
Graphics	_____	× 20 =	_____
Learning from Lectures	_____	× 20 =	_____
Recalling Information	_____	× 20 =	_____
Test-Taking	_____	× 20 =	_____
Library and Research	_____	× 20 =	_____

If your percentages were 80 percent or above, then your skills are strong in these areas. If you scored below 80 percent, then you need improvement in these areas.

Honest and careful reporting of symptoms helps a doctor make a correct diagnosis. In much the same way, honest reporting of your learning traits helps you correctly diagnose your learning strengths and weaknesses.

LEARNING STRATEGIES

Just as the purpose of the inventory is to determine your learning strengths and weaknesses, the goal of *CLASS* is to help you become the best learner you can be. In addition to text exercises, three specific strategies—**Write to Learn, Vocabulary Development,** and **Group Learning Activity**—facilitate your development.

Write to Learn activities appear in shaded boxes throughout each chapter. Although your writing may improve as a result of them, that is not their main purpose. Instead, they serve to focus your attention on important concepts and teach you to apply that information in new situations. In completing these activities, you also learn to monitor personal learning. You learn when you understand well enough to use information and when you need further review and reflection. Finally, **Write to Learn** activities help you strengthen your skills in communicating what you know.

Post-secondary education requires you to develop and refine your vocabulary in a variety of ways. For that reason, each chapter contains a **Vocabulary Development** section which focuses on different aspects of language acquisition related to the content of that chapter. These sections provide information and activities to foster your growth as a collegiate scholar.

In postsecondary settings, personal achievement is the basis of grades and other measures of performance. Yet, research indicates that working cooperatively with others in study groups aids learning—in some cases, more than independent study. Group learning provides you with a support group, different perspectives, and the subject-area strengths of others. For that reason, each chapter in *CLASS* includes at least one **Group Learning Activity** designed to help you form, maintain, and use groups to facilitate learning.

GROUP LEARNING ACTIVITY
GUIDELINES FOR ESTABLISHING ACTIVE STUDY GROUPS

A group consists of two or more persons whose contact, proximity, and communication produce changes in each other. As part of the group, you interact with and influence other students. The purpose of your group is the active discussion of information. Therefore, your group needs to have appropriate communication skills, a common purpose, the ability to set tasks, and the skills to accomplish those tasks. Unfortunately, acquiring these is easier said than done. The following guidelines can help you establish an effective study group.

1. *Select group members who have the academic interest and dedication to be successful.* Your friends do not always make the best study partners. Study group members must be prepared to discuss the topic at hand, not what happened at last night's party. You may not know which students in the class are interested in forming a group. Ask your instructor to announce the formation of a study group in class or place a sign-up sheet on a nearby bulletin board.

2. *Seek group members with similar abilities and motivation.* The group functions best when each member of the group contributes to the overall learning of the group, and no one uses the group as a substitute for personally learning the information.

3. *Limit group size to five or fewer students.* You don't want to restructure your entire class into a study group. Five or fewer members is more manageable in arranging schedules and setting goals. Larger groups also decrease the amount of time each member has to actively participate in the group.

4. *Two heads are better than one.* Although a group can consist of as many as five members, it can also contain just two. Lack of interest on the part of other committed members, lack of similar goals, or scheduling problems may preclude your participation in a larger study group. Work or other time commitments also limit the times at which you can meet on a regular basis. Two schedules generally have more in common than five.

5. *Identify the purpose and lifetime of the group.* Are you looking for a term-length group for in-depth study in a difficult course? Do you need pretest meetings to exchange ideas? Specific goals help prospective members decide if their investments of time will serve their purposes.

6. *If possible, schedule regular group meetings at the same place and time.* Group members can plan accordingly if they know that their study group meets every Tuesday afternoon at 2:00. If the group meets less frequently, members may forget which week the group meets. If you meet at different locations, members may forget where to go.

7. *Get acquainted.* You will be investing a great deal of time and effort with these people. Although you don't need to know their life histories, you do need to know something about their level of ability in the course (have they had six chemistry courses and this is your first?), their current time commitments (do they have jobs, family, social, or other activities that affect the times at which they can and cannot meet?), and their expectations of the group. At the very least, you need to exchange names and phone numbers so that you can contact members in case of an emergency.

Application

Form a study group for this class. Establish a purpose for the group and set a schedule for out-of-class meetings. As a group, create a checklist or survey to help you get acquainted with each other. Include questions that help you determine if group members have similar academic interests and levels of dedication. Make copies and exchange your group's checklist or survey with other groups in the class. Compare and determine which features are most appropriate.

SUMMARY OF MAIN POINTS

1. Winning the game of higher education depends on your desire, determination for success, and academic goals. Your aptitudes, abilities, interests, needs, and values play a role in setting these goals.

2. Computing your grade point average is one way to track your goals.

3. Certain campus offices are essential to your academic progress and success: business office, financial aid office, admissions office, dean's office, library, career guidance and placement office, correspondence and extension division, and student health service.

4. Interactions with instructors and other students affect your academic success and personal satisfaction.

5. Factors that contribute to postsecondary success are important for all students but are especially important for nontraditional students.

6. Honest, careful reporting of learning traits helps you determine your learning strengths and weaknesses and become a more skilled player in the game of higher education.

VOCABULARY DEVELOPMENT
TERMINOLOGY: THE LANGUAGE OF COLLEGE COURSES

Winning the game of higher education involves setting your own goals, as well as meeting those that your institution sets for you. It means knowing the people who work, teach, live, and study at school with you. Most of all, higher education provides you with opportunities—to assess yourself, enhance current abilities, learn new ideas, and grow in ways you've never even thought of. These changes will necessitate changes in your vocabulary to accomodate the new ways in which you think and communicate. From *academic year* to *astronomy*, from *GPA* to *Greek affairs,* from *provost* to *political science,* from *residential housing* to *religion,* you'll encounter new terminology in the game of higher education.

Since words are the currency of thought, the more words you master, the richer become your thought processes.

—JOSEPH BELLAFIORE, 1968

Words are the medium of exchange for the subjects you study. Without them, you can neither buy new ideas nor spend them in the form of written or verbal transactions. Just as sound financing forms the basis of any business, a sound understanding of course vocabulary underlies the business of learning that subject.

Just as your profession affects the terminology you use, the language of the courses in which you enroll varies according to the course. Basically, college courses fall into four categories: humanities, social studies, sciences, and applied or technical courses (see Table 1). The kinds of terms you encounter and the way in which you meet them vary according to the course type.

Course vocabulary generally takes three forms: **technical vocabulary, specialized vocabulary,** and **general vocabulary** (see Table 2). Your mastery of the vocabulary in a specific course depends on your prior knowledge of the course's content, the stages of your vocabulary development, and the depth of understanding required by the course.

Your knowledge of a word can range from no knowledge to the ability to use the word. Edgar Dale (1958) theorized four progressive stages of vocabulary development (see Table 3). In stage one, you have no knowledge of the word's meaning. You only realize that the word you encounter is new. At the second stage, you believe that the word is one you've seen or heard. However, you possess no real knowledge of its meaning. In stage three, you associate the word with a very general concept. For example, suppose you encounter the word *Protista* in biology class. You associate it with classifications of life. Further, you believe it to be a fairly simple form of life. Beyond that general concept, you have no clear understanding. At stage four, you attain an understand-

TABLE 1   Academic Disciplines and Subjects of Study

Humanities

Art	English	Journalism
Music	Philosophy	Classical languages
Speech	Religion	Foreign languages

Natural Sciences

Biological	*Mathematical*	*Physical*
Biology	Computer science	Astronomy
Botany	Mathematics	Chemistry
Marine science		Geology
Microbiology		Physics
Zoology		Physical science

Social Sciences

Anthropology	History	Psychology
Economics	Sociology	Political science
Geography		

Technical or Applied

Engineering	Education	Allied health
Agriculture	Physical education	Social work
Business	ROTC	

TABLE 2   Course Vocabulary

Type	Description	Frequent College Contexts	Examples
Technical	Specific to the course	Science Applied/Technical	ion lactose
Specialized	General vocabulary used in new or unfamiliar ways	Humanities Social studies Science	base core cell family rotation
General	Common words unfamiliar to you	Humanities Social studies	euthanasia laconic icon collate

TABLE 3	Stages of Vocabulary Development
1. You know that a word is new to you. You have no prior knowledge of the word.	
2. You recognize a word but are unsure about its meaning or any general associations with it.	
3. You recognize a word but have only vague associations with general concepts.	
4. You recognize a word and can use it in the context of the course.	

ing of the word in terms of the course and the manner in which it used. You know that *Protista* is a kingdom of single-celled organisms of such diversity that they include both plants and animals.

Making an effort to stop and learn the terminology in a course affects the depth of your understanding of the course. One way to estimate your understanding of a course is to identify the levels at which you understand its terms. Such identifications serve several functions. First, when you identify a word that you don't know, you focus your attention on it. This increases your chance of knowing the word in later encounters. Then, by attempting to determine the meaning, you increase your recall through association and active learning. Finally, the more you relate terms and ideas, the more effective you are at making future associations.

Activity 1
Words Can Make You Rich!

An exercise used with high school and college students for a number of years with interesting reactions is included here. The tongue-in-cheek idea is that you may determine your salary level based on your age and the number of words you can identify correctly. The terms come from a wide field.

1. Did you see the *clergy?*   a. funeral b. dolphin c. churchmen d. monastery e. bell tower

2. Fine *louvers.*   a. doors b. radiators c. slatted vents d. mouldings e. bay windows

3. Like an *ellipse.*   a. sunspot b. oval c. satellite d. triangle e. volume

4. *Dire* thoughts.   a. angry b. dreadful c. blissful d. ugly e. unclean

5. It was the *affluence.*   a. flow rate b. pull c. wealth d. flood e. bankruptcy

6. Discussing the *acme.*   a. intersection b. question c. birthmark d. perfection e. low point

7. How *odious.*   a. burdensome b. lazy c. hateful d. attractive e. fragrant

8. This is *finite*.
a. limited b. tiny c. precise d. endless
e. difficult

9. Watch for the *inflection*.
a. accent b. mirror image c. swelling
d. pendulum swing e. violation

10. The *connubial* state.
a. marriage b. tribal c. festive d. spinsterly
e. primitive

11. See the *nuance*.
a. contrast b. upstart c. renewal d. delinquent
e. shading

12. Where is the *dryad*?
a. water sprite b. fern c. dish towel d. chord
e. wood nymph

13. Will you *garner* it?
a. dispose of b. store c. polish d. thresh
e. trim

14. A sort of *anchorite*.
a. religious service b. hermit c. marine deposit
d. mineral e. promoter

15. *Knurled* edges.
a. twisted b. weather beaten c. flattened
d. ridged e. knitted

16. Is it *bifurcated*?
a. forked b. hairy c. two-wheeled
d. mildewed e. joined

17. Examining the *phthisis*.
a. cell division b. medicine c. misstatement
d. dissertation e. tuberculosis

18. *Preponderance* of the group.
a. majority b. heaviness c. small number
d. foresight

19. Ready to *expound*.
a. pop b. confuse c. interpret d. dig up
e. imprison

20. Starting at the *relict*.
a. trustee b. antique table c. corpse d. widow
e. excavation

Now, based on your raw score, find your salary level.

Number Correct

Age 13–16		Age 17–20	
20–12	$40,000 and up	20–15	$40,000 and up
11–10	32,000–$40,000	14–13	32,000–$40,000
9– 8	28,000– 32,000	12–11	28,000– 32,000
7– 6	25,000– 28,000	10– 9	25,000– 28,000
5– 4	20,000– 25,000	8– 7	20,000– 25,000
3– 2	15,000– 20,000	6– 3	15,000– 20,000
Below 2	Under 15,000	Below 3	Under 15,000

	Age 21–29		Age 30 and up
20–17	$40,000 and up	20–19	$35,500 and up
16–15	32,000–$35,500	18–17	32,000–$35,500
14–13	28,000– 32,000	16–15	28,000– 32,000
12–11	25,000– 28,000	14–13	25,000– 28,000
10– 5	20,000– 25,000	12–11	20,000– 25,000
Below 5	Under 15,000	10– 7	15,000– 20,000
		Below 7	Under 15,000

Activity 2

On a separate sheet of paper, copy the list of terms from Sample Chapter 1 in this text and from any chapter from a course in which you are now enrolled. Identify which are specialized, technical, or general terms. Then based on Dale's ranking system, identify your level of knowledge of each.

CHAPTER REVIEW

1. Consider your aptitudes, abilities, interests, needs, and values. Which one(s) impact your choice of majors and/or careers most and why?

   _____

   _____

   _____

2. Refer to Figure 1.2, Flowchart of Career Development. Imagine that you are in the stage of exploration. Using your college catalog, identify five services, options, or courses that your institution offers that could help you crystallize your career choice.

   _____

   _____

   _____

3. Refer again to Figure 1.2, Flowchart of Career Development and your college catalog. What services, options, or courses would provide you with vicarious experiences in your area of interest? Which could provide actual experiences in your area of interest?

   _____

   _____

   _____

4. Identify five places where students work on your campus and the kinds of work experiences available through each one.

   _____

   _____

   _____

5. Identify five special interest groups available on your campus.

   _____

   _____

   _____

6. Identify and give a brief description of the purpose of five service organizations available on your campus.

   _____

   _____

   _____

7. Identify five social organizations available on your campus.

   _____

   _____

   _____

8. Identify the building in which the following offices are found on your campus:

   a. Admissions office (registrar's office or office of records and registration)

   _____

   b. Financial aid office

   _____

   c. Business office (bursar's office or office of the treasurer)

   _____

9. What things can a returning older student and an ESL student do to improve their chances for academic success?

   _____

   _____

10. Why is participation in extracurricular affairs important?

   _____

   _____

REFERENCES

Brunvand, J. H. (1989) *Curses! Broiled Again!* W. W. Norton & Co. New York.

Ginzberg, E.; Ginsberg, S. W.; Axelrad, S.; & Herma, J. L. (1951). *Occupational Choice: An Approach to a General Theory.* New York: Columbia University Press.

Haggard, M. R. (1986). "The Vocabulary Self-Collection Strategy: Using Student Interest and Word Knowledge to Enhance Vocabulary Growth." *Journal of Reading* 29: 634–642.

Knox, D. (1990). *Sociology.* St. Paul, MN: West Publishers.

Maslow, A. H. (1954). *Motivation and Personality.* New York: Harper.

CHAPTER

2 Time Management: Put Yourself to Work

OBJECTIVES

By the end of this chapter you will be able to do the following:

1. Construct a class schedule which provides structure while retaining flexibility.

2. Set goals which enable you to avoid procrastination.

3. Implement goals through term, weekly, and daily time management.

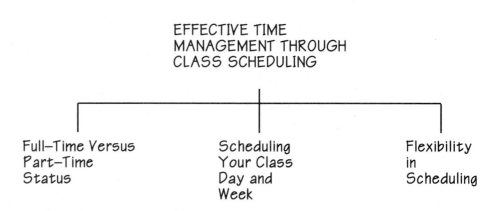

EFFECTIVE TIME
MANAGEMENT THROUGH
CLASS SCHEDULING

Full–Time Versus
Part–Time
Status

Scheduling
Your Class
Day and
Week

Flexibility
in
Scheduling

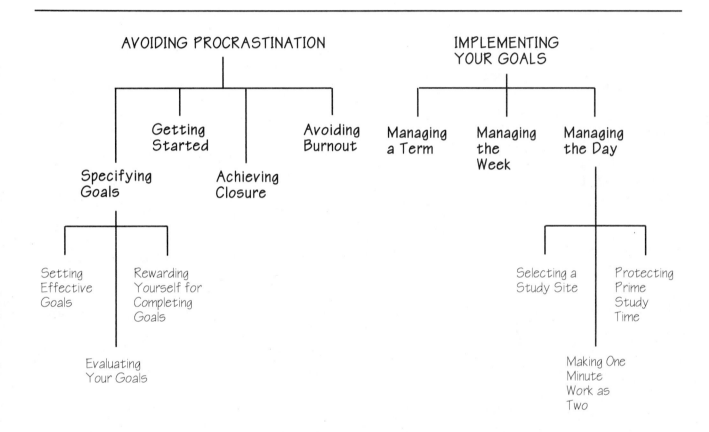

TERMS

behavior modification
burnout
closure
external motivation
full-time student
internal motivation
long-term goals
part-time student
peer pressure
prime study time
procrastination
rewards
schedule
short-term goals
time management

> HELP WANTED: Flexible hours. No supervision. Varied responsibilities. No experience necessary. Must be a self–starter. Apply at your POST–SECONDARY INSTITUTION, an equal opportunity employer.

EFFECTIVE TIME MANAGEMENT THROUGH CLASS SCHEDULING

Effective **time management** starts before a term begins. The way you organize your class **schedule** affects the success you achieve during the term. Your interests, physical and mental states, and abilities must be considered before scheduling classes.

FULL-TIME VERSUS PART-TIME STATUS

You have the choice of being a **full-time student** or a **part-time student.** Full-time enrollment usually means twelve or more hours in a quarter or semester system. This seems like a ridiculously short amount of time to be in class if you're used to a full-time 40-hour work week or a traditional high school schedule. The difference lies in where your work—in this case, your learning—is accomplished. Most high schools and employers expect you to work during class or on the job. In post-secondary education, most of the work you'll accomplish occurs on your own, after you leave the classroom. Some people say you should spend two hours out of class for every hour you are in class. Thus, for a fifteen-hour schedule, you spend thirty hours in study. Fifteen plus thirty equals forty-five hours per week, more than a full-time job. Of course, such estimates are just that—estimates. Perhaps you love math and finish an assignment in twenty minutes. On the other hand, you may be less proficient in English and spend six hours writing a two-page paper. The time you spend in learning must match your strengths and weaknesses, as well as your goals and priorities. Still, a full-time class schedule is generally a full-time job and should be approached in that manner.

Whether you enroll full time or not depends on your other commitments. If you work, have family responsibilities, or are involved in other fixed activities, then the number of courses you can successfully complete may be limited. Course difficulty also affects the total number of hours you schedule. If courses are less difficult, more can be scheduled. Another factor to consider is how experienced you are in a given subject or as a post-secondary student. A French course will be easier for students who have had previous course work in French or previous post-secondary experience.

SCHEDULING YOUR CLASS DAY AND WEEK

In the fifth century B.C., Solon, a wise lawmaker said, "Nothing in excess." That philosophy holds true for many experiences. Overwork leads to exhaustion. Overspending results in high bills. Too much food causes a stomachache. Even too much information is hard to digest at one time.

College classes often cause such information overloads. Because much of your learning occurs outside of class, the time you spend in class is especially valuable. Your professors may highlight only the most important concepts. They might elaborate on information found in assigned readings. They may shape and refine your understanding. They may focus on application, analysis, and synthesis of ideas. No matter how they approach their courses, they generally have one thing in common. They concentrate the information presented in class. The information you add through more reading, study, and thought dilutes it for your understanding. Because the concentration of information is so strong, packing idea upon idea often results in forgetfulness and confusion. After three classes in a row, you may find it hard to recall what occurred in the first. As a result, you spend additional time outside of class trying to figure out just what went on. Filling your class weeks and days often helps you solve information overload problems.

Some institutions schedule classes on alternating days so that a class meets two or three days per week. Some students think that by scheduling courses for only two or three days a week, they have time for concentrated study. Often this results in their being overworked and burned out on class days. They spend free days recuperating, rather than studying. If you do not work or have other fixed commitments, you should schedule your classes throughout the week.

A good schedule fills the day as well as the week. Time between classes gives you opportunities to consciously and subconsciously reflect on information. Reviewing information as soon as possible after class provides you with time to think through a lecture while the information is still fresh. Connections among information can be made before you have to go to another class and listen to another concentrated lecture.

Your most difficult courses should be scheduled during the times you are most alert. If you like getting up early, then morning is the time for your most difficult course. If you do your best work after lunch, then schedule your most difficult classes at this time. If you schedule classes on alternating days, consider the level of difficulty or your interest in that course. These factors affect the length of time you can concentrate. If you are very interested or the course is easy for you, then you can schedule it for longer time periods.

FLEXIBILITY IN SCHEDULING

The old adage "First things first" doesn't always apply to choosing your classes. Of course, certain courses must be taken in sequence. Some are prerequisites for courses that you'll need in the future. Few curricula, however, are completely rigid. Generally, the outline of courses in a catalog is just a suggested way to divide course work into years or terms (semesters or quarters), rather than a requirement. Thus, you have a great deal of flexibility in choosing when to take many of your courses.

While it would be wonderful if you liked and wanted to take every course in your curriculum, that is rarely the case. No matter what your major, you'll probably take some courses in which you feel you have little initial interest. In addition, based on your aptitudes and abilities, some courses will be more difficult for you than others. Too many difficult courses often overwhelm even the best students. Courses that you perceive as uninteresting may lead you to the conclusion that higher education as a whole is not worth the effort. Scheduling flexibility forms the solution to both problems. Your schedule should include courses that you look forward to attending, as well as those in which you have less interest. You should also balance difficult with easier course work.

Changes in your personal life can change your scheduling priorities. Perhaps you are an athlete. You may want to schedule more difficult classes during the terms in which your team is less active. Maybe you know that a family member will have surgery during a particular term so you adjust your schedule accordingly. You might have a job, hobby, or other interest with predictable highs and lows in effort during the year. You can accommodate such changes through flexible scheduling and thus affect how well you manage your time during the term.

Finally, flexibility in scheduling helps you choose from whom, as well as when, you will take a course. Interactions with faculty form one of the greatest benefits of a college career. Upper-class students often provide insights into who is considered to be the most outstanding teacher in the field. In addition, many student government associations monitor faculty performance and make the results available to students. These two sources provide you with views of how a professor is seen by other students. Once you decide whom you want for

a specific course, you must determine when that person teaches that course. Faculty courseloads vary by term. Although a specific instructor may or may not teach the same courses each term, course assignments are usually made a term, and sometimes a year, in advance. Thus, you can often find out when a specific person will be teaching and take advantage of the best that your institution has to offer.

AVOIDING PROCRASTINATION

If once a man indulge himself in murder, very soon he comes to think little of robbing; and from robbing he next comes to drinking, and Sabbath-breaking, and from that to incivility and procrastination.

—THOMAS DE QUINCEY
English author

How serious is the "crime" of **procrastination** (putting off activities until later)? The truth is that everybody—at one time or another—procrastinates on a project and feels guilty as a result. The question, then, is not "Do you procrastinate?" The question is, "What is your motive?"

Students—and others—procrastinate for a variety of reasons. One of the most common misconceptions about procrastination is that it is caused by laziness. Generally, if you've had enough drive and ambition to get to a post-secondary institution, laziness is not your problem.

Karen Coltharp of Louisiana State University describes procrastination based on Eric Berne's (1966) concept of transactional analysis. Coltharp suggests that you function in one of three modes: child, critic, or adult. The child is the part of ourselves that wants to have fun and have it now. When the child within you gains control, you avoid those tasks that seem dull, boring, or too difficult.

The inner voice of the critic causes you to doubt your abilities, goals, and yourself. The critic prophesies failure at every turn. The critic says that a task is too difficult for you or that you don't have the right background, experience, or intelligence to get the job accomplished. With such encouragement, why even try? Procrastination results.

The adult in you provides the voice of reason and logic. The adult knows that some tasks are no fun but that they must be completed. The adult then musters the internal motivation to begin dull and distasteful tasks and see them through. The adult must also be able to outtalk the inner critic in a stronger voice. "Yes, this is difficult, but

I've been successful before." "I lack experience in this particular area, but I have similar experiences upon which I can draw." "I don't have the right background, but I can learn it." "Others have been successful, and I can be, too."

Functioning in the role of the child, the critic, or the adult affects the way you work, as well as the ways in which you perceive problems. The child's primary behavior is lack of productive activity. Conversing with friends, partying, and doing other leisure activities prevent the child from ever getting to the business at hand. Worry is the critic's chief activity. Instead of studying, the critic worries about studying. This includes such self-questioning as "Can I learn this? What if I don't? If I don't, I may fail. What if I fail? What will I do?" and "What will other people think?" Problem-solving is the adult's forte. When the adult must study, the adult thinks, "What do I have to learn? What would be the best way to learn this? Am I learning it? If not, how can I rethink my understanding?"

Finally, the adult may appear to procrastinate at times. Weighing priorities and making choices about when and what to accomplish may seem like procrastination. The difference is in the motive. If your reasoning for putting off something is sound and appropriate, it may be the best plan of action. For example, you may be considering whether or not to drop a course after the first month of class. You've regularly attended class, and you have a good grade in it. However, your financial status indicates that you need to increase your work hours. Logically, you decide that you cannot do justice to the course and work more hours. What appears to be procrastination is actually a logical decision based on the reality of the situation.

EXCERPT 2.1   Overcoming the Deadline Dodge   by Barbara Smalley

- George, a junior at Queens College, rarely takes tests on time. Instead he invents a different excuse for each exam and begs for a second chance.

- Jim, a graduate student at the University of California at Berkeley, hasn't been seen on campus for months. "I'm avoiding my adviser," he explains, "because of all the outstanding commitments to him that I have."

- Kevin, a recent graduate of the City University of New York, is washing dishes because he has postponed making a career choice. "I always thought choosing a career would just happen, and I was having too much fun in school to think about it. One of these days I'll take a career-planning seminar," he vows.

Sound familiar? After teaching and counseling students for more than a decade, William Knaus, psychologist and author of *Do It Now: How to Stop Procrastinating*, estimates that a whopping 95 percent of college students put things off to some degree. And of that number, he says, some 25 percent are *chronic* procrastinators. "These are the ones who end up dropping out. Others finish school but begin postponing assignments when they're out on their own and no longer have the structure of college to rely on."

Procrastination on campus usually means that you delay doing a task that you have agreed to complete. Although the casual procrastinator postpones tasks *sporadically* and the chronic one does so *habitually,* Knaus points out that the differences between the two are not just a matter of degree. "Hard-core procrastinators usually have anxiety problems, may be depressed, or may suffer from acute self-doubt." And though casual delayers may start by putting off tasks now and then, many soon find themselves with a serious procrastination problem. "It's like being on a vicious merry-go-round," he explains, "because postponing tasks, even occasionally, can cause anxiety, self-doubt, and depression, which in turn provide the victim with even greater reasons to procrastinate."

Why You Put Off Projects

Procrastination can be remedied, but the cure often lies in first figuring out exactly why you are unable to complete your projects on time.

Are you just plain afraid?

Fear and anxiety cause many students to dodge deadlines. "Ask me to give a speech, and I'll do fine," says Luann Culbreth, a graduate student at Georgia State University, "but I'm so intimidated by grammar that I can't seem to get started on a writing assignment."

Actually, procrastinators often spend more time worrying about tasks than they would actually use completing them, reports Knaus. Thus the trick to breaking through the anxiety barrier is to stop worrying and start working. Practicing Knaus's "five-minute plan" is a good way to begin. It requires that you commit five minutes to a task that you have been putting off. When the time is up, decide if you can handle another five minutes of it. Chances are that you will have built up enough momentum to forge ahead.

Do you feel overwhelmed?

You have to take a biology test, turn in a history paper, and give a speech during the same week, but you are so behind that you don't know where to begin. Knaus advises setting mini-goals and deadlines for each project. "The satisfaction of accomplishing each small step should keep you going." The same principle holds if you are faced with a single but colossal project. First slice the task into more manageable pieces, then set up a schedule of clear and achievable goals.

Are you a perfectionist?

Surprisingly, perfectionists are especially vulnerable to procrastination. "They are terrified of getting anything less than 100 percent, because the tiniest flaw means an entire assignment is no good," claims Dr. David Burns, author of *Feeling Good: The New Mood Therapy* and *Intimate Connections.* Some perfectionists have trouble starting projects because they have set impossibly high standards. (Their rationale: "If I don't start, I can't fail.") Others refuse to recognize when a task is complete.

Burns concedes that if you are a perfectionist, you may require counseling to change, but he suggests that you try this introspective exercise in an attempt to do so on your own: "Make a list of the pros and cons of behaving flawlessly. Though there may be some pluses to being perfect, those are likely to be outweighed by a host of disadvantages that prevent you from growing and experimenting both with your schoolwork and in your personal life." The standards you have set for yourself, after all, are *guidelines* and not absolutes.

Are you unable to concentrate?

The environment in which you work can have an enormous effect on both your attitude and your productivity. Thus it pays to analyze *where* you typically study. "Students who work on cluttered desks and in areas open to a mass of interruptions are particularly prone to procrastination," says Knaus. He suggests that you choose a quiet workplace with room to spread out, stock it with reference materials you use regularly, and spend a few minutes setting goals. "Most people don't want to waste time getting organized, but spending 10 to 15 minutes a day doing so will save you hours of frustration later."

Do you feel indecisive?

Sometimes an uncertainty about your major or a strong desire to do something other than attend college can cause apathy, indecisiveness, and in turn, procrastination. When offered a one-month professional directing job, Natasha Shishkevish quit school 11 credits short of receiving her theater degree from Towson State University. "I fully intended to resume my studies afterward, but I just never got around to it."

Shishkevish has since held enough low-paying and unchallenging jobs to motivate her to return to college. "I'm finally happy with my career choice, and now that I've seen what work is like, I think I can discipline myself to do well in school."

But the transition between college and career may not be that easy for those whose habitual tardiness stems from a desire to be noticed. "I get more attention from professors when I have an excuse for being *late* with assignments than I do when I turn them in on time," admits one student. Although professors who accept excuses from students are merely reinforcing such behavior, students who squeak by on professorial pardons in school won't function well on the job. "Unless a company rides on you and your abilities," reports Knaus, "it simply won't put up with procrastination that causes a work slowdown."

When Postponing Isn't a Problem

Because setting priorities requires postponing activities and assignments, in some cases procrastination makes sense. "If you truly work better in spurts of massed time," admits Knaus, "holding off to do a term paper in the last week of a semester may work fine. Or if you forget things quickly, last-minute cramming rather than studying for days or weeks in advance of an exam may save you time and trouble."

How then can you tell when your stalling is "legit?" Knaus advises that you learn the difference between procrastination and a "strategic delay." Kim Bogert, for example, has purposefully put off taking freshman English in her first year at Northern Virginia Community College. "It's my worst subject," she explains, "and knowing that adjusting to college would be difficult in itself, I figured, why add more pressure up front?"

Because Bogert's postponement is not a cover-up for something like a fear of failure, Knaus believes her actions qualify as a sound strategy. "In each case you need to apply the definition of procrastination—putting off a relevant activity that *can* be and properly *should* be done today," he says. "Also, since most procrastinators tend to be self-cons, you should always be on the alert for irrational excuses."

New York career counselor and management consultant Janice LaRouche provides another clue. "Procrastination is a problem when you know you'll end up paying a high price as a result." For some, experiencing feelings of guilt for turning in mediocre work is too costly; others balk at receiving "incomplete" or failing grades.

Help Is on the Way

If you're prone to needless procrastination, psychologists and counselors suggest practicing these techniques:

- *Pinpoint where your delays typically start.* "Most procrastinators follow a pattern," Knaus reveals. Determine whether you put off beginning a project, fizzle out at the halfway point, or fade in the homestretch. After examining your behavior, become totally committed to altering it.

- *Discipline yourself to use your time wisely.* "Procrastinators are very bad at telling time," says Dr. Richard Beery, a procrastination workshop leader at the University of California at Berkeley. Most underestimate the time it takes to complete an assignment. Successful time management involves setting realistic deadlines, allowing extra hours for the unexpected, learning to use bits of time, and sticking steadfastly to your timetable.

- *Set priorities by making a list.* Force yourself to devote most of your efforts to the number-one task on that list. "Most procrastinators go to the bottom of the list," claims Knaus. "They'll have a history test and study biology instead."

- *Set a deadline and ask someone to hold you accountable for it.* In tight situations, promise to give up something meaningful if you fail to meet your goal. Pledging your front-row concert tickets to your roommate, for instance, might bring newfound motivation.

- *Beware of the inaction-exertion-inaction cycle.* Don't postpone a task and then become so immersed in playing catch-up that you become burned out and postpone your next assignment. Alternate periods of work with stretches of rest and recreation to prevent this vicious circle.

- *Don't wait until you finish a project to reward yourself.* "Most procrastinators value only the finished product," says Dr. Beery. "People need to realize that intermediate steps are also accomplishments."

MOST IMPORTANT, says Knaus, procrastinators must learn that it's *not* terrible to feel uncomfortable. "There are a lot of unpleasant things in life that must be done," he stresses. "The more people are willing to tackle those tasks, the more those jobs become less bothersome—and more routine."

SOURCE: Smalley, Barbara S. (1985, December–January). "Overcoming the Deadline Dodge." *Campus Voice*, pp. 55–56.

SPECIFYING GOALS

Lack of clear, specific goals is often a hidden cause of procrastination. If you are not sure of what your goals are, you will have little reason for beginning and completing a project. Goal interference also can causes you to neglect important tasks. If you become so involved in the process of working on an assignment, you may forget other due dates and important commitments.

A successful business principle also works during study time. That principle involves setting objectives or goals and then allocating time to complete them on schedule. This business principle is a management plan.

Setting Effective Goals

Management plans are organized from large to small commitments and from **long-term goals** to **short-term goals.** Long-term goals usually extend through a semester (for example, making the dean's list, completing all assignments on schedule) or even through an academic career (for example, finishing with a B average). Short-term goals usually span a day or a week (for example, writing an English paper or reading an assigned text). You usually use them to reach long-term goals. Setting achievable goals is no easy task. To be useful, a goal must describe specific measurable outcomes. Your goals need to measure observable, concrete facts, rather than your good intentions. Specific deadlines help you meet your goals and thus avoid procrastination. They offer you the inspiration to get to work.

Consider the following goals:

- **Study harder.**

- **Attend class more regularly.**

- **Take better notes in class.**

Such goals are too abstract to be useful. You have no way of knowing if and when you achieve them. You make these goals achievable by adding measurable outcomes and deadlines as follows:

- **Raise my grade point average by 0.2 by the end of the semester.**

- **Attend class each time it meets for the next quarter.**

- **Attend a note-taking seminar this term.**

Finally, your goals are best when they depend on you alone. "Practice vocal music twice a week with a quartet of singers" and "Complete assigned lab experiments with a partner" sound like achievable goals. However, because they rely on others' actions (and inactions), your goals may be sabotaged when others fail to do their parts or do not show up.

To know if a goal is achievable, ask the following questions:

- **How will I know if I attain this goal?**
- **When will I attain this goal?**
- **On whom do I depend to complete this goal?**

Evaluating Your Goals

Evaluation helps you determine where you may have gone wrong and how you can improve future goal-setting. To do this, ask the following questions:

- **What obstacles delayed the accomplishment of this goal?**
- **Who or what was responsible for these obstacles?**
- **How can these obstacles be eliminated in the future?**

EXERCISE 2.1   Use this key to describe each goal on the following page. If a goal is **not** satisfactory, more than one letter may apply. Then list five goals of your own and evaluate them.

    S—Satisfactory goal
    M—Measurable outcomes lacking
    D—Deadline lacking
    O—Others needed to achieve goal

_____ **1.** Define each biology term by the first exam.

_____ **2.** Know all math formulas by the end of next month.

_____ **3.** Appreciate art more fully as the result of visiting an art gallery.

_____ **4.** Identify the handouts that will be covered on the final exam by Tuesday.

_____ **5.** Learn more about construction engineering.

_____ **6.** Become a better reader.

_____ **7.** Improve my English grade by one quality point by participating in a group study project before the end of the term.

_____ **8.** Complete all assigned history readings by next Wednesday.

_____ **9.** Read geography notes immediately following each class in order to make additions and corrections.

_____ **10.** Improve my tennis grade by ten points from midterm to final by practicing with another student three days per week for the rest of the quarter.

_____ **11.** _____

_____

_____

_____ **12.** _____

_____

_____

_____ **13.** _____

_____

_____

_____ **14.** _____

_____

_____

_____ **15.** _____

_____

_____

_____

_____

Rewarding Yourself for Completing Goals

Imagine the following: You stand in a line in the rain for several hours. You pay money for the privilege of pushing your way into a crowded room. For the next two hours, you hear loud sounds and screams. It takes you twice as long as usual to get home because of traffic jams. Would you undergo such an experience? Yes, if the event were a concert you really wanted to attend. What makes you undertake such hardships? Motivation, either internal or external. Procrastination often results from a lack of motivation to complete a goal.

Motivation is an extension of the needs described by Maslow's hierarchy (See Chapter 1). Motivation at each level is based on an internal and/or external reward structure (see Table 2.1).

Internal motivation comes from within you. It is your desire to accomplish a task. It is more powerful than other forms of motivation. Perhaps your goal is to graduate and attend law school. The good grades you get when you finish a project affect your grade point average. Higher grades improve your chances of getting into law school. Internal motivation, then, corresponds to Maslow's levels of self-esteem or self-actualization.

TABLE 2.1   Internal and External Rewards in Terms of Maslow's Hierarchy.

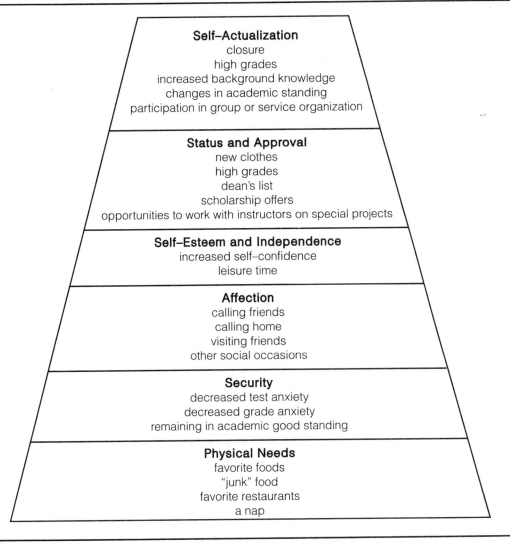

Self–Actualization
closure
high grades
increased background knowledge
changes in academic standing
participation in group or service organization

Status and Approval
new clothes
high grades
dean's list
scholarship offers
opportunities to work with instructors on special projects

Self–Esteem and Independence
increased self–confidence
leisure time

Affection
calling friends
calling home
visiting friends
other social occasions

Security
decreased test anxiety
decreased grade anxiety
remaining in academic good standing

Physical Needs
favorite foods
"junk" food
favorite restaurants
a nap

But what if you're not interested in attending the previously described concert? You may attend to please a date or other friend. Responding to **external motivation** is working for a reason other than yourself. Responding to such needs and desires of others corresponds to Maslow's levels of approval or affection. You might also devise artificial reasons for completing your goals. These might range from getting a candy bar for completing a math assignment to a new car for finishing your degree. These correspond to Maslow's lower physical and security needs.

Behavior modification is one way to use external motivation in the form of **rewards.** To be effective, the reward should be something you really enjoy or want (for example, an ice cream cone, a movie, a walk). Thus, you substitute desire for the reward for the dread of the task. However, the reward needs to fit the task. For example, if you have a five hundred-page novel to read for English, your reward should be great enough to make yourself complete the book (for example, a movie). If your task is to summarize a three-page article, an ice cream cone may be sufficient.

Other types of external motivation include **peer pressure** and punishment. By telling a friend you plan to accomplish a certain task by a certain time, you pressure yourself to perform. If you do not complete the task, you face your friend's disapproval, as well as your own. A final form of external motivation is punishment. Here, you take privileges (for example, going out with friends, having dessert, attending a ball game) from yourself if you fail to finish a task. This form of external motivation is generally ineffective and is not recommended. Unless you're a masochist, you won't punish yourself.

EXERCISE 2.2   Decide whether each of the following tasks is a short- or long-term goal. Identify an appropriate reward for each task. Indicate whether the reward is external or internal. Then identify five tasks that you need to complete. Identify an appropriate reward for each task. Indicate whether the reward is external or internal.

Task	Short/Long Term Goal	Reward	Internal/External Motivation
1. Read six chapters for a history assignment	_____	_____	_____
2. Make the dean's list	_____	_____	_____
3. Attend a classical concert for extra credit in Music Appreciation	_____	_____	_____
4. Complete half of a math assignment	_____	_____	_____
5. Complete the research for a twenty-page paper for psychology class	_____	_____	_____

Your Tasks

1. _____	_____	_____	_____
2. _____	_____	_____	_____
3. _____	_____	_____	_____
4. _____	_____	_____	_____
5. _____	_____	_____	_____

GETTING STARTED

Sometimes it is hard to get started on a project or an assignment, and this leads to procrastination. This problem surfaces in several ways, and each way requires its own solution. First, if a project seems too large or complex, you should cut it down to size. For example, you might have to design a school as a project for an architecture class. As a whole, the project might overwhelm you until you divide it into manageable parts. This might consist of researching the needs of the school, determining the price limitations, drawing a bubble diagram, and so on. In other words, use time management to locate the overall goal of the project and the steps needed to complete it. Second, you may not think of yourself as good at thinking of ideas for creative assignments (like speeches, and English themes). Brainstorming with others, asking your instructor for suggestions, or researching several topics to find one of interest often solves this problem. A final reason for procrastination is that the assignment may be beyond your skills in the subject. This occurs for any one of several reasons. You may have been ill or absent from class. Your high school preparation in the subject may have been inadequate. In any case, you can cope with this lack in skills by going to the campus learning lab, arranging for tutoring, or contacting your instructor.

EXERCISE 2.3   Think of the last major assignment you completed. List below any problems you faced getting started, how you solved these problems, and other solutions you could use in the future when similar problems arise.

Type of assignment: _____

Problems getting started: _____

_____

_____

_____

_____

_____

Solutions: _____

_____

_____

_____

_____

_____

_____

_____

Other alternatives: _____

_____

_____

_____

_____

_____

ACHIEVING CLOSURE

Closure is the positive feeling you get when you finish a task. Lack of closure results in the panicked feeling that you still have a million things to do.

"I think Harry's taking this concept of closure too literally."

One way to obtain closure is to divide a task into manageable goals, list them, and check them off your list as you finish them. For example, suppose your history teacher assigns three chapters to be read. If your goal is to read all three chapters, you may feel discouraged if you don't complete the reading at one time. A more effective way to complete the assignment is to divide the reading into smaller goals by thinking of each chapter as a separate goal. Thus, you experience success as you complete each chapter. Although you failed to complete the overall goal, you know you've progressed toward it.

A second block to obtaining closure is unfinished business. You may have several tasks with the same deadline. Although changing from one task to another serves as a break, changing tasks too often wastes time. Each time you switch, you lose momentum. You may be unable to change mental gears fast enough. You may find yourself thinking about the old project when you should be concentrating on the new one. In addition, when you return to your first task, you have to review where you were and what steps were left for you to finish.

Often you solve this problem by determining how much time you have free to work. If the time available is short (that is, an hour or less), you need to work on only one task. Alternate tasks when you have more time. Completing one task or a large portion of a task contributes to the feeling of closure.

Sometimes, when working on a long-term project, other tasks take precedence before the first one is completed. If this occurs, take time to write a few notes before moving on to the new task. Your notes could include the goal of the task and a list of questions to be answered or objectives to be completed. References, papers, and other materials concerning the task should be stored together, so you know where to begin when you return to it.

WRITE TO LEARN

"25 or 6 to 4"

Waiting for the break of day,
Searching for something to say,
Flashing lights against the sky,
Giving up, I close my eyes.
Sitting cross-legged on the floor,
Twenty five or six to four.
Staring blindly into space,
Getting up to splash my face,
Wanting just to stay awake,
Wondering how much I can take.
Should I try to do some more,
Twenty five or six to four.
Feeling like I ought to sleep,
Spinning room is sinking deep,
Waiting for the break of day,
Searching for something to say,
Twenty five or six to four;
Twenty five or six to four.
                              —ROBERT LAMM
Copyright © 1970 Lamminations Music
and Aurelius Music. Printed with
permission. All rights reserved.

Robert Lamm's song "25 or 6 to 4" tells of the plight of a person facing a deadline for writing music lyrics. The narrator faces a dilemma common to many college students. Should he continue working? Should he give up and get some sleep? Working against the clock often results from poor time management. Effective time management usually prevents a last-minute race with deadlines.

On a separate sheet of paper, write a song or poem similar to "25 or 6 to 4" describing a situation in which you are writing a paper or studying for a test. Include information on procrastination, motivation, and closure.

AVOIDING BURNOUT

Sometimes you procrastinate because you are burned out. **Burnout** results when you work without breaks. Burnout is unusual because its causes are the same as its symptoms. Fatigue, boredom, and stress are all signs of burnout.

A balance between break time and work time helps you avoid burnout. Therefore, you need to plan for breaks, as well as study

"Another classic case of student burnout."

time. A break does not have to be recreational. It simply can be a change from one task to another. For example, switching from working math problems to reading a book for English relieves boredom. Such planning also decreases interruptions during prime study time.

Another way to avoid burnout is to leave flexibility in your daily schedule. If you schedule commitments too tightly, you won't complete your goals and achieve closure. This defeats you psychologically because you fail to do what you planned.

IMPLEMENTING YOUR GOALS

Examine the figure below. It contains the numbers one through eighty. Giving yourself one minute, circle in numerical order as many numbers as you can.

76	4	48	28	64	5	77	33	53	45
56	32	16	44	72	17	37	69	29	1
20	36	8	24	52	21	61	13	57	49
68	60	12	80	40	9	41	65	25	73
3	67	47	79	23	70	22	38	14	54
19	31	55	51	71	6	62	2	46	50
59	7	63	27	39	74	10	42	66	26
35	75	15	43	11	78	18	34	30	58

How many numbers did you circle?

Now examine the figure below. It is the same as the preceding figure except that it has been divided into four quadrants. The number *1* can be found in the upper right quadrant, the number *2* in the lower right, the number *3* in the lower left, the number *4* in the upper left, and so on.

Now, giving yourself one minute, circle in numerical order as many numbers as you can.

76	4	48	28	64	5	77	33	53	45
56	32	16	44	72	17	37	69	29	1
20	36	8	24	52	21	61	13	57	49
68	60	12	80	40	9	41	65	25	73
3	67	47	79	23	70	22	38	14	54
19	31	55	51	71	6	62	2	46	50
59	7	63	27	39	74	10	42	66	26
35	75	15	43	11	78	18	34	30	58

How many numbers did you circle?

Knowing the plan in which the numbers are arranged aided you in your second attempt. Having a plan and implementing it is equally important in managing a term, a week, or a day.

MANAGING A TERM

The first thing to do to manage a school term is to get a calendar for the months during that term and a college catalog. The purpose of setting up this calendar is to get an overview of long-term goals and commitments. This aids you in planning your short-term and daily activities. Your calendar should include recreational as well as serious commitments. Table 2.2 provides steps for constructing a term calendar.

TABLE 2.2   Steps in Completing a Term Calendar

1. Obtain a college catalog for the current term, a monthly calendar, and course outlines.

2. Use the catalog to do the following:
   a. Record any holidays, school vacations, or social commitments.
   b. Record mid-term and final exam dates.
   c. Record dates for dropping and adding courses, and so on.

3. Use your course outlines to complete the following:
   a. Record test dates.
   b. Record due dates for papers or other projects.
   c. Set up deadlines for completing phases of lengthy projects.

4. Record important extracurricular and recreational events (for example, athletic events, concerts).

EXERCISE 2.4   Using a calendar for this year, label the months and days for the term in which you are currently enrolled on the following blank calendars. Using the process outlined in Table 2.2, construct a term calendar.

MONDAY	TUESDAY	WEDNESDAY	THURSDAY	FRIDAY	SAT/SUN

Month of _____

MONDAY	TUESDAY	WEDNESDAY	THURSDAY	FRIDAY	SAT/SUN

Month of _____

MONDAY	TUESDAY	WEDNESDAY	THURSDAY	FRIDAY	SAT/SUN

Month of _____

MONDAY	TUESDAY	WEDNESDAY	THURSDAY	FRIDAY	SAT/SUN

Month of _____

MONDAY	TUESDAY	WEDNESDAY	THURSDAY	FRIDAY	SAT/SUN

Month of _____

MANAGING THE WEEK

The span of time covered by a term calendar makes it unwieldy to use on a weekly or day-to-day basis. Thus, you need to review your commitments on a weekly basis. This helps you form weekly plans for managing the term.

A weekly plan consists of a weekly calendar of events and a daily "To Do" list. As a student, you have much to remember: course information, due dates for assignments, class meetings, appointments, and so on. Your weekly calendar of events helps you keep track of your fixed commitments. It also helps you find the most important items to record on your "To Do" list. Table 2.3 helps you set up your weekly calendar.

MANAGING THE DAY

In managing the day, you attempt to add hours through effective time management. After you complete your weekly calendar, construct a "To Do" list. Then organize your goals for each day. You need to remember two things when setting up your daily schedule. The first is that you don't have to plan each minute of each hour of each day. The second is that you don't have to stick to your schedule

TABLE 2.3   Steps in Constructing a Weekly Calendar

1. List fixed commitments first. This includes classes, meals, sleep, travel time to class, and so on. Allow a realistic amount of time for each activity. For example, daily travel times differ according to time of day, amount of traffic, and route taken. The time it takes to get to campus during rush hour may be very different from the time it takes to get home in the middle of the afternoon.

2. Set aside a few minutes before each class to review your notes and preview that day's topic. Leave a few minutes following each class to correct and add to your notes.

3. Identify blocks of free time.

4. Look for ways to group activities and schedule these in the blocks of free time. For example, if you have two papers to write, you can complete all your library work at once and avoid making two trips.

5. Plan to complete activities before the due date to allow for unexpected delays.

6. Schedule recreational breaks.

7. Schedule time for studying. Two hours of out-of-class study for every hour of in-class time is often advised. However, this rule varies according to your expertise in the subject and the course demands of the subject. Scheduling this much study time may be difficult for someone who works full-time and/or has family commitments. If you are such a student, you need to be careful not to overburden yourself. If you see you don't have enough time, you may need to drop one or more classes.

like glue. Be reasonable. Allow yourself the flexibility to relax and enjoy life.

Your items on the "To Do" list consist of that day's commitments transferred from your weekly calendar and any items left over from the previous day. You add other items as you think of them. Your next step is to rank the items on your "To Do" list by numbering each item in order of its importance. Chances are you won't get to the end of your "To Do" list by the end of the day. That's okay. If you placed your commitments in their order of importance, then you finished the most important goals first. To obtain closure, at the end of each day update that day's "To Do" list and construct a new list for the next day.

EXERCISE 2.5   List the courses you want to take next term and plan a schedule.

	SUN	MON	TUES	WED	THUR	FRI	SAT
6–7							
7–8							
8–9							
9–10							
10–11							
11–NOON							
NOON–1							
1–2							
2–3							
3–4							
4–5							
5–6							
6–7							
7–8							
8–9							
9–10							
10–11							
11–MIDNIGHT							
MIDNIGHT–1							
1–2							
2–3							
3–4							
4–5							
5–6							

	SUN	**MON**	**TUES**	**WED**	**THUR**	**FRI**	**SAT**
6–7							
7–8							
8–9							
9–10							
10–11							
11–NOON							
NOON–1							
1–2							
2–3							
3–4							
4–5							
5–6							
6–7							
7–8							
8–9							
9–10							
10–11							
11–MIDNIGHT							
MIDNIGHT–1							
1–2							
2–3							
3–4							
4–5							
5–6							

Weekly Planner   Week beginning _____

MONDAY _____
AM _____
_____
_____

Noon _____
_____
_____
_____

PM _____
_____
_____
_____

TUESDAY _____
AM _____
_____
_____

Noon _____
_____
_____
_____

PM _____
_____
_____
_____

WEDNESDAY _____
AM _____
_____
_____

Noon _____
_____
_____
_____

PM _____
_____
_____
_____

THURSDAY _____
AM _____
_____
_____

Noon _____
_____
_____
_____

PM _____
_____
_____
_____

FRIDAY _____
AM _____
_____
_____

Noon _____
_____
_____
_____

PM _____
_____
_____
_____

SATURDAY   **SUNDAY** _____
AM _____   _____
_____   _____
_____   _____
_____   _____

Noon _____   _____
_____   _____
_____   _____
_____   _____

PM _____   _____
_____   _____
_____   _____
_____   _____

TO DO

Protecting Prime Study Time

Prime study time is the time of the day when you are at your best for learning and remembering. This time differs from person to person. Your best time may be early in the morning, or you may learn more easily in the afternoon or at night. You determine your prime study time by observing when you get the most accomplished, when your studying results in higher grades, or when you feel most alert and able to concentrate.

Your best time of the day should be spent either in your hardest classes or on the class work that is more important or requires the most effort. Working on the hardest or most urgent task first allows you to work on that problem when you are most alert and fresh. Your one or two most important assignments should be scheduled for this time. By completing the hardest task first, one built-in reward is that you soon get to do an easier task.

Threats to prime time include mental distractions. You may find yourself thinking of other tasks you need to do. If so, keep a pad and

pen handy to make a list of your concerns as you think of them. By doing so, you literally put your problems aside until you are free to think about them. If you find yourself daydreaming, force your mind back to the task at hand.

Physical needs also affect prime study time. If you are too hungry or too full, concentration may be affected. If this occurs, you need to study at a different time. Fatigue is another factor that hinders study. A short nap often restores your stamina and memory. In addition, a well-balanced schedule that provides adequate time for sleep or rest limits fatigue.

Some threats to prime study time are less easily controlled. For example, you may find it difficult to rid yourself of friends concerned with your social life. All too often invitations to go out with the gang come at prime study times. The solution, although simple, is a hard one to implement. It involves saying "no" in such a way that you offend no one but make your point clear. Sometimes it's easier just to be unavailable. Taking the phone off the hook or closing the door to your room limits your availability. Another way to solve this problem is to hang a "Do Not Disturb" sign on your door. You can get one from a motel (usually free of charge), buy one at a card or stationery store, or make your own. A final option is to hide in the library or some other out-of-the-way place. Remember you will probably never rid yourself of all interruptions during prime study time, but you can reduce them.

Selecting a Study Site

Managing your day involves more than recognizing your best time of day. You must also manage your surroundings to maximize your study time.

The first thing you do is choose a place to study. Where you study needs to be environmentally comfortable. The temperature, furniture, and lighting should match your physical needs. If they don't, these factors will affect the quality of your work.

Where you study also should be free of distractions. It should be conducive to work, not relaxation or fun. For example, you may think the student center or your living room is a good place to review. However, if remembering information—not talking to others or watching TV—is your goal, you may be disappointed with the amount you recall later. In addition, the place you study should not hinder your alertness. Studying in bed may be comfortable but make you sleepy. Using music or television as a background for study sometimes affects your recall. If you find yourself singing along with a song or a television commercial, then your concentration leaves something to be desired.

The place you study should be free of clutter but should contain all the materials you need. Clutter affects your concentration because your eyes are drawn away from your notes. It also results in your feeling disorganized and overwhelmed. Your desktop should contain what you are studying, and nothing else. You need to distinguish between clutter and essentials, such as your text, notes, and so on. All study materials should be organized and within reach to make the best use of your prime study time.

Making One Minute Work as Two

On any one day, you may find yourself with spare minutes before you attack your next major goal. You might be waiting for the library to open, for class to begin, or for the bus to come. These spare minutes seem few when looked at separately. But when you add them up, they total more time than you would guess. Because you can't squeeze these minutes together, you need to do the next best thing. You need to develop a "quick-fix" for your free time. Table 2.4 lists some quick fixes for five-, fifteen-, and thirty-minute time periods. Once you get the idea, you'll think of others.

EXERCISE 2.7   Answer briefly but completely. Then categorize each one as five-, ten-, or fifteen-minute fixes.

1. List three times you have available for quick fixes.

   _____

   _____

   _____

   _____

2. Identify several tasks you can accomplish during these times.

_____

_____

_____

_____

_____

_____

_____

_____

_____

WRITE TO LEARN

Your younger brother is a junior in high school. He almost never completes assignments on time and crams for most of his exams. You think the information you've learned about managing a term and day could benefit him. On a separate sheet of paper, explain what suggestions you would give him for getting organized.

TABLE 2.4   Quick Fixes for 5-, 15-, and 30-Minute Time Periods

If you have a spare five minutes, you can:
   Review notes.
   Update your schedule or calendar.
   Skim newspaper headlines.
   Make a telephone call.
   Do a few sit-ups or other exercises.

If you have a spare fifteen minutes, you can:
   Straighten a room.
   Pay bills.
   Take a walk to relax.
   Survey a chapter.
   Read a magazine.

If you have a spare thirty minutes, you can:
   Run errands.
   Begin initial library research.
   Go to the grocery store.
   Brainstorm and/or outline a paper.
   Write a letter.

GROUP LEARNING ACTIVITY
BILL OF RIGHTS FOR GROUP MEMBERS

Time management strategies make or break study groups. Indefinite goals contribute to group, as well as individual, procrastination. Although the group should have a long-range purpose, it should have effective short-term goals that result in feelings of accomplishment and closure. The following bill of rights for group members requires commitment of both time and effort on the part of each person.

Bill of Rights for Study Groups

1. You have the right to limit group membership to no more than five and to dismiss members who consistently fail to meet their commitments as group members.

2. You have the right and responsibility to select a study site and time that are mutually beneficial to all members.

3. You have a right to contribute to the formation of group goals that have measurable outcomes and deadlines.

4. You have the responsibility to be an active participant, not a passive receiver, in the group process, and you have a right to expect active participation from other group members.

5. You have the right to have meetings begin and end promptly and to study sessions without needless interruptions.

6. You have the right to participate in a group that is free from arguing and competition.

7. You have the right to expect that the group will stay on the task it sets for itself and the responsibility for helping the group do so.

8. You have the right to take a break after an extended study session as long as the group resumes its study after the break.

9. You have the right to ask group members to limit socialization or discussion of off-the-subject topics to before and after study sessions.

10. You have the right to feelings of accomplishment at (1) the end of each study session and (2) the end of the group's life span.

SOURCE: Reprinted by permission of Longman, D. L., and Atkinson, R. H. (August, 1992). *The Teaching Professor.* 2718 Dryden Dr, Madison, WI: Magna Publications.

Application

In your class study group, identify additional rights that you expect in the study group. Are there any occasions for which you might give up your rights? Which ones and why?

Application

Maintain a log of all your academic and nonacademic activities for a week. In your study group, compare logs and identify ways in which group members could use their time more effectively.

SUMMARY OF MAIN POINTS

1. Time management is a means of controlling and organizing your schedule for maximum efficiency through careful planning of your class schedule.

2. Avoiding procrastination involves motivation, goals, getting projects started, achieving closure, and avoiding burnout.

3. Implementing goals involves effectively managing a term, a week, and a day.

VOCABULARY DEVELOPMENT
LEARNING THE LINGO WITH A SINGLE FLAME

The same time management principles you need for success in higher education aid you in vocabulary development. Modifications of the suggestions for avoiding procrastination and implementing your goals result in vocabulary development without cramming or burnout.

Learning the lingo—the language of the courses you take—is an overwhelming task. You might be tempted to ''burn the candle at both ends.'' Aside from a little more light, you won't accomplish much, and you'll run the risk of burning out twice as fast. How can you learn it all? Consider the following suggestions for managing your vocabulary development. Carrying out each individual suggestion requires relatively little time.

1. **Preview the text glossary before attending the first class.** Invest ten or fifteen minutes in getting a sense of the language of the course. Determine whether the words seem to be general, specialized, or technical terms. (See Vocabulary Development section in Chapter 1) Rate your general understanding of the vocabulary. Are they all new to you? Do you recognize some words? Can you form general associations? Are you able to use any of the words?

2. **Preview key terms before reading a text assignment.** Texts vary in the way they highlight important terms. These terms may appear in lists at a chapter's beginning or end, in a special typeface (for example, boldface or italics), or as marginal notations (sometimes with defini-

"Frankly, aside from a little more light, I don't see what they get out of it."

SOURCE: Reprinted by permission of Bill Maul. *Phi Delta Kappan,* October 1986.

tions). Again, check to see if they seem to be general, specialized, or technical in nature. Consider if you've already heard the terms in a lecture. Do you have any associations with the words? How do you think they will fit into the content of the chapter?

3. **Review key terms and concepts as soon as possible after each lecture.** After each lecture (and at least within twenty-four hours), review notes to identify key terms. How did the terms relate to each other? How would you define the terms in

your own words? How did they relate to the content of the lecture and/or reading assignment?

4. **Process terms weekly.** Recognition and memorization provide the raw materials for learning. Learning at these levels often results in a false sense of security because you think you know the information. In order to understand the language more fully, you must convert information to a form that you can use and understand. Such processing helps you become an owner, rather than a renter, of what you know. Effort forms the key. Such learning involves more than looking at words. It consists of active strategies to integrate information. These include:

* mapping (See Chapter 5)
* charting (See Chapter 5)
* discussing terms with a study group (See Chapter 7)
* creating note cards (See Chapter 8)

5. **Use terms in speaking and writing.** The old adage, "If you don't use it, you lose it" applies to vocabulary development. The words you use are those that you will retain.

6. **Don't be fooled.** Some students get misled by course content. Just because you've already had a biology class doesn't necessarily mean you already know the vocabulary as it will be applied to another biology course.

Activity 1

Using the following glossary, preview the terms and determine if they appear to be general, specialized, or technical in nature. How would you evaluate your overall understanding of these terms?

Example of a Glossary

Interpreter A high-level language translator that evaluates and translates a program one statement at a time; used extensively on microcomputer systems because it takes up less primary storage than a compiler.

Interrecord gap (IRG) A space that separates records stored on magnetic tape; allows the tape drive to regain speed during processing.

Interrupt A condition or event that temporarily suspends normal processing operations.

Inverted structure A structure that indexes a simple file by specific record attributes.

K (kilobyte) A symbol used to denote 1,024 (2^{10}) storage units (1,024 bytes) when referring to a computer's primary storage capacity; often rounded to 1,000 bytes.

Key The unique identifier or field of a record; used to sort records for processing or to locate specific records within a file.

Keypunch A keyboard device that punches holes in a card to represent data.

Keypunch operator Person who uses a keypunch machine to transfer data from source documents to punched cards.

Label A name written beside a programming instruction that acts as an identifier for that instruction; also, in spreadsheets, information used to describe some aspect of the spreadsheet.

Large-scale Integration (LSI) Method by which circuits containing thousands of electronic components are densely packed on a single silicon chip.

Laser printer A type of nonimpact printer that combines laser beams and electrophotographic technology to form images on paper.

Laser storage system A secondary storage device using laser technology to encode data onto a metallic surface; usually used for mass storage.

Librarian The person responsible for classifying, cataloging, and maintaining the files and programs stored on cards, tapes, disks, and diskettes, and all other storage media in a computer library.

Librarian program Software that manages the storage and use of library programs by maintaining a directory of programs in the system library and appropriate procedures for additions and deletions.

Light pen A pen-shaped object with a photoelectric cell at its end; used to draw lines on a visual display screen.

Linear structure A data structure in which the records in a computer file are arranged sequentially in a specified order.

Link A transmission channel that connects nodes.

Linkage editor A subprogram of the operating system that links the object program from the system residence device to primary storage.

LISP (LISt Processing) A high-level programming language commonly used in artificial intelligence research and in the processing of lists of elements.

Local system Peripherals connected directly to the CPU.

Logical file The combination of data needed to meet a user's needs.

SOURCE: Reprinted with permission of *Computers and Information Processing with BASIC Programming (SE)* by Mandell. © Copyright 1989 by West Publishing Company. All rights reserved.

Activity 2

Copy the terms from Sample Chapter 2, "The Planetary Setting." What associations do you have with these words? How do you think they fit into the chapter's content?

CHAPTER REVIEW

Answer briefly but completely.

1. What constitutes an effective class schedule?

   _____

   _____

2. Examine your current schedule. How long do you spend in study for each course per week? Using the following information, compute how long you should spend studying:

   Difficult course—three hours of study per each one hour of class per week

   Course with average level of difficulty—two hours of study per each one hour of class per week

   Easier course—one hour of study per each one hour of class per week

   _____

   _____

3. Consider your current schedule. How might you have better planned your courses to have more effectively filled the day and week?

   _____

   _____

4. How can you avoid procrastination? _____

   _____

   _____

5. List examples of ways in which you are externally motivated.

   _____

   _____

6. What is the difference between short-term and long-term goals?

   _____

   _____

7. List two ways to get started on a creative assignment.

   _____

   _____

8. What is the advantage of obtaining closure?

_____

_____

9. Contrast managing a term with managing a week.

_____

_____

10. What is prime study time? When is your prime study time? How can you protect and maximize your prime study time?

_____

_____

_____

_____

REFERENCES

Berne, Eric. (1966). *Principles of Group Treatment.* New York: Oxford University Press.

CHAPTER 3

Listening and Notetaking

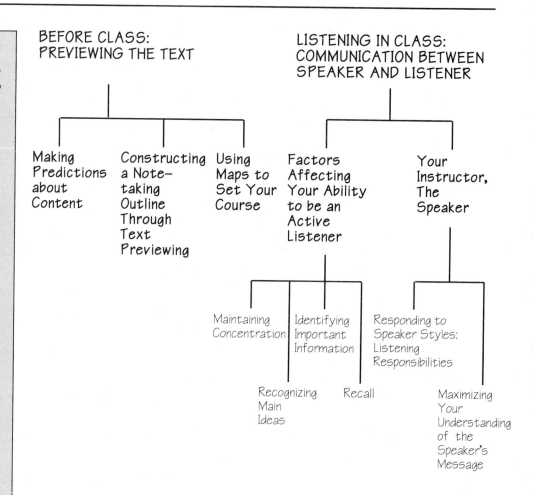

BEFORE CLASS: PREVIEWING THE TEXT

- Making Predictions about Content
- Constructing a Notetaking Outline Through Text Previewing
- Using Maps to Set Your Course

LISTENING IN CLASS: COMMUNICATION BETWEEN SPEAKER AND LISTENER

- Factors Affecting Your Ability to be an Active Listener
  - Maintaining Concentration
  - Identifying Important Information
    - Recognizing Main Ideas
    - Recall
- Your Instructor, The Speaker
  - Responding to Speaker Styles: Listening Responsibilities
    - Maximizing Your Understanding of the Speaker's Message

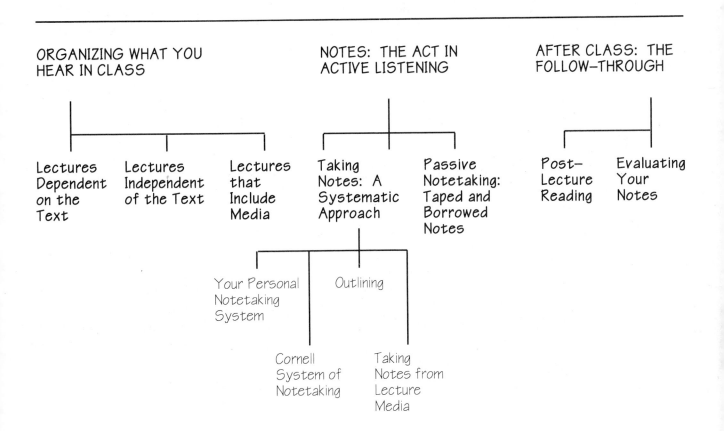

ORGANIZING WHAT YOU
HEAR IN CLASS

Lectures
Dependent
on the
Text

Lectures
Independent
of the Text

Lectures
that
Include
Media

NOTES: THE ACT IN
ACTIVE LISTENING

Taking
Notes: A
Systematic
Approach

Passive
Notetaking:
Taped and
Borrowed
Notes

Your Personal
Notetaking
System

Outlining

Cornell
System of
Notetaking

Taking
Notes from
Lecture
Media

AFTER CLASS: THE
FOLLOW–THROUGH

Post–
Lecture
Reading

Evaluating
Your
Notes

TERMS

active listening
background knowledge
chapter maps
curve of forgetting
distractions
lecture patterns
notetaking outline
outlining
previewing
self-talk
terms
transition words

There are others who think that the speaker has a function to perform, and the hearer none. They think it only right that the speaker shall come with his lecture carefully thought out and prepared, while they, without consideration or thought of their obligations, rush in and take their seats exactly as if they had come to dinner, to have a good time while others work hard.

—PLUTARCH, *MORALIA*, 45.14.E

P lutarch spoke of the same problem your instructors face each day. That problem is students who are not prepared and not ready to learn. Just as an instructor is responsible for preparing a lecture, you are obliged to be ready to process lecture information.

BEFORE CLASS: PREVIEWING THE TEXT

Your enjoyment and understanding of an activity often depend on your **background knowledge.** For example, most people who know nothing about sports fail to enjoy sporting events. Most people who know nothing about music fail to enjoy classical concerts. The same is true of academic activities. If you know nothing of a subject, you often fail to enjoy and understand that subject. On the other hand, the more background knowledge you have, the more easily you will enjoy and learn from lectures. One way to increase your background knowledge is to interact with the text.

Luckily for you, a process exists that helps you both predict chapter information, and then regulate or control your understanding of lecture content. Just as you examine the sky and check the wind for clues about the weather, **previewing,** or surveying, entails examining text features for clues about content.

Previewing is the first interaction between you and the text. When you survey before class, you think about what you already know about a subject. This lets you make the best use of background knowledge in learning and integrating what you hear in class. This information then can be related to what you know about the topic.

Previewing helps you create a mental outline for what the chapter contains. Once you get an overall picture of a chapter, you can see how details relate to major points. Previewing also improves your recall of what you read. This occurs because, rather than reading material that's unfamiliar to you, you read information you've seen before. Finally, previewing helps you set the speed at which you will later read and process information. The steps in previewing appear in Table 3.1.

TABLE 3.1   Steps in Previewing

1. Read the title. What is the chapter about? Recall what you already know about the topic.

2. Read the introduction or first paragraph. The main idea of the chapter is usually found here.

3. Read the boldfaced headings throughout the chapter.

4. Read the first paragraph or sentence under each heading. This gives you an overview of each section.

5. Look at accompanying graphs, charts, and pictures. Visual aids usually emphasize main points. They also summarize details.

6. Note any typographical aids (boldface, underlining, italics). In the body of the text, these aids highlight important terms. When found in the margins, they may outline important facts.

7. Read the last paragraph or summary. This often gives the main points or conclusions.

8. Read the objectives at the beginning of each chapter. Objectives help you set goals and purposes. Such goals help you determine what you should know or be able to do at the end of each chapter.

9. Read the vocabulary terms at the beginning or end of each chapter. You may recognize some of the terms. However, they may have specialized meanings for that topic.

10. Read the purpose-setting or review questions which accompany the chapter. These focus on key concepts.

MAKING PREDICTIONS ABOUT CONTENT

The most basic way to begin reading a chapter is to make predictions about what each section contains. This helps you interact more actively with the text. Instead of "just reading," you look for specific information. Predicting chapter content also helps you increase your understanding of lectures.

You can predict content in one of several ways. One way is to examine the chapter objectives provided by the author(s). Objectives specify what you should be able to do or understand after you read the chapter. Examining these objectives helps you set learning goals and compare chapter content to what you already know.

Another method is to preview the chapter summary or review questions. This helps you identify important information that forms the basis of the chapter.

A third method is to change headings and subheadings into questions. Certain questioning words help in identifying main ideas, and others help in locating details. Table 3.2 provides a key to these questioning words. In addition, the headings and subheadings guide your understanding of how information fits together. Perhaps in your psychology text, for example, the subheadings "Physical" and "Psychological" come under the heading "Stressors." Already, you know that there are two kinds of stressors, physical and psychological. As such, you know that you can compare and contrast the two. You do not know, however, if one causes the other to occur. You should expect the text to define and describe physical and psychological stressors and give examples of each.

TABLE 3.2   Questioning Words for Main Ideas and Details

QUESTIONING WORDS FOR MAIN IDEAS

If You Want to Know . . .	Then Ask . . .
a reason	why?
a way or method	how?
a purpose or definition	what?
a fact	what?

QUESTIONING WORDS FOR DETAILS

If You Want to Know . . .	Then Ask . . .
a person	who?
a number or amount	how many/how much?
a choice	which?
a time	when?
a place	where?

EXERCISE 3.1   Listed below are the boldfaced headings from Sample Chapter 3, "Nutrition and Digestion". Preview Sample Chapter 3, then write a purpose-setting question for each heading. Describe the connections you find for the headings and subheadings.

Heading	Question
1. A PRIMER ON HUMAN NUTRITION	_____
2. Macronutrients	_____
3. Micronutrients	_____

Connections

_____

_____

_____

_____

_____

_____

_____

Heading	Question
4. THE HUMAN DIGESTIVE SYSTEM	_____
5. The Mouth: Physical Breakdown of Food	_____
6. The Esophagus and Peristalsis	_____
7. The Stomach: Liquification, Storage, and Release of Food	_____
8. The Small Intestine and Associated Glands: Digestion and Absorption of Food	_____
9. The Large Intestine: Water Resorption	_____
10. Controlling Digestion	_____

Connections

_____

_____

_____

_____

_____

_____

_____

11. ENVIRONMENT AND HEALTH: _____
    EATING RIGHT/LIVING RIGHT
                                _____

CONSTRUCTING A NOTETAKING OUTLINE THROUGH TEXT PREVIEWING

Previewing to construct a **notetaking outline** before class (see Table 3.3) also provides you with the basics needed for understanding the lecture. Making a notetaking outline gives you a chance to locate what

TABLE 3.3   Constructing a Note-Taking Outline through Text Previews

Before beginning the previewing process, divide each page for your notes vertically into sections, with one third on the left and two thirds on the right. Record the following in the left-hand section as indicated:

1. Survey the physical characteristics of the chapter (that is, length, text structure, visual aids, or term identification).

2. Record the chapter title. Think about what you know about this topic. Consider how this information relates to the course content.

3. Read the chapter introduction or first paragraph. This gives you the overall main idea of the chapter.

4. Read and record each major and minor heading or subheading. Major headings express main ideas. Subheadings provide details to support major headings.

5. Estimate the amount of space for each section and skip lines accordingly.

6. Survey graphs, maps, charts, diagrams, and so on. These summarize details, emphasize main points, and highlight other important information.

7. Look for typographical aids (boldface, underlining, italics). In the body of the text, these highlight important new terms. In the margins, they outline important ideas. Record terms.

8. Read the last paragraph or summary. This generally reviews the main points or conclusions of the chapter.

appears to be important terms, concepts, and dates before the lecture. It helps you predict the content of the lecture. Figure 3.1 shows a notetaking outline, before and after the lecture.

Some text readings provide general background information, rather than a framework for the lecture information. Notetaking outlines, then, lose effectiveness for such lectures that are less dependent on information in your textbook. In these cases, skimming the chapter in its entirety or reading it more thoroughly may be needed.

EXERCISE 3.2   Preview Sample Chapter 2, "The Planetary Setting." On a separate sheet of paper, create a goal-setting question outline based on the headings and subheadings in the sample chapter. Then read the chapter summary and respond to the goal-setting questions based only on that information. Finally, identify which three of the four focus questions at the beginning of Sample Chapter 2 can be answered using the chapter's summary.

USING MAPS TO SET YOUR COURSE

Research in the functioning of the brain indicates that its two halves process information differently. The left half of the brain tends to think in analytical, logical, linear, and verbal terms. The right brain prefers holistic, nonverbal, and visual images.

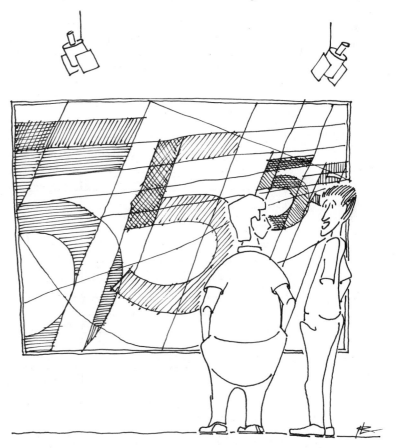

"I think the artist's left brain overpowered his right brain."

FIGURE 3.1   Example of a Notetaking Outline: Before and after the Lecture

Headings before

◯	headings ! Key concepts at end of chapter identify key points circled in notes CH1—Human perception: The Map of the Caribbean VS the Ducky	
P3 Intro		
◯	*Chap has 2 purposes	
Sees it w/own eyes:		
	(Perception/Truth Fallacy)	
◯	P6 Get what expect: (Perceptual Expectancy) *mental 'set'	

Headings after

◯	headings ! Key concepts at end of chapter identify key points circled in notes CH1—Human perception: The Map of the Caribbean VS the Ducky	
P3 Intro		1) be more aware of problems in how we
◯	*Chap has 2 purposes	see the world
		2) deal more effectively with these
		problems
Sees it w/own eyes:		Don't accept initial perceptions at face value—
	(Perception/Truth Fallacy)	Know Hoffer quote P.5
		Skip example
◯	P6 Get what expect: (Perceptual Expectancy) *mental 'set'	mental set causes us to anticipate future behaviors/events
		be able to tell why you see
		what you think you see from
		examples
		(TEST questions)

Doonesbury

BY GARRY TRUDEAU

TABLE 3.4	Steps in Constructing a Chapter Map

1. Turn a sheet of paper horizontally.

2. Write the first major heading in the top left corner.

3. Place the next-level headings (if any) underneath the major heading with lines showing their relationship to the major heading.

4. Place the next-level heading(s) (if any) underneath the second-level heading(s).

5. Continue the pattern until you come to the next major heading.

6. Repeat the process until the end of the chapter.

Chapter maps help you set your course with information for both sides of your brain. They provide verbal information in the context of a visual arrangement of ideas. They show relationships among concepts and express an author's patterns of thought. Each chapter of this text begins with a map for just these reasons.

You construct a chapter map by using headings and subheadings in a family tree-style branching format. Table 3.4 provides steps in constructing a chapter map. After you create your map, formulate some questions that analyze the links between information and synthesize the chapter as a whole and provide examples of questions that might accompany the chapter map for Sample Chapter 3. Figure 3.2 shows how these steps would be used to create the map for Sample Chapter 3.

LISTENING IN CLASS: COMMUNICATION BETWEEN SPEAKER AND LISTENER

Classroom communication takes place between your instructor, the speaker, and you, the listener. In the preceding *Doonesbury* cartoon, the cartoon's professor and his students are communicating at opposite ends of the continuum of listening (See Table 3.5). The students apparently are listening at the lowest end of the spectrum, the attention level. The lecturer tries desperately without success to entice them to evaluate what he says. Little communication occurs, no matter how hard the speaker tries.

Listening, then, is more difficult than it looks. It appears easy because it's something you've been doing all your life. It requires only the equipment you have with you, and you can use it in all your classes and at any time. One problem with learning from verbal information is your lack of training in being a good listener in the classroom. Educators take for granted that you know how to learn

FIGURE 3.2   Chapter Map for Sample Chapter 3

Step 1

Step 2

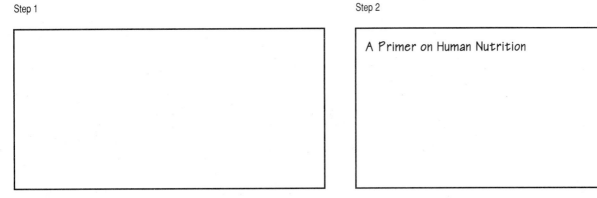

Step 3

Step 4

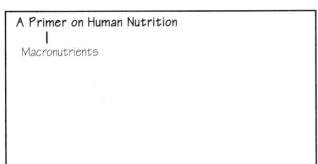

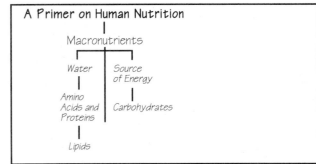

Step 5–6

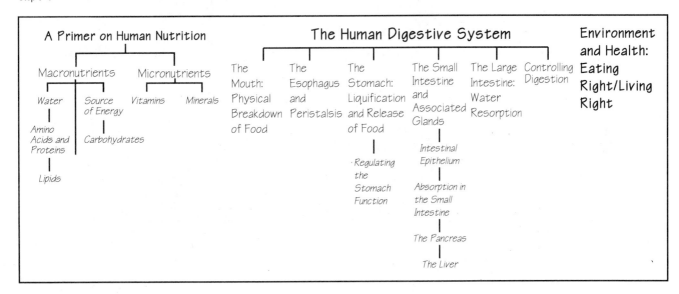

Examples of Questions

1. How do macronutrients compare with micronutrients? how are they different?
2. How do the different kinds of macronutrients compare with each other?
3. How do vitamins and minerals compare as micronutrients? what is the impact of micronutrients on nutrition?

Doonesbury

TABLE 3.5	Continuum of Listening
EVALUATION	Judging information in terms of accuracy and relevance
APPLICATION	Applying information to personal experience; using information in new situations
IMPLICATION	Drawing conclusions
INTERPRETATION	Synthesizing information; putting information into your own words
INTEGRATION	Relating new information to old learning
DEFINITION	Lowest level of active listening; giving meaning to isolated facts and details; no overall organizational plan
ATTENTION	Listening passively; no effort to relate or understand what is being said
RECEPTION	Hearing without thought

from lectures. That, however, is seldom the case. Since listening is a seemingly passive activity, you can appear to know how to listen even when you don't. You can appear to listen, even when you aren't. Listening, however, is not an all-or-nothing proposition. The level at which you listen depends on your background knowledge, the difficulty of the concepts, and your purpose in listening.

For most students, listening to lectures involves following a linear sequence of one idea after another. Like the students in the *Doonesbury* cartoon, they tend to take at face value what is being said. They passively accept any statement, evaluating little of what they hear. What a speaker says should elicit mental comments, if not spoken comments and questions. These comments should question what is said as well as what and how you think about it. In essence, you should always be asking, "What?" "So what?" and "Now what?" Table 3.6 modifies the continuum of listening to include the kind of mental comments that might be appropriate at each level.

WRITE TO LEARN

Examine Table 3.5. Compare your behavior in your favorite and least favorite classes. Consider the amount of time each of these classes lasts. On a separate sheet of paper, determine when and for how long you might be at each level of listening in each of these classes. What factors contribute to the level at which you listen and for how long you remain at a level in each class? Are there any differences? Why?

FACTORS AFFECTING YOUR ABILITY TO BE AN ACTIVE LISTENER

The student who spoke in the second *Doonesbury* cartoon demonstrates the alert and active process of listening. He related what the

TABLE 3.6	Mental Comments for the Continuum of Listening
Level	**Comments**
EVALUATION	Do I agree with . . . ? What information supports . . . ? Is this true and accurate? Why would . . . be so?
APPLICATION	How would . . . be used? How would . . . differ if one of its components changed? What situation would show . . . ?
IMPLICATION	What would be the result of . . . ? What would cause . . . ? So if . . . is true, then . . . follows.
INTERPRETATION	In other words, . . . To summarize, . . . That means . . . .
INTEGRATION	Then . . . relates to . . . . is part of . . . process. . . . could be organized like. . . . . . . could be classified as . . . .
DEFINITION	The meaning of . . . is . . . .
ATTENTION	Sure looks like a nice day outside.
RECEPTION	?????

instructor said to what he already knew. He took advantage of this knowledge by communicating with his instructor. He maintained eye contact and gave thoughtful responses. He seemed interested. As a result, the instructor took an interest in him and wanted to get to know him better.

You, too, should be like this student in *Doonesbury.* By combining what you learn from the instructor with what you know about yourself and the world, you become an active listener. Active listening occurs when you consciously monitor your listening and use pre-planned strategies for improving and maximizing these listening skills.

Are you an effective listener? Do you know what factors affect listening skills? The personal profile found in Figure 3.3 helps you rate your abilities as a listener.

Maintaining Concentration

Inactive listening results from **distractions.** These draw your attention from the subject being discussed. Some of these factors are beyond your control and others are not. All prevent you from fully focusing on the topic at hand.

Distractions beyond your control include traffic noises; sounds within the classroom, such as whispering, papers rattling, people moving, or hall noises; and other environmental interruptions. Your instructor's mannerisms pose another distraction you cannot control. Often an instructor's dialect, speech rate, and body language affect your concentration. Because you have no control over these distractions, you must learn to cope with them.

One way to cope is to increase your interest in the subject. You can try to become so interested in what is being said that you ignore what is bothering you. Another way to reduce environmental distractions is to move to a different seat. You may need to move away from a door or window. If you are in a large lecture class, moving closer to the instructor helps you hear better and focuses your attention.

Sometimes distractions are within you. These also prevent you from concentrating on the topic. Such distractions include physical discomforts, personal concerns, and daydreams. It is difficult to think when you are hungry, tired, or sick. Proper nutrition, rest, and exercise get rid of these physical distractions. Personal concerns, no matter how large or small, cannot be solved during a class. If your problem is a large one, consulting a counselor or talking with a friend before or after class may help reduce your anxiety. Worry about small problems (getting your laundry done, meeting a friend, running

---

FIGURE 3.3   Listening Questionnaire

The following two tests ask you to rate yourself as a listener. There are no correct or incorrect answers. Your responses, however, will extend your understanding of yourself as a listener and highlight areas in which improvement might be welcome . . . to you and to those around you.

When you've completed the tests, examine the Profile Analysis to see how your scores compare with those of thousands of others who've taken the same tests.

Quiz #1

1. Circle the term that best describes you as a listener.
   Superior
   Excellent
   Above Average
   Average
   Below Average
   Poor
   Terrible
2. On a scale of 0–100 (100 = highest), how would you rate yourself as a listener?

FIGURE 3.3   Continued

Quiz #2

Check (√) how frequently (almost always, usually, sometimes, seldom, almost never) you do the following listening behaviors:

LISTENING HABITS	FREQUENCY					SCORE
	Almost Always	Usually	Sometimes	Seldom	Almost Never	
1. Call the subject uninteresting	_____	_____	_____	_____	_____	_____
2. Criticize the speaker's delivery or mannerisms	_____	_____	_____	_____	_____	_____
3. Get overstimulated by something the speaker says	_____	_____	_____	_____	_____	_____
4. Listen primarily for facts	_____	_____	_____	_____	_____	_____
5. Try to outline everything	_____	_____	_____	_____	_____	_____
6. Fake attention to the speaker	_____	_____	_____	_____	_____	_____
7. Allow distractions to interfere	_____	_____	_____	_____	_____	_____
8. Avoid difficult material	_____	_____	_____	_____	_____	_____
9. Let emotion-laden words arouse personal antagonism	_____	_____	_____	_____	_____	_____
10. Daydream while the speaker is talking	_____	_____	_____	_____	_____	_____

TOTAL SCORE _____

KEY

For every "Almost Always" checked, give yourself a score of	2
For every "Usually" checked, give yourself a score of	4
For every "Sometimes" checked, give yourself a score of	6
For every "Seldom" checked, give yourself a score of	8
For every "Almost Never" checked, give yourself a score of	10

FIGURE 3.3   Continued

Profile Analysis

This is how other people have responded to the same questions that you've just answered.

Quiz #1

1. 85% of all listeners questioned rate themselves as Average or less. Fewer than 5% rate themselves as Superior or Excellent
2. On the 0-100 scale, the extreme range is 10-90; the general range is 35-85; and the average rating is 55.

Quiz #2

   All these habits get in the way of effective listening. Therefore, the higher your score (the more you *don't* fall into these habits), the better listener you are.

   The average score is 62 . . . 7 points higher than the average of 55 in Quiz #1. This suggests that when listening is broken down into specific areas of competence, we rate ourselves better than we do when listening is considered only as a generality.

   Of course, the best way to discover how well you listen is to ask the people to whom you listen most frequently—your spouse, boss, best friend, and so on. They'll give you an earful.

SOURCE: From Sperry Corporation Listening Program materials by Dr. Lyman K. Steil, Communication Development, Inc. for Sperry Corporation. Copyright © 1979. Reprinted by permission by Dr. Steil and Sperry Corporation.

---

errands) can be handled by listing them on a page in your notebook. Then you can forget about them until the end of class. Daydreaming is another common distraction. **Self-talk** can be used to force yourself back to attention. Self-talk involves your interrupting your daydream with a strong internal command like, "STOP! Pay attention now. Think about this later." Finally, you must maintain your stamina in listening to lectures. In general, students tend to take fewer and less comprehensive notes as a lecture progresses. Active listening and continued mental questioning helps you remain focused and attentive.

Recognizing Main Ideas

Every lecture has a plan, purpose, and structure that indicate the main idea of the talk. Learning to recognize the various patterns that lectures follow helps you distinguish between main ideas and details. It also aids you in recognizing examples and understanding the reasons for anecdotes.

   Lectures follow five basic patterns. Instructors either: 1) introduce new topics or summarize information; 2) list or rank details; 3) present two (or more) sides of an issue; 4) identify cause(s) and effect(s) or problem(s) and solution(s); or 5) discuss concepts with supporting details. These patterns vary as the instructor's purposes change in the course of a lecture. Identifying your instructor's mix of the patterns helps you predict the direction of the lecture. Signal words and other verbal markers help you identify the flow and content of these lecture patterns.

Listening for these signals makes you a kind of word detective. A detective follows a suspect, predicting where he or she will go based on clues left behind. You follow an instructor's lecture and predict the lecture's direction by identifying the **transition words** your instructor uses. These words also mark the end of a lecture. This is important because instructors often restate main ideas in their summaries. Becoming familiar with transition words helps you organize lecture notes and listen more actively. Table 3.7 compares transition words with **lecture patterns.**

TABLE 3.7   Lecture Patterns and Corresponding Signals

Pattern	Description	Signal Words
Introduction/Summary	Identifies main points	Identified by location, either at the beginning or end of a discussion of a topic; or by such words as: *in summary, in conclusion, as a review, to summarize, to sum up*
Enumeration/Sequence	Lists or orders main points or presents a problem and steps for its solution	*First, second, third, first, next, then, finally, in addition, last, and, furthermore, and then, most important, least important*
Comparison/Contrast	Describes ways in which concepts are alike or different or presents two or more sides of an issue	Comparison—*similarly, both, as well as, likewise, in like manner* Contrast—*however, on the other hand, on the contrary, but, instead of, although, yet, nevertheless*
Cause/Effect	Shows the result of action(s) or explains a problem and its solution	*Therefore, thus, as a result, because, in turn, then, hence, for this reason, results in, causes, effects*
Subject Development/ Definition	Identifies a major topic and describes or develops it through related details	Identified by terms denoting definition; types or kinds; characteristics, elements, and other kinds of supporting details

WRITE TO LEARN

On a separate sheet of paper, identify the lecture pattern in each of your classes today and tomorrow. Also list three to five of the signal words that each of your instructor(s) used to help you determine this pattern.

EXERCISE 3.3   Underline the transition words found in each lecture excerpt. Use the following key and write the lecture type in the space below the excerpt.
I/S: Introduction/summary
C/E: Cause/effect
E/S: Enumeration/sequence
C/C: Comparison/contrast
SD/D: Subject development/definition

---

1. Regardless of cultural or socioeconomic background, socialization has several common goals. The first goal is basic discipline of the individual. This discourages behaviors deemed unwanted by the group. Second, socialization inspires aspiration. In order for the group to prosper, people must continue to grow. Next, socialization forms identities. Who you are is often determined by how you fit into the context of the group. Fourth, social roles are learned from socialization. This includes external actions and internal values. Finally, socialization teaches skills necessary for the person to fit into the group.

   Lecture type: _____

2. In this case, both evaporation and condensation occur in the closed container. Condensation is an exothermic process. This means that it liberates heat. Condensation occurs when a gas or vapor is converted to a liquid or solid. Evaporation is, on the other hand, an endothermic process. In this process, heat is absorbed. Also called vaporization, evaporation occurs when particles leave the surface of a material. Equilibrium exists when two such opposing processes occur at equal rates.

   Lecture type: _____

3. In this problem, we are attempting to show the rate of growth for investments based on five-year intervals. As class ended last meeting, we had completed the majority of this programming example. Today, we will look at how to determine if a year is divisible by five. One way to accomplish this is to use the truncation property of integer division. If an integer is exactly divisible by a second integer—in this case, five—then the quotient times the second integer will produce the first as its value. If the value of the final result is not equal to the first integer, then the year is not divisible by five.

   Lecture type: _____

4. Clinical observation is what most of us think of as the case study method. This model comes from medicine. It is the foundation of the majority of the most popular and influential personality theories. The foremost strength of the clinical observation method is its great depth. The amount of time a clinical observation

devotes to each case possibly accounts for this advantage. A second strength is its realism, its lack of artificiality. Despite its popularity, however, clinical observation has its weaknesses. First, there is a possibility of observer bias. A second factor to consider is that clinical observation offers no possibility of replication. Should two observers agree on what they have seen, there is no way to duplicate the same set of circumstances for further study. Finally, there is a problem of sample bias. If observers see a sample of people not representative of the rest of humanity, then the observer finds information not generalizable to others.

Lecture type: _____

5. How does stress affect you physiologically? When you sense danger, your brain sends a message to the adrenal gland to secrete catecholamines, epinephrine, and norepinephrine into the bloodstream. This causes the liver to release glucose, which gives you more energy. It also decreases blood loss by increasing clotting time. It conserves fluid in the kidneys. Blood moves from the extremities of the body to the vital organs and legs. You breathe faster, which brings in more oxygen and allows you to rid yourself of carbon dioxide more quickly. Your heart rate also increases to provide more nutrients and oxygen to the body via the blood stream.

Lecture type: _____

6. Money and position affect life-styles in various ways. Upper-middle class females have more career opportunities. Wealthy women are more likely to combine marriage and work because of a commitment to their careers than are poorer women, who work out of necessity. Poorer families generally maintain the traditional division of labor within their household. Middle-class families exhibit more equal relationships between husbands and wives. Middle-class parents tend to be less strict than working-class parents. Thus, people in higher and lower socioeconomic classes act and react in different ways.

Lecture type: _____

7. Using statistics from law enforcement agencies across the nation, the Uniform Crime Reports (UCR) program provides assessments of crime in the country. Law enforcement agencies make these assessments by measuring the number of crimes that come to the attention of the police. The program's main goal is to generate reliable criminal statistics for use in law enforcement administration, operation, and management. Criminal justice professors, legislators, and scholars also use this data. The UCR also provides information to the public about levels of crime.

Lecture type: _____

8. Before we begin a discussion of the Basque language, you need to realize how few people actually speak it and why that number is so small. Only one language currently spoken in Europe, the Basque language, came there before the Indo-European invasion. Basque is spoken by about 2 million people in northern Spain and southwestern France. The uniqueness of the language reflects the isolation of the Basque people in their mountainous homeland.

Lecture type: _____

Identifying Important Information

Identifying important information is a third factor that contributes to your ability to be an active listener. Although instructors emphasize main points differently, there are some common ways that they let you know what's important. Instructors often use one or more kinds of emphasis. Careful observation of your instructor helps you know when your instructor is stressing a main idea.

First, some instructors write key information on the chalkboard. They often place lecture outlines on the board before class begins. Instructors also write **terms** or key points on the board as they lecture. Copying this outline or list of terms aids learning in three ways. Initially, you learn as you write. Next, copying the outline gives you an idea of the lecture's topic. Finally, the outline serves as a guide for study.

A second way an instructor stresses a point is by providing "wait time." When an instructor speaks more slowly, you have more time to write what is being said. Hesitations and pauses are forms of "wait time." In addition, you are given "wait time" when your instructor repeats information.

Third, your instructor may change tone of voice when stressing an important point. An instructor's voice could also change in volume or intensity. You need to listen for these changes.

A fourth way instructors emphasize main points is through body language. If your instructor pounds on the desk, moves closer to the class, or makes some other gesture to stress a point, it is often one essential to your understanding.

The next way instructors explain main ideas is by using visual aids. Films, overhead transparencies, videotapes, or other audiovisual materials signal important topics.

Sixth, some instructors refer to specific text pages. Information an instructor knows by page number is worth noting and remembering.

Finally, instructors stress information by referring to that information as a possible test question. Your instructor might say, "You may see this again," or "This would make a good test question."

WRITE TO LEARN

On a separate sheet of paper, list three ways the instructor for this class emphasizes information. Circle those mentioned in this text.

EXERCISE 3.4 Listen to the instructor on the videotape. Write down the main points. Following each point, list the cue used to emphasize the information.

Recall

Sometimes a lecture is like a movie that's continued for several nights. Often an instructor doesn't finish discussing a topic during one class. He or she begins with that same topic the next class meeting. You need a review, similar to the "scenes from last night's exciting episode." Without this review, you forget what happened in the notes, just as you might forget what happened in the movie. In either case, you lose continuity and interest. Recall is diminished.

Frequent reviews aid recall by transferring information from short-term to long-term memory (see Chapter 5). The more often you hear or read something, the easier it is to remember. The "Ebbinghaus curve" or **curve of forgetting** (Figure 3.4) shows the relationship between recall of information without review and time since presentation. The numbers along the left of the graph indicate the amount of material forgotten. The numbers along the bottom show the number of days since the material was presented. Note that on the basis of one exposure, most information is lost within the first twenty-four hours. This curve explains why you are sometimes confused by notes that seemed clear when you took them. Reviewing your notes within twenty-four hours after taking them slows down your curve of forgetting.

Reviewing your notes is your responsibility. After each day's class, reread your notes. Before the next class, review your notes again. Try to anticipate what the instructor will say next. This provides background information for you to use when listening to your

FIGURE 3.4   Curve of Forgetting

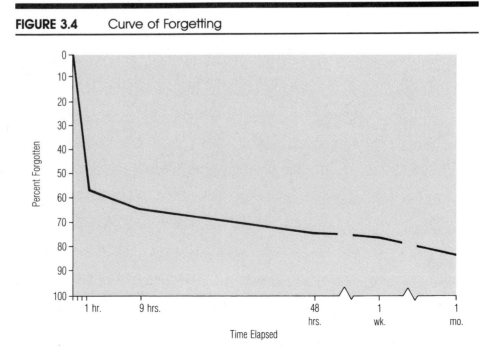

class lecture. It helps you relate information and remember more. In addition, it refreshes your memory of content you found confusing. You can begin the class by asking the instructor to clarify this material before he or she continues with the topic.

YOUR INSTRUCTOR, THE SPEAKER

The job of your instructor, the speaker, is to provide you, the listener, with information. College faculty spend their lives learning about their areas of expertise in order to share that information with you. As such, they are interested in talking about their topics and hope that you are interested in listening to what they have to say.

Instructors, like any other group, vary in ability. Some are excellent speakers. Others are mediocre at best. They vary in the ways in which they pace information. Some speak very rapidly, others more slowly. Information delivered at breakneck speeds often results in your feeling frustrated and lost. Information delivered too slowly tends to bore and therefore lose you.

Unlike a text, a lecture shifts between major and minor topics with few cues concerning which is which. Previewing the text chapter, having some ideas about how the content is organized, and re-organizing signal words help you determine a lecture's organization.

TABLE 3.8   Rating Checklist for Instructors

Indicate how often your instructor does each of the following by marking either A—Always; S—Sometimes; U—Usually; or N—Never.

DOES YOUR INSTRUCTOR . . .	A	S	U	N
1. Explain goals of the lecture?				
2. Review previous lecture material before beginning the new lecture?				
3. State main ideas in introduction and summary of lecture?				
4. Provide an outline of the lecture?				
5. Provide "wait time" for writing notes?				
6. Speak clearly with appropriate volume?				
7. Answer questions without sarcasm?				
8. Stay on topic?				
9. Refrain from reading directly from the text?				
10. Emphasize main points?				
11. Use transition words?				
12. Give examples to illustrate difficult ideas?				
13. Write important words, dates, etc., on board?				
14. Define important terms?				
15. Use audiovisual aids to reinforce ideas?				
Totals				

In general, your ability to distinguish good speakers from poor ones improves with practice. A rating system like the one in Table 3.8 helps you determine how effective your instructor is and how much you need to work to compensate. The more *A*'s your instructor receives, the more effective that instructor is.

Responding to Speaker Styles: Listening Responsibilities

How determined you need to be as an active listener depends in part on the effectiveness of your instructor. If your instructor is well organized and knows the subject, the amount of work you need to do lessens. Think again of the continuum on which listening takes place. With an effective instructor, you need only focus on the information that's presented. If, however, your instructor is less effective, then your responsibilities as an active listener increase. It becomes necessary for you to define, integrate, and interpret information. In addition, you must draw conclusions for yourself. Finding applications for information and judging its value become your job. The main way that you can cope with ineffective lecturers is to compensate for their deficiencies (see Table 3.9).

Maximizing Your Understanding of the Speaker's Message

**I know that you believe you understood what
you think I said, but I am not sure you realize that
what you heard is not what I meant.**
—QUOTE FROM THE '60s

The speaker controls what is said and how it is organized. To be sure you "realize that what you heard is what is actually meant," you need to control the way you listen to get the most from the lecture. You need to use what you know to interpret, organize, and store what you hear. Such information is then available for later retrieval and use. Whatever the lecture ability or style of your instructor, you need a way to understand and remember information. Table 3.10 shows a plan for maximizing your understanding of what you hear.

"I've spotted a Professor Emeritus—you can tell one by its tufted crown, bulging eyes, pointed beak, and garish plummage."

TABLE 3.9   How to Compensate for an Ineffective Lecturer

If Your Instructor Fails to . . .	Then You . . .
1. Explain goals of the lecture	Use your text and syllabus to set objectives.
2. Review previous lecture material before beginning new lecture	Set aside time before each class to review notes.
3. State main ideas in introduction and summary of lecture	Write short summaries of the day's lecture immediately after class.
4. Provide an outline of the lecture	Preview assigned readings before class or outline notes after class.
5. Provide "wait time" for writing notes	Politely ask instructor to repeat information or speak more slowly.
6. Speak clearly with appropriate volume	Politely ask instructor to repeat information or speak more loudly or move closer to him or her.
7. Answer questions without sarcasm	Refrain from taking comments personally.
8. Stay on topic	Discover how anecdotes relate to the topic or use anecdotes as a memory cue.
9. Refrain from reading directly from the text	Mark passages in text as instructor reads or summarize or outline these passages in text margin.
10. Emphasize main points	Supplement lectures through text previews and reading.
11. Use transition words	Supplement lectures through text previews and reading.
12. Give examples to illustrate difficult ideas	Ask instructor for a clarifying example, discuss idea with other students and/or create an example for yourself.
13. Write important words, dates, etc. on board	Supplement notes with terms listed in text and highlight information contained in lecture and/or text.
14. Define important terms	Use text glossary or a dictionary.
15. Use audiovisual aids to reinforce ideas	Relate information to what you know about the topic or create clarifying example for yourself.

TABLE 3.10   Method for Maximizing Your Understanding of the Speaker's
Message

1. Have a purpose for listening.

2. Pay careful attention to the instructor's introductory and summary statements. These usually state main points.

3. Take notes.

4. Sit comfortably erect. Slouching makes you sleepy and indicates to your
instructor your disinterest.

5. Look attentive. Show your interest by keeping your eyes on your instructor.

6. Concentrate on what the instructor is saying. Try to ignore external distractions. Try to eliminate internal distractions.

7. Think of questions you would like to ask or comments you want to make.

8. Listen for transition words that signal main points.

9. Mark words or references you don't understand. Do not attempt to figure
them out now—look them up later.

10. Be flexible—adjust your listening and note taking to the lecture.

11. If the instructor speaks too quickly or unclearly, then
    a. Ask the instructor to speak more slowly or to repeat information;
    b. Leave plenty of white space and fill in missing details immediately after
class;
    c. Exchange copies of notes with fellow classmates;
    d. Ask the instructor for clarification after class; and
    e. Be sure to preview lecture topic before class.

12. Avoid being a distraction (keep hands still, wait your turn in discussions,
avoid whispering, etc.).

EXERCISE 3.5   The instructions for this activity will be read aloud by your instructor. Listen and follow each
instruction carefully. Do not begin until you are told to do so.

_____

_____

_____

_____

_____

_____

_____

_____

_____

_____

ORGANIZING WHAT YOU HEAR IN CLASS

In learning, it is said that "we hear and we forget; we see and we remember; we do and we understand." Because this is true, you need to apply active listening techniques and take effective notes during class. These processes aid you in collecting information for later learning. They allow you to store data for future recall and use. They provide the oral and visual stimuli you need for remembering and understanding.

Lectures follow three general formats. In the first, lecture content corresponds closely to assigned textbook chapters. In the second, the content of the lecture is not necessarily contained in the text. Rather, the text provides additional information to help you better understand the subject. The third type can be either text-dependent or text-independent. It differs in that media is used to focus and enhance the delivery of information.

LECTURES DEPENDENT ON THE TEXT

When lectures are text-based, the way you use your text during the lecture depends on your preclass preparation. If you read the chapter in its entirety before class, you can record notes and instructions emphasized during the lecture directly in your textbook. As your instructor speaks, you can highlight or underline these items. You can cross out information your instructor tells you to omit and note important information in the margins of the chapter.

If you constructed a notetaking outline through text preview, you respond differently during the lecture. Using this method, you record class notes and instructions directly on your outline. You highlight important information and cross out sections that your instructor tells you to omit. You make notes in the larger section of your note-taking outline. When the instructor refers to specific graphics or quotations, you underline or mark these in your text.

LECTURES INDEPENDENT OF THE TEXT

When instructors lecture on information not contained in the text, your responsibility for taking notes increases. Because you do not have the text to use as a backup source, you need to be an especially active listener. After the lecture, you need to discover the plan of the lecture and outline or map its content. Your class notes and syllabus aid you in this attempt. Also, setting study objectives for yourself will help you create a purpose for learning and increase recall. To be sure you have fully grasped the content, discuss your notes with another classmate or do supplemental reading. Finally, when lectures are independent of the text, they are based on what your instructor feels is most important about the subject. For this reason, your instructor is a good source for clarifying confusing points. Feel free to ask questions.

LECTURES THAT INCLUDE MEDIA

Instructors use a variety of media—handouts, films, slides, models, and so on—to stimulate your visual and auditory senses during lectures. When the instructor selects media from published resources, the information tends to be more general. When an instructor creates the media, the information it contains is more course-specific. It corresponds closely to what you need to know for an exam.

Instructors use media to add knowledge and information, arouse emotion or interest, and increase skills and performance. Your responsibility is to recognize your instructor's purpose for using media and judge its worth in meeting your learning needs. For instance, suppose a psychology instructor shows a film introducing the concept of classical conditioning. How carefully you attend to the film depends on your prior knowledge of the topic. If you have extensive knowledge about classical conditioning, then the film serves only as a review for you. If classical conditioning is a new topic for you, then the film serves to build background knowledge. Table 3.11 is a list of media types and the corresponding purposes for their use.

TABLE 3.11   Media Types and Corresponding Purposes for Their Use

Purposes for Media	Chalk-board	Trans-paren-cies	Hand-outs	Audio-tapes	Films, Slides, Television	Models
To provide examples	X	X	X	X	X	X
To list characteristics	X	X	X	X	X	
To describe or define concepts	X	X	X	X	X	
To summarize notes	X	X	X			
To supplement information	X	X	X	X	X	X
To arouse emotion or interest				X	X	X
To document proof			X	X	X	X
To aid recall	X	X	X	X	X	X
To reinforce ideas	X	X	X	X	X	X
To provide background information	X	X	X	X	X	X
To provide a vicarious experience				X	X	X
To demonstrate a process				X	X	X
To introduce new concepts	X	X	X	X	X	X

EXERCISE 3.6   Circle the item that best answers or completes each of the following questions or statements.

1. An English literature professor begins a unit on Shakespeare by showing a film of life in sixteenth-century England. The purpose of this use of media is
   a. to provide contemporary examples of Shakespearean plays.
   b. to list characteristics of Shakespearean plays.
   c. to summarize notes.
   d. to provide background information about life in Shakespearean England.

2. A political science instructor wants to arouse interest in the development of political parties in the United States. Which of the following types of media could be used for this purpose?
   a. Transparencies
   b. Handouts
   c. Chalkboard presentations
   d. Audiotapes

3. A biology professor brings to class a model of the human heart. Which of the following is *least* likely to be a purpose for the use of this lecture media?
   a. To arouse emotion or interest in the processes of the human heart.
   b. To supplement information about the human heart and its processes.
   c. To aid recall of the human heart.
   d. To demonstrate how the human heart processes blood.

4. As a review, a history professor provides a handout of a timeline that includes all important events during the first twenty years of the American colonial period. The purpose of such a handout is most likely
   a. to arouse emotion.
   b. to provide a vicarious learning experience.
   c. to demonstrate a process.
   d. to summarize notes.

5. A mathematics professor shows how to work a complicated algebraic equation using a transparency. The purpose of the transparency is
   a. to describe concepts.
   b. to list characteristics.
   c. to provide an example.
   d. to provide background information.

6. A music history instructor provides tapes of Gregorian chants. The purpose of the tapes is least likely to be
   a. to summarize notes.
   b. to aid recall.
   c. to provide examples.
   d. to supplement information.

7. A chemistry instructor wants to teach a class the properties of solids. To ensure that each student has a complete summary of notes, the instructor provides which of the following?
   a. A film
   b. Models of solids
   c. A simulation of chemical processes
   d. A handout

8. A zoology professor asks students to view a public television special on primates. Which of the following would *not* be a logical purpose for such an assignment?
   a. To aid recall.
   b. To provide background information.

    c. To reinforce ideas.

    d. To summarize notes.

 9. An education instructor demonstrates the use of a braillewriter in a class on teaching the visually impaired. The purpose of this activity is

    a. to list characteristics of visually impaired students.

    b. to document proof.

    c. to supplement information.

    d. to provide a definition of visually impaired.

10. An astronomy professor wants to provide students with the experience of visiting the moon. Because he can't send them there, his next best opportunity for doing so is

    a. a handout describing the moon's rocks and craters.

    b. an example of a moon rock.

    c. a film of astronauts on the moon.

    d. a transparency of the solar system.

NOTES: THE ACT IN ACTIVE LISTENING

One of Aesop's fables tells of a blacksmith and his dog. The blacksmith, unhappy about the dog's laziness, said, "When I work, you sleep; but when I stop to eat, you want to eat, too." The moral of the fable is "Those who will not work deserve to starve." This moral holds true for notetaking. While the instructor "works," many students "sleep" passively receiving lecture information. Others actively take notes.

Notetaking supplements active listening in several important ways. First, some information in the lecture may not be found in the text or handouts. The lecture may be the only source for certain facts. Second, the information emphasized in a lecture often signals what will be found on exams. Next, class notes serve as a means of external storage. As a busy college student, it is impossible for you to remember everything you hear accurately. Thus, notes serve as an alternative form of memory.

The process of notetaking adds to learning independent of review. Notes often trigger your memory of the lecture or the text. Review, however, is an important part of notetaking. In general, students who review notes achieve more than those who do not (Kiewra, 1985). Researchers have found that if important information was contained in notes, it had a 34 percent chance of being remembered (Howe, 1970). Information not found in notes had only a 5 percent chance of being remembered.

TAKING NOTES: A SYSTEMATIC APPROACH

Peper and Mayer (1978) discuss three theories about notetaking: the attention theory, the effort theory, and the generative theory. The attention theory suggests that, by taking notes, you pay more attention and become more familiar with new material. The effort theory is based on the idea that notetaking requires more effort and thought than reading. The generative theory states that, as you take notes, you paraphrase, organize, and understand information. To do so, you relate this new information to your background knowledge. These three theories regard notetaking as an active process that results in learning. This process requires you to become an active listener. To do so, you need a plan. This plan can be an original creation or it can be a combination of parts of other plans.

Your Personal Notetaking System

Active listening requires more than passive reception of the speaker's voice. It is enhanced by action. Active listening requires you to recognize important concepts and supporting details. One way to make your listening active is by taking notes (see suggestions listed in Table 3.12).

As a knowledgeable notetaker, you need to selectively record only important information. What information is recorded is your choice. You make this decision based on what you know about the lecture topic, what subject you are studying, and what facts your instructor stresses. If you are familiar with a topic, your notes need not be as detailed as when you are less familiar with a subject. Active listening helps you find important information. Now you must get it written down.

Notes are not like a theme you turn in for a grade. They need not be grammatically correct. They don't even have to contain complete words. In fact, as a good notetaker, you need to develop your own system of shorthand to record your notes just as you developed a system for labeling what you read. In developing your system, you need to limit the number of symbols you use. After you thoroughly learn a few symbols, you can add others. Table 3.13 gives some rules for developing your own shorthand system.

TABLE 3.12   Suggestions for Taking Notes

1. Date each day's notes. The date serves as a reference point if you need to compare notes with someone or ask your instructor for clarification. If you are absent, the missing date(s) identifies which notes you need.

2. Develop a system for taking notes that best fits your learning style and course content.

3. Keep all notes together. You accomplish this in one of two ways. You can purchase a single spiral notebook or ring binder for each class. Or, you can purchase two multiple-subject notebooks or loose-leaf binders, one for your classes on Monday-Wednesday-Friday, and one for your classes on Tuesday-Thursday. This way you carry only one notebook each day. Notebooks with pockets are useful for saving class handouts.

4. Bring all necessary materials (notebooks, pencils and pens, text) to each class.

5. Develop a key for your symbols and abbreviations until you are comfortable using them. Without this, you may be unable to decode your notes.

6. Try to group and label information to aid recall.

7. Write down all terms, dates, diagrams, problems, etc., written on the board.

8. Use white space. Skip lines to separate important groups of ideas.

9. Write on only the front of your paper. This seems wasteful but makes reading your notes easier.

10. Write legibly. Notes are worthless if you can't read them.

11. If your instructor refers to specific text pages, turn to those pages and mark the information in your text rather than trying to duplicate information in your notes. Record in your notes the corresponding numbers of text pages.

12. Underline or mark important ideas and concepts with a different color ink than the one you used to take notes.

13. Compress your notes as you study. Underline or mark key words and phrases with a different color ink than the one you used to write the shorthand version.

14. Read over notes as soon as possible after class and make corrections and additions. If you have any gaps, check with another student, your instructor, or the text.

15. While you wait for class to begin, review notes to set up a framework for new material.

TABLE 3.13   Rules for Developing a Shorthand System

1. Limit the number of symbols you create.

2. Use the beginning letters of words.
   Examples   assoc/associated
   w/with
   geog/geography
   hist/history
   info/information
   intro/introduction

3. Use standard symbols.
   Examples   &/and
   #/number
   %/percent
   $/money, dollars
   ?/question
   +/plus
   ×/times, multiply
   < or > /less than or greater than

4. Use traditional abbreviations but omit periods.
   Examples   lb/pound
   ft/foot
   wt/weight
   mi/mile
   Dec/December
   US/United States

5. Omit vowels and keep only enough consonants to make the word recognizable.
   Examples   bkgd/background
   mxtr/mixture
   dvlp/develop

6. Drop endings that do not contribute to word meaning.
   Examples   ed
   ing
   ment
   er

7. Add "s" to show plurals.

8. Omit *a, an, the,* and unimportant verbs and adjectives.
   Example   Cause of CW = slavery. Instead of: A cause of the Civil War was the issue of slavery.

9. Write out terms and proper names the first time. Show your abbreviation in parentheses after the term or name. Then use the abbreviation throughout the rest of your notes.

10. Indicate dates numerically.
    Example   12/7/42 instead of December 7, 1942

TABLE 3.13   Continued

11. Use common misspellings of words.
   Examples   thru/through
                  nite/night
                  rite/right

12. Express numbers numerically.
   Examples   1/one
                  2/two
                  1st/first
                  2nd/second

EXERCISE 3.7   Use your personal shorthand system to transcribe the paragraphs in Exercise 3.3.

1. _____
   _____

2. _____
   _____

3. _____
   _____

4. _____
   _____

5. _____
   _____

6. _____
   _____

7. _____
   _____

8. _____
   _____

Cornell System of Notetaking

One system of notetaking that works well for students was developed at Cornell University. Because the system is not difficult, it saves time and effort. The step-by-step process brings efficiency to your notetaking. Walter Pauk (1984), director of the Reading Study Center at Cornell, identified five stages in notetaking. They are record, reduce,

FIGURE 3.5   Notes Written Using the Cornell Note Taking System

	[Shelters] topic
	Shelters are more efficient made of natural (raw) materials
Tropical shelters list types & quantities	Tropical Dwellers 1) Frequent rainfall 2) Bamboo – made of 3) Roof sloped for run off 4) Floor raised for dryness
Grassland Dwellers Types of weather cond. materials.	Grassland Dwellers 1) Winds, cold nights, & severe winters 2) Use animal hides stretched over wood 3) These tents are portable
Desert Dwellers Types of materials & quantities of	Desert Dwellers 1) Use mud masonry 2) Mud added to wood dries like brick 3) Mud insulates from severe climate changes (hot day— cool nights). 4) Most are farmers or nomadic. 5) Some dried brick shelters have lasted 1000 yrs.
Summary	Shelters are more efficient made of raw materials. There are 3 main types or areas where shelters are built. Tropical, Grassland & Desert regions.

SOURCE: Courtesy of Greg Jones, Metropolitan State College, Denver, Colorado.

recite, reflect, and review. Notes in Figure 3.5 are written according to the Cornell system of notetaking.

Stage 1 is to record. You prepare for this stage by drawing a vertical line about 2½ inches from the left edge of your paper. This column is your recall column. You leave it blank until Stage 2. During the lecture, you listen actively. You write in paragraph or outline form as much information as you think is important in the second, larger column.

Reduce is the key word in Stage 2. As soon after class as you can, you condense your notes and write them in the recall column. Your promptness in doing this is important because it helps you decrease your curve of forgetting. To condense notes, you omit adjectives and adverbs and leave nouns and verbs intact. It's important to use as few words as possible. If you wish, you can transfer these cues to index cards and carry them with you for quick and efficient review. The reduction stage increases your understanding and recall.

Recitation is Stage 3. During this stage, you cover your notes and try to say what's in them in your own words. You use the recall column to cue your memory. Then, you uncover your notes and check your accuracy. This review also aids in decreasing your curve of forgetting.

Stage 4 is reflect. After reciting your notes, you give yourself some "wait time." Then, you reread your notes and think about them. Next, you read your text to supplement and clarify your notes. You use your text and notes to discover the causes and effects of issues, define terms, and relate concepts. You make generalizations and draw conclusions. This helps you become a more active thinker.

Review is the goal of Stage 5. Briefly reviewing your notes several times a week helps you retain what you have learned. This distributed review keeps information fresh, provides repetition, and decreases your chances of forgetting what you've learned. (Chapter 5 discusses various memory techniques for rehearsing information.)

WRITE TO LEARN

On a separate sheet of paper or in the appropriate notebook, take notes in your next lecture using the Cornell system. Bring your notes to the next class for evaluation and discussion.

Outlining

The most common way to organize information you hear is through **outlining.** In this sequential process, you record major concepts and supporting details, examples, and other information in the same order as they appear in your text or the lecture. The disadvantage of this system is that you may record information without thought. Because you do not synthesize or relate the information you are writing, your understanding of key concepts remains superficial.

When the lecture is independent of the text, you combat this problem by active listening strategies. If the lecture reflects text content, your notetaking outline gives you a framework for recording information. With this framework, in-class notetaking becomes more active as you listen for details within subheadings.

Outlines use either formal or informal formats (See Figure 3.6). The formal format uses roman numerals (I, II, III, etc.) placed on the left side of the page or margin to note major concepts. You indent ideas that support the major concepts. You indicate these secondary points with capital letters. You show lesser supporting details with indented Arabic numerals (1, 2, 3).

Because notes are for your personal use, they need not be formally outlined. The key to an outline is to visually highlight information in some manner. For the sake of consistency, informal outlines

FIGURE 3.6   Formal and Informal Outline Formats

	Formal Outline
	I. Personality theorists
	A. Psychodynamic
	1. Freud
	2. Jung
	3. Erickson
	B. Behavior
	1. Skinner
	2. Bandura
	Informal Outline with Dashes
	Personality Theorists
	–Psychodynamic
	–Freud
	–Jung
	–Erikson
	–Behavioral
	–Skinner
	–Bandura
	Informal Outline with Symbols or Print Stlye Differences
	*PERSONALITY THEORISTS
	Psychodynamic
	Freud
	Jung
	Erickson
	Behavioral
	Skinner
	Bandura

retain the indented format of formal outlines. To make informal outlines clearer, you separate major headings and entire sections with a blank line. To construct informal outlines, you use symbols, dashes, various print types or other means of identifying differing levels of information.

EXERCISE 3.8   Outline the major headings and subheadings in Sample Chapter 2, "The Planetary Setting," using a formal outline style.

_____

_____

_____

_____

_____

_____

_____

_____

_____

_____

_____

_____

_____

_____

_____

_____

_____

_____

_____

_____

_____

EXERCISE 3.9   Using the major headings and subheadings, construct an informal outline of the information in Sample Chapter 3, "Nutrition and Digestion."

_____

_____

_____

_____

_____

_____

_____

_____

_____

_____

_____

_____

_____

_____

_____

_____

_____

_____

_____

_____

_____

Taking Notes from Lecture Media

You take notes from lecture media (for example, handouts, chalkboard, transparencies) in much the same way you take notes from lectures. You can do this because instructors control the pace of presentation and content. Conversely, taking notes from films, slides, or television differs from traditional notetaking in several ways. First, you may associate such formats with entertainment and fail to realize the importance of remembering the information they provide. Second, such media types take place in semidarkened rooms and encourage naps, rather than attention. Third, the fast pace and continuous action found in these formats often provide few pauses for taking notes. For this reason, taking notes immediately following the presentation sometimes provides the best alternative for recording new information.

PASSIVE NOTETAKING: TAPED AND BORROWED NOTES

In his poem "The Courtship of Miles Standish," Henry Wadsworth Longfellow tells of Miles Standish's courtship of a woman named Priscilla. Because Miles was such a shy man, he asked his friend John Alden to talk to Priscilla for him. John did so. During John's attempts to convince Priscilla of Miles's worth, Priscilla fell in love with John. John, however, was unaware of this. One night when he was trying to tell Priscilla of Miles's love of her, she said, "Speak for yourself, John." John did. Soon he and Priscilla were married, much to Standish's dismay.

Longfellow's poem shows that there are some tasks in life a person must do without help from others. For Miles Standish and John

*. . . and as time passed, technology overtook culture and
culture became extinct.*

Alden, that task was love. For you, it's notetaking. Borrowed or purchased notes reflect the person who took them. They require no effort
or action on your part. Thus, they are not part of active listening. The
most effective notes are personal and reflect your background knowledge and understanding.

Likewise, using a tape recorder to take notes seems a good solution. After all, a recorder copies every word the instructor says. A
recorder doesn't become bored, daydream, or doodle. It appears to be
the perfect notetaking solution. On the other hand, using a tape
recorder—like letting someone else speak for you—has drawbacks.
First, listening to tapes is too time-consuming. Transcribing them in
their entirety contributes little to understanding the lecture's main
ideas. Similar to underlining too much on a text page, writing each
word the lecturer says decreases your ability to highlight important
information. Second, because a tape recorder only records auditory
information, your notes lack diagrams, terms, and other information
that the instructor might have written on the board. Third, technical
difficulties sometimes arise. Problems like dead batteries or missing
tapes sometimes prevent you from getting the notes you need.
Fourth, the use of tape recorders sometimes offends or intimidates
instructors. Therefore, if you want to record notes, you need to get
your instructor's permission before recording any lecture. Fifth, your
reliance on recorders keeps you from learning good notetaking skills.
The sixth and most important drawback is that, as with using borrowed notes, you are a passive listener.

There is a place for borrowed or taped notes, however. If you are ill or absent from class, having someone else take or tape notes for you is better than not having notes at all. Another acceptable use of taped notes is to record the lecture while you take notes. Taped information allows you to fill gaps during review. Thus, this method is especially helpful if your instructor speaks rapidly. Like the telephone, taped notes are the next best thing to being there.

AFTER CLASS: THE FOLLOW-THROUGH

It is said that in the classroom there is more teaching than learning. Outside the classroom there is more learning than teaching. In class, you receive information from the instructor. After the lecture, your goal is to process that information. Thus, learning is not simply recording what you've seen or heard during the lecture. It's assimilating what you've seen and heard after the lecture. As a result what you learn becomes a part of you. Post-lecture reading and evaluating your notes are the follow-through that allows you to truly assimilate course information.

POST-LECTURE READING

After the lecture, you actually have been exposed to information on the lecture topic twice. First, you either previewed or read the chapter. Your second exposure was during the lecture. Postlecture reading helps you focus on the information emphasized in the lecture. If you previewed the text before the lecture, this final reading provides details, explanations, and examples to support the main ideas of the lecture. If you read the chapter in its entirely before the lecture, you should focus on the areas that confused you or that were emphasized in class. In both cases, post-lecture reading fills the gaps in your understanding.

EVALUATING YOUR NOTES

Notes organize the information you hear in a lecture—information that presumably will be the basis of a test. As a result, your notes need to be the best they can be for each course you take. Table 3.14 can be used to evaluate your notes. Assess your notes for each course you take. Notetaking ability varies according to the content and demands of the class.

TABLE 3.14   Notes Evaluation Criteria

Value points and descriptors of notetaking habits

Format	4	3	2	1	0
Use of ink	I use pen consistently.		I use pen and pencil.	I use pencil.	
Handwriting	Others can read my notes.		Only I can read my notes.	I can't read my notes.	
Notebook	I use a looseleaf binder.		I use a spiral notebook.	I don't use a notebook.	
Use of page	I leave enough space for editing.		I leave some space for editing.	My notes cover the page.	

Organization	4	3	2	1	0
Headings	I use new headings for each main idea.		I use headings inconsistently.	I don't use headings for changes in main ideas.	
Subtopics	I group subtopics under headings.		I don't indent subtopics under headings.	My subtopics are not grouped.	
Recall column	I use cue words and symbols to make practice questions.		I use cue words in a recall column.	I do not use a recall column.	
Abbreviation	I abbreviate whenever possible.		I use some abbreviation.	I don't abbreviate.	
Summaries	I summarize lectures in writing.		I write a list of summary lecture topics.	I don't summarize.	

Meaning	4	3	2	1	0
Main points	I identify main points with symbols and underlining.		I list main points.	I don't list main points.	
Supporting details	I show the relationships between main ideas and details.		My notes list details.	I don't list details.	
Examples	I list examples under main points.		I list some examples.	I don't record examples.	
Restatement	I use my own words.		I use some of my own words.	I use none of my own words.	

SOURCE: Reprinted with permission of Norman A. Stahl and the International Reading Association.

GROUP LEARNING ACTIVITY
EFFECTIVE NOTE TAKING—GOOD STUDENTS, TAKE NOTE!

Effective notetaking requires active listening. Active listeners know how to control their attention to avoid classroom daydreaming. Here's a listening/ notetaking plan that works for many students. The important steps are summarized by the letters LISAN, pronounced like the word listen (Carman & Adams, 1985).

L = *Lead. Don't follow.* Try to anticipate what the instructor is going to say. Try to set up questions as guides. Questions can come from the instructor's study guides or the reading assignments.

I = *Ideas.* Every lecture is based on a core of important ideas. Usually, an idea is introduced and examples or explanations are given. Ask yourself often, "What is the main idea now? What ideas support it?"

S = *Signal words.* Listen for words that tell you the direction the instructor is taking. For instance, here are some groups of signal words: *There are three reasons why* . . . Here come ideas, *Most important is* . . . Main idea, *On the contrary* . . . Opposite idea, *As an example* . . . Support for main idea, *Therefore* . . . Conclusion.

A = *Actively listen.* Sit where you can hear and where you can be seen if you need to ask a question. Look at the instructor while he or she talks. Bring questions you want answered from the last lecture or from your reading. Raise your hand at the beginning of class or approach your instructor before the lecture begins. Do anything that helps you to be active.

N = *Notetaking.* As you listen, write down only key points. Listen to everything, but be selective and don't try to write everything down. If you are too busy writing, you may not grasp what is being said. Any gaps in your notes can be filled in immediately after class.

Here is something more you should now: A revealing study (Palkovitz & Lore, 1980) found that most students take reasonably good notes—and then don't use them! Most students wait until just before exams to review their notes. By then, the notes have lost much of their meaning. This practice may help explain why students do poorly on test items based on lectures (Thielens, 1987). If you don't want your notes to seem like hieroglyphics or "chicken scratches," it pays to review them *on a regular basis.* And remember, whenever it is important to listen effectively, the letters LISAN are a good guide.

SOURCE: Coon, D. (1989). *Introduction to Psychology, Exploration and Application.* St. Paul: West Publishing.

Application

Use LISAN in the next lecture for this class or ask your instructor to give a brief sample lecture. In your study group, compare answers to the following questions:

1. What did you do to lead? What questions did you have? Where did you get your questions?

2. What was the core of the lecture's content? What details supported that idea?

3. What signal words were used in the lecture?

4. What did you do to actively participate in the lecture? Did other group members take note of your active participation?

5. Are you satisfied with your notes? What, if any, gaps occurred? What precipitated these gaps? What could you do differently?

SUMMARY OF MAIN POINTS

1. Strategies for previewing the text prior to class help you build background knowledge for course content. These include making predictions about content, constructing a notetaking outline through text previewing, and using chapter maps to direct your learning.

2. Several factors affect your ability to listen actively in class and communicate effectively with your instructor, the speaker. These include the abilities to maintain concentration, hear main ideas, identify important information, and recall what you hear. Although your listening responsibilities vary according to the speaker's style, you can develop a plan for maximizing your understanding of the speaker's message. As an active listener, you control the learning process and integrate what you already know with what you hear.

3. Lectures formats vary according to whether they are text-dependent, text-independent, or include media.

4. Taking notes enhances active listening. Your systematic approach to notetaking could be based on your personal system, the Cornell system, or another system. Taking notes from lecture media requires some alterations of your notetaking strategy. Passive notetaking methods are less effective because they fail to reflect your own background knowledge and purposes for learning.

5. The follow-through for notetaking occurs after class when you begin to assimilate information through post-lecture reading. Periodic evaluation of your notes for all your classes helps you assess weaknesses and formulate strategies for improvement.

VOCABULARY DEVELOPMENT
INTEGRATING LISTENING AND NOTETAKING: CONNECTING WHAT YOU LEARN WITH WHAT YOU KNOW

Consider Lincoln Logs. Some people think of college vocabulary development as a building process much as children build with Lincoln Logs. They think words are like logs that can be placed one on top of the other. Tinkertoys offer a better model for understanding how background knowledge contributes to vocabulary development. Words, like Tinkertoys, connect to each other in a variety of ways with many connections or only a few. The way you think about information and the connections you make affect what you hear and how you note it. Vocabulary development increases when you connect what you learn with what you know.

Background knowledge forms your personal set of mental Tinkertoys for connecting new information with what you already know. You make these connections as you listen to a lecture. You use the words you hear to cue the information you know. The information you know helps you make sense of and learn more about the topic. Vocabulary development is more efficient because learning something you already know about is easier than learning something you know nothing about. Notes that reflect your reactions, feelings, and connections, as well as lecture content, help you integrate new information more fully.

Background knowledge consists of everything you know about a topic. It is your knowledge of language and the world. Your knowledge of language consists of two areas: vocabulary and grammar.

Your vocabulary contributes to your knowledge of language. Your personal vocabulary consists of four subsets: listening, speaking, writing, and reading. Your listening vocabulary consists of words you understand when you hear them. Your speaking vocabulary includes words you use in talking, just as your writing vocabulary contains words you use in writing. Finally, the words you know when you see them comprise your reading vocabulary.

These four types of vocabulary can be divided into two groups, according to their use. The first group consists of those words you deposit in memory through listening and reading. The second group encompasses those words you use in speaking and writing (see Figure 1). You increase your listening vocabulary, the largest of the four types, with the least effort. Anything you hear (television, radio, teachers, friends, and so forth) enlarges your listening vocabulary. Similarly, your reading vocabulary increases each time you find the meanings of new words. Both reading and listening involve actively receiving new information. Speaking and writing are the ways you use the words you learn. If you make no deposits, you have no words to use.

The second area of language knowledge is grammar. Even if English isn't

FIGURE 1   Four Types of Vocabulary

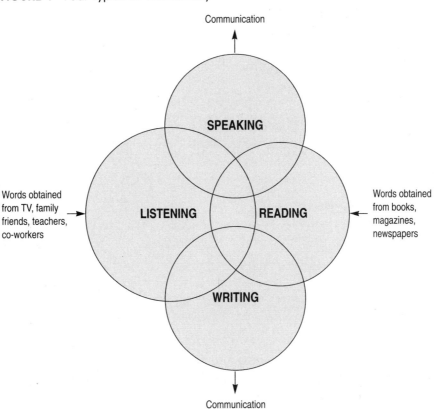

your favorite subject, you possess much knowledge about the English language. Your knowledge of words and their functions in sentences allows you to find meaning. Your knowledge of punctuation also helps you find meaning. This process is cyclical. The more you know about how language functions, the more you are able to learn. The more you are able to learn, the more you know. Knowledge of language aids you in becoming a more active listener. Active listening, in turn, helps you increase your language knowledge.

World knowledge comes from the sum of your experiences. It consists of what you know about the way people, places, things, and concepts work and relate to each other. It includes facts, opinions, inferences, and other information you get through direct experience or through vicarious learning.

For example, it's one thing to go to France. It's another to read about going to France. Although both provide you with information about the country, the direct experience of traveling to France provides you with more complete and direct information. The sights, sounds, and feelings you experience are your own. However, time, money, or other factors may keep you from taking such a trip. You can still learn about France vicariously through reading, television, movies, travel brochures, conversations with people who have been there, and so on. The quantity and quality of the information you get depends on the viewpoints, experiences, and perceptions of your sources. Active listening also increases your store of world knowledge.

Activity

In the space below, list the things you associate with the phrase

"Every man a king but no one wears a crown."

Now read the following passage from a biography of Huey Long, Louisiana governor in the 1930's. After reading, update your list in ink. On a separate sheet of paper, respond to the following question: How did the passage affect your consideration of the topic? What accounts for the differences in before and after reading? What happens when you connect what you learn with what you know? What happens if you fail to connect what you learn with what you know?

Above the platform stretched banners proclaiming the Long slogan: Every Man a King, But No One Wears a Crown." John H. Overton presided and introduced the dignitaries on the platform, among whom were John P. Sullivan and Swords Lee, and the candidate who was also the speaker of the evening. Huey gave the same kind of speech that he had given in launching his campaign four years before. . . . He wanted to make Louisiana into "a progressive, educated and modern commonwealth." He promised free textbooks, free bridges, surfaced roads ("practically every public road" should be surfaced), improved state hospitals and other institutions, natural gas for New Orleans and other cities, state warehouses to aid farmers in marketing their crops, vocational training for the deaf, dumb, and blind, and an expanded court system. He strongly implied that the state should supply financial assistance to local school units (every boy and girl should be able to live at home and have access to an education) and to students of poor families who wished to attend higher institutions. He denied that he was hostile to corporations. He had opposed only the evil ones, but he thought that all the big ones should bear a higher and fairer burden of taxation.

CHAPTER REVIEW

Answer briefly but completely.

1. Examine the textbooks you use for each of your classes (or the sample chapters in this text). How do factors within the text impact your choice of previewing strategy for making predictions about content?

_____

_____

_____

2. Compare and contrast Table 3.1, *Steps in Previewing*, with Table 3.3, *Constructing a Notetaking Outline through Text Previews*. How are the tables alike? How are they different? What accounts for their similarities and differences?

_____

_____

_____

_____

_____

3. Explain how differing lecture formats (text-dependent, text-independent, with media) might affect left- and right-brain learning.

_____

_____

_____

4. How do the listening habits in Quiz #2 of the Listening Questionnaire (Figure 3.3) affect your ability to understand and process a class lecture? Why?

_____

_____

_____

5. What is the relationship between the factors affecting your ability to be an active listener and the items in Table 3.8, Rating Checklist for Instructors?

_____

_____

_____

6. Which of Peper and Mayer's three theories of notetaking do you feel best supports the Cornell system of notetaking? Why?

_____

_____

_____

7. How do formal and informal outline formats (See Figure 3.6) affect right- and left-brain learning? Why?

_____

_____

_____

8. A notetaking service has just opened near your institution. It sells copies of the entire set of notes for each of the classes in which you are now enrolled. What might be the advantages of having a copy? What would be the disadvantages?

_____

_____

_____

9. How does the after-class follow-through affect the curve of forgetting (Figure 3.4)?

_____

_____

_____

10. Give a specific example of how course content and demands affect notetaking ability.

_____

_____

_____

REFERENCES

Howe, M. J. (1970). "Notetaking Strategy, Review and Long-Term Relationships between Notetaking Variables and Achievement Measures." *Journal of Educational Research* 63:285.

Kiewra, K. A. (1985). "Investigating Notetaking and Review: A Depth of Processing Alternative." *Educational Psychologist* 20(1): 23–32.

Pauk, W. (1984). *How to Study in College.* Boston: Houghton Mifflin, pp. 127–29.

Peper, R. J., and Mayer, R. E. (1978). "Notetaking as a Generative Activity." *Journal of Educational Psychology* 70(4): 514–22.

Williams, T. H. (1969). *Huey Long.* New York, NY: Alfred A. Knopf, Inc., pp. 262–63.

OBJECTIVES

By the end of this chapter, you will be able to do the following:

1. Survey a chapter to actively connect what you know with what you need to read.

2. Create questions to set goals for reading.

3. Actively read to find and summarize main ideas.

4. Recite information to check understanding.

5. Review information to lock it into long-term memory.

STEP ONE: SURVEY   STEP TWO: QUESTION   STEP THREE: READ   STEP FOUR: RECITE   STEP FIVE: PREVIEW

```
                              STEP THREE:
                              READ
                                 |
                    ┌────────────┴────────────┐
                 Text                      Text
                 Marking                   Labeling
                                              |
                                  ┌───────────┴───────────┐
                              Finding                  Identifying
                              Main                     Text
                              Ideas                    Structure
```

TERMS

cause/effect
comparison/contrast
enumeration/sequence
introduction/summary
subject development/
   definition
text labeling
text marking
text structure

The president was introducing the commencement speaker and Kate forced herself to concentrate. A plump woman in her fifties took the podium. Her plain, stern-lipped face was hazily familiar as that which in photographs of feminist rallies, usually appeared just behind that of Friedan or Steinem.

"I envy you women," she was saying. "The path is so clearly marked for you. There will be no need for you to repeat the mistakes of my generation. The obstacles that blocked us now exist only for you to hurdle. You will be free to go out and have anything and everything you want!"

Kate listened attentively. The message was clear: go out and do something and be sure that it is creative and meaningful, that it gives you power and above all makes you a success. But now the speaker was retiring from the podium. Wait! Kate shrieked silently. Don't go yet! You haven't told us what that something is, nor shown us how to get it. The path isn't clear . . . no, not clear at all.

SOURCE: Reprinted from *Everything We Wanted* by Lindsay Marcotta, © 1984 by Lindsay Marcotta. Used by permission of Crown Publishers, Inc.

As a student, you face a challenge in each class you take. Like Kate, you know what is expected of you—good grades, a degree, a new job. You probably have a general idea of what you need to do to meet your goals. You know that studying and preparing for class lead to success. Also like Kate, you may feel that you have no specific plan to help you accomplish the necessary tasks (reading texts, reviewing information) for achieving your goal.

Such a plan exists for using information from texts. Developed by Frances Robinson, the SQ3R study system has been used by countless students to help them read and recall text information. SQ3R involves five steps: *survey, question, read, recite,* and *review.*

These steps identify information presented in Chapters 3, 4, and 5 of this text. Table 4.1 defines all steps of the SQ3R process. It also provides a quick index of where information about each step is found in these chapters.

STEP ONE: SURVEY

Surveying, or previewing, is the first step in your interaction with the text. Surveying before reading accomplishes two goals. First, it makes reading an active, rather than a passive, process. It requires you to think about the topic of the chapter before you begin reading. Second, it provides you with an opportunity to connect what you already know about the topic, your background knowledge, with the new information you will be learning. How does your background knowledge affect your understanding? Read the passage below and answer the accompanying questions.

The procedure is actually quite simple. First you arrange things into different groups. Of course, one pile may be sufficient depending on how much

TABLE 4.1   Steps in SQ3R

SQ3R Step	Definition	Process Used
Survey	Previewing to find main ideas or get the gist of a chapter.	Previewing. See Table 3.1.
Question	Predicting chapter content or setting purposes for reading.	Making predictions about content. See Table 3.2.
Read	Checking your predictions through literal and inferential comprehension.	Reading or processing text and scanning. See Tables 4.3, 4.4, 4.5, and 4.6 and Figure 4.3.
Recite	Checking your understanding of the text.	Monitoring understanding. See Table 4.7.
Review	Transferring information from short-term to long-term memory.	Rehearsal through practice, organization, and association. See Chapter 5.

there is to do. If you have to go somewhere else due to lack of facilities that is the next step; otherwise, you are pretty well set. It is important not to overdo things. That is, it is better to do too few things at once than too many. In the short run this may not seem important but complications can easily arise. A mistake can be expensive as well. At first the whole procedure will seem complicated. Soon, however, it will become just another facet of life. It is difficult to foresee any end to the necessity for this task in the immediate future, but then one can never tell. After the procedure is completed one arranges the materials into different groups again. Then they can be put into their appropriate places. Eventually they will be used once more and the whole cycle will then have to be repeated. However, that is part of life.

SOURCE: Bransford, J. D., and Johnson, M. K. (1972). "Contextual Prerequisites for Understanding: Some Investigations of Comprehension and Recall." *Journal of Verbal Learning and Verbal Behavior* 2:6.

1. What is the topic of this passage?

2. What do you know about this topic?

3. In the first sentence, what procedure is being referred to?

4. How did you identify this procedure?

5. The passage states that after putting things into different groups, you might have to go somewhere else due to lack of facilities. What place does "somewhere else" refer to?

6. How do you recognize the location of "somewhere else?"

7. The passage states that mistakes could be expensive. What does that mean?

8. Why is there no foreseeable end to this procedure?

Some frameworks of the word score.

The topic of the passage is identified on the bottom of the last page in this chapter. After you have checked the topic, answer questions 2 through 8 again.

How was your understanding improved by knowing the topic? Although the passage contained no more information than when you first read it, you—the learner—provided the details needed to understand it. Before you knew the topic, you had no way to interact with the information. Without information supplied by you, it made no sense.

When you learn, information comes from two sources: one external, the other internal. The text is an external source of information. You, the learner, are the internal source.

Many students learn without making the most of the interaction of internal and external sources. Because you are a less obvious source of information, you may not have thought of yourself as a source.

The survey step in SQ3R allows you to maximize yourself as a source of information in learning. Surveying usually is part of your before-lecture preparation. As such, surveying, or previewing, was described in Chapter 3, Table 3.1.

WRITE TO LEARN

Consider the preceding cartoon. It shows how different people would define the word *score* based on their differing backgrounds. On a separate sheet of paper, write how the word *set* would be defined by each of the following: (1) a mathematician, (2) a jeweler, (3) a china salesperson, (4) a tennis pro, and (5) a cook. What accounts for differences among the definitions?

STEP TWO: QUESTION

I keep six honest servants
(They taught me all I knew);
Their names are *What* and *Why* and *When*
And *How* and *Where* and *Who*.

—RUDYARD KIPLING

For many students, the goal of reading is to finish. Whether or not they learn anything is beside the point as long as they meet their goal.

Your goals for learning should be part of a quest for knowledge. Employing Kipling's six servants assists you in your quest by helping you set goals for understanding what you read. Although you set your goals by asking questions as part of the before-lecture process as described on pp. 96–99 in Chapter 3, you find the answers to your questions through reading—Step 3 of the SQ3R process. Table 4.2 summarizes the kinds of information that each of your "honest servants" helps you find.

TABLE 4.2	Question Words and Corresponding Indicators
If your question begins. . .	**Look for. . . when you read.**
Why?	Words such as *because, for that reason, consequently, as a result*
How?	A sequence; a list; or words such as *by, through, as a result of*
What?	Nouns; linking verbs; punctuation symbols (commas, dashes, parentheses); words such as *involves, consists, includes*
Who?	Capitalized words or names of groups; nouns
How many? How much?	Numbers (written or Arabic)
Which?	Nouns and adjectives
When?	Capitalized words such as days, months, or other time periods; time of the day (written or Arabic); numerical symbols for months, days, and years; words like *before, during, after, soon, later, prior*
Where?	Capitalized places (cities, states, countries); addresses; words such as *behind, across, near, next to*

STEP THREE: READ

If you have ever bought a product marked "REQUIRES ASSEMBLY," you know how vital it is to preview the diagrams and read all of the directions before beginning. This thorough reading, in combination with your preview, provides you with all available information before you tackle your task.

Similarly, reading a chapter in its entirety before class helps you glean all important details and main ideas for use during class. Rather than encountering new ideas in the lecture, you affirm what you read and clarify misconceptions. Your background knowledge enables you to grasp new ideas more quickly and firmly.

To get the most from reading you must do more than simply sit and stare at a text. In the second step of SQ3R, you posed questions. Now you need to actively seek their answers. This means that you look for patterns, or connections, among information. You consider the meanings of terms in their surroundings. You try to summarize main ideas. You draw conclusions. You attend critically to the information in the text. One way to assure that you read actively is to mark your text as you read. Table 4.3 summarizes the reading process.

TEXT MARKING

The art of becoming wise is the art of knowing what to overlook.
—WILLIAM JAMES

Text marking sounds simple. You find important information and mark it. You highlight or underline what you want to remember. But what exactly do you mark? How do you know what is really important? How do you know what to "overlook?"

First, what you mark depends on how much you already know about the topic. Consider what might happen if you were studying about the settlement of Salt Lake City. If you're from Salt Lake City, you'd probably mark less. This is because you might already know some of the information. In contrast, if you know little about Salt Lake City, you'll probably mark more. In general, the less you know, the more you mark. The more you know, the less you mark.

Second, if you previewed and asked content-predicting questions, what you mark should answer your questions. As a result, you mark the information that highlights terms and main ideas.

You might also include other details that support your answers to your questions. These could be the steps in a sequence or other kinds of lists, reasons, conclusions, and so on. Knowing which and what

TABLE 4.3	Steps in the Reading Process

1. Keeping your purpose-setting question in mind, read the paragraph or passage.

2. Identify the topic by looking for the repetition of key words and phrases. If the main idea is unstated, identify the topic by retrieving background knowledge that seems appropriate until details confirm or disprove your choice.

3. Retrieve the background knowledge necessary to understand the text.

4. Based on elements in the text and your background knowledge, identify stated details and make inferences about new terms or concepts.

5. Make inferences about unstated details or the text pattern of the main idea.

6. Restate the main idea through paraphrasing, summarizing, or synthesizing.

7. Determine if the main idea answers your purpose-setting question.

---

kind of details your instructor deems most important helps you choose what to mark.

The difficulty of text language is a third factor to consider in text marking. Although how difficult you find a topic to be depends on your familiarity with that topic, its difficulty also depends on how it is written or presented. Such factors as subject depth, number of details, and vocabulary affect the ease with which you understand.

As you read the following excerpts, note their differing lengths. Although both passages are about the same topic, their content differs. The second passage includes more details and provides more information about the subject. In addition, the vocabulary (see bold-faced italicized words) is much more difficult.

PASSAGE 1

Babbage did not give up, however. In 1833 he developed a plan for building an *analytical engine.* This machine was to be capable of addition, subtraction, multiplication, division, and storage of intermediate results in a memory unit. Unfortunately, the analytical engine was also too advanced for its time. It was Babbage's concept of the analytical engine, though, that led to the computer more than a hundred years later. This earned him the title of ''the father of modern computers.''

SOURCE: Reprinted by permission from *Introduction to Computers and Basic Programming* by Brenan and Mandell; Copyright © 1984 by West Publishing Company. All rights reserved.

PASSAGE 2

One reason Babbage **abandoned** the Difference Engine was that he had been struck by a much better idea. Inspired by Jacquard's punched-card-controlled loom, Babbage wanted to build a punched-card-controlled calculator. He called his proposed automatic calculator the *Analytical Engine*.

The Difference Engine could only compute tables (and only those tables that could be computed by successive additions). But the Analytical Engine could carry out any calculation, just as Jacquard's loom could weave any pattern. All one had to do was to punch the cards with the instructions for the desired calculations. If the Analytical Engine had been completed, it would have been a nineteenth-century computer.

But, alas, that was not to be. The British government had already sunk thousands of pounds into the Difference Engine and had received nothing in return. It had no intention of making the same mistake with the Analytical Engine. And Babbage's **eccentricities** and **abrasive** personality did not help his cause.

Looking back, the government may have even been right. If it had **financed** the new invention, it might well have received nothing in return. For, as usual, Babbage's idea was far ahead of existing mechanical technology. This was particularly true because the design for the Analytical Engine was **grandiose.** For example, Babbage wanted his machine to do calculations with fifty-digit accuracy, an accuracy far greater than that found in most modern computers and far more than is needed for most calculations.

What's more, Babbage often changed his plans in the middle of a project, so that everything done previously had to be abandoned and the work started anew. How **ironic** that the founder of operations research, the science of industrial management, could not manage the development of his own inventions.

Babbage's **contemporaries** would have considered him more successful if he had stayed with his original plan and constructed the Difference Engine. If he had done this, however, he would have earned only a footnote in history. It is for the Analytical Engine he never completed that we honor Babbage as "the father of the computer."

SOURCE: Reprinted with permission from *The Mind Tool,* 3/e, by Graham; Copyright © 1983 by West Publishing Company. All rights reserved.

Your goal should be to mark amounts of information that are "just right." Consider the two examples of text marking found in Figure 4.1. In the first example, the student marked too much information to be useful for study. Remember that the purpose of text marking is to tell the difference between important and unimportant information. Here, there is no difference. Even if you know nothing about a subject, you should be marking half or less of the information.

In the second example in Figure 4.1, the student marked too little information. This could mean that the student already felt confident about understanding the information. It also could signal a lack of attention, poor understanding, or a lack of knowledge about what to mark.

Now consider the text marked in Figure 4.2. It shows the "just right" amount of text marking. Remember, while the amount you

FIGURE 4.1   Overmarking and Undermarking Text

The Problem of Obesity

However you define it, obesity does occur to an alarming extent and is increasing in the developed countries. For example, in the United States some 10 to 25 percent of all teenagers and some 25 to 50 percent of all adults are obese.

Obesity brings many health hazards with it. Insurance companies report that fat people die younger from a host of causes, including heart attacks, strokes, and complications of (type II) diabetes. In fact, among adults, gaining weight often appears to precipitate diabetes. Fat people more often have high blood cholesterol (a risk factor for coronary heart disease), hypertension, complications after surgery, gynecological irregularities, and the toxemia of pregnancy. For men, the risk of cancers of the colon, rectum, and prostate gland rises with obesity; for women, the risk of cancers of the breast, uterus, ovaries, gallbladder, and bile ducts is greater. The burden of extra fat strains the skeletal system, aggravating arthritis—especially in the knees, hips, and lower spine. The muscles that support the belly may give way, resulting in abdominal hernias. When the leg muscles are abnormally fatty, they fail to contract efficiently to help blood return from the leg veins to the heart; blood collects in the leg veins, which swell, harden, and become varicose. Extra fat in and around the chest interferes with breathing, sometimes causing severe respiratory problems. Gout is more common, and even the accident rate is greater for the severely obese.

Beyond all these hazards is the risk incurred by millions of obese people throughout much of their lives— the risk of ill-advised, misguided dieting. Some fad diets are more hazardous to health than obesity itself. One survey of 29,000 claims, treatments, and theories for losing weight found fewer than 6 percent of them effective— and 13 percent dangerous!

Social and economic disadvantages also plague the fat person. Obese people are less often sought after for marriage, pay higher insurance premiums, meet discrimination when applying for college admissions and jobs, can't find attractive clothes so easily, and are limited in their choice of sports. For many, guilt, depression, withdrawal, and self-blame are inevitable psychological accompaniments to obesity.

Although obesity is a severe physical handicap, it is unlike other handicaps in two important ways. First, mortality risk is not linearly related to excess weight. Instead, there is a threshold at which risk dramatically increases. Being

SOURCE: Reprinted by permission from *Understanding Nutrition*, 4th edition, by Whitney and Hamilton; © 1987 by West Publishing Company. All rights reserved.

mark depends on what you know about the topic, the difficulty of the text, the goal-setting questions you posed, and what you think your instructor will ask questions about, overmarking results in nothing gained but a neon-colored page.

FIGURE 4.1   Continued

The Problem of Obesity

However you define it, obesity does occur to an alarming extent and is increasing in the developed countries. For example, in the United States some 10 to 25 percent of all teenagers and some 25 to 50 percent of all adults are obese.

Obesity brings many health hazards with it. Insurance companies report that fat people die younger from a host of causes, including heart attacks, strokes, and complications of (type II) diabetes. In fact, among adults, gaining weight often appears to precipitate diabetes. Fat people more often have high blood cholesterol (a risk factor for coronary heart disease), hypertension, complications after surgery, gynecological irregularities, and the toxemia of pregnancy. For men, the risk of cancers of the colon, rectum, and prostate gland rises with obesity; for women, the risk of cancers of the breast, uterus, ovaries, gallbladder, and bile ducts is greater. The burden of extra fat strains the skeletal system, aggravating arthritis—especially in the knees, hips, and lower spine. The muscles that support the belly may give way, resulting in abdominal hernias. When the leg muscles are abnormally fatty, they fail to contract efficiently to help blood return from the leg veins to the heart; blood collects in the leg veins, which swell, harden, and become varicose. Extra fat in and around the chest interferes with breathing, sometimes causing severe respiratory problems. Gout is more common, and even the accident rate is greater for the severely obese.

Beyond all these hazards is the risk incurred by millions of obese people throughout much of their lives— the risk of ill-advised, misguided dieting. Some fad diets are more hazardous to health than obesity itself. One survey of 29,000 claims, treatments, and theories for losing weight found fewer than 6 percent of them effective— and 13 percent dangerous!

Social and economic disadvantages also plague the fat person. Obese people are less often sought after for marriage, pay higher insurance premiums, meet discrimination when applying for college admissions and jobs, can't find attractive clothes so easily, and are limited in their choice of sports. For many, guilt, depression, withdrawal, and self-blame are inevitable psychological accompaniments to obesity.

Although obesity is a severe physical handicap, it is unlike other handicaps in two important ways. First, mortality risk is not linearly related to excess weight. Instead, there is a threshold at which risk dramatically increases. Being

FIGURE 4.2 Text Marking

The Problem of Obesity

However you define it, obesity does occur to an alarming extent and is increasing in the developed countries. For example, in the United States some 10 to 25 percent of all teenagers and some 25 to 50 percent of all adults are obese.

Obesity brings many health hazards with it. Insurance companies report that fat people die younger from a host of causes, including heart attacks, strokes, and complications of (type II) diabetes. In fact, among adults, gaining weight often appears to precipitate diabetes. Fat people more often have high blood cholesterol (a risk factor for coronary heart disease), hypertension, complications after surgery, gynecological irregularities, and the toxemia of pregnancy. For men, the risk of cancers of the colon, rectum, and prostate gland rises with obesity; for women, the risk of cancers of the breast, uterus, ovaries, gallbladder, and bile ducts is greater. The burden of extra fat strains the skeletal system, aggravating arthritis—especially in the knees, hips, and lower spine. The muscles that support the belly may give way, resulting in abdominal hernias. When the leg muscles are abnormally fatty, they fail to contract efficiently to help blood return from the leg veins to the heart; blood collects in the leg veins, which swell, harden, and become varicose. Extra fat in and around the chest interferes with breathing, sometimes causing severe respiratory problems. Gout is more common, and even the accident rate is greater for the severely obese.

Beyond all these hazards is the risk incurred by millions of obese people throughout much of their lives— the risk of ill-advised, misguided dieting. Some fad diets are more hazardous to health than obesity itself. One survey of 29,000 claims, treatments, and theories for losing weight found fewer than 6 percent of them effective— and 13 percent dangerous!

Social and economic disadvantages also plague the fat person. Obese people are less often sought after for marriage, pay higher insurance premiums, meet discrimination when applying for college admissions and jobs, can't find attractive clothes so easily, and are limited in their choice of sports. For many, guilt, depression, withdrawal, and self-blame are inevitable psychological accompaniments to obesity.

Although obesity is a severe physical handicap, it is unlike other handicaps in two important ways. First, mortality risk is not linearly related to excess weight. Instead, there is a threshold at which risk dramatically increases. Being

SOURCE: Reprinted by permission from *Understanding Nutrition*, 4th edition, by Whitney and Hamilton;

TEXT LABELING

Imagine that you take a trip and have gotten lost. When you ask for directions, a friendly citizen gets a map and highlights the route you should take. Thanking your new friend, you start off once more. However, when you look at the map, you find no names for streets, buildings, or other locations. Although you may be able to reach your destination, it will take more effort to get there.

Much the same problem occurs in text marking. Many students read and mark information, just to find themselves somewhat "lost" when they have to study. Only with effort can they reconstruct why they marked their texts as they did.

Consider again the marked text in Figure 4.2. Most students would agree that, just by looking, it appears to be appropriately marked. The answer to the question "What is the problem of obesity?" ranges across much of the section. Reviewing for a test several weeks later, you might forget how the information relates. You would need to reread most of what you marked to reconstruct your thoughts.

Text labeling helps you identify relationships and summarize information. It does not replace text marking. Instead, you use it in addition to text marking. Text labeling forms a kind of index to help you locate information more quickly. You also use it to write yourself notes for later review.

Text marking and labeling require several steps (see Table 4.4). First, you read and mark your text. Then you look for patterns, main ideas, and ways to summarize information. Once you've thought of one or two summary words, you write them in the column next to that information. Finally, you include any notes to yourself about how and what to study (see Figure 4.3).

Finding Main Ideas

Every chapter and every paragraph of a text has a main idea, a central thought. The main ideas and supporting details of each paragraph support the key concept of the chapter. Sometimes, but not always, a topic sentence tells you the main idea; this sentence usually appears at the beginning or end of the reading but may appear anywhere. To answer your goal-setting questions and understand how information in a section relates to the chapter, you must locate and label main ideas.

Look at the paragraph below.

TWO THEORIES OF POWER

The two major *theories of power* are *pluralism* and *elitism*. According to the *theory of pluralism*, decision-making is the result of competition, bargaining, and compromise among diverse *special interest groups*. In this view, *power* is widely dis-

---

TABLE 4.4   Guidelines for Marking and Labeling Text

1. Read a paragraph or section completely before marking anything.

2. Mark those points that comprise the answer to your purpose-setting question.

3. Number lists, reasons, or other items that occur in a series or sequence.

4. Identify important terms, dates, places, names, and so on.

5. Be selective in marking. If you identify every line as important, you lose the benefit of text marking. If you are not good at being selective, mark your textbook in pencil first. Then, go back with a colored pen or highlighter and selectively mark important information.

6. Write main idea summaries, questions, or other comments in the margins.

7. Put a question mark beside unclear or confusing information.

8. Put a star or exclamation point beside information your instructor emphasizes in class, possible test questions, or what seems to be extremely important information.

9. Write comments on the table of contents or make your own table of contents of important topics inside the front cover or on the title page of the text.

10. When buying a used text, never choose one that's been underlined by another student.

---

tributed throughout a *society* or *community*. On the other hand, according to the theory of *elitism*, a *community* or *society* is controlled from the top by a few individuals or organizations. *Power* is said to be concentrated in the hands of an *elite* group with common interests and background.

To find the main idea of the preceding paragraph, you first create a purpose-setting question from the heading. Here, the question might be "What are two theories of power?" Then you read the paragraph to identify key words and phrases. (Italics highlight key words for you in the example.) You now look to see what idea the sentences share (that is, two theories of power—elitism and pluralism—affect societies and communities). Next, you decide if the key concept answers your purpose-setting question. Yes, your prediction is verified. Now, you create a label that states the key concept. In this case, your label might read: *Two theories of power—elitism and pluralism—affect societies and communities.*

FIGURE 4.3   Text Labeling

The Problem of Obesity

Rate of obesity– EX-U.S.

However you define it, obesity does occur to an alarming extent and is increasing in the developed countries. For example, in the United States some 10 to 25 percent of all teenagers and some 25 to 50 percent of all adults are obese.

Obesity brings many health hazards with it. Insurance companies report that fat people die younger from a host of causes, including heart attacks, strokes, and complications of (type II) diabetes. In fact, among adults, gaining weight often appears to precipitate diabetes. Fat people more often have high blood cholesterol (a risk factor for coronary heart disease), hypertension, complications after surgery, gynecological irregularities, and the toxemia of pregnancy. For men, the risk of cancers of the colon, rectum, and prostate gland rises with obesity; for women, the risk of cancers of the breast, uterus, ovaries, gallbladder, and bile ducts is greater. The burden of extra fat strains the skeletal system, aggravating arthritis—especially in the knees, hips, and lower spine. The muscles that support the belly may give way, resulting in abdominal hernias. When the leg muscles are abnormally fatty, they fail to contract efficiently to help blood return from the leg veins to the heart; blood collects in the leg veins, which swell, harden, and become varicose. Extra fat in and around the chest interferes with breathing, sometimes causing severe respiratory problems. Gout is more common, and even the accident rate is greater for the severely obese.

Health Hazards

Know Causes and Effects

Diets— Hazardous to Health!?

Beyond all these hazards is the risk incurred by millions of obese people throughout much of their lives— the risk of ill-advised, misguided dieting. Some fad diets are more hazardous to health than obesity itself. One survey of 29,000 claims, treatments, and theories for losing weight found fewer than 6 percent of them effective— and 13 percent dangerous!

Social, Economic, Psych disadv.

Social and economic disadvantages also plague the fat person. Obese people are less often sought after for marriage, pay higher insurance premiums, meet discrimination when applying for college admissions and jobs, can't find attractive clothes so easily, and are limited in their choice of sports. For many, guilt, depression, withdrawal, and self-blame are inevitable psychological accompaniments to obesity.

Compare

How unlike other handicaps

Although obesity is a severe physical handicap, it is unlike other handicaps in two important ways. First, mortality risk is not linearly related to excess weight. Instead, there is a threshold at which risk dramatically increases. Being

Now consider the following paragraph:

THE FIRST BUG
The first "bug" was found in the summer of 1945. The Mark II computer used by the Department of Defense suddenly stopped functioning. Routine checks found no problems. The search continued until a moth, which became stuck in one of the computer's relays, was located. Since then, the term has come to mean any hardware malfunction or software error which affects the ability of the computer to run.

Before reading, your purpose-setting question probably was "What was the first bug?" Perhaps you then inferred that the paragraph would have something to do with insects. Thus, you chose that background to use in understanding the text. As you read, you quickly found that you lacked details to support that topic. The second sentence probably led you to retrieve knowledge related to computers. Based on text elements and your knowledge about computers, you understood references to terms such as *hardware, software, computer relays,* and *run.* You inferred that the people who located the moth coined the term *bug,* filling that element by default. Therefore, you conclude that the main idea is that the first bug in computer technology was a moth and that the term *bug* became synonymous with a computer malfunction. This inferred main idea answers the question "What was the first bug?" Your label for this paragraph reads: *The first computer bug was a moth that caused trouble; now* bug *refers to a part of the computer process that causes trouble.*

The examples of labels for these paragraphs are complete sentences. When you label your text, often there is not room in the text or time in your life to write complete sentences. Then, you identify the main idea and abbreviate your main idea statement. For example, an abbreviation of the last example could be as follows: 1st computer bug = moth >>TROUBLE—now "computer bug" = TROUBLE.

A list of some simple shorthand symbols and their meanings appears in Table 4.5. This list changes depending on your needs and the course you take. Be careful not to abbreviate too much. You need to be able to decode your labels when studying.

WRITE TO LEARN

Consider again the quote by William James that begins the section on text marking: "The art of becoming wise is the art of knowing what to overlook." On a separate sheet of paper, explain this quote in light of what you have learned about text marking and labeling.

TABLE 4.5	Shorthand Symbols for Text Labeling
Symbol	**Meaning**
Ex	example or experiment
FORM	formula
Conc	conclusion
MI	main idea
! or *	important information
→	results, leads to, steps in a sequence
(1),(2),(3)	numbered points—label what points are important
circled word	summarizes process
?	disagree or unclear
TERM	important term
SUM	summary
{	indicates that certain pieces of information relate
OPIN	author's opinion, rather than fact

Identifying Text Structure

Text structure consists of how the vocabulary and topic of a text are organized. The patterns in which ideas, or details, are structured include introduction/summary, subject development/definition, enumeration/sequence, comparison/contrast, and cause/effect. Recognizing how ideas fit together helps you relate information more easily. Instead of having to recall isolated details, you fit them into an organized pattern. This helps you recall categories or blocks of information more easily within paragraphs, sections, and entire chapters.

Because text structure varies according to the topic and the author's purpose, there is seldom one single pattern. Features of various types of text structure usually are combined, with one predominant type. For example, a cause/effect passage may enumerate causes or effects. Nonetheless, patterns of text structure do exist, and identifying them aids you in reading and understanding texts. Special words signal the way the text is structured. These words show the direction and organization of the ideas being presented. Signal words within the passage, if present, help you draw conclusions and find main ideas. Table 4.6 gives a short description of each of the four types of text structure and lists examples of signal words. If no signal words are present, you determine structure by examining how the information is discussed.

Introduction/summary text structures differ from other text structures in that they are identified by their physical placement in a chapter or by headings such as "Introduction" or "Summary." Introduction/summary text paragraphs also may be found at the beginning or end of major sections. Once you have discovered the placement

TABLE 4.6   Text Structure Patterns and Signal Words

Pattern	Description	Examples of Signal Words
Introduction/ Summary	Identifies main points	Identified by location, either the beginning or end of a discussion of a topic, and by such words as *in summary, in conclusion, as a review, to summarize, to sum up*
Subject Development/ Definition	Identifies a concept and describes, develops, or explains it	Linking verbs, lists of facts related to the topic but unrelated to each other
Enumeration/ Sequence	Lists or orders main points or presents a problem and steps for its solution	*First, second, third . . ., first, next, then, finally, in addition, last, and, furthermore, and then, most important, least important*
Comparison/ Contrast	Describes ways in which concepts are alike or different or presents two or more sides of an issue	Comparison—*similarly, both, as well as, likewise, in like manner* Contrast—*however, on the other hand, on the contrary, but, instead of, although, yet, nevertheless, distinguish, alternative*
Cause/Effect	Shows the result of action(s) or explains a problem and its solution	*Therefore, thus, as a result, because, in turn, then, hence, for this reason, results in, causes, effects, leads to, consequently*

and identification of these passages in a textbook chapter, you probably will find them in the same place with the same identification throughout the other chapters of that text.

The content of an introduction or summary contains features of other structure types and aids you in choosing the information you need from memory. Many readers skip these sections, but they often concisely identify the main points of a chapter. To use an introduction/ summary text structure, you identify the placement of introductory and summary passages and the major points in the chapter or section.

Figure 4.4 provides an example of this structure type.

Subject development/definition text structure identifies a concept and lists its supporting details. Such paragraphs are usually found at the beginning of major sections.

A subject development/definition passage describes or explains a topic by providing a definition and/or listing characteristics. Often these facts relate to the topic but have little or no relationship with

FIGURE 4.4   Examples of Introduction and Summary Structures

Introduction Passage

The way anthropologists approach the study of humanity has undergone many changes since the discipline originated in the nineteenth century. Some ideas held by most scholars a century ago have been discarded today; others are still with us. In this chapter, we discuss some of the important scholars and schools of thought that shaped the way modern anthropologists approach their studies. For each approach, we emphasize its assumptions, its basic questions, its errors, and its contributions to the theoretical ideas of modern anthropology.

SOURCE: Reprinted with permission of Peoples and Bailey, *Humanity: An Introduction to Cultural Anthropology.* © 1991 by West Publishing Company. All rights reserved.

Summary Passage

In this chapter we have reviewed the functions of society, the ways in which societies are organized around food, the basis of social structure, and the process of social interaction. We have learned that society is an exceedingly complex phenomenon with its inner workings hidden from the casual view.

Individuals in every society must be socialized to behave in ways that are beneficial for that society. In the next chapter, we examine the process of socialization and consider how both the individual and society benefit from such socialization.

SOURCE: Reprinted with permission of Knox, *Living Sociology.* © 1990 by West Publishing Company. All rights reserved.

FIGURE 4.5   Example of Subject Development Structure

SLUMP.   A slump is the intermittent movement of a mass of earth or rock along a curved slip-plane. It is characterized by the backward rotation of the slump block so that its surface may eventually tilt in the direction opposite the slope from which it became detached. Slumps are most likely to occur on steep slopes with deep, clay-rich soils after a period of saturation by heavy rains. The movement generally takes place over a period of days or weeks and is nearly impossible to control or halt once it has begun.

Slumps are common along the California coast, where slopes have frequently been over-steepened by wave undercutting. They also occur along the sideslopes of river gorges in various parts of the western United States. Small slumps capable of blocking traffic frequently occur on steep roadcuts following heavy rains.

SOURCE: Reprinted with permission from *Essentials of Physical Geography*, by Scott; © 1991 by West Publishing Company.

---

each other. To locate subject development/definition passages, you look for a key concept and details that describe, develop, or explain it. Figure 4.5 provides an example of this structure.

Enumeration/sequence text structure lists major points. Although you may not be told initially how many points will be discussed, words such as "first, . . . second, . . . third" or "first, . . . next, . . . finally" often signal the number of points under discussion. The points are a list of equivalent items (enumeration structure) or a list of items in a progression (sequence structure). Such lists include information ar-

FIGURE 4.6   Examples of Enumeration and Sequence Structures

Enumeration Passage

Nerve cells can be categorized by structure or function. For our purposes, a functional classification is more useful. According to this system, nerve cells fall into three distinct groupings: (1) sensory neurons, (2) interneurons, and (3) motor neurons.

Sensory neurons carry impulses from body parts to the central nervous system, transmitting impulses from sensory receptors located in the body. Sensory receptors come in many shapes and sizes and respond to a variety of stimuli, such as pressure, pain, heat, and movement (Chapter 13).

Motor neurons carry impulses from the brain and spinal cord to effectors, the muscles and glands of the body. Sensory information entering the brain and spinal cord via sensory neurons often stimulates a response. A response is brought about by impulses transmitted via motor neurons to muscles and glands of the body. In some cases, intervening neurons—called interneurons or association neurons—are present. Interneurons transmit impulses from the sensory neurons directly to motor neurons and may also transmit impulses to other parts of the central nervous system.

SOURCE: Reprinted with permission from Chiras, *Human Biology.* © 1991 by West Publishing. All rights reserved.

Sequence Passage
OUTPUT

Once processing is complete, the results are available for output. There are three steps involved in the output phase of data flow. In retrieving information, the computer pulls information from storage devices for use by the decision maker. By converting information, the computer translates information from the form used to store it to a form understandable by the user (such as a printed report). Finally, communication occurs when the right information is in the right place at the right time.

SOURCE: Reprinted with permission from *Introduction to Computers,* by Brenan and Mandell; © 1984 by West Publishing Company. All rights reserved.

---

ranged alphabetically or in order of importance, direction, size, time, or other criteria. This structure also describes solutions to problems, answers to questions, or proofs of thesis statements. To use the enumeration/sequence text structure, you look for the overall concept, procedure, or problem; the total number of items in the list or steps in the sequence, whenever possible; the signal words that indicate the points in the list; and the relationship of items in the list or steps in the sequence. Figure 4.6 provides an example of this structure.

Comparison/contrast text structures express relationships between two or more ideas. Comparisons show how ideas are alike, whereas contrasts show how they differ. Signal words indicate whether likenesses or differences are being shown. Both comparisons and contrasts may be included, or the structure may consist of only comparisons or only contrasts. To use this type, you look for the items that are related and the signal words that indicate comparison and/or contrast. Figure 4.7 provides an example of this structure.

FIGURE 4.7   Example of a Comparison/Contrast Structures

A fault takes the form of a two-dimensional plane that typically extends from the earth's surface downward to a variable but often considerable depth. The trace of the fault on the surface is termed the fault line. Fault lines may extend for hundreds of miles, but lengths of a few tens of miles are more common. Most faults are nearly straight. This linearity, which results from the tendency of rock to fracture along straight lines, contrasts markedly with the irregularity of the features produced by most other geomorphic processes.

Geologists recognize four general categories of faults according to the nature of the displacements that occur; these are termed normal, reverse, transcurrent, and thrust faults. Relative motion is more vertical than horizontal, and an expansionary component is present, so the opposing sides also move apart, resulting in crystal extension. Normal faults are usually produced by broad regional arching in areas of tetonic stress.

Reverse faults are so-named because the movement of the opposing sides is reversed from that of normal faults. Like normal faults, reverse faults have deeply dipping fault planes and undergo predominantly vertical motion. Unlike normal faults, though, reverse faults are produced by regional compression. Crystal shortening results, and a net uplift of the surface normally occurs.

Transcurrent faults undergo a predominantly horizontal offsetting of their opposing sides. They are most frequently located along transform plate boundaries, where the relative motions of the opposing plate boundaries are essentially parallel. Most transcurrent faults are located on the floors of oceanic plates and are produced by seafloor spreading movements, but some, like California's San Andreas Fault, occur on land.

Thrust faults result from the extreme compression of rock strata produced by lisopheric plate collisons. The relative movements of the opposing sides is similar to that of a reverse fault. Relative motion, however is predominantly horizontal, as one side is thrust over the other, sometimes for considerable distances.

SOURCE: Reprinted with permission from *Essentials of Physical Geography*, by Scott; © 1991 by West Publishing Company. All rights reserved.

FIGURE 4.8   Example of a Cause/Effect Structures

Chemical weathering processes are considerably hampered by a lack of water in arid regions. As a result, the aridsols are shallow, stony, and mineralogically immature, with poorly developed horizons. Soil textures are generally coarse and sandy, leading to water retention ability even when water is available. The humus content is low to completely absent because of the sparseness of vegetation.

An important characteristic of the *aridsols* is their high alkalinity. Evapotranspiration exceeds precipitation, producing a surfaceward movement of ground water and dissolved minerals. Well-drained soils typically experience an accumulation of calcium carbonate and other soluble bases at the site of water evaporation, normally a few inches below the surface. Frequently, this produces a duricrust layer. In poorly drained depressions, the salinization process results in conditions toxic for most vegetables.

SOURCE: Reprinted with permission from *Essentials of Physical Geography*, by Scott (1991), West Publishing Company.

The **cause/effect** text structure shows an idea or event resulting from another idea or event. It describes what happens (the effect) and why it happens (the cause). To use this type of text structure, you look for the effect and the cause(s) of the effect. Figure 4.8 provides an example of cause/effect structure.

EXERCISE 4.1   Circle the signal words, if any, in the following paragraphs. Then identify the predominant text structure (introduction/summary, subject development/definition, enumeration/sequence, comparison/contrast, cause/effect) of each passage. Write your answer in the corresponding blanks below.

1. _____
2. _____
3. _____
4. _____
5. _____
6. _____
7. _____
8. _____
9. _____
10. _____

1. The duties of the bailiff vary. As sergeant-at-arms within the courtroom, he or she keeps watch over defendants and suppresses disorderly behavior among spectators. He or she summons witnesses when they are called to testify and maintains the legal proprieties pertaining to the actions of jurors and witnesses. When the jury is sequestered on the order of the judge, the bailiff accompanies the jurors and guards to prevent violations of trial secrecy—such as making unauthorized phone calls, reading an unedited newspaper, or listening to accounts of the trial on the radio or television. It is also the bailiff's job to see that the jury is suitably housed and fed during a trial.

2. But today's union member seeks need satisfaction on a wider range. Money or safety is no longer the dominant reason for joining a union. Most people earn a livable wage and work under reasonable conditions. Today, the need to join a union often stems from a higher level. Labor relations professors Arthur A. Sloane and Fred Witney tell us that "research suggests that dissatisfaction with

the extent of gratification of (1) safety, (2) social, (3) self-esteem needs—in approximately that order—has motivated many workers to join unions. To a lesser extent, status and self-fulfillment needs have also led to union membership."

3. Let us start with the religion most familiar to North American readers, Christianity. Christianity has approximately 1 billion adherents in the world, more than any other religion, and is the predominant religion in North America, South America, Europe, and Australia. In addition, countries with a Christian majority can be identified on every other continent. No other religion has such a widespread distribution.

4. Whether using the topical or regional approach, geographers can select either a descriptive or systematic method. Again, the distinction is one of emphasis, not an absolute separation. The descriptive method emphasizes the collection of a variety of details about the characteristics of a particular location. This method has been used primarily by regional geographers to illustrate the uniqueness of a particular location on the earth's surface. The systematic method emphasizes the identification of several basic theories or techniques developed by geographers to explain the distribution of activities.

5. Victims of crime and their relationships with criminals were briefly explored in this chapter. Beginning with a historical sketch of the ways in which various societies in the past have dealt with the victim of crime, the pioneering work of Hentig and Mendelsohn in the development of victim typologies was discussed and some consideration was given to the issue of victim compensation and restitution. Models for the delivery of victim services were also examined briefly. Victimization surveys and their significance for the assessment of crime were treated in some detail, and the chapter concluded with several observations on the bystander who remains a passive witness to someone else's victimization.

6. Three major aspects of communication must be understood for anyone to be an effective communicator: (1) people, (2) messages, and (3) the environment. In

communication, the person, or both *people,* is the focus of understanding. Communication really represents people in transaction. Second, although the people are of primary importance in a study of communication, *messages* mediate their transactions. Through sending or receiving messages, people make sense of one another. Third, communication takes place in a social environment. An organization where one works can be a major environment in which one communicates. How does this environment affect communication?

7. Fear is a basic ingredient of any psychological or social reaction to crime. It is a gut reaction that produces marked changes in individual behavior. The most intense fear is of the crimes least likely to occur: murder, assault, and forcible rape. Ironically, the perpetrator in such crimes is often a family member, close friend, or personal acquaintance. Nevertheless, what people fear most is violence at the hands of a stranger. Fear of an unknown assailant is prominent in both individual and collective responses to crime. Fear of strangers generalizes to fear of strange places, and people eventually see even public streets as unsafe. When fear of public places peaks, people avoid areas perceived as potentially hazardous. Consequently, normal activity is interrupted in various areas, removing one deterrent to criminal activity. Areas thus avoided are then increasingly frequented by persons bent upon crime.

8. **Modern Romance Languages.** The five most important contemporary Romance languages are Spanish, Portuguese, French, Italian, and Romanian. A reasonably close fit exists between the boundaries of these languages and the modern states of Spain, Portugal, France, Italy and Romania. An examination of a physical map of Europe provides ample evidence for the development of separate Romance languages, because the Spanish, Portuguese, French, and Italian language regions are separated from each other by mountains—the Pyrenees between France and Spain and the Alps between France and Italy. Romania is isolated from the other Romance language regions by Slavic-speaking people. Mountains serve as a strong barrier to communications between people living on opposite sides. Languages evolve over time. The distinct Romance languages did not suddenly appear. Instead, numerous dialects existed within each province, many of which still exist today. The creation of standard national languages, such as French and Spanish, was relatively recent.

9. Geographers face a choice between a topical or regional approach. The topical approach, which is used in this book, starts by identifying a set of important issues to be studied—for example, population distribution, migration, and settlements. Geographers using the topical approach would examine the location of different aspects of the topic and the reasons for the distribution.

The alternative approach is regional. Regional geographers start by selecting a portion of the earth and studying the people and activities within the area. The regional geography approach is used in courses on continents, such as Europe, Africa, and Asia. Although this book is organized by topics, geography students should be aware of the important world regions. One indispensable aid in the study of regions is an atlas, which can also be used to identify unfamiliar places that pop up in the news.

10. Several hundred Amish families migrated to North America, in two waves. The first group, primarily from Bern and the Palatine, settled in Pennsylvania in the early eighteenth century, enticed by low-priced land offered by William Penn. Because of lower land prices, the second group, from Alsace, settled in Ohio, Illinois, Iowa, and Ontario in the early nineteenth century. From these core areas, groups of Amish migrated to other locations where inexpensive land was available. Living in rural and frontier settlements relatively isolated from other groups, Amish communities retained their traditional customs, even as other European immigrants to the United States adopted new ones. Thus, the Amish customs can be observed on the landscape in such diverse states as Pennsylvania, Indiana, and Iowa, with each community relatively isolated from the others but sharing cultural traditions distinct from those of other Americans.

EXERCISE 4.2   Examine the text structures in Figures 4.4, 4.5, 4.6, 4.7, and 4.8. Identify the words which signal each particular type of text structure by circling them.

EXERCISE 4.3   Identify the text structure of each of the following paragraphs.

1. Page 521 (162), column 2, and continuing on page 522 (163), column 1, paragraphs 1 through 3, in Sample Chapter 3, "Nutrition and Digestion."

STRUCTURE TYPE _____

2. Page 518 (21), column 2, paragraphs 3 and 4, and page 519 (22), column 1, paragraphs 1 through 4 in Sample Chapter 2, "The Planetary Setting."

   STRUCTURE TYPE _____

3. Page 504 (7), column 1, paragraphs 1 through 3 in Sample Chapter 2, "The Planetary Setting."

   STRUCTURE TYPE _____

4. Page 531 (172), column 2, paragraph 2 in Sample Chapter 3, "Nutrition and Digestion."

   STRUCTURE TYPE _____

5. Page 537 (178), column 2, paragraph 2, and continuing on page 538 (179) in Sample Chapter 3, "Nutrition and Digestion."

   STRUCTURE TYPE _____

6. Page 522 (163), column 2, paragraph 3 and 4, and continuing on page 523 (164) in Sample Chapter 3, "Nutrition and Digestion."

   STRUCTURE TYPE _____

7. Page 495 (79), column 1 and column 2, paragraphs 1 and 2 in Sample Chapter 1, "Culture: The Ideas and Products People Adopt and Create."

   STRUCTURE TYPE _____

Exercise 4.4   Reread each paragraph in Exercises 4.1 and 4.3. Mark and label each one.

STEP FOUR: RECITE

If, at the end of each section of a chapter, you recite correct answers to your purpose-setting questions, then you continue reading.

What if you cannot completely answer your questions? One of two things has happened. Either you have asked the wrong questions or you have not understood what you read.

You decide where the problem lies by looking at your questions in light of the content of the passage. Does the content answer your questions? If not, you asked the wrong ones. Your skill in developing purpose-setting questions improves with practice.

Recitation becomes easier and more active when you study with someone. This helps you see how others develop questions and find answers. You can also practice by using a tape recorder. First, you record your purpose-setting questions. Then you read and record your answers. When you play your tape, see if your questions were appropriate and if your responses answered the questions correctly. Another way to practice involves writing your questions on index cards. Again, after reading, determine if your questions were appropriate. Then, write your answers on the back of the card.

If you find your questions are inappropriate, you form new questions and reread. If you still have problems understanding, you need to assess your reading in terms of the passage at hand. Do you know the terminology? Are you confused by the author's writing style? Table 4.7 provides a list of common comprehension obstacles and solutions.

Evaluating your text marking also helps you increase your understanding. If you marked too much, you may not be able to separate important from unimportant information. If this is a common problem for you, you need to use a pencil while marking and labeling. This allows you the freedom to rethink your notations. If you overmark only on occasion, you can remark text with a contrasting ink or highlighter. If you marked too little, you may not have enough information to comprehend fully. Thus, you need to reexamine the text and make more explicit notations. You need to be sure you have labeled all text markings. If you have done so, you can see at a glance where important information lies. If your labels are vague, then reread and relabel your text. Labels should concisely, yet completely, summarize what you've marked.

STEP FIVE: REVIEW

At this point in the SQ3R process, review seems redundant. You've already seen the information four times. You previewed the chapter to get the big picture. You began your analysis of content by asking questions. You examined each section by reading. You checked understanding. The review stage brings you full circle by allowing you to synthesize the chapter's meaning as a whole, see how information relates, and begin studying information for recall.

While Chapter 5 will provide many memory and study techniques, three strategies are immediately available to you as part of SQ3R. First, many chapters begin with objectives; you surveyed them during the first step of SQ3R. One way to review is to determine if you met all the objectives. A second way to review involves answer-

TABLE 4.7   Reasons and Solutions for Comprehension Failure

Reasons	Solutions
FAILURE TO ASK RIGHT QUESTION	
Lack of experience in questioning	Practice with index cards by putting a question on one side and the answer on the other. Practice with tape recorder. Practice with study partner. Review types of questioning words.
FAILURE TO UNDERSTAND TEXT	
Lack of concentration	Avoid external distractions. Study in short blocks of time over a longer period. Use a study system. Set learning goals. Keep a "worry list."
Unfamiliar terms	Use context and structural analysis to decode unknown terms. Use the text's glossary. Find the word in a dictionary or thesaurus. Actively consider new terms in context.
Lack of understanding	Reread or skim for main ideas. Scan for specific information. Verbalize confusing points. Paraphrase, summarize, or outline main ideas. Consult an alternate source. Reset learning goals.
Speed	Adjust speed to purpose. Take a speed-reading course. Use a study system. Practice with a variety of materials. Read recreationally.
Failure to identify text structure	Examine transition words as you reread. Outline the paragraph or passage.
Failure to locate main idea	Label the main idea of each paragraph. Identify text structure. Outline details. Summarize the main idea in your own words.
Insufficient background knowledge for understanding	Find alternative source of information. Obtain tutoring.
Inability to set appropriate purpose-setting questions	Practice with a tape recorder. Practice with a friend. Reset learning goals.

ing, without referring back to the text, any pre- or post-chapter questions posed by your author; these, too, should have been identified during your initial survey of the chapter. Both of these review strategies rely on the good graces of the text's author. Chapter objectives and questions may or may not be part of the text you are reading. The third review strategy depends solely on you. For this review, you return to the outline or map you created during the second stage of SQ3R and answer your goal-setting questions.

Any of these three study strategies—indeed, all three—allow you to test your recall and determine where you have memory deficits. This provides you with information about what and how much you need to study to complete the learning process.

EXERCISE 4.5 Survey, question, read, recite, and review Sample Chapter 1, "Culture: The Ideas and Products People Adopt and Create."

GROUP LEARNING ACTIVITY
READING STRATEGIES FOR GROUPS

An important phase of reading and learning information is monitoring. This stage helps you determine when you know information or when you need to reflect and review. However, many students lack the self-awareness to differentiate between when they know information from when they don't know it. The following group reading strategy helps you learn to monitor learning as well as practice summarization and memory skills. The group's goal is to master text information. This strategy incorporates visual, verbal, and aural components. It provides group members with opportunities to see how others identify, organize, and learn important information.

The following steps, based on cooperative learning instructions (Larson and Dansereau, 1986), can be used in your in-class study group:

1. Select and study a limited amount of text information. Initially, or when reading complex or unfamiliar information, this might be as little as a section in a chapter introduced by a minor subheading. It never should be more than two or three pages.

2. Each group member should practice appropriate marking and labeling strategies in reading the information.

3. Members continue to study and reflect on the information until everyone has completed the task.

4. Select one person to recall and summarize the information *without looking at the text*. That person should include important terms and

ideas in the summary, describing mnemonic devices, analogies, charts, drawings, or other visuals to reinforce and clarify information.

5. As the recaller summarizes information, group members *using their texts* check the accuracy and completeness of the summary. Group members correct errors and supply or elaborate on information following the summary, again using any mnemonic devices (see Chapter 5), analogies, charts, drawings, or other visuals to reinforce and clarify information.

6. The group then discusses the information, continues to clarify information, and suggests ways to consider and remember concepts.

7. During discussion, each person should notate important information, terms, visuals, or other information for later individual study.

8. Repeat the process with another member of the group serving as the recaller until all the information has been studied or all the members have had the opportunity to serve as recallers. To be most effective, group members need to actively facilitate the understanding of the recaller and themselves through questioning, elaborating, and otherwise amplifying information.

Application

Using the same text material, compare notes with other groups in the class, focusing on how others identify important information and facilitate learning.

SUMMARY OF MAIN POINTS

1. SQ3R is a systematic reading plan for studying text chapters. Its steps include *survey, question, read, recite,* and *review.*

2. Surveying, or previewing, is a strategy often used before attending a lecture. It helps you be an active learner and connect what you know with what you are learning.

3. The questioning stage concerns setting goals for reading.

4. Reading a chapter involves finding and recording main ideas.

5. When you recite information, you check your understanding and use strategies to solve comprehension problems, if they exist.

6. In the review stage, you attempt to see and remember how all information in the chapter relates. Additional strategies for learning information are included in Chapter 5.

VOCABULARY DEVELOPMENT
CONTEXT: TIME FLIES VERSUS FRUIT FLIES

Look around you. Are you in your room? Your car? A bus? A classroom? Outside? Your surroundings are your current context. What you see in that context often depends on those surroundings to make sense. The kind of seat you find in a car or bus differs from that found in a classroom or living area. Similarly, words differ according to the context in which they are found. Context helps you make sense of the new words you encounter when you read and forms a means of developing vocabulary.

Time flies like an arrow.
Fruit flies like a banana.
—Lewis Grizzard

What does *flies* mean in each of the sentences above? The meaning of many words change according to the words that surround them. These words—called context—give you the meaning and usage of the word in a realistic setting. For example, in psychology, the word *set* means orientation, as "mind set." In math, *set* refers to a group of things. *Set* refers to scenery in drama. As a result, context forms one of the most valuable aids to vocabulary development. Context consists of both stated and unstated clues to meaning.

While context is your first best choice in defining words you do not know, it is not foolproof. Sometimes authors embed words in weak context. That means, they provide too little information for you to identify the meaning of a new term. When that happens, your only alternative is to consult a dictionary or glossary. Then you need to reconsider the word in its original context.

STATED CONTEXT CLUES

Stated context clues consist of various punctuation marks and key words that signal meaning (see Table 1). In addition, they rely on your language knowledge to help you define unknown words. For

"Sure I've seen a good play . . . in the game on Sunday."

TABLE 1	Types of Stated Context Clues	
Stated Types	**Stated Clues**	**Examples**
Punctuation	commas ,,, parenthesis ( ) dashes - brackets [ ]	He also distinguished between *social statics*—the study of stability and order—and *social dynamics*—the study of change.[1]
Definition	*is, was, are, means, involves, seems, is called, that is, i.e., which means, resembles*	One of his enduring contributions is the idea that sociology should rely on *positivism;* that is, it should use observation and experimentation, methods of physical sciences, in the study of social life.[2]
Comparison	*similarly, both, as well as, likewise*	Similar in function to the parity bit is the *check digit.* Like a parity bit, a check digit is used to catch errors.[3]
Example	*such as, such, like, for example, e.g., other*	Have you ever watched people's eyes closely when they read? Their eyes don't flow smoothly over the words; instead they skitter or jump across the letters. Such motion is called *visual saccade.*[4]
Contrast	*however, on the other hand, on the contrary, while, but, instead of, although, nevertheless, yet*	Participants in an artificially created situation in a laboratory may not behave as they would in a real-life situation. In contrast, the *natural* experiment takes place in a real-life situation that is not totally created or controlled by the experimenter.[5]

[1]Reprinted with permission from *Sociology,* 2d ed., by Shepard. Copyright © 1984 by West Publishing Company. All rights reserved.

[2]Reprinted with permission from *Sociology,* 2d ed., by Shepard. Copyright © 1984 by West Publishing Company. All rights reserved.

[3]Reprinted with permission from *Understanding Computers,* by Hopper and Mandell. Copyright © 1984 by West Publishing Company. All rights reserved.

[4]Reprinted with permission from *Introduction to Child Development,* 2d ed., by Dworetzky. Copyright © 1984 by West Publishing Company. All rights reserved.

[5]Reprinted with permission from *Sociology,* 2d ed., by Shepard. Copyright © 1984 by West Publishing Company. All rights reserved.

example, punctuation clues actually identify appositives, words or phrases that restate or modify an immediately preceding term. Definition clues link nouns with describing or renaming words. Other clues indicate both synonymous (comparison and example) and antonymous (contrast) relationships among ideas within a sentence or paragraph. Finally, meanings may be located in other sentences.

UNSTATED CONTEXT CLUES

Unstated context clues require the use of your background knowledge to infer meaning. Key words and phrases identified within the text provide you with the clues necessary for decoding meanings. For example, consider the word *elite* in the paragraph below:

The existence of a surplus food supply explains why cities were able to develop but does not explain why people were attracted to them. Cities tended to attract four basic types of people: *elites*, functionaries (officials), craftsmen, and the poor and destitute. For elites, the city provided a setting for consolidating political, military, or religious power. The jewelry and other luxury items found in the tombs of these elites symbolize the benefits that this small segment of the population gained from their consolidation or power and control. Those who lived in cities as political or religious officials received considerably fewer benefits, but their lives were undoubtedly easier than those of the peasant-farmers in the countryside. Craftsmen, still lower on the stratification structure, came to the city to work and sell their products to the elites and functionaries. The poor and destitute, who were lured to the city for economic relief, were seldom able to improve their condition (Gist and Fava, 1974).

The text does not define *elite* for you or provide stated clues. The words *power*, *jewelry*, *luxury*, and *benefits* help you know that *elite* describes a wealthy class of people. In addition, by process of elimination, you may realize that a wealthy class of people is the only class that the text fails to mention.

Activity 1

Define any ten of the following words in context from Sample Chapter 2, "The Planetary Setting." Then identify the type of context clue that helps you determine the word's meaning. Words appear in boldface in the chapter in the same order as they appear in the activity.

1. Solar system

   Definition: _____

   _____

2. Milky Way galaxy

   Definition: _____

   _____

3. revolution

   Definition: _____

   _____

4. rotation

   Definition: _____

   _____

5. North Pole, South Pole

   Definition: _____

   _____

6. equator

   Definition: _____

   _____

7. parallelism

   Definition: _____

   _____

8. oblate ellipsoid

   Definition: _____

   _____

9. latitude

   Definition: _____

   _____

10. longitude

   Definition: _____

   _____

11. prime meridian

   Definition: _____

   _____

12. local time

   Definition: _____

   _____

13. standard time

   Definition: _____

   _____

14. International Date Line

   Definition: _____

   _____

15. daylight savings time

   Definition: _____

   _____

16. solstice

   Definition: _____

   _____

17. equinox

   Definition: _____

   _____

18. Tropics of Cancer and Capricorn

   Definition: _____

   _____

19. Arctic and Antarctic circles

   Definition: _____

   _____

Activity 2

Provide a definition for each of the words below. Then identify the meanings of these words from context from Sample Chapter 1, "Culture: The Ideas and Products People Adopt and Create." The words appear in the starred lines of the chapter in the same order as they appear in the activity.

1. race

Your definition: _____

_____

Definition in context: _____

_____

2. material

Your definition: _____

_____

Definition in context: _____

_____

_____

3. set

Your definition: _____

_____

Definition in context: _____

_____

4. codes

Your definition: _____

_____

Definition in context: _____

_____

5. minor

Your definition: _____

_____

Definition in context: _____

_____

ACTIVITY 3

Reconsider your responses in Activities 1 and 2. Respond to the following:

How did context affect your understanding of terms in Sample Chapter 2 and your understanding of general vocabulary in Sample Chapter 1?

_____

_____

_____

_____

_____

_____

_____

_____

_____

_____

_____

_____

_____

_____

_____

_____

_____

_____

CHAPTER REVIEW

Answer briefly but completely.

1. Complete the following analogy:
   goal : objective :: survey : _____

   _____

2. Which of Kipling's questioning words (*What, Why, When, How, Where,* and *Who*) might elicit main idea responses? Which would require details for answers?

   _____

   _____

   _____

   _____

   _____

3. Create a drawing that shows the role of *topic, main ideas,* and *details* in a paragraph or passage.

   _____

   _____

   _____

   _____

   _____

4. Think of the following subjects in light of the factors to be considered when marking text. Which factor might be most important to you in each area?

   a.   Freshman-level chemistry _____

   b.   music appreciation _____

   c.   European history _____

   d.   Junior-level trigonometry _____

   e.   Introduction to computer science _____

5. Create a cardinal rule for text marking that explains how much information should be marked.

   _____

   _____

   _____

   _____

   _____

6. Locate examples in this chapter for three of the five types of text structure.

    a. *Type:* _____

        Page: _____ *Paragraph:*_____

    b. *Type:* _____

        Page: _____ *Paragraph:*_____

    c. *Type:* _____

        Page: _____ *Paragraph:*_____

7. What are the functions of signal words?

_____

_____

8. Why should you monitor understanding?

_____

_____

9. Examine Table 4.7. Which of these comprehension obstacles, if any, do you feel you experience most often and why?

_____

_____

_____

_____

10. How do the three review strategies discussed in this chapter allow you to evaluate recall? What might you do if you find your recall failing in a given area?

_____

_____

_____

_____

REFERENCES

Larson, C.O., and Dansereau, D.F. (1986). "Cooperative learning in dyads." *Journal of Reading 29:,* 516–20.

KEY

The topic of the passage is "Washing Clothes."

5 Memory Techniques: The Process of Learning

OBJECTIVES

By the end of this chapter, you will be able to do the following:

1. Identify the stages in processing information.

2. Apply association techniques for recalling information.

3. Apply organizational techniques to analyze and synthesize ideas.

4. Compare and contrast various practice strategies.

5. Identify ways information is lost from long-term memory.

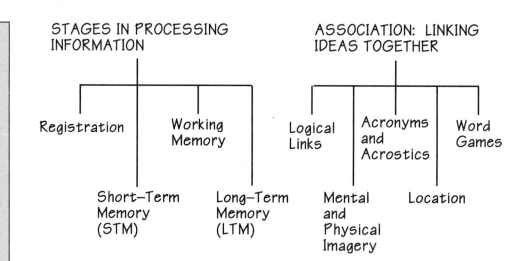

STAGES IN PROCESSING INFORMATION

Registration

Working Memory

Short-Term Memory (STM)

Long-Term Memory (LTM)

ASSOCIATION: LINKING IDEAS TOGETHER

Logical Links

Acronyms and Acrostics

Word Games

Mental and Physical Imagery

Location

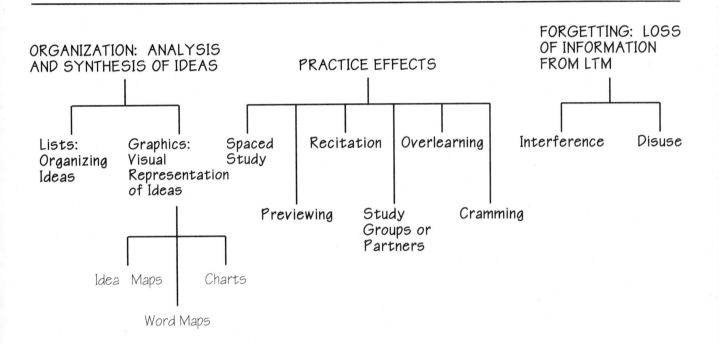

TERMS

auditory practice
behavior modification
charts
chunks
cramming
distributed practice
disuse
idea or concept maps
information matrices
interference
kinesthetic perception
long-term memory
mnemonigraph
overlearning
parodies
perception
puns
reception
recitation
registration
selection
semantic practice
short-term memory
spaced study
verbatim information
visual practice
working memory

A learned fool is one who has read everything and simply remembered it.

—JOSH BILLINGS
American humorist

The process of learning is far more than memorization. Memorization, or recall, is the lowest level of understanding in Bloom's taxonomy, a system developed in 1956 to describe levels of difficulty, sophistication, and thoroughness in thinking and reading (see Figure 5.1). Indeed, you can memorize information and not understand it at all. In memorization, what you "learn" is all there is. In general, you have no way to use the information other than the form in which you learned it.

That's why many students who had very good high school grades discover that the learning and memory strategies they used in high school often result in less-than-satisfactory grades in college courses. Although after studying for tests, they can define or recite almost any fact from the text or lecture, they often lack the ability to make important connections among information. This is a problem of depth. How deeply you process information impacts how well you understand it. The more you know about a concept, the better you can relate it to other ideas. This requires a deeper understanding. In high school, you are most often asked to think in words; in college, you must think in concepts.

Processing depth varies for a number of reasons. The strength of your interest in a subject and the amount of desire you have for learning affect how deeply you process information about the subject. Intense interest or desire causes you to process more thoroughly. Negative attitudes often result in superficial processing. Purpose and intention also influence depth of processing. Like setting purposes for reading, determining the level of understanding you need gives you a goal. In addition, how well you concentrate affects how deeply you process information. When you concentrate well, you make stronger and more numerous links among facts and ideas in the information for future applications. Finally, relating information to what you know—your background knowledge—affects processing. It allows you to form more connections between new information and what you already know.

For instance, consider what you know about Abraham Lincoln (sixteenth president of the United States) and Andrew Johnson (seventeenth president of the United States). If you are like most people, you can visualize Abraham Lincoln (tall, thin, bearded, black top hat). You associate several ideas with him (Civil War, Gettysburg Address, assassination, lawyer, log cabin). However, like most people, you may find that you recall little about Andrew Johnson, other than his

FIGURE 5.1   Bloom's Taxonomy of Thinking

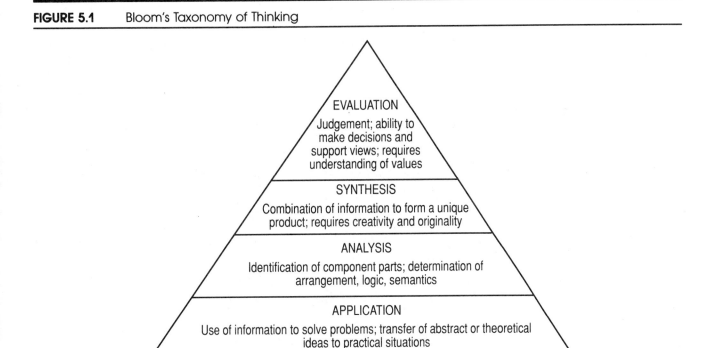

name and that he succeeded Lincoln as president. What you recall about each man reflects, to some extent, depth of processing. Because you know more about Lincoln and connect him to other concepts, you possess a deeper understanding of him. In contrast, if you know few details about Andrew Johnson, you make few connections between him and what you know. Your understanding of Andrew Johnson is shallowly processed.

As you use the various rehearsal techniques in this chapter to help you process information, you also must consider how you associate and organize information. Doing this allows you to develop the necessary links among information, thus increasing your ability to apply what you've learned.

For example, in a psychology course, you may be learning about the biological bases of behavior. As you study, you memorize the parts of the forebrain—thalamus, hypothalamus, limbic system, corpus callosum, cerebrum. You also learn a definition for each and can identify its function. With this information stored, you can answer questions, such as the following:

1. *What is the thalamus?*

2. *What part of the brain regulates autonomic functions?*

However, on the test you find the following questions:

1. *A classmate experiences memory lapses. Which part of the forebrain is most likely to contribute to this problem and why?*

2. *Hypothesize a time line for the development of forebrain structures and provide a rationale for the order of development.*

3. *As a research psychologist, devise a research question that you want to investigate for each of the components of the forebrain.*

4. *Which of the components of the forebrain have the most impact on the acquisition of knowledge for elementary school students?*

To answer the second set of questions, you must not only know the information but also be able to apply that knowledge to different situations. It requires you to have a deeper understanding of the biological bases of behavior.

Processing depth varies from person to person and from subject to subject. The way you practice, organize, or associate information depends on your personal learning preferences and goals, what your instructor emphasizes, and the content information and requirements.

Learning, then, involves a process or action which results in a product—knowledge. This process depends on your prior knowledge of the material, your reason for learning, and the level of understanding you need as well as the kind of material to be learned. You, the learner, control the process by understanding how memory enables you to select, assimilate, and retrieve and use information.

STAGES IN PROCESSING INFORMATION

Do you remember . . .
  your first birthday?
  your first kiss?
  where you found your keys the last time you lost them?

Do you ever wonder why you remember some things and not others? Because you store memories in different ways and forms, you remember some things more easily or clearly.

You probably cannot recall your first birthday. Two factors account for this lapse of memory. First, the brain structures used for remembering don't fully develop until you are about two years old. Second, because you had not learned to speak at one year old, you could not store information in words the way you do now. Thus, although that information is still stored in your brain, you cannot get to it.

You remember your first kiss, as opposed to your fifth, tenth, and twelfth kisses, because the first kiss was a new event that caused a new category to be formed in your memory. With each subsequent kiss, more information was added to that category, and kisses became less unique.

You probably don't recall where you found your keys the last time you lost them because you have no single specific place where lost keys are found. Because you have no general category for "lost keys" in memory for you to search, you don't recall where you found them.

Thus, how our memories work determines what we remember and what we forget. Because school courses require you to remember vast amounts of information, you need to understand the stages involved in processing information. These stages are **registration, short-term memory, working memory,** and **long-term memory** (see Figure 5.2).

REGISTRATION

Just as your first interaction with college classes is registration, your first interaction with information involves its registration. In this initial stage, you receive information but do not understand it.

Next, depending upon your background knowledge, you perceive information. For example, suppose you visit a foreign country whose language you do not speak. When you see signs and billboards there, you receive stimuli and recognize the symbols on them as words. However, you do not understand their meanings. This is similar to what happens when you first encounter information. If you do speak that country's language, however, you recognize the symbols as words. You understand their meanings. Thus, **reception** leads to **perception.**

The final phase of registration involves **selection.** What you select depends on you and the material at hand. Your purpose for learning and your background knowledge help you decide what to select. The content and difficulty of the information, as well as the way it is organized, also play a part in what you select. For example, suppose you need a place to sleep in the country you're visiting. As

---

FIGURE 5.2   A Model of Memory

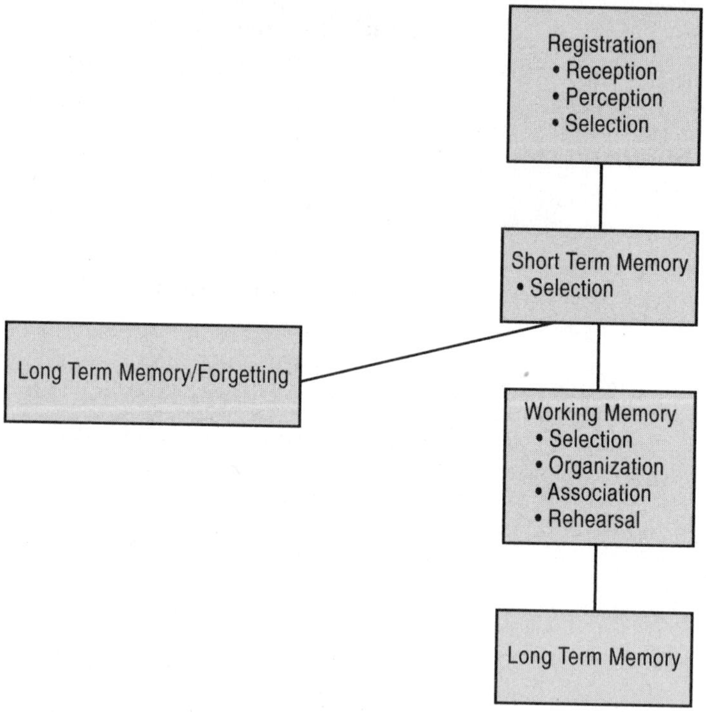

Registration
• Reception
• Perception
• Selection

Short Term Memory
• Selection

Long Term Memory/Forgetting

Working Memory
• Selection
• Organization
• Association
• Rehearsal

Long Term Memory

---

you look at the signs and billboards, you ignore ones advertising restaurants, tours, or shops. You concentrate on those for hotels. You selectively ignore or process depending on your purpose. You quickly forget what's ignored. The information you choose is transferred into your short-term memory—the second stage of memory processing.

SHORT-TERM MEMORY (STM)

All information you plan to remember goes through short-term memory (STM). When you try to remember a telephone number until you dial it, you use your STM. Its stay there is brief, lasting perhaps as little as fifteen seconds. This short duration results from the limited capacity of STM. This capacity resembles a library shelf that holds only a certain number of books. Miller (1956) found that STM could hold seven plus or minus two **chunks** of information. This varying capacity depends on how well or how poorly you "chunk," or group information for easier recall. The meaningfulness of the information chunks also affects capacity. For example, suppose you try to remember the numbers 1-8-6-0-1-8-6-4. If you chunk those numbers into dates—1860-1864—the numbers are easier to recall. This allows more memory space for other information. Factors such as age, maturation,

"Come on, Harold! The sign says 'Girls! Girls! Girls!'
but it's not the bathroom!"

practice, and the complexity of information also affect the size of STM. From its short stay in STM, information is either forgotten or moved to working memory.

WORKING MEMORY

Thinking takes place in working memory, the third stage of memory processing, through selection, association, organization, and rehearsal. Learning about working memory, then, helps you understand how and what you think about information.

Working memory is like a worktable on whose surface are the tools and materials you need. The tools and materials in your working memory include your intent for learning, your skills in processing information, relevant STM and background data, and the choices you make concerning how to process information. Thus, you take STM and background information, decide what you want from it, inventory your choices about how you could think and process the information, and choose the most appropriate one.

For example, you may need to evaluate various perspectives on U.S. foreign policy since World War II. You get your notes, text, and so on for reference and consider the background knowledge you already have. Then, you consider the ways in which you might process the information through association or organization. You decide to organize information so that you can identify the patterns of the perspectives and their effects in order to judge their worth. Rehearsal strategies help you encode the information—or place it in memory—more fully.

Like any worktable, working memory has a limited amount of space. Just as you clear table space to work on a project, you clear memory space to process information. For example, in learning a poem or in understanding U.S. foreign policy, you may find the information as a whole too complicated or unwieldy to think about at once. You need to divide the information and process a bit at a time. Just as you lose items on an overloaded table, memory processing becomes confused and information is lost when you think about too many ideas at one time or fail to clear memory space. Once information is processed at the level you intend, it is either forgotten or transmitted through rehearsal to long-term memory.

How rehearsal takes place depends on the type of information to be learned and your strategies for organizing and associating it with other information. The amount of time you spend rehearsing information is less important than what you do during that time.

WRITE TO LEARN

Two actors of the sixteenth century, Samuel Foote and Charles Macklin, reportedly argued about who had the better facility for learning lines. Macklin boasted that he could learn a speech after hearing it once. Foote then asked Macklin to repeat the following, "So she went into the garden to cut a cabbage leaf to make an apple pie; and at the same time a great she-bear, coming up the street, pops its head into the shop—What! No soap? So he died and she very imprudently married the barber; and there were present the Picninnies, the Joblillies, and the Garyalies, and the grand Panjandrum himself, with the little round button at top." Macklin could not remember the speech and was defeated. On a separate sheet of paper, explain how the factors that contribute to the process of learning—prior knowledge, intent, level at which information is to be learned—affected Macklin's inability to remember the speech.

LONG-TERM MEMORY (LTM)

If a library shelf represents STM, then the entire library corresponds to LTM. Following rehearsal, information enters LTM. It stays there until consciously or unconsciously recalled to working memory. Information in LTM is organized and stored for long periods of time. How long information remains there depends on how deeply you have processed or learned it and factors relating to forgetting. The apparent permanence of LTM is somewhat misleading, although the actual loss of information is slow. This loss results from variations in processing depth or forgetting.

ASSOCIATION: LINKING IDEAS TOGETHER

John Gilbert, an early twentieth-century actor, was once called upon at the last minute to play the role of the heroine's father. He succeeded in learning his lines but had great difficulty in remembering the name of the character he played—Numitorius. A fellow actor helpfully suggested that he associate the name with the Book of Numbers in the Bible. Confidence renewed, Gilbert rushed on stage and delivered his opening line, "Hold, 'tis I, her father—Deuteronomy."

Association forms links between familiar items and the items you want to remember. Once established, the links become automatic. Recalling a familiar item cues recall of the other item. Unfortunately for John Gilbert, he associated what he had to learn with the wrong book of the Bible.

This familiar mechanism is one you use every day. For example, perhaps you associate a certain song with a particular time, event, or person in your life. Hearing the song cues that memory. In much the same way, you form conscious associations between something familiar to you and the information you need to recall. Thus, to be effective, associations must be personal.

Logical links, mental imagery, physical imagery, acronyms and acrostics, and word games link information. The effectiveness of the various techniques depends on the type of information you need to learn and, most important, on you. Table 5.1 lists questions to help you choose the most appropriate technique.

WRITE TO LEARN

On a separate sheet of paper, select one of the association techniques to help you remember the names of each of your instructors. Explain how and why the technique cues your memory.

LOGICAL LINKS

Sometimes the logic or meaning of the information lends itself to memory. In this case, the whole may, indeed, be greater than the sum of its parts. For example, you may need to learn about the following aspects of aging: nutritional implications of aging, the effect of loneliness on nutrition, financial worries associated with aging and nutrition, assistance programs, and preparing for the later years. Such concepts would be difficult to learn in isolated parts. The sense of the concept as a whole forms the key. Consider the logic that links these

TABLE 5.1   Questions for Developing Associations

1. Does the item remind you of anything?

2. Does the item sound like or rhyme with a familiar word?

3. Can you visualize something when you think of the item?

4. Can you rearrange any letters to form an acronym?

5. Do you know of any gimmicks to associate with the item?

6. Can you draw a picture (mnemonigraph) to associate with the item?

7. Can you associate the item with any familiar locations?

8. Can you form logical connections among concepts?

ideas: What one eats (nutrition) impacts aging. Loneliness and lack of finances affect nutrition. Assistance programs provide adequate nutrition. One can prepare for aging if one knows what to expect and what assistance is available.

Understanding how concepts connect facilitates learning through the elaboration of ideas. Elaboration allows you to reframe information in terms of what you already know from experience. You provide the logic from your background knowledge of how information fits together.

MENTAL AND PHYSICAL IMAGERY

When you picture something in your mind, you experience mental imagery. Mental imagery is a natural occurrence because you often think in pictures, rather than words. For instance, think of an ice cream cone. Do you think i-c-e/c-r-e-a-m/c-o-n-e, or do you picture how an ice cream cone looks, smells, or tastes? This use of your visual and other senses aids your recall of both the familiar and unfamiliar. In addition, pictures are stored differently in the brain than words. Imagery provides an additional way to encode information. Table 5.2 lists suggestions for creating effective mental images.

Such mental associations link concrete objects with their images (for example, a picture of an apple with the word *apple*) or abstract concepts with their symbols (for example, a picture of a heart with the word *love*). Mental imagery also links unrelated objects, concepts, and ideas through visualization. For example, suppose you want to remember the name of the twenty-first president of the United States, Chester Arthur. You visualize an author writing the number *21* on a wooden chest. This mental picture helps you associate chest, author, and 21 to recall that Chester Arthur was the twenty-first president.

TABLE 5.2   Suggestions for Maximizing Mental Imagery and Examples

GOAL: To remember the four basic food groups: milk, meat, fruit and vegetables, and breads and cereals.

Suggestion	Example
1. Use common symbols, such as a heart for *love* or a dove for *peace*.	A cornucopia overflowing with cheese *(milk)*, sausages *(meat)*, fruits, and breads
2. Use the clearest and closest image.	Your family sitting at your dining table and eating fully loaded cheeseburgers (bread, meat, cheese, lettuce, tomatoes, onions, and so forth)
3. Think of outrageous or humorous images.	A *milk* cow *(meat)* eating a banana *(fruit)* sandwich *(bread)*
4. Use sexual connotations.	For males, seeing an attractive woman and thinking of the acrostic: "**M**omma **m**ia, look at that **f**oxy **b**road!" For females, seeing an attractive man and thinking of the acrostic: "That **m**acho **m**achine has a **f**antastic **b**uild!"
5. Create action-filled images.	See 2, 3, and 4 above

If you draw your mental image on paper, you make use of another sense, your **kinesthetic perception.** This type of memory aid is called a **mnemonigraph.** By actually making your mental image a physical one, you provide yourself with a form of repetition that reinforces your memory. Drawing or diagramming information also helps in another way. Rather than learning a list of details, you sketch a picture that includes the details you need to learn. For instance, suppose you need to remember the parts of an eye. Drawing and labeling the parts aid your recall.

ACRONYMS AND ACROSTICS

Forming acronyms and/or acrostics is most helpful for recalling lists of information (for example, the bones in the body).

Acronyms are words created from the first letter or the first few letters of the items on the list. *Roy G. Biv,* one of the most commonly used acronyms, aids you in recalling the colors of the rainbow in order (red, orange, yellow, green, blue, indigo, and violet). *HOMES,* another common acronym, cues your memory of the names of the Great Lakes (Huron, Ontario, Michigan, Erie, and Superior). Another acronym that aids your recall of the Great Lakes might be "Sho' me." Acronyms, then, need not be real words. Like others mnemonics, they work best when you create them for yourself.

"If only the test were just ten questions long!"

Acrostics are phrases or sentences created from the first letter or first few letters of items on a list you need to remember. For example, "George eats old gray rat at Paul's house yesterday" helps you spell "geography" correctly. Note that to be used as an acrostic, sentences need not be grammatically correct. They need only make sense to you. An acrostic ("Hot oatmeal makes eating sensational") cues your memory for the Great Lakes just as the acronym *HOMES* does.

LOCATION

The location method of mnemonics dates back to a gruesome event in ancient Greece. According to Cicero (Bower, 1970), Simonides, a Greek poet, had just finished reciting a poem when a messenger asked him to step outside the building. Just as he left the building, the roof collapsed. Everyone inside was killed. The guests' bodies were so mangled that they could not be identified. Simonides identified the corpses by remembering where each guest sat. Similarly, location memory occurs when you associate a concept with a place. This includes where you were when you heard the concept, how it looked in your notes, which graphics were on the page containing the information, and so on.

You can create location memory artificially as well. To create a memory map, you think of a familiar place. You associate the facts you need to know with features of that location. Then, you visualize yourself either walking around the place or looking at each feature of it. As you "see" the features, you recall the topic you've associated with it. For instance, suppose you want to learn a list of chemical elements. You choose a familiar route, like the route from the college bookstore to your math class. As you pass each building along the way, you assign it a chemical element. Later, in your class, you visualize your route. As you "see" each place, you recall the element it represents.

This same type of system works through visualizing a closet that contains many pegs or hooks for clothes. You "hang" information on each hook and then recall what's on each one.

WORD GAMES

Some memory aids involve what amounts to playing games with information. Such techniques aid your memory in two ways. First, they require you to actively think about the information in order to create the trick. Second, they provide clues that entertain you and stimulate your recall. Diverse in nature, word games can be both easy and difficult to create.

Advertisers realize the value of rhymes and jingles in making their products memorable. A common rhyme or jingle that aids recall of a spelling rule is "*I* before *E* except after *C* or when sounded like *A*, as in *neighbor* or *weigh*."

Puns and **parodies** are humorously copied common words, poems, stories, or songs. A pun is the humorous use of a word or phrase to suggest more than one meaning. Parodies copy serious works or phrases through satire or burlesque. The humor of puns and parodies brings cognitive benefits. Like other mnemonics, they make studying more imaginative and entertaining. For instance, suppose you want to learn the meaning of *numismatist* (a coin collector). You might parody the children's nursery rhyme "Four and Twenty Blackbirds." Instead of the king being in his counting house, counting all his money, you change the rhyme to "The numismatist was in his counting house, counting all his money." Or, you might make a pun to help you recall the definition. This could be something like "two numismatists getting together for old 'dime's' sake."

Many people create memory tricks to aid recall. Many such tricks have been created to teach the basics of common concepts. A good example of this is a trick for remembering the multiplication tables for nine (Table 5.3). Others you devise for yourself. For example, one student—needing to know the difference between *skimming* and *scanning*—decided to use the letters in the word to signal its purpose. The *mi* in *skimming* cued the purpose of finding main ideas. The *an* in *scanning* cued the purpose of finding specific answers.

TABLE 5.3   Memory Trick for Multiplying by Nine

1. List the numbers 0 to 9 in a column.

0
1
2
3
4
5
6
7
8
9

2. List the numbers 0 to 9 in a column beginning from the *bottom* beside the numbers you've already listed. Your combined columns form the products derived from multiplying 9 times 0, 1, 2, 3 . . . 9. (i.e., 9 × 0 = 00, 9 × 1 = 09, 9 × 2 = 18 . . .)

09
18
27
36
45
54
63
72
81
90

3. Note also that if you add the two digits in each product, you get 9.

9 × 1 = 09   (0 + 9 = 9)
9 × 2 = 18   (1 + 8 = 9)
9 × 3 = 27   (2 + 7 = 9)

EXERCISE 5.1   Respond to each of the following:

1. Create an acronym or acrostic to help you remember the difference between *values, norms, folkways, mores, taboos,* and *laws,* as described on pp. 485–488 (69–72) in Sample Chapter 1, "Culture: The Ideas and Products People Adopt and Create."

_____

_____

_____

_____

_____

2. Create a word game to help you remember two examples of *culture universals*, as described on page 495 (79) in Sample Chapter 1, "Culture: The Ideas and Products People Adopt and Create."

_____

_____

_____

_____

3. Create and draw a physical image to help you recall the concept of *cultural lag*, as described on pg. 497 (pg. 81) in Sample Chapter 1, "Culture: The Ideas and Products People Adopt and Create."

_____

_____

_____

_____

4. Create an acronym or acrostic to help you recall the major and trace minerals identified in Table 7–3, Important Information on Minerals, found on pg. 532 (pg. 173) in Sample Chapter 3, "Nutrition and Digestion."

_____

_____

_____

_____

5. Create and describe a mental image to help you tell the differences among local, standard, and daylight savings time, as described on pp. 512–515 (pp. 15–18) in Sample Chapter 2, "The Planetary Setting."

_____

_____

_____

_____

ORGANIZATION: ANALYSIS AND SYNTHESIS OF IDEAS

**Picasso, Monet, Rembrandt, Michelangelo
Donatello, Michaelangelo, Raphael, Leonardo
John, Paul, George, Ringo
Matthew, Mark, Luke, John
Cecil, Katy, Isaac, Regina**

Everything is organized in some way. Each of the lines above contains members of specific sets of information. The sense you make of each line depends on whether you can discern what concept organizes that set. Your ability to do so depends on your background knowledge. In analyzing line 1 you may realize that Picasso, Monet, Rembrandt, and Michelangelo are all artists. Michaelangelo, Raphael, Leonardo, and Donatello are the names of the Teenage Mutant Ninja Turtles, as well as artists. John, Paul, George, and Ringo were members of a musical group called the Beatles. Matthew, Mark, Luke and, John were apostles in the New Testament. Your analysis of the last line may not provide you with a single organizational format which includes all the names. Nothing in your background knowledge seems to fit. Indeed, the last line consists of names of pets of the authors of this text. So background knowledge forms one key to organizing information for learning. When you lack sufficient background knowledge, analysis of text organization or lecture content often provides you with the connections you need to categorize and organize new information.

LISTS: ORGANIZING IDEAS

People are often fascinated with lists of information. A popular best-seller, David Letterman's *Book of Lists* (1990), capitalized on such interests with lists of the "Top Ten Headlines in Hell," "Top Ten Things Lincoln Would Say if He Were Alive Today," and "Top Ten Least Loved Christmas Songs," to name a few. Newspapers contain lists of the top movies, books, stocks, and so on. Radio stations play from a list of most popular songs.

Lists, then, help you organize ideas by categorizing information according to some commonality. Recalling the name of the organizing concept helps you remember the details located within it. For example, the following items relate to the general subject of music.

tuba	violin	bassoon	bass drum
piccolo	trombone	viola	snare drum
kettle drum	trumpet	cymbals	clarinet
flute	French horn	oboe	double bass
tambourine	saxophone	cello	
	xylophone		

Remembering the individual instruments individually is more difficult than remembering a group of them. These items could be divided into the following various categories:

BRASS	WOODWINDS	PERCUSSION	STRINGS
tuba	piccolo	snare drum	cello
trombone	flute	xylophone	double bass
trumpet	saxophone	tambourine	viola
French Horn	oboe	kettle drum	violin
	clarinet	bass drum	
	bassoon	cymbals	

Or, the items could be rearranged in the following way:

HIGH VOICES	MEDIUM VOICES	LOW VOICES
trumpet	trombone	tuba
clarinet	kettle drums	bass drum
flute	bassoon	double bass
piccolo	French horn	
oboe	saxophone	
violin		
viola		
snare drum		
xylophone		
tambourine		

Organization of information depends on some sort of classification system. Because items relate to each other within the system, you can rearrange and reorganize information to aid your recall. The example shows musical instruments arranged in two different ways. Either would effectively aid memory by organizing instruments into a manageable number. In the first arrangement, four categories cued memory for the twenty-two instruments. In the second, three categories cued memory.

The arrangement that best suits your needs depends on learning goals, course emphasis, and course content. Sometimes an instructor suggests organizational structures by identifying types of information to remember (dates, names, places). An instructor might also provide the general categories of information you need to know. Other times,

"I think it's a bad omen to take a test on Friday the thirteenth on a chapter whose map looks like this!"

you need to do this for yourself. Like many other memory aids, the most effective organizational structures are those you make for yourself.

GRAPHICS: VISUAL REPRESENTATION OF IDEAS

The saying "one picture is worth a thousand words" applies to memory as well as art. Visual representations help you compress and synthesize notes. Because visual representations of ideas impact a different area of the brain than words, they provide another way for you to encode and recall information. Because you take an active part in organizing and visualizing the information, you remember more with less effort. Adding meaningful doodles, color, or symbols (for example, circles, squares, stars) also helps you remember information.

Visual representations of information include idea or concept maps, charts, and word maps. Some kinds of representations are more appropriate for certain kinds of information than others. Determining the graphic you need depends on the content of the information and your skill in representing ideas graphically.

Idea Maps

Idea or concept maps are pictures that show relationships among concepts. They express patterns of thought. Idea maps can be used to organize or condense text chapters or lecture notes. Because concepts and ideas are related in various ways, maps differ. Thus, you can be somewhat creative in your mapmaking. The text structure you've identified from the lecture or text helps you decide what concepts to map (see Table 5.4). In addition, if your instructor or text specifies elements or relationships, your map should reflect these.

Idea maps relate information to a central topic. They indicate major, minor, and equal relationships among details. Such maps show rankings of details by branching out from the central topic (see Figure 5.3). This text uses idea maps at the beginning of each chapter to show the relationship between chapter headings and subheadings. Another way idea maps show how details relate to a topic is by showing a progression of steps or chronological order of events or historical periods. Such maps show the logical flow of information (see Figure 5.4). A third idea map uses a web format to show how details relate to the topic but not to each other (see Figure 5.5 on page 208). The idea map you choose to use depends on the type of information you diagram and your preference (see Figure 5.6 on page 209). Table 5.5 explains the steps in drawing an idea map.

Charts

What you understand about the relationships of ideas can be indicated by charting, another method of graphic notetaking. **Charts,** or **information matrices,** help you recognize and remember how information is categorized. They also help you identify and compare the same factors of differing elements for most lecture and text topics. Table 5.6 explains the steps in charting information.

TABLE 5.4   Structure Patterns and Corresponding Elements in Idea Maps

Pattern	Examples of Elements	
Introduction/Summary	main ideas supporting details	
Subject Development/Definition	definitions supporting details examples	characteristics types or kinds elements
Enumeration/Sequence	main points details steps	elements procedures
Comparison/Contrast	similarities differences	pros cons
Cause/Effect	problems solutions elements	reasons procedures

TABLE 5.5   Steps in Constructing Idea Maps

1. Choose a word or phrase that represents the topic you wish your map to cover. This word could be the chapter title, a purpose-setting question, a heading, an objective, a term, or any other major concept.

2. Write this concept at the top of your notebook page.

3. List information about the concert. This could include descriptive details, definitions, functions, reasons, or any other listing of facts.

4. Examine the elements to determine how they relate to one another. Identify any associations between elements (least to most, largest to smallest, nonequivalent or nonsequential details, cause-to-effect, problem-to-solution, etc.).

5. Choose the type of idea map that can best represent the relationships you've identified.

6. Sketch the map.

7. Draw lines or arrows to indicate relationships among details and between the topic and details.

8. Judge the usefulness of your map by answering the following questions:
   a. Does the word you used to label the map accurately define the concept?
   b. Do the terms and ideas adequately support and describe the concept?
   c. Is the map logically organized?
   d. Is the map easy to read?

TABLE 5.6   Steps in Charting Information

1. Make a vertical list of the items you want to compare.

2. List horizontally the factors you want to know about each item.

3. Draw a grid by sketching lines between each element and each factor.

4. Locate and record the information that fills each box of the grid.

EXERCISE 5.2   Following the steps listed in Table 5.5, construct an idea map using the information contained in Table 7-1 of Sample Chapter 3, "Nutrition and Digestion."

Charts have several advantages. First, charting is probably a more familiar way to organize information (see Figure 5.7 on page 210). Because of their familiarity, you are better able to construct and understand charts. Second, charts concisely summarize large amounts of information on one page. Often, such summary sheets

FIGURE 5.3   Example of a Branching Idea Map

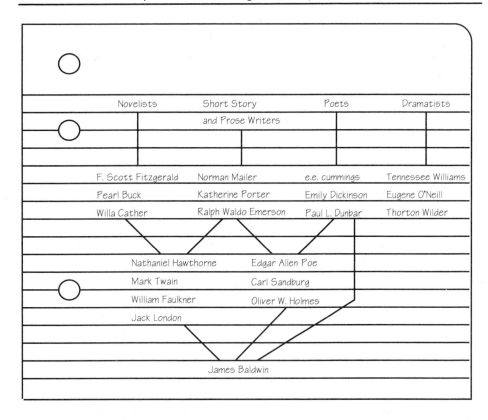

FIGURE 5.4   Example of a Flowchart Idea Map

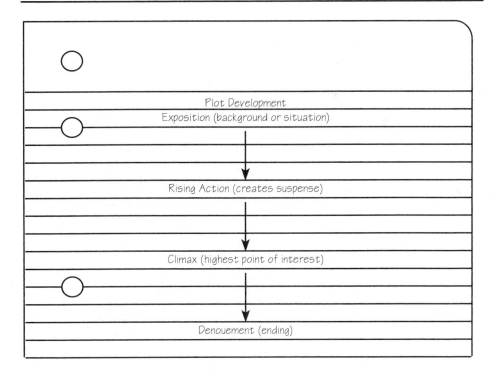

FIGURE 5.5   Example of a Web Idea Map

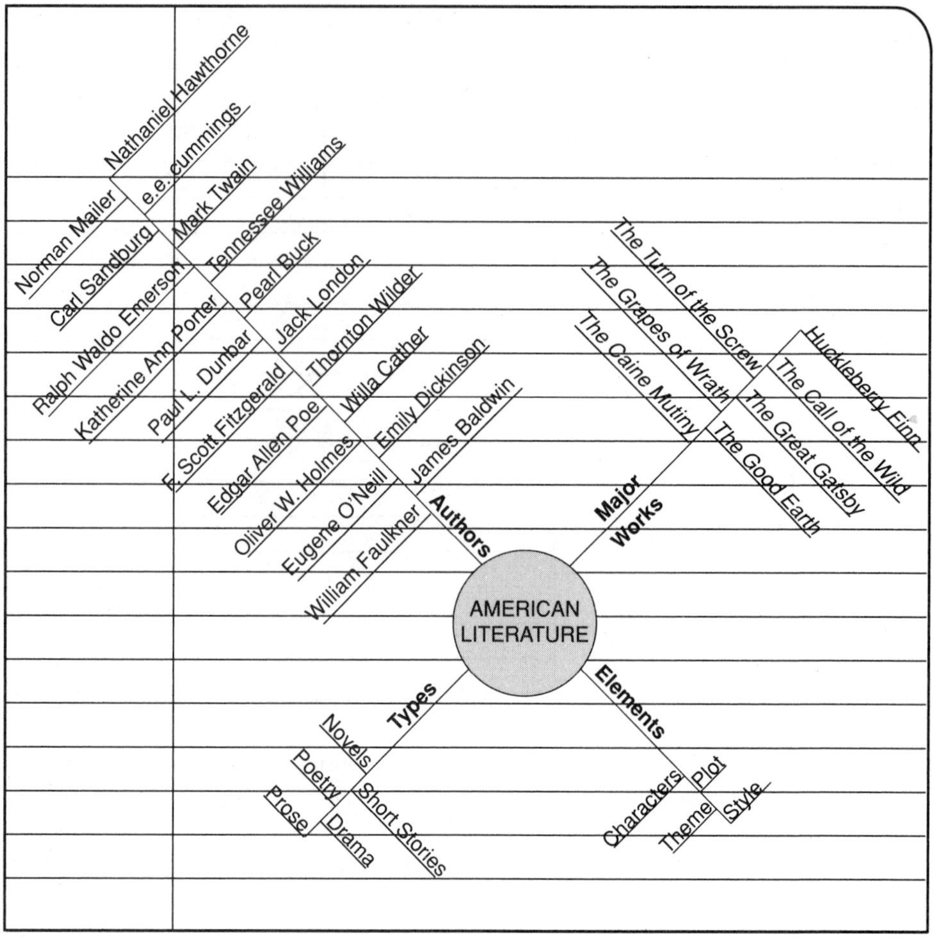

make information more manageable for study. Learning the information your notes contain becomes a more accomplishable goal. Third, like idea maps, charts graphically organize all sorts of information. You can chart any of the elements of a lecture or text (see Figure 5.8 on page 211). Finally, whereas idea maps concisely graph information on one topic, charts help you compare like features for different topics.

WRITE TO LEARN

On a separate sheet of paper, briefly explain the differences between outlines and graphic representations of information. Which appeal to you? Why?

FIGURE 5.6   Map Structures

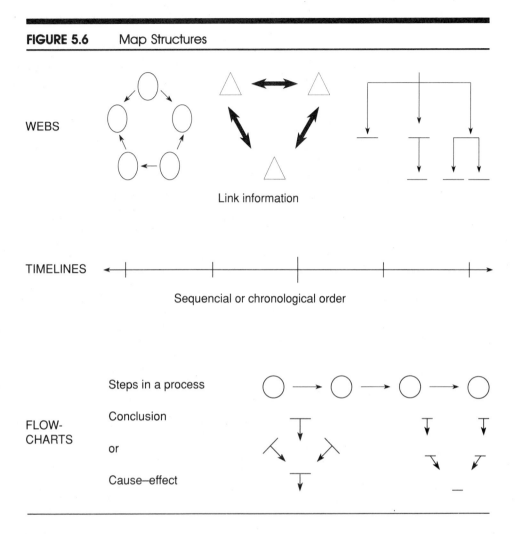

WEBS

Link information

TIMELINES

Sequencial or chronological order

FLOW-
CHARTS

Steps in a process

Conclusion

or

Cause–effect

Word Maps

Another way to aid recall of words is to draw or map the terms in a particular chapter. You do this by identifying general headings under which terms might fall. Then you draw a map showing these headings. Under each heading, you list the appropriate terms. Then you draw two lines under each term. On the first line, you draw a picture that you associate with the term and/or its meaning. On the second line, you write the term's meaning in your own words. Figure 5.9 (see page 212) provides an example of a word map.

When studying terms, you cover the information below the term. Then you try to remember the term's meaning. If you are not successful, you reveal the picture. Seeing your drawing should cue recall. If not, you uncover the definition. Your final step in using this memory technique is to spend a few seconds studying the term and recalling why you drew the picture you did.

FIGURE 5.7 Synthesis Charts

CHARTS FOR TERMS IN ANY SUBJECT

TERM	DEFINITION	CONNOTATION	PERSONAL EXAMPLE/ASSOCIATION

CHART FOR ARTISTS AND AUTHORS IN HUMANITIES CLASSES

TITLE	AUTHOR/ ARTISTS	THEME	SETTING	DESCRIPTION OF ACTION	MAIN CHARACTERS

CHARTS FOR DISCOVERIES IN APPLIED AND SOCIAL SCIENCES

WHO ?	FROM WHERE ?	WHAT ?	WHEN ?	HOW ?

EXERCISE 5.3 Complete the chart below that compares the functional, ecological, and evolutionary views of culture detailed on page 495 (79) of Sample Chapter 1, "Culture: The Ideas and Products People Adopt and Create."

View of Culture	Text Example	Personal Example

EXERCISE 5.4 Create your own chart to compare Revolution and Rotation on pages 504–507 (7–10) of Sample Chapter 2, "The Planetary Setting."

FIGURE 5.8   Classification Chart for Definitions of CITY

TYPE	DEFINITION	CHARACTERISTICS
Physical	territory of the city	1. boundary
		2. functional area
		3. metropolitan government
Environmental	atmosphere of the city	1. temperature differences
		2. pollution
		3. vulnerability to flooding
Ecological	relationships between people and environment	1. size
		2. density
		3. heterogeneity

PRACTICE EFFECTS

When the Polish pianist Ignacy Paderewski played before Queen Victoria, she said, "Mr. Paderewski, you are a genius!" Paderewski replied, "Perhaps, Your Majesty, but before that I was a drudge."

Learning is less genius and more drudgery. But rather than practice making perfect, as is does in music, practice makes permanent in learning.

This is because it aids storage in LTM. In addition, practice helps make retrieval from LTM to working memory more automatic.

You practice information visually, auditorily, or semantically. **Visual practice** usually involves the silent reading of information. Such practice often takes place in frantic, last-minute cramming sessions. **Auditory practice** occurs when you repeat information aloud or discuss it with another student. You practice information semantically when you write or diagram it. Both auditory and **semantic practice**

FIGURE 5.9   An Example of a Word Map

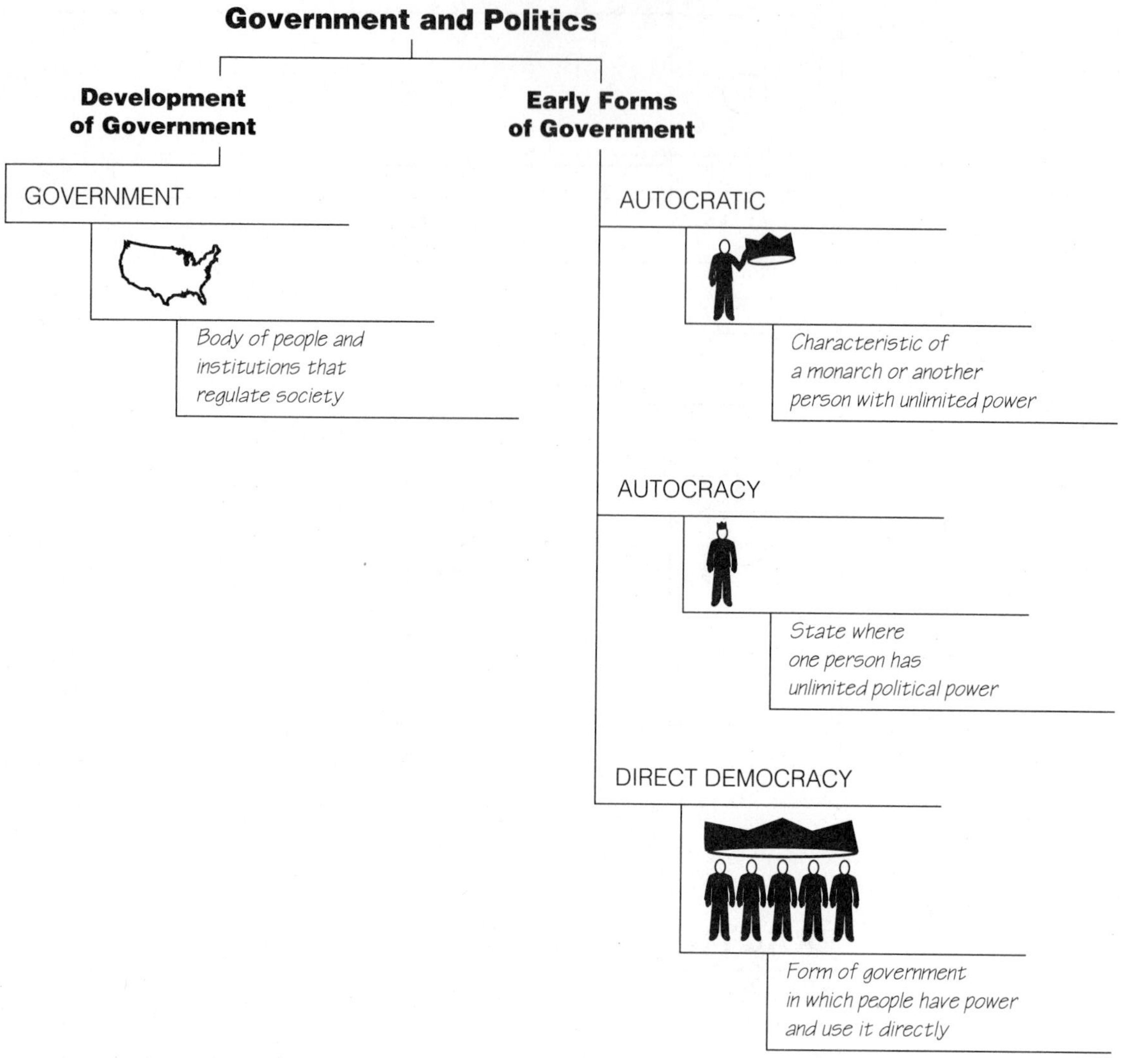

Government and Politics

**Development
of Government**

GOVERNMENT

*Body of people and
institutions that
regulate society*

**Early Forms
of Government**

AUTOCRATIC

*Characteristic of
a monarch or another
person with unlimited power*

AUTOCRACY

*State where
one person has
unlimited political power*

DIRECT DEMOCRACY

*Form of government
in which people have power
and use it directly*

yield better results because they involve active processes. And, as with any learning process, the more actively you are involved, the more learning takes place.

Practice methods assume many forms. They vary in amount of time involved, depth of learning, and manner in which information is learned. When you choose a practice method, you should consider your purpose for learning the information and the way you learn most effectively. No matter which method you choose, you will be repeating information in some way.

SPACED STUDY

Spaced study consists of alternating short study sessions with breaks. This method is also known as **distributed practice.** You set study goals by time (for example, fifteen minutes) or task (for example, three pages) limits. After reaching these goals, you allow yourself a short amount of free time. You could take a walk, have a soft drink, or call a friend. This method helps you process information into LTM.

Spaced study works for many reasons. First, spaced study rewards hard work. This form of study involves **behavior modification.** This type of learning is based on research by B. F. Skinner, an American psychologist. In his studies with animals, Skinner found that they respond best when rewarded with food. The breaks in spaced study serve as your reward for completing a set amount of study. Second, because you work under a deadline of time or task limits, you complete quality work. Knowing you have a certain amount of time or work to study motivates you. Third, because working memory has limited capacity, breaks provide time for information to be absorbed into LTM. Fourth, when studying complex, related information, study breaks keep you from confusing similar details. Avoiding this **interference** is best accomplished by sleeping between study sessions. It is for this reason that cramming seldom works well as a form of practice.

PREVIEWING

As discussed in Chapters 3 and 4, many study strategies suggest that you preview information before reading a text or hearing a lecture.

The primary purpose of previewing is to access what you already know about a topic. Previewing also provides a form of practice, because it requires you to analyze information before you read or study it. As a result, you increase the amount of details you can recall.

RECITATION

Recitation involves silent, oral, or written repetition of the answers to study questions. These questions can come from the text, the instructor, or yourself. Thus, the first step of recitation is to locate or set study questions. Next, you read or study information to answer these questions. Third, you recite answers. Fourth, you use your text or notes to check the accuracy of your answers. This process keeps information in your working memory. Repeated recitation transfers information to LTM.

STUDY GROUPS OR PARTNERS

The old saying "Two heads are better than one" describes the purpose of study groups or partners. The purpose of such groups is discussion of information. Therefore, learning becomes an active, rather than passive, process. In a group, members explain and listen to explanations from each other, which allows them to use their auditory, visual, and physical senses. Combining these sensory impressions not only enhances the active learning process but also helps transfer information to LTM. Finally, group discussions motivate members. This happens because members make commitments to prepare for and come to study sessions.

Study groups learn a variety of information. Group members provide drill in learning **verbatim information,** such as definitions of terms or lists of names or dates. In addition, group members practice skills, such as solving math problems or learning foreign languages. Analysis and organization of complex or confusing information enhances the understanding of group members. Finally, creating and discussing test questions provides practice of test-taking skills and reduces test anxiety.

One note of caution concerns the way in which groups practice. Because most groups discuss information orally, members may neglect practicing their writing skills. If you have difficulty composing written responses to test items, you also need to practice your skills in putting information on paper.

OVERLEARNING

Overlearning, most appropriate for verbatim information, consists of overlapping study. This form of practice continues to reinforce information after you've first seen it (Tenney, 1986). For example, suppose you need to learn a list of forty terms for a history course. You can overlearn the list in one of two ways, which is described in Table 5.7.

TABLE 5.7   Methods of Overlearning

Method I	Method II
1. List each item separately on note cards.	1. Divide the list into manageable units (three to five items per unit, depending on the difficulty of the material).
2. Learn the first three cards.	
3. Add one card.	2. Learn one set by practicing it orally.
4. Practice all four cards orally.	
5. Add one card.	3. Add another set.
6. Practice all five cards orally.	4. Practice all sets orally.
7. Delete the card from the original set that you know the best and add one new card.	5. Repeat steps 3 and 4 until you know all the items.
8. Practice with all five cards.	
9. Repeat steps 7 and 8 until you know all the items.	

CRAMMING

It's the night before the test. You have twelve chapters left to read. You missed the last week of classes but borrowed a friend's notes. Unfortunately, your friend doesn't take very good notes.

What to do? Cram for the exam! **Cramming** involves frantic, last-minute (and sometimes all-night) memorization. Such learning rarely results in complete success. Such learners have no time to learn information. They simply try to memorize everything. As a result, they become renters, rather than owners, of information. Short-term benefits rarely translate into long-term results. Since students fail to learn the information, they must memorize it over and over. Cramming, then, is one of the least effective means of study.

But, what if it *is* the night before the exam and you really do have twelve chapters left to read? Your best bet is to use parts of the SQ3R process to maximize your efforts. You begin by reading all chapter introductions and summaries. These provide you with the most basic condensation of information. Then you construct chapter maps or outlines. These show you the connections among ideas. Finally, you examine the terms to see how they support chapter concepts. These measures will not ensure a good grade. They only represent a more informed means of cramming.

FORGETTING: LOSS OF INFORMATION FROM LTM

**The more we study, the more we know.
The more we know, the more we forget.
The more we forget, the less we know.
The less we know, the less we forget.
The less we forget, the more we know.
So why study?**

Once information is processed, it may or may not remain in LTM. You, too, may wonder "why study?" When you lose information from LTM, more commonly known as forgetting, you do so because of interference and/or **disuse.** Which of these two occurs more often depends on four factors: your interest in learning, your purpose for learning, the frequency you use information, and the number of connections you make with other information. For instance, suppose you hear a funeral home ad the same day you meet an attractive member of the opposite sex. Whose name are you more likely to recall? Because you have greater interest in meeting new people than in visiting funeral homes, your recall of the person's name is stronger. If you

"If she can remember our credit card number, looks like she could remember our phone number."

plan to contact the person at a later date, your purpose for remembering also strengthens recall. If you date the person often, remembering the person's name becomes automatic. This is because you use it so frequently. As you learn more about the person, you associate these pieces of information in your background knowledge with the person. This, too, strengthens recall.

INTERFERENCE

Have you ever been listening to your favorite radio station when another station broke into your station's frequency? That's called interference. This happens in your memory, too. Interference occurs because new, conflicting information affects background knowledge. It hinders memory for specific details more often than it does memory for main ideas.

Interference occurs for two reasons. Either new information confuses existing knowledge or existing knowledge confuses new learning. For example, suppose you are taking courses in both sociology and psychology. Because the content of these courses is somewhat alike, interference is more likely to occur. As previously stated, interference is best avoided by alternating study periods with at least a short nap.

DISUSE

"Who was President Carter's vice-president?" "What does M*A*S*H* mean?" "How do you write fifty-one in Roman numerals?" Part of the fun and frustration in answering these and other trivia questions is remembering information learned long ago. The answers to such questions depend on your ability to recall seldom-used information. Such information is sometimes difficult (or even impossible) to locate in memory because you have not used it for a long time. Because of its disuse, you no longer remember where the information is stored. Or you forgot many of the details concerning it. In a way, "use it or lose it" applies to memory.

WRITE TO LEARN

On a separate sheet of paper, explain the logic in the poem at the beginning of this section ("The more we study . . :'). What is illogical about it?

GROUP LEARNING ACTIVITY
MEMORY DETECTIVES

You may not think of yourself as a "memory detective," but active probing often helps improve recall. A case in point is the *cognitive interview*, a technique used to jog the memory of eyewitnesses. The cognitive interview was created by R. Edward Geiselman and Ron Fisher to help police detectives. When used properly, it produces 35 percent more correct information than standard questioning (Geiselman et al., 1986).

By following four simple steps, you can apply cognitive principles to your own memory. The next time you are searching for a "lost" memory—one that you know is in there somewhere—try the following search strategies.

1. Say or write down everything you can remember that relates to the information you are seeking. Don't worry about how trivial any of it seems; each bit of information you remember can serve as a cue to bring back others.

2. Try to recall events or information in different orders. Let your memories flow out backward or out of order, or start with whatever impressed you the most.

3. Recall from different viewpoints. Review events by mentally standing in a different place. Or try to view information as another person would remember it. When taking a test, for instance, ask yourself what other students or your professor would remember about the topic.

4. Mentally put yourself back in the situation where you learned the information. Try to mentally re-create the learning environment or relive the event. As you do, include sounds, smells, details of weather, nearby objects, other people present, what you said or thought, and how you felt as you learned the information (Fisher & Geiselman, 1987).

These strategies help re-create the context in which information was learned, and they provide multiple memory cues. If you think of remembering as a sort of "treasure hunt," you might even learn to enjoy the detective work.

Application

As a preexam activity, use the preceding strategies to assist recall when you or another member of your study group becomes stumped on a question. Compare memories among group members. Once you learn to use these strategies, you can use them to aid recall on exams.

SUMMARY

1. The process of learning includes the ability to evaluate, synthesize, analyze, apply, interpret, and translate, as well as recall, information.

2. The stages of processing information are registration of information, transference to short-term memory, manipulation in working memory, and transference to long-term memory.

3. Logical links, mental and physical imagery, acronyms and acrostics, location, and word games are associational techniques for linking ideas.

4. Information can be organized into lists or through visual representations, such as idea maps, charts, and word maps.

5. Rehearsal occurs through practice strategies, such as spaced study, previewing, recitation, study groups or partners, and overlearning. Cramming is also a way of rehearsing information, but it is not as effective as other means.

6. Forgetting, or the loss of information from long-term memory, results from interference and/or disuse.

VOCABULARY DEVELOPMENT

WORD HISTORIES: USING THE RESULTS OF REASONING, BELIEF, ACTION, AND PASSION

Numerous supermarket tabloids appeal to the public's desire for gossip. "Is Elvis still alive?" "Was there a conspiracy to assassinate Kennedy?" "Are aliens living and working in the United States?" The stories are often more interesting, and therefore memorable, than the people they describe. And so it goes with words. Word histories provide you with many of the same sort of stories. They whet your interest and help you remember the meanings of the words you encounter.

> **What is all knowledge too but recorded experience,
> and a product of history; of which, therefore,
> reasoning and belief, no less than action and passion,
> are essential materials.**
>
> **—Thomas Carlyle**

Knowledge springs from a variety of sources. According to Carlyle, reasoning, belief, action, and passion form the essential materials for its development. The words that define and describe that knowledge also find their roots in these essential materials. And just how do these materials create words? *The Mother Tongue: English and How It Got That Way* (1990) provides some answers. According to Danish linguist Otto Jespersen, words form by adding or subtracting from current words, by making them up, or by having new meanings attached to them. Bill Bryson, the book's author, adds two other ways words are developed: borrowing them from other languages and creating them by accident.

And so it goes throughout history. People acted and reacted according to their thoughts, beliefs, and passions. The names of some of these people became so intertwined with their actions that they now refer to that action. For example, Vidkun Quisling was a leader of Norway in 1940. He undermined his country by collaborating with the Nazis during World War II. Today, *quisling* means "traitor." Josh Billings, a humorist in the 1800's, popularized a bantering comedy style now known as joshing.

Words from other countries also contribute to the English language. For example, the meaning of *calculate* dates back to ancient Rome. Romans often hired carts to take them where they wanted to go. The cart was equipped with a kind of taxi meter. A cylinder filled with pebbles was attached to the wheel. Each time the wheel turned, a pebble dropped through a slot into a separate container. The fare was computed based on the number of pebbles that fell into the container. The Roman word for pebble was *calculus*. Thus, calculate means to count. As a second example, in the 1812 campaign against Napoleon's armies, Russian soldiers got as far as Paris. They patronized sidewalk cafes and shouted "Bistro!"—or "hurry up"—to the slow-moving waiters. Today, *bistro* is a synonym for a sidewalk cafe.

Words often reflect current interests, trends, and innovations. These include such words as *feminist, New Wave, planned parenthood,* and *rap music.* New products of technology also result in new words. These include *astronaut, lunar module, user-friendly, byte, nylon, yo-yo,* and *trampoline.*

Words also come from abbreviations when the abbreviation is commonly used as the word itself. These include *IQ* (intelligence quotient), *TV* (television), and *CD* (compact disk). Words also come from acronyms (words formed from the first letter or first few letters of several words). The word *posh* originally stood for "port outbound, starboard home." Passengers traveling through the Suez Canal in the 1800s ordered cabins on the left side of the ship for the trip out and ones on the right for the return trip. This kept their staterooms in the shade both ways. Records for these very desirable accommodations noted them as "P.O.S.H."

The creation and development of a word is its etymology—the word's history. Found in dictionary entries, etymologies tell information about a word's evolution, how it was first used, and how it is used now. Knowing a word's etymology serves as another mechanism to expand your connections with and understanding of that word.

Activity

Look up the etymology of the boldface words in a large collegiate dictionary. Describe the history or origin of each. Then define it. In the sample dictionary entry, the history of the word has been underlined.

> **hip-pi-pot-a-mus** (hip -a pat'-a mas) *n.* a very large pachydermatous African quadruped frequenting rivers. *pl.* -es or hippopotami (hip a pat' a mi) [Gr. *hippos,* a horse; *potamos,* a river].

1. Convert 45° on the Celsius scale to its **Fahrenheit** equivalent.

    etymology _____

    _____

    definition _____

    _____

2. **Gremlins** are fictitious creatures.

    etymology _____

    _____

    definition _____

    _____

3. Prisoners who **escape** are generally recaptured within a short period of time.

   etymology _____

   _____

   definition _____

   _____

4. **Radar** enables ships to navigate treacherous seas.

   etymology _____

   _____

   definition _____

   _____

5. Few people know what **RSVP** means.

   etymology _____

   _____

   definition _____

   _____

6. **Luscious** fruits come from tropical regions.

   etymology _____

   _____

   definition _____

   _____

7. The owner of the company was a **shyster**.

   etymology _____

   _____

   definition _____

   _____

8. The **Miranda warning** must be given to each suspect.

   etymology _____

   _____

   definition _____

   _____

9. **Sequoya** forests flourish in California.

   etymology _____

   _____

   definition _____

   _____

10. Oil **derricks** dotted the countryside.

    etymology _____

    _____

    definition _____

    _____

Activity

Read the following essay, "A Few Famous Trips of the Tongue," by Jack Smith. On a separate sheet of paper, describe the histories of each of the following words: *spoonerism, sandwich, boycott, wellington, cardigan, raglan,* and *bowdlerize*. Identify the dictionary definition and check the history for each one. Give one of Smith's examples of a spoonerism. Create a spoonerism of your own to help you remember any concept from one of the sample chapters.

EXCERPT 5.1   A Few Famous Trips of the Tongue   by Jack Smith

For no discernible reason other than sheer whimsy, John Liddle of San Diego has sent me a London-dateline story from the Los Angeles Times of Sept. 11, 1977, about the inimitable Rev. William Archibald Spooner (1884–1930).

No reason other than whimsy prompts me to recall that otherwise extraordinarily dull man's one endearing service—his gift to the English language of that slip of the tongue known, in his honor, as a spoonerism.

Thus, Spooner joins the small company whose names, usually because of some personal quirk or invention, have become common nouns. It was John Montagu, 4th Earl of Sandwich (1718–1792), who invented the sandwich to avoid having to leave the gaming tables, and hence gave his name to that handy meal.

Boycott comes from Capt. C. C. Boycott (1832–1897), an Irish land agent who was boycotted by his tenants when he refused to lower their rents in 1880.

Wellingtons are the boots named after Arthur Wellesley, 1st Duke of Wellington (1769–1852), who bested Napoleon at Waterloo—and wore that type of boot.

Cardigan—a long-sleeved, collarless knitted sweater that buttons down the front—was named after James Thomas Brudenell, 7th Earl of Cardigan (1797–1868), a vainglorious martinet who led the foolhardy charge of the Light Brigade at Balaklava, in which Errol Flynn was a film hero. A notorious dandy, Cardigan evidently favored that garment.

Raglan, an overcoat or topcoat with sleeves that continue in one piece to the collar, was named after FitzRoy James Henry Somerset, 1st Baron Raglan (1788–1855). He was the British commander in chief during the Crimean War who issued the ambiguous order sending Cardigan on his disastrous charge.

And a verb:

Bowdlerize, to damage a literary work by censoring lines that one finds offensive, comes from an English editor, Thomas Bowdler (1754–1825), who had the effrontery to publish an expurgated Shakespeare.

Spooner's gift was his habit of transposing the initial or other sounds of words. For instance, it is said that Spooner once referred to Queen Victoria as "the queer old dean," when he meant to say "the dear old Queen."

Spooner's slips were never deliberate, though they brought him a strange sort of fame. He lived in dread of making the next error and remained modest about his accomplishment.

Finding his name in a newspaper, he noted, "But of course they thought me most famous for my spoonerisms, so I was not greatly puffed up."

For 60 years Spooner was a member of New College, Oxford, and served as its warden from 1903 to 1924. He was a small man and colorless, in fact an albino, and had cruelly been called "this shrimp-like creature."

That this remarkably unprepossessing Anglican clergyman should be remembered with such reverence today is owed entirely to his oral lapses.

He was likely to drop them in church and once assured his flock that "the Lord is a shoving leopard." Also, he once announced that the next hymn would be "Kinkering Kongs Their Titles Take."

It is said that he once told a lady, "Mardon me, padam; this pie is occupued; allow me to sew you to another sheet," but that sounds too contrived to be authentic.

Perhaps his most famous was a quadruple—a prodigious accomplishment even for the gifted Spooner. While lecturing a delinquent undergraduate, he is said to have told him: "You have tasted a whole worm. You have hissed my mystery lectures. You were fighting a liar in the quadrangle. You will leave by the town drain."

The complexity of that quadruple suggests that it was invented by one of Spooner's contemporaries or perhaps even put together from remarks Spooner made to different students at different times. But there is evidence that Spooner himself was capable of such an achievement.

This is one of my favorite spoonerisms, perhaps because it was spoken during World War I, when the dean was getting on in years, and it suggests that age had not diminished his powers.

When Brits were fighting across the channel, he told the Home Front: "When the boys come back from France, we'll have the hags flung out." Typical of the kind of British spunk that helped them survive the deaths and mutilations of two world wars.

Perhaps Spooner hoped wistfully to be eulogized for a more scholarly skill. "We all know what it is," he once told his flock, "to have a half-warmed fish within us."

SOURCE: © 1990 Los Angeles Times. Reprinted by permission.

CHAPTER REVIEW

Answer briefly but completely.

1. Using the levels of understanding in Bloom's taxonomy (Figure 5.1), determine the level for each of the following sample questions:
   a. State exactly the meaning of *secondary reinforcer*.

   _____

   b. Compare your text definition of visual thinking with that of the supplemental reading.

   _____

   c. You are an advisor to the president. After considering the four futures of U.S. foreign policy identified in the text, what other future would you conceptualize?

   _____

2. Choose any two courses in which you are not enrolled. Compare the depth at which you have processed information for each. How do you account for these differences?

   _____

   _____

   _____

   _____

   _____

3. How does working memory differ from long- and short-term memory?

_____

_____

_____

_____

_____

4. Organize the following list of locations for recall: Las Vegas, Brazil, Alabama, Utah, Canada, Greenland, Connecticut, London, and Munich.

_____

_____

_____

_____

_____

5. Locate a list of information you need to remember for a course you are taking. Devise and show an acronym or acrostic to aid you in recalling this list.

_____

_____

_____

_____

_____

6. What is the relationship between association techniques and information you already have in LTM?

_____

_____

_____

_____

_____

7. In what ways are visual representations of ideas improvements on lists?

_____

_____

_____

_____

8. Create a chart using the information on American Literature found in the web map in Figure 5.5.

   _____

   _____

   _____

   _____

   _____

9. Create a chart for practice strategies (spaced study, previewing, recitation, study groups or partners, overlearning, and cramming) and give examples of how they can include visual, auditory, and semantic practice.

   _____

   _____

   _____

   _____

   _____

   _____

   _____

   _____

   _____

   _____

10. Identify the reason why each of the following people forgot information:

    a. Meguami cannot remember the name of the person who sat behind her in first grade.

    _____

    b. Mrs. Johnson cannot recall if the education's department's number is 757-0349 or 759-0346.

    _____

    c. Kate has difficulty remembering the difference between inductive and deductive reasoning.

    _____

    d. Lee failed to remember what he received as graduation gifts.

    _____

REFERENCES

Bower, G. H. (1970). "Analysis of a Mnemonic Device." *American Scientist* 58:496.

Letterman, D. (1990). *David Letterman's Book of Lists.* New York: Pocket Books.

Miller, G. A. (1956). "The magical number seven, plus or minus two: Some limits on our capacity for processing information." *Psychological Review* 63:81–97.

Tenney, J. (1986, March). "Keyword Notetaking System." Paper presented at the nineteenth annual meeting of the Western College Reading Association, Los Angeles.

6 Thinking Critically: Analysis, Synthesis, and Evaluation

OBJECTIVES

By the end this chapter, you will be able to do the following:

1. Describe the requisites for critical thinking.

2. Analyze information to determine relevance or fact/opinion.

3. Synthesize ideas to identify issues and problems, draw conclusions, and demonstrate creativity.

4. Identify ways to evaluate information when checking consistency or making decisions.

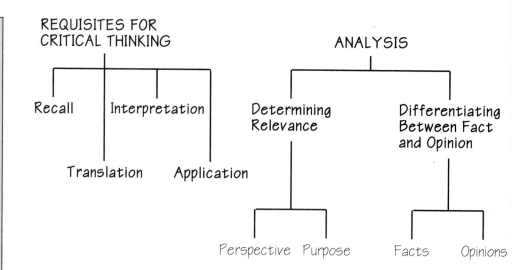

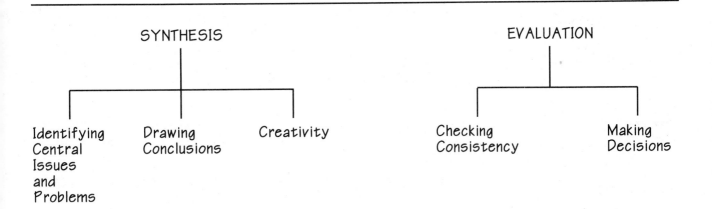

TERMS

analysis
application
assumptions
conclusions
consistency
creativity
critical thinking
evaluation
expert opinions
facts
hypothesis
interpretation
logical inferences
non sequiturs
opinions
perspective
recall
relevance
synthesis
translation

What do you think about when you order a pizza? You probably consider which vendor's pizza you like best. Your choice may also be determined by price, delivery capabilities, and discount coupons you may have. You choose thick or thin crust, heavy or light sauce. You select the toppings. When the pizza arrives, you assess its adequacy based on past experience. Is your order correct? How does it compare to other pizzas? Does it taste like you think it should? If you can think critically about ordering a pizza, you can transfer that kind of thinking to other areas of your life. From the groups you join to the classes you take, from the friends you choose to the way you study, from the degree you pursue to the job you accept, everything you do depends on your ability to think critically.

Critical thinking may be defined as disciplining and taking control of your thinking so you can process information more easily. (Paul, 1990). How you discipline and control your mind depends on your purpose and subject. Thus, as a political science major, you might be particularly good at analyzing the platforms of various candidates. That analytical process, however, would not transfer automatically to determining which insurance policy you should purchase. In addition, you may not consciously choose to accept critical judgments in each and every circumstance. For example, in choosing what to eat, you might correctly discern that a piece of fruit is more nutritionally sound than a piece of cake. Still, you may decide to eat cake.

Critical thinking involves thinking about thinking and, as such, spans the stages of Bloom's Taxonomy (See Figure 5.1 on page 189). Each successive stage depends on the knowledge and ability at the preceding stage(s) (See Figure 6.1). This chapter summarizes the kinds of thinking you must do at the **recall, translation, interpretation,** and **application** stages. It expands the kinds of thinking you need to analyze, synthesize, and evaluate information. Although the topics within each of the following sections address various aspects of critical thinking, critical thinking is not and should not be considered equivalent to the mastery of a few isolated and specialized techniques. Critical thinking goes beyond any one technique to become a way of life. Thus, critical thinking is not something you only read about; it is something you experience and practice.

REQUISITES FOR CRITICAL THINKING

The loftiest edifices need the deepest foundations.
—GEORGE SANTAYANA

Large buildings require great structural support, or they fall. The taller the building, the deeper its foundation must be. Similarly, great

FIGURE 6.1   Requirements for Understanding Determined by Bloom's Taxonomy

RECALL	TRANSLATION	INTERPRETATION	APPLICATION	ANALYSIS	SYNTHESIS	EVALUATION
	depends	depends	depends	depends	depends	depends
	on	on	on	on	on	on
	Recall	**Translation**	**Interpretation**	**Application**	**Analysis**	**Synthesis**
		depends	depends	depends	depends	depends
		on	on	on	on	on
		Recall	**Translation**	**Interpretation**	**Application**	**Analysis**
			depends	depends	depends	depends
			on	on	on	on
			Recall	**Translation**	**Interpretation**	**Application**
				depends	depends	depends
				on	on	on
				Recall	**Translation**	**Interpretation**
					depends	depends
					on	on
					Recall	**Translation**
						depends
						on
						Recall

ideas require understanding at many lower levels, or they fall apart. Just as learning the *ABCs* was the foundation for your ability to read difficult texts, the ability to work with ideas in basic ways is your foundation for more lofty thoughts.

RECALL

The ability to recall information is the lowest level of understanding and requires little more than auditory or visual memory skills. While recall is the lowest level of understanding, it is the only level appropriate for some concepts, such as phone numbers, addresses, and chemical formulas. Table 6.1 provides additional examples of tasks found at the recall level.

   If you've ever taken a test and been able to respond correctly to questions without really understanding the question or the answer, then you've used the recall level of understanding.

TABLE 6.1	Recall Level Tasks

1. Foreign language equivalents
2. Addresses, phone numbers, names, places, and so on.
3. Poetry
4. Songs
5. Music
6. Mathematical formulas and equations
7. Lists or other exact sets of information (see Chapter 5)
8. Quotations

The key is whether or not you know how much you understand. This kind of thinking about thinking forms the basis of critical thinking—the ability to know when you understand something and when you do not.

TRANSLATION

A translator converts one language into another while remaining true to what's said or written. In translation, you convert information from one form into your own words while retaining the essence of the idea. This level of understanding requires that you not only hear or see information but also that you manipulate it in some way. Taking notes, summarizing, and paraphrasing are common forms of translation. Additional translation tasks appear in Table 6.2.

Translation is not as easy as it appears. In the childhood game "gossip," one child whispers a sentence to another child, who whispers it to someone else and so on. The fun of the game is seeing how the original sentence ultimately becomes something entirely different. This, too, is the danger in the translation of information. Something is often lost in translation.

You hold the key to keeping translations faithful to the original. You must determine if your translation is equivalent to the original information. Your ability to determine whether translations are accurate increases with your familiarity with the subject and your skills in translating information in different ways.

INTERPRETATION

Consider the statement "Doreen is going to the hospital." What does this mean? Doreen could be having surgery, having a baby, working at the hospital, undergoing medical tests, or just visiting. Each of

TABLE 6.2	Translation Level Tasks

1. Paraphrase (see Chapter 3).

2. Summarize (see Chapter 3).

3. Reduce equations to the lowest terms.

4. Illustrate information based on the written text.

5. Interpret art, music, process, or other event.

6. Create a chart, diagram, or map based on written information (see Chapter 5).

7. Convert a formula or other symbol to verbal information.

these responses is an interpretation of what the event means. Interpretation is based, then, on your ability to explain events through your knowledge of the connections that exist among ideas. For example, after ordering a sandwich in some places, you may be asked, "Do you want that dressed?" Your background knowledge may leave you without a response unless you know that *dressed* means with all the trimmings (tomato, lettuce, pickle). Background knowledge—and your ability to use it— forms the key to your ability to interpret people, things, ideas, experiences, words, and so on. Interpretation tasks appear in Table 6.3.

Compared to recall or translation, interpretation leaves more room for error. Because background knowledge plays such a part in interpretation, interpretations are often open to question. The connections you make can be incorrect. You control this problem by first examining information and then determining if what you find is consistent with what you know and the rest of the situation. Next, try to explain the situation. Is any information missing? Are any meanings hidden? If so, can you find out what you need? Remain open to ideas and refrain from making decisions based on insufficient evidence.

APPLICATION

When you apply for a job, you are saying that you have the ability to do whatever work is required. When you apply information, you are saying that the process, idea, theory, and so on you have is also appropriate to accomplish what is required. Your understanding has to be such that you can use an idea in a new situation or solve real-life problems. This may require your ability to recall exact information, put the information in your own words (translation), and determine if the information you have fits the situation at hand (interpretation). Other tasks for application appear in Table 6.4.

TABLE 6.3   Tasks for Interpretation

1. Generalize.

2. Draw analogies.

3. Compare and contrast ideas (see Chapter 3).

4. Determine causes and effects (see Chapter 3).

5. Develop spatial relationships.

6. Determine numerical relationships (see Chapter 3).

7. Identify denotations and connotations (see the Vocabulary Development section in this chapter).

TABLE 6.4   Tasks for Application

1. Solve problems that are somewhat different than those previously seen.

2. Solve math and logic word problems.

3. Use a theory or formula to solve a problem.

4. Follow directions to complete a task or project.

5. Group or classify information according to a rule or principle.

WRITE TO LEARN

Your best friend missed the lecture on recall, translation, interpretation, and application. You volunteer to help your friend learn about each concept. On a separate sheet of paper, define each of these levels of thinking, provide examples of each (other than those used in the text), and explain how each lower-level thought process supports the next level of thinking. Create and explain a mnemonic to help you recall the levels of thinking in order.

ANALYSIS

> **If you gave Ruth a rose, she'd peel all the petals off to make sure there weren't any greenfly. And when she'd done that, she'd turn around and say, "Do you call that a rose? Look at it, it's all in bits."**
>
> **—ALAN AYCKBOURN**

> **There is no trusting appearances.**
>
> **—RICHARD BRINSLEY SHERIDAN**

Quick, can you follow the spiral to the center of the whirlpool? (Answer appears on the last page of this chapter.)

Sometimes things are not what they seem. Some people, like Ayckbourn's Ruth, twist and change things until they don't appear to be what they really are. Your powers of observation are tested and sometimes swayed. You must be able to identify the component parts (for example, petals) and then perceive arrangements of data based on your background knowledge. Is a rose still a rose, even if all the petals are gone?

Whether you're analyzing an event, person, place, or thing, you must observe carefully, determine the meaning of the words involved, and continually compare, contrast, and refine your findings. Your **analysis** of a text chapter or lecture ranges from the viewpoint to the very words used by an author or speaker. Determining relevance and adequacy, as well as differentiating between fact and opinion, provides you with the information you need for synthesis and the support you need for evaluation. Examples of analysis-level tasks appear in Table 6.5.

DETERMINING RELEVANCE

Lectures often contain more words than you can immediately note. Textbooks often contain more concepts than you can initially grasp. Experiences contain more sensory impressions than you can quickly process. Even people are far more complex than you can easily discern. How can you choose the right words, important concepts, memorable moments, and friends you need? The answer is in **relevance**. Relevance concerns the appropriateness of information in relation to your purpose. Information that's relevant to one person may be completely irrelevant to another. Information that's critical to the solution of one problem has no bearing on another. Relevance is determined

---

TABLE 6.5   Analysis-Level Tasks

1. Identify stated and/or inferred details that support a main idea or conclusion.

2. Examine the form and/or style of music, poetry, literature, or art.

3. Identify library references and other sources that support a paper's topic and thesis statement.

4. Identify a math or science problem by type.

5. Identify information relevant for the solution of a problem.

6. Identify statements of fact, opinion, or expert opinion.

7. Compare a word's denotation with its connotation.

8. Identify kinds of figures of speech.

9. Identify gaps in logical sequences or arguments.

10. Determine how text format (headings, subheadings, italics) affects the organization of information.

---

by analyzing what is available and choosing what is appropriate to your needs.

Anderson and Pichert (1978) conducted a research study in which they examined how relevance affects recall. Subjects read a passage about what two boys did at one boy's home while playing hooky from school. Some readers were asked to read the passage as if they were burglars. Others were asked to read as if they were home buyers. A third group read with no particular point of view. Researchers found that the reader's point of view affected what was considered relevant and later recalled. For example, those readers who read as burglars were more likely to recall where money was kept. That's what was relevant to them. Readers who read as home buyers recalled more about the house's landscape. That's what was relevant to them. Relevance, then, depends on your point of view or your purpose.

Perspective

Perspective concerns point of view. Clashes of understanding occur when the perspective of the reader or listener differs from that of the author or speaker. Analysis of an author's or speaker's perspective provides you with insights concerning the way the author or speaker thinks about information. Perspectives come from roles (parent, employer, employee, physician, teacher), politics (Republican, Democrat, independent), religion (Christian, atheist, Buddhist, Jewish), social views (communist, libertarian, conservative, liberal), or from a variety of other information that affects beliefs, values, and biases.

EXERCISE 6.1   Use Sample Chapter 1, "Culture: The Ideas and Products People Adopt and Create," to respond to each of the following:

1. You are an artist. You want to create a painting that includes three material aspects of culture that relate to sex or marriage. According to the text, what might you use?

_____

_____

_____

_____

2. You are a historian. You want to credit other cultures for the objects that they contributed to American culture. What table in this chapter could you use?

_____

_____

_____

_____

3. You are indexing the terms in this chapter. On what pages do you find each of the following terms: *mores, sanction, invention, cultural lag.*

_____

_____

_____

_____

4. You are a xenocentric person. Put a check mark by each of the items you would probably prefer.

_____ Chevrolet Corvette	_____ Mazda Miata
_____ Italian Chianti	_____ California chardonnay
_____ American literature	_____ English literature
_____ Empire State Building	_____ Eiffel Tower
_____ Reggae	_____ Jazz

5. You are a cultural anthropologist. Which of the following would be cultural universals in any group?

_____ marriage

_____ money

_____ funerals

_____ division of labor

_____ literacy

_____ government

EXERCISE 6.2   Respond to each of the following:

1. Using the material items in Table 3.1, Material and Nonmaterial Aspects of Culture, in Sample Chapter 1, "Culture: The Ideas and Products People Adopt and Create," identify the perspectives that you would like or dislike.

   _____

   _____

   _____

   _____

   _____

   _____

   _____

2. Read the "Values in the United States," section in Sample Chapter 1, "Culture: The Ideas and Products People Adopt and Create." Create a chart that compares and contrasts those values (success, money, job/career, freedom, equality, and education) for each of the following perspectives: chief executive officer (CEO), teacher, priest, and lawyer.

   _____

   _____

   _____

   _____

   _____

   _____

   _____

3. Read the "The Farm: A Commune Subculture" section in Sample Chapter 1, in "Culture: The Ideas and Products People Adopt and Create." What indicators do you find that give you a sense of their perspective? Does their perspective appeal to you? Why or why not?

   _____

   _____

   _____

   _____

   _____

   _____

   _____

> **WRITE TO LEARN**
>
> Consider the following: Two roommates move into a new apartment, where pets are not allowed. After living there for one month, one roommate buys a cat and brings it home. The other roommate is unhappy about having the cat in the apartment. An argument ensues. At its end, the cat's owner accuses the roommate of kicking her cat. The roommate insists she merely nudged the cat away from the leg of her chair with her foot. On a separate sheet of paper, explain how point of view could account for the difference in the two stories.

Purpose

Radio commentator Paul Harvey reports on people, places, and events that possess elements of intrigue. Just when his listeners think they discern the main idea, Harvey provides a particularly interesting detail that changes the listeners' analysis of what the person, place, or event was all about. Harvey concludes by saying, "And, now you know the rest of the story."

Sometimes, as a critical thinker, you must determine if you need "the rest of the story." Facts, opinions, conclusions, observations, and so on must be analyzed to determine if what you have is enough for your purpose. As in many other critical-thinking abilities, background knowledge plays a part in determining whether you have sufficient information. Eighteenth-century English poet William Blake said, "You never know what is enough unless you know what is more than enough." To paraphrase Blake, you must know if you have more than enough to determine if you have enough information.

EXERCISE 6.3   Read Sample Chapter 4, "Managing Stress," and respond to the following statements. Place an X by the statements that lack adequate information for a response.

_____ 1. Selye would agree that stress can classified as eustress or distress.

_____ 2. The effects of eustress are always positive.

_____ 3. The general adaptation syndrome involves physiological and psychological responses to stress.

_____ 4. Stress is causing increases in occupational disease claims.

_____ 5. Selye would agree that the more LCUs in a population, the higher the mortality and morbidity rates.

_____ 6. Stressful life events cause disease.

_____ 7. According to Table 3.1, Common Sources of Stress, intrapersonal conflict, interpersonal relationships, and family are the top three causes of stress.

_____ 8. Effective time management is a key factor in coping with stress.

_____ 9. Increases in scores on the Social Readjustment Rating Scale (Self-Inventory 3-1) often result in increased chances of illness.

_____ 10. Carl's grades dropped in his sophomore year due to illness, and he lost his scholarship. He got a part-time job and finished school in five years, rather than four. This would be a good example of salutogenesis.

DIFFERENTIATING BETWEEN FACT AND OPINION

When Mark Twain was a reporter, he was told never to state as fact anything that he could not personally verify. Following this instruction to the letter, he wrote the following account of a social event: "A woman giving the name of Mrs. James Jones, who is reported to be one of the society leaders of the city, is said to have given what purported to be a party yesterday to a number of alleged ladies. The hostess claims to be the wife of a reputed attorney." Twain was careful not to confuse **facts,** or statements of reality, with **opinions**— viewpoints, judgments, or beliefs. You, too, must be careful to distinguish between facts and opinions in texts and lectures.

Facts

Facts often describe concepts that are universally held or easily agreed upon. "The first month of the year is January"; "The boiling point of water is 212 degrees Fahrenheit"; "3 + 5 = 8"; "The time is now 2 P.M."; "The accident occurred at the corner of Fourth and Main" are all examples of facts. Words that tell about facts are often descriptive. They provide details without being judgmental or opinionated. They express absolutes. Words such as _dead, freezing,_ and _wet_ are examples of such words. Other words limit statements of fact. They show the possibility of other options. Consider the difference between these two statements: "I make good grades" and "At times, I make good grades." _Frequently, sometimes,_ and _seldom_ are examples of or words that limit information.

Opinions

Opinions, like facts, are also forms of truth. Unlike facts, they are the truth as perceived by one person. Opinions represent a judgment, attitude, feeling, or perception of a person, place, thing, or event. Words describing opinions are more interpretive. Words such as *dangerous, attractive, confusing,* and *distant* all imply opinion.

The background of the person giving an opinion affects the value of the opinion. Anyone can give an opinion, but some are **expert opinions.** Your dentist might say, ''This is a good car.'' An auto mechanic might say, ''This is a good car.'' Which person would you trust to know more about cars?

An expert opinion depends on many factors. In reading, you judge an author's educational and professional backgrounds. Often an author's background affects point of view, what is said about a topic, and the way in which facts are reported. You find background information about an author in the preliminary or concluding statements of an article or a book. A biographical dictionary or an encyclopedia also contains such information. You also gain this knowledge through discussions with others in the field. You judge where the author works and the reputation of that institution.

You also judge the reputation of the author. However, this works both as an advantage and a disadvantage. Sometimes authors who are well-known authorities in one field write below their standards in another. As a critical reader, you need to know the difference.

Sometimes information about the author's credentials is missing. You then need another way to judge the information. For example, suppose an article in *Today's Science* compares the incidence of cancer in the United States with that of France. The author, who is unknown to you, concludes that the air in France is cleaner than that in the United States and that this keeps the French in better health. Since you have no information about the author's background, you cannot evaluate the author's qualifications or bias. In this case, you judge the standards and credibility of the journal containing the article.

WRITE TO LEARN

On a separate sheet of paper, respond to the following: In your American history class, a graduate student in history guest lectures. She asserts that Grover Cleveland was the most effective president. Do you consider hers an expert opinion? Justify your answer.

Authors and lecturers often appear to report facts when what they really describe are their opinions and expert opinions about the information. You can discern the difference by considering the questions in Table 6.6.

TABLE 6.6   Differentiating between Fact and Opinion

1. Which statements appear to be facts?

2. How can these statements be proven?

3. Which statements are opinions?

4. Which statements represent expert opinions?

5. What is the expertise and reputation of the person giving an expert opinion?

EXERCISE 6.4   Use Sample Chapter 4, "Managing Stress," to respond to the following:

1. Using Self-Inventory 3-1, The Social Readjustment Rating Scale, identify three life events that represent facts and three that represent opinions.
   FACTS

   _____

   _____

   _____

   OPINIONS

   _____

   _____

   _____

2. Using Self-Inventory 3-2, The Social Readjustment Rating Scale for College Students, identify three life events that represent facts and three that represent opinions.
   FACTS

   _____

   _____

   _____

   OPINIONS

   _____

   _____

   _____

3. The chapter's author states that the information from Table 3-2, Perceived Intensity of Stress Factors for College Students, is based on a study in which college students in Kentucky rated the factors they thought were most stressful for them. Do you think their responses represent facts, opinions, or expert opinions? Explain your response.

_____

_____

_____

_____

4. Review the section "Keeping a Journal," including the "Guidelines to Your Good Health." How do facts, opinions, and expert opinions enter into the process of keeping a journal?

_____

_____

_____

_____

5. This chapter discusses the following social supports: esteem, status, social companionship, information, and material support. If possible, identify one opinion and one fact for each social support. Would you assess this section as primarily opinionated or factual? Provide a rationale for your decision.
   Esteem

_____

_____

   Status

_____

_____

   Social Companionship

_____

_____

   Information

_____

_____

   Material Support

_____

_____

   Rationale:

_____

_____

WRITE TO LEARN

On a separate sheet of paper, categorize the following words as fact or opinion: *pregnant, humid, blond, green, wealthy, prejudiced, large, size 8, old.*

SYNTHESIS

The mind of men is a mystery; and like the plant, each one of us naturally appropriates and assimilates that about him which responds to that which is within him.

—JOSEPH ROUX

Synthesis is the assimilation of knowledge to create a new idea. The way you synthesize depends on your background knowledge and the way in which you recall, define, translate, apply, and analyze information. More than an additive process, synthesis allows you to literally transform knowledge into a different form. In synthesizing, you take everything you know and come up with something you didn't know you knew.

Synthesis is the essence of looking at something or putting pieces together in a new way. It may involve examining a vast amount of information and a variety of situations in order to identify issues and problems. Sometimes, some of the information you need for understanding will be missing. This means you will need to draw logical conclusions. Finally, the hypotheses you pose and the answers you find may call for real ingenuity—the ability to be creative. Table 6.7 shows tasks which require you to synthesize.

WRITE TO LEARN

The French word *ingenue* means a young girl who is innocent and free-spirited. Your text tells you that the ability to create calls for *ingenuity.* On a separate sheet of paper, explain the relationship between these words in terms of youth and creativity.

IDENTIFYING CENTRAL ISSUES AND PROBLEMS

The following story is adapted from a popular book of experiential training exercises for staff development programs (Newstrom and Scannel, 1980).

I sat next to a man in the doctor's office who was wearing a very nice shirt with his suit. When I complimented the man on the shirt, he said that it was one

---

TABLE 6.7   Tasks Requiring Synthesis

1. Writing fiction.

2. Writing poetry.

3. Creating visual works of art.

4. Composing music.

5. Solving a problem or mystery.

6. Designing an experiment.

7. Writing a research paper (see Chapter 10).

8. Drawing conclusions to form a main idea.

9. Drawing conclusions from given details.

10. Summarizing information (see Chapter 3).

11. Predicting information (see Chapter 3).

12. Creating a title for a book, chapter, song, or other information (see Chapter 10).

13. Identifying the main idea of graphics (see Chapter 8).

---

of several he had purchased months ago. He said he wore a very unusual shirt size (14 ½ × 36) and found it difficult to find shirts that fit. But, he had found a new clothing store which had just what he wanted.

He said that one salesperson had been particularly helpful. The salesperson had asked if she could help him and said that the store carried several shirts in his size.

The man said he had replied by asking, "Do your shirts have collars that don't wrinkle when stuffed in a suitcase, buttons that won't crack when laundered, and cuffs that won't fray?"

The salesperson brought out several shirts in the correct size. She twisted the collar—no wrinkles. She got a hammer and hit the buttons—no cracks. She got sandpaper and rubbed the cuffs—no fraying. The man admitted that shirts were expensive—over $100 each—but they answered all the questions he had about shirt construction. He had purchased five of them. I looked at the collar, cuffs, and buttons—they were in perfect shape.

"And," said the man, "I really learned something from the salesperson. The person who asks the right question at the right time will not only be in control of the conversation but will get what he wants in the bargain. Say, it's getting hot. Do you mind if I take off my jacket?"

When he turned to hang his jacket on the back of his chair, I saw that the back of the shirt was worn to threads!

Identifying issues and problems is a refinement of your ability to identify main ideas in lectures (see Chapter 3) and in reading (see Chapter 4). While this requires you to analyze the component parts of information, you must also be able to synthesize a variety of main

---

TABLE 6.8   Identifying Central Issues and Problems

1. What is the point, issue, or problem?

2. What is the point of view?

3. What other points, issues, or problems are relevant but not the central point, issue, or problem?

4. Which questions will give you the most relevant information about this issue or problem?

5. What is the best question to ask?

---

ideas in order to identify overall importance. Identifying central issues and problems often requires the ability to ask the right—and most important—questions. It helps you focus on essential and basic information (shirt fronts and backs) and avoid emphasizing less important details (collars, buttons, and cuffs). Examples of questions that help you synthesize central issues and problems appear in Table 6.8.

EXERCISE 6.5   Respond to each of the following:

1. Read the "Applying Sociological Research, Culture and Life Expectancy" section in Sample Chapter 1, "Culture: The Ideas and Products People Adopt and Create," then answer the following questions.

   a. What is the point, issue, or problem?

   _____

   _____

   b. What is the point of view?

   _____

   _____

   c. What other points, issues, or problems are relevant but not the central point, issue, or problem?

   _____

   _____

   d. Construct 3 questions that will give you the most relevant information about this issue or problem.

   _____

   _____

   e. What is the single best question to ask to find the central issue?

   _____

   _____

2. Read Health Note 7-1, "Lowering Your Cholesterol," in Sample Chapter 3, "Nutrition and Digestion."
   a. What is the point, issue, or problem?

   _____

   _____

   b. What is the point of view?

   _____

   _____

   c. What other points, issues, or problems are relevant but not the central point, issue, or problem?

   _____

   _____

   d. Construct 3 questions that will give you the most relevant information about this issue or problem.

   _____

   _____

   e. What is the single best question to ask to find the central issue?

   _____

   _____

3. Read the "Exercise Your Critical Thinking Skills" section at the end of Sample Chapter 3, "Nutrition and Digestion."
   a. What is the point, issue, or problem?

   _____

   _____

   b. What is the point of view?

   _____

   _____

   c. What other points, issues, or problems are relevant but not the central point, issue, or problem?

   _____

   _____

   d. Which of the questions—if any—in paragraphs 4 and 5 will give you the most relevant information about this issue or problem?

   _____

   _____

   e. What is the single best question you could ask to find the central issue?

   _____

   _____

4.

Classroom Types

BY VAL CHEATHAM

$ $ $ $ $

$ $ $ $ $

$ $ $ $ $

$ $ $ $ $

$ $ $ $ $

¢

"I called all you teachers together to tell you about next year's raise."

SOURCE: Reprinted by permission of Val R. Cheatham.

a. What is the point, issue, or problem?

_____

_____

b. What is the point of view?

_____

_____

c. What other points, issues, or problems are relevant but not the central point, issue, or problem?

_____

_____

d. Create three questions that will give you the most relevant information about this issue or problem.

_____

_____

e. What is the best question to ask to find the central issue?

_____

_____

5.

SOURCE: Reprinted by permission of George Abbott.

a. What is the point, issue, or problem?

_____

_____

b. What is the point of view?

_____

_____

c. What other points, issues, or problems are relevant but not the central point, issue, or problem?

_____

_____

d. Create three questions that will give you the most relevant information about this issue or problem.

_____

_____

e. What is the best question to ask to find the central issue?

_____

_____

DRAWING CONCLUSIONS

Sir Arthur Conan Doyle's character of Sherlock Holmes was known for his ability to draw conclusions. In the story "The Sign of Four," Doctor Watson, Sherlock Holmes's associate, showed Holmes a watch and reminded him that Holmes had said that when a person uses an object every day, he or she leaves identifying marks on it.

Holmes looked at the watch. He said that although the watch has been recently cleaned, the initials and date of manufacture on the back of the watch indicated that it had belonged to Watson's late brother, who had inherited it from their father. He added that Watson's brother was probably an untidy and careless man who had thrown away good financial prospects. He indicated that Watson's brother had lived in poverty with intermittent periods of prosperity, abused alcohol, and later died.

Watson confronted Holmes. How could he have known this? Did he guess? Was he a mindreader?

Holmes apologized saying,
No, no: I never guess. It is a shocking habit—destructive to the logical faculty. What seems strange to you is only so because you do not follow my train of thought or observe the small facts upon which large inferences may depend. For example, I began by stating that your brother was careless. When you observe the lower part of that watch case you notice that it is not only dented in two places but it is cut and marked all over from the habit of keeping other hard objects, such as coins or keys, in the same pocket. Surely it is no great feat to assume that a man who treats a fifty-guinea watch so cavalierly must be a careless man. Neither is it a very far-fetched inference that a man who inherits one article of such value is pretty well provided for in other respects.

. . . It is very customary for pawnbrokers in England, when they take a watch, to scratch the number of the ticket with a pin-point upon the inside of the case. It is more handy than a label as there is no risk of the number being lost or transposed. There are no less than four such numbers visible to my lens on the inside of this case. Inference—that your brother was often at low water. Secondary inference—that he had occasional bursts of prosperity, or he could not have redeemed the pledge. Finally, I ask you to look at the inner plate, which contains the keyhold. Look at the thousands of scratches all round the hole—marks where the key has slipped. What sober man's key could have scored those grooves? But you will never see a drunkard's watch without them. He winds it at night, and he leaves these traces of his unsteady hand. Where is the mystery in all this?

SOURCE: Doyle, Arthur Conan. (1960).*The Complete Sherlock Homes*, vol. I. Garden City, N.Y.: Doubleday & Company, Inc.

A **conclusion** is a decision, judgment, or opinion reached by reasoning or inferring. It's your best estimate based on both observable facts and logical inferences. Sometimes conclusions are easy to make. Sometimes they are not. Drawing conclusions improves with practice. Using the knowledge you have and thinking actively helps you draw valid conclusions. Four types of conclusions are possible: **hypotheses, logical inferences, assumptions,** and **non sequiturs.**

A hypothesis is your idea of what will happen next in a particular situation or what might the consequences of a given action. For example, suppose your co-worker often misses work. When he returns to work, he brings cookies for the staff. When he misses work the next time, what will your hypothesis be about the snacks available at work that day? Or, suppose your best friend fails to pass any of her chemistry exams. What do you hypothesize about her final grade in the class?

A logical inference is a conclusion that cannot be avoided. Once you consider the facts, you can infer nothing else. This inference is somewhat like the reflective theorem in geometry that says, "If $a = b$ and $b = c$, then $a = c$." For example: Sophomores must have at least thirty hours of college credit. Juan is a sophomore. Therefore, Juan has at least thirty hours of college credit.

Assumptions form the third and most common type of conclusion. This conclusion is based on given facts and your background knowledge. Such an inference will often be true, but it could also be false. For example, if one instructor's sections of a class on your campus are always filled, then you can assume that the instructor is very good or very easy. One, both, or neither of these assumptions may be accurate.

Non sequiturs are the fourth type of conclusion. Non sequiturs are not supported by facts, nor do they follow from given evidence. Indeed, they are inferences that make no sense. For example, consider again your friend in the chemistry class. If you examined her failing performance on all her tests and inferred that she would pass chemistry with a final grade of B, you would be making a non sequitur.

EXERCISE 6.6   Respond to each of the following:

1. Read the "Values in the United States" and "The Farm: A Commune Subculture" sections in Sample Chapter 1, "Culture: The Ideas and Products People Adopt and Create." Given Williams's analysis of the more important values in our society in terms of success, money, job/career, freedom, equality, and education, what do you think the values of a Farm member are for each one? Would you characterize your conclusions as hypotheses, logical inferences, assumptions, or non sequiturs? Why?

_____

_____

_____

_____

2. Examine Table 3.3, "Life Expectancy of Whites and Blacks in the United States," at the end of Sample Chapter 1, "Culture: The Ideas and Products People Adopt and Create." Using the chart format, hypothesize what the life expectancy for the years 1994, 1995, and 1996 might be for whites and blacks.

_____

_____

_____

_____

_____

_____

_____

CREATIVITY

Creativity is the ultimate form of synthesis. It is taking all the available information, creating hypotheses, drawing conclusions, and coming up with a new idea or product or a new way of looking at an idea of product. If you've ever solved a problem, told a story in oral or written form, drawn a picture, created a song, made do with something because you didn't have the right equipment (for example used a knife as a screwdriver), then you used your abilities of creativity.

According to Roger van Oech (1986, 1990), creativity begins with exploration to see what ideas, materials, processes, and situations are available. Then, he says, the artist in you takes over to design a new product or idea. Your ability to judge helps you identify the merits of that product or idea. Your ability to fight for your idea aids in implementation. The creative person looks at information in different ways. According to Dr. Paul Torrance (Kincher, 1990), creative thinking depends on four factors: fluency, flexibility, originality, and elaboration. Fluency concerns the quantity of ideas you generate. Flexibility relates to the variety of ideas you formulate. If your ideas are your own, then you are thinking with originality. Finally, elaboration describes the amount and quality of details you include. Figure 6.2 contains an inventory to help you assess your creative abilities.

FIGURE 6.2	Estimating Your Creative Quotient

What's Your C.Q. (Creativity Quotient)?
Give yourself anywhere from 1–10 points for each of these creativity characteristics.

- 10 points = you're very much the way the question describes

- 9, 8, 7, or 6 points = you're pretty much that way

- 5 points = you're average for that characteristic

- 4, 3, or 2 points = you're lower than average for that characteristic

- 1 point = you aren't that way at all

Highest possible score: 100 points
Lowest possible score: 10 points

1. *Are you a curious cat?* Do you wonder why, how, why not? Do you enjoy collecting bits of information? Do you ask questions? Do you question the obvious?

2. *Are you observant?* Did you notice when the house down the street was painted? When the market got a new sign? When your aunt got a new hairdo? When the newspaper changed its column width?

3. *Do you see other points of view?* When you disagree with people, are you able to understand their side? Can you see new ways of looking at old problems.

4. *Are you willing to change your ideas?* Are you open to new ideas? If someone can add to your idea and improve it, will you change it? Do you search for the best idea rather than stick to your idea?

5. *Can you learn from your mistakes and move on?* Do you accept failure without just giving up? Do you realize that if you don't give up, then you haven't really failed?

6. *Do you use your imagination and dreams?* Do you say "What if . . . ?"

7. *Do you see connections between things that seem unrelated?* (For example, do a desert plant and a tough person have anything in common?) Do you recombine ideas in new ways (like using a glass for a flower vase)?

8. *Do you believe in yourself?* Do you have a can-do attitude? Do you expect to find solutions to problems?

9. *Do you try to keep from judging other people, ideas, and situations?* Do you wait until all the evidence is in before making up your mind?

10. *Do you have a fun attitude?* Will you do things even if they look silly? Do you trust yourself enough to be adventurous and take risks? Will you suggest a solution that might be rejected by others, or do you usually play it safe?

Creativity aids learning in that the more ways you have to think about information, the better you understand it. For example, creativity assists you in forming acrostics, acronyms, mnemonigraphs, and other memory devices (see Chapter 5). Creativity helps you form analogies and other figures of speech (see Chapter 10). Creativity aids you in solving problems, forming concept maps, writing papers, and giving impromptu speeches.

EXERCISE 6.7   Respond to each of the following:

1. Examine the symbol on p. 505 (p. 8) of Sample Chapter 2, "The Planetary Setting." What do you think it is? What other things might it symbolize?

_____

_____

_____

2. Examine the symbol in Health Note 7-1 on p. 527 (p. 168) of Sample Chapter 3, "Nutrition and Digestion." What do you think it is? What other things might it symbolize?

_____

_____

_____

3. Examine the symbol in the Vocabulary Development section at the end of this chapter. What do you think it is? What other things might it symbolize?

_____

_____

_____

4. In the left margin, create a symbol that could be used to identify the Living Sociology boxes found in Sample Chapter 1, "Culture: The Ideas and Products People Adopt and Create."

5. In the left margin, create a symbol that could be used to identify the Guidelines to Your Good Health boxes found in Sample Chapter 4, "Managing Stress."

EXERCISE 6.8

1. Create your own imaginary society. Using the information from Sample Chapter 1, "Culture: The Ideas and Products People Adopt and Create," give an example of a material and a nonmaterial aspect of culture in that society. In a paragraph, describe the society's values, norms, folkways, mores, taboos, and laws and how they came to be that way.

_____

_____

_____

_____

2. Sample Chapter 4, "Managing Stress," provides a paradigm for the effect of balancing factors in a stressful event in Figure 3-3 and a case study in Figure 3-4. Create another example of the paradigm in the space below.

3. Examine the symbols you created and interpreted in Exercise 6.7. Why did you create the ones you did? Why do you think the publishers used the ones they did? How can such symbols to aid recall?

_____

_____

_____

_____

WRITE TO LEARN

Examine Figure 6.1, "Bloom's Taxonomy." Read the information that explains it on the first page of this chapter. On a separate sheet of paper, create a symbol that explains it. How will your recall of information in Figure 6.1 be aided by your creating a symbol?

EVALUATION

> **We are mistaken in believing the mind and the judgment two separate things; judgment is only the extent of the mind's illumination.**
> **—LA ROCHEFOUCAULD**

Evaluation, also called judgment, is the highest level of thinking. As La Rochefoucauld noted over three hundred years ago, it is not separate from the other processes of thinking. Rather, it builds on all the other levels of thinking to become the highest extension of thinking. Thus, to evaluate, you first possess basic understanding (recall) and the ability to put information in your own words (translation). You discern how one piece of information connects with other pieces (interpretation). You are able to use it (application) and examine its components (analysis). You find ways to recombine it in a variety of ways and re-structure it (synthesis). Then, you are ready to judge the information for consistency with other information or what you already know, make decisions, and rethink the decisions that you make.

CHECKING CONSISTENCY

Almost more than they want fairness, people want to live in a world of **consistency.** If you know your neighbor is always grouchy, you know what to expect. It's the people who are friendly one minute and vicious the next who pose problems because you never know what to expect from them. While extraordinary occurrences are interesting, consistency is the quality that gives life balance.

Consistency is essentially quality control. It concerns the reliability of information in both written and spoken forms. In judging consistency, you evaluate not accuracy or worth as much as you determine agreement.

In general, a text or lecture possesses several kinds of internal consistency. The style and general sentence structure remains constant throughout. The author or speaker does not use contradictory information. All of the information in a single document or speech agrees and makes some sort of logical sense.

Determining consistency is most difficult when you must examine the same concept from different sources. The perspective, structure, and even content of the information can vary from author to author, speaker to speaker.

EXERCISE 6.9   You are writing a paper on cultural rules and American values based on the information in Sample Chapter 1, "Culture: The Ideas and Products People Adopt and Create." You use the following article—"Moral Growth Stages" by Lawrence Kohlberg for reference. Read, mark, and label this source. Then respond to the following:

1. Although the article did not identify specific behaviors as being cultural rules, laws, taboos, and so on, some could be classified as such. Find an example of each kind of cultural rule and cite its source.

---

2. Consider the "Values" section in the sample chapter. According to the article, how are moral values developed?

_____

_____

_____

_____

_____

3. Are moral growth stages according to Kohlberg and cultural rules according to the sample chapter synonymous? Explain.

_____

_____

_____

_____

_____

_____

4. How are the viewpoints and content of the article and the chapter similar?

_____

_____

_____

_____

_____

5. How are the viewpoints and content of the article and the chapter different?

_____

_____

_____

_____

_____

6. How does understanding the differences between rules, laws, taboos, and so on help you comprehend the article?

_____

_____

_____

_____

_____

EXCERPT 6.1   MORAL GROWTH STAGES   Lawrence Kohlberg

The cognitive-developmental approach was fully stated for the first time by John Dewey. The approach is called *cognitive* because it recognizes that moral education, like intellectual education, has its basis in stimulating the *active thinking* of the child about moral issues and decisions. It is called developmental because it sees the aims of moral education as movement through moral stages. According to Dewey:

The aim of education is growth or *development*, both intellectual and moral. Ethical and psychological principles can aid the school in the *greatest of all constructions—the building of a free and powerful character*. Only knowledge of the *order and connection of the stages in psychological development can insure this*. Education is the work of *supplying the conditions* which will enable the psychological functions to mature in the freest and fullest manner.

Dewey postulated three levels of moral development: 1) the *pre-moral* or *preconventional* level "of behavior motivated by biological and social impulses with results for morals," 2) The *conventional* level of behavior "in which the individual accepts with little critical reflection the standards of his group," and 3) the *autonomous* level of behavior in which "conduct is guided by the individual thinking and judging for himself whether a purpose is good, and does not accept the standard of his group without reflection."[1]

Dewey's thinking about moral stages was theoretical. Building upon his prior studies of cognitive stages, Jean Piaget made the first effort to define stages of moral reasoning in children through actual interviews and through observations of children (in games with rules). Using this interview material, Piaget defined the pre-moral, the conventional, and the autonomous levels as follows: 1) The *pre-moral stage*, where there is no sense of obligation to rules; 2) the *heteronomous stage*, where the right was literal obedience to rules and an equation of obligation with submission to power and punishment (roughly ages 4–8); and 3) the *autonomous stage*, where the purpose and consequences of following rules are considered and obligation is based on reciprocity and exchange (roughly ages 8–12).[2]

In 1955 I started to redefine and validate (through longitudinal and cross-cultural study) the Dewey-Piaget levels and stages. The resulting stages are presented in Table 1.

We claim to have validated the stages defined in Table 1. The notion that stages can be *validated* by longitudinal study implies that stages have definite empirical characteristics. The concept of stages (as used by Piaget and myself) implies the following characteristics:

1. Stages are "structured wholes," or organized systems of thought. Individuals are *consistent* in level of moral judgment.

2. Stages form an *invariant sequence*. Under all conditions except extreme trauma, movement is always forward, never backward. Individuals never skip stages; movement is always to the next stage up.

3. Stages are "hierarchical integrations." Thinking at a higher stage includes or comprehends within it lowerstage thinking. There is a tendency to function at or prefer the highest stage available.

TABLE 1   Definition of Moral Stages

I. Preconventional level

At this level, the child is responsive to cultural rules and labels of good and bad, right or wrong, but interprets these labels either in terms of the physical or the hedonistic consequences of action (punishment, reward, exchange of favors) or in terms of the physical power of those who enunciate the rules and labels. The level is divided into the following two stages:

Stage 1: *The punishment-and-obedience orientation.* The physical consequences of action determine its goodness or badness, regardless of the human meaning or value of these consequences. Avoidance of punishment and unquestioning deference to power are valued in their own right, not in terms of respect for an underlying moral order supported by punishment and authority (the latter being Stage 4).

Stage 2: *The instrumental-relativist orientation.* Right action consists of that which instrumentally satisfies one's own needs and occasionally the needs of others. Human relations are viewed in terms like those of the marketplace. Elements of fairness, or reciprocity, and of equal sharing are present, but they are always interpreted in a physical, pragmatic way. Reciprocity is a matter of "you scratch my back and I'll scratch yours," not of loyalty, gratitude, or justice.

II. Conventional level

At this level, maintaining the expectations of the individual's family, group; or nation is perceived as valuable in its own right, regardless of immediate and obvious consequences. The attitude is not only one of *conformity* to personal expectations and social order, but of loyalty to it, of actively *maintaining,* supporting, and justifying the order, and of identifying with the person or group involved in it. At this level, there are the following two stages:

Stage 3: *The interpersonal concordance or "good boy-nice girl" orientation.* Good behavior is that which pleases or helps others and is approved by them. There is much conformity to stereotypical images of what is majority or "natural" behavior. Behavior is frequently judged by intention—"he means well" becomes important for the first time. One earns approval by being "nice."

Each of these characteristics has been demonstrated for moral stages. Stages are defined by responses to a set of verbal moral dilemmas classified according to an elaborate scoring scheme. Validating studies include:

1. A 20-year study of 50 Chicago-area boys, middle- and working-class. Initially interviewed at ages 10–16, they have been reinterviewed at three-year intervals thereafter.

2. A small, six-year longitudinal study of Turkish villages and city boys of the same age.

3. A variety of other cross-sectional studies in Canada, Britain, Israel, Taiwan, Yucatán, Honduras, and India.

With regard to the structured whole or consistency criterion, we have found that more than 50% of an individual's thinking is always at one stage,

---

TABLE 1   Definition of Moral Stages   *(continued)*

Stage 4: *The "law and order" orientation.* There is orientation toward authority, fixed rules, and the maintenance of the social order. Right behavior consists of doing one's duty, showing respect for authority, and maintaining the given social order for its own sake.

III. Postconventional, autonomous, or principled level

At this level, there is a clear effort to define moral values and principles that have validity and application apart from the authority of the groups or persons holding these principles and apart from the individual's own identification with these groups. This level also has two stages:

Stage 5: *The social-contract, legalistic orientation,* generally with utilitarian overtones. Right action tends to be defined in terms of general individual rights and standards which have been critically examined and agreed upon by the whole society. There is a clear awareness of the relativism of personal values and opinions and a corresponding emphasis upon procedural rules for reaching consensus. Aside from what is constitutionally and democratically agreed upon, the right is a matter of personal "values" and "opinion." The result is an emphasis upon the "legal point of view," but with an emphasis upon the possibility of changing law in terms of rational considerations of social utility (rather than freezing it in terms of Stage 4 "law and order"). Outside the legal realm, free agreement and contract is the binding element of obligation. This is the "official" morality of the American government and constitution.

Stage 6: *The universal-ethical-principle-orientation.* Right is defined by the decision of conscience in accord with self-chosen *ethical principles* appealing to logical comprehensiveness, universality, and consistency. These principles are abstract and ethical (the Golden Rule, the categorical imperative); they are not concrete moral rules like the Ten Commandments. At heart, these are universal principles of *justice,* of the *reciprocity* and *equality* of human *rights,* and of respect for the dignity of human beings as *individual* persons. ("From Is to Ought," pp. 164, 165)

—Reprinted from *The Journal of Philosophy,* Inc. Lawrence Kohlberg

---

with the remainder at the next adjacent stage (which he is leaving or which he is moving into).

With regard to invariant sequence, our longitudinal results have been presented in the *American Journal of Orthopsychiatry,* and indicate that on every retest individuals were either at the same stage as three years earlier or had moved up. This was true in Turkey as well as in the United States.

With regard to the hierarchical integration criterion, it has been demonstrated that adolescents exposed to written statements at each of the six stages comprehend or correctly put in their own words all statements at or below their own stage but fail to comprehend any statements more than one stage above their own. Some individuals comprehend the next stage above their own; some do not. Adolescents prefer (or rank as best) the highest stage they can comprehend.

To understand moral stages, it is important to clarify their relations to stage of logic or intelligence, on the one hand, and to moral behavior on the other.

Maturity of moral judgment is not highly correlated with IQ or verbal intelligence (correlations are only in the 30s, accounting for 10% of the variance). Cognitive development, in the stage sense, however, is more important for moral development than such correlations suggest. Piaget has found that after the child learns to speak there are three major stages of reasoning: the intuitive, the concrete operational, and the formal operational. At around age 7, the child enters the stage of concrete logical thought: he can make logical inferences, classify, and handle quantitative relations about concrete things. In adolescence individuals usually enter the stage of formal operations. At this stage they can reason abstractly, i.e., consider all possibilities, form hypotheses, deduce implications from hypotheses, and test them against reality.[3]

Since moral reasoning clearly is reasoning, advanced moral reasoning depends upon advanced logical reasoning: a person's logical stage puts a certain ceiling on the moral stage he can attain. A person whose logical stage is only concrete operational is limited to the preconventional moral stages (Stages 1 and 2). A person whose logical stage is only partially formal operational is limited to the conventional moral stages (Stages 3 and 4). While logical development is necessary for moral development and sets limits to it, most individuals are higher in logical stage than they are in moral stage. As an example, over 50% of late adolescents and adults are capable of full formal reasoning, but only 10% of these adults (all formal operational) display principled (Stages 5 and 6) moral reasoning.

The moral stages are *structures of moral judgment* or *moral reasoning*. *Structures* of moral judgment must be distinguished from the *content* of moral judgment. As an example, we cite responses to a dilemma used in our various studies to identify moral stage. The dilemma raises the issue of stealing a drug to save a dying woman. The inventor of the drug is selling it for 10 times what it costs him to make it. The woman's husband cannot raise the money, and the seller refuses to lower the price or wait for payment. What should the husband do?

The choice endorsed by a subject (steal, don't steal) is called the *content* of his moral judgment in the situation. His reasoning about the choice defines the structure of his moral judgment. This reasoning centers on the following 10 universal moral values or issues of concern to persons in these moral dilemmas:

1. Punishment

2. Property

3. Roles and concerns of affection

4. Roles and concerns of authority

5. Law

6. Life

7. Liberty

8. Distributive justice

9. Truth

10. Sex

A moral choice involves choosing between two (or more) of these values as they *conflict* in concrete situations of choice.

The stage or structure of a person's moral judgment defines; 1) *what* he finds valuable in each of these moral issues (life, law), i.e., how he defines the value, and 2) *why* he finds it valuable, i.e., the reasons he gives for valuing it. As an example, at Stage 1 life is valued in terms of the power or possessions of the person involved; at Stage 2, for its usefulness in satisfying the needs of the individual in question or others; at Stage 3, in terms of the individual's relations with others and their valuation of him; at Stage 4, in terms of social or religious law. Only at Stages 5 and 6 is each life seen as inherently worthwhile, aside from other consideration.

Moral Judgment vs. Moral Action

Having clarified the nature of stages of moral *judgment*, we must consider the relation of moral judgment to moral *action*. If logical reasoning is a necessary but not sufficient condition for mature moral judgment, mature moral judgment is a necessary but not sufficient condition for mature moral action. One cannot follow moral principles if one does not understand (or believe in) moral principles. However, one can reason in terms of principles and not live up to these principles. As an example, Richard Krebs and I found that only 15% of students showing some principled thinking cheated as compared to 55% of conventional subjects and 70% of preconventional subjects. Nevertheless, 15% of the principled subjects did cheat, suggesting that factors additional to moral judgment are necessary for principled moral reasoning to be translated into "moral action." Partly, these factors include the situation and its pressures. Partly, what happens depends upon the individual's motives and emotions. Partly, what the individual does depends upon a general sense of will, purpose, or "ego strength." As an example of the role of will or ego strength in moral behavior, we may cite the study of Krebs: Slightly more than half of his conventional subjects cheated. These subjects were also divided by a measure of attention/will. Only 26% of the "strong-willed" conventional subjects cheated; however, 74% of the "weak-willed" subjects cheated.

If maturity of moral reasoning is only one factor in moral behavior, why does the cognitive-developmental approach to moral education focus so heavily upon moral reasoning? For the following reasons:

1. Moral judgment, while only one factor in moral behavior, is the single most important or influential factor yet discovered in moral behavior.

2. While other factors influence moral behavior, moral judgment is the only distinctively *moral* factor in moral behavior. To illustrate, we noted that the Krebs study indicated that "strong-willed" conventional stage subjects resisted cheating more than "weak-willed" subjects. For those at a preconventional level of moral reasoning, however, "will" had an opposite effect. "Strong-willed" Stages 1 and 2 subjects cheated more, not less, than "weak-willed" subjects, i.e., they had the "courage of their (amoral) convictions" that it was worthwhile to cheat. "Will," then, is an important factor in moral behavior, but it is not distinctively moral; it becomes moral only when informed by mature moral judgment.

3. Moral judgment change is long-range or irreversible; a higher stage is never lost. Moral behavior as such is largely situational and reversible or "loseable" in new situations.

Aims of Moral and Civic Education

Moral psychology describes what moral development is, as studied empirically. Moral education must also consider moral philosophy, which strives to tell us what moral development ideally *ought to be*. Psychology finds an invariant sequence of moral stages; moral philosophy must be invoked to answer whether a later stage is a better stage. The "stage" of senescence and death follows the "stage" of adulthood, but that does not mean that senescence and death are better. Our claim that the latest or principled stages of moral reasoning are morally better stages, then, must rest on considerations of moral philosophy.

The tradition of moral philosophy to which we appeal is the liberal and rational tradition, in particular the "formalistic" or "deonotological" tradition running from Immanuel Kant to John Rawls. Central to this tradition is the claim that an adequate morality is *principled*, i.e., that it makes judgments in terms of *universal* principles applicable to all mankind. *Principles* are to be distinguished from *rules*. Conventional morality is grounded on rules, primarily "thou shalt nots" such as are represented by the Ten Commandments, prescriptions of kinds of actions. Principles are, rather, universal guides to making a moral decision. An example is Kant's "categorical imperative," formulated in two ways. The first is the maxim of respect for human personality, "Act always toward the other as an end, not as a means." The second is the maxim of universalization, "Choose only as you would be willing to have everyone choose in your situation." Principles like that of Kant's state the formal conditions of a moral choice or action. In the dilemma in which a woman is dying because a druggist refuses to release his drug for less than the stated price, the druggist is not acting morally, though he is not violating the ordinary moral rules (he is not actually stealing or murdering). But he is violating principles: He is treating the woman simply as a means to his ends of profit, and he is not choosing as he would wish anyone to choose (if the druggist were in the dying woman's place, he would not want a druggist to choose as he is choosing). Under most circumstances, choice in terms of conventional moral rules and choice in terms of principles coincide. Ordinarily, principles dictate not stealing (avoiding stealing is implied by acting in terms of a regard for others as ends and in terms of what one would want everyone to do). In a situation where stealing is the only means to save a life, however, principles contradict the ordinary rules and would dictate stealing. Unlike rules which are supported by social authority, principles are freely chosen by the individual because of their intrinsic moral validity.[4]

The conception that a moral choice is a choice made in terms of moral principles is related to the claim of liberal moral philosophy that moral principles are ultimately principles of justice. In essence, moral conflicts are conflicts between the claims of persons, and principles for resolving these claims are principles of justice, "for giving each his due." Central to justice are the demands of *liberty, equality,* and *reciprocity.* At every moral stage, there is a concern for justice. The most damning statement a school child can make about a teacher is that "he's not fair." At each higher stage, however, the conception of justice is reorganized. At Stage 1, justice is punishing the bad in terms of "an eye for an eye and a tooth for a tooth." At Stage 2, it is exchanging favors and goods in an equal manner. At Stages 3 and 4, it is treating people as they desire in terms of the conventional rules. At Stage 5, it is recognized that all rules and laws flow from justice, from a social contract between the governors and the governed designed to protect the equal rights of all. At Stage 6, personally chosen moral principles are also principles of justice, the principles any member of a society would choose for that society if he did not know what his position was to be in the society and in which he might be the least advantaged. Principles chosen from this point of view are, first, the maximum liberty compatible with the like liberty of others and, second, no inequalities of goods and respect which are not to the benefit of all, including the least advantaged.

As an example of stage progression in the orientation of justice, we may take judgments about capital punishment. Capital punishment is only firmly rejected at the two principled stages, when the notion of justice as vengeance or retribution is abandoned. At the sixth stage, capital punishment is not condoned even if it may have some useful deterrent effect in promoting law and order. This is because it is not a punishment we would choose for a society if we assumed we had as much chance of being born into the position of a criminal or murderer as being born into the position of a law abider.

Why are decisions based on universal principles of justice better decisions? Because they are decisions on which all moral men could agree. When decisions are based on conventional moral rules, men will disagree, since they adhere to conflicting systems of rules dependent on culture and social position. Throughout history men have killed one another in the name of conflicting moral rules and values, most recently in Vietnam and the Middle East. Truly moral or just resolutions of conflicts require principles which are, or can be, universalizable.

Alternative Approaches

We have given a philosophic rationale for stage advance as the aim of moral education. Given this rationale, the developmental approach to moral education can avoid the problems inherent in the other two major approaches to moral education. The first alternative approach is that of indoctrinative moral education, the preaching and imposition of the rules and values of the teacher and his culture on the child. In America, when this indoctrinative approach has been developed in a systematic manner, it has usually been termed "character education."

Moral values, in the character education approach, are preached or taught in terms of what may be called the "bag of virtues." In the classic studies of character by Hugh Hartshorne and Mark May, the virtues chosen were honesty, service, and self-control. It is easy to get superficial consensus on such a bag of virtues—until one examines in detail the list of virtues involved and the details of their definition. Is the Hartshorne and May bag more adequate than the Boy Scout bag (a Scout should be honest, loyal, reverent, clean, brave, etc.)? When one turns to the details of defining each virtue, one finds equal uncertainty or difficulty in reaching consensus. Does honesty mean one should not steal to save a life? Does it mean that a student should not help another student with his homework?

Character education and other forms of indoctrinative moral education have aimed at teaching universal values (it is assumed that honesty or service are desirable traits for all men in all societies), but the detailed definitions used are relative; they are defined by the opinions of the teacher and the conventional culture and rest on the authority of the teacher for their justification. In this sense character education is close to the unreflective valuings by teachers which constitute the hidden curriculum of the school.[5] Because of the current unpopularity of indoctrinative approaches to moral education, a family of approaches called "values clarification" has become appealing to teachers. Values clarification takes the first step implied by a rational approach to moral education: the eliciting of the child's own judgment or opinion about issues or situations in which values conflict, rather than imposing the teacher's opinion on him. Values clarification, however, does not attempt to go further than eliciting awareness of values; it is assumed that becoming more self-aware about one's values is an end in itself. Fundamentally, the definition of the end of values education as self-awareness derives form a belief in ethical relativity held by many value-clarifiers. As stated by Peter Engel, "One must contrast value clarification and value inculcation. Value clarification implies the principle that in the consideration of values there is no single correct answer." Within these premises of "no correct answer," children are to discuss moral dilemmas in such a way as to reveal different values and discuss their value differences with each other. The teacher is to stress that "our values are different," not that one value is more adequate than others. If this program is systematically followed, students will themselves become relativists, believing there is no "right" moral answer. For instance, a student caught cheating might argue that he did nothing wrong, since his own hierarchy of values, which may be different from that of the teacher, made it right for him to cheat.

Like values clarification, the cognitive-developmental approach to moral education stresses open or Socratic peer discussion of value dilemmas. Such discussion, however, has an aim: stimulation of movement to the next stage of moral reasoning. Like values clarification, the developmental approach opposes indoctrination. Stimulation of movement to the next stage of reasoning is not indoctrinative, for the following reasons:

1. Change is in the way of reasoning rather than in the particular beliefs involved.

2. Students in a class are at different stages; the aim is to aid movement at each to the next stage, not convergence on a common pattern.

3. The teacher's own opinion is neither stressed nor invoked as authoritative. It enters in only as one of many opinions, hopefully one of those at a next higher stage.

4. The notion that some judgments are more adequate than others is communicated. Fundamentally, however, this means that the student is encouraged to articulate a position which seems most adequate to him and to judge the adequacy of the reasoning of others.

In addition to having more definite aims than values clarification, the moral development approach restricts value education to that which is moral or, more specifically, to justice. This is for two reasons. First, it is not clear that the whole realm of personal, political, and religious values is a realm which is nonrelative, i.e., in which there are universals and a direction of development. Second, it is not clear that the public school has a right or mandate to develop values in general.[6] In our view, value education in the public schools should be restricted to that which the school has the right and mandate to develop: an awareness of justice, or of the rights of others in our constitutional system. While the Bill of Rights prohibits the teaching of religious beliefs, or of specific value systems, it does not prohibit the teaching of the awareness of rights and principles of justice fundamental to the Constitution itself.

When moral education is recognized as centered in justice and differentiated from value education or affective education, it becomes apparent that moral and civic education are much the same thing. This equation, taken for granted by the classic philosophers of education from Plato and Aristotle to Dewey, is basic to our claim that a concern for moral education is central to the educational objectives of social studies.

Notes

1. These levels correspond roughly to our three major levels: the preconventional, the conventional, and the principled. Similar levels were propounded by William McDougall, Leonard Hobhouse, and James Mark Baldwin.

2. Piaget's stages correspond to our first three stages; Stage 0 (pre-moral), Stage 1 (heteronomous), and Stage 2 (instrumental reciprocity).

3. Many adolescents and adults only partially attain the stage of formal operations. They do consider all the actual relations of one thing to another at the same time, but they do not consider all possibilities and form abstract hypotheses. A few do not advance this far, remaining "concrete operational."

4. Not all freely chosen values or rules are principles, however. Hitler chose the "rule," "exterminate the enemies of the Aryan race," but such a rule is not a universalizable principle.

5. As an example of the "hidden curriculum," we may cite a second-grade classroom. My son came home from this classroom one day saying he did not want to be "one of the bad boys." Asked "Who are the bad boys?" he replied, "The ones who don't put their books back and get yelled at."

6. Restriction of deliberate value education to the moral may be clarified by our example of the second-grade teacher who made tidying up of books a matter of moral indoctrination. Tidiness is a value, but it is not a moral value. Cheating is a moral issue, intrinsically one of fairness. It involves issues of violation of trust and taking advantage. Failing to tidy the room may under certain conditions be an issue of fairness, when it puts an undue burden on others. If it is handled by the teacher as a matter of cooperation among the group in this sense, it is a legitimate focus of deliberate moral education. If it is not, it simply represents the arbitrary imposition of the teacher's values on the child.

MAKING DECISIONS

To be, or not to be: That is the question.
—WILLIAM SHAKESPEARE

The difficulty in life is the choice.
—GEORGE MOORE

Choice is the most wonderful, and often the most terrible, freedom. To choose one thing often means you cannot choose something else. To choose to spend your money on one purchase often means you have no money left for something else. To choose to marry someone means that you choose not to marry someone else. To attend one college, to major in a particular area, to enroll in a specific class are all choices you make. The success of these choices—whether they involve the money you spend, the people you see, or the college life you pursue—depends on the way that you weigh the alternatives and make decisions.

Decision making is an exercise in evaluation. You identify a problem, look at the information you have, draw conclusions, and formulate a variety of hypotheses about what to do. You identify the advantages and disadvantages of each hypothesis. Then, you decide.

Decision making is a skill that applies to information, situations, and people. Some people make excellent choices in situations and information but choose unwisely in their personal relationships. Others have excellent interpersonal skills but are unable to generalize that ability to information and situations. Decision making can be learned and refined. The process you use in making one decision can be transferred to other situations (See Figure 6.3).

FIGURE 6.3   The Decision-Making Process

STEP	EXAMPLE
1. Perceive a problem.	1. You are a sophomore and you are still undecided about a major.
2. Define the problem.	2. You need to select a major.
3. Collect data.	3. You seek information through career decision-making workshops, volunteer work, part-time employment, interviews with professionals in selected fields, and so on.
4. Associate bits of data.	4. Compare first-person reports and workshop information with actual experiences.
5. Measure various variables.	5. Assess how job interests compare with your values and needs and the educational requirements of the field.
6. Estimate data.	6. Identify employment trends and resources for education and training.
7. Classify data.	7. List pros and cons.
8. Integrate data.	8. Determine which of the fields best fit your needs and have the most pros, as well as the ones for which employment opportunities exist and for which you can get education and training.
9. Generalize.	9. Identify which majors fit the identified fields.
10. Conceptualize a hypothesis.	10. Identify which specific major will lead you to the career of your choice.
11. Evaluate the hypothesis.	11. Discuss your choice of major with a professional in the field and counselors and instructors at your school.
12. Make a decision.	12. Choose a major.
13. Implement the decision.	13. Enroll in the appropriate courses and seek additional work experiences.
14. Evaluate the decision.	14. Determine if your course work and work experience indicate your decision was a good one.

GROUP LEARNING ACTIVITY
STEREOTYPES: DEBUNKING ARCHIE BUNKER

Archie Bunker, a character in the TV's "All in the Family," was known for branding people and behavior. Uncritical thinkers—like Archie—often think in stereotypes. These are typical images or conceptions held by members of a specific group or applied to a person, group, or idea. Like Archie, you probably belileve some form of stereotypes. That's because you've never examined these ideas to find why you hold them.

What stereotypes do you hold? What stereotypes might apply to you?

Determine how each person in your group defines each person in the following pairs. What does each one do? How would he/she or they act? What facts and opinions apply to each one? How does the concept of relevance apply to each one? Discuss your responses and conclusions with the group.

1. College Student/Retiree

2. Employer/Employee

3. American/Foreigner

4. Gang Member/Police

5. Priest/Atheist

6. Kindergarten Teacher/Professor

7. Two-Year-Old Child/Adult

8. Democrat/Republican

9. Men/Women

10. Vietnam Veteran/Desert Shield Veteran

How do stereotypes impact your ability to think critically? What examples could debunk these stereotypes? How does this activity change the way you think about these groups and yourself?

SUMMARY OF MAIN POINTS

1. Critical thinking is more than a set of separate skills and is best represented as a cumulative thought process that becomes a way of life.

2. Recall of information forms the basis of ability to think at higher levels.

3. Translation of information involves the ability to convert information without distortion or loss.

4. Interpretation requires the use of background knowledge and given information to identify connections among ideas.

5. Application requires the ability to use information to solve problems.

6. Analysis of information involves careful observation and determination of meaning. It also requires determining relevance through identifying perspective and purpose and differentiating between fact and opinion.

7. Synthesis is the assimilation of knowledge to create a new idea. Identifying issues and problems, drawing conclusions, and creativity require the ability to synthesize.

8. Evaluation forms the highest level of critical thinking. It concerns the ability to judge the worth or validity of information.

9. Evaluation is used to check the consistency of information and make decisions.

VOCABULARY DEVELOPMENT
CONNOTATION: KNOW WHAT I MEAN?

An elderly woman watched MTV for a long time. She turned to her son and asked, "But what does it all mean?" College course work and life exposes you to a variety of situations, people, and ideas. Appearances are often deceiving, and things are not always what they seem. You, too, may find yourself wondering just what everything means.

Post secondary education helps you refine your ability to analyze and evaluate experience and find meaning. Words, too, represent a variety of situations, people, and ideas. Your ability to think critically about their meanings, both in connotation and denotation, helps you understand the courses you take, as well as life in general.

Jim Varney, star of such movies as "Ernest Goes to Camp" and "Ernest's Christmas," first created the character of Ernest P. Worrell for an amusement park commercial. A country bumpkin, Ernest constantly harasses an off-screen character named Vern with the phrase, "Know what I mean, Vern?" Vocabulary development is a constant analysis to discover the answer to "Know what I mean?" in college course work.

Words actually have two meanings. The first is the denotation—the literal, or dictionary definition. The second is the connotation. This includes the way a word is understood and used by the text or lecturer, as well as your own understanding of what a word means. You derive these implied meanings from hearing, reading, speaking, writing, and experiencing the word in everyday life. For example, a sociology class might study labor unions. The denotation of *labor union* would be "an organization of wage earners designed to improve the economic interests and general working conditions of its members." Your experiences might provide you with your own connotations. If your experiences were good, you might define a labor union as a benevolent group that works for the common good and supports its members. If your experiences were not favorable, for example, your family's company was financially ruined by a union strike), you might think of a labor union as a ruthless group that destroys companies and the people associated with it.

The words an author or lecturer chooses and uses provide insights into what they really mean—both in literal meaning and implied connotations. The words you use in responding to class discussions or writing assignments similarly require the listener or reader to know what you mean. Vocabulary development occurs when you critically consider connotation as well as denotation in listening, reading, speaking, and writing.

Activity 1

For each of the following excerpts from Sample Chapter 1, "Culture: The Ideas and Products People Adopt and Create," list your connotation for the boldface words or phrases. Then, using a dictionary, provide the word's denotation. Contrast your connotation and the word's definition.

Derek Freeman, another ethnographer who studied the Samoan culture between 1940 and 1967, reported evidence that contradicted Mean's findings (Freeman, 1983). Contrary to Mead's report, the Samoan **adolescents** that Freeman describes are aggressive, **impulsive,** status-hungry, violent, and sexually "hung up."

1. **adolescents**

   Connotation _____

   _____

   Denotation _____

   _____

   Contrast _____

   _____

2. **impulsive**

   Connotation _____

   _____

   Denotation _____

   _____

   Contrast _____

   _____

In his Inaugural Address, George Bush suggested what he hoped to be the values of his Presidency," a **summons** back to the **patrician** values of restraint and responsibility.

3. **summons**

   Connotation _____

   _____

   Denotation _____

   _____

   Contrast _____

   _____

4. **patrician**

   Connotation _____

   _____

Denotation _____

_____

Contrast _____

_____

The youth movement of the 1960s, the Hare Krishna religious **sect,** and the **Amish** are examples of countercultures. The theme of the youth movement of the sixties was that success and materialism were misguided goals for individuals in society. Love, peace and sharing was the suggested alternative. The **"hippies"** (as they were called) who flourished in such communities as Haight-Ashbury in San Francisco and the East Village in New York have virtually disappeared.

5. **sect**
    Connotation _____

    _____

    Denotation _____

    _____

    Contrast _____

6. **Amish**
    Connotation _____

    _____

    Denotation _____

    _____

    Contrast _____

7. **"hippies"**
    Connotation _____

    _____

    Denotation _____

    _____

    Contrast _____

Activity 2

How did the differences between your connotations and the word's denotation change your understanding of the word's meaning? Give one example and explain.

CHAPTER REVIEW

Answer briefly but completely.

1. Consider the following passage:

   Isokinetic Programs. Weight training programs that are **isokinetic** enable muscles to contract against the same level of resistance (on Nautilus or Cybex or some other specialized equipment) throughout a full range of motion. Many experts believe that isokinetic programs are the best for developing both muscular strength and endurance. One of the disadvantages of an isokinetic program is that it requires specialized equipment, such as Nautilus and Cybex, which is expensive. This equipment can be found not only in spas and health clubs but also on college campuses in the physical education department.

   Isotonic Programs. Exercise that is **isotonic** involves lifting a constant weight through a full range of motion. Isotonics entail the use of free weights (such as barbells and dumbbells) or machines, and they can help you to develop both muscular strength and endurance. You should use free weights which have equal weight for right and left sides. This will allow for equal distribution in both arms and legs.

   Isometric Programs. Weight training that is **isometric** involves the individual pushing or pulling against a fixed resistance or an immovable object. This requires a steady muscle contraction against an immovable resistance object, like a wall or a door jamb. The range of motion is restricted, which results in the muscle becoming strong at a particular angle only.

   SOURCE: Reprinted with permission from Boskin, W., Graf, G., & Kreisworth, V. (1990) *Health Dynamics Attitudes and Behaviors.* West Publishing Company. All rights reserved.

   Identify a concept appropriate for recall, a concept appropriate for translation, and a concept appropriate for interpretation.

   _____

   _____

   _____

2. How does the concept of relevance affect test construction as perceived by students? As perceived by instructors?

   _____

   _____

   _____

3. How is an expert opinion like a fact? Is this a non sequitur? Explain your response.

   _____

   _____

   _____

4. Provide an example of how you would use synthesis in each of the following courses: English composition, introduction to public speaking, intermediate French, art history, music appreciation, and political science.

   _____

   _____

   _____

5. How does point of view impact identification of central issues and problems?

   _____

   _____

   _____

6. Which of the four kinds of conclusions identified in this chapter (hypotheses, logical inference, assumptions, and non sequiturs) are easiest for you to draw? Why? Which are most difficult to draw? Why?

   _____

   _____

   _____

7. What do drawing conclusions and creativity have in common, other than being mechanisms for synthesis?

   _____

   _____

   _____

8. Choose a product or idea. How does it rate according to Dr. Paul Torrance's factors of creativity? Explain your response.

   _____

   _____

   _____

9. A thirty-year-old man decides to enter college and takes introductory psychology for his first course. How would his evaluation of course content compare with an evaluation of the same course made by a thirty-year-old man who is working on a graduate degree? Explain your response.

   _____

   _____

   _____

10. Choose a problem other than the one identified in Figure 6.3 and apply the decision-making steps to solving it.

_____

_____

_____

REFERENCES

Anderson, R.C. and Pichert, J.W. (1978). Recall of previously unrecallable information following a shift in perspective. *Journal of Verbal Learning and Verbal Behavior, 17,* 1–12.

Paul, R.W. (1990). *Critical Thinking: What every person needs to survive in a rapidly changing world.* Rohnert Park, CA: Center for Critical Thinking and Moral Critique.

Kincher, J. (1990). *Psychology for Kids.* Minneapolis: Free Spirit.

Newstrom, J.W. and Scannel, E.E. (1980). *Games Trainers Play.* New York: McGraw Hill.

von Oech, R. (1986). *A Kick in the Seat of the Pants.* New York: Harper and Row.

von Oech, R. (1990). *A Whack on the Side of the Head.* New York: Warner Books.

ANSWER FOR ANALYSIS FIGURE

No. Because you are looking at concentric circles, *not* a spiral.

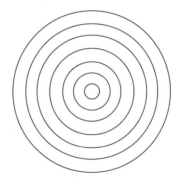

OBJECTIVES

By the end of this chapter, you will be able to do the following:

1. Utilize general suggestions for taking exams.

2. Apply strategies for preparing for and taking subjective exams.

3. Apply strategies for preparing for and taking objective exams.

4. Apply strategies for preparing for and taking specialized exams.

5. Manage stress through mental preparation.

6. Manage stress through physical preparation.

7. Analyze test preparation and performance through an after-exam evaluation.

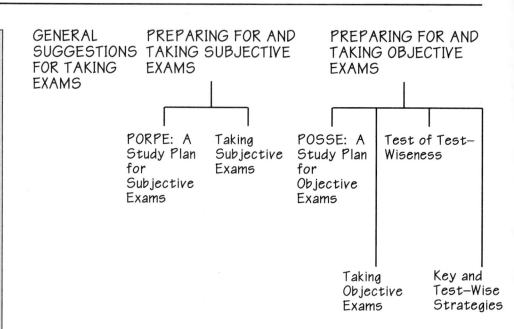

GENERAL SUGGESTIONS FOR TAKING EXAMS

PREPARING FOR AND TAKING SUBJECTIVE EXAMS

PREPARING FOR AND TAKING OBJECTIVE EXAMS

PORPE: A Study Plan for Subjective Exams

Taking Subjective Exams

POSSE: A Study Plan for Objective Exams

Test of Test-Wiseness

Taking Objective Exams

Key and Test-Wise Strategies

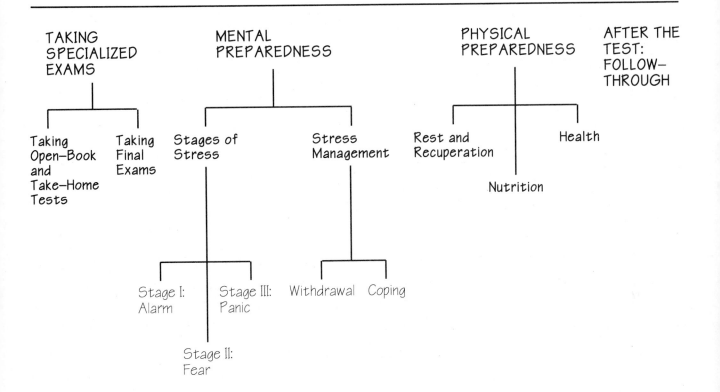

TAKING SPECIALIZED EXAMS

- Taking Open–Book and Take–Home Tests
- Taking Final Exams

MENTAL PREPAREDNESS

- Stages of Stress
  - Stage I: Alarm
  - Stage II: Fear
  - Stage III: Panic
- Stress Management
  - Withdrawal
  - Coping

PHYSICAL PREPAREDNESS

- Rest and Recuperation
- Nutrition
- Health

AFTER THE TEST: FOLLOW–THROUGH

TERMS

comprehensive tests
coping
denial
noncomprehensive
    tests
objective tests
projection
rationalize
repression
subjective tests
stress

"Now, let's see. Tomorrow, I'll put D for #1, A for #2, and E for #3!"

S uccessful test-taking involves what someone once called "that old *ABC*—ability, breaks, and courage." Luckily, you can acquire these. Successful test-taking abilities include knowing about kinds of tests and how to alter your studying to accommodate the differences among them. Being test-wise means that you take advantage of breaks and avoid any pitfalls you might encounter during a test. Having the courage you need to be a successful test-taker means identifying and effectively managing the stress that comes with exams. Just as the *ABCs* are the basics of language, these *ABCs* are the basics you need to maximize your test performances.

GENERAL SUGGESTIONS FOR TAKING EXAMS

Tests consist of two types: **subjective** and **objective.** Subjective tests require you to supply the answers in your own words. They measure your recall of information, your skills in organizing and expressing yourself, and your ability to relate ideas. Types of subjective test questions include short-answer, essay, and fill-in-the-blank (see Table 7.1). Objective tests involve your choosing among provided answers. Instructors frequently give objective exams because they allow for the quick testing of a large amount of material and are easy to grade. Types of objective test questions include multiple choice, matching, and true-false (see Table 7.2). Some students think objective tests are a fairer judge of their abilities because these exams are free from grader bias.

TABLE 7.1 Subjective Test Formats

Example of an essay question:
  Compare and contrast Emily Dickinson's "Because I Could Not Stop for Death" with Hilda Doolittle's "Evening."
Example of a short-answer question:
  Briefly describe the hydrologic cycle.
Example of a fill-in-the-blank question:
  A _____ is a form of figurative language in which two dissimilar objects are compared using the words *like* or *as.*

TABLE 7.2 Objective Test Formats

Example of a true-false question:
  T F Soil fertility depends upon relative amounts of gravel, sand, silt, and clay.
Example of a multiple-choice question:
  Sources of vitamin A include all of the following except:
  a. dark green leafy vegetables.
  b. yeast.
  c. fish liver oils.
  d. yellow and orange fruits.
Example of matching questions:

1. Johannes Guttenberg	_____ Electric self-starter
2. Guglielmo Marconi	_____ Mimeograph machine
3. Charles F. Kettering	_____ Printing press
4. Thomas Edison	_____ Wireless telegraph

To prepare for a test, you need to know what to expect from it. Because most exams are written by the instructor, the instructor is a prime source of information about them. Most instructors want you to do well. Thus, they are willing to answer questions about test content and format. Instructors can tell you if a test is **comprehensive** (covering all material presented since the beginning of the term) or **noncomprehensive** (covering only that information presented since the last exam).

Extensive preparation alone is not all you need to pass an exam. Special test-taking skills enhance your carefully acquired knowledge. No matter how well you are prepared, you should use the following general suggestions for taking exams (see Table 7.3).

All exams test the way you process information. Some questions ask you to define or remember information exactly as it was presented in your text or the lecture. Other questions demand you link information to form conclusions about a topic. You may also be asked to use information in a new way. Questions that ask you to think criti-

---

TABLE 7.3   Steps in Taking Exams

1. Bring the appropriate materials for the test (pencil, paper, blue book, calculator).

2. Arrive at the test on time.
   a. If you are early, do not discuss the test with other students. Their concerns and worries will increase any anxieties you have.
   b. If you are late, you may miss important verbal directions. Arriving late also makes you feel rushed and anxious. If so, take a minute to relax and organize your thoughts. Ask your instructor for clarification if you feel confused.

3. If you are trying to keep a difficult formula or process in mind, jot it down after you get your test paper.

4. Preview the test. Note the total number of items. Identify variations in point values. Estimate the amount of time to spend on each item. Spend the most time on questions receiving the most credit.

5. Read all directions slowly and carefully. When given a test, many students ignore the directions. However, directions often state information you need to receive full credit. They also provide information about the way answers should be marked. Although you may have all the right answers, selective instructors may not give full credit when responses are not correctly marked.

6. Underline key terms and steps in the directions.

7. Answer the easiest questions first. This builds your confidence and triggers your memory for other information. Also, if you run out of time before you complete the test, you will have answered the questions you knew.

8. Expect memory blocks. Mark difficult questions, but skip them and go on. Return to these questions, if time permits.

9. Answer every question, if possible. If incorrect answers are not penalized, guess at all objective and subjective questions.

10. Make your responses as neat and legible as possible.

11. Work at your own pace. Do not be concerned when other students finish and leave before you.

12. If time permits, review questions and answers. Be sure you understood the question and marked the correct response. Some students think it is better to always stay with their first answer. You can determine what's best for you by examining some of your old tests. Count the number of questions you changed to correct answers. Compare that total with the number of those you changed to incorrect answers.

---

cally require you to analyze, synthesize, and evaluate information. Both subjective and objective exams often test your ability to remember and manipulate concepts in a variety of ways. The kinds of knowledge required for different kinds of questions appear in Figure 6.1, Bloom's Taxonomy on page 233.

PREPARING FOR AND TAKING SUBJECTIVE EXAMS

"Writing is hell," someone once said. This certainly seems true to many students who face subjective exams. These exams require you to understand major concepts and describe them in a coherent written form. Your essay must state main points and contain the facts that support the ideas you express. It must show your analysis and/or synthesis of ideas and application of knowledge. Taking such exams requires careful preparation and confidence in your test-taking skills.

PORPE: A STUDY PLAN FOR SUBJECTIVE EXAMS

If you wish to be a writer, write.
—EPICTETUS

Often students fear subjective exams because they are uncertain of their writing skills. A study plan exists that helps you become a better writer by asking you to practice writing. This plan, PORPE, consists of five stages: Predict, Organize, Rehearse, Practice, and Evaluate (Simpson, 1986). When put into motion at least three days before an exam, PORPE helps you predict possible essay questions, organize your thoughts, and find strategies for recalling information.

Even if you do not predict the exact test questions, PORPE will not be a waste of time for several reasons. First, your predicted questions will probably reflect the content, if not the wording, of the test. Second, you often can use the information you rehearsed and practiced in answering questions you may not have predicted. Third, the practice you give yourself in writing increases not only your self-confidence but also your writing ability. Remember the quote from Epictetus that began this discussion of PORPE: "If you wish to be a writer, write."

To follow the stages in PORPE, you answer a series of questions and complete the steps at each stage (Table 7.4).

TAKING SUBJECTIVE EXAMS

Freshmen who are preppies have a great advantage. . . . They . . . arrive at college well-versed in the techniques of the essay question, and could pad their paragraph with such useful phrases as "from a theoretical point of view," or "on first inspection we may seem to discern a certain attitude which may well survive even closer scrutiny," and so forth. This sort of wind can sail you halfway through an hour test before you have to lay a single fact on paper.

SOURCE: Reprinted from *The Class* by Erich Segal, Bantam Publishers.

TABLE 7.4   Stages of PORPE

Three days before the exam:

PREDICT

Predict information about the test by answering these questions:

   What does the test cover?

   Is the test comprehensive or noncomprehensive?

   How many questions will the test contain?

   Will the test require me to apply information?

   How much does this test count in my final course grade?

   When is the test?

   Where will the test be given?

   What special material(s) will I need to take the test?

Predict essay test questions by answering the following questions:

   What information did the instructor stress during the lectures?

   What information did the text emphasize?

   What questions appeared in both my initial preview and the chapter's
      review or study guide?

   What terms did the instructor emphasize during the lectures?

Predict at least three times as many questions as your instructor has indicated
will be on the exam.

Two days before the exam:

ORGANIZE

Organize information by answering the following questions:

   What type of text structure will best answer each of these questions
      (problem-solution/cause/effect, subject development, enumeration/
      sequence, or comparison/contrast)?

   What is the best way to organize this information (outline, idea map, note
      cards, chart)?

   What information is essential for answering this question?

   What information adds relevant, supporting details or examples?

   What is the source of this information:

      textbook?

      handouts?

      lecture notes?

      supplemental readings?

The great advantage that Segal describes is part of what preppies learn at college-preparatory schools. They learn the art of taking subjective tests—a skill you, too, can learn.

Essay exams require special test-taking considerations. Because answering them is much like writing short papers on assigned topics, there is more work involved. The procedure outlined in Table 7.3 is important to follow, but other steps are also necessary (see Table 7.5). The wording of essay questions helps you organize and write your answers (see Table 7.6).

TABLE 7.4   Stages of PORPE *continued*

REHEARSE

Lock information into your memory by answering these questions:

How much time each day will I study?

What mnemonic techniques (acronyms, acrostics, word games, etc.) can I use to practice this information?

When will I study?

How will I distribute my study time?

Where will I study?

If necessary, when will my study group/partner and I meet?

What obligations do I have that might interfere with this study time?

Construct mnemonic aids.

Use overlearning to help you practice mnemonic aids overtly (writing or speaking them).

One day before the exam:

PRACTICE

Practice writing your answers from memory.

EVALUATE

Judge the quality of your answer as objectively as possible by answering the following questions:

Did I answer the question that was asked?

Did my answer begin with an introduction?

Did my answer end with a conclusion?

Was my answer well organized?

Did I include all essential information?

Did I include any relevant details or examples?

Did I use transition words?

Is my writing neat and easily read?

Did I check spelling and grammar?

If you answered any of these questions negatively, you need to continue practicing your answers. Repeat the final four stages of PORPE until you answer all of these questions positively.

After the exam has been returned, read your instructor's comments and compare them with the last evaluation you made during your study sessions. Look for negative trends you can avoid or positive trends you can stress when you study for your next exam. File your PORPE plan, course materials, study aids, and evaluation data for future reference.

The wording you use to answer the questions determines the quality of the responses. Figure 7.1 shows examples of good and poor responses to an essay question. How do they differ?

The good response begins with an introductory sentence that identifies the three symptoms of Parkinson's disease. The second sentence identifies early symptoms of the disease. Sentences 3 and 4 identify and describe the first major symptom. Sentences 5 and 6 identify and describe the second major symptom. The next three sen-

---

TABLE 7.5   Taking Essay Exams

1. Choose a title. Even though you won't necessarily entitle your paper, a title helps you focus your thoughts and narrow your subject.

2. Outline your response or list main points before you begin. This keeps you from omitting important details.

3. Have a beginning, a middle, and an end. Topic and summary sentences are important in making your answer seem organized and complete.

4. Use transitional words. The key words in each question help you identify the transitions you need for clarity.

5. Attempt every question. If you run out of time, outline the remaining questions. This shows your knowledge of the content. Partial responses often result in partial credit.

6. Proofread your answers. Check spelling, grammar, and content.

TABLE 7.6   Key Terms in Essay Questions

If You Are Asked To . . .	Then . . .
compare or match,	identify similarities.
contrast or distinguish,	identify differences.
discuss or describe,	provide details or features.
enumerate, name, outline, or list,	identify major points.
sequence, arrange, trace, or rank,	list information in order.
explain, defend, or document,	give reasons for support.
relate or associate,	show connections.
summarize, paraphrase, or compile,	provide a short synopsis.
outline,	list major points.
apply,	show use for.
construct, develop, or devise,	create.
criticize or analyze,	review features or components.
demonstrate, illustrate, or show,	provide examples.

---

tences identify and describe the third major symptom. The last sentence summarizes the effects of variations in these symptoms.

At first glance, the second response appears to be a good one. It is well written and appropriate in length. It appears to be the work of a student who knows something about Parkinson's disease, but it lacks the specific information required for a correct response to this question. Closer inspection reveals several weaknesses. Sentences 1 and 2 could be considered introductory sentences; however, sentence 3 is the only sentence that identifies (and not by correct terminology) and describes the three major symptoms of Parkinson's disease. Sentence 4 incorrectly identifies the disease as a mental, rather than a

Figure 7.1   Examples of an Essay Question and Responses

QUESTION: Identify and describe the symptoms of Parkinson's disease.

RESPONSE 1

Parkinson's disease is a neurological disease characterized by gradual changes in three fundamental symptoms: tremor, rigidity, and bradykinesia. Although the onset of this disease is so gradual that neither the patients nor the people close to them notice it, early symptoms include fatigue and complaints of mild muscular aches. Tremor is often the first real symptom to appear. Conspicuous, but rarely disabling, tremor usually begins in one hand and occurs when the limb is at rest. Rigidity, the second major symptom, is muscular stiffness. This results in slow movement, muscle cramps, and resistance against passive movement. The most disabling symptom is bradykinesia. This describes slowness and poverty of voluntary movements. It also leads to difficulty in performing rapid or repeated movements. It underlies facial masking and involuntary hesitations. Variations in these three symptoms cause the variety of disabilities associated with Parkinson's disease.

RESPONSE 2

Parkinson's disease was first described by Dr. James Parkinson, an English physician. Parkinson wrote an essay entitled, "Essay on the Shaking Palsy," which described the symptoms he saw in six patients. He described the three primary symptoms as involuntary shaking movements of the limbs, muscular stiffness, and slowness and poverty of movement. Because the entire body was involved, Dr. Parkinson theorized that it was a mental illness resulting from a dysfunction in the brain. Parkinson's disease can affect anyone—men, women, children. Various theories account for the symptoms, including genetic links, viral causation, stress, neurotransmitter damage, and environmental causes.

RESPONSE 3

Parkinson's disease is a terrible disease. It affects millions of people. Parkinson's disease has many symptoms. One symptom is shakiness. Some people become very shaky. Their hands shake most. This makes it difficult to pick up things or hold things. Another symptom is that you can't move very well anymore. You have difficulty climbing stairs or walking. So, these symptoms are very terrible.

neurological, illness. Sentence 5 describes who is affected by Parkinson's disease. The last sentence—an attempt at a summary—actually lists the theories that account for the symptoms.

The last example, another poor response, is more clearly identifiable as such. The writer uses the word *symptom* frequently to disguise the fact that he or she really has little understanding of what the symptoms are. Sentences 1, 2, and 3 are feeble introductory attempts. Sentence 4 identifies one symptom as shakiness, without using the appropriate terminology. While the writer apparently knows that the hands are often affected, he or she does not realize that this occurs most often when the limb is at rest. Sentences 8 and 9 identify mobility impairments and their effects. The reader cannot tell if this refers to the symptom of rigidity or that of bradykinesia. The last sentence attempts to conclude the paragraph by restating the main idea of sentence 1.

PREPARING FOR AND TAKING OBJECTIVE EXAMS

Find a perfect star in the pattern below. As you look for it, try to be aware of the search strategies you use.

SOURCE: Figure from *A Kick in the Seat of the Pants* by Roger von Oech. Reprinted by permission of Harper Collins Publishers.

Did you find the star? If not, reexamine the lower-right quadrant. If you did, how did you go about finding it? (A key appears at the end of this chapter.) According to Roger von Oech, who originated this exercise in his book *A Kick in the Seat of the Pants*, the point of the exercise is that you have to know what you're looking for in order to find it. To locate the star, you first have to determine what kind of star you're seeking. The star could be a regular five-pointed star, a Star of David, a seven-pointed sheriff's star, or the Chrysler star. It could be large or small. It could be composed entirely of white pieces, black pieces, or a combination of both. In other words, to locate the star, you need the ability to recognize it when you see it. You also need a strategy for finding it.

The same is true when preparing for and taking objective exams. When you take an objective exam, your job is to search among the answers provided by the instructor for the correct one. If you've studied carefully and are more than familiar with the information covered on the exam, you are able to focus on the one or two choices that are most appropriate. Test-wise strategies aid you in making the best choice possible.

POSSE: A STUDY PLAN FOR OBJECTIVE EXAMS

Our plans miscarry because they have no aim. When a man does not know what harbor he is making for, no wind is the right wind.

—SENECA

In preparing for an objective test, you need to know the harbor you are making for and how you intend to get there. POSSE (Plan, Organize, Schedule, Study, and Evaluate) is a system to help you identify your study goals and make plans for achieving them. To follow the stages of POSSE, you answer a series of questions and complete the steps at each level (Table 7.7). Responding to the questions in written form forces you to concentrate on each question. It also keeps you from inadvertently omitting one. You will obtain many answers from either your syllabus, your instructor, or your experience in the class. Other questions, however, will force you to examine your study strengths and weaknesses. Your success on your upcoming test depends on your honesty in dealing with such issues. It is also important that you begin the POSSE process at least a week before the test is scheduled. If you work through POSSE with care and determination, you will make the best of your study time and efforts.

WRITE TO LEARN

On a separate sheet of paper, compare and contrast PORPE and POSSE.

TAKING OBJECTIVE EXAMS

When to elect there is but one, 'Tis Hobson's choice, take that or none.

—THOMAS WARD

"Hobson's choice" refers to Tobias Hobson, a stablekeeper who made his customers take whatever horse was nearest the door when they came into his stable. Hobson's choice, then, refers to the only choice possible. In taking objective exams, your goal is to find Hobson's

---

TABLE 7.7   Stages of POSSE: Questions to Be Answered

PLAN

Answer these questions:

What does the test cover?

Is the test comprehensive or noncomprehensive?

Will the test questions be multiple-choice, true-false, and/or matching?

How many questions (of each type) will the test contain?

Will the test require me to apply information or think critically?

How much does this test count in my final grade?

When is the test?

Where will the test be given?

What special material(s) will I need to take the test?

ORGANIZE

Answer these questions:

What information do I predict will be on the test?

What materials do I need to study:

textbook?

handouts?

lecture notes?

supplemental readings?

old exams?

What study and memory methods will work best with this material?

Can I find partner or group to study with?

Gather materials together.

Construct study and memory aids.

SCHEDULE

Answer these questions:

How much time do I have before the exam?

How much time will I need to study for this test?

How much time each day will I study?

When will I study?

How will I distribute my study time?

Where will I study?

When will my study group/partner and I meet?

What obligations do I have that might interfere with this study time?

Construct a time schedule.

STUDY

At the end of each study session, answer these questions:

Am I studying actively, that is, through writing or speaking?

Am I distributing my study time to avoid memory interference and physical fatigue?

Am I following my schedule? Why or why not? What adjustments do I need to make?

Am I learning efficiently? Why or why not? What adjustments do I need to make?

TABLE 7.7	Stages of POSSE: Questions to Be Answered *continued*

EVALUATE

After the test has been returned, complete the worksheet in Table 7.10. Answer these questions:

What pattern(s) emerge(s) from the worksheet?

What type of questions did I miss most often?

What changes can I make to my study plan to avoid these trends in the future?

File your POSSE plan, course materials, study aids, exam, worksheet, and evaluation for future reference.

---

choice among the answers provided by the instructor. You seek to locate the one alternative that answers the question completely. Even when you've adequately prepared for the test, finding Hobson's choice isn't always easy. You need test-taking tips to help you find the correct answer among the alternatives. The following Test of Test-Wiseness shows you these strategies.

TEST OF TEST-WISENESS

The test below measures your test-wiseness. Little content knowledge is required and the answers to all questions can be determined through test-taking skill.

After finishing the exam, score it using the key that begins on page 296. Specific test-taking strategies are explained there. Follow specific directions given for each section.

Multiple-Choice Questions

Credit: 2 points each

Circle the correct answer for each multiple-choice question.

1. SQ3R is
   a. a study plan.
   b. a kind of test.
   c. a course number.
   d. none of the above.
2. The first thing you should do when taking a test is
   a. has a sharpened pencil.
   b. looks over all questions.
   c. read the directions.
   d. asks the teacher for clarification of directions.

3. Which of the following is true of standardized reading exams?
   a. Standardized reading tests require no special test-taking skills.
   b. A score on a standardized reading test may equal the number of right answers minus a percentage of the number of wrong answers.
   c. Always guess on standardized tests.
   d. Standardized tests are never timed tests.
4. If you do not understand a question during a test, you should
   a. ask a friend to explain it to you.
   b. skip that question.
   c. look it up in your textbook.
   d. ask the instructor for clarification.
5. Response choices are found on
   a. an objective test.
   b. a multiple-choice test.
   c. an essay test.
   d. all of the above.
   e. a and b only.
6. All of the following are parts of a study plan *except*
   a. reviewing information frequently.
   b. copying another person's notes.
   c. surveying a chapter.
   d. reading assignments.
7. Which of the following should *not* be done before taking a final exam?
   a. Review study notes.
   b. Find out when and where the test will be given.
   c. Determine if the test will be comprehensive or noncomprehensive.
   d. Become anxious.
8. An illusion is
   a. something that is not really there.
   b. an allusion.
   c. the same as elusive.
   d. another word for illustration.
9. The capital of Canada is
   a. New York City.
   b. Paris.
   c. Ottawa.
   d. Dallas.
10. The SQ3R study plan was developed in the 1940s by
    a. Francis Robinson.
    b. George Washington.
    c. Michael Jackson.
    d. Christopher Columbus.
11. The chemically inactive substances used in experiments to determine drug effectiveness are _____ .

    a. prescription medications
    b. federally controlled pharmaceutical products
    c. similar to physician-prescribed drugs
    d. placebos
12. Who was the third president of the United States?
    a. Lyndon Baines Johnson
    b. Franklin Delano Roosevelt
    c. Rutherford B. Hayes
    d. Thomas Jefferson

True-False Questions

Credit: 5 points each
Respond to each question by writing the word true or false in the blank.

_____ 1. You should always answer every question on every test.

_____ 2. All exams are comprehensive.

_____ 3. Never study with a partner.

_____ 4. Some tests are too lengthy to complete in the allotted time.

_____ 5. A test may not be without poorly worded questions.

_____ 6. Following directions is not unimportant.

Matching Questions

Credit: 4 points each
Write the letter of the correct answer in the blanks. Answers may be used more than once.

_____ 1. George Washington   a. a study plan

_____ 2. SQ3R   b. multiple-choice

     c. essay

_____ 3. example of an objective test   d. president

_____ 4. example of a subjective test

_____ 5. a written theme

Math Questions

Credit: 10 points each
Write your answers in the blanks.

_____ 1. A container holds 20 gallons. It is ⅗ full. How many gallons do you need to fill the container?

_____ 2. 20,819 + 74,864 =
    a. 10,993
    b. 95,683
    c. 95,666
    d. 85,333

KEY AND TEST-WISE STRATEGIES

The Test of Test-Wiseness helps you examine your test-taking skills. When taking any test, it is important that you preview the test and carefully follow directions. If you previewed this test, you probably realized that the test contained more multiple-choice questions than any other type. However, the multiple-choice questions received the least amount of credit. If you spent too much time on these questions, you might have failed to complete questions with higher point values.

Directions had to be followed exactly. If you failed to underline answers to the multiple-choice section, count them as incorrect. If you responded to the true-false questions with letters instead of the entire word, count them as incorrect. All other answers should have been written in the blanks to the left of the questions for you to receive credit.

Responses on any test often are designed to be similar and confusing. Whenever possible, after you read the question, you should answer it in your own words without looking at the responses given. Then, you should search for a response that matches your answer.

The following test-wise principles are no substitute for study and preparation. They can, however, help you eliminate choices and make educated guesses. The principle to remember is italicized.

Multiple-Choice Questions

Question 1. *If you don't know an answer, skip it and go on.* Don't waste time mulling over an answer. Go on to the questions you know. Sometimes a clue to the answer you need is found elsewhere in the test. In this case, the clue is in question 10. The answer is *a*.

Question 2. *Eliminate grammatically incorrect responses.* Sometimes, questions are poorly worded. The only grammatically correct choice in this question is answer *c*. Misuse of *a* or *an* is also a common grammatical error found in test questions.

Question 3. *Often the longest choice is correct.* For a correct answer to be absolutely clear, a response may need to be lengthy. The correct answer is *b*.

Questions 4 and 5. *Be sure the right choice is the best choice.* At first glance, answer *b* seems correct for question 4; however, further examination of choices reveals that answer *d* is a better choice. Watch for "all of the above," "none of the above," and paired choices. Answer *d* is the correct answer for question 5.

Questions 6 and 7. *Read questions carefully.* Not and except are small words, but they completely change the meaning. The careless reader might interpret question 6 as asking for a part of a study plan. Such

"You may be wise to the test, but is this test-wise?"

a reader might also interpret question 7 as asking for a procedure to be done before taking a final exam. The correct response for question 6 is *b*. The correct response for question 7 is *d*.

Question 8. *Responses that look like the word to be defined are usually incorrect. Allusion, elusive,* and *illustration* all resemble the word *illusion.* These are called "attractive distractors" because they look so appealing. Attractive distractors are almost always poor choices. The answer, therefore, is *a*.

Questions 9 and 10. *If you do not know what the answer is, determine what the answer is not.* Eliminate silly choices and use common sense. You may not know the capital of Canada. However, you should realize that New York City and Dallas are in the United States and Paris is in France. Only answer *c* remains. For question 10, answer *c* is silly. Answers *b* and *d* are wrong because neither Christopher Columbus nor George Washington was alive in the 1940s. Answer *a* is correct.

Question 11. *Watch for responses that are essentially the same.* A careful reading of choices *a*, *b*, and *c* reveals that they restate the same idea in a variety of ways. In this case, a physician-prescribed drug is a prescription medication. It is also federally controlled and a pharmaceutical product. Because these answers are synonymous, none of them can be the correct answer. The correct answer is answer *d*.

Question 12. *Use what you know to analyze and make decisions about information.* At first glance, you may not recall who the third U.S. president was. And, unlike the responses in questions 9 and 10, all of the men identified in the responses have served as president of the United States. But when were their terms of office? You reflect on what you know about each man. You might think of Lyndon Baines Johnson as a recent president, recalling that he took office after the assassination of John F. Kennedy and that the nation was involved in the Vietnam War during his presidency. Clearly a president of the twentieth century, he could not have been the third president. You might associate Franklin Delano Roosevelt with the Great Depression and World War II. Thus, he, too, was also a relatively modern president. You might have little knowledge about Rutherford B. Hayes, so you go on to Thomas Jefferson. You recall that he signed the Declaration of Independence and visualize him in colonial-era clothing. Logically, then, *d* is the correct choice.

True-False Questions

Questions 1, 2, 3, and 4. *Look for words that determine limits.* Words such as *always, never, none, every,* and *all* place no limitations on meaning. Words such as *some, few, often, many,* and *frequently* limit meaning and are better choices. If you can think of one example that contradicts an unlimited meaning, then it is false. For example, the answer to question 1 is false. This is because you wouldn't answer every question if a percentage of wrong responses were to be subtracted from the total of correct choices. The answers to questions 2 and 3 are also false. The answer to 4 is true.

Questions 5 and 6. *Watch for double negatives.* Just as multiplying two negative numbers equals a positive number, two negative words in a sentence indicate a positive relationship in standard English usage. In question 5, *not* and *without* cancel each other. The gist of the sentence is that a test may have poorly worded questions. The answer to question 5, then, is true. In question 6, the word *not* and the prefix *un-* cancel each other. The gist indicates that following directions is important. The answer to question 6 is true.

Matching Questions

Matching sections are somewhat like multiple-choice tests. Thus, the same principles apply. However, there are some special strategies for matching sections.

Often the two items being matched rely on an implied rather than a stated association. These relationships include a word and its definition, a person and a noted accomplishment, a step in a process and the process from which it comes, and so on. As with other test questions, complete items you know first. Use the side with the longer responses as your question side. This keeps you from repeatedly reading through numerous lengthy responses. When responses are used only once, do not blindly fill in the last question with the only remaining choice. Check to make sure it fits. If not, recheck all answers.

The answers to the matching section are as follows: question 1, *d;* question 2, *a;* question 3, *b;* question 4, *c;* and question 5, *c.*

Math Questions

Many good math students have difficulty with word problems. Panic prevents them from translating a word problem into a numerical one. Thus, the first step in solving math problems is to remain calm and avoid negative thinking. Second, picture the problem in your mind. This allows you to determine what the question asks. Next, identify your facts and the processes required. If possible, estimate the response. Work the problem and check it against your estimate. Recheck if necessary.

Problem 1. Picturing the problem reveals an everyday situation. You have a container that is partially filled, and you want to know how much more is needed to fill it. You have the following facts: a 20-gallon container that is ⅗ filled. You will need to multiply ⅗ and 20 to find out how much is in the container. Then you subtract that amount from 20 to find out how much more can be put in the container. You know that the container is more than half full but less than ¾ full; ½ of 20 is 10 and ¾ of 20 is 15. The container holds between 10 and 15 gallons now. Subtracting those amounts from the total results in an estimate of 5 to 10 gallons. The problem is worked in the following manner:

$$⅗ \times 20 = 12$$
$$20 - 12 = 8$$

The answer is 8; 8 is within the estimated range.

Problem 2. Standardized math tests provide a choice of answers. You can save time by estimating answers and eliminating responses. In this problem, adding the final digits (9 + 4 = 13) indicates that the response must end in 3. This eliminates answer *c.* Rounding off the two figures results in 21,000 and 75,000. The sum of the rounded figures is 96,000. The answer that is closest to the estimate is answer *b.*

TAKING SPECIALIZED EXAMS

Marathon runners often talk about "hitting the wall." This happens when runners get to the point where they feel they can no longer keep going. While some runners may routinely cover several miles each day with ease, the length or difficulty of some race routes can sometimes seem insurmountable.

You, too, may feel like you've "hit the wall" when it comes to taking specialized exams. The strategies you successfully use in subjective and objective test are not sufficient. Just as runners develop specialized techniques to help them pass "the wall," you need special strategies for specialized tests, open-book, take-home, and final exams.

Skyler might not believe it, but in many ways a final exam is just like all the other tests you take. However, finals usually are longer than regular exams. In a way, this works to your advantage. Longer exams cover more information. You get a better chance to get answers correct because there are more questions to attempt. The same strategies and suggestions for taking other tests apply to final exams (see Table 7.3).

Finals are often given in places and at times that differ from your regular class schedule. Final exam locations and schedules are printed in campus newspapers, posted in each department, and announced by your instructor. If more than two of your exams occur on the same day, you can sometimes ask to reschedule one of them. Procedures for such requests vary. Seeing your advisor is the first step in the process.

SOURCE: *Shoe*. Reprinted by permission; Tribune Media Services

TABLE 7.8	Steps in Taking Open-Book and Take-Home Exams

1. Familiarize yourself with your text. Tab sections of the text that deal with major topics or contain important formulas or definitions.

2. Organize your notes. Mark them in the same way you tabbed your text.

3. Highlight important details in both your text and notes.

4. Know how to use the table of contents and index to locate information quickly.

5. Paraphrase information. Unless you are quoting a specific source, do not copy word-for-word from your text.

6. Use other applicable test-taking strategies.

TAKING OPEN-BOOK AND TAKE-HOME EXAMS

Open-book and take-home tests are types of finals that sound too good to be true. You might think that these tests require no study at all. In fact, they require as much studying as any other exam. Such tests are easier when you have the appropriate strategies for taking them (see Table 7.8).

An open-book exam tests your ability to locate, organize, and relate information quickly. Such tests also measure how quickly you can read and process information. Thus, the open-book test may be biased toward well-prepared students. This is another reason why you need to study thoroughly before taking this type of exam. Next, insufficient studying results in your wasting test time while you decide what the question means or where to find the answer.

The take-home exam also evaluates your ability to locate, organize, and relate information. Because you are not expected to take the test during class, it measures your knowledge more fairly, although spelling and neatness generally count more. In most cases, a take-home test allows you to avoid the stress associated with in-class exams. On the other hand, setting your own pace has drawbacks, particularly if you tend to procrastinate. Waiting until the last minute to begin working on such a test results in the same stressful feelings you get during an in-class test. Such scheduling also results in work of lesser quality.

"Did your instructor say to take home the library, too?"

MENTAL PREPAREDNESS

Stress is known by many names, including pressure, worry, concern, anxiety, and nervousness. *Stress* comes from the word *distress*. Distress is emotional or physical strain caused by an external but short-term event. You and many other students face stress whenever you take a test. Believe it or not, instructors realize this (see Figure 7.2).

FIGURE 7.2   Exam Anxiety and Grandma's Health

Every student knows that examination time can be a source of great stress. In the following article, Professor John J. Chiodo of Clarion University describes some truly extraordinary effects of exam-related stress and suggests a variety of ways in which faculty members can help to alleviate the problem.

I entered the ranks of academe as well prepared as the next fellow, but I was still unaware of the threat that midterm exams posed to the health and welfare of students and their relatives. It didn't take long, however, for me to realize that a real problem existed. The onset of midterms seemed to provoke not only a marked increase in the family problems, illnesses, and accidents experienced by my students, but also above-normal death rates among their grandmothers.

In my first semester of teaching, during the week before the midterm exam, I got numerous phone calls and visits from the roommates of many of my students, reporting a series of problems. Mononucleosis seemed to have struck a sizable portion of my class, along with the more common colds and flu.

A call from one young woman awakened me with the news that her roommate's grandmother had died, so she (my student) would be unable to take the exam. I expressed my condolences, and assured the caller that her roommate would not be penalized for such an unexpected tragedy.

Over the next few days I received many more calls—informing me of sickness, family problems, and even the death of a beloved cat. But the thought of three grandmothers passing away, all within the short exam period, caused me a good deal of remorse. But the term soon ended and, with the Christmas break and preparations for the new semester, I forgot all about the midterm problem.

Eight weeks into the second semester, however, I was once again faced with a succession of visits or phone calls from roommates about sick students, family problems, and, yes, the deaths of more grandmothers. I was shaken. I could understand that dorm meals and late nights, along with "exam anxiety," might well make some students sick, but what could account for the grandmothers? Once again, though, other things occupied my mind, and before long I had stopped thinking about it.

I moved that summer to a large Midwestern university, where I had to reconstruct my teaching plans to fit the quarter system. I taught three classes. By the end of the first midterm exams two of my student's grandmothers had died; by the time the year was over, a total of five had gone to their reward.

I began to realize the situation was serious. In the two years I had been teaching, 12 grandmothers had passed away; on that basis, if I taught for 30 years 180 grandmothers would no longer be with us. I hated to think what the universitywide number would be.

I tried to figure out the connection. Was it because grandmothers are hypersensitive to a grandchild's problems? When they see their grandchildren suffering from exam anxiety do they

STAGES OF STRESS

In 1936, Hans Selye developed a theory about stress called the "General Adaptation Syndrome." He suggested that stress builds in three progressive states that are characterized by both physical and emotional symptoms. A variation of this theory describes the characteristics that you might experience in stressful testing situations (Table 7.9).

Test-induced stress includes both physical and emotional symptoms. You may have one or more of the symptoms at a stage. You

---

FIGURE 7.2   Exam Anxiety and Grandma's Health *continued*

---

become anxious too? Does the increased stress then cause stroke or heart failure? It seemed possible; so it followed that if grandmothers' anxiety levels could be lowered, a good number of their lives might be prolonged. I didn't have much direct contact with grandmothers, but I reasoned that by moderating the anxiety of my students, I could help reduce stress on their grandmothers.

With that in mind, I began my next year of teaching. On the first day of class, while passing out the syllabus, I told my students how concerned I was about the high incidence of grandmother mortality. I also told them what I thought we could do about it.

To make a long story short, the results of my plan to reduce student anxiety were spectacular. At the end of the quarter there had not been one test-related death of a grandmother. In addition, the amount of sickness and family strife had decreased dramatically. The next two quarters proved to be even better. Since then, I have refined my anxiety-reduction system and, in the interest of grandmotherly longevity, would like to share it with my colleagues. Here are the basic rules:

- Review the scope of the exam.
- Use practice tests.
- Be clear about time limits.
- Announce what materials will be needed and what aids will be permitted.
- Review the grading procedure.
- Review the policies on makeup tests and retakes.
- Provide study help.
- Make provision for last-minute questions.
- Allow for breaks during long exams.
- Coach students on test-taking techniques.

I have been following these rules for 13 years now, and during that time have heard of only an occasional midterm-related death of a grandmother. Such results lead me to believe that if all faculty members did likewise, the health and welfare of students—and their grandmothers—would surely benefit.

SOURCE: Morris, C. G. (1988). *Psychology: An Introduction.* Englewood Cliffs, N.J.: Simon & Schuster.

TABLE 7.9	Progressive Stages of Stress
STAGE I: ALARM	STAGE III: PANIC
Initial feelings of anxiety	Feelings of intense anxiety
Emotional or physical reactions	Emotional or physical reactions
"Butterflies"	"Butterflies"
Perspiration	Perspiration
Dryness of mouth	Dryness of mouth
Ability to concentrate	Pounding of heart
STAGE II: FEAR	Breathlessness
Feelings of fearful anxiety	Tremors
Emotional or physical reactions	Nausea
"Butterflies"	Faintness
Perspiration	Inability to concentrate
Dryness of mouth	Disorganization of thoughts
Pounding of heart	
Breathlessness	
Muscle tension	
Frustration	
Reduced ability to concentrate	

could also have hidden symptoms. Often stress reactions build without your knowledge. Hidden or apparent, the symptoms of stress need management. How and when you manage stress determine if its effect is negative or positive.

Stage I: Alarm

Alarm, the first stage, mobilizes your body for action. You feel nervous anticipation. This alarm focuses your energies on handling the stress. Although you may question your degree of preparedness for the test, you feel confident. At this point you get your first chance to manage stress. When you control stress in its first stage, it motivates you to think more clearly and work harder or longer. Actors, athletes, and public speakers use the effects of the alarm stage to stimulate better performances. The alarm stage can give you the same kind of "natural high" for test performance.

Stage II: Fear

Stress also can be managed in the second stage, fear. When the symptoms described above increase in intensity, feelings of anxiety become feelings of fear. Fear of the unknown, of failure, of disappointing yourself or others, and of competition instill personal doubts. This apprehension is harder to control. If you fail to overcome stress at this stage, stress overcomes you.

Stage III: Panic

Stress in its final stage becomes panic. You no longer control the situation. Your thought processes break down. Disorganization and chaos result in careless errors and loss of memory. When you panic during a test, you think, "I don't know any of these questions;" "I'm going to fail this test and fail the course;" "My mind is blank." When the test is returned to you, you find you misread questions and forgot information you really knew. You were the victim of panic—the third stage of stress.

WRITE TO LEARN

On a separate sheet of paper, identify a time when you experienced test anxiety. Describe how you felt during this time.

STRESS MANAGEMENT

You cope with stress by either withdrawing from it or learning to manage it. Withdrawal from stress does not solve anything. It is just an escape. **Coping,** or managing stress, is a more difficult but longer-lasting solution.

Withdrawal

Obviously, you can physically withdraw by dropping a class or dropping out of school. You also can withdraw psychologically from a situation in several ways.

Blocking the cause of stress from your memory is one way you withdraw from anxiety. Called **repression,** this method involves your doing nothing to solve the problem. You think about more pleasant things, instead of whatever is bothering you.

A second way to withdraw is **denial.** You pretend taking tests doesn't bother you. Again, you fail to prepare. By denying the test's existence or its importance to you, you withdraw from the stress it creates within you.

Another way to avoid stress is **projection.** Here you blame someone or something else for your failure. For example, when you are unprepared for a test, you blame your friends, your roommate, your teacher, or your job.

A fourth way to withdraw from stress is to **rationalize,** or find acceptable excuses, for being unprepared. You might rationalize flunking out of school by saying, "Having experience in the field will help me get a high-paying job."

"A score of 7.5 isn't earth shattering unless I grade it on the Richter scale."

Coping

Coping with stress requires that you anticipate and prepare for it before, during, and after tests. The first and best way to accomplish this is to study. If you feel confident about yourself, stress symptoms occur less often.

Relaxation is another way to cope with test anxiety. Instead of last-minute cramming, spend ten or fifteen minutes alone in a quiet place before an exam. Simply flexing and releasing the muscles of your neck and shoulders reduces stress. During an exam, you can manage stress by pausing and taking a few deep breaths. This calms your nerves and steadies your mind. A second way to manage stress while taking a test is to answer questions you are sure you know or make notes of information you feel you might forget. Such activity reduces your anxiety and builds confidence. Third, the way a test is constructed or a question is worded often causes stress. Asking your instructor for clarification helps you cope. Self-talk is a fourth way to reduce anxiety during a test. Self-talk involves your recognizing negative thoughts and feelings and forcing yourself to change them. Typical negative thoughts and feelings during a test include worry about your performance, indecision between possible answers, concern with the physical symptoms of stress, and anxiety about the consequences of failing the test. To talk yourself out of a negative frame of mind, think, "STOP. I *do* know this information. I *am* prepared for this exam." This helps to clear your mind from worry so you can concentrate on remembering the information.

"Let me get this straight. You flunked English because your electric typewriter broke down, you flunked Math because your electric calculator broke down, and you flunked everything else because the electrical system in your car broke down and you couldn't get to your classes."

SOURCE: Button, Ford. *Phi Delta Kappan.*

PHYSICAL PREPAREDNESS

One of the most important and least considered aspects of test-taking is your physical well-being. Maslow's hierarchy of needs (see Figure 1.2 in Chapter 1) theorizes that physical needs must be satisfied before other needs can be met. Physical preparedness is the basis of test-taking skills. Physical well-being allows you to meet higher-level needs, such as self-esteem and self-actualization.

REST AND RECUPERATION

Battle-fatigued soldiers get leave for R & R, rest and recuperation. You, too, get fatigued in the battle for grades and need R & R. Constructive recuperation helps you regain your mental and physical well-being. When you return to your studies, you can accomplish more.

Fatigue results from mental and physical effort. The amount of effort it takes for a person to tire varies. Your physical condition and the task you are attempting affect fatigue. If you are physically fit, you can achieve more with less fatigue. If you are interested or have skill in the task before you, you also can achieve more with less fatigue.

Like the causes of fatigue, methods of rest and recuperation also differ from person to person. In addition, they vary in quality and effectiveness. Sleep is not the only way to get constructive R & R. Changing activities—for example, studying different subjects—also rests your mind. Moreover, exercise works off pent-up frustration and stress. Other effective ways to relax include watching television, listening to music, talking to friends, and reading a book.

This price seems too steep to some students. They take shortcuts by using tranquilizers to relax and amphetamines to stimulate themselves. These artificial means are quick but costly. They create dependencies and are study crutches, not study supports.

NUTRITION

Just as fuel powers your car, food powers you. Because nutrition affects your physical well-being, it ultimately also affects your study habits and grades. What you eat and when you eat probably matter more than you think. You must satisfy your physical need for nutrition. This, in turn, ensures good health.

What you eat affects your stamina and behavior. Foods in the four basic food groups (fruits and vegetables, breads, dairy products, and protein) supply the nutrients you need. They serve not only as a foundation for good health but also as a reserve of energy.

In college, when you eat is not always in your control. Classes, work, and study time alter regular mealtimes. You need to plan for adequate nutrition even when you miss meals. For example, your lab class may extend past the hours that the cafeteria serves lunch. Eating a later breakfast or an earlier dinner helps you cope. Often college cafeterias will prepare sack lunches for students whose classes conflict with scheduled mealtimes.

HEALTH

Every instructor has heard the excuse "I was too sick to take the test." Although this line is well worn, there really may be times when you will be too sick to take a test. Many students simply skip class and confront the instructor later. A better solution is to contact the instructor as soon as possible. Making this special effort shows your concern for your grade and your respect for the instructor. Arranging for makeup work at this time decreases stress. You know if and when you'll be able to make up work.

If you are ill for a lengthy period of time, you need to discuss with your instructor the possibility of receiving an incomplete or *I* grade. This enables you to complete the work when you recover.

TABLE 7.10   Worksheet for Examining Returned Tests

Test Item Missed	Insufficient Information						Test Anxiety					Lack of Test-Wisdom						Test Skills					Other		
	I did not read the text thoroughly.	The information was not in my notes.	I studied the information but could not remember it.	I knew main ideas but needed details.	I knew the information but could not apply it.	I studied the wrong information.	I experienced mental block.	I spent too much time daydreaming.	I was so tired I could not concentrate.	I was so hungry I could not concentrate.	I panicked.	I carelessly marked a wrong choice.	I did not eliminate grammatically incorrect choices.	I did not choose the *best* choice.	I did not notice limiting words.	I did not notice a double negative.	I changed a correct answer to a wrong one.	I misread the directions.	I misread the question.	I made poor use of the time provided.	I wrote poorly organized responses.	I wrote incomplete responses.			
Number of Items Missed																									

AFTER THE TEST: FOLLOW-THROUGH

What do you do when a test is returned to you? Do you throw it away? Or do you carefully examine it? A review of your test paper provides information about your skills. You use this information to improve your future performance on tests. Such an analysis helps you decide which of your study and test-taking strategies were most successful and which ones need more emphasis.

Table 7.10 is a worksheet for examining your test paper. To complete this worksheet, you list each item that you missed in the first column. Then you mark an X under the description that best explains why you missed that question. If the reason is other than one of those identified in this chart, list it in the *Other* column. Sometimes you will have to mark more than one reason for missing a question. Next, you tally the number of Xs under each reason. These numbers indicate the areas of study and test-taking strategies on which you must place more effort in the future.

After you have determined information about your study and test-taking habits, look for information about how your instructor constructs exams. You should be able to see patterns in the types of questions asked, the emphasis placed on lecture or text notes, grading patterns, and so forth. This valuable information will serve you in preparing for the next exam.

WRITE TO LEARN

Photocopy Table 7.10. Complete the table using a test from any of your courses. On the back of the sheet, indicate the patterns you discovered and how you plan to alter your study habits to overcome these obstacles.

EXERCISE 7.1   Respond to each of the following scenarios:

1. Your calculus instructor has assigned a midterm test for next Tuesday. The test will be given as part of the course's group exams from 6 to 8 P.M. The test will cover chapters 7, 9, and 16. According to PORPE and POSSE, what questions should you ask your instructor in order to adequately prepare for the exam?

----

2. Your biology test will cover Sample Chapter 3, "Nutrition and Digestion." The test will consist of three essay questions. How many questions should you predict in preparing for the test? List them below.

_____

_____

_____

_____

_____

_____

_____

_____

_____

3. You are preparing for your essay test in biology (see question 2). Describe how you will learn and recall the information for any three questions you predicted using the memory techniques found in Chapter 5.

_____

_____

_____

_____

_____

_____

_____

_____

_____

4. Your sociology test will cover Sample Chapter 1, "Culture: The Ideas and Products People Adopt and Create." Your instructor has implied that one of the essays will require you to analyze the meaning of the chapter's title. What might your response be?

_____

_____

_____

_____

_____

5. You are taking a political science test. You preview the test and find the following: three essay questions worth ten points each, ten short-answer questions worth five points each, and ten multiple-choice questions worth two points each. You have ninety minutes to complete the test. Estimate the amount of time you plan to spend on each item and explain your rationale.

_____

_____

_____

_____

_____

_____

6. You read the following question on a computer science test. What is most likely to be the correct answer? Why?

The Hollerith Code
A. use 0 and 1 only.
B. was used to sort census data.
C. developed by Charles Babbage in 1822.
D. forerunner of the Mark I.

_____

_____

_____

_____

_____

_____

7. Your professor returned your last psychology test. You see that you received no credit for the following:

Respond to the following essay question: Trace the development of IQ tests.

Your response:
The Wechsler Adult Intelligence Scale—Revised (WAIS-R) measures performance and verbal abilities. It contains ten subtests—five of each ability. The WISC-R is a form of the test used for children. The Stanford-Binet is similar but consists of thirty tests arranged in order of increasing difficulty. Some tests, such as the Seguin Board and the Porteus Maze, only evaluate performance abilities. Some people consider tests like the Progressive Mazes and the Goodenough-Harris Intelligence Test to be more culturally fair. Group tests of ability, such as the California Test of Mental Maturity are also available.

Explain why you failed to receive credit for this response.

_____

_____

_____

_____

_____

8. Your score on the last microbiology test was 57 percent. Your average is 43 percent. You think your problem is that your high school preparation was not sound. What kind of withdrawal would your theory exemplify?

_____

_____

_____

_____

9. You stayed up until 3 A.M. working on your architecture project. You overslept and didn't have time for breakfast. You were late to your algebra final and didn't hear the directions for the test. You forgot your calculator and had to perform calculations without it. When you examine your returned test, which factors probably affected your performance?

_____

_____

_____

_____

10. You are taking a political science test. You see the following question:

Name two presidents who were members of the Whig Party.

You know you studied that information, but your mind is blank. What should you do and why?

_____

_____

_____

_____

_____

EXERCISE 7.2 Read Sample Chapter 4, "Managing Stress," before completing the rest of this exercise. As you read, note the information that might be on an exam. Below you will find sample test questions. Read each. Then answer the questions that follow each test item by either circling the correct response or filling in the blanks.

1. *What is the parasympathetic nervous system?*
   a. Did you predict this as a test question?   Yes   No
   b. What type of question is this: definition, translation, interpretation, application, analysis, synthesis, or evaluation?
   c. On what page(s) would the answer to this question be found?
      Page(s) _____

2. *Other than an athlete, what profession might experience eustress? When?*
   a. Did you predict this as a test question?   Yes   No
   b. What type of question is this: definition, translation, interpretation, application, analysis, synthesis, or evaluation?
   c. On what page(s) would the answer to this question be found?
      Page(s) _____

3. *When confronted with a problem, how might you restore equilibrium to your system?*
   a. Did you predict this as a test question?   Yes   No
   b. What type of question is this: definition, translation, interpretation, application, analysis, synthesis, or evaluation?
   c. On what page(s) would the answer to this question be found?
      Page(s) _____

4. *Define crisis.*
   a. Did you predict this as a test question?   Yes   No
   b. What type of question is this: definition, translation, interpretation, application, analysis, synthesis, or evaluation?
   c. On what page(s) would the answer to this question be found?
      Page(s) _____

5. *A friend of yours has just found out she has tested HIV-positive. What sort of social supports might be of help to her?*
   a. Did you predict this as a test question?   Yes   No
   b. What type of question is this: definition, translation, interpretation, application, analysis, synthesis, or evaluation?
   c. On what page(s) would the answer to this question be found?
      Page(s) _____

6. *Which group in each of the following pairs would you expect to exhibit more emotional closeness? Explain your choices.*
   (a) a Girl Scout troop or cheerleaders?
   (b) a collegiate baseball team or a physical education class?
   (c) roommates or co-workers?

    a. Did you predict this as a test question?   Yes   No
    b. What type of question is this: definition, translation, interpretation, application, analysis, synthesis, or evaluation?
    c. On what page(s) would the answer to this question be found?
      Page(s) _____

7. *Provide an example of one of your social networks.*
    a. Did you predict this as a test question?   Yes   No
    b. What type of question is this: definition, translation, interpretation, application, analysis, synthesis, or evaluation?
    c. On what page(s) would the answer to this question be found?
      Page(s) _____

8. *Your father has just lost his job; this is the first time this has ever happened to him. You know that he needs some ideas for relieving the stress he feels before going job hunting. What suggestions do you make?*
    a. Did you predict this as a test question?   Yes   No
    b. What type of question is this: definition, translation, interpretation, application, analysis, synthesis, or evaluation?
    c. On what page(s) would the answer to this question be found?
      Page(s) _____

9. *What is the relationship between time management and stress?*
    a. Did you predict this as a test question?   Yes   No
    b. What type of question is this: definition, translation, interpretation, application, analysis, synthesis, or evaluation?
    c. On what page(s) would the answer to this question be found?
      Page(s) _____

10. *Compare the information in Figure 3–2 on page 550 (60) with Selye's general adaptation syndrome (GAS).*
    a. Did you predict this as a test question?   Yes   No
    b. What type of question is this: definition translation, interpretation, application, analysis, synthesis, or evaluation?
    c. On what page(s) would the answer to this question be found?
      Page(s) _____

GROUP LEARNING ACTIVITY
TEST-TAKING STRENGTH IN NUMBERS

A recent study (Shanker, 1988) examined reasons why some post-secondary students consistently had better mathematics grades than others. Results indicated that the critical difference was study groups. Those students who participated regularly in a study group understood and performed better than those who studied independently. When independent learners formed study groups, their grades improved to the level of those already involved in group study.

In terms of preparing for tests, study groups offer the following advantages:

1. **Active Learning.** Because you discuss information with others, you participate more fully than in individual study for exams. Being with others focuses your attention and efforts. You have more opportunities to see, hear, verbalize, and otherwise come in contact with the information you study.

2. **Commitment.** People often break promises to themselves and delay test preparation until it's too late. If you make a commitment to others that you will be prepared to study with them at a specific place and time, you will be more likely to keep that promise.

3. **Increased links among information.** Studying with others gives you new insights and conclusions that increase your associations with a concept. You not only have your own ideas but the ideas of others from which to draw when recalling information on an exam.

4. **Psychological support.** A study group helps you realize that you're not alone. Knowing that others are having difficulty or have been successful lessens your anxiety and provides encouragement.

5. **Monitoring.** Sometimes it's difficult to predict what and how information will appear on an exam. The suggestions and views of others gives you more ways in which to direct study efforts.

Application

Using Exercise 7.2 as a guide, each group member should individually construct a test for this chapter. In your study group, exchange copies of each test and compare questions predicted by each person. How did each member select questions? How did each member choose the information to be tested? Discuss other ways in which each member's test questions might be phrased.

SUMMARY OF MAIN POINTS

1. All exams require certain test-taking strategies (getting to the test on time, reading the directions, and so on).

2. Because subjective exams require you to provide your own answers, you need to be well-versed in the subject matter and skilled in writing.

3. Objective exams force you to select an answer from a set of instructor-made choices. Your selection needs to be based on both your knowledge of content and test-wise strategies.

4. Finals are longer forms of subjective and objective exams; they require no special test-taking strategies, unless they are open-book or take-home exams.

5. Mental preparedness involves eliminating stress. Stress caused by test anxiety occurs in progressive stages and can be managed before, during, and after exams.

6. Your physical needs for rest, proper nutrition, and health must be met to achieve maximum test performance.

7. You prepare for future testing successes by learning from your mistakes when exams are returned to you.

VOCABULARY DEVELOPMENT
STRUCTURAL ANALYSIS: WORDS IN YOUR POCKET

Test taking requires a calm hand and a cool wit. It calls for strength and perseverance. It takes steady nerves and courage. But, most of all, it requires knowledge and the words that reflect that knowledge. Sometimes knowing a part of a word's meaning allows you to eliminate distractors on exams. Other times, it helps you understand words in questions that seem tricky or ambiguous. Knowledge of word parts, then, aids you in determining correct answers on exams and in showing the knowledge you have gained in a course.

A word is not the same with one writer as with another. One tears it from his guts. The other pulls it out of his overcoat pocket.

—CHARLES PEGUY

Using the parts of words to determine meaning is called structural analysis. Pats of a word fit together much as parts of a car do. As with a car, some parts are essential to the functioning of a word. Called bases, these word parts give you an overall meaning. Affixes (prefixes and suffixes) accessorize the word and affect the overall meaning. Prefixes occur at the beginning of words. Suffixes are found at their ends. Affixes sometime help identify the subject area of a word. They can also help determine the part of speech or use. The following charts show common roots (Table 1), prefixes (Table 2), suffixes (Table 3), and

TABLE 1	General Roots	
Root	**Example**	
script (write)	manuscript	_____
vert (turn)	convert	_____
ject (throw)	eject	_____
port (carry)	transport	_____
vis/vid (see)	video	_____
rupt (break)	interrupt	_____
dict (say)	dictionary	_____
aud (hear)	auditory	_____
cede (go)	recede	_____
junct (join)	junction	_____
pseudo (false)	pseudonym	_____
mem (mind)	memory	_____

TABLE 2   Prefixes

Prefix	Example	
be (by)	beloved	_____
pre (before)	prehistoric	_____
de (away, from)	detract	_____
inter (between)	intervene	_____
ob (against)	obstruction	_____
in, il, ir (not)	illegible	_____
a (not)	asexual	_____
un (not)	unconnected	_____
ad (to, toward)	adhere	_____
contra (against)	contraband	_____
en, in (in)	encapsule	_____
com/col/con/co (together, with)	coauthor	_____
non (not)	nonexistent	_____
auto (self)	autonomy	_____
ex (out of)	exit	_____
re (again)	repeat	_____
pro (forward)	proponent	_____
homo (same)	homogeneous	_____
hetero (different)	heterosexual	_____
dis (apart from)	disjointed	_____
over (above)	overwhelm	_____
super (above)	superscript	_____
sub (under)	subscript	_____
mis (bad, wrong)	mistaken	_____
trans (across)	transfer	_____

math and science roots (Table 4). Knowing how word parts fit together saves your guts and puts words in your pocket.

Structural analysis is an important tool in preparing for and taking a test. Because it is an active process, it stimulates you to use what you know to analyze new words and understand familiar words more fully.

When preparing for a test, you may be struggling with learning the meanings of a large number of words. Structural analysis helps you connect and organize meaning. For example, consider the following words and meanings:

macrophage—a cell derived from the white blood cells called monocytes whose function is to consume foreign particles, such as bacteria and viruses.

monocyte—one type of white blood cells; produces macrophages

lymphocyte—white blood cell produced by the lymphatic system.

TABLE 3   Suffixes

Root	Example	
Noun		
ane/ine/ene (forms a name of a chemical)	butane	_____
ade (act of; result or product of)	blockade	_____
age (state or condition of)	blockage	_____
arch/archy (rule)	monarchy	_____
ard/art (one who does something not admirable to excess)	braggart	_____
arian (age, sect, or social belief; occupation)	agrarian	_____
asis/osis/ysis (condition characterized by)	paralysis	_____
tion (state of being)	elation	_____
cide (kill)	homocide	_____
ory (place or state of; ability in)	laboratory	_____
ster (one who is or does)	youngster	_____
wright (one who builds or makes)	playwright	_____
hood (state of being)	statehood	_____
ship (state of being)	leadership	_____
ance/ence (state of being)	absence	_____
ism (state of being)	communism	_____
ness (state of being)	kindness	_____
sion (act of)	conversion	_____
ation (act of)	jubilation	_____
ity/ty (state or condition)	creativity	_____
ist (one who does)	journalist	_____
or/er (one who)	inventor	_____
ment (action or state of)	government	_____
Adjective		
able (able to/capable of being)	remarkable	_____
ible (able to)	divisible	_____
ful (full of)	beautiful	_____
ous (having)	advantageous	_____
ive (having the quality of)	creative	_____
al (pertaining to)	comical	_____
ic (pertaining to)	academic	_____
Verb		
en (belonging to/cause to be)	roughen	_____
ize (to become/to make)	maximize	_____
fy (to make)	unify	_____
Adverb		
ly (in the manner of)	carefully	_____

TABLE 4	Math and Science Roots and Affixes	
Root	**Example**	
mono (one)	monograph	_____
aqua (water)	aquatic	_____
hydro (water)	hydrolic	_____
hemi (half)	hemisphere	_____
semi (half)	semicircle	_____
equi (equal)	equidistant	_____
tele (far off)	telescope	_____
some (body)	chromosome	_____
sphere (ball, globe)	biosphere	_____
quad (four)	quadrant	_____
bi (two)	bisect	_____
geo (earth)	geology	_____
micro (small)	microscope	_____
onomy (science of)	astronomy	_____
ology (study of)	biology	_____
uni (one)	universe	_____
tri (three)	triangle	_____
octa (eight)	octagon	_____
dec (ten)	decimal	_____
centi (hundred, hundredth)	centigrade	_____
milli (thousand, thousandth)	millimeter	_____
bio (life)	biology	_____
astro (star)	astronomy	_____
thermo (heat)	thermal	_____
meter (measure)	kilometer	_____
ped/pod (foot)	arthropod	_____
kilo (thousand)	kilogram	_____
botan (plant)	botanist	_____
cyto (cell)	cytoskeleton	_____
lymph (water)	lymph nodes	_____

lymphatic system—the system that helps protect the body against infection and returns excess fluid to the blood circulatory system.

At first glance, they may seem a bit confusing. Consider the following map with meanings (in parentheses) derived from structural analysis:

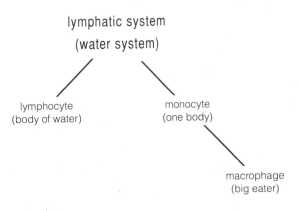

Now you see the relationships. The lymphatic system produces both lymphocytes and monocytes. Monocytes produce macrophages, which "eat up" foreign bodies in the body.

How does structural analysis aid you in test-taking? Consider the following test questions:

1. Which of the following is a *pseudopod?*
   a. amoeba
   b. horse
   c. spider
   d. anteater

2. Unlike in the aristocracies of Europe, the founders of the United States believed that all humans are of the same worth. As a result of this _____ philosophy, anyone can rise to power.
   a. egalitarian
   b. diversify
   c. coordinator
   d. unification

Your recall of word parts aids you in answering question 1. But if you cannot think of a specific meaning of a word part, you can attempt to think of other words that contain that particular part. So, if you couldn't think of the meaning of *pseudo* or *pod,* you might think of such words as *pseudonym* or *tripod.* From this, you might generalize that *pseudo* means *false* and that *pod* means *foot.* Thus, *pseudo pod* means "false foot." Since spiders, horses, and anteaters all have some sort of foot, the answer must be *a,* amoeba.

In question 2, the correct answer depends on two factors. First, the word that fits in the blank must modify the noun *philosophy.* Thus, it must be an adjective. Second, you must recall how suffixes change part of speech. If you recall that *tion* and *or* indicates nouns and that *ify* indicates verb forms, then answer *a* is the correct choice. This will be verified when you recall that some adjectives end in *ian.*

Activity

Fill in the blanks in Tables 1, 2, 3, and 4 with your own examples of words with these parts.

CHAPTER REVIEW

Answer briefly but completely.

1. Describe the differences between objective and subjective tests. Which kind do you personally find easier to prepare for and take? Why?

   _____

   _____

   _____

   _____

   _____

2. Identify what the text describes as the *ABCs* of successful test taking. Which one(s) do you possess? Which one(s) do you need to improve? Give examples of each for a specific course in which you are enrolled.

   _____

   _____

   _____

   _____

   _____

3. Identify the stages of PORPE. At which stage do you foresee yourself having the most difficulty? Why? At which stage do you foresee yourself having the least difficulty? Why?

   _____

   _____

   _____

   _____

   _____

4. Identify any four of the steps in taking exams found in Table 7.3. Explain why you need to use each one.

   _____

   _____

   _____

   _____

   _____

5. Using the information in Table 7.5, Taking Essay Exams, respond to the following in essay form:
   Describe the strategy you used in finding the star in the picture on page 290.

   _____

   _____

   _____

   _____

   _____

6. Relate time management to the use of PORPE and POSSE.

   _____

   _____

   _____

   _____

   _____

7. Describe the advantages and disadvantages of finals, take-home exams, and open-book exams.

   _____

   _____

   _____

   _____

   _____

8. Identify the irony found in Figure 7.2, Exam Anxiety and Grandma's Health. Which of Professor Chiodo's thirteen basic rules were not covered in another part of this chapter? Why might they have been omitted?

   _____

   _____

   _____

   _____

9. Review your responses to the Write to Learn on page 305. What might you do to control feelings of anxiety in the future?

   _____

   _____

   _____

10. This chapter identifies rest and recuperation and proper nutrition as factors necessary in physical preparedness. As a college student, which of these are you most likely to neglect? Why? How can you realistically adjust your life-style to meet these physical needs?

_____

_____

_____

_____

REFERENCES

Shanker, A. (1988, Fall). "Strength in Numbers." _Academic Connections_ p. 12.

Simpson, M. L. (1986). "PORPE: A Writing Strategy for Studying and Learning in the Content Areas." _Journal of Reading_ 29:407–14.

Van Oech, R. (1986). _A Kick in the Seat of the Pants._ New York: Harper and Row.

Using Graphics in Texts

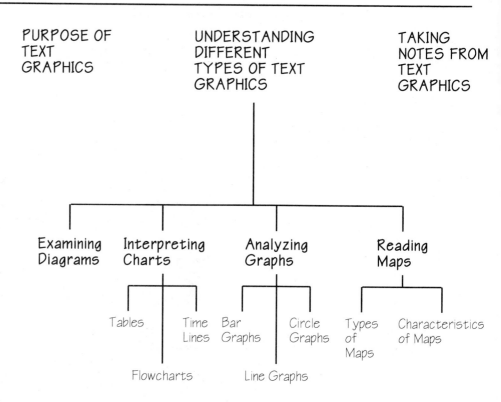

PURPOSE OF TEXT GRAPHICS

UNDERSTANDING DIFFERENT TYPES OF TEXT GRAPHICS

TAKING NOTES FROM TEXT GRAPHICS

Examining Diagrams

Interpreting Charts

Analyzing Graphs

Reading Maps

Tables

Time Lines

Flowcharts

Bar Graphs

Circle Graphs

Line Graphs

Types of Maps

Characteristics of Maps

TERMS

bar graphs
cartographers
charts
chronology
circle graphs
diagrams
feature analysis table
flowcharts
general reference
maps
graphics
graphs
histograms
key
legend
line graphs
pictorial graphs
quality table
scale of distance
special purpose maps
symbols
symbol graphs
tables
time lines
thematic map
trends

B efore the development of written language, ancient people communicated through pictures they carved or painted. These pictures helped Egyptians, Aztecs, Native Americans, and other early societies to express ideas and concepts. Today, authors use both words and pictures to express and relate their ideas and concepts.

To quote the English author and critic, Anthony Burgess, "Art never imitates. It merely takes over what is already present in the real world and makes an aesthetic pattern out of it, or tries to explain it, or tries to relate it to some other aspect of life." In much the same way, text **graphics** never imitate. They merely take over what is already present in the text. They organize it, or try to explain it, or try to relate it to some other aspect of the text.

PURPOSE OF TEXT GRAPHICS

What do you see when you look at this drawing? Some people see a vase. Others see two faces. What makes one person view the figure one way while another person sees something else? What you see in a picture depends on both the artist's and your own perspective.

Graphics refer to text representations such as diagrams, charts (tables, flowcharts, and time lines), graphs (bar, line, and circle), and maps (general reference and special purpose). The type of information determines the graphic format to some degree. For example, a chart or graph summarizes or classifies data whereas diagrams illustrate complex ideas. Authors include graphics, therefore, to exemplify, clarify, organize, and further illustrate the key ideas they want you to know (see Table 8.1).

TABLE 8.1   Purposes of Text Graphics

	Diagram	Table	Flow-Chart	Time Line	Bar or Line Graph	Circle Graph	Map
Summarize	X	X	X	X	X	X	
Organize		X	X		X	X	
Illustrate	X		X	X	X	X	
Demonstrate	X		X				
Compare		X	X	X	X	X	
Contrast		X	X	X	X	X	
Show parts of a whole	X		X	X		X	
Sequence	X		X	X			
Depict location	X						X

As a reader, you view these graphics carefully in an attempt to see why the author included them. Your goal is to find their main ideas. Your success depends on the information in them and your store of background knowledge. Much like the title, headings, and subheadings of a chapter, the title of a graphic identifies its subject and, thus, the information you need to draw from your background to understand it. Authors usually identify the purpose and subject of untitled graphics in the text. Because you must recognize and evaluate this information for yourself, processing untitled graphics requires higher-level thinking and the ability to draw conclusions.

UNDERSTANDING DIFFERENT TYPES OF TEXT GRAPHICS

A red sports car drove up to our town filling station, stopping a good distance from the pumps. The driver shouted to the attendant, "Which way to the lake?" The attendant called back, "North to 12th Street, make a right and watch for the signs."
Turning to me as the car drove off, he said, "Actually there aren't any signs, but if a guy can't get out of his car, come over and ask you nice, he doesn't deserve any better directions."

SOURCE: Reprinted with permission from the February 1990 Reader's Digest. Copyright © 1990 by The Reader's Digest Assn., Inc. Contributed by Charles Grisham.

People ask for directions for many reasons. Sometimes they lack a map. Other times they have a map but think it's too difficult to read. Maybe you, too, skip or give superficial attention to maps and other text graphics because you think that they require too much time and effort or are unimportant.

Text graphics usually illustrate complex information. Many students conclude that the graphics, too, must be complex—probably too complex to understand. Once you learn how to decipher graphics, you will find that reading them is actually faster and easier than understanding written information. This is because graphics focus attention and provide visual reinforcement. Graphics give authors ways to make abstractions more real.

Understanding graphics helps you learn information in another way. Your brain consists of two halves. One side, the left side, processes text and data in a logical, systematic fashion. The other side, the right side, processes information that has a more artistic, visual nature. Graphics appeal to the right side of your brain. By attending to both text and graphic information, you use both sides of your brain to aid learning and memory.

EXAMINING DIAGRAMS

A dignified old lady, attending a contemporary art exhibition, was caught staring at a painting by its artist. "What *is* it?" she inquired. The artist smiled condescendingly.

"That, my dear woman, is supposed to be a mother and her child."

"Well, then," asked the lady, "why isn't it?"

Often you encounter **diagrams** in text which make you, similar to the woman in the story, wonder "What is it?" That's because diagrams often represent complex concepts. They are designed to help you picture the events, processes, structures, relationships, or sequences described in the text. Both the written description and the visual picture are necessary for your complete understanding. For instance, consider the following description of the visual cliff:

The visual cliff—a tool for studying depth perception—consists of a center board on top of a glass table. On one half of the board, a patterned surface is directly below the glass, whereas on the other half of the board the patterned surface is several feet below the glass table. This gives the illusion of a cliff.

This somewhat confusing description makes it difficult to understand the concept of the visual cliff (unless you are already familiar with it). Now, consider the diagram in Figure 8.1. The precision with which the diagram has been drawn and labeled allows you to better understand the concept of the visual cliff.

FIGURE 8.1   Example of the Use of a Diagram

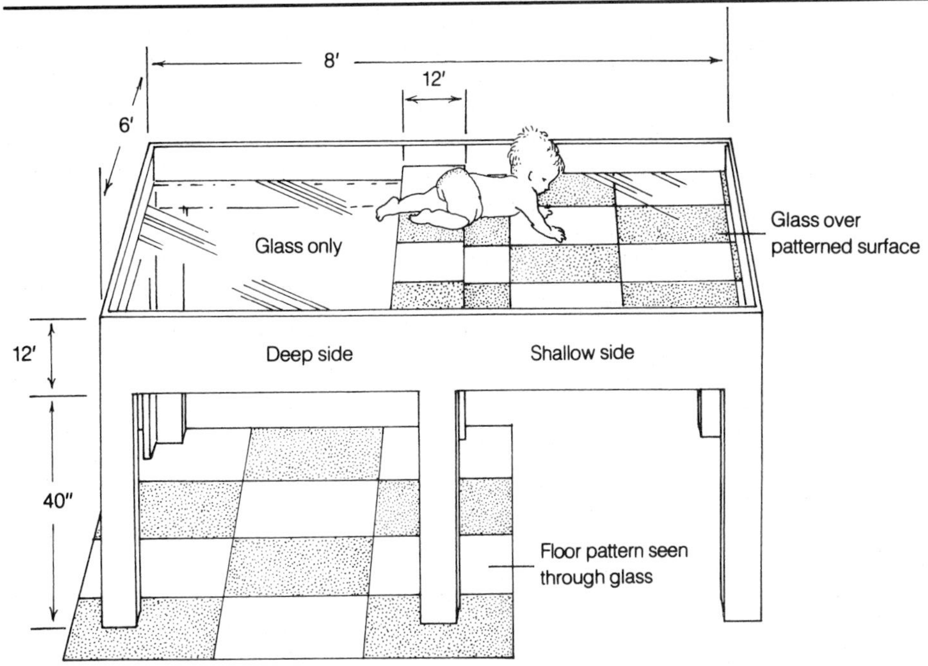

SOURCE: Reprinted with permission from *Introduction to Child Development,* 2d ed., by Dworetzky.
© 1984 by West Publishing Company. All rights reserved.

EXERCISE 8.1   Read the introduction to Sample Chapter 2, "The Planetary Setting" before answering the following questions about Figure 1.3.

1. To the nearest million, what is the approximate number of miles in the earth's orbit?

2. Consider the distance of the earth from the sun at the aphelion and the perihelion. What is ironic about the correlation between distance and time of year?

3. How many solstices are there in a year?

4. How many equinoxes are there in a year?

_____

_____

5. What is the relationship between a solstice and its corresponding aphelion and perihelion?

_____

_____

_____

6. Approximately how much time elapses between an equinox and a solstice?

_____

_____

_____

7. Is the earth's orbit clockwise or counterclockwise? How do you know?

_____

_____

_____

8. What is the shape of the earth's orbit? What is its focus?

_____

_____

9. What percentage is the variation in the earth's distance to the sun?

_____

_____

10. What would be the Greek meaning of *aphelion?*

_____

_____

_____

INTERPRETING CHARTS

Like diagrams, **charts** show information too complex to be easily understood in oral or written forms. Charts condense and simplify information. They also emphasize important points. Common types of charts include **tables, flowcharts,** and **time lines.** Examples of common charts are class schedules and academic calendars.

Tables

Tables indicate relationships among pieces of information. To permit direct comparisons, tables organize information into rows and columns. A row runs horizontally across the page (left to right). A column runs vertically down the page (up to down). Headings or labels identify rows or columns.

A special type of table shows the presence or absence of common features for the items being analyzed (see Figure 8.2). If a feature is possessed by an item, a mark fills the box or space where the item and feature intersect or meet. If the feature is not possessed by that item, the box or space is left blank. This type of table is called a **feature analysis table.** This chart allows you to find details related to the items being compared, infer unstated information, and summarize information.

A second kind of table shows the amount or quality of the items being compared (see Figure 8.3). This table allows you to locate details about each item or feature, infer unstated information, and identify **trends** (directions in which features change). Such a chart is called a **quality table.**

Table 8.2 lists steps in reading both feature analysis and quality tables.

FIGURE 8.2   Example of a Feature Analysis Table

Comparison of Programming Languages

FEATURE	ASSEMBLY LANGUAGE	FORTRAN	COBOL	PL/I	RPG	BASIC	PASCAL	APL
Strong math capabilities	X	X		X		X	X	X
Good character manipulation capabilities	X		X	X		X	X	X
English-like			X	X		X	X	
Available on many computers	X	X	X		X	X	X	
Highly efficient	X							
Standardized		X	X	X		X		
Requires large amount of storage			X	X				X
Good interactive capability						X	X	X
Procedure oriented		X	X	X		X	X	X
Problem oriented					X			
Machine dependent	X							

SOURCE: Reprinted with permission from *Understanding Computers,* by Hopper and Mandell. © 1984, West Publishing Company. All rights reserved.

FIGURE 8.3   Example of a Quality Table

Mean Annual Income by Sex, Race, and Education

Demographic Group	Overall Median Income	YEARS OF SCHOOLING*					
		7 or Less	8	9–11	12	13–15	16 or More
White males	$16,267	$7,004	$8,948	$12,053	$16,622	$18,574	$23,556
Black males	10,109	4,686	6,623	9,172	12,074	13,803	16,811
White females	5,487	3,425	3,820	4,233	5,774	7,342	10,813
Black females	5,338	2,963	3,423	4,282	6,856	8,910	13,767

Note: These figures include the total money income of full-time and part-time workers, ages twenty-five and over, as of March 1981.

*In terms of highest grade completed.

Source: U.S. Department of Commerce, Bureau of the Census, *Money Income of Households, Families, and Persons in the United States: 1980,* Current Population Reports, Series P-60, No. 132 (Washington, D.C.: U.S. Government Printing Office, 1982), pp. 174, 178.

SOURCE: Reprinted with permission from *Sociology,* 2d ed., by Jon M. Shepard. © 1984, West Publishing Company. All rights reserved.

TABLE 8.2   Steps in Reading Tables

1. Read the title. This tells you the subject or general content of the table.

2. Identify the type of table. This helps you determine the kind(s) of information given. A table shows the presence or absence of a feature, or it shows the quantity or quality of a feature.

3. Look at the labels or headings in the table. These tell you what items are being compared and what features are being used to compare them. You need to keep the items and features in mind to recognize when and how the relationships change.

4. Note any general trends.

5. If you are looking at a table as part of a chapter survey, stop your examination of this graphic. Continue previewing the chapter.

6. When you reach the section of the text that refers to the table, identify the purpose before turning to the table. Does the author want you to note specific facts, generalizations, or trends?

7. Turn back to the table. Use the purpose set in the text to look at specific areas of the table.

8. Reread the section of the text that referred to the table. Make sure you understand the points and relationships noted by the author.

EXERCISE 8.2   Read pages 526–531 (167–172) on vitamins and use Table 7.2 in Sample Chapter 3, "Nutrition and Digestion," to answer the questions below.

1. How many vitamins are fat soluble? How many are water soluble? Explain the difference between the two types.

   _____

   _____

   _____

2. Which vitamins are still under intense study?

   _____

   _____

3. Which vitamins are co-enzymes in energy metabolism?

   _____

   _____

   _____

4. Which vitamins are widely distributed in foods?

   _____

   _____

   _____

5. What are the effects of taking too much pantothenic acid and biotin?

   _____

   _____

   _____

6. A patient exhibits upset stomach. What might be the cause?

   _____

   _____

7. You eat a salad of lettuce only. What vitamins are you most likely to get?

   _____

   _____

8. How is vitamin D acquired?

   _____

   _____

   _____

9. Name three countries in which a person would be most likely to be deficient in vitamins. Name three countries in which a person would be most likely to get too many vitamins and have vitamin poisoning.

_____

_____

_____

10. How are vitamins absorbed in the body?

_____

_____

_____

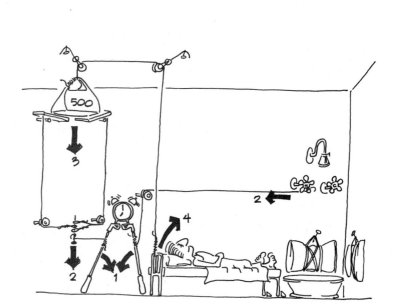

Flowcharts

Flowcharts diagram the sequence of steps in a complex process. Arrows show the route through the procedure. Circles, boxes, or other shapes tell what should be done at each step. Flowcharts also depict ordered associations among elements. In such an arrangement, a ranking of information shows superior, equal, and lesser relationships. Some flowcharts show both sequence and hierarchical relationships. The flowchart in Figure 8.4 indicates the process for advancement in the field of law enforcement and the progressive ranks in law enforcement. Table 8.3 depicts the steps in reading a time line.

FIGURE 8.4   Example of a Flowchart

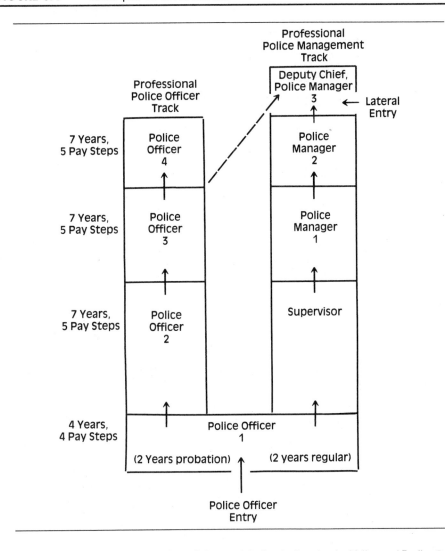

EXERCISE 8.3   Use the flowcharts in Figure 7.1 in Sample Chapter 3, "Nutrition and Digestion," to answer the following questions. Read "Sources of Energy" on pages 523–524 (164–165) before answering.

1. Where is glucose stored in the body?

_____

_____

_____

2. What happens when muscle glucose stores are depleted?

_____

_____

_____

3. Once glucose enters the bloodstream, what are the three ways in which it is used?

_____

_____

_____

4. How do cells use glucose?

_____

_____

_____

5. What foods provide glucose to the body?

_____

_____

_____

6. What is the significance of the arrows that lead and return from the blood to the liver and muscle?

_____

_____

_____

7. How is excess glycogen removed from the body?

_____

_____

_____

8. A football player uses a certain percentage of energy to mow the lawn. How would the percentage for a computer programmer compare for the same activity?

_____

_____

_____

_____

Time Lines

Suppose that a local radio station intends to spotlight musical acts from the fifties, sixties, and seventies—one act per night. Its advertisement of this musical revival is a series of posters, each with a rebus

TABLE 8.3 Steps in Reading a Flowchart

1. Look at the caption to determine the subject of the flowchart.

2. Note the beginning and ending points on the flowchart.

3. Infer trends and/or any breaks in trends by identifying the regularity or irregularity of steps.

4. If you are looking at a flowchart as part of a chapter preview, stop your examination of this graphic. Continue previewing the chapter.

5. When you reach the section of the text that refers to the flowchart, determine the author's purpose before turning to the flowchart. Does the author want to emphasize specific facts, generalizations, or trends?

6. Turn to the flowchart. Use the purpose set by the author to look at specific areas of the chart.

7. Reread the section of the text that referred to the flowchart. Make sure you understand the information noted by the author.

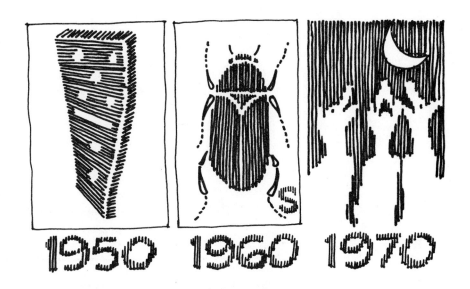

indicating the band that will be featured that night. Because the posters appear in chronological order, they form a sort of time line of music. Can you decipher the rebuses in the cartoon above to determine who has been chosen to perform? (The answers appear on the last page of this chapter.)

A time line is a graphic **chronology** (time-ordered sequence) or outline of important dates or events. It relates these features to the overall time frame in which they occur. Thus, time lines indicate order. A time line, like the one in Figure 8.5, describes the history of a topic or the sequence in which things happen. Table 8.4 lists the steps in reading a time line.

FIGURE 8.5   Example of a Time Line

The Evolution of Life

Number of Years Ago	Evolutionary Advances
3.6 billion	Primitive one-celled organisms that obtained energy through the method of fermentation
3 billion	Sulfur bacteria that used hydrogen sulfide to conduct photosynthesis
	Single-celled organisms able to use water in photosynthesis instead of sulfur. These were the ancestors of the blue-green algae and green plants
2 billion	Oxygen atmosphere
1.6 billion	Bacteria able to use nonsulfur photosynthesis and oxygen in respiration. These bacteria could extract 19 times more energy from food than could the first primitive bacteria
1.3 billion	Cells with nuclei evolved
1 billion	Multicelled organisms. Plant and animal kingdoms divide
500 million	Many marine animals, corals, clams, and fish
300 million	Amphibians, ferns, spiders, insects, and first reptiles (over 800 species of cockroach)
150 million	Dinosaurs and reptiles rule the land, sea, and air
	First birds evolve from smaller dinosaurs
	Modern insects (bees, moths, flies)
70 million	Dinosaurs extinct
	Marsupials and primitive mammals
	Flowering plants
	Deciduous trees
	Giant redwoods
	50 percent of North America under water; Rocky Mountains are formed
50 million	Modern birds
	The early horse (only 1 foot high)
	The ancestors of the cat, dog, elephant, camel, and other mammals
	Seed-bearing plants and small primates
40,000	Modern man

SOURCE: Reprinted from *Introduction to Child Development,* 2d ed., by Dworetzky. © 1984, West Publishing Company. All rights reserved.

TABLE 8.4   Steps in Reading a Time Line

1. Look at the caption to determine what time period is being covered.

2. Note the beginning and ending points on the line.

3. Infer trends and/or any breaks in trends by identifying the regularity or irregularity of events.

4. If you are looking at a time line as part of a chapter preview, stop your examination of this graphic. Continue previewing the chapter.

5. When you reach the section of the text that refers to the time line, determine the author's purpose before turning to the time line. Does the author want to emphasize specific facts, generalizations, or trends?

6. Turn to the time line. Use the purpose set by the author to look at specific areas of the chart.

7. Reread the section of the text that referred to the time line. Make sure you understand the points and relationships noted by the author.

EXERCISE 8.4   Examine the time line below to answer the following questions:

The Technology Race: Generations of Computer Development

PERIOD	CHARACTERISTICS
First Generation 1951–1958	Vacuum tubes for internal operations. Magnetic drums for internal storage. Limited internal storage. Heat and maintenance problems. Punched cards for input and output. Slow input, processing, and output. Low-level symbolic languages for programming.
Second Generation 1959–1964	Transistors for internal operations. Magnetic cores for internal storage. Increased internal storage capacity. Magnetic tapes and disks for external storage. Reductions in size and heat generation. Increase in processing speed and reliability. Increased use of high-level languages.
Third Generation 1965–1970	Integrated circuits on silicon chips for internal operations. Increased internal storage capacity. Compatible systems. Introduction of minicomputers. Emergence of software industry. Reduction in size and cost. Increase in speed and reliability. Operating systems on external storage media.

Fourth Generation	Large-scale integration for internal operations.
1971–Today	Development of the microprocessor.
	Introduction of microcomputers and supercomputers.
	Greater versatility in software.
	Introduction of very-large-scale integration.
	Increase in speed, power, and storage capacity.

SOURCE: Reprinted with permission from *Computers and Information Processing* by Mandell. Copyright © 1989 by West Publishing Company. All rights reserved.

1. Trace the development of internal operations from the first through the fourth generations.

   _____

   _____

   _____

   _____

2. Trace the development of internal storage from the first through the fourth generations.

   _____

   _____

   _____

   _____

3. Which generation spanned the greatest length of time?

   _____

   _____

   _____

   _____

4. Compare languages in the first and second generations.

   _____

   _____

   _____

5. Why are the periods of development called *generations?*

   _____

   _____

   _____

6. How many decades of growth are shown by the time line?

   _____

ANALYZING GRAPHS

Samuel Johnson once said, "Painting can illustrate, but it cannot inform." Graphs both illustrate and inform. They allow large amounts of information to be organized into a more manageable form. **Graphs** show quantitative comparisons between two or more sets of information. By looking at comparable amounts or numbers, you determine relationships. The most common types of graphs are **bar graphs** (or **histograms**), **circle graphs,** and **line graphs.** Table 8.5 lists the steps in analyzing graphs.

Bar Graphs

Bar graphs (see Figure 8.6) compare and contrast quantitative values. They show the amount or quantity of an item. Although the units in which the items are measured must be equal, they can be of any size and can start at any value. If the units are large, the bar graph may show approximate rather than exact amounts.

TABLE 8.5   Steps in Analyzing Graphs

1. Read the title, heading, or caption to identify the general group of objects being compared.

2. Note labels or headings for each item or unit to identify the specific objects being compared or contrasted.

3. Determine the units used to measure the items in a bar or line graph. Identify the number that each symbol represents in a symbol graph.

4. Note any general trends.

5. If you are looking at a graph as part of previewing a chapter, stop your examination of this graphic. Continue previewing the chapter.

6. When you reach the section of the text that refers to the graph, identify the text's purpose before turning to it. Does the author want you to note specific facts, generalizations, or trends?

7. Turn to the graph. Use the purpose set by the author to look at specific areas of the graph.

8. Reread the section of the text that referred to the graph. Make sure you understand the points and relationships noted by the author.

FIGURE 8.6   Example of a Bar Graph

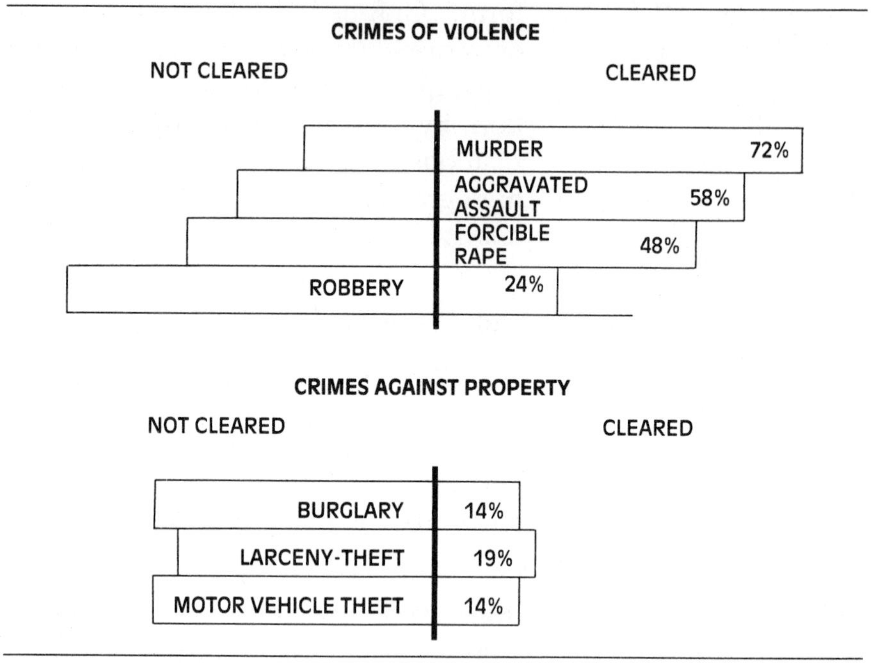

CRIMES OF VIOLENCE

NOT CLEARED   CLEARED

MURDER		72%
AGGRAVATED ASSAULT	58%	
FORCIBLE RAPE	48%	
ROBBERY	24%	

CRIMES AGAINST PROPERTY

NOT CLEARED   CLEARED

BURGLARY	14%
LARCENY-THEFT	19%
MOTOR VEHICLE THEFT	14%

SOURCE: Note: Crimes cleared by arrest, 1981. Data from Federal Bureau of Investigation, Crime in the United States, FBI Uniform Crime Reports [Washington, D.C.: U.S. Government Printing Office,] p. 152. Reprinted with permission from *Crime and Justice in America: A Human Perspective,* by Vetter and Territo. Copyright © 1984 by West Publishing Company. All rights reserved.

EXERCISE 8.5   Answer these questions about the bar graphs that follow.

1. Without reading the caption, define *total engagement* and *caregiving*.

_____

_____

_____

_____

2. Now read the caption and define *total engagement* and *caregiving*. How closely did your definitions resemble the ones used in the caption?

_____

_____

_____

_____

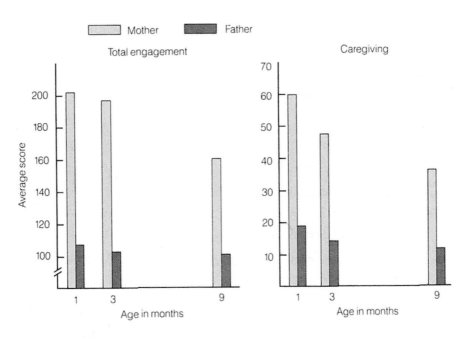

SOURCE: Reprinted with permission of *Introduction to Psychology* by Coon. © 1989 by West Publishing Company.
All rights reserved.

3. After reading the caption, explain what the two graphs indicate.

_____

_____

_____

_____

4. Who tends to spend most time with an infant? Do you find this surprising or not surprising in today's society? Why or why not?

_____

_____

_____

_____

5. What trend occurs in the father's total engagement time as the child grows older? In his caregiving time? What might account for these trends?

_____

_____

_____

_____

6. What trend occurs in the mother's behavior as the child grows older? What might account for this trend?

_____

_____

_____

_____

_____

Line Graphs

Line graphs (see Figure 8.7) show quantitative trends for an item over time. Each line on the graph represents one item. When one or more lines are shown, a **key** or **legend** tells what each line represents. Lines

FIGURE 8.7   Example of a Line Graph

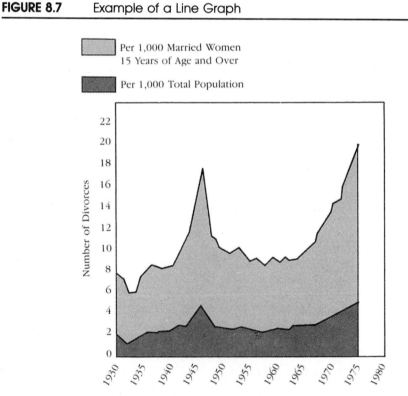

Annual divorce rate for the United States. _Source:_ National Center for Health Statistics, _Advance Report: Final Divorce Statistics, 1975,_ May 19, 1977 (Vol. 26, No. 2, Supplement 2).

show increases, decreases, or no directional changes. Line graphs often are thought to be more accurate than bar graphs because they represent amounts more precisely.

Symbol or **pictorial graphs** (see Figure 8.8) are specialized types of bar graphs. They use **symbols** to show quantitative amounts. A key or legend tells what each symbol represents. You multiply the number of symbols by the value of the symbol to determine totals.

FIGURE 8.8   Example of a Symbol Graph

Estimated retention rates, fifth grade through college graduation: United States 1972 to 1984

For every 100 pupils in the 5th grade in fall 1972

99 entered the 9th grade in fall 1975

89 entered the 11th grade in fall 1978

75 graduated from high school in 1980

46 entered college in fall 1980

23 are likely to earn bachelor's degrees in 1984

= 10 persons

EXERCISE 8.6 Read the passage to answer the questions which follow:

■ Alcohol and the Law

Learn The Law

As of 1988, all fifty states have limited the purchase of alcoholic beverages to people 21 years of age or older. Some state legislatures are considering lowering the drinking age to 19, but pressure is being exerted by the federal government to maintain the 21-year-old limit. In some states, drivers are permitted to drink while driving, whereas in others they are not. Some states have open container laws, which prohibit the possession of an open container of an alcoholic beverage in the passenger compartment of a vehicle even if the driver or passengers have had nothing to drink. There are many places where the possession of an open container on a public street, even by a pedestrian, is illegal. Most states require drivers to have proof of adequate insurance in case of accidents. It is important that you learn the law in your locality.

Drinking and Driving

The leading cause of death for persons in the fifteen- to twenty-four-year-old age group is motor vehicle accidents (see Figure 12–3). Many of us have been to a party where someone has had enough to drink to impair his or her ability to drive. What do we do in such situations? One solution is to choose a designated driver, someone who is willing to not drink at the party, to drive everyone home. Certainly, we would not get into a car as a passenger with someone who has been drinking. Students Against Driving Drunk (SADD) has developed a contract for young people to sign with their parents or friends in which the young person agrees to call the parent or friend if he or she is

FIGURE 12–3 ■ **Drinking and Highway Safety: Odds of a Crash after Drinking.**

SOURCE: National Highway Traffic Safety Administration.

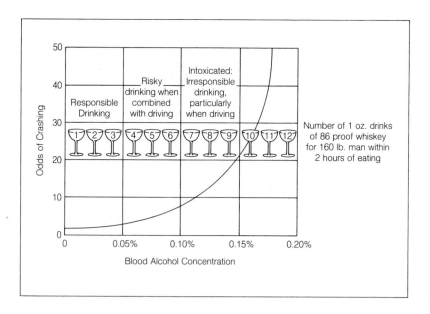

FIGURE 12–4 ■ SADD "Contract for Life"

CONTRACT FOR LIFE

THE COLLEGE CONTRACT FOR LIFE
BETWEEN FRIENDS

As students at _____, we recognize that many of our fellow students and friends choose to use alcoholic beverages and, that on occasion, some students may find themselves in a potential DWI situation.

Therefore, we have entered into a contract in which we agree that if we are ever in a situation where we have had too much to drink, or a friend or date who has had too much to drink, we will seek safe and sober transportation home.

We, the undersigned, also agree that we will provide or arrange safe, sober transportation home for each other should either of us face a situation where we have had too much to drink.

If we cannot find safe transportation, we will contact a taxi service, walk or stay the night.

_____
Signature of 1st Party

_____
Signature of 2nd Party

_____
Date

COPYRIGHT 1987 - All Rights Reserved
This contract may not be duplicated.

S.A.D.D. does not condone drinking by those below the legal drinking age. S.A.D.D. encourages all young people to obey the laws of their state, including laws relating to the legal drinking age.

Distributed by S.A.D.D., "Students Against Driving Drunk"

SADD and the SADD logo are registered with the United States Patent and Trademark Office. All rights reserved by S.A.D.D. — Students Against Driving Drunk, Inc., a Massachusetts non-profit corporation. Trademark registration is pending in other jurisdictions.

SOURCE: Reprinted with permission of Students Against Driving Drunk.   TM 1984

FIGURE 12–5 ■ Tips to Help Avoid "Driving Under the Influence of Alcohol" (DUI)

There is no safe way to drive after drinking. These charts show that a few drinks can make you an unsafe driver. They show that drinking affects your **Blood Alcohol Concentration (BAC)**. The **BAC** zones for various numbers of drinks and time periods are printed in yellow, orange, and red. **How to use these charts:** First, find the chart that includes your weight. For example, if you weigh 160 lbs., use the "150 to 169" chart. Then look under "Total Drinks" at the "2" on this "150 to 169" chart. Now look below the "2" drinks, in the row for 1 hour. You'll see your **BAC** is in the orange shaded zone. This means that if you drive after 2 drinks in 1 hour, you could be arrested. In the orange zone, your chances of having an accident are 5 times higher than if you had no drinks. But, if you had 4 drinks in 1 hour, your **BAC** would be in the red shaded area, and your chances of having an accident, 25 times higher. What's more, it is illegal to drive at this **BAC** (.10% or greater). After 3 drinks in 1 hour, the chart shows you would need 3 more hours, with no more drinks, to reach the yellow **BAC** zone again.

- Set a safe limit in advance and don't go above it.
- Space your drinks, try not to have more than one drink per hour.
- Taper off and STOP DRINKING at least one hour before you drive.
- Eat before and during drinking.
- Don't drink alcohol if you're taking medicine or drugs.

By strictly following these tips, you can greatly lower your chances of being arrested or having an accident.

Remember, coffee can't help, ONLY TIME CAN LOWER YOUR BLOOD ALCOHOL CONCENTRATION (**BAC**). Some drivers can even be under the influence at .03% **BAC**.

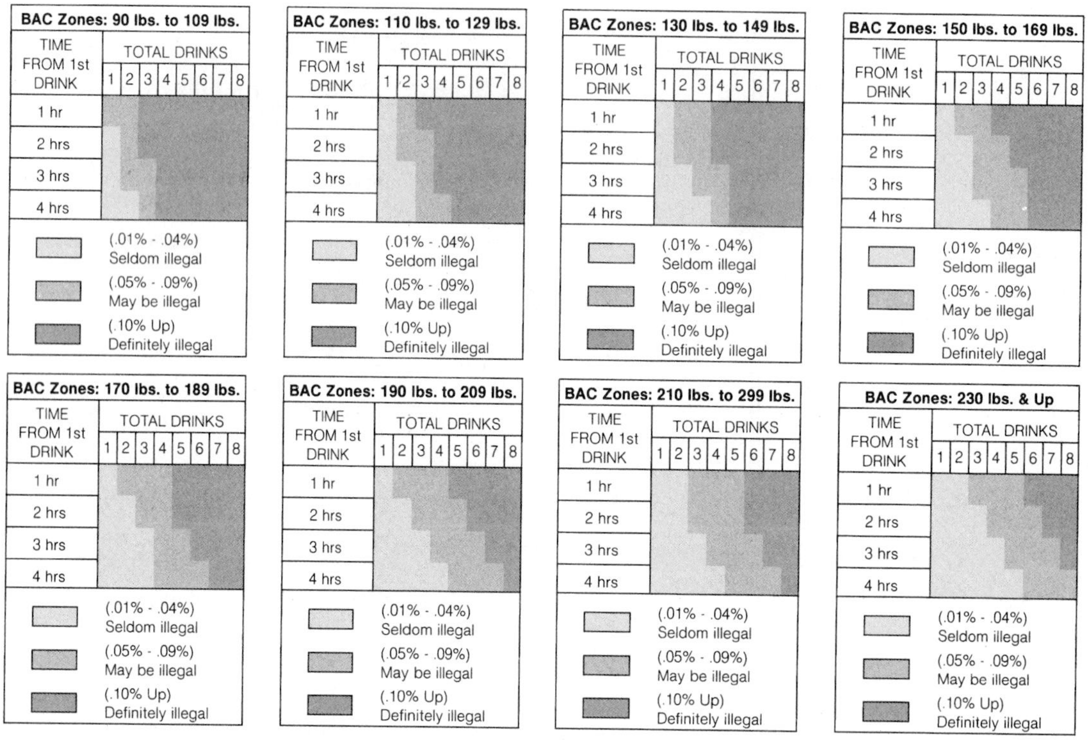

BAC Zones: 90 lbs. to 109 lbs.	BAC Zones: 110 lbs. to 129 lbs.	BAC Zones: 130 lbs. to 149 lbs.	BAC Zones: 150 lbs. to 169 lbs.

BAC Zones: 170 lbs. to 189 lbs.	BAC Zones: 190 lbs. to 209 lbs.	BAC Zones: 210 lbs. to 299 lbs.	BAC Zones: 230 lbs. & Up

Each chart: TIME FROM 1st DRINK (1 hr, 2 hrs, 3 hrs, 4 hrs) / TOTAL DRINKS (1 2 3 4 5 6 7 8). Legend: (.01% – .04%) Seldom illegal; (.05% – .09%) May be illegal; (.10% Up) Definitely illegal.

REMEMBER: "One drink" is a 12-ounce glass of beer, or a 4-ounce glass of wine, or a 1¼-ounce shot of 80-proof liquor (even if it's mixed with non-alcoholic drinks). If you have larger or stronger drinks, or drink on an empty stomach, or if you are tired, sick, upset, or have taken medicines or drugs, you can be unsafe with fewer drinks.

TECHNICAL NOTE: These charts are intended to be guides and are not legal evidence. Although it is possible for anyone to exceed the designated limits, the charts have been constructed so that fewer than 5 persons in 100 will exceed these limits when drinking the stated amounts on an empty stomach. Actual values can vary by body-type, sex, health status, and other factors.

Distributed by the Department of Motor Vehicles and prepared in cooperation with the California Highway Patrol, The Office of Traffic Safety, the Department of Alcohol and Drug Programs and the Department of Justice.

incapable of driving and the parent or friend agrees to pick the young person up and bring him or her home with no questions asked at the time. The college "Contract for Life" is illustrated in Figure 12–4.

The amount of alcohol in a person's bloodstream is expressed as the blood alcohol level (BAL) or blood alcohol concentration (BAC). There is one drop of alcohol per thousand drops of blood for each 0.1 percent increase in BAL. It takes approximately three drinks in a one-hour period to cause a 110-pound person to reach a BAL of 0.1 percent. For a 150-pound person, it would take approximately four drinks, and for a 200-pound person, approximately six drinks (see Table 12–2). The BAL is affected by how much alcohol is consumed, the time that has elapsed since the first drink, the time that has elapsed since the last drink, and the drinker's body weight. The amount of alcohol that is considered to be lethal is a BAL of 0.4 to 0.6.

As the blood alcohol level increases, visual acuity decreases, making it more difficult for the driver to see. Glare recovery time after passing the headlights of an oncoming car increases. Coordination is impaired and reaction time increases, making the driver less able to respond quickly to an emergency. Peripheral or side vision decreases so that the driver may not see things such as a car entering an intersection from the right or left or a child running into the street. Refer to Table 12–2 to see how drinking can affect your driving.

> ■ *PROBLEM SITUATION*   You are at a party with several of your friends. The person you drove with has had too much to drink. He refuses to give you or anyone else the keys to his car and intends to drive home. Since no one else at the party is going in your direction, he is your only way back. What do you do?

The Maryland Institute for Emergency Medical Services in Baltimore reported that 67 percent of all young people treated in its center have been involved in alcohol- or drug-related traffic accidents.

TABLE 12–4 ■ **Years of Potential Life Lost (YPLL) before Age 65 and YPLL Rates from Total and Alcohol-Related Motor Vehicle Traffic (MVT) Fatalities, by Sex—United States, 1987**

MVT Fatalities	YPLL[a]		
	Number	**Percent**	**Rate[b]**
Total[a]	**1,416,806**	**100.0**	**663**
Male	1,027,956	72.6	966
Female	388,780	27.4	363
Alcohol-related[c]	**783,304**	**100.0**	**367**
Male	603,944	77.1	568
Female	179,333	22.9	167
Alcohol intoxication–related[c]	**609,346**	**100.0**	**285**
Male	476,662	78.2	448
Female	132,661	21.8	124

[a]Estimates provided by the Fatal Accident Reporting System. Infants dying before age 1 year were assigned age 0. Total YPLL includes a few persons of unknown sex.

[b]Rate per 100,000 persons under age 65. 1987 population estimates obtained from the Bureau of the Census Current Population Reports.

[c]Blood alcohol concentration of ≥0.01% for alcohol-related and ≥0.10% for alcohol intoxication–related fatalities.

SOURCE: *Morbidity and Mortality Weekly Report* 37 (December 16, 1988).

FIGURE 12–6 ■ **Number of Highway Fatalities by Day of Week, Time of Day, and Alcohol Involvement, 1981.**

SOURCE: *Fifth Special Report to the U.S. Congress on Alcohol and Health, U.S. Department of Health and Human Services, December 1983.*)

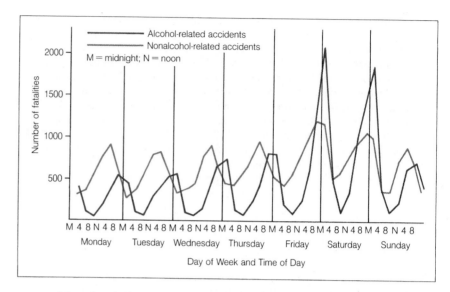

More than half of all highway deaths—approximately 25,000 each year—are related to drinking and driving (See Table 12–4). Although, in most states, it takes a BAL of 0.10 percent for a person to be considered legally drunk, many people are not capable of driving a car with far less alcohol in their bloodstreams. At a BAL of 0.10 percent, a driver is ten times more likely to have an accident than a nondrinker. At a BAL of 0.15 percent, the likelihood of an accident increases by twenty-five times and at 0.20 percent by one hundred times. Most drunk-driving accidents occur at about midnight on weekdays and at about 2 A.M. on Friday and Saturday nights (See Figure 12–6). Beer is the beverage most frequently associated with drinking and driving. Accidents not involving motor vehicles are also significantly higher when alcohol is involved.

1. What is the time span covered in the figure in hours? In days?

_____

_____

_____

2. What is the significance of the time of day and day of week when the incidence of alcohol-related accidents is greatest?

_____

_____

_____

3. Explain the horizontal labels on the graph (M, 4, 8, N, 4, 8).

_____

_____

_____

4. What is confusing about the title and the legend of the figure?

   _____

   _____

   _____

5. What age group is most likely to be involved in motor vehicle accidents?

   _____

   _____

   _____

6. What two solutions does this text offer for the problem of alcohol-related accidents?

   _____

   _____

   _____

7. According to the text, what four physical functions decrease with alcohol use? What is the implication of this to driving?

   _____

   _____

   _____

8. What BAL is considered to mean that one is legally drunk? What level is considered lethal?

   _____

   _____

   _____

Circle Graphs

Probably the most common circle graph resembles something you may have had for lunch today—a pizza. Because circle graphs so closely resemble pies, they often are called pie charts.

A circle graph (see Figure 8.9) represents only one unit. It shows the relationship of parts of one unit to the whole of that unit. Because all of the parts equal the whole unit, or 100 percent of the unit, percentages and/or fractions measure the parts of the graph. Contrasting colors or shading often denote these components in pie-shaped wedges.

FIGURE 8.9   Example of a Circle Graph

Types of Study Habits

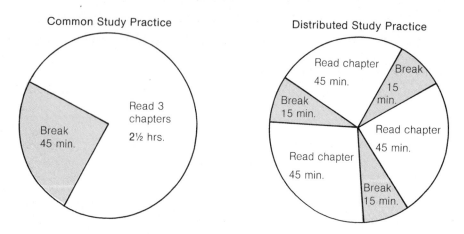

Common Study Practice

Distributed Study Practice

Circle graphs deal with fractions of a whole, instead of units on a continuum. Thus, the steps involved in reading them differ somewhat from those for reading other kinds of graphs. Table 8.6 lists the steps in reading circle graphs.

TABLE 8.6   Steps in Reading Circle Graphs

1. Read the title, heading, or caption. These identify the whole unit whose parts are being shown and compared.

2. Look at the labels for each part of the circle.

3. Identify the general sizes for each of the parts. Note relationships between and among the parts.

4. Note any general trends.

5. If you are looking at a circle graph as part of a chapter preview, stop your examination of this graphic. Continue previewing the chapter.

6. When you reach the section of the text that refers to the graph, identify the text's purpose before turning to the graph. Does the author want you to note specific facts, generalizations, or trends?

7. Turn to the graph. Use the purpose set by the text to look at specific areas of the graph.

8. Reread the section of the text that referred to the graph. Make sure you understand the points and relationships noted by the author.

EXERCISE 8.7   Answer these questions using the circle graphs that follow.

1. What is the title of the graph on the left? On the right? From what source did the information in each originate?

2. In what specialty do most psychologists study? In what specialty does the smallest percentage of psychologists study?

3. In what field do most psychologists work? In what specialty does the smallest percentage of psychologists work?

_____

_____

_____

_____

_____

4. Compare the percentage of psychologists who specialize in school and educational psychology with the percentage of those who work in academic settings. How might you account for the disparity in these figures?

_____

_____

_____

_____

_____

5. Compare the percentage of psychologists who specialize in counseling with the percentage of those who work in private practice. In what other field(s) might psychologists who specialize in counseling work?

_____

_____

_____

_____

_____

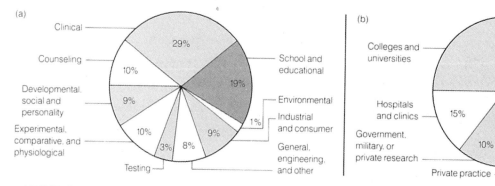

SOURCE: Coon, D., (1989). *Introduction to Psychology.* St. Paul: West, p. 16. (a) Specialties in psychology. Percentages are approximate (from Howard et al., 1986). (b) Where psychologists work (from Pion, 1986).

WRITE TO LEARN

On a separate sheet of paper, use the following information to construct a line graph, a bar graph, and a circle graph.
Students at Northeast College:

Freshmen	350
Sophomores	250
Juniors	200
Seniors	150
TOTAL	950

READING MAPS

"You want to know how to get to the library? Well, first you go past Jones Hall, or is it Smith? Anyway, then you pass three, or maybe four more buildings, turn right, go straight for another two buildings, and turn left. You can't miss it."

If you've ever received directions like these, you probably wished you had a map. **Maps** provide information about places and their characteristics in a two-dimensional format.

Most commonly found in geography or history texts, maps are sometimes found in science, math, or literature texts and recreational reading books. Map-reading skills add to your understanding of the text by giving you visual representations of what's been written. Steps for reading maps appears in Table 8.7.

TABLE 8.7   Steps for Reading Maps

1. Locate and read the title, heading, or caption. This identifies the geographical area represented by the map.

2. Read the key or legend to identify symbols that are used on the map. Check the scale to get an idea of how much area the map covers.

3. If you are looking at a map as part of a chapter preview, stop your examination of the map. Continue previewing the chapter.

4. When you reach the section of the text that refers to the map, identify the text's purpose before turning to the map. What information does the map illustrate?

5. Turn to the map. Use the purpose set by the text to look at specific features of the map.

6. Reread the section of the text that referred to the map. Make inferences about information provided by the map and the text.

Types of Maps

The **general reference map** and the **special purpose map** (also known as a **thematic map**) are the most common types found in texts. The general reference map (see Figure 8.10) gives general geographical information. This includes surface features (rivers, plains, mountains), places and their distances from each other, political data such as boundaries between states or countries, and urban population data. Special purpose or thematic maps (see Figure 8.11) highlight a particular feature of a geographical region. They show variations among other regions with respect to this feature. Such maps include information on scientific data (for example, ocean currents and climate), social or cultural data (people and customs), political data (boundaries, governments), and economic data (expenditures and finances).

FIGURE 8.10   Example of a General Reference Map (Political)

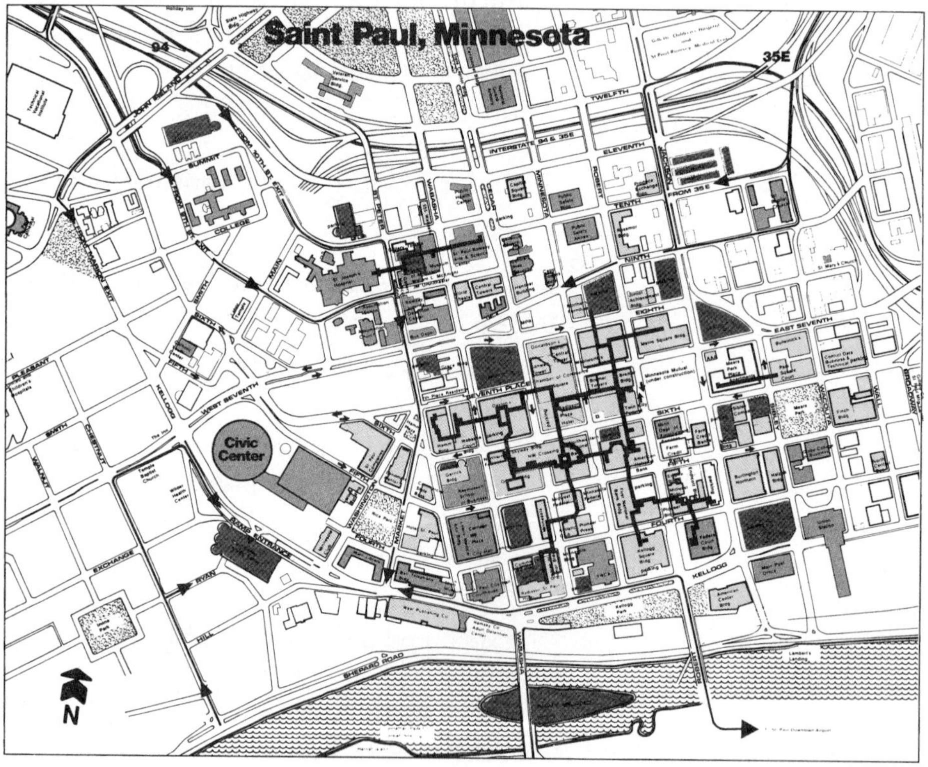

Figure 8-10. The CBD of St. Paul, Minnesota. Note the relatively large percentage of land devoted to public and semi–public buildings as well as to transportation. The map also shows the city's second–level pedestrian–only walkway system.

Commercial buildings

Public & semi public buildings

Parking

SOURCE: © 1979 by the Board of Trustees of the University of Illinois, reprinted by permission of the University of Illinois Press.

FIGURE 8.11   Example of a Special or Thematic Map (Physical)

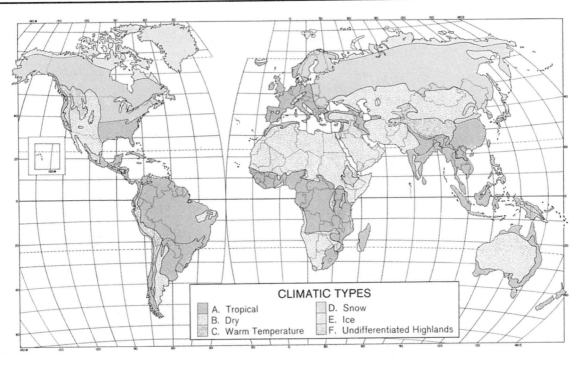

CLIMATIC TYPES

A. Tropical
B. Dry
C. Warm Temperature
D. Snow
E. Ice
F. Undifferentiated Highlands

General reference and thematic maps come in two types: physical—showing the natural features of an area—and political—indicating manmade features of an area. City, state, or national boundaries comprise the only political information found on physical maps. Mountains or major bodies of water (rivers, oceans) comprise the only physical information found on political maps.

Characteristics of Maps

Special characteristics of maps include a **scale of distance**, symbols, and keys or legends. Although while these may seem to add to the complexity of maps, such devices let authors provide vast amounts of information concisely. They also help you recognize the features highlighted by maps and make comparisons among these.

Because it would be unrealistic to make a map the actual size of the area it represents, **cartographers** (mapmakers) draw maps according to a set scale. A scale of distance, found on most maps, shows the relationship between distances on a map and distances in real life. Scales can be shown in the following three ways:

Fraction	1" : 50 miles	
Written Statement	1 inch equals 50 miles	
Graphic Scale	/_____/_____/__/____	
	0 50 100 150	

Symbols, contrasting colors, or shading represent natural or manmade details. Thorough reading of a map depends on a thorough understanding of the ways in which features are represented. This understanding is accomplished with the aid of a key or legend that shows each symbol, color, or shade used on a map and its corresponding explanation. Figure 8.11 shows a key ("Climatic Types") on a thematic map.

WRITE TO LEARN

A friend of yours needs directions from your house to the nearest grocery store. On a separate sheet of paper, provide: 1) written directions and 2) a map (including landmarks, scale of distance, and key). Compare the two. Which provides the clearest instruction? Why? Which type of map did you draw? How is this type different from the other type?

EXERCISE 8.8   Answer these questions using the excerpt and map that follow.

1. Is this map a physical map, a political map, or both? Cite map features that support your response.

   _____

   _____

   _____

2. Provide a written description of the location of the Homestake Formation.

   _____

   _____

   _____

3. Based on conclusions drawn from reading and map study, identify two states that are depicted in the map.

   _____

   _____

   _____

4. Other than the designation "Black Hills," identify four terms from the map that lead you to believe that this is a mountainous region.

_____

_____

5. In kilometers, what is the approximate combined area of the schist and granite regions depicted on the map?

_____

_____

Archean Gold and the Battle of the Little Bighorn

The Black Hills of South Dakota are an eroded domal uplift with a central core of Archean rocks (Fig. 1). A gold rush into the Black Hills began in 1876, and what had been a wilderness was quickly transformed into a major mining center. Events leading to this gold rush began in 1874, when Lieutenant Colonel George Armstrong Custer led an army expedition into the Black Hills, the Holy Wilderness of the Sioux Indians. For three months Custer and the 1,000 soldiers, engineers, and gold miners that accompanied him explored the region, and in his official report Custer said that "gold in satisfactory quantities can be obtained in the Black Hills."

News of gold in the Black Hills spread rapidly. Many people believed that a gold rush would cure the economic problems that resulted in the "Panic of 1873," and soon the U.S. government was besieged with demands by thousands of voters to acquire the Black Hills. According to the treaty of 1868, however, the Black Hills were to forever belong to the Sioux, and they refused to sell their Holy Wilderness. The breakdown of negotiations to purchase the Black Hills led to the Indian War, during which Custer and some 260 of his men were annihilated in June, 1876, at the Battle of the Little Bighorn in Montana. Despite this stunning victory, the Sioux could not sustain a war against the U.S. Army, and in September, 1876, they were forced to relinquish their claim to the Black Hills.

Miners and settlers began entering the Black Hills in early 1876, and by the following year several mining towns were thriving. During the next 50 years more than $230,000,000 worth of gold was recovered. Indeed, large-scale mining still continues today. In fact, the Homestake Mining Company at Lead, South Dakota is one of the largest producers of gold in the Western Hemisphere.

Most of the Black Hills' gold comes from the Homestake Formation, an Archean rock unit composed of iron- and carbonate-rich rocks

FIGURE 1

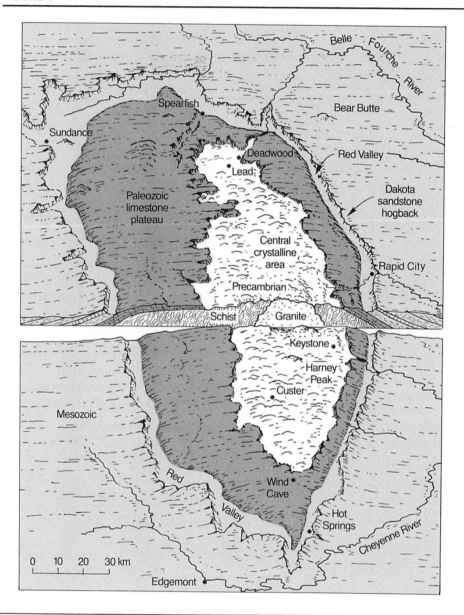

altered to schist by regional metamorphism. The Homestake Formation has been badly deformed, and the gold ores are concentrated along fold axes, especially the axes of synclines. Mining of these ores began at the surface, but now they are being recovered from depths as great as 2.5 km. Huge quantities of rock must be mined and processed, because only about one-third ounce of gold is recovered from each ton of rock. Nevertheless, production since 1953 has been about 600,000 ounces of gold annually.

The time of emplacement of the gold ores in the Homestake Formation was debated for several decades. Some geologists thought it was emplaced during the Tertiary Period when the formation was intruded by rhyolite dikes, while others believed it was emplaced during the Proterozoic when intrusions of large granitic bodies occurred. Detailed geochemical studies seem to have resolved the problem; the ores and rocks of the Homestake Formation formed at the same time by hot spring processes.

However, regional metamorphism later in the Precambrian concentrated the ores along fold axes.

SOURCE: Wicander, Reed, and Monroe, James S. (1989). *Historical Geology: Evolution of the Earth and Life Through Time.* St. Paul: West, pp. 200-202.

EXERCISE 8.9   Use Figure 1.9 and the section on standard time, pages 512–514 (15–17), in Sample Chapter 2, "The Planetary Setting," to answer the following questions.

1. What time zone covers the most states? What time zone covers the fewest?

   _____

   _____

   _____

2. If it is five o'clock in the Eastern time zone, what time is it in California? In Utah? In Missouri?

   _____

   _____

   _____

3. How many time zones are shown on the map? How might having this many time zones affect the business of the nation?

   _____

   _____

   _____

4. How many degrees are shown in a single time zone?

   _____

   _____

   _____

5. How many time zones are on the earth?

_____

_____

_____

6. United States : 7: : former Soviet Union : _____

7. Why do time zone boundaries not correspond directly to meridians?

_____

_____

_____

8. Name three states that span two time zones.

_____

_____

_____

9. How do you think the names of the time zones originated?

_____

_____

_____

10. What is the basis of all time zones?

_____

_____

_____

TAKING NOTES FROM TEXT GRAPHICS

You process graphic information to your brain through an overt action—writing. Taking notes from text graphics involves six steps. First, you decide why you think the author included this graphic. Because publishers pay illustrators or others for permission to print graphics, if it's there, it's there for a reason. Second, you identify important details or features of the graphic. From these, you determine the graphic's main idea. In other words, you summarize the information the graphic includes. Then you note your summary in the margin beside the graphic. The fourth step is to draw conclusions about the importance of the graphic to your overall understanding. Next, you check your understanding of the graphic with information presented in the text or emphasized in class. Sixth, you record in your notes where important text graphics are located.

GROUP LEARNING ACTIVITY
A Picture or 1,000 Words

Consider again the job of cartographers. They observe, plot, survey, photograph, and otherwise describe the locations of places by measuring distances, directions, and elevations. The maps they draw contain lines, words, symbols, and colors that describe new places to us or help us move from place to place.

The following activity provides you with the opportunity to create a map and interpret both written and graphic information.

Application

Step one: Create a map of a mythical country. Include information about the size and shape of the country; number and location of large cities; descriptions of natural formations; and names, sizes, and shapes of border countries and their locations. Select your own symbols for major highways, cities, natural formations, and so forth.

Step two: Pass your map to the person on your left and take the map from the person on your right. Write a one- to two-paragraph description of the mythical country based on this map.

Step three: Give this description to the person on your left and take the description from the person on your right. Now draw a map of the country that that person has described.

Step four: Return the maps and accompanying description to the original owner. Provide time for each person to compare his or her map with the corresponding description and map.

Step five: Discuss as a group how people interpret written and graphic material.

SUMMARY OF MAIN POINTS

1. Variations in the way graphics are interpreted depend on learner characteristics and the purpose set by the person who selects the graphic.

2. Visual literacy is essential for processing graphics.

3. Text graphics include diagrams, charts (tables, flowcharts, and time lines), graphs (bar, line, and circle), and maps (general reference and special purpose). Purposes of text graphics include explanation, clarification, organization, and illustration.

4. Note taking from text graphics requires different strategies than note taking from lecture media.

VOCABULARY DEVELOPMENT
RIGHT-BRAIN NOTE CARDS: PICTURE THIS!

Think of your instructor for this course. Did you think of a name or a face? Authors know that verbal and visual information impacts learning and memory differently. A combination of text and graphic information provides you with stimuli for both kinds of understanding. Similarly, vocabulary development can be enhanced through the use of visual as well as verbal information.

One picture is worth ten thousand words.
—FREDERICK R. BARNARD

In many ways, Barnard's view of pictures has been scientifically validated. In the 1960s Roger Sperry conducted research with epileptics. He theorized that if he surgically split their brains, their seizures would be more manageable because they would be confined to only one half of the brain. In effect, these individuals then had two separate brains. Sperry found that in most cases, lack of communication between the halves did not have any effect because both sides of the brain received the same information. However, he did find striking differences when he controlled the way the information was presented.

Prior to Sperry's research, science had already discovered that the right side of the brain controlled the left side of the body and vice versa. Thus, a stroke or other damage on he left side of the brain produced paralysis on the right side of the body. Sperry also found functional differences between the two halves. He found the left half focused on analysis, sequencing, and verbal expression. The right half was more visual and spatial in nature, focusing on patterns and on the whole, rather than the part.

Wittrock (1977) put Sperry's findings to work in a study of memory and learning. He found that students remembered vocabulary words better when they drew pictures to represent them than when they read and wrote the words and the definitions. Tracing a picture of a definition resulted in better recall than writing the definition. Creating a personal visual image for the word proved to be more effective than tracing.

The work of Sperry and Wittrock has clear implications for college vocabulary development. Pictures capture the attention of the right brain. The left brain focuses on the words. Like text graphics, pictures impact your brain, your learning, and your memory differently than do words alone. Using both sides of the brain—instead of relying only on the left side—increases your potential for learning. While your pictures may not be worth ten thousand words, they will help you picture—and learn—the words you need.

FIGURE 1   Example from Sample Chapter 3, "Nutrition and Digestion"

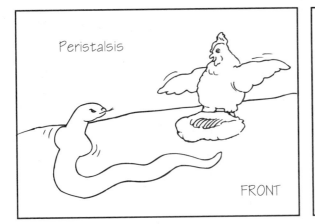

Use the following suggestions and Figure 1 to picture words with note cards that appeal to the right brain.

1. Write the word on the front of the card.

2. On the front of the card, draw a picture that represents its meaning. Form personal associations. Use humorous or outrageous images. Use common symbols.

3. Write the word's meaning on the back of the card.

4. Use the front of the card for recall. If you cannot recall the meaning, look at your drawing. Try to remember why you drew what you did. If you still cannot recall the meaning, refer to the definition.

Activity

Choose five of the following terms from Sample Chapter 3, "Nutrition and Digestion"and create a right-brain note card for them.

macronutrients	lipids
polysaccharide	glycogen
diverticulitis	vagus nerve
micronutrients	amylase
micronutrients	trypsin
ribonuclease	gastrin
trypsinogen	secretin
cholecystokinin	

CHAPTER REVIEW

Answer briefly but completely.

1. Understanding graphs depends on an interaction between what two sources?

   _____

   _____

   _____

2. Design a flowchart for how to study for an exam.

   _____

   _____

   _____

3. Select a graphic of your choice and use it to demonstrate a feature of your class (the number of males to females, the number of people who wear glasses to those who don't, or so on).

   _____

   _____

   _____

4. What is a time line?

   _____

   _____

   _____

5. Examine Table 8.1. Which graphic is most versatile? Least versatile? Why is this so?

   _____

   _____

   _____

6. What is the difference between general reference and special purpose maps? Contrast physical and political maps.

   _____

   _____

   _____

7. Complete the following analogy: left brain : written information :: right brain : _____ .

   _____

8. Examine Figure 8.3. List three trends you observe from its data.

_____

_____

_____

_____

9. What is the purpose of keys or legends in reading graphs or maps?

_____

_____

_____

10. Identify and define two types of tables.

_____

_____

REFERENCE

Wittrock, M. C. (1977). "The generative processes of memory." In M. C. Wittrock, ed., _The Human Brain_. Englewood Cliffs, N.J.: Prentice-Hall.

KEY

The singers and/or groups in the time line are Fats Domino, the Beatles, and Three Dog Night.

CHAPTER

9

Making Your Way through the Maze: Library and Research Skills

SOMEONE TO ASSIST YOU: THE LIBRARIAN

A THREAD TO GUIDE YOU: LIBRARY ORGANIZATION

The Card Catalog

The Computerized Card Catalog

Systems of Organization

Searching for Authors and/or Titles

Conducting a Keyword Search

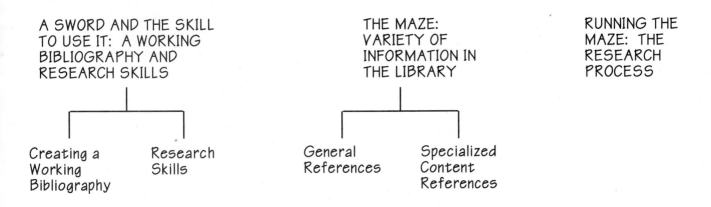

A SWORD AND THE SKILL
TO USE IT: A WORKING
BIBLIOGRAPHY AND
RESEARCH SKILLS

Creating a
Working
Bibliography

Research
Skills

THE MAZE:
VARIETY OF
INFORMATION IN
THE LIBRARY

General
References

Specialized
Content
References

RUNNING THE
MAZE: THE
RESEARCH
PROCESS

TERMS

almanacs
atlas
antonyms
author card
call number
card catalog
clipping file
cross-references
data base
derivations
Dewey decimal system
direct quote
ellipsis
entry
etymology
fiction
gazetteer
government
   documents
guide words
interlibrary loan
Library of Congress (LC)
system
main entry card
microfiche
microfiche reader
microforms
newspaper index
nonfiction
paraphrase
periodical indices
ready reference
reserve books
scan
skim
stacks
subject card
summary
synonyms
thesaurus
title card
unabridged dictionary
vertical file
working bibliography
yearbooks

A Greek myth tells how the Minotaur, a creature with a man's body and a bull's head, was imprisoned in a maze by King Minos of Crete. The Minotaur, the strongest creature of the time, was fed seven young men and seven young women each year. A young prince named Theseus posed as one of the young men so he could kill the Minotaur. He took with him a sword given to him by his father. He also carried a ball of thread given to him by Ariadne, daughter of Minos. He used the thread to help him mark his way. After a systematic search, he found the Minotaur and killed it with his sword. Then, using the thread as a guide, he returned to freedom.

If you have ever spent time trying to find information in a library, you know how Theseus felt. You, too, were trapped in a maze, facing what seemed to be dead ends. You needed what Theseus had—someone to assist you, a thread to help you find information and guide you through a library's maze of materials, and a sword and the skill to use it.

SOMEONE TO ASSIST YOU: THE LIBRARIAN

If you are confused by a library's maze of information, you need the assistance of someone like Ariadne to help you find your way in the library. That person is the librarian or librarian assistant.

A librarian or a librarian assistant is one of the most helpful people you can know on campus. Asking politely for assistance and remembering to thank the librarian for help pay off. The librarian knows what sources of information and services the library offers. The librarian can direct you to ones you may overlook. Often a librarian who knows you personally is willing to find information in response to a phone call from you. This saves you time and a trip to the library. Librarians also know about materials and services of other

libraries. Often they can help you secure materials from them through an **interlibrary loan.**

The librarian spent years learning about a wide variety of reference materials. Trained to aid students who are looking for specific information, the librarian is much more than a clerical person who keeps up with the library's inventory. The librarian is more like a travel agent who guides you in your library search. Perhaps the most valuable travel advice the librarian has to offer is the way your campus library is organized.

EXERCISE 9.1   Provide the following information about your campus library:

1. Library's hours.

2. Policy on overdue books.

3. Five books found in the ready reference section.

4. The names of three indices.

5. The names of three computerized indices.

6. The location of current and bound periodicals.

7. Available media services.

_____

_____

_____

8. The location of a map of the library holdings.

_____

_____

_____

9. The location of the card catalog or computerized card catalog.

_____

_____

_____

10. The name of your librarian.

_____

_____

_____

11. The location of the microfiche reader.

_____

_____

_____

12. The location of general collection books.

_____

_____

_____

A THREAD TO GUIDE YOU: LIBRARY ORGANIZATION

The thread that marks your way through the maze of library information is the **card catalog.** It is organized by either the **Library of Congress (LC)** or the **Dewey decimal** system. Libraries create and use variations of the card catalog and these classification systems. That's not a problem for you, however. You need only know the general framework of the system your library uses. The card catalog provides an organized inventory of the library's information to help you locate what you need quickly and easily. Such inventories are stored either in files or in a computerized **data base.** Because the catalog is crucial to finding materials, libraries usually place the files or computer terminals in the front or center of the library.

THE CARD CATALOG

Catalogs kept in files require you to manually search for information. Sets of drawers contain cards, at least one for each book in the library. Drawers are labeled on the outside, much like encyclopedias, to tell you what they contain. Cards, filed alphabetically, help you find what you need. Three cards for each **nonfiction** publication in the library are made before the book is shelved: the **author card** or **main entry card,** the **subject card,** and the **title card.** The catalog usually contains only title and author cards for **fiction.**

Each card provides information about the author, publisher, contents, and **call number** of the book. Each type of card gives this information in a different order (see Figure 9.1). Author information includes the author's name (last name first) followed by the dates of the author's birth and death. Publishing facts tell who published the book and when and where it was published. Content information consists of the number of pages, if there are maps and illustrations, a brief description of the contents, and **cross-references** (related sources of information). The call number, formed from either the Dewey decimal or the Library of Congress system, reflects content, author's name, and publication date. It is found in the upper left corner of each catalog card and on the spine or cover of each publication. The call number not only indicates where the material is kept in the library but also identifies how your library is organized.

To save space, some libraries store their card listings on **microfiche.** Microfiche, one of many types of **microforms,** is a piece of photographic film usually four-by-six inches. Such film is kept in files similar to those containing cards. However, one piece of film actually holds dozens of cards, greatly reduced in size. To read it, you enlarge the print with a machine called a **microfiche reader.** Like other microforms, a microfiche card catalog saves space, is cheaper to produce, and can be updated quickly.

THE COMPUTERIZED CARD CATALOG

In many libraries, the card catalog has been replaced either partially or entirely by an on-line catalog accessible through a computer terminal.

FIGURE 9.1   Example of Author, Subject, and Title Cards

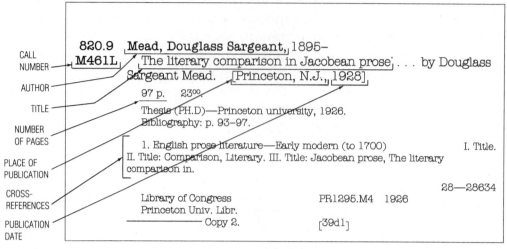

Author Card

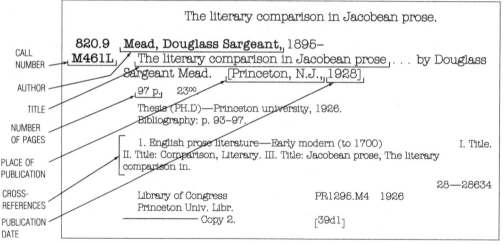

Title Card

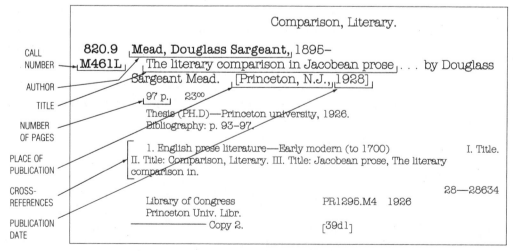

Subject Card

A computerized card catalog allows you to find information more quickly because the computer does the work for you. It searches all entries for the author, subject, or title you need. Sometimes such a system uses specialized subject headings. A list of these is kept in a manual near the computer terminal. Some libraries develop their own catalog systems, but many others alter ready-made software to fit their collections. The examples in this text are from NOTIS, a widely used system developed at Northwestern University.

The features and commands for differing on-line systems vary. The commands are the symbols and/or terms that are used to access information (see Figure 9.2). Figures 9.3 through 9.8 show how to access information from the NOTIS system.

Searching for Authors and/or Titles

Although you don't have to be a computer whiz to use a computerized data base, exact spelling is essential. While some data bases allow you to abbreviate or omit words or parts of words, you need to follow standardized rules for doing so. Table 9.1 supplies some of those rules.

Conducting a Keyword Search

A keyword search is different from searching for a specific author or title. You perform a keyword search for one of two reasons. First, you use one when you have incomplete or uncertain information about an author or title. Second, you perform a keyword search when you are unsure of the correct subject heading or when the most appropriate subject heading is not included in the data base.

Keyword searches are executed the same way as title, author, and subject searches. When the search is completed, what you have is every record in the data base that contains the key word. Figure 9.9 shows a partial listing of what you might get if you typed the command "k = dog." Because keyword searches retrieve so much information, it is important that you carefully select your key words. Doing so limits the number of entries you must read to find the information you seek. Table 9.2 provides you with some suggestions for limiting your keyword search.

FIGURE 9.2   Commands for Retrieving Information Using NOTIS

Author search	a = author's name; last name first
Title search	t = exact title of the publication; ignore *a*, *an*, and *the* if they are the first word in a title
Subject search	s = appropriate subject heading
Keyword search	k = important ideas or concepts

FIGURE 9.3   Introductory Screen

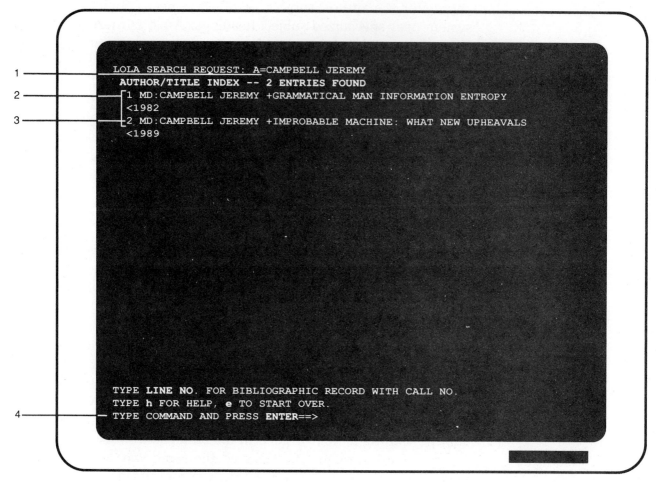

```
LOLA SEARCH REQUEST: A=CAMPBELL JEREMY
 AUTHOR/TITLE INDEX -- 2 ENTRIES FOUND
1 MD:CAMPBELL JEREMY +GRAMMATICAL MAN INFORMATION ENTROPY
 <1982
2 MD:CAMPBELL JEREMY +IMPROBABLE MACHINE: WHAT NEW UPHEAVALS
 <1989




TYPE LINE NO. FOR BIBLIOGRAPHIC RECORD WITH CALL NO.
TYPE h FOR HELP, e TO START OVER.
TYPE COMMAND AND PRESS ENTER==>
```

1. Acronym used for Library On-Line Access.
2. Introductory information provides general data about the system. Since this is necessarily brief, libraries often provide more comprehensive written instructions.
3. List the kinds of searches available on the system and the commands needed to find materials by author, title, subject or keyword.
4. Information needed to access the database.

1. Figures 5.18–5.34 are screen reproductions from the NOTIS System currently being used in the Louisiana State University Libraries. (Copyright 1990 by NOTIS Systems, Inc. Material reproduced by permission of the copyright holder and the Louisiana State University Libraries.)

SOURCE: The figures 9.3, 9.4, 9.5, 9.6, 9.7 and 9.8 are reprinted with permission from Bolner, et. al.; *Library Research Skills Handbook.* Copyright © 1990 by Kendall/Hunt Publishing Company. Used with permission.

FIGURE 9.4   Author and Title Index Screen

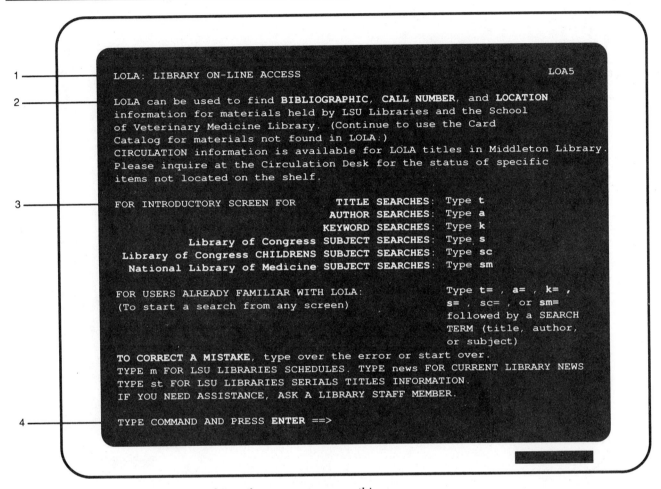

1 ——
2 ——

3 ——

4 ——

```
LOLA: LIBRARY ON-LINE ACCESS                                        LOA5

LOLA can be used to find BIBLIOGRAPHIC, CALL NUMBER, and LOCATION
information for materials held by LSU Libraries and the School
of Veterinary Medicine Library. (Continue to use the Card
Catalog for materials not found in LOLA.)
CIRCULATION information is available for LOLA titles in Middleton Library.
Please inquire at the Circulation Desk for the status of specific
items not located on the shelf.

FOR INTRODUCTORY SCREEN FOR          TITLE SEARCHES: Type t
                                    AUTHOR SEARCHES: Type a
                                   KEYWORD SEARCHES: Type k
            Library of Congress SUBJECT SEARCHES: Type s
  Library of Congress CHILDRENS SUBJECT SEARCHES: Type sc
   National Library of Medicine SUBJECT SEARCHES: Type sm

FOR USERS ALREADY FAMILIAR WITH LOLA:              Type t= , a= , k= ,
(To start a search from any screen)                s= , sc= , or sm=
                                                   followed by a SEARCH
                                                   TERM (title, author,
                                                   or subject)
TO CORRECT A MISTAKE, type over the error or start over.
TYPE m FOR LSU LIBRARIES SCHEDULES. TYPE news FOR CURRENT LIBRARY NEWS
TYPE st FOR LSU LIBRARIES SERIALS TITLES INFORMATION.
IF YOU NEED ASSISTANCE, ASK A LIBRARY STAFF MEMBER.

TYPE COMMAND AND PRESS ENTER ==>
```

1. Command entered into the system to access this screen.
2. Numbers 1–2. List of book titles available in the database under the author's name.
3. Number entered to access the complete bibliographic record for the book, *The Improbable Machine* by Jeremy Campbell.
4. Instructions needed to enter the database.

WRITE TO LEARN

A friend of yours is not in this class but is taking a course in which he must write a term paper. On a separate sheet of paper, explain to him how to use a card catalog or a computerized data base, whichever your college library has.

FIGURE 9.5   Author or Main Entry Bibliographic Record Screen

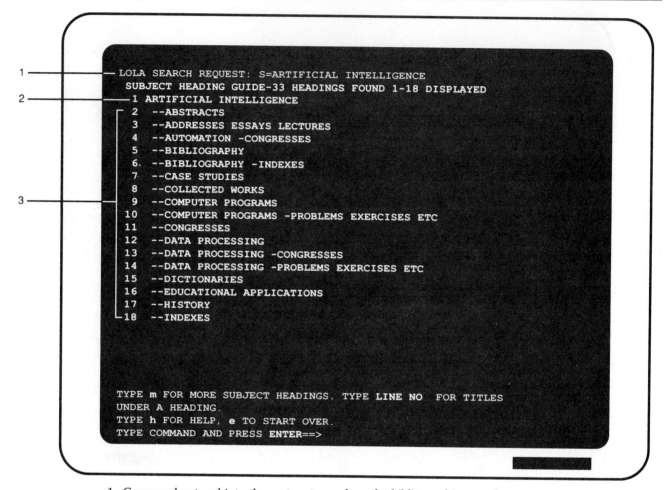

1. Command entered into the system to produce the bibliographic record.
2. Author of the book.
3. Title of the book. This includes both the short title and subtitle.
4. Place of publication.
5. Publisher and copyright date.
6. Physical description. The book has 334 pages and is 23 cm. tall.
7. Book includes bibliographical references.
8. Subject headings under which this book and ones like it can be found.
9. Book is located in the Middleton Library.
10. Call number of the book.
11. Circulation information. Book checked out to user/due date.
12. Type "i" to go back to the author/title index screen (Figure 9.4).
13. Type "e" to go back to the introductory screen (Figure 9.3).
14. Type "h" to access the help screen. Help screens provide useful information for interpreting the system.
15. Type next command and press ENTER to access the system for another record.

FIGURE 9.6   Subject Heading Guide Screen

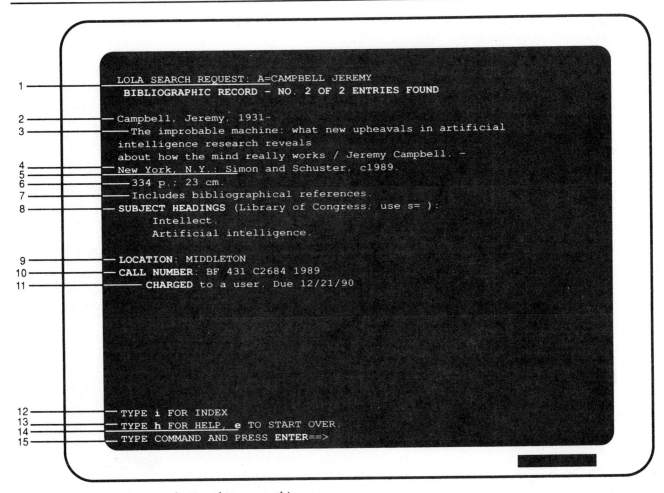

1. Command entered to access this screen.
2. Number entered to go to the subject/index screen.
3. Possible subheads available under this subject.

FIGURE 9.7   Subject and Title Index Screen

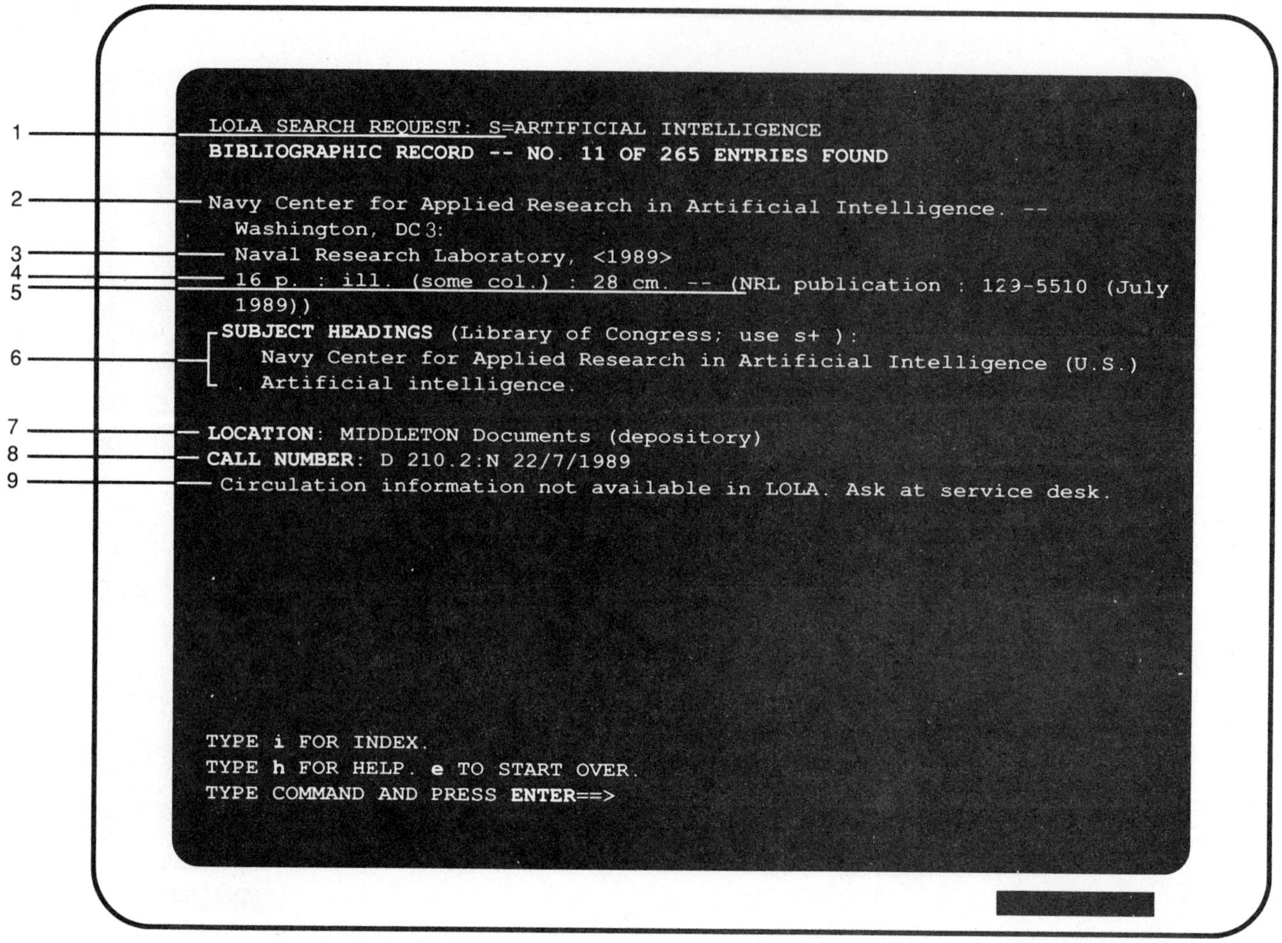

```
LOLA SEARCH REQUEST: S=ARTIFICIAL INTELLIGENCE
BIBLIOGRAPHIC RECORD -- NO. 11 OF 265 ENTRIES FOUND

Navy Center for Applied Research in Artificial Intelligence. --
   Washington, DC 3:
Naval Research Laboratory, <1989>
16 p. : ill. (some col.) : 28 cm. -- (NRL publication : 129-5510 (July
   1989))
SUBJECT HEADINGS (Library of Congress; use s+ ):
   Navy Center for Applied Research in Artificial Intelligence (U.S.)
   . Artificial intelligence.

LOCATION: MIDDLETON Documents (depository)
CALL NUMBER: D 210.2:N 22/7/1989
Circulation information not available in LOLA. Ask at service desk.




TYPE i FOR INDEX.
TYPE h FOR HELP. e TO START OVER.
TYPE COMMAND AND PRESS ENTER==>
```

1. Number 1 entered to go from subject heading guide (Figure 9.6) to the subject/title index (Figure 9.7)
2. Number 7 selected to go to the bibliographic record screen (Figure 9.5)
3. Number 11 selected to go to the bibliographic record screen (Figure 9.8)
4. Example of a reference to a government publication. Call number is a SuDocs number. GP, dodd indicates that the book is in the documents collection.
5. Both MD and midl indicate that book is in the Middleton Library.

FIGURE 9.8   Bibliographic Record for a Government Publication

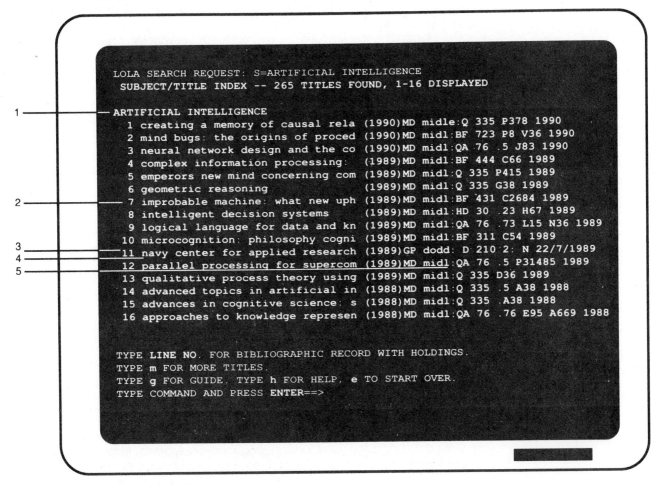

```
LOLA SEARCH REQUEST: S=ARTIFICIAL INTELLIGENCE
  SUBJECT/TITLE INDEX -- 265 TITLES FOUND, 1-16 DISPLAYED

ARTIFICIAL INTELLIGENCE
   1 creating a memory of causal rela (1990)MD midle:Q 335 P378 1990
   2 mind bugs: the origins of proced (1990)MD midl:BF 723 P8 V36 1990
   3 neural network design and the co (1990)MD midl:QA 76 .5 J83 1990
   4 complex information processing:  (1989)MD midl:BF 444 C66 1989
   5 emperors new mind concerning com (1989)MD midl:Q 335 P415 1989
   6 geometric reasoning              (1989)MD midl:Q 335 G38 1989
   7 improbable machine: what new uph (1989)MD midl:BF 431 C2684 1989
   8 intelligent decision systems     (1989)MD midl:HD 30 .23 H67 1989
   9 logical language for data and kn (1989)MD midl:QA 76 .73 L15 N36 1989
  10 microcognition: philosophy cogni (1989)MD midl:BF 311 C54 1989
  11 navy center for applied research (1989)GP dodd: D 210 2: N 22/7/1989
  12 parallel processing for supercom (1989)MD midl:QA 76 .5 P31485 1989
  13 qualitative process theory using (1989)MD midl:Q 335 D36 1989
  14 advanced topics in artificial in (1988)MD midl:Q 335 .5 A38 1988
  15 advances in cognitive science: s (1988)MD midl:Q 335 .A38 1988
  16 approaches to knowledge represen (1988)MD midl:QA 76 .76 E95 A669 1988


TYPE LINE NO. FOR BIBLIOGRAPHIC RECORD WITH HOLDINGS.
TYPE m FOR MORE TITLES.
TYPE g FOR GUIDE. TYPE h FOR HELP, e TO START OVER.
TYPE COMMAND AND PRESS ENTER==>
```

1. Subject heading.
2. Title of publication.
3. Place of publication publisher, and publication date.
4. Physical description. Publication has 16 pages; illustrated, some in color; 28 centimeters tall.
5. Part of the NRL publication series.
6. Subject headings under which book can be found. Note that Navy Center for Applied . . . is an added entry for a subject corporate name.
7. Located in Middleton Library Documents department. Library is a depository for U.S. Government publications.
8. SuDocs call number for book.
9. Circulation information not available.

TABLE 9.1   Rules for Abbreviating Reference Titles

- Abbreviate from right to left. For example, *Dictionary of Recreational Education* becomes *Dictionary of Recreational Ed.*
- Use standard abbreviations, for example, Psyc psychology and *J* for journal.
- Omit *a*, *an*, and *the* (and foreign language equivalents) from titles and begin the search command with the first word that follows the article.
- Enter initials, acronyms, abbreviations, numbers, and dates exactly as they appear in the title. For example, if you are looking for the book *100 Ways to Manage Time Better*, type *100 Ways to Manage Time Better*, not *One Hundred Ways to Manage Time Better.*
- Type two dashes between the primary subject heading and all subdivisions.
- To avoid confusion and save time in searches, avoid using common last names without first names or initials.

FIGURE 9.9   Partial Listing for "k = dog"

- Titles: *Dog Days of Summer*
- Authors: Dog, Ima
- Subjects: Dogs—greyhounds
- Publishers: International Dog Owners Association, Inc.

TABLE 9.2   Suggestions for Limiting Your Keyword Search

- Omit *a*, *an*, and *the* (and foreign language equivalents) from titles and begin the search command with the first word that follows the article.
- Avoid common words such as *and, by, from, for, in, not, of, or, same, to,* and *with.* These words are so common the computer cannot search for them and may actually stop the search.
- Avoid broad, general words such as *geography* and *music.*

EXERCISE 9.2   Answer briefly.

1. Which of the following books are in your library? List call numbers and dates of publication for each one.
   The Chinese Welfare System—John E. Dixon

   _____

   Early American Furniture—Morton Yamon

   _____

   Challenges in Mental Retardation—Geimar Dybward

   _____

Law and the Jungle—Harvey Ellsworth Newbranch

_____

A General Income Tax Analyzer—John Bossons

_____

2. Who wrote *One Man's America?*

_____

3. List the call numbers of each of the following subjects: architecture, music, education, computer science, and psychology.

_____

_____

_____

4. How many books does your library hold under the listing "pineapple"? What types of books (that is, fiction, nonfiction, reference, and so on) are included under this listing?

_____

_____

_____

5. List three books that your library has on nuclear energy.

_____

_____

_____

6. List three periodicals that are found on microfiche or microfilm in your library.

_____

_____

_____

7. Photocopy the title page from one article found on microfiche or microfilm.

8. Do your library holdings include ERIC documents? If so, what are they used for?

_____

_____

9. On separate sheets of paper, copy one author, one title, and one subject card and label their parts.

10. Identify three daily newspapers to which your library subscribes.

_____

_____

_____

SYSTEMS OF ORGANIZATION

Libraries use the Library of Congress and/or the Dewey decimal systems to organize nonfiction materials. The numbers in these systems form the call number of the material and indicate where the material is shelved.

Many large research and university libraries use the LC system. Its advantages over the Dewey decimal system include its precision and capability for expansion. A combination of capital letters and numbers classify and identify books. The first letter indicates the general topic (see Table 9.3). The second letter represents a subject of that topic. The numbers further specify the subject. A second line identifies the book's author and edition.

Some libraries use an older but just as effective system of classifying materials called the Dewey decimal system. This method classifies materials into ten major categories (see Table 9.3). Its call numbers also are written in two lines. The top line is the Dewey decimal classification number (three digits with decimals indicating more specific classifications). The bottom line identifies the book's author and edition.

TABLE 9.3   Comparison of the Dewey Decimal and Library of Congress Systems

Subject	Dewey Decimal	Library of Congress
General works	000	A
Philosophy and psychology	100	B
Religion	200	BL-BX
History	900	C-E
Geography	910	G
Social science	300	H
Political science	320, 350	J
Law	340	K
Education	370	L
Music	780	M
Fine arts	700	N
Language	400	P
Literature	800	P
Pure science	500	Q
Medicine	610	R
Agriculture	630	S
Applied science and technology	600	T
Military science	355	U
Naval science	359	V
Bibliography	010	Z

A SWORD AND THE SKILL TO USE IT: A WORKING BIBLIOGRAPHY AND RESEARCH SKILLS

To reach his goal of killing the Minotaur, Theseus needed a weapon and the skill to use it. In meeting your goal of finding information within the library, you also need a weapon—a **working bibliography**—and the skill to use it—research skills.

CREATING A WORKING BIBLIOGRAPHY

A working bibliography consists of a list of materials found on a topic after a survey of the card catalog. To compile this list, you record the titles, authors, dates of publication, and call numbers of materials that seem relevant to your topic and worth your consideration (see Table 9.4). Writing each item of this list on an index card provides a permanent record of possible references.

Another way to develop a working bibliography is through the use of a computer search of special data bases. Such a search generally requires the assistance of the librarian or other staff member in identifying the most appropriate data base and explaining necessary procedures for its use. The computer printout serves the same purpose as the self-made notebook of references. The computer search has two advantages over the self-prepared working bibliography. First, it identifies references you may overlook. Second, it takes you less time and effort to find possible sources of information. The major disad-

---

TABLE 9.4   Checklist for Judging the Relevance of References

1. Who is the author? Do you know anything about the author's reputation?

2. If you cannot judge the author's qualifications or reputation, does the author have more than one publication on this topic?

3. If you cannot judge the author's qualifications, depth of writing experience, or reputation, what is the reputation of the publisher?

4. When was the material published? Is information of this time period relevant to your research?

5. Does the material contain a bibliography?

6. Does the material contain appendices?

7. Does the material contain illustrations?

8. Was this publication considered worthy of reprinting?

9. Have you seen other publications reference this publication?

10. If a book, has the information in it been updated through the publication of subsequent editions?

vantage of computer searches is cost. Unless you consider time equal to money, the self-made working bibliography is free compared to the fees charged for computer searches. Rates vary from one data base service to another. Rates also vary within services depending on the time of day or day of the week.

EXERCISE 9.3 Using the catalog cards on the following pages, complete the chart below. If information is not specifically noted on the card, assume that it is not available.

AUTHOR	TYPE OF CARD	COPTRIGHT DATE	CALL NUMBER	ILLUS-TRATED?	NUMBER OF PAGES	BIBLIO-GRAPHY?	PUBLISHER	NUMBER OF CROSS-REFERENCES	INDEXED?
Bladen, Ashby									
Blackwell, James & Janowitz, M. (Ed.)									
Birren, James E.									
Beyer, Jinny									
Birmingham, Stephen									
Groves, Marjorie P. (Ed.)									
No Author									

HJ8119-B57

Blades, Ashby.
    How to cope with the developing financial crisis / Ashby Bladen. — New York : McGraw-Hill, c1980.
    xiii, 178 p. ; 21 cm.

    Includes bibliographal references and index.
    ISBN 0-07-005547-5 : $8.95

    1. Debts, Public—United States.   2. Finance—United States.   3. International finance.   I. Title

Library of Congress   79

HM22.U5B55

Black sociologists : historical and contemporary perspectives /
edited by James E. Blackwell and Morris Janowitz. — Chicago
: University of Chicago Press, 1974.

xxii, 415 p. ; 21 cm. — (The heritage of sociology)

Papers based on a National Conference on Black Sociologists, University of
Chicago, May 5–6, 1972.
Includes bibliographies and index.
ISBN 0-226-05565-5

1. Negro sociologists—United States—Congresses.   I. Blackwell, James
Edward, 1925–   II. Janowitz, Morris.   III. National Conference on
Black Sociologists, University of Chicago, 1972.

Library of Congress   75

136.53

Birren, James E.
  The psychology of aging [by] James E. Birren. Englewood
Cliffs, N.J., Prentice-Hall [1964]

ix, 303 p. illus. 24 cm.

Includes bibliographical references.

1. Aging.   2. Developmental psychology.   I. Title.

Library of Congress   [74]

TT835.B44

Beyer, Jinny.
  The quilter's blocks and borders : more than 750 geometric
designs, illustrated and categorized for easy identification and
drafting / Jinny Beyer : ill. by Jinny Beyer and Dan Ramsey. —
McLean, Va : EPM Publications, c1980.

ix, 198 p. : ill. ; 29 cm

Grids, 1 sheet and 1 transparent overlay, inserted.
Bibliography: p. 191-192.
Includes index.
ISBN 0-914440-32-2 : $15.95 (est.)
1. Patchwork—Patterns.   2. Quilting—Patterns.   I. Ramsey, Dan, 1945-
    . II. Title.
Library of Congress

974.4'1

Birmingham, Stephen.
    Life at the Dakota : New York's most unusual address /
Stephen Birmingham.—1st ed.—New York : Random House,
c1979.

    xii, 241 p., [8] leaves of plates : ill. ; 25 cm.

    Includes index.
    ISBN 0-394-41079-3 : $12.50

    1. New York (City). Dakota.   2. New York (City)—Social life and customs.
3. Social classes—New York (City)   I. Title.

Library of Congress   79

635

Better homes and gardens complete guide to gardening / [editor:
Marjorie P. Groves]. — 1st ed. — Des Moines : Meredith Corp.,
c1979.

    551 p. : ill (some col.) ; 26 cm. — (Better homes and gardens books)

    Includes index.
    ISBN 0-696-00041-5

    1. Gardening.   I. Groves, Marjorie P.   II. Better homes and gardens.   III.
Title: Complete guide to gardening.

Library of Congress   80

F341.B6 1978

Biographical and historical memoirs of Mississippi : embracing
an authentic and comprehensive account of the chief events in the
history of the state and a record of the lives of many of the most
worthy and illustrious families and individuals. — Spartanburg.
S.C. : Reprint Co. 1978.

    2 v. : ports. ; 24 cm.

    Reprint of the 1891 ed. published by Goodspeed Pub. Co., Chicago.
    Includes index.
    ISBN 0-87152-267-5 (set) : $90.00

    1. Mississippi—History.   2. Mississippi—Biography.
Library of Congress   72

EXERCISE 9.4   Using the directions for charting found in Table 5.6, create a chart that compares and contrasts the information found in the three references in Exercise 9.5.

RESEARCH SKILLS

After acquiring your working bibliography, you are ready to begin searching for and evaluating materials. First, you locate the references on the shelves. Then, you survey the pertinent features of the material. Next, you **skim** or **scan** these features to decide if the material fits your needs. Skimming and scanning speed the process of selecting or eliminating materials. Skimming is a means of quickly understanding what a publication is generally about, its main idea. Scanning helps you find specific details. In evaluating the relevance of material, you use your skimming and scanning skills at the same time (see Table 9.5). Finally, you note information beside the reference or eliminate unsuitable materials.

After you survey materials and decide that you want to use information contained in them in your paper, take notes, or make photocopies of the information for later use. Whatever method you choose, it's important to reference your notes or photocopies with

TABLE 9.5   Important Features to Survey in Evaluating References

1. Survey the title page and copyright page (the back of the title page) to answer:
   a. What is the complete title of this material?
   b. Who wrote the material?
   c. What is the author's title and professional affiliation?
   d. What occupation, position, titles, education, experience, and so forth qualifies this author to write on topic?
   e. Is this material collected from other sources?
   f. If so, who edited the collection?
   g. Who is the publisher of the material?
   h. When and where was the material published?
   i. Have there been other editions or revisions?

2. Scan the table of contents to determine:
   a. How is the book organized?
   b. Are topics important to you covered and how many pages are devoted to them?
   c. How does the coverage in this material compare with other references?

3. Scan the preface or introduction to discover:
   a. What is the author's point of view?
   b. Why did the author write this material?
   c. What information is covered in the material?
   d. Does the author's experience and scholarship seem sufficient for a thorough discussion of the topic?
   e. What method of research or data collection was used—personal opinions, personal experience, interviews, library research, surveys, clinical experiments, or other?
   f. To what audience is this material addressed?

4. Scan the bibliography, a listing of references used in the material, to answer:
   a. Does the author give primary sources (the actual words of an identified person, a historical document, a literary work, and so on) rather than secondary sources (other authors' descriptions of the original events)?
   b. Does the length of the bibliography indicate the scholarship of the author?
   c. Does the bibliography contain references you can use to further research your topic?
   d. Does the bibliography include articles by other authorities in the field besides the author?

5. Scan the index (an alphabetical listing of important topics included in the material) to answer:
   a. Are topics important to you covered? And how many pages are devoted to them?

6. Scan, then skim, important terms in the material's glossary (a small dictionary of terms used in the material) to decide:
   a. Do terms have specialized definitions?
   b. Are terms defined clearly and completely?
   c. Do the meanings of terms provide new insights into the topic?

complete bibliographical information (title, author, publisher, place and date of publication, volume or issue number, and page numbers) for later identification.

If you only need a small amount of information, note taking is sufficient (see Table 9.6). If you need a larger amount or complex graphics, photocopying may be more useful. You need to be aware that laws limit the number of photocopies made from a single source. However, for educational research purposes, the laws allow single copies to be made of a small percentage of the total material.

Notes consist of two basic types: **direct quotes** and summaries or paraphrases of main ideas and specific details (see Figure 9.10). Direct quotes are exactly what an author says about a topic. They leave no room for your opinion or thoughts. A **summary** or a **paraphrase,** likewise, contains an unbiased version of what the author said. This version, however, is written in your own words. It is your attempt to condense and clarify information.

You record a direct quote exactly as it is written and note its original source. You identify a direct quote as such by using quotation marks to set it apart from other statements. When a quote contains information that you think is unnecessary or unimportant, you may omit it only if you indicate that you are doing so. You show this omission by placing an **ellipsis,** three dots (. . .), where the missing information normally would appear.

Summaries or paraphrases state main ideas and supporting details or examples in your own words. They include specific details that are new or important points or concepts. Van Dijk and Kintch (1978) identified five basic rules essential to summarization. Table 9.7 lists these as steps—with slight variations—for you to follow in summarizing or paraphrasing information.

TABLE 9.6   Steps in Taking Research Notes

1. Use note cards or regular-sized pieces of paper to record important information.

2. Write all notes about one topic on the same piece of paper or note card. If you need additional space, be sure to keep notes on the same topic together.

3. Write notes using a standard format.

4. If taking notes on large amounts of information, use the same shorthand system you use when taking notes in class (see Chapter 3).

5. Cross-reference information.

FIGURE 9.10   Examples of Direct Quotes and Summaries or Paraphrases

---

Intact Text

Most messages are sent with signals. Animals use singing, growling, chirping, roaring, and other sounds to warn and attract others. Baboons display their huge canine teeth to threaten one another. Dogs and other animals raise their hackles to intimidate; some apes pound their chests. Animals also use gestures to attract mates. Dances, feather displays, and other signals convey mating intentions.

Sloshberg, W. and NesSmith, W. (1983). *Contemporary American Society: An Introduction to the Social Sciences*. St. Paul, MN: West Publishers, p. 65.

Direct Quote

"Animals use singing, growling, chirping, roaring and other sounds to warn and attract others. Animals also use gestures to attract mates."

Sloshberg, W. and NesSmith, W. (1983). *Contemporary American Society: An Introduction to the Social Sciences*. St. Paul, MN: West Publishers, p. 65.

Summary/Paraphrase

Animals use sounds and gestures as signals to warn and attract other animals.

Sloshberg, W. and NesSmith, W. (1983). *Contemporary American Society: An Introduction to the Social Sciences*. St. Paul, MN: West Publishers, p. 65.

TABLE 9.7   Steps in Writing Summaries or Paraphrases

1. Delete unimportant information.

2. Delete repeated information.

3. Group similar objects and concepts; find an identifying word for this group. (For example, group *pears, bananas, apples,* and *peaches* as *fruit.*)

4. Write important details in your own words.

5. Locate the topic sentence of the passage.

6. Once you locate the topic sentence, restate it in your own words. If you cannot locate the topic sentence, compose your own.

EXERCISE 9.5   Choose one of the following topics. Go to your college library and find three references on this topic. List these references in the spaces below. Evaluate them using the criteria in Table 9.5.

Topics
1. Ozone layer
2. Landscape architecture
3. Music composition
4. Presidential elections
5. American history
6. Medical technology
7. Nuclear weapons
8. Forestry
9. Economic recession
10. Industrial Revolution

Reference 1

_____

_____

_____

_____

_____

_____

_____

_____

_____

_____

_____

_____

Reference 2

Reference 3

EXERCISE 9.6   Use Sample Chapter 1, "Culture: The Ideas and Products People Adopt and Create," to identify two pieces of information that you could use as direct quotes. Then summarize or paraphrase this same information.

_____

_____

_____

_____

_____

_____

_____

_____

_____

_____

_____

_____

_____

_____

_____

_____

_____

_____

_____

_____

EXERCISE 9.7   In the space provided below, use the rules in Table 9.7 to write a summary or paraphrase of "Health Note 7.1—Lowering Your Cholesterol," in Sample Chapter 3, "Nutrition and Digestion."

_____

_____

_____

_____

_____

_____

_____

_____

_____

_____

_____

_____

_____

_____

_____

_____

_____

_____

WRITE TO LEARN

On a separate sheet of paper, compare and contrast the characteristics of a working bibliography and the bibliography which should be included with your final draft.

THE MAZE: VARIETY OF INFORMATION IN THE LIBRARY

To many students, the **stacks** in the library resemble Minotaur's maze. In the past, knowing your way through the stacks was sufficient for doing library research. However, modern libraries reflect the ever-increasing influx of knowledge, both in the size and formats of their collections. Although materials in the stacks remain a major part of today's libraries, a variety of other collections and sources provide you with innumerable references.

GENERAL REFERENCES

General references are vast in number and scope. Because of their utility to large numbers of students, they need to be kept available. Most libraries store these books in **ready reference.** They keep others in a reserved section of the library. Libraries either do not allow such books to be checked out or check them out only for limited periods of time.

"Medieval history . . . on a bearing of N37°E go 400 feet, then S15°E 175 feet."

Reserved books are books that are temporarily removed from the stacks at the request of faculty member. This is done to ensure that a book is not checked out for a long period of time, making it unavailable as a reference for their students.

General **periodical indices** do for journals what the card catalog does for other materials. They list authors, titles, and subjects of articles in many periodicals. They also include cross-references. The *Reader's Guide to Periodical Literature* is a common index of general and nontechnical journals and magazines. An alphabetical listing includes authors and subjects of articles. Entries provide information for finding specific articles (see Figure 9.11).

Accurate research often depends on knowing exactly what is meant by the words that describe the topic. A library's holdings usually include two general sources about word meanings. The first source is the **unabridged dictionary,** the most comprehensive general dictionary found in a library. It lists all words used in the English language, including obsolete words, scientific terms, and proper names. Definitions include word histories, quotations, related terms, and other information. A **thesaurus** provides a second general source for finding words. It identifies synonyms, antonyms, and related words for specific headings. Like a dictionary, this aids you in finding other key words that identify your topic.

Some types of information cannot be put in book form. The **vertical file** or **clipping file** holds materials of this type. These include pamphlets, newspaper and magazine clippings, pictures, circulars, and bulletins. Such materials are stored in large manila folders or envelopes. The envelopes are arranged alphabetically by subject in a vertical file cabinet.

FIGURE 9.11   Example of *Reader's Guide* Entry

Marketing

See also
Booksellers and bookselling
Market group to launch book coupon drive. *Publ Wkly* 230:19 Ag 8 '86
MPBA research explores independent bookstore customer. *Publ Wkly* 230:48 S 26 '86
The power of positive marketing [Guideposts home Bible study program marketed by mail] E. Bence. *Publ Wkly* 230:43–4 O 3 '86

Preservation

See Books—Conservation and restoration.

Prices

U.S. book title output and average prices. 1983–1985. C. B. Grannis. il *Publ Wkly* 230:89–92 O 3 '86

Statistics

Best sellers
Paperback books
Royalties
Talking books
Textbooks
The yestermorrow of the book [reprint from January 1972 issue] M. McLuhan. il *UNESCO Cour* 39:50-1 My/Je '86

Advertising

Giveaways, gimmicks and gizmos [children's book promotions] A. M. Martin. il *Publ Wkly* 230:164-6, Jl 25 '86.
Mine the midlist [promoting trade novels] K. Ray. por *Publ Wkly* 230:76 Ag 15 '86

(Labels: ARTICLE TITLE, VOLUME NUMBER, MONTH/DATE/YEAR, CROSS-REFERENCE, SUBJECT, PERIODICAL, ILLUSTRATIONS, AUTHOR)

Care

See Books—Conservation and restoration

Censorship

See Censorship

Collectors and collecting

See also
Libraries. Private
Oliver Optic (William T. Adams): nineteenth-century novelist's books are collectible. D. E. Matter and R. M. Matter. il *Hobbies* 91:52–4 S '86

Conservation and restoration

Rescuing old papers [deacidification] S. Budiansky. il *U S News World Rep* 101:84 S 22 '86

Dedications

See Dedications (in books)

FIGURE 9.11   Continued

Exhibitions
See Book exhibits
Export-import trade
Beyond the 10% tariff [tariff on books exported to Canada] P. Yaffe. por *Publ Wkly* 230:76 Ag 1 '86
Canada's writers oppose 'free trade' talks [trade with U.S.] P. Adams. *Publ Wkly* 230:98 Jl 25 '86
Eight firms win against California importer [copyright infringement lawsuit against J. B. Stark] M. Yen. *Publ Wkly* 230:14 Ag 1 '86
Selling books in China. J. Chan. il *Publ Wkly* 230:23–6 Ag 8 '86
U.S. exports, imports, UNESCO reports. C. B. Grannis. il *Publ Wkly* 230:96–8 S 19 '86
Illustration
See Illustration
Manufacture
See Book industries

Almanacs or **yearbooks** provide information about government, industry, politics, commerce, world events, sports, and almost any other topic. Updated yearly, they contain statistical, tabular, and general information.

The most logical sources of current information are daily and/or weekly newspapers. Current issues of local, state, and national papers are shelved or hang on racks in your library. Some libraries also display newspapers from other countries. Newspapers may or may not be indexed. This causes no problems, however. If you find the date of a particular event in any **newspaper index,** other papers probably carried reports of that event the same day. Examples of such indices include *Facts on File* (weekly summaries of world news), the *New York Times Index* (summaries of *New York Times* articles), and the *Wall Street Journal Today* (a yearly list of its financial and business articles).

Atlases and **gazetteers** provide geographical information. An atlas contains a collection of topographical, climatic, geological, economic, and political maps. These maps are arranged alphabetically according to region. Atlases often include gazetteers, which are general dictionaries of geographical names. A gazetteer lists names of places, seas, mountains, and so on. Entries cover pronunciation, classification, population, height, length, area, and points of interest.

Books of quotations identify well-known or important statements by general topic and by their sources. *Bartlett's Familiar Quotations* indexes information by subject and author.

General biographical indices or dictionaries report information about the lives of important people. Facts include birth and death dates, nationality, profession, accomplishments, and other personal and professional information. Examples of such dictionaries include *Who's Who in America, Who Was Who in America*, and *Current Biography. Who's Who in America*, updated every other year, contains information about notable living Americans. *Who Was Who in America*, similar to *Who's Who in America*, includes information on important deceased Americans. Published since 1940, each year's volume of *Current Biography* contains an illustrated description and a short biography about living important world figures.

Government documents are materials published by municipal, state, and federal governmental agencies. They include detailed information on governmental policies and procedures as well as almost any other topic. Because of the volume and variety of publications, identifying the agency that publishes the one you need poses a problem. Writing to your representative or senator or the Government Printing Office aids in finding the proper department and the publication you need. In addition, some libraries possess a collection of government documents. *The U.S. Government Organization Manual* and the *Monthly Catalog of United States Government Publications* index federal government publications.

EXERCISE 9.8   Match each reference with its corresponding phrase.

_____ 1. Periodical

_____ 2. *Reader's Guide*

_____ 3. Reserve books

_____ 4. Microforms

_____ 5. Vertical file

_____ 6. Newspaper

_____ 7. Gazetteer

_____ 8. Almanac

_____ 9. *Who Was Who in America?*

_____ 10. Newspaper index

a. Temporarily removed from stacks at instructor's request.

b. Index of general and nontechnical journals and magazines

c. Materials in reduced format

d. Dictionary of geographical names

e. Index of the most up-to-date information

f. Clipping file

g. Contains biography of Martin Luther King

h. Current events published annually

i. Provides the most up-to-date information

j. Magazines or journal

EXERCISE 9.9 Answer the following questions using references in your campus library. Indicate the title of the reference that you used to locate the answer.

1. Which city is farther north: Duluth, Minnesota, or Toronto, Canada? Which city is farther south: Tijuana, Mexico, or Houston, Texas?

   _____

   _____

   *Reference type:*_____

2. What lines from Dorothy Parker's *Resume* describe her feelings about suicide?

   _____

   _____

   *Reference type:*_____

3. On what day in October 1987 did the stock market suffer a 508-point drop?

   _____

   _____

   *Reference type:*_____

4. What was the leading cause of death among Americans in 1985?

   _____

   _____

   *Reference type:*_____

5. List three synonyms for *ghat*.

   _____

   _____

   *Reference type:*_____

6. What magazine in August 1987 contained the article "God and Money"? Who wrote the article?

   _____

   _____

   *Reference type:*_____

7. What is the title of the microfiche that has the ERIC Document Reproduction Service number 136189?

   _____

   _____

   *Reference type:*_____

8. Who said, "The cruelest lies are often told in silence"?

_____

*Reference type:*_____

9. Define *paparazzi*.

_____

_____

*Reference type:*_____

10. Who was Clarence Darrow?

_____

_____

*Reference type:*_____

SPECIALIZED CONTENT REFERENCES

The sources of general and specific information you'll use depend upon your interests and the courses you are taking. You need not be familiar with every publication your library owns, but you need to know how to find the information for your particular course.

Specialized content reference books list and briefly describe various sources on a particular subject. Two such references many libraries keep on ready reference are A. J. Walford's *Guide to Reference Material* and Eugene P. Sheehy's *Guide to Reference Books*, both published by the American Library Association. *Guide to Reference Material* consists of three volumes. Volume one deals with science and technology; volume two concerns social and historical sciences, as well as philosophy and religion; and volume three includes generalities, languages, the arts, and literature. *Guide to Reference Books* is a one-volume index of general references, humanities, social sciences, history and area studies, and pure and applied science. Another guide that is briefer and less costly than library sources is *Reference Books: A Brief Guide*, published by Enoch Pratt Free Library (400 Cathedral Street, Baltimore, MD 21201). Every four or five years, Enoch Pratt Free Library updates this helpful 180-page booklet. With it, you have a personal reference book at your fingertips.

WRITE TO LEARN

On a separate sheet of paper, identify the general reference that would be of most use to you in your chosen major. Explain your choice.

RUNNING THE MAZE: THE RESEARCH PROCESS

To know you've found the most information you possibly can, you need to look at every resource alternative. Because of the overwhelming size of this task, it sometimes helps to know where you're going and where you've been. The flowchart in Figure 9.12 looks much like the maze Theseus faced. With someone to assist you (the librarian), a thread to guide you in locating information (library organization), and a sword and the skill to use it (a working bibliography and research skills), you, too, can run the maze and kill the Minotaur.

FIGURE 9.12   A Flowchart of Library Information

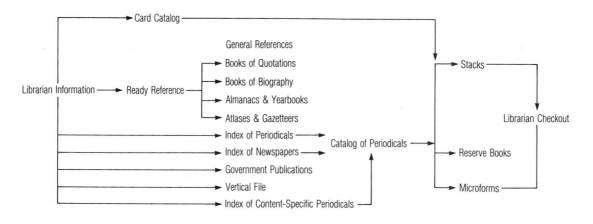

GROUP LEARNING ACTIVITY
Approaching Library Research

Just as you can take different routes to get to a specific location, you can use different routes to approach library research. These approaches do not have to be used exclusively. You can choose to use one as a starting point until you have enough information to try something else. The following eight standard approaches often are suggested (Morse, 1975).

Bibliographic. This approach is the most basic. A bibliography is a list of all materials consulted in your search for information. References all relate to the topic in some way, although that relationship can differ. Thus, the result of a bibliographic approach in an annotated list of books, articles, and other related materials.

Biographical. Biographies concern people—their lives and accomplishments. Thus, if a particular person is associated with a topic, the story of that person's life may be an appropriate starting point for the context of your paper. Although this approach is not suitable for all topics, it is appropriate for some.

Chronological. Chronological order concerns the time line of events associated with your topic. This approach is particularly suitable for historical events, current events, and other topics that have a beginning, middle, and, sometimes, end.

Geographical. Sometimes you want to know where or in what locations an event occurred. In this approach, you use a map to focus on specific areas, locations, or countries.

Linguistic. Linguistics refers to the study of language. This approach focuses on definition of key words and ideas as the basis for beginning research. Other words or terms in the definition, or the etymology of the word, can be a springboard to other references. The meanings you find help you clearly define your topic and the words you intend to research.

Practical. The sequence or order of a process can be the focus of your research. This method is particularly appropriate for "how to do it" topics that focus on the step-by-step progression of an action or idea.

Statistical. Some topics are best described by data. Here, you search for information that tells you how many, how much, who, where, and why in numerical terms. This collection of facts forms the basis for analysis and interpretation of information to form new conclusions.

Theoretical. Sometimes exact answers to life's questions are not available. In those cases, the theories that answer those questions suffice. These can be compared, contrasted, or related in other ways.

Application

As a group, complete the following activity and compare your results.

1. The group as a whole should select one of the following topics: AIDS research and treatment, automobiles, the brain, gymnastics, voting rights, or war veterans of the twentieth century.

2. Each group member should select one of the eight approaches described above. No two group members should use the same approach.

3. Each group member should find and annotate five references for that topic and approach.

4. As a group, compare the information you located.

SUMMARY OF MAIN POINTS

1. The librarian assists your research by identifying appropriate sources and services.

2. Understanding the organizational system that your library uses helps you locate materials efficiently. The card catalog is a file or computerized data base that indexes nonfiction library holdings by author, title, and subject, and fiction holdings by author and title. Two classification systems are used to identify library holdings: the numerically based Dewey decimal system and the alphabetically based Library of Congress system.

3. A working bibliography, created through a systematic search of the card catalog or a computer search, provides you with a list of possible research references. Searching, evaluating, and recording information from reference sources requires skills in skimming, scanning, and note taking.

4. Modern libraries contain a variety of materials for both general and content-specific research purposes. General references include unabridged dictionaries, thesauruses, vertical files, almanacs, yearbooks, atlases, gazetteers, biographies, books of quotations, government documents, and indices to magazines and newspapers. The specific subject references you need depend on your interests and course work. You use indices to content-specific sources to find them.

VOCABUARLY DEVELOPMENT
READY REFERENCES FOR WORDS: DICTIONARY, GLOSSARY, AND THESAURUS

*". . . 98, 99, 100! Here I come, ready, prepared, anticipated, girded,
on the alert, provided for—or not."*

SOURCE: Use by permission of Frank Hauser.

Like Roget, you, too, need to be ready, prepared, apt, and all set to seek whatever your college course work has hidden. Luckily for you, three references found in all libraries—the dictionary, the glossary, and the thesaurus—are ready for your use in learning the meaning of unfamiliar terms.

Using the Dictionary. What do you do when you see a word you don't know? Most students define words by looking them up in the dictionary. After all, for years parents and teachers have said, "You don't know how to spell that word? You don't know what it means? Well, look it up!" Using the dictionary, then, becomes second nature to you. This often-used method works best when you know how to use the dictionary effectively.

To find word entries quickly in the dictionary, use the **guide words** at the top of each page. They indicate the words that appear between them. Arranged in alphabetical order, definitions contain much more than correct spellings, pronunciations, and meanings.

A dictionary **entry** follows a general format (see Figure 1). First, the word is spelled and divided into syllables. Second, the word's phonetic pronunciation

---

FIGURE 1   Example of a Dictionary Entry

library (lī'brer'ē) *n., pl.* -les [< L. *liber.* book] **1.** a collection of books, etc. **2.** a room or building for, or an institution in charge of, such a collection

Source: Webster's New World Dictionary of the American Language, Simon & Schuster © 1982.

---

is given. (A key to phonetic symbols usually appears at the bottom of the page.) Next appears an abbreviation of the word's part of speech followed by its **etymology.** This is the word's origin or history and tells how or why the word became a word. The word's definition comes after the etymology. Usually the longest and most often used part of the entry, the definition is the word's meaning(s). If the word has several different and distinct meanings, these are numbered separately. Some entries also include **synonyms** (words with the same meaning) and/or **antonyms** (words with the opposite meaning). Finally, the entry shows the **derivations** of the word and their parts of speech. Derivations are words formed from the entry word. Although entry formats vary slightly from one dictionary to another, their general consistency allows you to use a variety of dictionaries easily.

Resorting to a dictionary is not always the best solution. First, because many words have specialized meanings, you may have difficulty locating the meaning you need. By the time you find the one you need, you may forget why you needed it. This break in concentration leads to a loss of understanding. This increases study time and decreases study efficiency. Thus, glossary usage, context, and structural analysis are alternatives for understanding.

Using a Glossary. When a glossary is included in a textbook, it stands as your greatest resource in understanding the language of the course. An entry in this dictionary-like listing of words generally consists of only the term and its course-specific definition (see Figure 2). Examining the glossary before the beginning of a course provides you with an introduction to the language of the course. Referring to the glossary during reading requires less time than using a dictionary. It also assures that you get the correct meaning. Reviewing glossary entries before exams helps you determine which words and concepts require further study.

Using a Thesaurus. Once you have a sense of what a word means, using a thesaurus provides you with other words with similar meanings (synonyms). First compiled by Peter Mark Roget in 1852, a thesaurus is a collection of words that enhances vocabulary development.

As in a dictionary, the information found in a thesaurus entry varies (see Figure 3). A thesaurus entry is less complicated than a dictionary entry. It omits a word's pronunciation, etymology, and derivations. Consistently, however, entries contain a word's part of speech, synonyms and related words or phrases, and cross-references. Some also include

FIGURE 2   Example of a Glossary

Interpreter A high-level language translator that evaluates and translates a program one statement at a time; used extensively on microcomputer systems because it takes up less primary storage than a compiler.

Interrecord gap (IRG) A space that separates records stored on magnetic tape; allows the tape drive to regain speed during processing.

Interrupt A condition or event that temporarily suspends normal processing operations.

Inverted structure A structure that indexes a simple file by specific record attributes.

K (kilobyte) A symbol used to denote 1,024 (2^{10}) storage units (1,024 bytes) when referring to a computer's primary storage capacity; often rounded to 1,000 bytes.

Key The unique identifier or field of a record; used to sort records for processing or to locate specific records within a file.

Keypunch A keyboard device that punches holes in a card to represent data.

Keypunch operator Person who uses a keypunch machine to transfer data from source documents to punched cards.

Label A name written beside a programming instruction that acts as an identifier for that instruction; also, in spreadsheets, information used to describe some aspect of the spreadsheet.

Large-scale Integration (LSI) Method by which circuits containing thousands of electronic components are densely packed on a single silicon chip.

Laser printer A type of nonimpact printer that combines laser beams and electrophotographic technology to form images on paper.

Laser storage system A secondary storage device using laser technology to encode data onto a metallic surface; usually used for mass storage.

Librarian The person responsible for classifying, cataloging, and maintaining the files and programs stored on cards, tapes, disks, and diskettes, and all other storage media in a computer library.

Librarian program Software that manages the storage and use of library programs by maintaining a directory of programs in the system library and appropriate procedures for additions and deletions.

Light pen A pen-shaped object with a photoelectric cell at its end; used to draw lines on a visual display screen.

Linear structure A data structure in which the records in a computer file are arranged sequentially in a specified order.

Link A transmission channel that connects nodes.

Linkage editor A subprogram of the operating system that links the object program from the system residence device to primary storage.

LISP (LISt Processing) A high-level programming language commonly used in artificial intelligence research and in the processing of lists of elements.

Local system Peripherals connected directly to the CPU.

Logical file The combination of data needed to meet a user's needs.

FIGURE 2   Continued

Logo An education-oriented, procedure-oriented, interactive programming language designed to allow anyone to begin programming and communicating with computers quickly.

Loop A structure that allows a specified sequence of instructions to be executed repeatedly as long as stated conditions remain constant.

FIGURE 3   Examples of Various Thesaurus Entries

rumble, *n.* roll, hollow roar, reverberation. See LOUDNESS.

rumble, *v.* boom, thunder, roll (RESONANCE, LOUDNESS).

rumble *verb*
1. To make a continuous deep, reverberating sound: *heard the convoy rumbling in the distance.* **Syns:** boom, growl, grumble, roll.
2. MUTTER.
rumble *noun* MUTTER.

antonyms. Figure 4 shows a common thesaurus entry and its parts.

Thesauruses use the same labels for parts of speech as dictionaries. Again, these labels tell how a word functions in language. Because many words can be used as more than one part of speech, a thesaurus lists synonyms for each function. Thus, when looking for words in a thesaurus, you need to know how a word is to be used in a sentence.

Because it would be redundant to reprint every term associated with each entry, an entry sometimes includes cross-references. Found at the end of an entry, these either begin with the words "See also" or are written in all caps. Cross-references direct you to other entries that contain additional synonyms or to antonyms.

Choosing Ready References. A glossary is your first and best choice for

---

FIGURE 4   Example of a Thesaurus Entry

Gratitude

Nouns—gratitude, gratefulness, thankfulness; indebtedness; acknowledgement, recognition, thanksgiving; thanks, praise; paean, *Te Deum*, WORSHIP, grace; thank-offering; requital.

Verbs—be grateful, thank; give, render, return, offer, *or* tender thanks; acknowledge, requite; thank *or* bless one's [lucky] stars.

Adjectives—grateful, thankful, appreciative, obliged, beholden, indebted to, under obligation.

Interjections—thanks! much obliged! thank you! thank Heaven! Heaven be praised! thanks a million! *gracias! merci!*

            Antonyms, see INGRATITUDE.

SOURCE: *The New American Roget's College Thesaurus in Dictionary Form*, 4th ed. New American Library © 1985. Reprinted by permission.

---

determining the meaning of the terms you encounter because their meanings are specific to your course of study. Nonetheless, a personal dictionary and thesaurus are imperative for continued vocabulary development. Contrary to popular opinion, all dictionaries and thesauruses are not alike. Most are abridged versions containing a limited number of entries. When determining what to purchase, you need to base your choice on more than size alone. Indeed, large unabridged dictionaries would be inappropriate for everyday use but would be the best choice for an extensive etymology search. How, then, do you decide which reference book you need? Table 1 provides guidelines for your selection.

TABLE 1   Guidelines for Purchasing a Dictionary and Thesaurus

---

Dictionary

1. What size is the dictionary? Will you use it at home or in class? If you plan to use the dictionary at home, it can be larger than if you will be carrying it to class each day.

2. How many total entries are included? Within the limits of size manageability, the more entries, the better.

3. What is the copyright date of the dictionary? More up-to-date dictionaries contain new words that older dictionaries do not contain.

4. What is the quality of the entries given? Contrast the entries of several dictionaries to determine which would best fit your needs.

5. Is the type clear and easy to read?

6. Does the dictionary include a clear guide to aid you in using information contained in it? Skim it to determine how easy it is to use.

7. What additional information is included in the dictionary? Many contain such features as a periodic table, sections on punctuation and language usage, lists of foreign words or spellings, and a table of weights and measures. The components you need depend on how you plan to use your dictionary.

Thesaurus

1. Are entries listed alphabetically or by subject? Thesauruses with an alphabetical format are easier to use.

2. How many total entries are included? Within the limits of size manageability, the more entries, the better.

3. Are cross-references included? Cross-references are necessary in helping you locate the exact synonym you need.

4. Does the entry include antonyms when possible? Thesauruses with antonyms are helpful because sometimes you need a word that means the opposite of a word you know.

5. Is the type clear and easy to read?

6. Does the thesaurus include a clear guide to aid you in using information contained in it? Skim it to determine how easy it is to use.

Activity

I.   Define each of the following words using a dictionary. Then define them using the glossary in Figure 2. Using a thesaurus, find three to five words that would generally be considered synonyms of these words. Compare the glossary, dictionary, and thesaurus meanings. What differences do you find?

1. *interpreter*

Dictionary:_____

_____

Glossary:_____

_____

Thesaurus:_____

_____

Comparison:_____

_____

_____

2. *key*

Dictionary:_____

_____

Glossary:_____

_____

Thesaurus:_____

_____

Comparison:_____

_____

_____

3. *label*

Dictionary:_____

_____

Glossary:_____

_____

Thesaurus:_____

_____

Comparison:_____
_____
_____

4. *link*
Dictionary:_____
_____

Glossary:_____
_____

Thesaurus:_____
_____

Comparison:_____
_____
_____

5. *loop*
Dictionary:_____
_____

Glossary:_____
_____

Thesaurus:_____
_____

Comparison:_____
_____
_____

II.   How does using these references as combined sources affect your vocabulary development?

CHAPTER REVIEW

Answer briefly but completely.

1. Compare and contrast the role of Ariadne with that of the librarian. Be specific.

2. What is the purpose of a call number?

3. Contrast the advantages of microfiche with its disadvantages.

4. You plan to write a research paper on music in the 1920s. List three key words you might use to access this information in your library's data base.

5. Contrast the Dewey decimal system with the Library of Congress system. Which system does your library use?

_____

_____

_____

_____

6. When might you use direct quotes instead of summaries? Why?

_____

_____

_____

_____

7. Using the microfiche or microfilm in your library, copy the front page of the *New York Times* on the day you were born.

8. How do skimming and scanning aid you in researching a paper?

_____

_____

_____

_____

9. Identify two of each of the following found in your library:
   a. general references and their call numbers

   _____

   _____

   b. general biographical indices

   _____

   _____

10. Compare and contrast an atlas, a gazetteer, and a globe.

   _____

   _____

   _____

   _____

REFERENCES

Morse, G. W. (1975). *Concise Guide to Library Research* (2d ed.). New York: Fleet Academic Editions.

Van Dijk, T. A., and Kintch, W. (1978). "Cognitive Psychology and Discourse: Recalling and Summarizing Stories." In W. V. Dressler, ed., *Trends in Text Linguistics*. New York: DeGruyter.

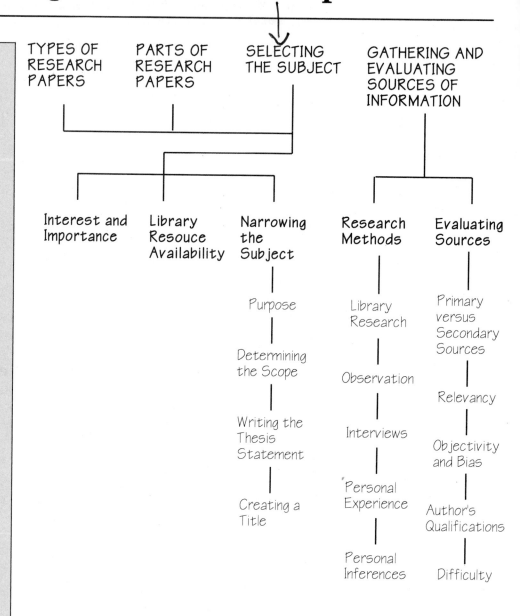

TYPES OF RESEARCH PAPERS

PARTS OF RESEARCH PAPERS

SELECTING THE SUBJECT

GATHERING AND EVALUATING SOURCES OF INFORMATION

Interest and Importance

Library Resouce Availability

Narrowing the Subject

Purpose

Determining the Scope

Writing the Thesis Statement

Creating a Title

Research Methods

Library Research

Observation

Interviews

Personal Experience

Personal Inferences

Evaluating Sources

Primary versus Secondary Sources

Relevancy

Objectivity and Bias

Author's Qualifications

Difficulty

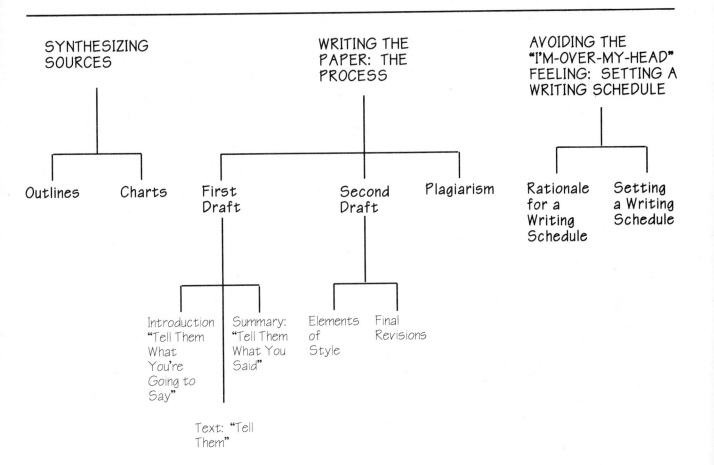

The deadline would strike in exactly twenty-one days. I had to start writing. The next morning, a beauteous one in June, I woke up, washed my face and brushed my teeth in a hurry, made a pot of coffee, tightened the sash on my bathrobe, snapped my typewriter out of its case, carefully placed it on the kitchen table, unwrapped the pack of bond paper I had purchased the day before, retrieved my notes from the floor where they were stacked tidily in manila folders . . . opened the first folder, put the top sheet of paper in the typewriter, looked at it, put my head on the keys, wrapped my arms around its base, and cried.

If I had known then how many times, during the next fifteen years, I would have the same feeling—the I'm-over-my-head-and-this-time-they're-going-to-catch-me feeling—I might have become a receptionist in a carpeted law office and married the first partner in a three-piece suit who asked me. But I didn't know. I thought, if I get through this, it'll be over.

—BETTY ROLLIN

SOURCE: Reprinted with permission from *Am I Getting Paid for This?* by Betty Rollin, Little, Brown and Company, Publishers.

No matter if your assignment comes from an editor or an instructor, the "I'm-over-my-head-and-this-time-they're-going-to-catch-me feeling" often prevails. Unlike Betty Rollin, you may have no clear idea of what's involved in researching and writing a paper. Perhaps the writing process confuses and frustrates you. If so, you—like Betty Rollin—probably feel like crying.

Writing a paper is much like cooking. If a chef follows the recipe, everything goes as planned. If the chef leaves something out or fails to follow directions, the recipe is ruined. A paper has a recipe, too. As with cooking, leaving out a part of the paper or a step in the writing process results in a paper that's not all you hoped it would be.

The recipe for your paper depends on the type of paper you need to write and the parts you plan to include. It also consists of other key ingredients and steps for you to follow. These help you find where you are in the process and what you need to do next. You complete four steps when writing a paper: selecting a topic, narrowing your subject, gathering information, and actually writing the paper.

TYPES OF RESEARCH PAPERS

There are almost as many types of papers as there are types of food. Instructors often assign **themes** or **essays, reports,** and **research papers** or **term papers.** Themes require little or no research. Somewhat short in length, they usually contain your personal opinions about a single topic. Other kinds of papers vary in length and purpose. Reports narrate or describe something that you have experienced firsthand. They sometimes include information that you derive from the accounts of others. Research papers are required assignments, written as a culmination or synthesis of a course's content. They often require supporting research. Called term papers by some instructors, research papers involve much library work. They focus on either part or all of a course's content or a related topic.

PARTS OF THE RESEARCH PAPER

Regardless of the purpose or topic, all research papers include the same basic parts: the title page, body of the paper and **bibliography,** in that order. In addition, they often contain a table of contents, an **abstract,** and **appendices** (see Figure 10.1).

The title page lists the paper's title, your name, the course and the instructor for whom the paper is written, and the date. Second is the body of the paper. It contains the introduction of the topic, synthesis of information, and summary or conclusions. Third, your paper includes a list of references, sometimes called a bibliography.

Whether or not your paper contains additional information depends on the options your instructor wants and the scope of the paper. The first optional item is a table of contents, often used in

"A fill-in-the-blank research paper is a unique idea, but. . . ."

FIGURE 10.1   Parts of a Research Paper

TITLE

The State of Education:
Comparisons between Louisiana
and Maryland

Henry Brandt

Professor Miles Jeffrey
Education 4443
Trends in Education
Spring 1984

ABSTRACT

ABSTRACT

The State of Education:
Comparisons between Louisiana
and Maryland

Henry Brandt

The purpose of this paper is to provide a descriptive examination of factors relating to education in the states of Louisiana and Maryland.

The context of the situation in each state will be developed through a discussion of population characteristics, state history, political history, economic trends, and readership data.

The scope of this paper focuses on the following aspects of the educational system in each state: enrollment, public elementary and secondary schools, private elementary and secondary schools, teachers, adult literacy, and post-secondary institutions.

SAMPLE PAGE FROM BODY

Population Characteristics

The population of Maryland is comparable to that of Louisiana (4,265,000 VS. 4,362,000), although Maryland is much more densely populated than Louisiana (431.2 persons per square mile VS. 97.1 per square mile). Louisiana is 68.7% urban as compared to Maryland's urban population of 80.3%. Louisiana's racial make-up is 69.2% white, 29.4% black, and 1.4% other. Only two other states have black populations higher than Louisiana. The racial make-up of Maryland is 74.9% white, 22.7% black, and 2.4% other. (Feist, 1983; American Almanac, 1983).

Maryland's physical density and urban atmosphere would seem to be advantageous for its residents. This would facilitate accessibility to formal educational resources (i.e. libraries and schools). In addition, opportunities for participating in non-school educational/cultural activities (i.e., museums, plays, concerts, exhibitions, etc.) would be increased.

History

Louisiana was first visited by Spanish explorers in 1530 but was claimed for France in 1682. French control of the state

APPENDIX

APPENDIX A. Readership Data

	LOUISIANA	MARYLAND
Newsweek (7/30/83)		
Subscriptions	55,025	60,000
Single Copy Sales	2.933	4.535
Total	57,958	65,535
Time (7/30/83)		
Subscriptions	53,700	79,036
Single Copy Sales	3,542	3,216
Total	56,242	82,252
U.S. News and World Report (7/30/83)		
Subscriptions	39,162	44,775
Single Copy Sales	924	1,644
Total	40,086	46,419
Sports Illustrated (7/30/83)		
Subscriptions	62,741	58,149
Single Copy Sales	1,391	2,126
Total	64,132	60,275
House Beautiful (7/30/83)		
Subscriptions	18,725	19,048
Single Copy Sales	4.600	5,016
Total	23,326	24,064
Reader's Digest (6/30/83)		
Subscriptions	244,603	286,333
Single Copy Sales	15,235	10,333
Total	232,538	296,666

FIGURE 10.1   Continued

TABLE OF CONTENTS

TABLE OF CONTENTS

REFERENCES

BIBLIOGRAPHY

Ashworth, J., (1980). *Education in Louisiana.* Baton Rouge, Louisiana; University Press.

Craig, F.J. (ed.). (1983). *American Almanac* Boston: Ginn Co.

Feist, J.T., (1983). *General Education Facts and Figures* New York: Holt.

Jones, E.M. (1982). "Maryland's Push for Better Education." *Journal of General Education, 21,* pp. 192–193.

Stoll, E.P., & Bradley, A.C. (1984). *Readership Data for Popular Magazines.* New York: Hill & Smith.

papers that are lengthy or segmented. An abstract—a second optional element—briefly summarizes the content of your paper. Both the table of contents and abstract follow the title page. A final optional element consists of appendices that contain supplementary material (for example, illustrations, figures, charts). These are placed at the end of your paper.

SELECTING THE SUBJECT

A chef's library contains many specialized cookbooks. For example, when planning to bake a cake, the chef selects a cookbook containing cake recipes. The choice of a specific recipe depends on the ingredients on hand, the amount of preparation time involved, the number it will serve, and so on. The subject of your paper, much like a specialized cookbook, is the general area that you plan to research. Your instructor sometimes assigns specific topics. If this is the case, your job is to find information on that topic and write about it. If not, your job is more difficult. You then choose a subject from either a list of subjects supplied by the instructor or from your own research. Subject selection depends on your interest, the importance of the subject, and the availability of resources.

INTEREST AND IMPORTANCE

The subject you choose needs to be one of interest or importance to you, the course content, and your audience. Because writing a paper requires much work, you stand a better chance of doing a good job if you care about the subject that you select. The subject of your paper also should be relevant to the course. Finally, the content of your paper needs to meet the demands of your audience, whether that be your instructor, your peers, or others.

Finding a subject that relates to you, the course, and your audience requires effort. By scanning your text's index or table of contents, you can identify topics that interest you or appeal to your audience. Skimming your notes or class handouts also helps you pinpoint likely subjects. Talking with your instructor or classmates is a third means of finding possible areas of research. Finally, subject areas surface through vicarious and direct experiences. These include books, magazines, television, newspaper accounts, travel, and work.

LIBRARY RESOURCE AVAILABILITY

The availability of library resources is a second consideration in subject selection. Consulting the card catalog helps you determine if your library owns books or other references on your subject. If your library contains limited information, choosing another subject may be advisable. In addition, checking the location of such resources helps you determine the availability of those references to you. If the ones you want are checked out or are otherwise unavailable, again you may need to find another subject.

NARROWING THE SUBJECT

Narrowing your subject into a manageable topic is much like a chef deciding what kind of cake to bake. Because you can't write about every aspect of a subject, you need to decide specifically what you plan to cover. The narrower the topic, the better your chance of covering it.

Purpose

Establishing the purpose of a paper aids you in narrowing the subject. Purposes are sometimes set by instructors; however, you often must set them yourself. Determining the purpose helps you determine the type of information you need to collect (see Table 10.1).

TABLE 10.1   Identifying Research Purposes

If Your Purpose is to . . .	You Collect . . .
define or describe,	details, characteristics, features, qualities, relationships.
compare/contrast,	similarities and differences.
analyze,	factors or elements that comprise the totality of the topic.
explain or interpret,	reasons, causes, effects, data.
persuade,	facts that support or refute an argument.
chronicle,	sequence, process, or history.
relate,	spatial or geographical associations or patterns.
infer,	evidence to make predictions or conclusions.

*"I don't think that's what your instructor meant
by reducing the scope of your paper."*

To identify your purpose, you ask questions about the subject. Asking "Who?" elicits information describing a person or a group. Asking "What?" requires you to find information defining a process, an event, a place, or an object. Asking "Why?" involves your finding information that explains the importance of the person or group, a process, an event, a place, an object, or the relationships among these. Asking "When?" helps you pinpoint the time frame you want to cover. Asking "How?" helps you focus on process.

Determining the Scope

Once you identify your purpose, you determine the **scope** of your paper. This refers to the general size and specification of your topic.

FIGURE 10.2   Example of Progressively Limiting a Subject's Scope

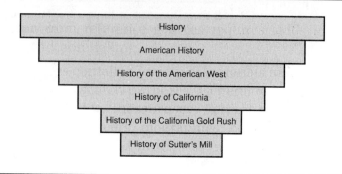

The scope of your topic needs to be neither too broad nor too specific but "just right." Your paper reflects its scope. Its contents, too, must be neither too broad nor too specific but "just right."

Scope involves setting limits on the amount of information covered and the number of details included. It also depends on your expertise, the amount of time you have to spend on the topic, and the type of paper you are writing. Once you determine your scope, you refrain from exceeding these limits. You set these limits by progressively narrowing your topic until it becomes a manageable size (see Figure 10.2). In doing so, you move from general to specific. Encyclopedias and textbooks do this when they divide information into sections or chapters. You can use these as a guide when setting the scope of your paper.

EXERCISE 10.1   Select five of the ten broad subjects below that most interest you. Go to your campus library and locate two references that pertain to each topic. Skim the references to help you narrow the scope to a workable topic.

1. Sexual harassment
2. Medical insurance
3. Computers
4. Gambling
5. Inventions

6. Abortion
7. Presidential campaigns
8. Educational costs
9. Automobiles
10. Monopolies

1. Subject:_____

    Subtopic:_____

    Subtopic:_____

    Subtopic:_____

    Workable Topic:_____

2. Subject:_____

    Subtopic:_____

    Subtopic:_____

    Subtopic:_____

    Workable Topic:_____

3. Subject:_____

    Subtopic:_____

    Subtopic:_____

    Subtopic:_____

    Workable Topic:_____

4. Subject:_____

    Subtopic:_____

    Subtopic:_____

    Subtopic:_____

    Workable Topic:_____

5. Subject:_____

    Subtopic:_____

    Subtopic:_____

    Subtopic:_____

    Workable Topic:_____

Writing the Thesis Statement

The scope of a paper's contents often determines the **thesis statement.** Because it defines the limits of your research, the thesis statement guides and controls your research, your writing, and—later—your audience. The thesis statement of your paper is much like a topic sentence in a paragraph. It states your paper's purpose and your major assertions or conclusions. You write your thesis statement in the form of a complete, declarative sentence. It restates your title or topic, states major assertions or conclusions (not minor details, illustrations, quotations), and establishes the purpose of your research.

For example, suppose you are researching the topic ''Rising Health Costs for Big Businesses'' to analyze results of increases in the cost of health care. You assert that the rising cost of health care results in lower dividends for stockholders. Based on this, your topic sentence could be: ''The rising cost of health care for employees threatens to wipe out many companies' profits.''

Creating a Title

Like the thesis statement, your title identifies the contents of your paper. Also, it needs to appeal to your readers, spark their interest in your topic, and motivate them to read your paper. According to the author Walker Percy, "A good title should be like a good metaphor; it should intrigue without being too baffling or too obvious." Often, your narrowed topic serves as the title of your paper. On the other hand, composing the thesis statement sometimes helps you form a more appropriate title. Such titles are precise and state your topic in a few key words. Wordy, overly cute, or fancy titles often detract from the seriousness of your research. Finally, it really doesn't matter if you title your paper before or after you write it. Sometimes you find through research or **synthesis** (concise, unified compilation of ideas) a title that perfectly fits your paper. Until then, your thesis statement serves as your composition guide. A good title is worth the wait. As Tennessee Williams once said, "The title comes last."

EXERCISE 10.2 Given the following topics, major assertions or conclusions, and purposes of research, construct a thesis statement for each topic.

1. *Topic:* The American Presidential Election of 1864
   Major assertions: Out of their desire for an end to the Civil War, many leading Republicans refused to support Abraham Lincoln in his bid for renomination to the presidency.
   Purpose of research: To analyze the political scene.

   *Thesis statement:*_____

   _____

2. *Topic:* Choosing a Personal Computer
   Major assertions: Choosing a personal computer is based on the software you want to use, the amount of money you have to spend, and the recommendations you receive from other users.
   Purpose of research: To compare and contrast features of Apple and IBM personal computers.

   *Thesis statement:*_____

   _____

3. *Topic:* Increasing Unemployment Rates in Urban Poverty Areas
   Major assertions: Unemployment rates in urban poverty areas have increased in the past five years.
   Purpose of research: To analyze reasons for the increase in unemployment rates in urban poverty areas.

*Thesis statement:*_____

_____

4. *Topic:* Quality of Health Care in Public Health Facilities
   Major assertions: Patient care in public health facilities is of a lower standard than that in private facilities.
   Purpose of research: To compare health care in public and private institutions.

   *Thesis statement:*_____

   _____

5. *Topic:* The Origin of the Universe
   Major assertions: One of the fundamental problems in astronomy is to develop a theory describing the origin of the universe.
   Purpose of research: To analyze various theories describing how the universe was formed.

   *Thesis statement:*_____

   _____

6. *Topic:* U.S. Space Program's Unmanned Interplanetary Missions
   Major assertions: Unmanned interplanetary missions are a major component of the U.S. space program. This is based on the fact that they began with the program's inception and continue today.
   Purpose of research: To chronicle the history of the U.S. space program's unmanned interplanetary missions.

   *Thesis statement:*_____

   _____

7. *Topic:* Comparing the Netherlands and My Home State
   Major assertions: The terrain of the Netherlands varies from low and flat to hilly.
   Purpose of research: To compare the Netherlands with my state.

   *Thesis statement:*_____

   _____

8. *Topic:* Cable Television: The Pros and Cons
   Major assertions: The local cable television company celebrated its tenth anniversary with the usual insincere promises of expansions and breakthroughs.
   Purpose of research: To analyze propaganda techniques used in advertisements to persuade people to subscribe to cable television.

   *Thesis statement:*_____

   _____

9. *Topic:* Rebuilding the Statue of Liberty
   Major assertions: The rebuilding of the Statue of Liberty was financed through contributions of patriotic Americans.

Purpose of research: To list the sources of contributions for the refurbishing of the Statue of Liberty.

*Thesis statement:*_____

_____

10. *Topic:* UFOs: Sightings as Proof
    Major assertions: Since 1947, reports of UFOs have been increasing. Large numbers of sightings in varied locations prove their existence.
    Purpose of research: To persuade the reader to believe in UFOs.

    *Thesis statement:*_____

    _____

GATHERING AND EVALUATING SOURCES OF INFORMATION

After you choose your subject, narrow your topic, and write your thesis statement, you gather information about your topic. You become the chef, locating ingredients and organizing what you find. After you find the data you need, you judge the integrity of the source in which it is found. Then you determine its usefulness as a **primary source** or **secondary source.** You take notes by carefully summarizing information or writing exact quotes. The process of gathering information is time-consuming but, if done correctly, makes writing the paper an easier task.

RESEARCH METHODS

There are numerous research methods you can use to locate information. As a researcher, you choose the method or methods that result in your finding the most information. Your skill in using these methods improves with practice, just as a chef's cooking improves with each dish.

Library Research

Locating, examining, and taking notes from library sources is probably the research method most often used (see Chapter 9). Your library's holdings include a vast array of written information on almost any topic. In addition, your library probably contains films, tapes, photographs, and materials in microform.

Observation

Observation is a second way to obtain information. It is the process of purposefully watching and noting what you see. The main problem with observation is that it's hard to see everything. The second is that your mind interprets what it sees. Thus, two people seeing the same event may note different details. Although observation is a subjective process, you can make it more objective by setting up a checklist before beginning your observation. You base this checklist on the details you plan to observe and, if possible, on prior research in your subject area. This increases the chances of your having a reliable observational checklist. Such a checklist helps you monitor the situation precisely and accurately. When reported in your paper, your checklist reflects your commitment to observing as objectively as possible.

Interviews

Conducting interviews is another way to acquire information. Deciding who to interview is your first step. You often find potential interviewees through library research or by talking with others. Once you decide who to interview, you schedule the interview. You can conduct interviews in person, by phone, or even by mail. Your most important responsibility is to be prepared for the interview. Not only should you know about the person you are interviewing, you need to know the questions you plan to ask. Asking questions becomes easier if you take a reporter's perspective. Asking *who, where, when, what, how,* and *why* helps you explore all areas of a topic. Most people enjoy talking about subjects that interest them and sharing their knowledge with you. However, most people lead busy lives. They don't have time for your lack of preparation. Like an observational checklist, a set of interview questions increases the chances that you will precisely and accurately get the information you need. Your main job in an interview is to listen actively (see Chapter 3). Your interview depends on your ability to hear and focus on what is said. Using a tape recorder helps you concentrate on what your subject is saying. It allows you to note nonverbal communication (such as gestures and expressions). A guide for interviewing is found in Table 10.2.

Personal Experience

Relating your personal experiences is an additional way of getting information. Personal examples add interest and realism to your writing. When narrating such an experience, you first decide what to

---

TABLE 10.2 Guide for Interviewing

Before the Interview You Should . . .

1. Decide who to interview.

2. Contact the person and arrange for a meeting.

3. Learn about the person to be interviewed.

4. Develop a list of questions to guide your interview.

5. Obtain a tape recorder for use in the interview. Be sure you have extra batteries and cassettes.

During the Interview You Should . . .

1. Establish rapport by talking informally before beginning the interview.

2. Ask permission to use the tape recorder.

3. Use your list of questions as a guide but be flexible.

4. Observe and make notes about nonverbal behavior (gestures, expressions).

5. Write down particularly important statements or conclusions.

6. At the end of the interview, indicate your gratitude and your intention to provide a copy of your paper to the interviewee.

After the Interview You Should . . .

1. Listen to the tape(s) to get the gist of the overall interview.

2. Transcribe the entire interview.

3. Decide what information to omit or stress.

4. Organize notes according to your thesis statement and the structure of your paper.

5. Draw conclusions and synthesize.

6. Mail or hand deliver a copy of your paper to the interviewee.

---

emphasize. Then you select the details which convey that impression. When writing, you organize these details to describe the incident accurately and briefly. However, you need to proceed carefully. Overuse of personal examples negates your paper's worth as scholarly research.

Personal Inferences

Drawing conclusions about what you've read, seen, or heard is a final way of gathering information. Inferring relationships between two known factors or between the known and unknown provides new insights into familiar topics. Such guesses, as with stories of personal experience, require supporting judgment and thought. Hypotheses

"But how will we footnote this source?!"

about information require research. You make such assertions only when you present evidence to support your opinions.

EVALUATING SOURCES

Because you want your research to be accurate, you evaluate the information you gather. This involves assessing the value of a particular book, article, or example to your paper.

Evaluating sources is difficult if you are unfamiliar with the information. Thus, you first should examine several general or introductory discussions of the topic. You may not use that general information in your paper, but it will provide the context for understanding more complex information.

Primary versus Secondary Sources

In evaluating references, you first determine if a source is a primary source or secondary source. Primary sources are original documents (speeches, research, writings) or first-person accounts of an event. Secondary sources interpret, evaluate, describe, or otherwise restate the work of primary sources. If a document cites references from another source, it's best to locate and read the original document for yourself. Because information may be lost in translation, primary sources are generally preferred. Identifying a source as primary or secondary often depends on the content of your research (see Table 10.3).

TABLE 10.3   A Guide to Primary and Secondary Sources in Content Areas

	Primary Sources	**Secondary Sources**
Literary Topics	novels, poems, plays, short stories, letters, diaries, manuscripts, autobiographies	journal articles, reviews, biographies, critical books about writers and their works
Government, Political Science, History	speeches, writings by presidents and others, the *Congressional Record*, reports of agencies and departments, documents written by historic figures	newspaper reports, newsmagazines, political journals and newsletters, journal articles, and history books
Social Sciences	case studies, findings from surveys and from questionnaires, reports of social workers, psychiatrists, and lab technicians	commentary and evaluations in reports, documents, journal articles, and books
Sciences	tools and methods, experiments, findings from tests and experiments, observations, discoveries, and test patterns	interpretations and discussions of test data as found in journals and books (note that scientific books, which are quickly dated, are less valuable than up-to-date journals)
Fine Arts	films, paintings, music, sculptures, as well as reproductions and synopses of these for research purposes	evaluations in journal articles, critical reviews, biographies and critical books about the artists and their works
Business	market research and testing, technical studies and investigations, drawings, designs, models, memoranda and letters, computer data	discussion of the business world in newspapers, business magazines and journals, government documents, and books
Education	pilot studies, term projects, sampling results, tests and test data, surveys, interviews, observations, statistics, and computer data	analysis and evaluation of educational experimentation in journals, reports, pamphlets, and books

SOURCE: From *Writing Research Papers: A Complete Guide,* by James B. Lester. Copyright © 1986 by Scott Foresman & Co. Reprinted by permission of HarperCollins Publishers.

Relevancy

You judge the **relevancy,** or usefulness, of each source to your paper in two ways.

First, you decide if information is needed for your paper's arguments, conclusions, or summary. In determining relevancy, you ask if the information provides new or important supportive data about your topic. If so, you include it. If not, you omit it from your working bibliography.

Second, you determine if the publication date of the source is current enough for inclusion. Some content areas require historical perspectives, but others—like science or technology—change rapidly. If the information you find is outdated, then its worth to your paper is limited. In general, you want the most current research available.

EXERCISE 10.3   Identify each of the following as a primary (P) or secondary (S) source.

1. _____
   Author: Dr. John Doe, noted educator
   Title: "Education in the One-Room School: A Treatise on Education in the 1800s"
   Publication: *Connecticut Education Quarterly*
   Date Published: 1990
   Publisher: Connecticut Education Association

2. _____
   Author: Dr. Jane Doe, noted electrical engineer
   Title: "Solar Energy: The Hope of the Nineties"
   Publication: *American Scientific Magazine*
   Date Published: 1992
   Publisher: Science Associates Press

3. _____
   Interviewee: Mrs. Jane Doe, veteran of World War II
   Title: Untitled notes from 1943–1945
   Publication: Unpublished
   Date of Interview: December 1986
   Publisher: None

4. _____
   Author: John Doe, Army private killed in Vietnam
   Title: "Letters Home: A Wartime Correspondence 1968–1970"
   Publication: *Read*, a bimonthly publication of award-winning fiction and nonfiction
   Date Published: 1972
   Publisher: American Press

5. _____
Author:	Jane Doe, professor of political science
Title:	"Economic Effects of the Civil War"
Publication:	*National Encyclopedia*
Date:	1983
Publisher:	National Encyclopedia, Inc.

7. _____
Author:	Jane Doe, survivor of breast cancer
Title:	"How Cancer Changes Your Life"
Publication:	*Woman's Monthly Journal*
Date Published:	April 1991
Publisher:	Woman's Monthly, Inc.

8. _____
Author:	Jane Doe
Title:	"In the War Zone"
Publication:	*1776: Poetry about the American Revolution*
Date:	1959
Publisher:	University Press

9. _____
Author:	John Doe
Title:	*We Went Hungry*
Publication:	Diary written during the Great Depression
Date Published:	1990
Publisher:	Haliburton Press

10. _____
Author:	John Doe, feature reporter
Title:	"Reunion at Dover: War Veterans Return for Fortieth Anniversary–1984"
Publication:	*Contemporary News*, a daily national news publication
Date:	1984
Publisher:	U.S. Contemporary, Inc.

Objectivity and Bias

Objectivity refers to the author's ability to report information without expressing unsubstantiated, personal opinions. When writing objectively, an author presents facts without letting personal feelings or **bias** (prejudice or slanted interpretations) distort what is written. Bias is difficult to identify unless you are familiar with the subject or the author's background and qualifications.

For example, suppose an author who has published several books about Freudian psychology states, "Freud was the greatest psychologist of modern times. Only a few ignorant souls know nothing about him. A student's greatest learning experience is reading about Freud." Clearly, the statement contains author bias, the author's beliefs about the subject. Although this author is qualified to discuss Freud, the information provided about Freud is slanted. The inclusion of biased material undermines the validity and academic integrity of your research.

Author's Qualifications

An author's qualifications depend on many factors. First, you must judge an author's educational and professional background. This is important because an author's background often affects **point of view**—perspective—and the manner in which data are reported. You can find background information in an article or book's preliminary or concluding statements or in a biographical dictionary or encyclopedia. Discussions with professionals in the field also help you obtain information about an author.

Second, you judge where the author works and the reputation of that school, company, or other institution. You also evaluate the author's professional reputation. Usually, the works of a well-respected, widely published author contain useful and pertinent information. Sometimes, however, authors who are well-known authorities in one subject publish information below their normal standards in another. As a critical reader, you need to be able to distinguish between solid gold and gold-plated information.

Sometimes the background information you need about an author is unavailable. Then, you need an alternative plan for judging the reliability of the information. Suppose that an article in *Today's Health* compares the high incidence of heart disease in America with the low incidence in Norway. The author, whom you know nothing about, concludes that the climate of Norway keeps its people healthy. Because the weather there is often cold, the author suggests that Americans move from southern states. The statements made in *Today's Health* may be as unreliable as those made earlier about Freud. Because the article gives no background information about the author, you cannot judge author qualifications or bias. In fact, the author might be the owner of condominiums in the Northeast! You can, however, judge the reputation of the journal that contains the article. You examine its professionalism and the standards it sets for its articles. You determine what type of publication the journal is by seeing if it appeals to academic or professional readers or a more general audience. Information reported in academic or professional publications is generally well grounded in research.

Difficulty

Journal articles and technical papers are written for people in the field who have significant expertise on the subject, not students writing research papers. This doesn't mean that you must exclude this information. You just need to approach it in a different manner.

If you lack the background knowledge and/or vocabulary to understand the information, try reading encyclopedia entries, textbook sections, or other introductory information on the subject. Identify key words and look them up for future reference. Discuss the information with your instructor. Your instructor should be able to clarify the information or tell you if the information is beyond the scope of your paper. Finally, put this source aside until you have read and considered other sources. They may provide the background information necessary for understanding the more complex information.

When you feel ready to attempt to work with the information, review the concepts and terms you learned in introductory readings. Read the introduction and summary or conclusion first. Read more slowly and carefully than usual and monitor your understanding. Stop periodically and summarize what you read. Highlight and label text when possible. Finally, avoid taking or using notes when you do not fully understand.

EXERCISE 10.4 You are writing a research paper on the history of U.S. armed forces (1800–1990) for history class. Using the sources in Exercise 10.3, identify, by number, the sources that would be suitable for inclusion in your paper.

_____

_____

_____

_____

_____

_____

_____

SYNTHESIZING SOURCES

It's a great feeling. You have completed your research. You have taken your last note. No more searching through stacks of books and articles for information. You have everything you need. All you have to do is combine the information and write the paper.

For some people, the moment of elation over completing their research turns to one of dread. Like Betty Rollin, they suddenly have that "I'm-over-my-head-and-this-time-they're-going-to-catch-me" feeling. You, too, may experience these "what-do-I-do-now" feelings when you begin the actual writing process.

As in identifying and collecting research information, your thesis statement guides the process of writing your paper. It reminds you of the original purpose of your research and the limits you set for its scope. Knowing your purpose and limits helps you organize the information you've collected. Outlining and charting major sections provides you with the means of establishing the framework for the development of your topic.

OUTLINES

Outlining—organizing information in a sequence—is the first step in synthesis. Because research usually is collected from a variety of sources at different times, information may seem disjointed and isolated. Thus, in completing an outline, you first review your notes. This helps you become familiar with what they contain.

The second stage of outlining—determining relevance—depends on how well you know what your references contain. Now you judge their importance to your paper. One way to do this is to randomly list important terms and concepts necessary to the understanding of your topic. Next, determine the relative importance of each term and concept. You do this by making inferences about the relationships between common themes found in your research and your paper's purpose. These themes become the main headings or subheadings of your outline, depending upon their complexity. If the remaining terms and concepts further develop your topic, they become supporting details. You omit unnecessary information.

The third stage of outlining begins the charting process in synthesis. Once you identify the main headings and subheadings you wish to include, you search for information on these themes in your different sources.

CHARTS

As discussed in Chapter 5, charts help you identify and categorize information. As you write your research paper, they aid you in comparing themes from various sources.

To construct a synthesis chart for writing (see Figure 10.3), you first list horizontally the sources you plan to use as references. Then, you list vertically the themes you've identified. Third, you construct a grid by drawing lines between each theme and each source. Now, you determine if the source contains information about a specific theme and briefly note that information. Fifth, you look at your chart to categorize sources based on likenesses and differences of information contained in them. This helps you to see patterns and relationships. Finally, you use the chart to write your paper.

FIGURE 10.3   Example of Synthesis Chart, Sources, and Resulting Paper (*Source 1 begins here*)

INTRODUCTION

The hardware of the computer is the physical devices that comprise the computer system: the central processing unit, the input devices, the output devices, and the storage devices. Basically, hardware includes all parts of the computer that are tangible. Hardware is *not* operating systems, concepts, or programs (these are software). Hardware consists of only those parts of the computer that one could reach out and touch.

THE CENTRAL PROCESSING UNIT

The **central processing unit**, or **CPU**, is the essence of the computer's hardware. It is the "brain" of the computer. It tells the other parts of the computer what to do; it decides what to do with the instructions that the programmer gives it; and it ensures that the tasks assigned to it are properly carried out.

    The CPU is composed of three separate units—the control unit, the arithmetic/logic unit, and the primary storage unit (Figure 2-1). The **control unit** is, quite literally, in control of the operations. It reads the actual instructions and tells the other computer parts what to do. The control unit directs the appropriate input device to send the necessary data. It keeps track of what parts of the program have already been executed and which ones are left to be done. Finally, it controls the execution of the specific instructions, collects the output, and sends the output to the designated output device.

    The **arithmetic/logic unit (ALU)** is the computer's own personal mathematician. It executes all arithmetic and logic statements. Logic statements aren't quite so straightforward as arithmetic statements, but they are equally easy to understand. A logic statement is a statement that makes a comparison and then does something based on the result. For example, if today is Friday, then pick up paycheck and go to the bank; if not, don't. Obviously, this isn't quite the type of logic statement that the computer would work with, but the idea is the same. More likely, the computer would want to know: If this is the end of the input data, then make the calculations and output the results. If not, read the rest of the input. Arithmetic and logic operations are the only type of instructions that the ALU can execute. But when you think about it, you will realize that almost everything you want the computer to do is either an arithmetic or logic problem. The only noticeable exceptions are reading input and printing output. (These are controlled by the control unit.)

    The **primary storage unit** is in charge of storing data and programs in the computer's internal memory. It is very important to distinguish this internal memory, called primary storage, from external memory, called auxiliary storage. The primary storage unit is a part of the actual internal hardware of the computer. Without the primary storage unit, the computer could not work because it would not be able to store the programs. Auxiliary storage is not necessary for the computer to function; it is not part of its internal hardware. The CPU can access only primary storage; information between primary and auxiliary storage is transferred through electrical lines.

    Most current primary storage hardware consists of **semiconductors** which have their memory circuitry on silicon chips. The data are stored in **bit cells,** located on the chips, which can be in either an "on" or an "off" state. Each cell holds a BInary digiT (bit). The cells are arranged so that they can be written to or read from as needed.

CENTRAL PROCESSING UNIT (CPU)
Acts as the "brain" of the computer.

CONTROL UNIT
Controls the execution of programs.

ARITHMETIC/LOGIC UNIT (ALU)
Executes mathematical and logic statements.

PRIMARY STORAGE UNIT
The computer's internal memory.

SEMICONDUCTOR
A type of primary storage that stores data in bit cells located on silicon chips.

FIGURE 10.3   Continued (*Source 1 ends here*)

Basically, the primary storage unit holds the program that is being executed, as well as its input, output, and intermediate results of any calculations. When a program is entered into the computer, the control unit sends the program to the primary storage unit. The control unit then retrieves one line at a time from the primary storage unit. Therefore, the primary storage unit acts somewhat like a shelf upon which statements, instructions, and results are placed when they aren't being read by the control unit.

All three parts of the central processing unit work together to enable the computer to function. Together they are often called the "computer proper" because in some microcomputers, they *are* the computer. In any computer, the CPU is the central core.

Computers derive most of their amazing power from three features; speed, accuracy, and memory. Generally, computer speed is expressed as the time required to perform one operation. The following units of time apply:

BIT CELL
Used in semiconductors; stores data by designating each cell as "on" or "off."

UNIT	SYMBOL	FRACTIONS OF A SECOND	
Millisecond	ms	one-thousandth	(1/1,000)
Microsecond	μs	one-millionth	(1/1,000,000)
Nanosecond	ns	one-billionth	(1/1,000,000,000)
Picosecond	ps	one-trillionth	(1/1,000,000,000,000)

Today's computers can complete computations in a matter of **nanoseconds.**

A nanosecond is one-billionth of a second. The best way to comprehend just how small a nanosecond is is to compare it visually with one second. In the computer, computations are made electrically. The speed of electricity is approximately the speed of light. Thus, in one second the electricity used for computations will travel 186,000 miles. In one nanosecond that electricity will travel 11.8 inches.

NANOSECOND
One-billionth of a second.

MORE ON INTERNAL STORAGE
Storage Locations and Addresses

When the CPU stores programs, input data, and output, it does not do so randomly. These items are stored in specific memory locations that can then be accessed by their addresses to retrieve their contents.

To process information, the CPU's control unit must first locate in storage each instruction and piece of data. Computer storage can be compared with a large array of mailboxes. Each mailbox is a specific location and can hold one item of information. Since each location in storage has a distinct address, stored-program instructions can locate particular items by giving their addresses.

Suppose, for instance, the computer is instructed to calculate an employee's salary by subtracting TOTAL TAX from his or her GROSS PAY.

FIGURE 10.3   Continued (*Source 2 begins here*)

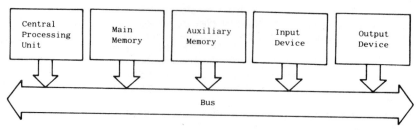

Fig. 3-1. The hardware components of a computer system.

- *Main memory.* The data that the computer is manipulating and the program that it is executing are both stored in main memory. In many respects, main memory serves as the computer's scratch pad or blackboard.

- *Input and output devices.* Input and output devices convert data between the binary codes that computers use and forms suitable for human use—such as pictures, sounds, and printed text.

- *Auxiliary memory.* Auxiliary memory is used for long-term storage of data files and program libraries. If main memory is the computer's scratch pad, auxiliary memory is its filing cabinet.

For large computers, the central processor and main memory usually occupy one centrally located cabinet, around which are arranged the input, output, and auxiliary memory devices. For this reason, the input, output, and auxiliary memory devices are often called *peripherals.* In small computers, however, some or all of the "peripherals" may be installed in the same cabinet as the central processor and main memory.

The Central Processing Unit

The central processing unit is *the* essential component of a computer because it is the part that executes the program. Other components—such as auxiliary memory, input and output devices, or even main memory—can sometimes be omitted. But without a central processor, there is no computer.

Not surprisingly, in view of the job it has to do, the central processor is the most complex part of a computer. This is why the development of the microprocessor, a central processor on a single silicon chip, was such an important advance. Microprocessors make it possible to buy the complex central processor as a single, inexpensive component, instead of having to build it out of thousands of individual transistors and integrated circuits.

The central processor is itself made up of two components—*the arithmetic-logic unit,* which does the calculations, and the *control unit,* which coordinates the activities of the entire computer.

The arithmetic-logic unit

The arithmetic-logic unit performs the same jobs for a computer that a pocket calculator performs for a human being. It can perform arithmetical operations, comparisons, and logical operations.

Arithmetical operations. The arithmetic-logic unit adds, subtracts, multiplies, and divides. On some computers, only addition and subtraction are built into the arithmetic-logic unit. Such machines need programs to tell them how to multiply and divide.

Comparisons. The arithmetic-logic unit can determine such things as whether two alphabetic characters are the same or whether one number is less than, equal to, or greater than another. The results of these comparisons are made available to the control unit, which can use them to determine which instruction to execute next. Under the control of its program, the computer can "decide" what action to take next depending on the input it has received and on the outcome of previous calculations.

FIGURE 10.3   Continued (*Source 2*)

This decision-making capability allows a computer to be far more responsive to its user's requests than is possible with most other machines. Indeed, one reason computers are often installed in machines such as household appliances is to endow these machines with some of the computer's flexibility and responsiveness.

Logical operations. Sometimes we want to use complicated criteria to determine the action a computer will take. For example, we may ask a computer to print the names of every employee of a company who has been with the company more than ten years *and* who makes less than twenty thousand dollars *and* who has not had a raise in the last three years.

In general, such criteria consist of simple conditions (such as ''the employee has been with the company more than ten years'') joined by *and, or,* or *not.* Given whether each of the simple conditions is true or false for a particular individual, the program must calculate whether or not the overall criterion is satisfied. To simplify this kind of calculation, the arithmetic/logic unit provides *logical operations*, which correspond to the English words *and, or,* and *not.*

The control unit

The control unit fetches instructions one by one from main memory. Like everything stored in memory, instructions are represented by binary codes. The control unit decodes each instruction, then sends the necessary control signals to other units (such as the arithmetic-logic unit or a peripheral device) to get the instruction carried out.

The control unit is said to work in a *fetch-execute cycle* because it fetches each instruction from main memory and then executes the instruction. When an instruction has been executed, the control unit fetches the next instruction, executes it, and so on. (To speed things up, some computers fetch the next instruction while the previous instruction is being executed.)

It's important to realize that no matter how complex or subtle the job is that the program is doing, the control unit is still working in a simple, repetitive cycle—fetching and executing instructions, one after another. Herein lies the real power of programming: A machine that works in a very simple, repetitive cycle can nevertheless exhibit very complicated behavior by following suitable instructions. People who sneer that a computer can only do what it is told to do completely miss this point.

Computer Memory   *Memory* is the part of the computer that stores information for later use. Most computers have both *main memory* and *auxiliary memory.* Main memory is sometimes referred to as *main storage, primary memory,* or *primary storage.* In the past, because of the widespread use of the now-obsolete magnetic-core technology, main memory was often called *core.* Auxiliary memory is sometimes referred to as *auxiliary storage, secondary memory, secondary storage,* or *mass storage.*

Main memory

A computer's main memory is divided into a large number of individual *memory locations*, each of which can hold a certain amount of data. Each location has an *address*, which the central processor uses to designate which location to store data in or retrieve data from. We can picture a computer's memory as an array of post-office boxes, each having a unique address and containing an item of data.

Access to data stored in main memory is very fast. The time required to store a data item in main memory or to recall an item from main memory is measured in billionths of a second. Main memory also allows

FIGURE 10.3   Continued (*Source 2 ends here*)

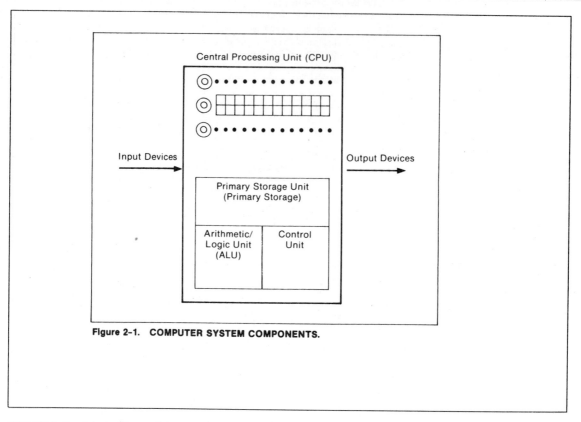

Figure 2-1. **COMPUTER SYSTEM COMPONENTS.**

FIGURE 10.3 Continued (*Source 3 begins here*)

The Central Processing Unit

The **central processing unit (CPU)** is the heart of the computer system. It is composed of three units: the control unit, the arithmetic/logic unit (ALU), and the primary storage unit. Each unit performs its own unique functions.

The **control unit**, as its name implies, controls what is happening in the CPU. It does not process or store data; rather, it directs the sequence of operations. The control unit retrieves one instruction at a time from the storage unit. It interprets the instruction and sends the necessary signals to the ALU and storage unit for the instruction to be carried out. This process is repeated until all the instructions have been executed.

Another function of the control unit is to communicate with the input device in order to transfer program instructions and data into storage. Similarly, it communicates with the output device to transfer results from storage to the output device.

The **arithmetic/logic unit (ALU)** handles the execution of all arithmetic computations. It does not store data; it merely performs the necessary calculations. Functions performed by the ALU include arithmetic operations (addition, subtraction, multiplication, and division) and comparisons. Since the bulk of computer processing involves calculations or comparisons, the capabilities of a computer often depend upon the capabilities of the ALU.

The **primary storage unit (internal storage** or **main storage)** holds all the instructions and data necessary for processing. These are transferred from an input device to the primary storage unit, where they are held until needed for processing. Data that are being processed and intermediate results from ALU calculations are also held in primary storage. After all processing is completed, the control unit directs the final results to be transferred to an output device.

A **microprocessor** is the CPU of a microcomputer. It performs arithmetic operations and control functions, much as the CPU of a large computer does; however, a microprocessor fits on a single silicon chip the size of a nailhead (see Figure 2-2).

CENTRAL PROCESSING UNIT The heart of a computer system, consisting of three components.

CONTROL UNIT The part of the CPU that directs operations.

ARITHMETIC/ LOGIC UNIT The part of the CPU that executes arithmetic computations and comparisons.

PRIMARY STORAGE Part of storage inside the CPU.

The CPU in Operation

Let us examine a simple problem. Assume we want the computer to add two numbers and print the result. The following series of steps demonstrates the flow of program instructions and data through the CPU.

Step A: The control unit directs an input device to transfer program instructions to primary storage. (As will be shown later, some data and instructions may be stored outside of the CPU and transferred to primary storage when needed.) Since this is a simple problem, there may be only two instructions—one to add and one to print.

Step B: The control unit examines the first instruction and interprets it as addition.

Step C: The control unit sends an electronic signal for the data (the two numbers) to be brought into primary storage from an input device, or for data already in primary storage to be transferred to the ALU.

FIGURE 10.3   Continued (*Source 3 ends here*)

Step D: The ALU performs the necessary calculation (addition).

Step E : The results are transferred back to the primary storage unit.

Steps B through E: These steps are repeated until all instructions are executed. (In this simplified example, steps B through E are not repeated.)

Step F : The control unit signals the primary storage unit to transfer the results to an output device to be printed.

"It looks like Coach Henson's been using my terminal again."

SOURCE 3: Reprinted with permission from *Introduction to Computers and BASIC Programming,* by Brenan and Mandell. © 1984 by West Publishing Company. All rights reserved.

FIGURE 10.3   Continued

Synthesis Chart:

Topic: Central Processing Unit

	BRENAN/MANDELL	HOPPER/MANDELL	GRAHAM
CONTROL UNIT			
DIRECTS PROCESSES	X	X	X
Retrieves instructions	X	X	X
Interprets instructions	X	X	X
Sends instructions	X	X	X
COMMUNICATES W/INPUT & OUTPUT	X		
Reads input		X	
Prints output		X	
DECISION-MAKING CAPABILITY			X
USES BINARY CODES			X
EXECUTES "FETCH, EXECUTE CYCLES"			X
ARITHMETIC LOGIC UNIT			
PERFORMS ARITHMETICAL CALCULATIONS	X	X	X
COMPARES INFORMATION	X		X
$<, >, =$			X
CARRIES OUT LOGICAL OPERATIONS		X	X
"and," "or," "not"			X
DEFINITION OF LOGIC STATEMENT		X	
PRIMARY STORAGE			
SAME AS INTERNAL OR MAIN STORAGE	X	X	
FUNCTIONS OF PRIMARY STORAGE	X	X	
Holds program being executed	X	X	
Holds results	X	X	
PRIMARY STORAGE HARDWARE		X	

Paper:

The Central Processing Unit

A computer's central processing unit consists of three components: the control unit, the arithmetic logic unit, and primary storage.

In general, the control unit directs the computer's processes by retrieving instructions from storage, interpreting and sending instructions back to storage (Brenan and Mandell, 1984; Graham, 1983; and Hopper and Mandell, 1984). These form "fetch-execute" cycles (Graham 1983). It also communicates with input and output devices by reading input and printing output (Hopper and Mandell, 1984). The control unit utilizes binary codes and has decision-making capability (Graham, 1983).

The second component of the central processing unit is the arithmetic logic unit (ALU). As its name suggests, the ALU performs arithmetical calculations (Brenan and Mandell, 1984; Graham, 1983; and Hopper and Mandell, 1984). It also compares information (Brenan and Mandell, 1984; Graham, 1983) by determining if one piece of information is equal to, greater than, or less than another piece of information (Graham,

1983). The ALU also carries out logical operations (Graham, 1983; Hopper and Mandell, 1984). A logic statement is "a statement that makes a comparison and then does something about it based on the results" (Hopper and Mandell, 1984).

Primary storage (also called internal or main storage) is a final component of the central processing unit. It holds both the program being executed and the results of processing (Brenan and Mandell, 1984; Hopper and Mandell, 1984). Here data is stored as binary digits (bits) in the computer's hardware (Hopper and Mandell, 1984).

EXERCISE 10.5   On a separate sheet of paper, construct a synthesis chart and write a paper comparing and contrasting information found in the following sources. (Sample pages from the *Sociology* source begin here)

Biological, Psychological, and Sociological Aspects of Aging

Aging occurs in three ways: biological, psychological, and sociological.

BIOLOGICAL ASPECTS OF AGING. There are various views about how the body ages (Birren 1986):

1. *Tissue organ deficiency*. Tissues and organs of the body may become diseased, so that the body becomes debilitated. This view is too limiting and does not address the issue of whether the diseased tissues/organs cause aging or are the result of aging. Also, there is considerable variability between people regarding the rate at which these tissues/organs alter with time.

2. *Hardening of the arteries*. This view emphasizes that as individuals age, their arteries become clogged, preventing the blood from taking oxygen and nutrients to the vital organs of the body. Decline in alertness, for example, would be explained as a consequence of inadequate oxygen to the brain. This focus also has limitations because changes in the blood vessels are currently viewed as an avoidable condition.

3. *Endocrine gland malfunction*. Another biological view of aging suggests that it is tied to the breakdown of the endocrine glands (including thyroid, pancreas, gonads, adrenals). However, researchers have discovered that hormone levels, by themselves, do not have inevitable predictable effects on the body.

4. *Immunity system changes*. Another aspect of aging suggests that "the debilitated older person may not only come to forget events, names, and familiar faces, but may also gradually lose the biological memory necessary to recognize and fight previously encountered viruses and 'unfriendly' proteins" (Birren 1986, 271). However, lower forms of life without specialized immune systems also show characteristics of aging. Hence, the breakdown of an immune system does not automatically lead to aging.

5. *Genetic diseases*. Longevity is an inherited trait. While diet, exercise, and lack of stress all play a role in avoiding disease and living a long time, individuals whose parents and grandparents have lived a long time are more likely to have a similar lifespan than are those whose ancestors died relatively early.

These biological changes emphasize that although the body does alter with time, it does so in different degrees and at different rates. Hence, any statement that a person will experience a specific biological decline at a specific age must be considered tentative.

PSYCHOLOGICAL THEORIES OF AGING. In studying aging, psychologists look at changes in the speed of behavior, and changes in perception, memory, and depression.

1. *Speed of behavior*. As an individual ages, so it is assumed, it takes longer to register incoming information, process it, and act. But the degree to which there is slowing of behavior, and whether this change is inevitable, are controversial. In some cases, with extensive and concerted effort to master a specific task, speed of response can increase.

2. *Perception*. Perception, both visual and auditory, may change with age. Our eyes and ears are not immune to generalized decline. However, independent of disease (glaucoma, cataracts), visual perceptual functioning may remain substantially intact. The ability to hear higher tones, and every syllable of what someone is saying, generally declines with age. The psychological effect of such loss may be the development of mild paranoia. The elderly may assume others are talking about them.

3. *Memory*. Short-term memory functions also decline with age. The elderly take slightly longer to retrieve information.

▼   LIVING SOCIOLOGY   ▼

In our society, mistakes in memory on the part of the elderly are labeled differently than similar mistakes on the part of young people. If a young person forgets something, we say that he or she simply forgot. If an old person forgets something, we say that he or she is old. The way our society regards "memory mistakes" is another illustration of its prejudice against the elderly.

(Sociology, continuing)

4. *Depression.* Depression is the most common psychological complaint of the elderly. Feelings of hopelessness, worthlessness, and despair characterize depression. Depression can be mild, lasting a few days; or debilitating, requiring hospitalization. The causes of depression may be physiological (brain cell degeneration) or cultural (social changes in the person's life, such as loss of spouse, job, or children). Treatment may involve taking medication and increasing their involvement in meaningful relationships, social positions, and roles.

Psychological variables influence biological outcomes. For example, feelings of not being in control of one's life circumstance or of feeling helpless or hopeless have been correlated with an increase in reported physical symptoms (Pennebaker et al. 1977).

SOCIOLOGICAL ASPECTS OF AGING. The concept of social aging refers to the arbitrary social definitions of what is appropriate or expected of people at various ages. Definition of the situation and status-role connections become important in discussing how individuals age sociologically.

If people define themselves as old (Thomas and Thomas 1928), the consequences of their doing so are to limit what they do. People who define themselves as too old to be a romantic lover, a hang-glider flyer, or a race-track driver tend to avoid these roles. Others may also define the elderly as persons who should engage in certain behaviors (play canasta) and not others (use a skateboard).

The status a person is in implies certain role behaviors. People whose status is elderly (that is, elderly people) are expected to act certain ways. Although some elderly people like to skydive and some young people like to play canasta, age tends to limit the range of behavior considered appropriate. A 10-year-old can be a member of a neighborhood skateboard group, a cub scout, and a fourth grader. A 16-year-old can be a driver, an 18-year-old a voter, a 21-year-old a legal alcohol drinker, and a 65-year-old a retiree. Each age status provides eligibility for some roles and closes eligibility for other roles. An 18-year-old cannot be a grandparent and a 90-year-old cannot compete in the Olympics.

One consequence of accepting social definitions of status positions is to restrict people into interactions in subgroups with others who approve of their role choices. The young and the old keep to themselves (have a disproportionate level of interaction within their own groups) because their peers approve of their role behavior.

Aging brings new statuses. Although there are various status paths, a typical one involves being a child, teenager, spouse, parent, empty nester, grandparent, retiree, and widow or widower. Other statuses some assume along the way are divorced person, single parent, and stepparent.

The culture an individual lives in defines the value of that person. In our youth-oriented culture, the elderly are more likely to feel devalued. "Evidence indicates that young adults view the life circumstances of older adults more negatively than do older adults themselves. Hence, the young regard aging as moving from, rather than toward, an ideal state" (Birren 1986, 277). Sociologists suggest that as people adopt statuses that have traditionally been associated with being old, they inadvertently adopt the values associated with those statuses. For example, because the retired are stereotyped as being bored, some people may adopt those feelings once they assume the status. Sometimes the elderly are subjected to worse treatment than negative social reflections. They are abused (see the feature on the next page).

▼ GERONTOLOGICAL THEORIES OF AGING

Gerontology is the study of the process of aging and of the elderly. Social gerontology focuses on the social changes that occur as individuals age. Five general theories of aging follow.

Disengagement Theory

The earliest and most controversial theory of aging, disengagement theory, was developed by Cumming and Henry (1961). They took the view that as people age and move toward death they gradually disengage from all social attachments, obligations, and activities. The researchers viewed the process as natural and emphasized that the process of withdrawal was functional both for society and the elderly.

Reaction to the theory was immediate and negative. The theory (as originally proposed) did not

(Sociology, continuing)

acknowledge that individuals in different cultures vary in how much they "disengage." Indeed, in some cultures, the elderly stay very much involved in social relationships and in society. In addition, many people in our society do not typically disengage. We discuss one such group, the centenarians, later in this chapter.

Exchange Theory

Dowd (1980) argues from an exchange theory perspective that the elderly withdraw because they have nothing to offer other people as an incentive to interact with them (the elderly). Young people are generally not interested in interacting with the elderly because they (the young) look to peers for companionship. Corporations also tend to favor young rather than old employees. Exchange theory says that the elderly are usually forced into a lower devalued social position because they have nothing of value to offer society.

This theory is flawed because the elderly do offer skills others regard as rewarding. For example, grandparents provide invaluable child care for their children and grandchildren. The elderly as workers also have shown themselves to be responsible and productive.

EXERCISE 10.5   Continued (Sample pages from the *Psychology* source begin here)

Chapter 4: From Birth to Death: Life-Span Development   131

▪▪▪ Aging—Will You Still Need Me When I'm 64?

Some years ago, students at Long Beach City College in California elected Pearl Taylor their spring festival queen. Ms. Taylor had everything necessary to win: looks, intelligence, personality, and campus-wide popularity. At about the same time, citizens of Raleigh, North Carolina, elected Isabella Cannon as their mayor.

Question: What's so remarkable about these events?

Not too much really, except that Pearl was 90 years old when elected, and Isabella was 73 (Barrow & Smith, 1979). Both are part of the graying of America. Currently, some 30 million Americans are over the age of 65. By the year 2020, some 50 million persons, or *1 out of every* 5, will be 65 years of age or older. These figures make the elderly the fastest-growing segment of society. Understandably, psychologists have become increasingly interested in aging.

Question: What is life like for the aged?

There are large variations in aging. Most of us have known elderly individuals at both extremes: those who are active, healthy, and satisfied and whose minds are clear and alert; and those who are confused, childlike, dependent, or senile. Despite such variations, some generalizations can be made.

Aging   **Biological aging** is a gradual process that begins quite early in life. Peak functioning in most physical capacities reaches a maximum by about 25 to 30 years of age. Thereafter, gradual declines occur in muscular strength, flexibility, circulatory efficiency, speed of response, sensory acuity, and other functions.

Biological aging Physiological changes that accompany increasing age and alter a variety of physical and psychological functions.

Maximum life span The biologically determined maximum number of years humans could live under optimal conditions.

Life expectancy The average number of years a person of a given sex, race, and nationality can expect to live.

Question: So people are "over the hill" by 30?

Hardly! Prime abilities come at different ages for different activities. Peak performances for professional football and baseball players usually occur in the mid-20s; for professional bowlers, the mid-30s; for artists and musicians, the 50s; and for politicians, philosophers, business or industrial leaders and others, the early 60s.

For those who are still young, the prospect of aging physically may be the greatest threat of old age (see Highlight 4-2). However, it is wrong to believe that most elderly people are sickly, infirm, or senile. Only about 5 percent of those over 65 years old are in nursing homes. As for the possibility of a mental slide, physician Alex Comfort (1976) comments, "The human brain does not shrink, wilt, perish, or deteriorate with age. It normally continues to function well through as many as 9 decades." As a **gerontologist** (jer-ON-TOL-o-jist: one who studies aging), Comfort estimates that only 25 percent of the disability of old people is medically based. The remaining 75 percent is social, political, and cultural.

Gerontologist One who scientifically studies aging and its effects.

Comfort's view is backed by studies of the intellectual capacities of aging individuals. Little overall decline occurs in intelligence test scores with aging. Although it is true that **fluid abilities** (those requiring speed or rapid learning) may decline, **crystallized abilities,** such as vocabulary and stored-up knowledge, actually improve— at least into the 70s (Baltes & Schaie, 1974). The general intellectual decline attributed to old age is largely a myth.

Fluid abilities Innate abilities based on perceptual, motor, or intellectual speed and flexibility; abilities that are not based on prior intentional learning.

(Psychology, continuing)

132

Essentials of Psychology

Crystalized abilities Abilities that a person has intentionally acquired in the past and has practiced to a high level of mastery; accumulated knowledge and skills.

Disengagement theory of aging Theory stating that as people age it is normal and desirable for them to withdraw from society and from roles they held earlier.

Activity theory Theory of aging stating that the best adjustment to aging occurs for individuals who remain active mentally, socially, and physically.

Ageism Discrimination or prejudice based on a person's age.

Critical Thinking Exercise

In Japan, aging is seen as positive, and growing older brings increased status and respect. Is this an example of ageism?

Answer

Yes it is. Even when the elderly are revered, they are being prejudged on the basis of age (Kimmel, 1988). Also, giving higher status to the elderly relegates the young to lower status—another instance of ageism.

Question: What kind of person adjusts most successfully to aging?

Activity and Disengagement   Two principal theories have been proposed to explain successful adjustment to the physical and social changes of aging. **Disengagement theory** assumes that it is normal and desirable for people to withdraw from society as they age (Cumming & Henry, 1961). According to this theory, elderly persons welcome disengagement since it relieves them of roles and responsibilities they have become less able to fulfill. Likewise, society benefits from disengagement as younger persons with new energy and skills fill positions vacated by aging individuals.

Certainly we have all known people who disengaged from society as they grew older. Nevertheless, disengagement theory can be criticized for describing successful aging as a retreat. While disengagement may be common, it is not necessarily ideal.

Question: What does the second theory say?

A second view of optimal aging is provided by **activity theory,** a sort of "use-it-or-lose-it" view that assumes activity is the essence of life for people of all ages. Activity theory predicts that people who remain active physically, mentally, and socially will adjust better to aging (Havighurst, 1961).

Proponents of activity theory believe that aging persons should maintain the activities of their earlier years for as long as possible. If a person is forced to give up particular roles or activities, it is recommended that these activities or roles be replaced with others. In so doing, the aging person is able to maintain a better self-image, greater satisfaction, and more social support—resulting in more successful aging.

Question: Which theory is correct?

The majority of studies on aging support the *activity theory*, although there have been exceptions (Barrow & Smith, 1979). At the same time, some people do seek disengagement, so neither theory is absolutely "correct." Actually, successful aging probably requires a combination of activity and disengagement. For example, one researcher found that the elderly tend to disengage from activities that are no longer satisfying while maintaining those that are (Brown, 1974). In the final analysis, it seems that life satisfaction in old age depends mainly on how much time we spend doing things we find meaningful (Horn & Meer, 1987) (Fig. 4-9).

Ageism   In one way or another you have encountered ageism. **Ageism** refers to discrimination or prejudice on the basis of age. It applies to people of all ages and can oppress the young as well as the old. For instance, a person applying for a job may just as likely be told, "You're too young," as "You're too old." In most Western nations, ageism tends to have a negative impact on older individuals. Usually, it is expressed as an aversion, hatred, or rejection of the elderly. As Alex Comfort (1976) points out, the concept of "oldness" is often used to expel people from useful work. According to Comfort, retirement is frequently just another name for dismissal and unemployment.

Another facet of ageism is stereotyping of the aged. Popular stereotypes of the "dirty old man," "meddling old woman," "senile old fool," and the like, help perpetuate the myths underlying ageism. Contrast such images to those associated with youthfulness: The young are perceived as fresh, whole, attractive, energetic, active, emerging, appealing, and so forth. Even positive stereotypes can be a problem. If older people are perceived as financially well-off, wise, or experienced, it can blind others to the real problems of the elderly (Gatz & Pearson, 1988). The important point, then, is to realize that there is a tremendous diversity among the elderly—ranging from the infirm and senile, to aerobic-dancing grandmothers.

(Psychology, continuing)

Chapter 4: From Birth to Death: Life-Span Development   133

Highlight 4-2	Biological Aging—How Long Is a Lifetime?

Whatever the biological causes of aging, humans seem to grow, mature, age, and die within a set time. The length of our lives is limited by a boundary called the **maximum life span.** Humans, like other animals, appear to live a limited number of years, even under the best of circumstances. Estimates of the average human life span place it around 95 to 110 years (Botwinick, 1984).

For most people, **life expectancy** (the actual number of years the average person lives) is shorter than a life span. In the 1800s the average life expectancy was 36 years. Now, average life expectancy for American males is 72 years and for females it is 79 years. With improved health care, life expectancy should move even closer to the maximum life span.

At present there is no known way to extend the human life span. On the other hand, there is every

reason to believe that life expectancy can be increased. If you would personally like to add to a new, higher average, here are some deceptively simple rules for living a long life (Coni et al., 1984):

1. Do not smoke.
2. Use alcohol in moderation or not at all.
3. Avoid becoming overweight.
4. If you suffer from high blood pressure, have it treated.
5. Remain socially and economically active in retirement.
6. Exercise regularly throughout life.

To this we can add: Get married (married persons live longer), learn to manage stress, and choose long-lived parents!

Question: What can be done about ageism?

One of the best ways to combat ageism is to counter stereotypes with facts. For example, studies show that in many occupations older workers perform better at jobs requiring *both* speed and skill (Giniger et al., 1983). Gradual slowing with age is a reality. But often, it is countered by experience, skill, or expertise (Schaie, 1988). One study, for example, showed that older typists responded slower on reaction-time tests than younger typists. Nevertheless, there was no difference in the actual typing speeds of younger and older typists (Salthouse, 1987).

Taking a broader view, Bernice Neugarten (1971) examined the lives of 200 people between the ages of 70 and 79. Neugarten found that 75 percent of these people were satisfied with their lives after retirement. Neugarten's findings also refuted other myths about aging.

Countering Myths About Aging

1. Old persons generally do not become isolated and neglected by their families. Most *prefer* to live apart from their children.
2. Old persons are rarely placed in mental hospitals by uncaring children.
3. Old persons who live alone are not necessarily lonely or desolate.
4. Few elderly persons ever show signs of senility or mental decay, and few ever become mentally ill.

In short, most of the elderly studied by Neugarten were integrated, active, and psychologically healthy. Findings such as these call for an end to the forced obsolescence of the elderly. As a group, older people represent a valuable source of skill, knowledge, and energy that we can no longer afford to cast aside. As we face the challenges of this planet's uncertain future, we need all the help we can get!

Living will A written declaration stating that a person prefers not to have his or her life artificially prolonged in the event of a terminal illness.

EXERCISE 10.5   Continued (Sample pages from the *Nutrition* source begin here)

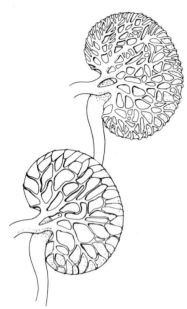

As the heart pumps less blood into an organ, the capillary trees within that organ recede, leaving some of the cells without nourishment. Exercise promotes maintenance, and even growth, of capillaries.

cardiac index: the cardiac output per square meter of body surface area. The **cardiac output** is the quantity of blood pumped into the aorta each minute. Cardiac output is responsible for transport of substances to and from the tissues; it changes markedly with body size.

vital capacity: the maximum volume of air that can be inhaled into or exhaled from the lungs.

Aging of Systems

The aging of cells is reflected by changes in the organs they are a part of. The most visible changes take place in the skin. As people age, wrinkles increase, partly because of a loss of elasticity and of the fat that lies under the skin. Scars accumulate from many small cuts and roughen the skin's texture. Exposure to sun, wind, and cold hastens wrinkling.

Less visible, but much more important to nutrition, are the changes that take place in the digestive system. The gums deteriorate, causing loss of teeth; gum disease afflicts 90 percent of the population in the decade after age 65. The senses of taste and smell diminish, reducing the pleasure of eating. The stomach's secretions of hydrochloric acid and enzymes decrease, as do the secretions of digestive juices by the pancreas and small intestine, impairing the digestive process. The digestive tract muscles weaken with reduced use, so that pressure in the large intestine causes the outpocketings of diverticulosis. Constipation becomes a problem.

The liver is somewhat different. Liver cells regenerate themselves throughout life, but even with good nutrition, fat gradually infiltrates the liver, reducing its work output. The pancreatic cells become less responsive to high blood glucose levels, and the body's cells become resistant to insulin, so that it takes more to make them respond.

The heart and blood vessels age similarly. All organs and tissues depend on the circulation of nutrients and oxygen, so degenerative changes in the cardiovascular system critically affect all other systems. The decrease in blood flow through the kidneys makes them gradually less efficient at removing wastes and maintaining the blood's normal composition. As the heart pumps blood less forcefully, the capillary trees of the kidneys diminish in size; some kidney cells die. This degenerative process can be retarded by regular exercising, which ensures that an ample volume of blood is pumped into the kidneys, keeping the capillaries open.

The body's systems age at different rates and to different extents. In a lifetime, nerve conduction velocity appears to be affected least and lung function most, with other functions between the extremes:

- Nerve conduction velocity and cellular enzyme activities decline about 15 percent.
- Cardiac index falls 30 percent.
- Vital capacity and renal blood flow decrease by 50 percent.
- Maximum breathing capacity, maximum work rate, and maximum oxygen uptake fall by 60 to 70 percent.[1]

Like the body's organ systems, the skeletal system is subject to change with the passage of time. Bone-building and bone-dismantling cells are constantly remodeling this structure, but after 40, bone loss becomes more rapid than bone building. The result is osteoporosis—a disease that afflicts close to half of all people over 65. Arthritis, a painful swelling of the joints, is another problem that troubles many people as they grow older. During movement, the bones must rub against each other at the joints. The ends are protected from wear by cartilage and by small sacs of fluid that act as a lubricant. With age, the ends

(Nutrition, continuing)

of the bones become pitted or eroded as a result of wear and the loss of cartilage and fluid. The cause of arthritis is unknown, but it afflicts millions around the world and is a major problem of the elderly.

Can Aging Be Prevented?

What can we do to avoid growing old? Is there a magic potion we can drink, a food we can eat, a pill we can swallow? Or, on a more down-to-earth level, are there any lifestyle habits we can adopt to prolong our youth?

As far as potions, foods, and pills go, the answer seems to be no, although the search has gone on since the dawn of human history. We are still looking for the fountain of youth, and quacks who claim to have found it have been selling its waters for centuries. A recent candidate for prevention of aging is superoxide dismutase (SOD).

Another approach to prevention of aging has been to study other cultures in the hope of finding an extremely long-lived race of people and then learning

superoxide dismutase (SOD): an antioxidant enzyme. Purified from animal tissues and sold in powder form, it is one of many fraudulent antiaging products on the popular market.

SOD deserves a moment's notice here. It is an enzyme that occurs naturally in the cells of animals, including humans. It acts as an antioxidant, as do vitamin C, vitamin E, and the selenium-containing enzyme described in Chapter 11. Animal species that live the longest, such as human beings, have the highest concentrations of SOD in their tissues, and it has been hoped that the concentration of this enzyme in the human body could be raised and would prolong life.

It doesn't work.[2] Like any other enzyme taken orally, SOD is digested in the stomach and intestine to fragments that the body uses to make its own proteins. If it were injected, it would still be external to cells, and could cause irritation and allergic reactions, but not longer life. The trick would have to be to induce the cells to make more of it themselves (genetic engineering)—and even then, who is to say that higher levels would have a beneficial effect? The body tends to make the right amount of what it needs, as this book has shown in countless examples, and "more" SOD would probably not be "better." Still, many health-food stores and other establishments are doing a brisk business selling it.

WRITING THE PAPER: THE PROCESS

What is written without effort is in general read without pleasure.
—SAMUEL JOHNSON

The effort you put into writing a research paper shows in the quality of what you've written. Often *how* you write your paper is graded as much as *what* you write in your paper. It pays, then, to spend whatever effort and time is necessary to master the two main steps of the writing process: writing the first draft and revising it in the second draft. Your final version, the product of your effort, will deserve the grade it receives.

FIRST DRAFT

Your first writing effort is often called a **rough draft,** and with good reason. Its goal is simply to get your ideas on paper. As Jackie Collins once said, "If you want to be a writer, stop talking about it and sit down and write!" No one reads your first draft but you. To some extent, you write without worrying about neatness. However, writing only on the front of your paper aids you in later constructing your second draft.

The flow of words forms your most important consideration. Because your objective is to sketch your paper, you might try following the advice given to speakers. In the introductory paragraph, "Tell them what you're going to say." In the text, "Tell them." And, in the summary, "Tell them what you said." Although this seems redundant, most papers take this form.

Although you should keep the basic format of introduction-body-summary in mind, many writers find starting and completing a paper to be the hardest parts. Because your thesis statement guides your writing, sections need not be written in a set order. As you write the body of your paper, you may think of the perfect beginning or ending for it. Otherwise, you may stare at a blank page for a very long time.

Introduction: "Tell Them What You're Going to Say"

In telling your audience what you're going to say, you set the stage for the rest of your paper. The introduction informs readers of your paper's general content and tells them why they will want to read your paper. The introduction lets you be creative, an important trait in capturing an audience's attention. A new approach, perfect example, or clever phrase won't always come easily. You need to keep an open mind and a patient outlook in searching for ideas.

By getting your readers' interest, you motivate them to continue reading. Briefly summarizing your most important sources provides a background for your specific subject. The reader then sees how your paper relates to a larger context of information. Interest also may be elicited by focusing the reader's attention on a particularly relevant or surprising aspect of your topic. This could be a question, generalization, viewpoint, definition, quotation, problem, conflict, or other pertinent factor. A related way to motivate the reader is to note the significance of your research. Here you tell the contribution (answers to questions, facts that support a generalization or viewpoint, new insights) that your paper proposes to make.

In telling your readers what you're going to say, you want to familiarize them with your topic. Your thesis statement tells them your purpose and plan for your paper. A summary of the main headings to be discussed in the paper expands the thesis statement. It provides a preview of important ideas.

Text: "Tell Them"

The bulk of your paper consists of the text. Here you provide a detailed synthesis of your information. When you synthesize information, you identify patterns and relationships among supporting details found through charting. Thus, the end result of your research is a concise, unified combination of ideas, rather than a summary or collection of facts.

Your most important consideration in writing the text of your paper is its organization. How you order the points you make in your text depends on your purpose and the research you collect. Several patterns of organization are possible (see Table 10.4). Once again, you rely on your inferential skills to determine which pattern best fits your paper. Following an organizational pattern helps you include all the

---

TABLE 10.4   Organizational Patterns

Inductive/Deductive (specific to general/general to specific)
Hierarchical (most to least or least to most)
Chronological (time order)
Sequential (process order)
Part to Whole/Whole to Part
Spatial (top to bottom, left to right, etc.)
Categorization
Alphabetical
Comparison/Contrast
Problem-Solution
Cause-Effect

information you've identified for a specific point. It also makes corrections in the second draft easier.

No matter what your topic and organizational pattern are, your paper needs to conform to a research paper format, which includes **footnotes** or **endnotes** with an accompanying bibliography or **parenthetical references** with an accompanying list of references. Rules for making these notations depend on the style that your instructor demands or that you choose. Specific books describe and provide examples for your reference. Table 10.5 identifies some of the most common **style manuals**.

Summary: "Tell Them What You Said"

The summary paragraph(s) provides closure for the text of your paper. It is especially important in lengthy papers. In the summary paragraph(s), you restate your thesis and the purpose of the research. In addition, you highlight the major points that supported your topic. You indicate the relationship between headings and how these prove the points you've made. You also identify the need for further research. You raise new questions or speculate on information or conclusions in your paper.

SECOND DRAFT

Have you ever talked with a friend, left, and then thought of a forgotten detail, an omitted point, or a perfect example, and thought, "I wish I'd said that." Your second draft gives you that chance. Allowing some time between writing the first draft and starting the second lets your ideas gel. Thus, when you begin to revise your paper, you have a fresh perspective.

One way to revise your first draft involves scissors and tape. Instead of rewriting, you simply cut apart sentences, paragraphs, or sections, and tape them in the order you desire. This patchwork manuscript forms the basis for writing your final draft.

Using a personal computer for writing your rough draft decreases the time it takes for revisions. Word processing programs allow you to change sentence or paragraph order, style, spelling, and punctuation without having to retype the entire manuscript. Some programs even check your grammar and writing style.

Two drawbacks hinder the use of word processing programs. Luckily, they are not insurmountable ones. First, using a word processor takes more skill than using a standard typewriter. Learning a word processing program involves time and practice. When planning to use a word processor, you need to allow time for learning the program. Second, word processing requires access to personal com-

TABLE 10.5   Style Manuals for Various Content Areas

American Mathematical Society. *A Manual for Authors of Mathematical Papers,* 7th ed. Providence, R.I.: American Mathematical Society, 1990.

American Psychological Association. *Publication Manual of the American Psychological Association,* 4th ed. Washington, D.C.: American Psychological Association, 1988.

A Uniform System of Citation, 13th ed. Cambridge, Mass.: Harvard Law Review Association, 1991.

The Chicago Manual of Style, 13th ed. Chicago: Univ. of Chicago Press, 1982.

Cochran, Wendell, Peter Fenner, and Mary Hill, eds.

Geowriting: A Guide to Writing, Editing, and Printing in Earth Science. Alexandria, Va.: American Geological Institute, 1984.

Council of Biology Editors. Style Manual Committee. *CBE Style Manual: A Guide for Authors, Editors, and Publishers in the Biological Sciences,* 5th ed. Bethesda, Md.: Council of Biology Editors, 1983.

Day, Robert A. *How to Write and Publish a Scientific Paper.* 3d ed. Phoenix, Ariz.: Oryx Press, 1988.

Dodd, Janet S., ed. *The ACS Style Guide: A Manual for Authors and Editors.* Washington, D.C.: American Chemical Society, 1986.

Garner, Diane L., and Smith, Diane H. *The Complete Guide to Citing Government Documents: A Manual for Writers and Librarians.* Bethesda, Md.: Congressional Information Service, 1984.

Gibaldi, Joseph, and Achtert, Walter S. *MLA Handbook for Writers of Research Papers,* 2d ed. New York: Modern Language Association, 1988.

Huth, Edward J., M.D. *How to Write and Publish Papers in the Medical Sciences.* 2nd ed. Philadelphia: ISI Press, 1987.

International Steering Committee of Medical Editors. "Uniform Requirements for Manuscripts Submitted to Biomedical Journals." *Annals of Internal Medicine* 90: 95–99 (1982).

Michaelson, Herbert B. *How to Write and Publish Engineering Papers and Reports.* 2d ed. Philadelphia: ISI Press, 1986.

Rosnow, R. L. & Rosnow, M. (1992) *Writing Papers in Psychology.* Wadsworth, Belmont, CA.

Skillin, Marjorie E., and Gay, Robert M., eds. *Words into Type,* 3d ed. Englewood Cliffs, N.J.: Prentice-Hall, 1986.

Society of Mining Engineers. *Author's Guide.* Littleton, Colo.: Society of Mining Engineers/AIME, 1983. Includes supplement entitled "Suggestions to Authors of Papers Intended for Society of Mining Engineers Publications."

Steffens, H. J. & Dickerson, M. J. (1987) *Writers Guide: History.* D. C. Heath: Lexington, MA.

U.S. Department of the Interior. Bureau of Reclamation. *Style Guide for Technical Publications.* Denver: Bureau of Reclamation, 1989.

U.S. Geological Survey. *Suggestions to Authors of Reports of the United States Geological Survey,* 6th ed. Washington, D.C.: Government Printing Office, 1991.

U.S. Government Printing Office. *Style Manual.* Washington, D.C.: GPO, 1984.

Note: More recent editions of these manuals may be available upon request of their publisher.

puters. If you do not own a computer, one may be available through local computer rental agencies or your institution's computer center.

Elements of Style

Regardless of the subject of your research, to write a well-organized, readable paper, you must remember the three elements of style: conciseness, clarity, and cohesion. Each is easier if you consider order when compiling your first draft. These elements demand much of your writing ability.

First, conciseness demands brevity. If you've got something to say, you need to say it clearly and quickly without omitting important details. Adding extra details detracts from the quality of your paper. Undue padding contributes nothing to your topic.

Second, clarity means writing clearly and logically to clarify vague or complex information. It also involves rewriting stilted sentences and omitting trite expressions.

Clarity relates to coherence, or cohesion, the "glue" that holds your paper together. The topic and summary sentences of paragraphs or sections and transition words build coherence. They help the parts of your paper "stick together."

Writing a research paper, or any paper, is difficult. Some students choose to take composition courses to improve their skills. Others use style manuals to develop better writing styles. Table 10.6 is a list of such manuals.

Final Revisions

I think of being a child in my family at the dinner table, with seven kids and hubbub and parents distracted by worries and responsibilities. Before I would say anything at the table, before I would approach my parents, I would plan what I wanted to say. I'd map out the narrative, sharpen the details, add color, plan momentum. This way I could hold their attention. This way I became a writer.

—PEGGY NOONAN

Final revisions consist of editing, rewriting, and polishing your second draft into the final draft. You reread, looking for both structural and grammatical errors. You check the paper's structure by looking at organization and transition. You look at your choice of words and use of details and examples. To check for grammatical errors, you inspect words, sentences, and paragraphs for mistakes in spelling, punctuation, etc.

TABLE 10.6   Guide to General Manuals of Writing Style

Standard Handbooks of Composition

Baker, S. *The Complete Stylist and Handbook.* New York: Harper, 1984.

Elsbree, et al. *Health Handbook of Composition,* 10th ed. Lexington, Mass.: Heath, 1981.

Gefvert, C. J. *The Confident Writer: A Norton Handbook.* New York: W. W. Norton, 1988.

Hodges, J. C., and Whitten, M. E. *Harbrace College Handbook,* 10th ed. New York: Harcourt Brace Jovanovich, 1990.

Kirszner, L. G. and Mandell, S. R. (1986). *The Holt Handbook,* CBS College Publishing, New York.

Leggett, G. C., Mead, D., and Charvat, W. *Prentice-Hall Handbook for Writers,* 8th ed. Englewood Cliffs, N.J.: Prentice-Hall, 1988.

McCrimmon, J. M. *Writing with a Purpose: Short Edition.* Boston: Houghton, 1988.

Neeld, E. C. *Writing Brief,* 2d ed. Glenview, Ill.: Scott, Foresman, 1986.

Guides to Writing Style

Chicago Guide to Preparing Electronic Manuscripts. University of Chicago Press, Chicago, 1986.

Chicago Manual of Style, 13th ed. Chicago: University of Chicago Press, 1982.

Eastman, R. M. *Style: Writing as the Discovery of Outlook,* 2d ed. New York: Oxford University Press, 1978.

Elbow, P. *Writing with Power: Techniques for Mastering the Writing Process.* New York: Oxford University Press, 1981.

Howell, John Bruce. *Style Manuals of the English-Speaking World: A Guide.* Phoenix, Ariz.: Oryx Press, 1983.

Strunk, W., Jr., and White, E. B. *The Elements of Style,* 3d ed. New York: Macmillan, 1982.

Turabian, K. L. *A Manual of Style for Writers of Term Papers, Theses, and Dissertations.* 5th Ed. Chicago: U of Chicago P, 1987.

University of Chicago Press. *The Chicago Manual of Style.* 13th ed. Chicago: University of Chicago Press, 1982.

U.S. Government Printing Office Style Manual. Rev. ed. Washington, D.C.: Government Printing Office, 1984.

Walker, Mellisa. *Writing Research Papers: A Norton Guide.* New York and London: W. W. Norton & Company, 1984.

Webster's Standard American Style Manual. Springfield, Mass.: Merriam-Webster, 1985.

Weidenborner, Stephen, and Domenick Caruso. *Writing Research Papers: A Guide to the Process.* New York: St. Martin's Press, 1982.

Williams, N. M. *Style: Ten Lessons in Clarity and Grace.* Glenview, Ill.: Scott, Foresman, 1989.

When you select a book to read, does its cover affect your choice? What about the size of the print? Do you consider how well it's packaged? Just as these external factors color your perception about a book, they affect the way your instructor perceives your paper. Your final draft needs to be a revised copy, as error-free as possible. Papers neatly written in ink or typed receive higher grades than those written without care. Margins should be wide enough for your instructor's comments. However, they should not be so wide that your instructor suspects that you're padding your work. Your final draft should include a title page, body, references, and any other elements required by your instructor. Table 10.7 is a checklist for locating errors that need correcting.

"Your writing isn't very creative, but your spelling certainly is."

SOURCE: Jack Corbett. Reprinted from *Phi Delta Kappan*.

TABLE 10.7   Checklist for Revisions

	Revise	Leave as is
1. Structure		
a. Appropriate title	_____	_____
b. Thesis statement	_____	_____
• Purpose		
• Audience appeal		
c. Introductory paragraph(s)	_____	_____
d. Logically organized text	_____	_____
e. Supporting research or examples	_____	_____
f. Summary or concluding paragraph(s)	_____	_____
2. Grammar		
a. Spelling	_____	_____
b. Sentences (complete? run-ons?)	_____	_____
c. Punctuation	_____	_____
d. Paragraphs (indented? topic and summary sentences?)	_____	_____
e. Tense (past, present, future)	_____	_____
f. Subject-verb agreement	_____	_____
3. Style		
a. Conciseness	_____	_____
b. Clarity	_____	_____
c. Cohesion (transition)	_____	_____
d. Word choice	_____	_____
e. Format of footnotes and bibliography (as required by style book of choice)	_____	_____
4. References		
a. Identification of direct quotes or other referenced information	_____	_____
b. Complete citations	_____	_____
c. Relevancy	_____	_____
d. Objectivity	_____	_____
e. Author's qualifications	_____	_____
f. Primary sources	_____	_____
g. Secondary sources	_____	_____
h. Adequate number of references	_____	_____
i. References from a variety of sources	_____	_____
5. Form		
a. Title page	_____	_____
b. Table of contents	_____	_____
c. Abstract	_____	_____
d. Bibliography or references	_____	_____
e. Appendices	_____	_____

EXERCISE 10.6 Revise the following paper according to the standards indicated in the checklist in Table 10.7.

Countries and Their Constitutions

A constitution is a statement which outlines the basic principals of formal organizations. Such organizations include countries, political associations, and private groups. A constitution can be written or unwritten. It sets up the way the organization will function in terms of rules and purposes, etc

The first kind of American Constitution was a document called the Articles of Confederation. It granted freedoms to each state, but this document was inadequate for governing the country. The new country of america faced many problems left unresolved by the Articles. The document did not contain means for getting states to work together. It lacked provisions for an executive branch and a national court system. The Articles of Confederation made no allowances for regulating trade among states. No means for getting taxes.

At first statesman such as George Washington and Alexander Hamilton planned to meet to rewrite the Articles into a stronger document but then they decided to write the Constitution of the United States. A Constitutional Convention got together in 1787. Twelve of the thirteen colonies attended.

Only Rhode Island didn't. George Washington was president of the convention.

Fifty-five men attended the convention, but only thirty-nine signed the Constitution. The ones that did not sign disagreed with some of the things it said. But just because these men signed it, it did not represent the wishes of American yet. It had to be voted on and approved by nine states. This kind of approval was called ratification. People who liked the Constitution and supported it were called Federalists. Those that opposed it were Anti-Federalists. These groups formed the basis of the first political parties in the U.S.

The Constitution consist of the preamble, seven articles, and twenty-six amendments. The preamble a short introduction which explains the overall purposes of the Constitutuion. The Constituion established a federal government which divided power between the states and the national government.

The first three articles establish the branches of the government. So there are three branches of the national govenment. Including the executive, legislative, and the judicial. The executive branch enforces the laws made by the legislative

branch which are explained by the judicial branch. The fifth article provides for future amendments or changes in the Constitutuion. The sixth article concerns the national debt. The fourth article tell how states will relate to each other. The last article tells how the constitution was to be ratified.

After the Constitution was ratified. It was amended by a document called the Bill of Rights. These were the first ten amendments to the Constitutuion. They protect citizens from unfair governmental acts. In all there have been twenty-six additions or amendments to the Constitutions covering everything from individual freedoms to voting procedures. Everyone agrees that the American Constitution is the best document for running a country.

WRITE TO LEARN

On a separate sheet of paper, explain how the old saying, "Making a silk purse out of a sow's ear" is analogous to writing a research paper.

PLAGIARISM

Plagiarism is stealing another person's work and presenting it as your own. Plagiarism comes in two forms: unintentional and intentional. Unintentional, or accidental, plagiarism occurs through inaccurate note taking or through incorrect citation of references. Intentional plagiarism is deliberate, premeditated theft of published information. Intentional plagiarism also includes getting a paper from a friend or "term paper service." The article reprinted in Figure 10.4 describes the hazards of buying term papers.

When you plagiarize, you run the risk of disciplinary action. You avoid plagiarism by carefully noting and documenting reference materials.

WRITE TO LEARN

On a separate sheet of paper, create an analogy that defines or explains plagiarism.

AVOIDING THE "I'M-OVER-MY-HEAD" FEELING: SETTING A WRITING SCHEDULE

All authors experience the "I'm-over-my-head-and-this-time-they're-going-to-catch-me" feeling. Knowing what's involved in writing a paper helps you avoid the writer's block that comes with this feeling. Table 10.8 outlines the writing process.

Once you know the process of writing a research paper, you realize that you cannot write a paper in a day or a week. Avoiding the "I'm-over-my-head-and-this-time-they're-going-to-catch-me" feeling involves scheduling enough time to complete the writing process. Setting specific objectives and completion dates helps you budget time and make the best use of resources.

RATIONALE FOR A WRITING SCHEDULE

You need a writing schedule for several reasons. First, research takes time in what is probably a full schedule of academic, personal, and perhaps work commitments. Without a time line for beginning, con-

FIGURE 10.4   Buying a Term Paper Could Turn Out to Be the First Step to Academic Bankruptcy

"Tired of typing? Is your research wretched? When term paper trauma sets in, call us! 15,483 papers to choose from. All subjects from Anthropology to Zoology. Call Researchers to the Rescue now! 555–3211."

The end of the semester. It's 3:00 in the morning. You've already gone through two pots of coffee and a box and a half of cookies. Your eyes are bloodshot. You've been staring at that blank sheet of paper so long you've memorized the number of lines.

Worst of all, you still don't know what you're going to write for your Econ paper.

When academic deadlines have you stressed out, an ad like the one above could have you dialing in desperation. But, beware! Before you send up an S.O.S. to "Researchers to the Rescue," consider what happened to Suzy B.

"I went to an organization that advertised in the classified section of the campus paper," she confessed. "Since I had a paper due on one of Shakespeare's plays, which is a pretty universal topic, I figured they could whip out a great essay. At $10 a page, it was worth its weight in gold for the amount of aggravation it saved me. Worth in gold until I showed it to a friend of mine who went to the same place last semester and found parts of her paper in mine!"

Although Suzy's lack of originality went unnoticed, her story points out one of the major hazards of buying a term paper. The biggest risk, or course, is getting caught at what clearly is cheating. We'll deal with that biggie in a moment, but it's not the only risk. Another is being accused of plagiarism.

For instance, let's say the one paper you choose out of the fifteen written on Shakespeare was submitted to your prof by another student last semester. Your professor might spot this repeat or even discover your paper contains a few lines of famous criticism copied verbatim.

Other things can go wrong. You always run the risk that the style of a purchased paper will clash with the rest of your semester's work. When you suddenly start sounding like Hemingway, your professor will notice. And you might find that you can do a better job yourself.

"Often the papers aren't that good," one student pointed out. "The companies that write these papers don't know the focus of the course or the teacher's expectations. I paid $120 for a 10-pager and only got a C +."

Which brings up another issue: cost. Any paper longer than a few pages is a costly investment for a questionable return. At $10–$12 a page, wouldn't it be better to do the research yourself and spend the money on the finer things in life?

The biggest hazard, of course, is getting caught. One university alone reported fifteen cases last year. If you do get caught, the price is a lot more than just a slap on the hand.

Robert Brooks, Associate Dean of Students at the University of Massachusetts, warns, "Not only is it in violation of our code of student conduct, but in Massachusetts it is a statutory offense to sell plagiarized goods, punishable by fine and imprisonment."

Care to know the procedure you'll go through if you're caught plagiarizing? Robert Mannes, Dean for Student Life at the University of Southern California, says that the faculty member who teaches the course the student is enrolled in makes the initial decision. "For a paper that doesn't count as a major portion of the course grade, the student will usually receive an 'F' for the paper alone, particularly if it's a first offense. However, if the paper is more heavily weighted in the course, if it is a student's second offense or if the degree of plagiarism is severe, then the student will usually receive an 'F' in the course and go before a review board."

Proving plagiarism, Mannes continues, can be tough. "If we're not sure if a paper has been plagiarized, we'll compare it to the catalog from one of these organizations. In one case, the student didn't even change the title of the paper!"

Okay, okay. So you're smart enough to change the title. What else can happen?

At the University of Arizona, a charge of plagiarism is also worked out as much as possible between faculty member and student. However, if the case does go through a formal committee hearing (profs and peers present), several things can happen.

FIGURE 10.4   Continued

According to Dean Glenn Smith, Administrator of the Code of Academic Integrity, "the student can be suspended for a semester or more, expelled from the university altogether, have an academic dishonesty clause placed on his transcripts or be refused a degree from that particular department."

While writing a paper on the imagery and style of Shakespearean tragedy might take a lot of effort on your part, the alternative of buying a paper can take a lot more out of you. Getting caught will not only contribute to the decline of that GPA you worked so hard for, but will cause a lot of embarrassment. It may also bias the teacher against the rest of the work you do in that class.

And, in the end, you have to live with the fact that you compromised your integrity by taking credit for someone else's work.

The risks are real. So, even if it takes two typewriter ribbons, three pots of coffee and forsaking your cherished sleep, work until you rip your hair out and write your own paper.

SOURCE: Gina Renée Gross, "Buying Term Papers." Reproduced by permission of *College Woman Magazine* 1 (3):48 (Summer 1986).

tinuing, and completing your research, your paper may not reflect the quality of work you wish.

Second, the resources you need may not be readily available. Interlibrary loans help you obtain materials that are not part of the library's holdings. If a book you need is checked out, you can ask the library to request that it be returned as soon as possible. Copy machines may be out of order, preventing you from obtaining information for later study. Whatever the case, you need to plan for such delays.

Finally, you need time to reflect on the information you gather. This time gives you opportunities to consider your information in different ways and get fresh perspectives. Such reflection helps you determine the commonalities of your ideas and your organizational structure.

SETTING A WRITING SCHEDULE

Suppose that on the first day of class your instructor says that a research paper will be due at mid-term. Your first task in completing this assignment would be to set a writing schedule. Table 10.9 lists the steps in setting a schedule.

You need to modify the steps according to your own research and writing strengths or weaknesses. If you are familiar with your library's holdings and your subject, you may complete your task more quickly. If you lack such background information, your task will probably take more time. If writing comes easily to you, you may not

---

TABLE 10.8   Steps in Writing a Research Paper

1. Identify type of paper
   a. Theme or essay
   b. Report
   c. Term paper
   d. Research paper
2. Determine format of paper
   a. Title page
   b. Table of contents
   c. Abstract
   d. Body
   e. References
   f. Appendices
3. Select subject
   a. Identify interest and importance of topic
   b. Estimate availability of library resources
4. Narrow subject into manageable topic
   a. Establish purpose of paper
   b. Set scope of paper
      • Write thesis statement
      • Select title
5. Gather sources
   a. Library research
   b. Observation
   c. Interviews
   d. Personal experience
   e. Personal inferences

6. Evaluate sources
   a. Determine primary sources versus secondary sources
   b. Judge relevancy
   c. Estimate objectivity and bias
   d. Evaluate author's qualifications
7. Avoid plagiarism
8. Synthesize sources
   a. Outline
   b. Chart
   c. Revise thesis statement and/or title
9. Write first (rough) draft
   a. Introduction
   b. Text
      • Determine organizational pattern
      • Select style manual
   c. Summary
10. Write second draft
   a. Check style
   b. Make final revisions

---

require as much time. On the other hand, if writing is difficult for you, you need to budget extra time.

In most procedures, you begin at the beginning. Here you begin at both the beginning and the end. You begin at the beginning by setting your schedule as soon as a research paper is assigned. You begin at the end by plotting the activities you need to complete in relationship to the paper's final due date.

TABLE 10.9   Setting a Writing Schedule

Using your term calendar, mark the following dates:

1. Due date for the paper.

2. If the paper needs to be typed, identify a completion date for getting your final draft to the typist, whether the typist is you or someone else. You may need to call a typist and reserve time if your final due date is close to midterm, finals, or other busy time in the term. Determine how the length of your paper will affect the time it will take to be typed.

3. Your personal due date for the final draft. Leave ample time for typing or rewriting your draft.

4. Your personal due date for completing a rough draft. The rough draft should be completed approximately ten days to two weeks before the final due date.

5. Due date for completing your research. Allow time to evaluate and synthesize your sources before beginning your rough draft. Your research should be completed approximately two-and-a-half to three weeks before the due date.

6. Due date for beginning your research. This should be the day the research paper is assigned. Within the first week, you should determine the type and format of the paper, select a subject, and narrow your subject into a manageable topic.

GROUP LEARNING ACTIVITY
NOTETAKING AS A CAUSE OF UNINTENTIONAL PLAGIARISM

Although the consequences of intentional and unintentional plagiarism are the same, their causes differ greatly.

Intentional plagiarism has deceit as its purpose. But could people accidentally copy information and plagiarize without realizing it? Yes, it is easier than you think. The following group exercise (Nienhuis, 1989) can be used to demonstrate how unintentional plagiarism might occur.

1. Divide the group into two parts.

2. Individually, group members should go to the campus library and observe other students taking notes. Observe the methods that students use most often in taking notes from reference materials.

3. Compare observations in the group. Did you see students looking back and forth between the reference source and their paper? Did they seem to look at the source, write, look at the source, and write again? Did it appear as if they were copying almost directly from the text?

4. Half of the study group should take notes from the "Formation of the universe, solar system, and Earth," which begins Sample Chapter 2 as

described in Step 3. The other half of the group should take notes on the same material in the following manner. Put pencils and pens down and read without taking notes. Mentally summarize information that you think is important. Close the book and summarize on paper without looking back at the source. Open the book and check what you've written against the original source. Add quotation marks around direct quotes that you recalled. Note bibliographic citations.

Application

Compare the notes taken according to each of the two methods. Use the following questions as springboards for group discussion. What differences can you find? What do you think accounts for the differences? How would these differences be manifested if the material were more difficult? Less difficult?

Application

The two subgroups should exchange notes. Underline any phrases or sentences in the notes that are uncited direct quotations from the passage. Compare results.

SUMMARY OF MAIN POINTS

1. Instructors usually assign themes or essays, reports, and research papers or term papers.

2. A research paper includes a title page, table of contents, abstract, body, references, and appendices.

3. Selecting the subject depends on its interest and importance and the availability of library resources.

4. Narrowing the subject is done by determining the purpose of the paper. The scope determines the thesis statement and title.

5. Gathering sources depends on the method used to research the subject and your evaluation of the sources.

6. Outlining and charting are used to organize information for synthesis.

7. The first draft of your paper includes an introduction, the text of the paper, and a summary.

8. Your second draft should follow an established style. Revisions occur until the paper is error-free.

9. To complete your paper, you first set a writing schedule and then follow the steps in the writing process.

VOCABULARY DEVELOPMENT
FIGURATIVE LANGUAGE: JUST LIKE HOME

Y ou can only analyze and measure knowledge and experience against what you already know. If you don't have prerequisite knowledge, you must get a sense of how an experience is like something else you already know. Because authors are well-acquainted with their subjects, they can draw comparisons between a subject's features and features of some other, more common, concept or process. They often use figurative speech to make such comparisons. In writing a paper, your role is that of an author. You must inform your reader—who may or may not be familiar with your subject. Figurative language helps you refine your own thoughts about a concept and facilitates communication with your reader.

Analogies, it is true, decide nothing, but they can make one feel more at home.
—SIGMUND FREUD

The problem with a new idea is often your unfamiliarity with it. You many not understand the processes involved. You might lack the terms to describe those processes. Everything seems strange. In short, you just don't know what the new idea is like. And that is the solution to your dilemma. In order to learn new information, you must link it to something you do know. You have to figure out what the new information is like.

The authors of your textbooks and the faculty in your classrooms also want you to know what new information is like. They often describe new and unfamiliar concepts by relating them to common items and processes with which you are familiar. Such comparisons often take the form of figures of speech: similes, metaphors, symbols, and analogies. Like Freud, they know that these can help you feel more at home with unfamiliar subject matter.

Similes and metaphors. Similes and metaphors are figures of speech that state or imply that two unlike ideas are comparable. At first glance, the two ideas may seem so totally different that they could have nothing in common. However, a closer look reveals a basic relationship between them.

The words *like* or *as* signal the use of a simile. For example, in describing an atom, you might describe the movement of electrons around a nucleus as being "like planets around the sun." Thus, if you know how a solar system moves, you know that the parts of an atom move in a similar fashion.

In a metaphor, one idea is described as if were another without the use of *like* or *as*. For example, a biology professor might describe glucose as the gasoline that powers the human engine. That means that glucose performs the same function in the body as gasoline performs in a car.

Symbols. Symbols are like metaphors and similes with one major difference. Similes and metaphors name both ideas being compared. In symbolism, the comparison between two ideas became so well-known that one part of the comparison is no longer used. Thus, you are given one idea. You must infer the other. For example, the sentence "A rainbow is like a promise of better times for the coalition" would be a simile. "A rainbow is a promise of better times" is a metaphor. A rainbow alone symbolizes a promise of better times.

Symbols are based on background knowledge and experiences. In general, they are universally understood due to years of association between the symbol and the object it represents; however, symbols mean different things in different cultures. The flag that inspires patriotism in one country evokes little sentiment in another. A symbol's meaning also varies according to context. Symbols in one time and place (for example, X as in "X marks the spot", "X-tra Savings," size XXXL, and so on) may have a different meaning in another time and place.

Analogies. An analogy is a kind of expanded simile. Instead of comparing items as a whole, analogies compare specific features of a concept, process, person, place, or thing. For example, suppose you need to understand the relationship between a *secondary trait* (a characteristic that affects personality only under certain conditions) and *personality*. You might think of this concept as being like a knock that you get in your engine when you forget to add oil. This comparison is clarified by an analogy: A secondary trait is to personality as a knock is to a car's engine. The order of the ideas expressed in the analogy is important. Analogies can show any kind of relationship. These include synonyms, antonyms, parts to whole, age or size, or object to use.

Using figurative language in writing. Just as authors and faculty use figurative language to make you feel at home with an idea, you, too, can use such language to help the reader feel at home with the concepts in your research paper.

Your own understanding of the topic increases as you think of clear and appropriate examples. The metaphor, simile, symbol or analogy you choose should include the following characteristics described by Yelon and Massa (1990):

- **Accuracy.** The ideas being compared should be similar in definition, composition, function, or description. The comparison should be believable and realistic.

- **Clarity.** Whenever possible, use words, images, or actions that are observable and evoke sensory images. The connection between the example and the topic should be emphasized so that the reader easily grasps the relationship.

- **Brevity.** Examples need to be short enough so that their connection to the topic is not lost.

Activity

Following the guidelines presented in this chapter, use figurative language in creating an example to explain each of the following paragraphs.

1. Simple sequence is one of the four major logic patterns in computer programming. In simple sequence, the computer executes one statement after the other in the order in which they are listed in the program.

    EXAMPLE _____

    _____

    _____

2. In exploitation, one person or party controls the "rules" for access to rewards while keeping the second party or person naive or helpless concerning such access.

    EXAMPLE _____

    _____

    _____

3. The vascular, or blood circulatory, system is a closed system of vessels through which blood flows continuously in a figure eight, with the heart serving as a pump at the crossover point. As the blood circulates through the system, it picks up and delivers materials as needed.

    EXAMPLE _____

    _____

    _____

4. Pinocytosis involves a large area of the cell membrane, which actively engulfs liquids and "swallows" them into the cell. Occasionally, an entire protein can enter the body this way.

    EXAMPLE _____

    _____

    _____

5. The concept of nuclear reactions emerged following research into atomic structure in the 1920s. In fusion reactions, nuclei merge to create a larger nucleus representing a new chemical element. In fission reactions, a single nucleus splits into two or more smaller nuclei.

    EXAMPLE _____

    _____

    _____

CHAPTER REVIEW

Answer briefly but completely.

1. Complete the following analogy:
   reports : narration :: research papers :: _____

   _____

2. On what factors do you base the decision to include a table of contents, abstract, and/or appendices?

   _____

   _____

   _____

3. Your instructor has asked you to write a paper on any aspect of environmental pollution. Identify a topic that would be of interest to you and your classmates. Explain the factors on which you based your topic selection. Then narrow this topic into one of suitable scope.

   _____

   _____

   _____

   _____

   _____

   _____

4. Complete the following analogy:
   topic sentence : _____ :: thesis statement : research paper

   _____

5. Contrast primary and secondary sources.

   _____

   _____

   _____

6. How can using a tape recorder help the interview process? How can it hinder it?

   _____

   _____

   _____

7. Contrast outlines and charts as methods for synthesizing sources of information. Which method do you prefer? Why?

_____

_____

_____

8. Reread the quotation by Samuel Johnson on page 458. Use this quote to write an argument in favor of writing first and second drafts and for using word processing programs.

_____

_____

_____

9. Complete the following analogy: plagiarism : _____ :: grand theft auto : cars

_____

10. Examine Table 10.9. How would you modify the steps shown here to accommodate your research and writing strengths and weaknesses?

_____

_____

_____

REFERENCES

Nienhuis, T. (1989). "Curing Plagiarism with a Note-taking Exercise." *College Teaching* 37(3): 100.

Yelon, S., and Massa, M. (1990). "Heuristics for Creating Examples." In R. A. Neff and M. Weimer (Eds.) *Teaching College: Collected Readings for the New Instructor.* (Madison, WI: Magna Publications.

1 Sample Chapter

Culture: The Ideas and Products People Adopt and Create

C H A P T E R 3

▼

We shape our dwellings, and afterwards our dwellings shape us . . .

WINSTON CHURCHILL

Imagine that you are alone with a person that you love, and who loves you. You are holding his or her face in your hands as you look intently into his or her eyes. Slowly you move your lips toward your partner's, and the two of you share a passionate kiss.

You probably view the act of kissing and the feelings associated with it as "natural." To a sociologist, kissing and many other common behaviors and experiences are viewed as cultural rather than natural. We are not born with an innate knowledge of how to kiss or what it means to kiss. Rather, we learn about kissing from our culture. For example, you may have learned that kissing someone of a certain age, race, social class, and level of attractiveness is an enjoyable experience.

Culture is pervasive and powerful in the lives of every person in a society. Your culture determines many of the experiences you have, and the meaning you attribute to them. Kissing is neither a positive nor negative experience. Its enjoyment depends on the "definition of the situation" (W. I. Thomas 1923) that you and your partner have learned and adopted from the culture you live in. In this chapter we review what culture is, how it influences our daily lives, and how cultures vary throughout the world.

▼ THE MEANING OF CULTURE

The term *culture* has different meanings for lay people and for sociologists. In everyday speech, people sometimes use culture to refer to the use of proper manners. *High culture* refers to the display of manners found among the upper class, such as the use of finger bowls at the dinner table. Another typical use of the word culture is to imply an interest in elite art: museums, theaters, orchestras, opera, and dance companies (Blau 1986). Those who have and enjoy such interests are said to be "cultured." In sociology, the meaning of the term culture is much broader.

Sociological Meaning of Culture

To the sociologist, **culture** is everything that human beings are socialized to do, think, use, and make. Culture may be thought of as containing two levels: material and nonmaterial. **Material culture** refers to all objects (also known as **artifacts**) that have meaning to and are used by the members of a society. Artifacts include tools, clothes, buildings, weapons, and art objects. **Nonmaterial culture** refers to the intangible aspects of culture, such as norms, customs, beliefs, values, attitudes, knowledge, and language. Table 3.1 illustrates some examples of the material culture in the United States, and the nonmaterial values associated with them.

Importance of Culture

Much of what humans think and do is learned from the culture they have lived in. Because humans live in groups and communicate with each other, they pass on what they know to their offspring and to each other. Human knowledge, and the languages used to transmit knowledge, represent the nonmaterial aspect of culture. Other aspects of nonmaterial culture, such as values and

T A B L E   3.1   **Material and Nonmaterial Aspects of Culture**

Material	Nonmaterial
Football stadium	Value of recreation
Textbook	Knowledge and language
Wedding ring	Custom of marriage ceremony
Test tube	Value of science
Church	Belief in sacred and holy
Clothes	Norms for appropriate dress
Statue of Liberty	Value of freedom
Abortion clinics	Pro-choice value
Condom	Value of "safe" sex

▼   LIVING SOCIOLOGY   ▼

What we do for recreation or fun is dictated by our culture. Writing poems about cows, cutting large trees, and dancing are regarded as fun in some, but not all, cultures. Regarding dancing, "Among the Masai of Kenya, young men enjoy leaping up and down in the air. This custom is apparently being duplicated in Great Britain where some of the followers of English rock groups enjoy themselves by jumping up and down during rock concerts" (Cohen and Eames 1982, 272).

One of the latest culturally defined "fun toys" for kids is "Nintendo." This arcade video game machine can be played on one's own television. Children define for each other the importance of having the "right" type of fun. For example, "Super Mario Brothers 2" became one of the most desired "Nintendo" games in 1989.

---

norms, are important in guiding the behavior of members of a society.

The behavior of individuals and the characteristics of whole societies are also greatly determined by the artifacts, or material aspects of culture.

Countless artifacts influence the daily lives of individuals. In modern societies, cars, light bulbs, refrigerators, and computers are just a few of the artifacts that affect us daily.

Ethnography: The Study of Culture

The study of a culture involves describing the material and nonmaterial aspects of that culture. The descriptive study of individual cultures is referred to as **ethnography.** Researchers who conduct the descriptive studies of cultures are known as **ethnographers.** An ethnographer may be either a sociologist or an anthropologist. Ethnographers gather data on a culture by conducting field research (refer to chapter 2), which usually involves living among the various people they report on.

Two ethnographers who study the same culture may present different versions. Perhaps the most well known example involves Margaret Mead's *Coming of Age in Samoa* (1928), in which Mead describes adolescent Samoan females as sexually relaxed, carefree, peaceful, loving, and free of psychological conflict. Derek Freeman, another ethnographer who studied the Samoan culture between 1940 and 1967, reported evidence that contradicted Mead's findings (Freeman 1983). Contrary to Mead's report, the Samoan adolescents

(continued)

(*continued*)

that Freeman describes are aggressive, impulsive, status-hungry, violent, and sexually "hung up."

In reading about different cultures, we should not only keep in mind that ethnographers may disagree, but why such disagreement occurs. The reasons why ethnographers may present different versions of the same culture include the following (Heider 1988):

1. One researcher is wrong. "Ethnographies can contain information that is wrong, whether through deliberate falsification or otherwise" (p. 75).

2. Different subpopulations of a culture are being studied. In studying the same culture, one ethnographer may focus on people of a particular gender, class, age, or occupation, whereas another ethnographer may have a different focus. Studying different subpopulations may lead to differing views of a culture. Formulating a description of an entire culture based on the observation of one particular subset of the population is misleading.

3. The same culture is being studied at different times. Culture is not static, but rather changes across time. Ethnographies of the same culture done at different times are likely to differ. Part of the reason why Freeman's description of adolescent Samoans differed from Mead's account is that Mead's study took place in the 1920s, whereas Freeman's study did not begin until the 1940s (Scheper-Hughes 1987).

4. The theoretical orientation of the researchers may differ. A researcher will tend to "see" those aspects in a culture he or she studies that support his or her theoretical orientation. For example, a sociologist who believes that functionalism best explains social behavior may emphasize those aspects of a culture that can be explained by the functionalist viewpoint.

5. Researchers have varying degrees of knowledge of the language. An accurate description of a culture greatly depends on how well the researcher knows the language of the culture. "I once heard two people who both claimed linguistic competence give drastically different translations of a phrase shouted at a ceremony" (Heider 1988, 77).

Most of us do not have the opportunity to experience other cultures firsthand, and therefore we must rely on the research of ethnographers. The five variables just described remind us to view accounts of other cultures with caution.

▼ CULTURAL RULES

Every society has a complex set of rules that are based on the shared expectations of behavior.

▼ Values in the United States ▼

Robin Williams, Jr. (1970) conducted a systematic analysis of values in the United States. Other studies on values have been conducted by *U. S. News and World Report* (McBee 1985) and the American Council on Education in conjunction with UCLA's Higher Education Research Institute (1989). The latter is based on questionnaires completed by 222,296 freshmen entering 402 two- and four-year colleges in 1988. Following are some of the more important values in our society.

SUCCESS

Desire for success in wealth, power, or fame are basic contemporary American values.

MONEY

Notice that success, as just defined, begins with the pursuit of money. "Making more money" was the reason 72.6 percent of college freshmen gave for attending college. This percentage is up from 49.9 percent in 1971 (Higher Education Research Institute 1989). Among high school seniors, evidence suggests that the goal of "having lots of money" has risen in importance, whereas "finding purpose and meaning" in life has decreased in importance (Easterlin and Crimmins 1988). Indeed, the accumulation of money is a dominate value in our society.

JOB/CAREER

The avenue to "enough" money is often thought of as being a good job. Although the value of play and recreation is gaining popularity, there is still broad-based support for the value of work. This value is embedded in the Protestant ethic, which views hard work as its own reward and suggests that success in one's work is evidence of being counted among God's chosen. The value of work has become a trait of American culture and is no longer considered solely as a Protestant religious tenet.

FREEDOM

With the Japanese attack on Pearl Harbor, America entered World War II. It was a time

Americans literally felt that their freedom to worship, to read, and to move in an unrestricted society might come to an end. The reaction of Americans to this possibility was to pull together as a society for the war effort. Men volunteered to fight, women joined the work force, and industry converted from making "butter to guns." These efforts reflected how much our society values freedom (even to burn the flag).

Societies vary in how much they value or allow freedom. For example, in China, governmental policy put into effect in 1954 limits anyone from moving away from their established residence and workplace without official approval. Similar mobility is restricted in the Soviet Union.

EQUALITY

Our society has become very equality conscious. Women, blacks, and other minorities in our society have judicial support to obstruct any attempt to deny their equal access to employment, education, or housing. As a society, we take the position that everyone has the right to pursue opportunities with equal access.

EDUCATION

Although Williams (1970) did not specifically identify education as a top U. S. value, at the end of the eighties it appears to have become one. Concern for certification standards for teachers, bond bills to finance new schools, and the requirement that student athletes maintain a reasonable grade point average reflect the importance our society places on education. The value behind the value for education is that it provides industry with an educated work force, which results in greater economic efficiency.

We have noted only a few of the cultural values in our society. Other U. S. values include individualism, democracy, practicality, romantic love, and heterosexuality (McBee 1985). An emerging new value is controlling AIDS through education and "safe sex" practices.

Higher Education Research Institute, 1989.

(continued)

These rules or standards of behavior are referred to as social **norms.** Norms define what is socially acceptable and provide guidelines for appropriate behavior in particular social situations. Norms usually reflect the values that either exist in the culture, or existed at some time in the history of the culture. Next we discuss values, and then look at specific types of norms, including folkways, mores, taboos, and laws.

Values

Values may be thought of as standards of behavior that identify something as desirable or undesirable. In his Inaugural Address, George Bush suggested what he hopes to be the values of his Presidency: "a summons back to the patrician values of restraint and responsibility" (Clift, et al., 1989, 24). Some of the more prominent values in our culture are reflected in the feature on "Values in the United States" on the previous page.

Norms

You may recall from chapter 1 that the concept of **norms** refers to social rules or expectations of

▼   LIVING SOCIOLOGY   ▼

To what extent do you adopt the values of achievement, money, job, freedom, equality, and education? One way to assess your values is to examine the behaviors you engage in that reflect each value. For example, regarding achievement, what are your goals and what are you doing daily to accomplish those goals? Your value for freedom would become evident in your reaction to someone breaking into your apartment and demanding to go through your personal belongings without a warrant. Your value for equality is reflected by how much you are willing to give to others the same benefits and privileges you want for yourself. Your value for education may be indicated by the amount of time you spend studying for tests, and the amount of time you spend reading, watching documentaries on television, and attending lectures on campus that you will not be tested on. Your value regarding money would be reflected in the amount of time you spend worrying about it or seeking ways to get more of it.

behavior. When norms are violated, there may be some form of consequence or sanction. A **sanction** may be either a penalty or a reward that discourages or encourages socially expected behavior.

Norms make social interactions easy, since they prescribe who is to do what. Most of us have been socialized to the extent that we have internalized many of our society's norms and behave according to them without awareness. For example, in answering the telephone, you automatically say, "Hello." It never occurs to you to say anything else (unless you are George C. Scott, who reportedly answers with a "Who the hell is it?").

Norms are culturally determined and are greatly varied throughout the societies of the world. Differences in cultural norms are reflected in the wide variations in the ways that members of different cultures perform daily activities, such as eating and dressing. One may observe, for example, that "Clothing in a hot climate ranges from a penis gourd and necklace for a man in New Guinea to layers of cloth covering the body from head to toe in the Arab world" (Schusky and Culbert 1987, 114).

The norms of a culture change across time. During the Puritan era, people kissing in public were viewed as lacking constraint and were penalized by the male being locked in the stocks. Today, it is not unusual to see lovers kissing in public.

▼   LIVING SOCIOLOGY   ▼

The rules of sports, which may be thought of as norms guiding the behavior of each player, also change across time. In the late 1800s, there were less than 80 rules governing a football game. Today, over 700 rules apply to the sport of football.

Folkways

Folkways are norms that are not considered to be crucial for society, but define what is considered "proper" behavior in a given culture. Literally, the term *folkways* refers to "ways of the folk," or the customs and courtesies that members of a group are expected to abide by. Examples of folkways include dress codes (wearing black clothes at a funeral) and etiquette (saying "excuse me" when you burp). Folkways may be considered to be minor rules, because they have weak penalties for violations (Sumner 1906). Folkways are not enforced by law, but by informal social control. Punishment for violating a folkway may involve a dirty look, a chastising remark, or the severance of a social relationship.

Mores

Mores are social norms that provide the moral standards of behavior for a group or society. The singular form of *mores* is *mos*. Mores involve an emotional element and carry heavier penalties for violations than do folkways. The severe sanctions for violating mores are frequently informal, rather than legally enacted. For example, although there are no laws against middle-aged men dating adolescent girls (assuming the relationship is nonsexual), there is a mos in our culture against this behavior. Anyone violating this mos would not be breaking the law, but would nonetheless experience strong negative reactions from others in his or her social group. There are also mores, such as parents taking care of their children and driving only when sober, that are legally enforced. The state may take children away from parents who neglect and abuse them and may take away the driver's license of someone driving under the influence.

Taboos

A taboo refers to a strong social norm that prohibits or forbids a certain activity, food, or place. Prohibitions against incest and murder are examples of taboos in our society. Taboos vary from culture to culture. This variation is illustrated in the following excerpt, which discusses taboos against certain foods (Schusky and Culbert 1987, 115).

Probably every digestible food is eaten somewhere by some group of people [e.g. the eyeballs of sheep are considered a gourmet's delight in some North African societies], but when it comes to animals, someone somewhere says the flesh is taboo—that is it should not be

(*continued*)

eaten. Hindus will not eat beef while Moslems scorn pork, creating a problem for the British in feeding their Indian troops. Most Westerners reject the idea of eating horses, dogs, or insects. Fish with scales are rejected by Tasmanians while Jews are forbidden fish without scales. . . . The reasons people give for their taboos vary as much as the forbidden foods. Proscribed foods may be 'unnatural,' 'dirty,' or cause illness or skin blemish;

their consumption may offend the supernatural in a variety of ways.

Laws

Folkways, mores, and taboos that are formalized (written) and carry legally imposed sanctions for their violations are known as **laws.** Laws are enacted and enforced by political authority, rather than by custom.

▼ LIVING SOCIOLOGY ▼

A basic dilemma of every society is how much legal control to exercise over its members. For example, should states require motorcycle riders to wear helmets? In 1988, 28 states did not have such a requirement. However, the near-fatal crash of Gary Busey in December 1988 revived the debate.

Many cyclists insist the decision to wear a helmet is a matter of personal freedom. "A motorcyclist should be able to feel the wind through his hair if that's what he wants," says Wayne Thomas of the California Motorcyclists Association. But the price of such freedom can be high not only for the individual cyclist but for society at large. A study of 105 bike-accident victims hospitalized in Seattle during 1985 found that of the $2.7 million they incurred in medical bills, 63% was paid out of public funds. Says John Cook of the Insurance Institute for Highway Safety: "This is a social issue. When you have a seriously brain-injured person, all of us pay" (*Time* 1988, 65).

Laws permeate our society. Government buildings must have access facilities for the handicapped; factories are limited in the amount of waste they can dump into public waterways, and neighborhood residents are under the restriction of local fire codes to burn leaves only under certain conditions.

Although we tend to think of laws as more powerful than folkways, the opposite may be true. Drinking alcohol as a minor is against the law, but refusing to drink among friends may be a violation of a folkway. Gaining approval of one's friends and avoiding their disapproval may be more motivating than avoiding the threat of penalty from the law.

▼ CULTURAL CONCEPTS

A number of concepts help to clarify several aspects of culture: ethnocentrism, cultural relativism, xenocentrism, and cultural meshing.

Ethnocentrism

Ethnocentrism involves the attitude that one's own culture is superior. We are being ethnocentric when we judge another culture by the standards in our own culture. We divide the world into "we" and "they." Everything about "us" seems right and proper, while everything about "them" seems unusual and wrong.

Paul (1988) observed that ethnocentrism expresses itself in three ways. First, individuals view the beliefs and habits of other cultures as being odd or peculiar, while viewing their own cultural beliefs and habits as normal. Second, individuals assume that the ways and ideas of their own culture are more advanced and superior than those of other cultures. Finally, we tend to view customs and beliefs as isolated elements rather than as parts of a system or pattern. But Paul notes that "it frequently turns out that people cling to a particular practice or belief not merely because it is familiar and traditional but because it is linked to other elements of the culture" (pp. 57–58).

An example of ethnocentrism is found in the following illustration (Campbell 1972, xviii):

In much of Africa, including the Arabic cultures, children are systematically trained to use their left hands after urination and defecation, and their right hands for eating. Harsh punishment and scandalized rejection may be used in such training, so that absent-minded substitutions of the wrong hand is entirely eliminated. When such a person for the first time sees a European or an American put food in his mouth with his left hand, the sight is vividly disgusting, fully as revolting as it would be for us, for example, to see someone wipe his mouth with dirty toilet paper.

Ethnocentrism performs several functions. It provides group members with a feeling that they are "right" in how they think and behave. In this way, ethnocentrism strengthens group solidarity—the feelings the group members have for each other and for their group. Football coaches talk of preparing team members "mentally" for the next game. Such preparation involves getting each member to feel a part of the team and to "pull together." Phrases such as "we're number 1" and "we're the best" are designed to make team members (as well as fans) feel strongly about identifying with the group.

▼   LIVING SOCIOLOGY   ▼

Games and sports represent an important part of the culture in most societies. Some cultures feature professional athletes, such as the gladiators in Ancient Rome, the Aztecs of Mexico, and the Sumo wrestlers of Japan. Olympic games are viewed as more than games. Victory is seen as an index of superiority among competing social groups and political/economic systems, and provides a source of national pride.

Ethnocentrism also helps group members to fight against those who try to question their beliefs or practices. Wars typically originate in the "rightness" a group feels about a particular point of view and the desire to impose that view on the opposition.

Ethnocentrism may result in the limited ability to explore and understand ways of thinking and behaving that are different from our own. Because we unconsciously adopt the standards of our culture, it is difficult to view other cultures from a neutral standpoint.

Xenocentrism

Xenocentrism is the opposite of ethnocentrism. It is the belief that what is foreign is best, and that one's own way of life, artifacts, or values are inferior. Some Americans feel that the best place to live is in Australia, not the United States. Others believe that the best cars are made in Japan, the best watches in Switzerland, and the best beer in Germany. Xenocentrism can become so extreme

that an individual denounces his or her own country and seeks citizenship in another.

Cultural Relativism

The principle of **cultural relativism** suggests that to understand other cultures, we must view them according to their own standards. Those who adopt the principle of cultural relativism view the beliefs and practices of another culture according to the norms and values of that culture.

In India, cows regularly roam the streets while much of the population is starving. Such starvation amid plenty of beef seems silly to Westerners. Yet, the cultural context in which this situation occurs provides a rational explanation for why cows are not slaughtered for food (Harris 1974). Cows produce oxen, which are necessary for the small farming communities in India. If Indians eat all the cows, they will have no animal labor to plow the fields and their food shortage will get worse. Also, while the cows are alive, they provide manure to fertilize the crops; and when they die, they provide leather. Finally, cows consume food that is not physiologically digestible by humans (so they are not a threat to the food supply of the Indians), they provide an important protein food source (milk), and their dung is used as a fuel source. Not eating cows "makes sense" from the perspective of an Indian.

Even cannibalism, when viewed in the context of the culture it occurs in, is understandable. A chief of a cannibalistic tribe was once asked why his people practiced cannibalism. The chief indicated surprise at the fact that some people viewed this practice as abominable.

You whites . . . will not eat crocodiles or apes, although they taste well. If you did not have so many pigs and crabs you would eat crocodiles and apes, for hunger hurts. It is all a matter of habit. When I have killed an enemy, it is better to eat him than to let him go to waste . . . I know of no game which tastes better than men. You whites are really too dainty (Sumner 1906, 331).

A major criticism of cultural relativism is that it encourages tolerance of repressive practices such as genocide and slavery. But the challenge to understand the beliefs and practices of another cultures does not require us to totally abandon the notions of right and wrong, good and bad.

Cultural Meshing

Also referred to as *cultural integration*, the concept of **cultural meshing** refers to the degree to which the various elements of a culture mesh, or fit together. Pig breeding among the Kapauku Papuans in West Irian, Indonesia represents an example of cultural integration (Harris, 1979). To raise a lot of pigs, a great deal of sweet potatoes must be raised. This is often done by women, who also tend pigs. Polygyny, the practice of one man having more than one wife, is socially approved of and provides a way for one man to have plenty of wives to tend his pigs. To get a wife he must pay a hefty bride price, in the form of pigs. The interrelatedness of the economy (pigs) and marriage patterns (polygyny) demonstrates how different aspects of a culture fit together or mesh.

Language

Language is an extremely important aspect of every culture. It is language that to a great degree distinguishes humankind from other animal forms. Although we can hardly imagine what human life would be like without language, most of us take language for granted. We do not fully realize how much our behavior, perceptions, and experiences are influenced by the language of our culture.

Learning a foreign language is one way to develop an appreciation for the role language plays in determining our perceptions and experiences. For example, if you studied the Eskimo language, you would discover that Eskimos have over 20 words for snow (including dry-wind-driven snow, powder-snow, wet-packed-snow, and dry-packed-snow-suitable-for-cutting-into-blocks). When most Americans see snow, they do not perceive snow as one of 20 types of snow, because the American language has only one word for snow. What the Eskimo "sees" is different from what the American "sees" because of the difference between the American and Eskimo languages. Of course, you are capable of defining and seeing (with the use of modifiers) all the different types of snow Eskimos see. You are not likely to want

to do that, because snow is not as significant to your life as it is to the Eskimo.

The idea that our language predisposes us to perceive, interpret, and experience life in a particular way is known as the **linguistic relativity hypothesis.** This idea is also known as the *Sapir-Whorf hypothesis*, after Edward Sapir (1929) and Benjamin Lee Whorf, who developed it.

Our language influences even the most basic aspects of our experience, such as the concept of time. In America we organize time into the past, present and future. We talk about where we have been, where we are, and where we are going. To the Hopi Indians, all of life is viewed as an unbroken, continuous movement in which everything is forever becoming, and nothing is thought of as being or having been.

▼ CULTURAL CONFUSIONS

Our culture sometimes confuses us by socializing us with two sets of incompatible values and norms. Police officers are often caught between the expectation that they obtain evidence against suspected criminals and the expectation to obtain such evidence by legal means. Some undercover police officers feel pressure to "plant" drugs on people and arrest them, and then to perjure themselves in court when asked to tell how they obtained the evidence.

Politicians are often caught between the desire to be honest and the desire to get elected. To get

---

▼   LIVING SOCIOLOGY   ▼

You have probably experienced what it is like to be caught between two sets of cultural expectations. For example, your parents expect you to study and earn good grades in school. They also want you to have friends and not be a social isolate. So, what do you do when your friends want you to join them in a party the night before you have a test? How will you resolve this role conflict that results from your culture creating two sets of incompatible expectations?

votes, some politicians may feel pressure to say things they don't believe, unfairly criticize opponents, and give political favors to supporters.

"Ideal" Culture vs. "Real" Culture

Aside from personal dilemmas, which are the result of two competing norms, there are an array of cultural inconsistencies. The "ideal" culture consists of the cultural ideals that are publicly supported. Behind the ideal culture is the real culture, which is what people actually do.

As an example of the inconsistency between the ideal culture and the real culture, consider taxes. Most people publicly agree that honesty is important and that taxes are necessary for the functioning of our government. We know that without taxes we would not have "free" public schools, interstate highways, and garbage pickup. However, at least a fourth of Americans cheat on their taxes (McBee 1985).

The discrepancy between our sexual values and behavior also illustrates inconsistency between ideal culture and real culture. Most brides and grooms value being involved in a monogamous marital relationship and literally stand before witnesses and agree that they will "hold ourselves only unto each other as long as we both shall live." However, the data on extramarital sexual behavior reveal that about half of both husbands and wives have intercourse with someone other than their spouse at least once during the marriage (Thompson 1983).

Subcultures

A **subculture** is the culture of a segment of a society. Subcultures are part of the total culture of a society, but they differ from the larger culture in certain respects. For example, subcultures may diverge from the larger culture in their customs, languages, values, religion, or norms. American subcultures include various racial, ethnic, religious, and economic groups. The feature about "The Farm" describes a rural commune, which is a type of subculture in the American society.

Countercultures

Subcultures may also be countercultures. **Countercultures** are groups that actively reject the norms and values of the larger culture. The youth movement of the 1960s, the Hare Krishna religious sect, and the Amish are examples of countercultures. The theme of the youth movement of the sixties was that success and materialism were misguided goals for individuals in society. Love, peace, and sharing was the suggested alternative. The "hippies" (as they were called) who flourished in such communities as Haight-Ashbury in San Francisco and the East Village in New York have virtually disappeared. As they grew older, they married, had children, and got jobs. Being in the roles of spouse, parent, and employee influenced their perceptions and behaviors to become consistent with those roles. Spouses can't love "everybody" (at least in a physical sense), parents of young infants can't spend all day at a youth rally, and employees are expected to be at work on time.

Members of the Hare Krishna religious sect can be seen proselytizing in airports. Their goal is to save the world through conversion to the Krishna

(*continued*)

The Farm: A Commune Subculture

The Farm is a cooperative community of families and friends living on 1750 acres in southern middle Tennessee. We started the Farm in 1971 with the hope of establishing a strongly cohesive, outwardly-directed community, a base from which we could, by action and example, have a positive effect on the world as a whole. Among ourselves we try to use agreement and mutual respect to generate a friendly working environment. We recognize that there are many paths toward realizing personal ideals and that people have a wide range of individual social values, but as a group, we do not accept the use of violence, anger or intimidation for solving problems. The fabric of our community is created by our friendship and respect for one another. The institutions we have developed to organize our community have changed over the years and will probably change more. The Farm is not really *what* we are doing—it is how we are currently doing it. It is a process, rather than an end-result.

WHY DID WE COME TO TENNESSEE?

In the mid-1960s, many people went through a cultural change that took them away from their roots and cast them adrift, searching for something better. They were disillusioned by the Vietnam War, disturbed by increasing violence and injustice in the nation, encouraged by the successes of the Civil Rights and other movements, and empowered by the strength of their numbers. Many gravitated toward the West Coast, looking for alternatives. In 1970, Stephen Gaskin led a caravan of more than 300 of us from California to start an experimental community where our ideals could find expression in our daily lives.

WHAT ARE THE FARM'S RELIGIOUS BELIEFS?

The Farm is a nondenominational church. We like to call ourselves "free thinkers," because we discuss religion and philosophy in terms that do not exclude any possibilities. People come to the Farm from a variety of religious traditions and disciplines and find those views treated with honor and respect. While individual practices may vary, our group practice is an on-going, free-ranging discussion. We consider ourselves to be a *spiritual* community. In keeping with our deep reverence for life, we are pacifists, conscientious objectors, and most of us are vegetarians. On Sunday mornings many of us like to gather for group meditation and church services in an open-meeting style.

HOW IS THE COMMUNITY MANAGED?

All members of The Farm are expected to contribute to the financial upkeep of the community through their earnings. Since our community operates like a small town, it has some of the same needs. We maintain our own roads, municipal buildings, and public water system. Community policies are arbitrated and implemented through an elected board. Important questions are discussed at town meetings and decided by community votes. We don't always reach complete consensus, but we generally have a high level of agreement in everything we decide.

HOW DO PEOPLE SUPPORT THEMSELVES?

About a third of the adults in the community work in nearby towns to support themselves and their families. Some are members of our construction company, and some are medical, financial, or legal professionals. Some work as independent contractors, while others work in local shops and industries.

About half of us make our living right on the Farm. Some of us work for community-based businesses like the Book Publishing Company, the Good Tasting Food Company, the Dye Works, our electronics business, or our Soy Dairy. Others are involved in community services such as The Farm School, the store, the gatehouse, our clinic, or our community government. Still others work for the international relief and development organization, Plenty, or its One World Trading Company.

Jobs within the Farm have been developed over many years, often by the people that hold them. Since new job openings are not readily available within the community, we advise prospective members to consider job alternatives in the surrounding area or bring with them a reliable source of self-employment.

WHAT ARE THE LIVING ARRANGEMENTS?

Most of us live in one- or two-family households or as single people living alone or with friends. Presently we hold our land in common and are discussing ownership in regard to homes. We have run electricity and water mains to most accessible parts of the land and encourage new home construction, within reasonable zoning limits and building standards. We have a strong affinity for the beauty of nature and are trying to protect our forests, creeks, and wilderness as we gradually develop our community.

WHAT WAS THE CHANGE THE FARM WENT THROUGH IN 1983?

From 1971 to 1983, the Farm had a traditional communal economy like the Shakers or the Hutterites. Anyone joining the Farm gave everything they owned to the common treasury and anything developed or received by any member belonged to the whole group. A recession, several business reverses, overcrowding, lack of experience, and mismanagement brought about a severe financial crisis. Extreme austerity, which we tried for some years, was not enough to keep the Farm from the threat of bankruptcy, and so in October, 1983, we reorganized our communal economy. Individual members were made responsible for providing for their own living expenses *and* contributing to the support of the community. The effect of the austerity measures, the loss of jobs in community services, the need to find outside income and other contributing factors took the Farm's population down from its peak of about 1400 in 1981 to 300 by 1986. Although this change was difficult for all of us, we

succeeded in retiring the debt, saving our 1750 acre freehold, and putting the community back on a solid financial footing.

WHAT IS THE ECONOMIC COMMITMENT OF MEMBERSHIP?

Members of The Farm pay weekly or monthly dues which contribute to the upkeep of the community. We call it our "rent." The level of individual contribution, which is usually between $100 and $125 per adult per month, is based on a budget that is drafted and re-drafted at town meetings and voted on, line-by-line, once a year.

In addition, new members are also asked to provide a one-time membership fee, which may be paid in installments over time. This money goes to our capital fund, which is used to maintain the land, improve the community's facilities, stimulate cottage industries, and otherwise help the Farm develop.

WHY ARE WE HERE?

Since we first came here, we've had the satisfaction of realizing many of the dreams and aspirations with which we began. After more than a decade on this land, we appreciate even more the security of a tight-knit, compassionate, community environment. Our children have the freedom to explore the woods or go anywhere in our town in safety. The adults they interact with are honest and caring. We have very nurturing and healthful surroundings. No one has to carry the burden of his or her problems alone, or to bear the entire brunt of some catastrophe.

We hold as a common belief that our outward works and goals should be seamless with how we choose to live—and we choose to live in community with one another.

Consciousness. By shaving their heads, dressing in white, developing elaborate rituals, and actively trying to convert members of the larger society, the Hare Krishna are one of the more visible countercultures in our society.

The Amish are a religious sect (about 100,000 members) who have lived in America for over 250 years (Hostetler 1980). A large Amish settlement in Lancaster, Pennsylvania is noted for its beautiful farmlands, horsedrawn carriages, and dark-

(continuing)

colored clothes. The Amish want to be separate from the larger culture. They take the Bible seriously when it says "Be not conformed to this world . . ." (Romans 12:2). The Amish strongly discourage marriage to those who are not Amish; they also discourage becoming involved in a business partnership with outsiders. They view themselves as "chosen people" and want no part of violence or war. They are exempt from military service as conscientious objectors, and their children do not have to attend public schools. They also wanted to avoid paying Social Security taxes on those they employ, but the Supreme Court ruled against this. The larger culture will tolerate some deviation from countercultures, but there are usually limits.

▼   LIVING SOCIOLOGY   ▼

You can observe these subcultures and countercultures yourself. Information can be obtained by writing to the following and arranging to visit: The Farm, Route 1, Box 197A, Summertown, Tenn. 38483; International Society for Krishna Consciousness, c/o David Schiller, Jr., International Office of Public Affairs, P.O. Box 7030, Laguna Niguel, Calif. 92677; Amish Information, Chamber of Commerce, Lancaster, Pa. 17604.

▼ CULTURAL VARIATION

One benefit of being in college is being exposed to people who have been reared in different parts of the country and who have mannerisms, speech patterns, and values different from your own. One "northerner" went to school in Texas and said of her southern classmates that they "talk funny ('yall'), dress funny (wear cowboy hats), and have strange values (everybody has or wants to own a horse)." Although her description does not fit all Texans, she perceived them to be different.

Just as Texans have their own culture, so do people in different ethnic groups (Italians are known for their distinctive foods and patterns of expression), occupations (physicians, attorneys, meat cutters), and sexual life-styles (homosexuals, heterosexuals). The cultures in these groups are all different. Why are they different? Why aren't all people the same everywhere? Three explanations for cultural differences are offered by the viewpoints of functionalism, ecologism, and evolutionism.

A Functional View

From chapter 1, you recall that functionalists describe how one part of society functions for the whole. A functional view of cultural variation explains the existence of a particular aspect of the culture on the basis of how that aspect benefits the rest of the culture. For example, satellite dishes in the yards of American homes function to express the American value of individualism. "I'll get my own dish and tune in my own programs without sending monthly checks to the local cable company" illustrates the basic values of freedom and frugality.

There are no privately owned satellite dishes in Russia. Russian values are generally not those of individual freedom and possessions, but of restricted freedoms and community property. Although satellite dishes would be functional in America, they would be dysfunctional to political values in Russia, where access to unedited media is restricted.

An Ecological View

Some aspects of a culture develop to help members adapt to their physical environment. An ecological view suggests that some differences between cultures are due to variations in the physical environment. Snowshoes for Eskimos, thatch huts for hunting and gathering societies in west Africa, and tents among the Bedouin Arabs illustrate the enormous impact of the environment on what people wear and how they live. Because the nomadic Bedouin Arabs live in desert terrain, they must continually search for food and water. This lifestyle requires them to be highly mobile, hence their tents are light and their possessions are few.

Every culture exists in a physical environment, so there is necessarily a relationship between any particular culture and its environment. However, it has been pointed out that very different cultures can exist in similar environments (White and Dillingham 1973). For example, the Indians of Tierra del Fuego live in an environment that is very similar to that of the Eskimos, yet the cultures of these two groups are very different. This leads to the conclusion that although the environment does influence a culture, it does not totally determine it. "The habitat may permit certain things and prohibit certain others, but there is still room for a great deal of variation" (White and Dillingham 1973, 19).

An Evolutionary View

An evolutionary view suggests that cultures evolve, or develop from simpler to more complex forms. According to this view, those characteristics of a culture that increase the survival of its members tend to endure, and those that are dysfunctional tend to disappear. Societies whose people gather berries and hunt food (more about this in chapter 4) for their survival have not, according to the evolutionary perspective, evolved to the stage where cultivating crops or domesticating animals for a food supply have been integrated into their cultural system.

Whereas human evolution according to Darwin involves genetic changes, cultural evolution may involve individuals teaching each other that there are different and sometimes more efficient ways of doing things (Lenski and Lenski 1987). It is not easy to predict the course of how any given culture evolves over time. "A deadly new disease could sweep through human societies, and in a short time, reverse most of the trends of the last ten thousand years" (p. 75).

Cultural Universals

Although most societies are different in the cultural patterns they display, there are **cultural universals:** traits found in all cultures. Earlier in this chapter, we referred to ethnocentrism as a universal culture trait. The institution of marriage is another example of a cultural universal. In all societies there is some form of bonding males and females together to produce offspring. Although the nature of marriage may vary from monogamy (one husband, one wife) to polyandry (one wife, two or more husbands) to polygyny (one husband, two or more wives), the existence of marriage is universal. Other cultural universals include a division of labor, funeral rites, and religious rituals.

Cultural Change

The material and nonmaterial aspects of cultures undergo varying degrees of change across time. In modern cultures, change is rapid and widespread. New products, services, technology, and fashions are continually being introduced into modern cultures. Values such as those related to being single (less stigma), children (childfree marriages) and sexuality (greater fear of contracting AIDS) are also changing. In more primitive cultures, material and nonmaterial aspects of culture may also change, but at a much slower rate.

The mechanisms by which cultures change include invention (and/or innovation), discovery, diffusion, and acculturation. **Invention** is the putting together of existing phenomena to produce something new. Music television (MTV) and nuclear energy are inventions in which existing technology and artifacts were combined in a unique way to produce new phenomena.

▼   LIVING SOCIOLOGY   ▼

Inventions may affect the social roles and relationships in a culture. The invention of the steam engine resulted in factories, which required workers to operate them. Many of these workers were women who became independent from their fathers and husbands as a result of earning their own money outside the home.

Discovery is finding something in the environment that is already there. The discovery of the Grand Canyon (or some other natural beauty) can influence the availability of jobs for individuals in the nearby community. Rafting, helicopter and mule tours, lodging facilities, and restaurants result from such a discovery, thus altering the economy and culture of the community.

Diffusion is the borrowing of a cultural trait or object from another culture. Linton (1937) observed in his work, "One Hundred Percent American," that many common American objects have been borrowed from another culture. Table 3.2 reflects the origin of some objects that are common in America.

Another mechanism of culture change is **acculturation,** which is a restructuring process that results when two cultures come into contact with

TABLE   3.2   Common "American" Objects Borrowed from Another Culture

Object	Place of Origin
Bathroom	
Glazed tile	Near East
Mirror	Mediterranean
Soap	Gaul
Bathtub	Rome
Towel	Turkey
Food	
Coffee	Arabia
Waffle	Scandinavia
Butter	Near East
Utensils	
Spoon	Rome
Fork	Italy
Glass	Egypt
Clothes	
Pajamas	East India
Necktie	Croats
Cotton	India
Wool	Asia Minor
Recreation	
Alcohol	Near East
Other items	
Clock	Medieval Europe
Umbrella	India
Coins	Lydia

Source: From Linton, Ralph. 1937. "One Hundred Percent American." *The American Mercury* 40:427–29. Used by permission.

each other and they exchange cultural traits. When Cortes (along with 2,500 other Spaniards) arrived in Mexico in 1519, they brought a culture that soon mixed with the already-developed culture of the Aztec Indians. Over a period of years, the Spaniards adopted the agricultural practices, food habits, and architectural techniques of the Indians; in turn, the Indians adopted the language, dress, and life-styles of the Spaniards. Today, the basic distinctions between the respective cultures has been lost; through the process of acculturation, Mexico has become a blend of Spanish and Indian culture.

Changes in the material aspect of a culture often involve changes in cultural values. For example, a cultural value supporting population control may either lead to or result from the introduction of contraceptive techniques and devices (which may be acquired through invention, discovery, of diffusion). In an attempt to slow China's population (estimated to be 1.3 billion by the year 2000), the Chinese government adopted a policy whereby couples were encouraged to have only one child. This new cultural policy, adopted in 1980, contradicted 2000 years of Chinese Confucian belief that couples were to have large families because sons were necessary to carry on the family name. If a couple had only one child, and that child was a daughter, the family name would die. To help change this perspective, the Chinese government passed a law that allows daughters to keep their family name when they marry. Despite this change, the one-child policy in China is only slowly gaining acceptance.

Cultural Lag

In his work on social change, Ogburn (1932) observed that **cultural lag** exists when some aspect of a culture changes at a faster rate than other related aspects of the culture. Cultural lag often creates a sense of imbalance and disrupts the equilibrium of the culture. The concept of cultural lag is often used to refer to the delay between the rapid advances made in science and technology, and our adjustment to these advances. For example, medical technology makes it possible to keep a brain-dead person alive almost indefinitely. This medical advance requires adaptations in the philosophical, theological, and legal aspects of our culture. But it takes time for the larger culture—the patients, spouses, physicians, ministers, and judges—to adapt to the new possibilities and problems created by this new medical technology.

Cultural lag does not only occur in modern industrial societies. In rural India, for women who had previously defecated in open fields, sanitation experts provided latrines in an attempt to avoid the unsanitary conditions this practice creates. Their efforts were unsuccessful, however, because the women went to the field in groups not only to defecate but to gossip, exchange advice, and take a break from toil (Paul 1988). Before women in rural India will consistently make use of latrines, other cultural changes must occur. Knowledge concerning the relationship between sanitation and disease

must be made public, the culture must support sanitation and disease control, and new social patterns must develop in which Indian women may gossip, exchange advice, and relax. Because these changes will take time, we see the occurrence of cultural lag.

Sometimes individuals in a culture that is rapidly changing develop physiological reactions to such change. One such change is elevated blood pressure, which alters life expectancy. We discuss culture and life expectancy in our research section.

▼   PERSPECTIVE   ▼

We have emphasized that culture includes everything we are socialized to do, think, use, and make. Our skills, language, ideas, possessions, and behaviors are reflections of our culture. Humans are unique from other species in that they have culture and transmit it to others.

In the next chapter we look at the people in the culture and the societies that they develop. We are all familiar with the society we are a part of. By examining other societies, we become aware of the many variations in patterns of food acquisition, language, values, and behavior.

▼ **MAIN POINTS**

1. Sociologists define culture as everything that human beings are socialized to do, think, use, and make.

2. Cultural products are both material (concrete artifacts) and nonmaterial (values, norms, customs).

3. Ethnographers sometimes give conflicting reports of a culture, which could be due to giving selective attention to a particular aspect of culture, studying the culture at different times, and having different theoretical orientations.

4. Norms—in the form of folkways, mores, taboos, and laws of a society—help to ensure that the members of society act in predictable ways to facilitate the functioning of society.

5. Ethnocentrism means evaluating others on the basis of the norms, values, and beliefs that are held in one's own group. Ethnocentrism may encourage self-confidence, group solidarity, racism, and narrow-mindedness.

6. The language of a culture greatly determines how members of that culture perceive and experience the world.

7. There are contradictions in all cultures. What a culture says that it values ("ideal" culture) and what the culture actually values ("real" culture) may be quite different.

8. All cultures have subcultures that do not participate fully in the larger society. Some subcultures are also countercultures—they reject the values of the larger culture.

9. The causes of cultural change include invention, discovery, and diffusion. Much of what is evident in a culture has been borrowed from other cultures.

10. Cultural lag exists when one aspect of a culture changes more rapidly than other related aspects of the culture. For example, the medical institution can develop ways to prolong life faster than the religious and political institutions can decide how to use the technology.

11. Some aspects of culture are related to life expectancy. For example, the stress associated with modernization has been related to elevated diastolic blood pressure. In addition, blacks live in a culture that suggests they are disadvantaged when compared to whites in regard to life expectancy. (See Applying Sociological Research.)

▼ GLOSSARY

Acculturation A restructuring of two cultures that come into contact with each other. The result is a new culture that is a blend of the two original cultures.

Artifacts Objects that have meaning and are used by members of a culture.

Counterculture A subculture that rejects the beliefs, norms, and values of the larger culture. The Amish and members of the youth movement of the sixties are examples of countercultures.

Cultural lag Ogburn's term for the social disequilibrium that occurs when some aspect of a culture changes at a faster rate than other related aspects of the culture.

Cultural meshing Also known as *cultural integration;* the extent to which the various elements of a culture complement each other or "fit together."

Cultural relativism The view that values and customs of a society can only be understood within the context of the culture in which they exist.

Cultural universal A cultural pattern or trait that is found in all cultures.

Culture Everything that a group of human beings learns to do, think, use, and make.

Diffusion The borrowing of a cultural trait or object from another culture.

Ethnocentrism The tendency to judge other cultures according to the standards of one's own culture and to view one's own culture as superior.

Ethnographer A researcher, usually a sociologist or anthropologist, who gathers data about a culture through field research.

Ethnography The descriptive study of individual cultures.

Folkways A type of norm in which an informal understanding by the members of society has developed about the usual patterns of expected behavior (for example, Speak when spoken to). Folkways carry only informal sanctions.

Laws Norms that are formalized (written) and have been approved by the political or legal authority.

Linguistic relativity hypothesis The idea that the way a person experiences his or her environment is a result of the words or labels that person has of the environment.

Material culture All man-made objects as well as objects found in nature that have meaning to and are used by the members of a society.

Mores A set of norms involving a moral sentiment that members of society take seriously (homicide is wrong), and that has attached to it severe penalties for not behaving as expected.

Nonmaterial culture The intangible aspects of culture, including norms, customs, beliefs, values, attitudes, knowledge, and language.

Norms Rules or standards of behavior that define what behavior is socially acceptable in particular social situations.

Sanction Either a penalty or a reward that discourages or encourages certain socially expected behavior.

Subculture A culture of a segment of a society that deviates from the larger culture in certain respects; for example, in customs, language, religion, values, or norms.

Taboo A strong social norm that prohibits or forbids a certain activity, food, or place.

Values Standards of behavior that identify something as desirable or undesirable.

Xenocentrism The belief that foreign values, life-styles, patterns of behavior, and material goods are superior to those in one's own society.

▼ REFERENCES

Billingsley, Andrew. 1988. "The Impact of Technology on Afro-American Families." *Family Relations* 37:420–25.

Campbell, Donald. 1972. "Herskovits, Cultural Relativism and Metascience." In *Cultural Relativism: Perspectives in Cultural Pluralism,* edited by M. Herskovits. New York: Random House, pp. v–xxiv.

Clift, Eleanor; Thomas M. DeFrank; Howard Fineman; and Ann McDaniel. 1989. "Bush Reaches Out." *Newsweek* January 30, 22–26.

Cockerham, William C. 1986. *Medical Sociology.* (3d ed.) Englewood Cliffs, N.J.: Prentice-Hall.

Cohen, Eugene N., and Edwin Eames. 1982. *Cultural Anthropology.* Boston: Little, Brown.

Dressler, William W.; Jose Ernesto Dos Santos; Philip N. Gallagher, Jr.; and Fernando E. Viteri. 1987. "Arterial Blood Pressure and Modernization in Brazil." *American Anthropologist* 89:398–407.

Easterlin, Richard A., and Eileen M. Crimmins. 1988. "Recent Social Trends: Changes in Personal Aspirations of American Youth." *Social Science Review* 72, no. 4: 217–27.

Freeman, Derek. 1983. *Margaret Mead and Samoa: The Making and Unmaking of an Anthropological Myth.* Cambridge: Harvard University Press.

Harris, Marvin. 1974. *Cows, Pigs, Wars, and Witches: The Riddles of Culture.* New York: Random House.

————. 1979. *Culture, People, Nature.* (3d ed.) New York: Crowell.

Heckler, M. 1985. *Report of the Secretary's Task Force on Black and Minority Health,* Vol. 1, *Executive Summary.* Washington, D.C.: Department of Health and Human Services.

Heider, Karl G. 1988. "The Rashomon Effect: When Ethnographers Disagree." *American Anthropologist* 90:73–81.

Higher Education Research Institute. 1989. "The American Freshman: National Norms for Fall 1988." University of California, Los Angeles, 405 Hilgard Avenue, Los Angeles, California 90024. Used by permission.

Hostetler, John A. 1980. *Amish Society.* (3d ed.) Baltimore: Johns Hopkins University Press.

Lenski, Gerhard, and Jean Lenski. 1987. *Human Societies: An Introduction to Macrosociology.* (5th ed.) New York: McGraw-Hill.

Linton, Ralph. 1937. "One Hundred Percent American." *The American Mercury* 40:427–29.

McAdoo, H. P. 1982. "Stress-absorbing Systems in Black Families." *Family Relations* 31:478–88.

McBee, Susanna. 1985. "The State of American Values." *U.S. News and World Report* 99:52–58.

McBroom, William H.; F. W. Reed; C. E. Burns; J. L. Hargraves; and M. A. Trankel. 1985. "Intergenerational Transmission of Values: A Data-Based Reassessment." *Social Psychology Quarterly* 48:150–63.

Mead, Margaret. 1973. (originally published in 1928). *Coming of Age in Samoa.* New York: Morrow.

Ogburn, William F. 1932. *Social Change.* New York: Viking Press.

Paul, Benjamin D. 1988. "The Role of Beliefs and Customs in Sanitation Programs." In *Social Interaction* (3d ed.), edited by Candace Clark and Howard Robboy. New York: St. Martin's Press, pp. 56–63.

Sapir, Edward. 1929. "The Status of Linguistics as a Science." *Language* 5:207–14.

Scheper-Hughes, Nancy. 1987. "The Margaret Mead Controversy: Culture, Biology and Anthropological Inquiry." In *Perspectives in Cultural Anthropology,* edited by Herbert Applebaum. Albany: State University of New York.

Schusky, E. L., and T. P. Culbert. 1987. *Introducing Culture.* (4th ed.), Englewood Cliffs, N.J.: Prentice-Hall.

Statistical Abstract of the United States: 1989. (109th ed.) Washington, D.C.: U.S. Bureau of the Census, 1989.

Sumner, William G. 1960. (originally published in 1906). *Folkways.* New York: New American Library.

Thomas, William I. 1923. *The Unadjusted Girl.* Boston: Little, Brown.

Thompson, A. P. 1983. "Extramarital Sex: A Review of the Research Literature." *Journal of Sex Research* 19:1–22.

Time. 1988. "Head Gear: The Bike-helmet Battle." December 19, p. 65.

White, Leslie A., and Beth Dillingham. 1973. *The Concept of Culture.* Minneapolis: Burgess Publishing.

Williams, Robin M., Jr. 1970. *American Society: A Sociological Interpretation.* (3d ed.) New York: Knopf.

APPLYING SOCIOLOGICAL RESEARCH

▼

Culture and Life Expectancy

Sociologists study groups of people in different cultures and ask why some live longer than others. One predictor of a shortened life expectancy is high blood pressure, because of its association with heart attacks and strokes. Although blood pressure is an aspect of biology, it is influenced by the culture an individual lives in. Researcher William W. Dressler and his colleagues (1987) hypothesized that as a culture becomes more modernized, there is increased stress, which will be reflected in the blood pressure readings of the people in that culture. To test their notion, the researchers identified 139 individuals in four occupational categories in the city of Ribeirão Prêto in Brazil:

- day laborers (sugar-cane cutters with no guarantee of stable employment)
- agricultural workers (employed full-time and living in housing provided by the plantation owners)
- factory workers (living on the outskirts of the city)
- bank employees (living in middle-and upper-middle-class neighborhoods)

From these individuals they selected 20 in each group, interviewed them, and took blood pressure readings.

Blood pressure was taken by an automatic device, which eliminated interobserver variability. Although blood pressure is an expression of both the systolic (contraction of heart) and diastolic (dilation or relaxing of the heart) pressure, only diastolic pressure was used in the study, because it has been associated with hypertension and cardiovascular disease. Life stress was assessed by weighing the material possessions of the individuals (color televisions, cars, stereos, etc.) against the material resources available to afford these items.

Analysis of the data revealed that when there was a discrepancy between what individuals owned and what their economic resources could realistically pay for, they experienced "life-style stress." This stress was reflected in elevated diastolic blood pressure readings.

The difficulty arises when individuals are attempting to attain and maintain a particular style of life that is inconsistent with their economic resources. In this circumstance persons are likely to experience frustration, anger, uncertainty in social interaction, and a symbolic discordance in their person identities; also a person may have to work long hours or multiple jobs to try to amass economic resources (p. 399) . . . The model of the high blood pressure risks associated with modernization has received additional empirical support here (p. 404).

Blacks and whites in the United States also live in different "cultures" that affect their life expectancy. Table 3.3 shows the life expectancy of whites and blacks in selected years.

Although life expectancy has been increasing for both whites and blacks, the gap between the groups has continued. Black culture (when compared to white culture) involves a dietary pattern (e.g., more fat in the diet) that encourages the development of high blood pressure and heart attacks.

In addition, black culture involves a great deal of stress, frustration, and anxiety resulting from racial discrimination. Many blacks feel powerless to defend

T A B L E 3.3	**Life Expectancy of Whites and Blacks in the United States**	
Year	**White**	**Black**
1970	71.7	64.1
1975	73.4	66.8
1980	74.4	68.1
1985	75.3	69.5
1986	75.4	69.4
1987	75.5	69.7

Source: Statistical Abstract of the United States: 1989. Table No. 106. National Center for Health Statistics. 1988. "Advance report of final mortality statistics, 1986." *Monthly Vital Statistics Report* 37, no. 6, Supp. DHHS Pub. No. (PHS) 88–1120. Hyattsville, Md.: Public Health Service.

CHAPTER 3   Culture: The Ideas and Products People Adopt and Create   ▼   85

themselves against pervasive racism. One black remarked:

They cut off expectations. I mean no matter how good you are, you will always be a nigger. Hey, that puts strains on people. I mean you can be smart, have a lot of bread, but you know that you will not be able to give your children or yourself an equal chance, and that takes its toll. A lot of really good people have a lot on the ball, end up on dope, alcohol, or one thing or another. I mean everyone that I know has one of these problems because of this racist society. Let me tell you, I do not have any hope for the future (McAdoo 1982, 484).

Black culture also involves greater unemployment. Blacks suffer disproportionately more deaths from cirrhosis of the liver, by homicide, and by suicide; and more blacks are admitted to mental hospitals and prisons (Billingsley 1988). Black men die at higher rates than all other groups from six of the seven leading causes of death (heart disease, stroke, cancer, homicide, accidents, and cirrhosis of the liver). Only with respect to diabetes do black men take second place to black women (Heckler 1985).

Other minority groups in America also have a disproportionately high incidence of health problems. American Indians "have the poorest health of all Americans" (Cockerham 1986, 46). Diabetes, tuberculosis, alcoholism, and suicide are much more prevalent among native Americans compared to whites.

The relevance of this research is to be aware of how life expectancy is affected by culture. Awareness of the causes and consequences of stress may be the first step toward controlling the level of stress in our own lives. In addition, as a culture we should examine the wisdom of implementing social policies to reduce the social stresses of racism and unemployment. ▼

2 Sample Chapter

The Planetary Setting

SOURCE: Reprinted by permission of *Essentials of Physical Geography* by Ralph Scott. Copyright 1991 by West Publishing Company. All photographs and captions have been deleted.

Chapter One

The Planetary Setting

Outline

Focus Questions

1. What is the geographical setting of the earth in space, and what movements is it making through space?
2. How is the global system of time zones organized?
3. What causes the changing seasons?

The Planetary Setting

THE PLACE OF THE EARTH IN THE UNIVERSE

The earth is the third of nine known planets orbiting the star we call the sun. Sharing our **solar system** with the sun and planets are a number of planetary satellites or moons as well as asteroids, comets, dust, gases, and a great deal of empty space. Two opposing factors are responsible for the maintenance of stability in the solar system. One is the outward thrust of centrifugal "force" caused by the inertia of the planets as they orbit the sun; the second is the inward pull of gravity. The revolution of the planets around the sun, and of the moons around the planets, is made possible by the precise balance between these forces.

The sun is only one relatively undistinguished member of a giant assemblage of stars called the **Milky Way galaxy**. Galaxies are large groups of stars held together by their mutual gravitational attraction. They vary tremendously in size, shape, and density and contain anywhere from a few thousand to hundreds of billions of stars. Most galaxies also contain extensive clouds of gases and dust out of which new stars constantly form. The Milky Way is a large, discus-shaped galaxy consisting of more than 100 billion (or 10^{11}) stars. Despite its enormous stellar population, the great preponderance of the galaxy consists of virtually empty space containing only the most rarefied concentrations of gas and dust.

Our solar system is located near the outer fringe of the Milky Way on a spiral arm an estimated 30,000 light years from the galactic center. The center of the galaxy is rendered invisible to us by vast clouds of interstellar gas and dust. The stars that so liberally sprinkle the sky on a clear night are our stellar neighbors, occupying nearby portions of our arm of the galaxy.

PLANETARY MOTIONS

The earth is engaged in several motions through space, each at a differing level of magnitude. These movements can be divided into two categories—large-scale movements and small-scale movements. The large-scale movements are of limited direct significance to the earth because millions or even billions of years are needed for them to produce major changes. The earth's small-scale movements, however, critically affect nearly every aspect of our environment and will be discussed in greater detail. For clarity, the various earth motions will be discussed in order of decreasing magnitude.

Large-scale Motions

The largest-scale motion of all is the movement of the earth, along with the rest of the solar system and galaxy, away from the center of the universe—that is, from the site of the Big Bang (see the Focus box on page 8). The universe is still expanding at great speed.

The second large-scale motion is the revolution of our solar system around the center of the Milky Way galaxy. The time required for one full revolution is estimated to be 230 million years.

Small-scale Motions

The small-scale motions cause the earth to change its position constantly with respect to the sun. Because the sun is our only major source of planetary heat and light, and because it powers external earth processes such as the weather, plant growth, and erosion, these movements are extremely crucial to the earth and its lifeforms. The small-scale motions are also responsible for the changing seasons and the alternation of day and night and form the basis of our system of keeping time.

Revolution

The larger of the two primary small-scale motions of the earth is its **revolution** around the sun. This motion is made possible by the combined effect of centrifugal force generated by the inertia of the earth as it travels in a curved orbit around the sun and the inward pull of the sun's gravitational force.

The earth's revolution is the basis of our calendar year. To be precise, the period of time needed for one complete revolution around the sun is 365 days, 5 hours, and 49 minutes. For the sake of convenience, though, calendar years are defined in whole day increments. Thus, most years are 365 days long. Because the extra 5 hours and 49 minutes required for a full revolution is very close to an extra quarter of a day, every fourth year has an added day (February 29) and is termed a *leap year*.

The earth orbits the sun on an angular plane termed the *plane of the ecliptic* in the same direction as all the other planets (see Figure 1.1). This direction appears as counterclockwise when earth is viewed from a point in space above the northern hemisphere. The vantage point in space is crucial because the direction of revolution becomes clockwise when earth is viewed from above the southern hemisphere.

Physical Geography

Formation of the Universe, Solar System, and Earth

Astronomical observations have revealed that the universe is composed of vast expanses of nearly perfectly empty space, as well as the widely separated clouds of gases, dust, and stars we call galaxies. Within the known universe are many billions of galaxies, each containing, on the average, tens of billions of stars. The number of stars in the universe is, for all practical purposes, limitless. It has been said that there are more stars in the universe than grains of sand on all the beaches of the world, and this is apparently a great understatement. Moreover, a large proportion of these stars may have planetary systems similar to our own solar system.

The origin of the universe is one of the great mysteries facing humanity, and numerous theories concerning its formation have been developed over the centuries. Any modern scientific theory, however, must take into account a startling fact revealed through the spectrographic analysis of the light from distant galaxies. This fact is that the galaxies are rushing away from one another. In general, the farther apart two galaxies are, the faster their rate of recession seems to be. The only way astronomers can explain this phenomenon is by theorizing that the occupied universe is expanding in all directions, much like an inflating balloon, as the result of a titanic explosion.

The Big Bang Theory

Over the past few decades a theory of the origin of the universe—the so-called "Big Bang Theory"—has been developed and refined. It seems to fit most known facts, and is now generally accepted by the scientific community. According to this theory, some 15 or so billion years ago, all matter in the known universe was concentrated into one tiny and inconceivably dense "cosmic egg." How it formed, and what events occurred prior to this time, nobody knows. The universe as we know it was initiated by the explosion of this egg. The explosion, the "big bang," destroyed the egg and hurled all the matter it contained into space in all directions, much like shrapnel from a detonating bomb. The violence of the explosion was so great that the super-dense matter of the cosmic egg was reduced to its constituent atomic particles, which soon reassembled to form only two elements, hydrogen and helium. Shortly after the explosion, then, the universe consisted of an expanding cloud of gas composed of approximately 73 percent hydrogen and 27 percent helium.

Gravity, however, began to alter the characteristics of the cloud. The expanding cloud gradually lost its homogeneity as it was drawn into many smaller gas clouds, each held together by internal gravitational attraction. Within these gas clouds, or proto-galaxies, gravity produced much denser and more localized concentrations of gas. As these gas clouds con-

continued on next page

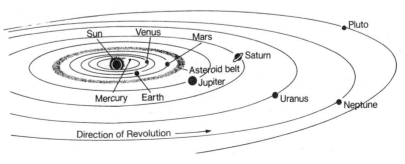

Figure 1.1 The planets of our solar system all orbit the sun in the same direction and, except for Pluto, on nearly the same orbital plane.

8

The Planetary Setting

tracted, their central cores were gradually heated by compression until thermonuclear fusion reactions were spontaneously initiated; and stars were born. The basic thermonuclear reaction that powers the stars, including the sun, involves the conversion of hydrogen to helium. A series of other stellar fusion reactions are believed to have produced all the elements heavier than helium.

The earliest stars formed under highly favorable conditions and were large, extremely hot, and short-lived. These massive stars became increasingly unstable as their fuel supplies were exhausted and eventually exploded as supernovas, spewing throughout the galaxy a portion of the heavy elements they had produced. Succeeding generations of stars, including our sun, thus formed from concentrations of gas containing not only hydrogen and helium, but the heavier elements as well. It is believed that the elements that constitute most of the earth, and even our own bodies, originated in the cores of these supernova stars!

Formation of the Solar System and Earth

When a cloud of gas contracts to form a star, any initial rotational motion is magnified because of the conservation of angular momentum. (This is the same principle that causes ice skaters to spin faster when their arms are drawn in.) The generated centrifugal force draws the contracting gases into a disk shape. The major concentration of gases at the center of the disk is under enough gravitational pressure to initiate thermonuclear reactions and become a star, while it is believed that smaller nodes of gases form on the rotating rim of the disk to produce planets. This would explain why the planets of our solar system all orbit the sun on roughly the same angular plane and why they revolve around the sun in the same direction. If this system operates everywhere, most stars would have planetary systems, and, of course, the chances of earth-like planets and the existence of life elsewhere in the universe would greatly increase.

In the case of our solar system, it is believed that the weaker gravity of the earth and the other inner planets, coupled with intense radiation emanating from the nearby sun (the so-called "solar wind"), drove off the hydrogen and helium that formed the initial bulk of the masses of these planets. The inner planets therefore consist primarily of the heavier residual elements that originated in supernova stars. The massive outer planets, though, were able to retain most of their light gases. They still consist largely of hydrogen and helium, which probably surround small solid cores of heavier elements.

The earth's orbital path is roughly circular, but actually forms a broad ellipse. The mean radius of this ellipse, which represents the average distance between the earth and sun, is approximately 93 million miles (150 million km). At its closest approach to the sun, the earth is said to be at *perihelion* (from the Greek *peri,* or "near," and *helios,* or "sun"). At this point in its orbit, which occurs about January 3 each year, the earth is only 91.5 million miles (147.5 million km) from the sun (see Figure 1.3). Six months later, on or about July 4, the earth is at its farthest point from the sun, or at *aphelion* (from the Greek *ap,* or "away from"). Our distance from the sun is then approximately 94.5 million miles (152.5 million km). Therefore, the earth's distance from the sun varies by about 3 percent during the course of a year.

Rotation

Rotation, the most small-scale motion of the earth, involves the spinning of our planet on its *axis*. The rotation of the earth on its axis is similar to the rotation

Physical Geography

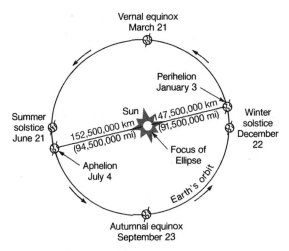

Figure 1.3 The earth's orbit is slightly elliptical. As a consequence, we are approximately three million miles nearer the sun in early January than in early July.

of a model globe on its axis bar except that, of course, the real earth's axis is not a physical entity and provides no support. The rotational motion of the earth allows for the definition of three important and very basic locations. The **North Pole** and **South Pole**, located on opposite sides of the planet, are the two points where the axis intersects the earth's surface. Midway between the poles, and exactly equidistant from both along its entire length, lies the **equator**. This is the line of the fastest rotational speed on the earth.

Rotation is the basis of our calendar day and is the primary reason for the apparent westward motion of the sun, moon, and stars through the sky. (The situation is analogous to riding eastward in an automobile and watching the outside scenery apparently rushing by to the west.) The earth rotates in the same direction as it revolves; this rotational direction can be described as counterclockwise from north, clockwise from south, or eastward if the earth is viewed from a point in space above the equator.

Because all places on earth complete one 360° rotation in a 24-hour period, they rotate through an angle of 1° every 4 minutes. The linear speed of rotation, however, is highly variable and is dependent upon distance from the equator. The speed of rotation is at its maximum value of approximately 1040 miles per hour (465 meters/sec) at the equator, but diminishes to 0 miles per hour at the poles.

Earth's axis is not oriented at a perpendicular angle to the plane of the ecliptic, but instead is inclined from the perpendicular at an angle of approximately $23\frac{1}{2}°$ (see Figure 1.4). Because this value does not change significantly over the short term as the earth revolves around the sun, the earth's axis is described as exhibiting **parallelism**, and the poles remain directed toward essentially the same points in space for extended periods of time. This is why the North Star, or Polaris, occupies a fixed position above the North Pole.

SIZE AND SHAPE OF THE EARTH

It is common knowledge that the earth is approximately spherical in shape. The shape of the earth, however, is not readily apparent from observation and was the

Figure 1.4 The earth's axis is tilted at a constant angle with respect to the plane of the ecliptic as it revolves around the sun during the course of the year.

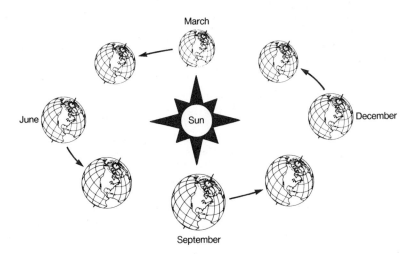

The Planetary Setting

subject of speculation and debate for centuries. Most early scientists and philosophers believed that the earth was flat. This view was based on the physical appearance of the earth's surface, just as the early belief that the rest of the universe revolved around the earth was based on the apparent motion of the sun, moon, and stars. Modern science, however, has produced many proofs of the sphericity of the earth. These include the virtual equality of gravitational attraction at all points on the earth's surface, numerous precise surface and astronomical measurements of distances and directions, and the visual evidence provided by high altitude and space photography.

Earth's spherical shape is produced by gravity. This incompletely understood force causes all matter to have an attraction for, and to be attracted by, all other matter. The mutual gravitational attraction of the earth's matter has caused the planet to assume a spherical form—the most compact form that exists. Gravity has also produced a layering of the earth by density, with lighter materials tending to overlie heavier ones. (Fortunately for us, this layering is far from perfect.) All other known astronomical objects of large size are also essentially spherical, indicating that gravity is apparently a universal force that operates wherever a sufficient mass of matter has assembled.

The three basic measurements of the size of a sphere are its radius, diameter, and circumference. For a given sphere, if any one of the measurements is known, the other two can be readily calculated. The radius of the earth, or the distance from its surface to its center, is approximately 3950 miles (6350 km). Earth's diameter, the linear distance from any point on its surface through the center of the earth to its opposite (antipodal) point,

is equal to two radii, or 7900 miles (12,700 km). Finally, earth's circumference, the length of a line drawn on the surface that bisects the planet, is 24,900 miles (40,000 km).

Departures from Perfect Sphericity

Although gravity causes the earth to be approximately spherical, it is not perfectly so because other forces also influence the shape of our planet. The effects of two of these forces are sufficiently important to merit discussion. They are the outward thrust of centrifugal force generated by the earth's rotation on its axis and tectonic forces produced deep within the earth.

The centrifugal force of rotation is much too weak to overcome the binding force of gravity and cause the earth to fly apart. It is, however, sufficient to slightly distort our planet's shape. In the vicinity of the equator, where the speed of rotation is greatest, the earth is bulged out from its spherical form. In contrast, the slowly rotating polar areas are somewhat flattened as the earth's rotational inertia displaces their mass equatorward (Figure 1.5). The earth thus assumes the shape of an **oblate ellipsoid**, a three-dimensional ellipse that is flattened at the poles. The amount of bulging and flattening is too small to be visually perceptible, and from space the earth looks perfectly spherical. However, this departure from perfect sphericity affects the precise calculations required for surveying and mapping and also influences the force of gravity on different parts of the earth.

A second, more important departure from perfect sphericity (discussed at length later in this book) results from the earth's variable surface features. If our planet

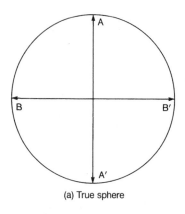

(a) True sphere

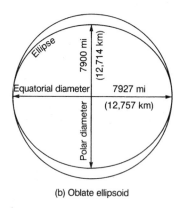

(b) Oblate ellipsoid

Figure 1.5 The earth's shape is somewhat distorted from that of a true sphere (Figure a) because of the centrifugal force of the earth's rotation on its axis. This motion causes our planet to assume the shape of an oblate ellipsoid (Figure b), with its equatorial diameter slightly larger than its polar diameter.

11

Physical Geography

were a perfect sphere, or even a perfect oblate ellipsoid, its surface would be smooth and would appear flat to an observer at ground level. Instead, the surface is highly wrinkled and contorted in places, exhibiting a great variety of landforms of many sizes and shapes. Total surface irregularity increases if we consider the sea floor, rather than the ocean surface, as comprising more than 71 percent of our planet's surface. Thus the earth, when examined in sufficient detail, has a unique shape, undoubtedly duplicated by no other planet in the universe.

How great a departure from perfect sphericity do earth's surface features represent? One way of judging is by determining the total vertical distance between the world's highest mountain and its greatest ocean depth. Mt. Everest in the Himalayas is the highest peak on earth, reaching an elevation of 29,028 feet (8847 m) above sea level. Challenger Deep in the western Pacific is the deepest known point of any ocean, with a maximum depth of 36,198 feet (11,033 m) below sea level. The total vertical difference between these two extreme points is 65,226 feet (19,880 m), or about $12\frac{1}{3}$ miles. This value is less than one-third of 1 percent of the earth's total radius of 3950 miles.

Despite the relatively diminutive size of the earth's surface features when compared to the size of the entire planet, they are extremely important to humankind because we happen to live just where these features are located—at the surface. As a result, the earth's surface features have strongly influenced most major aspects of human society, including population distributions, transportation routes, and agricultural patterns. In addition, earth's landforms profoundly influence global patterns of climate, vegetation, and soils.

DIRECTIONS

The concept of direction is vital to the field of geography because of the discipline's emphasis on location. Unfortunately, due to a lack of reference lines or surfaces, no natural "universal" directions exist in space. In outer space, in fact, even the words "up" and "down" are meaningless.

The basis for the horizontal directional systems used on earth is our planet's rotational orientation. Rotation has established the positions of the North and South Poles and the equator. These locations enable us to construct reference lines for stating horizontal directions. Vertical directions are based on the orientation of the earth's gravitational force, which is considered to pull directly downward toward the center of the earth.

North, often considered the most basic of all directions, is by definition the straight-line direction from any point toward the North Pole. Likewise, *south* is the direction from any point toward the South Pole. These two directions, of course, are always 180° apart with respect to a given starting point because the poles are on opposite sides of the earth. *East* and *west* may either be defined as those directions lying perpendicular to north and south, or as those lying parallel to the orientation of the equator. The earth rotates in an eastward direction, and when an observer stands facing northward, east is on his right and west on his left. Any other direction can be determined by reference to these four cardinal directions.

It is important to note that the directions north, south, east, and west are all equally horizontal. Expressions such as "up North" and "down South" are strictly figures of speech and are probably based on the fact that many maps showing these areas are displayed vertically, as on classroom walls.

Magnetic North and South

The exact determination of direction is difficult or impossible without reference to an accurate map or the availability of surveying equipment, although estimates can often be made from the position of the sun, the North Star, or other celestial objects. The most commonly employed method for determining direction in the field is the use of a magnetic compass. A compass does not point toward the geographic (rotational) North Pole, however, but instead aligns itself with the magnetic field extending outward from the magnetic North Pole.

The magnetic North and South Poles, unlike the geographic poles, are not fixed in position, but drift slowly about. The magnetic North Pole is currently located in the Canadian Arctic, north of the Hudson Bay, at a point some 1000 miles (1600 km) south of the geographic North Pole. The magnetic South Pole is located near the coast of Antarctica south of Sydney, Australia, at a point about 1800 miles (2900 km) from the geographic South Pole. Because the magnetic poles are at considerable distances from the geographic poles, compass directions can differ greatly from geographical directions, and corrections are generally needed.

The Planetary Setting

LATITUDE AND LONGITUDE

Geographers are concerned with understanding spatial phenomena and interactions over the entire earth. It is therefore necessary for them to employ locational systems that can accurately describe the geographic position of any point on the earth's surface.

A number of global locational systems have been devised, but the most widely used, by far, is the system of **latitude** and **longitude**. This system is based on the locations of the North and South Poles and the equator. Related to these locations are the directions established by the earth's rotational orientation. All lines in the system of latitude and longitude are oriented either due north-south or east-west. The system will be examined by discussing first the characteristics of lines of latitude, then lines of longitude. Finally, the two will be put together to show how these lines form a system for describing locations.

Latitude

Lines of latitude have the following characteristics, as illustrated in Figure 1.6.

1. They extend in an east-west direction but are used to state locations in a north-south reference frame.
2. Lines of latitude are really circles of latitude if viewed in their entirety, because they form full circles on the globe.
3. Lines of latitude are parallel, or equidistant to one another, along their entire lengths. For this reason, they are commonly termed *parallels*.
4. Lines (or circles) of latitude vary greatly in length (circumference), but do so in an orderly fashion. The longest circle of latitude is the equator. Progressing poleward, the circumferences of the circles of latitude become progressively shorter until at the poles they have shrunk to a point.
5. An unlimited number of parallels exist, but on a map they are usually spaced at set intervals, decided upon by the cartographer (mapmaker) in view of the map's intended purpose.

By international agreement the equator is used as the starting line for the determination of latitude values. Parallels of latitude are identified by their angular distance, in degrees, north or south of the equator. As the starting line, the equator is assigned a value of 0° latitude. The half of the earth's surface located north of

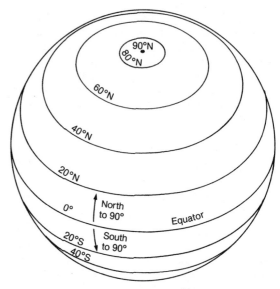

Figure 1.6 The globe with selected lines of latitude. These lines actually take the form of concentric circles, numbered from the equator.

the equator is termed the *northern hemisphere,* and all lines of latitude here contain an "N" after their value. Likewise, the half of the earth's surface located south of the equator is termed the *southern hemisphere;* and all latitude values here end with an "S." If we took a large globe and drew a parallel for each degree of curvature north of the equator, we would find that the fortieth line we drew would pass through Philadelphia, Pennsylvania. Philadelphia therefore has a latitude of 40° N. So do Columbus, Ohio; Boulder, Colorado; Ankara, Turkey; Beijing (Peking), China; and many other cities and towns. It is therefore evident that a statement of latitude is insufficient by itself to pinpoint a location.

The higher the numerical value of a line of latitude, the farther it is from the equator. The point farthest north is the North Pole, which is 90 degrees north of any point on the equator. Its latitude is therefore 90° N. By the same token, the latitude of the South Pole is 90° S. Because all low-numbered parallels are near the equator, areas within about 30° of the equator are frequently referred to as the *low latitudes.* Areas between about 30° and 60° N and S latitude have intermediate values and are referred to as the *middle latitudes.* Most of the United States and Europe lie within this zone. Areas poleward of about 60° N and S are considered to be in the *high latitudes.*

13

Physical Geography

Lines of latitude are parallel to one another, and, if the earth is considered to be a sphere with a circumference of 24,900 miles, the length of one degree of latitude can be calculated readily. A circle contains 360° of arc. The length of one degree of latitude must therefore be 24,900/360 or 69 miles (111 km). Actually, since the earth is not perfectly spherical, a degree of latitude is slightly longer at the poles (69.4 miles, or 111.7 km) than it is at the equator (68.7 miles, or 110.6 km).

For greater precision, a degree of latitude or longitude can be subdivided into sixtieths, termed *minutes* ('), and each minute, in turn, can be divided into sixtieths, termed *seconds* ("). Minutes and seconds of curvature therefore subdivide degrees as minutes and seconds of time subdivide hours. One minute of latitude is approximately 1.15 miles (2.85 km) long, and one second of latitude is about 100 feet (31 m) long. A latitudinal reading is given from left to right in progressively smaller units, as in the following example:

39° 07′ 15″ S.

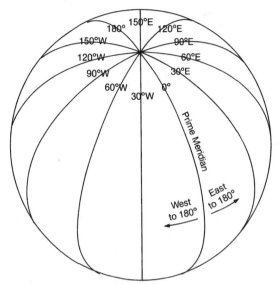

Figure 1.7 Lines of longitude are half circles with their end points at the poles. They are spaced farthest apart at the equator and are numbered in degrees east and west of the prime meridian.

Longitude

Lines of longitude, or *meridians,* are similar to lines of latitude but they also possess a number of unique characteristics (see Figure 1.7). The term "meridian" means "noon" or "midday," and, as we shall see, longitude is the basis of our system of time.

Lines of longitude have the following characteristics:

1. They extend in a north-south direction but are used to state locations in an east-west reference frame.
2. Each meridian has its endpoints at the North and South Poles and its midpoint at the equator.
3. Meridians are *not* parallel to one another; they are spaced farthest apart at the equator and converge northward and southward to meet at the poles. Because meridians converge, the surface length of a degree, minute, or second of longitude depends on its latitude. The length of one degree of longitude at the equator is approximately the same as that of a degree of latitude: 69.2 miles (111.1 km). This length decreases to 0 at the poles.
4. Meridians always intersect parallels at 90° angles.
5. No limitation exists as to the number of meridians that may be placed on a map, but, like parallels, they are usually spaced at set intervals.

The numbering of meridians is accomplished in the same way as is the numbering of parallels—by choosing a starting 0° line and measuring subsequent lines in degrees of surface curvature, this time to the east and west. A problem long existed, though, in choosing an appropriate starting meridian because no one meridian differs from the rest in any geometrical manner. As a result, many countries that made maps established 0° meridians through their own capital cities or other points of national importance. This practice resulted in a great deal of confusion because longitude values for the entire world depended upon the country of origin of the map or book being consulted. It was finally decided at an international meeting in 1884 to adopt the English system, in which the starting or **prime meridian** passed through Greenwich Observatory on the outskirts of London.

From the prime meridian (also called the *Greenwich meridian*) westward, longitude values increase from 0° W to a maximum of 180° W halfway around the world from Greenwich. Similarly, going eastward, values of longitude increase from 0° E to 180° E. The numerical values of meridians therefore go twice as high as values for parallels. (The two 180° lines are actually one and the same, and thus two meridians, 0° and 180°, can be labeled either E or W.)

Longitude divides the world into the *eastern hemisphere* and the *western hemisphere*. These terms are not as frequently employed as the terms northern hemisphere and southern hemisphere, but such longitudinally derived expressions as the Western World and the Middle East are in common usage.

Determining Geographical Coordinates

Taken together, the latitude and longitude of any location describe its geographical position. A given parallel intersects a given meridian at only one point on the earth, so if the correct value of each line is given, the position of any place can be pinpointed. The accuracy of placement of any point depends on the accuracy with which its position is stated. Locations stated to the nearest whole degree contain a potential margin of error of many miles, while those stated to the nearest second of latitude and longitude are accurate to within 50 feet.

When the geographical coordinates of a site are given, latitude is always given first. An example of a location stated to the nearest second is as follows:

39° 22′ 18″ N 76° 38′ 05″ W

It must be remembered that each number is always followed by the letter, N, S, E, or W, and that minutes and seconds are sixtieths, not hundredths. Most maps have selected lines of latitude and longitude either drawn on them or indicated by tick marks on their margins. The spacing of lines of latitude is not necessarily the same as that for lines of longitude.

TIME

Our system of keeping time is based on the east-west (or longitudinal) position of the sun. The sun's position and apparent motion during the course of a day are associated primarily with the earth's axial rotation but are also slightly affected by the earth's revolution around the sun. The basic unit of time is the *solar day*, which is the period of time needed for the sun to make one apparent 360° circuit of the sky. The solar day is, of course, divided into units of hours, minutes, and seconds.

Local Time

The event historically used for establishing the time of day has been *solar noon*. Solar noon occurs the instant the sun reaches its daily high point in the sky. For centuries, until the late 1800s, communities made the time of the mean occurrence of solar noon the official instant of noon and then simply subdivided the periods between solar noons into the appropriate hours, minutes, and seconds. This system of **local time** was highly accurate with respect to the position of the sun, because the time was individually adjusted to each locality. During the nineteenth century, however, a major shortcoming in the local time system became increasingly evident and eventually led to its discontinuance over most of the world. The problem was that different places, even those located near one another, inevitably had somewhat different times. Because the local time system used the precise east-west position of the sun in the sky, only places on precisely the same meridian had exactly the same time at any one instant.

Prior to the nineteenth century, time differences between nearby localities using the local time system were only a minor inconvenience. Timepieces were rare and rather inaccurate, appointments were not generally made for exact times, and means of transport were so slow that it took a long period to reach a location with a significantly different time. In the nineteenth century, however, the advent of the railroads provided a rapid and long-distance means of transportation, while the telegraph offered a means of instantaneous long-distance communication. The railroad and telegraph companies, as might be imagined, experienced serious difficulties because of the multiplicity of times existing throughout the world. As a result, they increasingly pressured government agencies to develop standardized time zones.

Standard Time

Our present **standard time** system was officially established for the United States in November 1883 and was soon adopted by most other countries. The standard time system, like the local time system, is based on the position of the noon sun, but only at selected meridians of longitude rather than at each specific site. The areas surrounding these standard meridians all have the same official time. Because the earth rotates 15° in one hour, the standard time zones differ by exact one-hour intervals. Thus, 24 time zones cover the earth (see Figure

Physical Geography

1.8). In changing from local time to standard time, a decision was made to sacrifice accuracy of time determination for much greater convenience.

The meridians used as the centers of their respective time zones are multiples of 15°. The meridian that provides the basis for all the time zones is the Greenwich meridian, and the time zone established by this meridian is called Greenwich mean time (GMT). Many people employed in fields such as transportation and communications base their activities directly on Greenwich mean time.

If the standard time system were rigorously followed, each time zone would be exactly centered on its standard meridian and would extend 7° 30′ both east and west from the meridian to the borders of the adjacent time zones. For example, the 75° W meridian is used as the basis for the Eastern Time Zone of the United States. In theory, Eastern Time should extend westward to 82° 30′ W, changing to Central Time from that line westward to 97° 30′ W. In reality, though, the time zone boundaries are generally drawn along state or county lines and are sometimes quite distant from the theoretical 7° 30′ boundaries (see Figure 1.9). The rationale for this, of course, is to avoid the problems that arise when time lines pass through the middle of a county, town, or other political unit. Internationally, time zone boundaries have also been adjusted considerably, as is evident from Figure 1.8. In many cases, entire countries use the same time, and the time changes as the international boundary is crossed. Most large countries, especially those of great longitudinal extent, have multiple time zones. The United States, for example, has 7

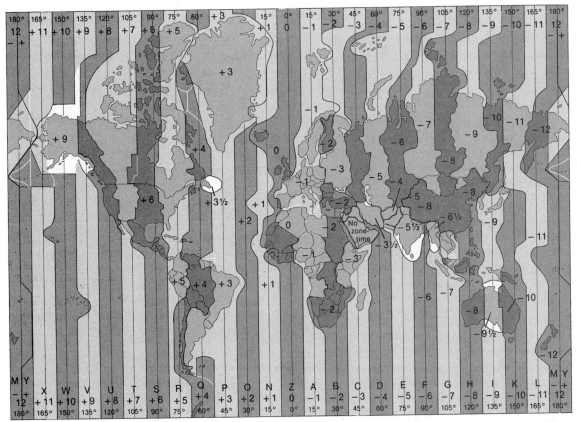

Figure 1.8 The global system of time zones. The International Date Line appears near the left and right margins of the map.

The Planetary Setting

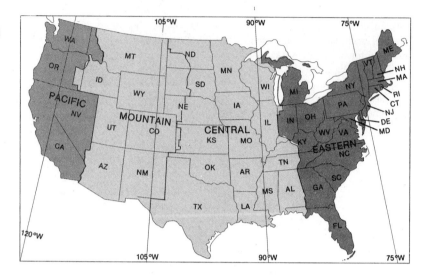

Figure 1.9   The standard time zones of the coterminous United States. The central Meridian of each time zone is indicated.

different time zones (4 in the coterminous United States) and the Soviet Union has 11! Over the open oceans, the official time boundaries are generally used because no practical advantage is gained from shifting them.

The International Date Line

The **International Date Line** is a unique line in the world standard time system. When it is crossed, time changes by a full 24 hours. Therefore, although the hour of the day remains the same, the calendar date and day of the week both change. In addition, the direction of the time change is the opposite of all those established by the 24 one-hour time zone boundaries. Crossing the Date Line from east to west causes the time to become one day later, and crossing it from west to east causes the time to become one day earlier.

The International Date Line is closely associated with the 180th meridian, and the two lines run together along much of their lengths through the Pacific. For the sake of convenience, though, the Date Line contains three major longitudinal digressions that allow portions of continents or island groups crossed by the 180th meridian to remain entirely on one side or the other. The 1883 decision to extend the 0° longitude line through England was at least partially made so as to place the International Date Line, with its potentially confusing

date changes, in as remote a portion of the earth as possible.

Daylight Saving Time

For most people, the daylight hours are those around which most activities, especially work-related ones, are centered. Certainly, major advantages exist in concentrating our waking periods and activities during the day; these include the presence of light to see by and the economic benefits derived from decreased fuel needs for lighting and heating. Yet, in many societies, especially in more technologically developed countries, the waking hours of most individuals are considerably offset from the daylight period. To illustrate this point, consider that on a typical day the sun is above the horizon from 6 A.M. to 6 P.M. The average adult in Europe or North America, however, is likely to awaken at perhaps 7 A.M. or later and to retire at 11 P.M. or later. This results in an hour or more of daylight being wasted in the morning, while nearly half the night is spent in wakefulness. **Daylight saving time** represents an attempt to achieve a greater correlation between the daylight hours and the human activity period.

To convert from standard time to daylight saving time, the official time is simply moved forward by one hour. This obliges individuals with set time schedules to do everything an hour earlier with respect to solar time. The implementation of daylight saving time changes no

17

Physical Geography

Determining Times

Because time is based on the apparent westward movement of the sun in the sky, time zones to one's east are progressively later in hour while those to one's west are progressively earlier in hour regardless of the longitude. For example, the time in California is three hours earlier than on the East Coast. Announcements concerning the times of television programs have familiarized much of the American public with this fact. Conversely, standard time is five hours later in Great Britain than in the eastern United States.

The simplest method of calculating the difference in time between any two points is to determine their differences in longitude and then to divide this difference by 15 to determine the difference in hours. The time in the location farthest east in longitude is always the latest. When determining the difference in longitude between two places in opposite longitudinal hemispheres for the purpose of comparing their times, you should measure by way of the prime meridian in order to avoid the potential confusion encountered when crossing the International Date Line. The following two time problems should serve to clarify the methodology involved:

■ *Problem 1:* If it is 10 P.M., Sunday, at 135° W, what is the time and day at that same instant at 15° W?
■ *Analysis:* In going from 135° W to 15° W, we are traveling eastward; therefore, the time gets later. Since both points are in the same longitudinal hemisphere, we subtract their numerical values to determine their longitudinal separation. Since 135 − 15 = 120, the time must be 120/15 or 8 hours later at 15° W. Eight hours later than 10 P.M., Sunday, is 6 A.M., Monday.
■ *Problem 2:* If it is 9 A.M., Tuesday, at 105° E, what is the time and day at that same instant at 150° W?
■ *Analysis:* In going from 105° E to 150° W, we are traveling far west in longitude, so the time must become much earlier. (Actually, a much shorter distance would be involved if we traveled *eastward* past 180° longitude to reach 150° W. This direction, however, includes the complication of crossing the International Date Line.) Since the two given longitudes are in opposite longitudinal hemispheres, their total longitudinal separation is calculated by adding their numbers. Thus, we must go 105° + 150°, or 255°, westward from 105° E to reach 150° W. The time at 150° W must therefore be 255/15 or 17 hours earlier than 9 A.M., Tuesday. Subtracting, our new time and day becomes 4 P.M. Monday.

time zone boundaries; only the time within each time zone is changed.

Although it had long been in use in some parts of the United States, daylight saving time was adopted nationwide in 1966 for six months of the year, and this period was increased slightly in 1986. (A few localities have elected not to use the system.) Daylight saving time begins at 2 A.M. on the first Sunday in April (when the time is moved ahead to 3 A.M.) and ends at 2 A.M. on the last Sunday in October (when the time is moved back to 1 A.M. and standard time is resumed). A phrase sometimes employed to help keep track of the necessary clock adjustments is "spring forward and fall back." The reason for using daylight saving time only during what is essentially the summer half of the year is that the sun rises earliest during this period and, correspondingly, the greatest loss of daylight hours is likely to occur.

THE SEASONS

Over most of the earth's land surface, including nearly all areas lying outside the tropics, the seasonal climatic changes are one of the most important aspects of the natural environment. All lifeforms, both plant and animal, have had to adjust to the seasonal rhythm of the climate in these areas, and most species have evolved biological cycles that cause them to depend on the orderly seasonal progression of climatic changes.

Cause of the Seasons

The seasonal climatic changes are caused by the inclination of the earth's axis. This results in a yearly cycle of change in both the angle and duration of sunlight for all places on the earth (see Figure 1.4). The resulting changes in solar energy produce annual cycles of higher and lower temperatures over most of our planet.

Before the earth-sun relationships associated with each of the four seasons are examined, it is necessary to discuss the key factor responsible for the relationship between the sun's angle and its heating ability. The angle of the sun in degrees above the horizon is termed its *altitude*. The altitude of the sun is the most important factor controlling the amount of solar heating received at the earth's surface in all but the high latitudes. When the sun is directly overhead, or at an altitude of 90°, its heating power is greatest; as its altitude decreases, its rays gradually lose intensity. This loss of intensity occurs because a decrease in the sun's altitude causes an equivalent amount of solar energy to strike a larger earth surface area, spreading and reducing the energy received per unit area (see Figure 1.10). A further reduction in solar energy reaching the earth's

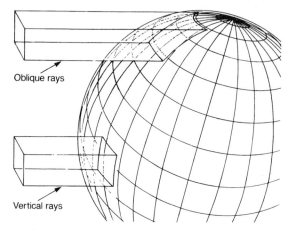

Figure 1.10 The intensity and heating power of the sun's rays are directly related to the sun's altitude. The same amount of energy is contained in both "boxes" of incoming radiation above, but the oblique rays striking the higher latitudes are spread over a larger area, resulting in lower temperatures.

surface occurs when the sun is at a low altitude because of increased scattering and absorption of sunlight resulting from its oblique passage through the atmosphere.

The tilt of the earth's axis causes the noon sun to vary in altitude at any place during the course of the year. This results in a considerable variation in the concentration and heating ability of the solar energy received. As the earth revolves around the sun, the North and South Poles constantly point toward the same two locations in space. The inclination of the poles, or of any other location on earth, is *not* constant, though, with respect to the sun. In fact, the combination of rotation and revolution constantly shifts both the latitude and longitude of the point on the earth's surface that has the sun directly overhead. Tracing the position of this point through the course of a year would show that the point shifts alternately northward and southward because of the earth's axial inclination (Figure 1.11) and moves constantly westward because of the earth's rotation.

The four seasons are based on the changing orientation of the earth's axis with respect to the sun during the course of a year. The official beginning of each season marks the instant that a key earth-sun positional relationship occurs.

Summer officially begins in the northern hemisphere when our hemisphere reaches its maximum inclination of $23\frac{1}{2}°$ toward the sun (see Figure 1.11). When this occurs, the sun is at its *summer* **solstice** position, and at solar noon is directly overhead at a point $23\frac{1}{2}°$ north of the equator. The northern hemisphere at this time receives a larger proportion of the earth's total allotment of solar energy than at any other time of the year. Because the southern hemisphere is on the opposite side of the earth, it receives a smaller amount of solar energy than at any other time during the year. Therefore, the northern hemisphere's summer solstice marks the beginning of winter in the southern hemisphere, where the sun is at its *winter solstice* position. All the seasons are exactly reversed between the two hemispheres, so that when any seasonal event occurs in one, the opposite event occurs in the other.

In the northern hemisphere, the summer solstice occurs on, or within two days of, June 21. In fact, each of the four seasonal positions occurs between the nineteenth and twenty-third day of its respective month. The exact time and date vary in different years because of leap years and slight variations in the orbital path of the earth from year to year. The decision to begin each of the four seasons at the four "quarter positions" of the

Physical Geography

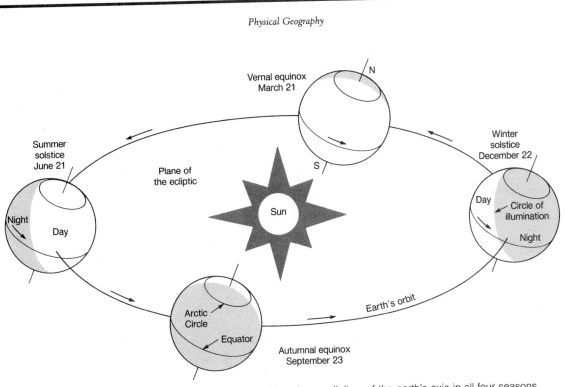

Figure 1.11 The four seasonal positions of the earth. Note the parallelism of the earth's axis in all four seasons.

earth's orbit around the sun was an arbitrary one; no natural law mandates this. As a consequence, the change of seasons often does not lead immediately to the changes in weather that some people seem to expect.

During the three months of summer that follow the summer solstice, the earth revolves so that the inclination of the North Pole toward the sun is progressively reduced. Consequently, the sun's vertical rays gradually shift southward from $23\frac{1}{2}°$ N until they reach the equator. When this occurs, between September 19 and 23, the sun is at its *autumnal* **equinox** position for the northern hemisphere, and the fall season begins. In the southern hemisphere, where spring is beginning, the sun is in its *spring* (or *vernal*) *equinox* position. At this time the axial tilt of the earth is precisely perpendicular to the sun's rays, and the amount of solar energy reaching both hemispheres is equal.

As the fall season progresses, the continued revolution of the earth causes the northern hemisphere to be inclined more and more away from the sun. Finally, between December 19 and 23, the entire $23\frac{1}{2}°$ tilt of the axis is directed away from the sun in the northern hemisphere and toward the sun in the southern hemisphere (see Figure 1.12). Winter now begins in the northern hemisphere as it began six months earlier in the southern hemisphere. At this time, the sun follows its lowest course through the southern sky and provides less energy to the northern hemisphere than at any other time of the year.

During the three months of the winter season, the sun's vertical rays gradually progress northward from their initial position at $23\frac{1}{2}°$ S to reach the equator as the earth's inclination again becomes perpendicular to the sun's rays. Between March 19 and 23, the northern hemisphere spring equinox occurs as the sun crosses the equator; and both hemispheres again receive equal energy. The following three months of spring witness the increasing tilt of the northern hemisphere toward the sun until once again the summer solstice position is reached.

Two lines of latitude achieve importance as a result of the earth-sun relationships involved in the changing of the seasons. The **Tropic of Cancer** ($23\frac{1}{2}°$ N) and the **Tropic of Capricorn** ($23\frac{1}{2}°$ S) mark, respectively, the highest latitudes north and south that the sun's vertical rays ever reach. Stated differently, the sun is always directly overhead somewhere between $23\frac{1}{2}°$ N and $23\frac{1}{2}°$ S. Places between these two parallels have the sun directly over-

The Planetary Setting

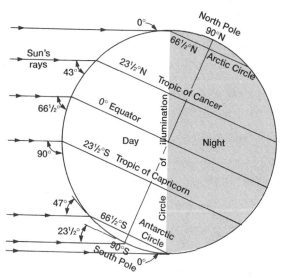

Figure 1.12 The northern hemisphere winter solstice. The sun is directly overhead at the Tropic of Capricorn. Days are longer than nights in the southern hemisphere, while nights are longer than days in the northern hemisphere.

head on two occasions during the year—once while the sun shifts northward toward the Tropic of Cancer and once while it shifts southward toward the Tropic of Capricorn. More than half the world is poleward of these lines (or outside the *tropics*) and never has the sun directly overhead. For nontropical locations, the sun reaches its highest altitude at solar noon on the date of the summer solstice.

Lengths of Day and Night

The changing of the seasons involves not only constant changes in the sun's noon altitude, but also variations in the lengths of day and night for all places on earth except the equator. All locations in the northern hemisphere experience longer days than nights during the spring and summer seasons, when the northern hemisphere is inclined toward the sun. Days are shorter than nights during the fall and winter seasons, when the northern hemisphere is tilted away from the sun. The lengths of day and night at equivalent latitudes in the southern hemisphere are exactly reversed from those in the northern hemisphere because the seasons are reversed. Only the equator, the line separating the two

hemispheres, experiences equal 12-hour lengths of day and night throughout the year.

The length of daylight is not evenly distributed by latitude, but becomes progressively less equal poleward. Figure 1.12 shows that more of each·line of latitude north of the equator is on the night side than on the day side of the earth. North of the **Arctic Circle**, at $66\frac{1}{2}°$ N, all parallels are entirely in darkness. The sun therefore does not rise in this area at the time of the winter solstice. Conversely, increasing proportions of parallels progressively south of the equator (and experiencing the summer solstice) are in daylight until south of the **Antarctic Circle**, at $66\frac{1}{2}°$ S, continuous daylight prevails. Of course, the situation is exactly reversed six months later, so that both hemispheres (indeed, all places on earth) receive six months of day and six months of night over the course of a year.

The Arctic and Antarctic Circles therefore mark the equatorward limits of the two portions of our planet in which day and night periods exceed 24 hours at the times of the summer and winter solstices. All other parts of the world experience both day and night each calendar day. The situation is most extreme at the North and South Poles, where day and night each last for six months. The sun at these two locations remains constantly below the horizon during the fall and winter seasons, but is continuously above the horizon during the spring and summer seasons. On the dates of the equinoxes, all places on earth experience 12 hours of day and 12 hours of night.

Summary

This chapter has examined the earth's origin, position, and movements in space, as well as the size and shape of our planet. These factors have enabled us to devise systems for describing locations and determining times on the earth's surface; they are also responsible for the changing of the seasons.

The earth is the third planet from the sun in a solar system that contains nine known planets. The solar system is located in the outer portion of a spiral arm of the Milky Way galaxy—a rotating collection of many billions of stars. The earth is involved in several movements through space, occurring at greatly differing orders of magnitude. At the largest scale, we, along with the entire galaxy, are moving away from the center of the universe as an apparent consequence of the "big bang." We are also revolving around the center of the

Physical Geography

Milky Way galaxy. On a smaller scale, earth revolves around the sun once each year and rotates on its axis once each day.

The earth is roughly spherical because of the inward pull of gravity and has a diameter of approximately 7900 miles (12,700 km). The centrifugal force of earth's axial rotation, however, has caused the equatorial regions to bulge outward and the polar regions to become flattened, so that the earth is more accurately described as an oblate ellipsoid. Forces above and below the earth's surface have also produced landforms of many sizes and shapes, so that in detail the shape of the earth is complex and undoubtedly unique.

The system of latitude and longitude is the most important locational system currently in use. Degrees of latitude are measured north and south of the equator, and degrees of longitude are measured east and west of the prime meridian.

The standard time zones are swaths of longitude 15 degrees wide, each centered on a meridian divisible by 15. Each of the 24 time zones differs in time by one hour from adjacent zones. Over land areas, the zones are usually adjusted to coincide with existing political boundaries. Across the International Date Line, located in the central Pacific, a 24-hour time difference exists.

The changing seasons occur because the earth's axis is inclined at $23\frac{1}{2}°$ from a perpendicular angle to the plane of the ecliptic. As the earth revolves around the sun during the course of the year, the northern and southern hemispheres alternately incline at varying angles toward and away from the sun. Spring and summer occur when a hemisphere is inclined toward the sun; the sun is therefore higher in the sky, periods of daylight longer, and the hemisphere's total energy receipt greater. Conversely, fall and winter occur when the hemisphere is inclined away from the sun.

Review Questions

1. Draw diagrams illustrating the revolution of the earth around the sun and the rotation of the earth on its axis. Be sure to indicate the correct directions of motion.

2. Why is the earth spherical in shape? What two major departures from a perfect spherical shape exist? Why do they occur?

3. What is the purpose of the system of latitude and longitude? What similarities and differences exist between parallels and meridians? How are degrees of latitude and longitude subdivided for greater precision?

4. Why was the system of local time discontinued? What advantages and disadvantages does the standard time system offer? Explain how this system is organized.

5. If it is 3 A.M., Thursday, at 30° E, what are the time and day at that same instant at 120° E?

6. If it is noon, Monday, at 135° W, what are the time and day at that same instant at 165° E?

7. What is the justification for the use of daylight saving time? Why is it used in the United States during only part of the year?

8. Draw a single diagram illustrating the parallelism of the earth's axis and the position of the earth with respect to the sun at the times of the solstices and the equinoxes. Label each position.

9. Describe the locations and explain the significance of the Arctic and Antarctic Circles and of the Tropics of Cancer and Capricorn.

Key Terms

Solar system
Milky Way galaxy
Revolution
Rotation
Geographic North and South Poles
Equator
Parallelism
Oblate ellipsoid
Latitude
Longitude

Prime meridian
Local time
Standard time
International Date Line
Daylight saving time
Solstice
Equinox
Tropics of Cancer and Capricorn
Arctic and Antarctic Circles

3 Sample Chapter

Nutrition and Digestion

7 Nutrition and Digestion

I t must be a law of human nature. Ask almost any couple and they will tell you: she lies shivering under the covers on a cold winter night while he bakes. Out on a hike in winter, he wears a light jacket and is warm, while she bundles up in stocking cap, down coat, and gloves to keep warm. What causes this marked difference in many men and women?

New research suggests that part of the answer lies in iron—not pumping iron, but dietary iron. Many American women do not consume enough iron to offset losses that occur during **menstruation**, the monthly discharge of blood and tissue from the lining of the uterus (Chapter 16). Iron deficiencies in women may reduce internal heat production.[1]

John Beard, a researcher at Pennsylvania State University, recently reported on a study that supports this conclusion. In his research, Beard compared two groups of women, one with low levels of iron in the blood and the other with normal iron levels. Beard found that body temperature drops more quickly in iron-deficient women exposed to cold than those with normal iron levels. He also found that iron-deficient women generated 13% less heat. Furthermore, iron-deficient women warm themselves less efficiently than women with normal levels. For reasons not yet well understood, iron-deficient women rely more on

[1]Critical thinking suggests that the difference in body temperature between men and women may also result from other factors, such as body mass and surface area.

SAMPLE CHAPTER 3

glucose than fat for energy production. Ounce for ounce, glucose provides half the energy of fats. After 12 weeks of iron supplements, though, women who were formerly iron-deficient responded normally to cold.

At least two hypotheses can explain these results. The first hypothesis is that iron deficiencies may reduce the amount of oxygen available for metabolism, thus lowering heat production. Iron is a vital component of the hemoglobin molecule (a protein) in the red blood cells (RBCs). RBCs transport oxygen from the lungs to body tissues. Iron in the hemoglobin molecule binds to oxygen, which is required for cellular respiration (Chapter 3). Cellular respiration, in turn, produces ATP and heat. Reduced oxygen transport could result in reduced body heat.

The second hypothesis is based on the role of iron in energy production. Iron is also a vital component of the electron transport proteins found in the mitochondria. As noted in Chapter 3, these proteins are part of the electron transport system, which produces most of the ATP in the cell. If iron levels are low, electron transport and energy production could be impaired. ATP production releases heat. Iron deficiencies, therefore, could reduce internal heat.

The research on iron may help explain not only why many women experience cold feet in bed at night, but also why many women who take iron supplements during pregnancy report an improvement in heat production. This example also illustrates how important a healthy, balanced diet is to normal physiological function. This chapter introduces other examples of the dependence of our health on our diet as it outlines the major nutritional requirements of humans and describes the process of digestion.

A PRIMER ON HUMAN NUTRITION

Some people eat to live and a great many others seem to live just to eat. No matter what your orientation, food probably occupies a central part of your day-to-day activities. Without food, you could survive six to eight weeks, but much of that time you would be too weak to move.

In our study of nutrition, however, we will be concerned not just with survival, but with living and eating well—thriving. The Greek philosopher Socrates put it best, "Not life, but a good life, is to be chiefly valued." Despite the increased emphasis on nutrition, most Americans still pay little attention to their diet. To perform our very best, though, we must eat well,

TABLE 7−1	Macronutrients and Micronutrients	
NUTRIENTS	**FOUND IN**
Macronutrients	
Water	All drinks and many foods
Amino acids and proteins	Cheese, meats, eggs
Lipids	Cheeses, meats, eggs
Carbohydrates	Breads, pastas, cereals
Micronutrients	
Vitamins	Many vegetables
Minerals	Many vegetables

acquiring a full complement of the nutrients required by our cells, tissues, and organs each day.

Humans require two basic types of nutrients: macronutrients and micronutrients (Table 7−1). This section describes these nutrients and notes their importance in human physiology.

Macronutrients

Macronutrients are required in relatively large quantities and include four substances: water, proteins, lipids, and carbohydrates.

Water.   Water is one of the most important of all nutrients. Without it, a person can only survive one or two days. Despite its importance, water does not usually show up on the nutrition charts. In part, that is because water is supplied in so many different ways. For example, water is in the liquids we drink and in virtually all of the solid foods we eat; water is even produced internally during cellular metabolism (Chapter 3).

Evolution has provided humans (and other organisms) with a variety of mechanisms to control the amount of water in the body (Chapter 11). Adequate water intake is important for several reasons. First, water participates in many chemical reactions in body cells. Thus, a decrease in water levels may impair metabolism, including energy production. According to some studies, athletic performance may drop significantly when water levels fall even slightly. Maintaining an adequate water volume is also important because water helps maintain normal body temperature. A decline in body water decreases the volume of the blood and the volume of the extracellular fluid. A decrease in body fluids can cause body temperature to rise, because the heat normally produced by the cells is being absorbed by a smaller volume of water. A rise in body temperature may impair cellular function and can lead to death. Maintaining an adequate water intake also helps maintain normal concentrations of nutrients and toxic waste products in the blood and extracellular fluid. Urine becomes more concentrated when a person fails to drink enough liquid; the increased concentration of wastes in the urine increases the likelihood of developing kidney stones. Kidney stones are deposits of calcium and other materials in the kidney that can block the flow of urine, causing extensive damage to this organ (Chapter 11).

Sources of Energy.   The body also requires a continuous supply of energy. Energy is provided by three macronutrients: carbohydrates, lipids, and, to a lesser degree, protein. Cells require energy to carry out thousands of functions needed to maintain homeostasis, to grow, and to divide. All cells need energy to transport molecules across their membranes. Surpris-

ingly, 70 to 80% of the total energy required by humans goes to perform basic functions—metabolism, food digestion, absorption, and so on. The remaining energy is used to power body movements, such as walking, talking, and running. For more active people, though, these percentages shift considerably. A basketball player, for example, uses proportionately more energy for vigorous muscular activity than a sedentary office worker.

At rest, the body relies on nearly equal amounts of fat and carbohydrate to supply basic body needs. Contrary to popular myth, proteins provide energy only under certain circumstances, described later in the chapter. As you may recall from Chapter 3, carbohydrates are catabolized during cellular respiration. They provide about 4 calories per gram. Lipids (fats) are also catabolized in cells to provide energy. The by-products of fat catabolism enter the biochemical pathways of cellular respiration, yielding—gram-for-gram—twice as much ATP as carbohydrates.

Carbohydrates come in many forms and from many different foods (Table 7–1). Starch from plants (grains and vegetables), for instance, contributes about 45% of the total energy requirements of humans. Much of the rest of our energy comes from glycogen (a polysaccharide) in meat, simple sugars in fruits, and lactose (a disaccharide) in milk.

Glycogen and starch are broken down into glucose molecules in the digestive system and are absorbed into the bloodstream for distribution to body cells. Most of this glucose is stored as glycogen in muscle and the liver for later use. Some is catabolized immediately by the cells to produce energy; and a small amount is excreted in the urine.

Figure 7–1 illustrates the homeostatic balance of body carbohydrates, showing the inputs and outputs that determine the level of blood glucose. Since most of us eat only a few times a day, body stores of glucose play a crucial role in maintaining homeostasis. Between meals and during exercise, glycogen is broken down to provide glucose. When muscular activity is prolonged, however, as in the case of a long-distance runner, glycogen stored in the liver and muscle may be depleted. Eighteen to twenty miles into a marathon, runners become exhausted and weak, a sensation they describe as "hitting the wall," as a result of muscle glycogen depletion.

A knowledge of energy metabolism is more than an academic exercise. Consider an example. Determined to lose a few extra pounds, two friends of mine spent a year working out in a health club. They exercised hard and often—running, swimming, and bicycling

FIGURE 7–1   Glucose Balance   Glucose levels in the blood result from a balance of input and output.

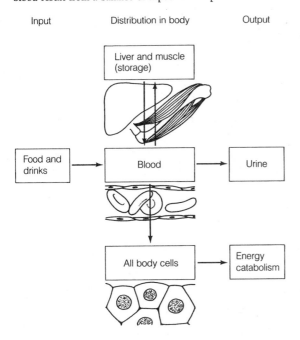

three or four nights a week. At the end of the year, though, they both weighed about the same as they had on the day they began their program. Disappointed, they turned to an exercise physiologist for help. She explained an often-overlooked fact about energy metabolism: heavy exercise depletes muscle oxygen levels, and when muscles become anaerobic, they use carbohydrates—mostly glucose—to generate energy. Body fat stores are relatively untouched. Try as you may, you generally do not lose weight if your exercise program is so vigorous that it depletes muscle oxygen levels.

The exercise physiologist advised my friends to tone down their program—to work out often and long, but not quite so hard. The object? To avoid depleting muscle oxygen during exercise. This is called **aerobic exercise**. It helps the heart and cardiovascular system and also helps people "burn off" weight because it relies primarily on the body's fat reserves. Soon after the couple shifted to aerobic workouts, the weight started disappearing.

Amino Acids and Protein.   *Although many people think of protein as a source of energy, it is really only important under two conditions: either when dietary intake of carbohydrates and fats is severely restricted or when protein intake far exceeds demands.* Dietary deficiencies occur in millions of children throughout the world. The arms and legs of children deprived of protein are often thin and emaciated, because their muscle cells break down protein in an effort to provide energy (Figure 7–2). Their abdomens are bloated because of fluid accumulation, caused by the decreased levels of protein in their blood.

On the other end of the spectrum are the well-fed populations of the world. Many Americans eat far more food than they need. On average, U.S. protein intake is twice the daily requirement. Amino acids released from the surplus dietary protein are broken down in the body to generate energy and to make fat.

Protein in the food we eat is used to synthesize enzymes and structural proteins. Dietary proteins cannot be used directly by cells, but must first be broken down into their constituent amino acids in the digestive tract. Amino acids liberated during this process are absorbed into the bloodstream and distributed throughout the body.

In cells, some amino acids are used to make body protein directly. Others are converted into different amino acids, then used in protein synthesis. Proteins are synthesized from 20 different amino acids. Humans can make 11 of the 20 different types of amino

acids needed to produce protein. The remaining nine amino acids must be provided by the diet (that is, they are not synthesized from other amino acids) and are called **essential amino acids**. A deficiency of even one of the essential amino acids can cause severe physiological problems. Nutritionists, therefore, recommend a diet containing many different protein sources. In this way, individuals can be assured they are getting all of the amino acids they need. Milk and eggs provide the best assortment of essential amino acids. These proteins are, therefore, said to be **complete**. Unfortunately, many American adults lack the enzyme (lactase) needed to digest milk sugar (lactose), and many people avoid eggs to reduce cholesterol levels in their blood (Health Note 7–1). These individuals get their proteins from other sources. The next best sources of proteins are meats, fish, poultry, cheese, and soybeans. Each of these has low levels of several (but not all) essential amino acids. To avoid deficiencies, nutritionists recommend combining these protein sources. The lowest quality proteins are in legumes (peas, beans), nuts, seeds, grains, and vegetables. Each of these foods contains low levels of only one or two essential amino acids. Care must be exercised to prevent deficiencies. Vegetarians, for instance, can acquire all of the amino acids they need by

(continuing)

SAMPLE CHAPTER 3

FIGURE 7–3   Complementary Protein Sources By combining protein sources, a vegetarian can be assured of getting all of the amino acids needed. Legumes can be combined with foods made from grains or nuts and seeds.

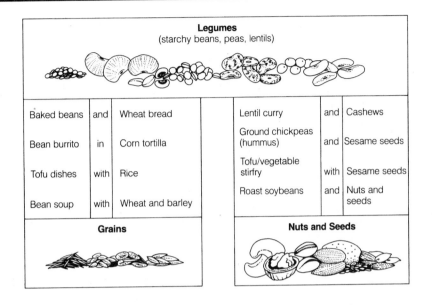

(continuing)

combining protein sources. Figure 7–3 shows how this is done.

Lipids. Although lipids provide cellular energy, they serve other functions as well. The layer of fat beneath the skin in humans, for instance, helps insulate the body from heat loss. Certain lipids are used to synthesize hormones, and lipids are a principal component of the plasma membrane. Lipids in the intestine increase the intestinal uptake of the fat-soluble vitamins (A, D, E, and K).

Lipids are consumed in excess by most Americans. On average, fats provide about 45% of the dietary caloric intake, but to lower the risk of heart attack, fat intake should only be about 30%. (For more on the effects of lipids on the circulatory system, see Health Note 7–1.)

Carbohydrates. Carbohydrates, like lipids, are a principal source of energy. However, carbohydrates are important for other reasons as well. Dietary **fiber**, for example, is nondigestible polysaccharide (such as cellulose) found in fruits, vegetables, and grains. As noted in Chapter 2, cellulose cannot be digested because the body lacks the enzymes needed to break the covalent bond joining the monosaccharide units (glucose) in the molecule. In humans, fiber passes through the intestine largely unaffected by enzymes or stomach acidity.

Fiber exists in two basic forms: water soluble and water insoluble. Water-soluble fibers are gummy polysaccharides in fruits, vegetables, and some grains, including apples, bananas, carrots, barley, and oats. In contrast, water-insoluble fibers are rigid cellulose molecules in celery, cereals, wheat products, and brown rice. Some foods, such as green beans and green peas, contain a mixture of both types.

Water-insoluble fiber increases the water content of the **feces**, the semisolid waste produced by the large intestine. This makes the feces softer and facilitates their transport through the large intestine. Increasing the water content also reduces constipation and helps prevent pressure from building up in the large intestine. In some cases, pressure from constipation causes small pouches, or diverticulae, to form in the wall of the large intestine, resulting in a condition known as **diverticulitis**. The pouches in the intestinal wall often become inflamed. Bacteria may enter the bloodstream, causing high fever. Occasionally, the diverticulae burst, releasing feces into the abdominal cavity. Since feces contain billions of bacteria, their release into the abdominal cavity results in a massive infection that is difficult to treat and may result in death.

Diverticulitis, although not common, has increased substantially in America since the introduction of white flour. Flour is made from wheat, a grain grown in many states. When wheat grain is ground, it produces whole wheat flour, a powdery mixture containing the entire products of the wheat grain. White flour, however, is produced from wheat whose shells have been removed. Removing the shells eliminates most, if not all, of the fiber. With the widespread use of white flour, several problems, such as diverticulitis, arose. Not surprisingly, diverticulitis is rare in areas, such as Africa, where fiber intake is higher.

Water-insoluble fiber is thought to reduce colon cancer, which afflicts about 3% of the U.S. population. In rural Africa, colon cancer is practically unheard of. Although critical thinking skills suggest that other differences may also be responsible for the difference, this and other evidence led researchers to recommend an increase in the amount of fiber we eat. How does fiber protect us from colon cancer?

A recent study showed that some bacteria in the large intestine produce a potent chemical mutagen that may cause cancer. Researchers suggest that, by accelerating the transport of wastes through the intestine, fiber may decrease colon cancer by reducing the formation of the mutagen or by reducing the time in which the intestinal cells are exposed to it.

Water-soluble fiber is also beneficial to our health; several studies suggest that it helps lower blood cholesterol. Some water-soluble fibers act as sponges, absorbing cholesterol inside the digestive tract and preventing it from being absorbed into the bloodstream. Others change the pH of the intestine, making cholesterol insoluble and difficult to absorb. (The chemical action of water-soluble fibers is discussed in more detail in the section on the liver.)

Micronutrients

Micronutrients are substances needed in small quantity and include two broad groups: vitamins and minerals.

Vitamins.   Vitamins are a diverse group of organic compounds that occur in foods in small quantities and play an important role in many metabolic reactions. Vitamins serve as **enzyme cofactors**, chemicals required by a number of enzymes for proper functioning. Since *vitamins are recycled many times during these reactions, they are only needed in small amounts.* One gram of vitamin B-12, for example, would supply over 300,000 people for a single day.

Vitamins are absorbed in the digestive tract without being broken down and generally cannot be synthesized in the body cells in sufficient amounts to satisfy cellular demands, making dietary intake essential. Vitamin D, for instance, is manufactured by the skin when exposed to sunlight. However, most Americans spend so much time indoors that dietary input is essential to good health. Table 7–2 lists vitamins and their functions.

Vitamins are needed in almost all cells of the body. As a result, a dietary deficiency in just one vitamin can cause wide-ranging effects in the body. Vitamins also interact with other nutrients in the dynamic balance of the body. Vitamin C, for example, increases the absorption of iron in the small intestine. Large doses of the vitamin, however, decrease copper utilization by the cells. *Maintaining good health, therefore, requires the proper balance of vitamins and other nutrients.*

Vitamins fall into two broad categories: water soluble and fat soluble. Water-soluble vitamins include vitamin C and 11 different forms of vitamin B. Water-soluble vitamins are transported in the blood plasma and are eliminated by the kidneys. Because they are water soluble, they are not stored in the body in any appreciable amount.

Water-soluble vitamins generally work in conjunction with enzymes, promoting the cellular reactions that supply energy or synthesize cellular materials. Contrary to common myth, the vitamins themselves do not provide energy.

Experts long believed that megadoses of water-soluble vitamins were harmless because these vitamins were excreted in the urine and did not accumulate in the body. New research, however, shows that this is not entirely true. *Some water-soluble vitamins, such as vitamin C, when ingested in excess, can be toxic* (see Table 7–2 for some examples).

The fat-soluble vitamins are vitamins A, D, E, and K. They perform many different functions. Vitamin A, for example, is converted to a light-sensitive pigment present in receptor cells of the retina, the light-sensitive layer of the eye (Chapter 13). These pigments play an important role in vision. Like other vitamins, vitamin A exists in several forms, serving many different functions. One member of the vitamin A group, for example, removes harmful oxidants from the body. Retin-A, a derivative of vitamin A, is used by dermatologists to treat acne and reduce wrinkling that occurs with aging and exposure to sunlight (Chapter 17).

Unlike water-soluble vitamins, the fat-soluble vitamins are stored in body fat and accumulate in the fat reserves. The accumulation of fat-soluble vitamins

HEALTH NOTE 7–1
Lowering Your Cholesterol

Let there be no question about it: diseases of the heart and arteries are leading causes of death in the United States.

Atherosclerosis, the buildup of plaque on artery walls, and the problems it creates are responsible for nearly two of every five deaths in the United States each year. Thanks to improvements in medical care and diet, the death rate from atherosclerosis has been falling steadily in recent years, but it is still a major concern. New research, in fact, shows that atherosclerotic plaques are present even in children. Researchers believe atherosclerotic plaques begin to form after minor injuries to the lining of blood vessels. High blood pressure, they think, may damage the lining, causing platelets and cholesterol in the blood to stick to the injured site. The blood vessel responds by producing cells that cover the fatty deposit. This thickens the wall of the artery, reducing blood flow. Additional cholesterol is then deposited in the thickened wall, forming a larger and larger obstruction to blood flow. Cholesterol deposits impair the flow of blood in the heart and other organs, cutting off oxygen to vital tissues. Blood clots may form in the restricted sections of arteries, further obstructing blood flow. When the oxygen supply to the heart is disrupted, cardiac muscle cells can die, resulting in heart attacks and death. Blood clots originating in other parts of the body may also lodge in the diseased vessels, obstructing blood flow.

Oxygen deprivation can weaken the heart, impairing the heart's ability to pump blood. When the oxygen supply to the heart is restricted, the result is a type of heart attack known as a **myocardial infarction**. Victims of a myocardial infarction feel pain in the center of the chest and down the left arm. If the deprived area is extensive, the heart may cease functioning altogether.

Atherosclerotic plaque also impairs the flow of blood to the brain, which can cause cell death. Victims often lose the ability to speak or to move limbs. If the damage is severe enough, they may die. Thanks to advances in medical treatment, however, many victims can be saved. Over time, they can recover many lost functions as other parts of the brain take over the functions of destroyed regions. Atherosclerosis also affects other organs, such as the kidneys.

Atherosclerosis and cardiovascular disease are the result of nearly 40 factors, some more important than others. Several of these risk factors, such as old age and sex (being male), cannot be changed. Other factors are controllable. These include high blood pressure, high blood cholesterol, smoking, inactivity, and excessive food intake. Of all the risk factors, three emerge as the primary contributors to cardiovascular disease: elevated blood cholesterol, smoking, and high blood pressure.

Consider cholesterol. It may surprise you, but for most of us the cholesterol in our blood is produced by the liver. The liver synthesizes and releases about 700 milligrams of cholesterol per day. Only about 225 milligrams of cholesterol are derived from the food we eat each day. Normally, the concentration of cholesterol in the blood is constant. If dietary input falls, the liver increases its output. If the amount of cholesterol in the diet rises, the liver reduces production. So what's all the fuss about cholesterol in a person's diet?

Even though the liver regulates cholesterol levels, it cannot work fast enough. It may simply be unable to absorb, use, and dispose of cholesterol quickly enough. Consequently, excess cholesterol circulates in the blood after a meal and is deposited in arteries.

Cholesterol is carried in the bloodstream bound to protein. These complexes of protein and lipid fall into two groups: **high-density lipoproteins (HDLs)** and **low-density lipoproteins (LDLs)**. LDLs and HDLs function very differently. LDLs, for example, transport cholesterol from the liver to body tissues. In contrast, HDLs are scavengers, picking up excess cholesterol and transporting it to the liver where it is removed from the blood and excreted in the bile. Research shows that the ratio of HDL to LDL is an accurate predictor of cardiovascular disease. The higher the ratio, the lower the risk of cardiovascular disease.

High cholesterol level (or hypercholesterolemia) tends to run in families. Thus, if a parent has died of a heart attack or suffers from this genetic disease, his or her offspring are more likely to have high cholesterol levels than others.

For many years, physicians have advised cutting back on high-cholesterol foods, especially eggs and red meats, to reduce cholesterol levels. However, a reduction in dietary cholesterol in one individual

Research on mice shows that a diet rich in omega-3 fatty acids doubles life span. One of the conclusions of the study, though, is that omega-3 fatty acids, which are extremely susceptible to oxidation, are only effective if oxidation can be prevented. Mincing fish prior to cooking increases oxidation and lowers the levels of omega-3 fatty acids.

Cholesterol levels can be lowered with drugs, diet, and exercise. Research spanning several decades shows that lower cholesterol levels translate into a decline in cardiovascular disease. Unfortunately, experts disagree on several key issues. One is exactly who will benefit from a reduction in cholesterol. Some researchers say that only high-risk people with cholesterol levels over 250 milligrams per 100 milliliters of blood should take steps to cut back. Since two-thirds of the American adult population have blood cholesterol levels over 200 mg/100 ml, some experts believe that the entire adult population should take steps to reduce cholesterol.

High cholesterol is also surprisingly common in children, leading many health experts to believe that steps should be taken to prevent problems later in life. In children under the age of two, however, diets should not be restricted. A diet that is too restrictive may actually impair physical growth and development. What children need is a well-balanced diet, low in fats, with sufficient calories from other sources. If nothing else, it could help create the good eating habits necessary for good health throughout adult life.

(continuing)

may result in very little decline in total blood cholesterol, but in another a reduction may result in a much larger drop. The difference in response can be attributed to exercise, genetics, initial cholesterol levels, and age.

Despite the differences in response, the American Heart Association recommends (1) limiting dietary fat to less than 30% of the total caloric intake, (2) limiting dietary cholesterol to 300 milligrams/day, and (3) acquiring 50% or more of one's calories from carbohydrates, especially polysaccharides. Reductions in saturated fatty acids (animal fats) can also help lower cholesterol levels for reasons not fully understood. You can cut back on saturated fat by using margarine instead of butter, reducing your consumption of red meat, and trimming the fat off all meats before cooking. You can also increase your consumption of fruits, vegetables, and grains, letting these low-fat foods displace some of the fatty foods you might otherwise eat.

New and still controversial research also indicates that a diet rich in fish oils can help reduce blood cholesterol. Fish oils contain polyunsaturated fatty acids called omega-3 fatty acids. These fatty acids stimulate the release of prostaglandin, which increases the flexibility of the red blood cells and reduces their stickiness, which is essential for blood clotting.

TABLE 7–2 Important Information on Vitamins

VITAMIN	MAJOR DIETARY SOURCES	MAJOR FUNCTIONS	SIGNS OF SEVERE, PROLONGED DEFICIENCY	SIGNS OF EXTREME EXCESS
Fat soluble				
A	Fat-containing and fortified dairy products; liver; provitamin carotene in orange and deep green produce	Component of rhodopsin; still under intense study	Keratinization of epithelial tissues including the cornea of the eye (xerophthalmia); night blindness; dry, scaling skin; poor immune response	From preformed vitamin A: damage to liver, kidney, bone; headache, irritability, vomiting, hair loss, blurred vision. From carotene: yellowed skin.
D	Fortified and full-fat dairy products; egg yolk	Promotes absorption and use of calcium and phosphorus	Rickets (bone deformities) in children; osteomalacia (bone softening) in adults	Gastrointestinal upset; cerebral, CV, kidney damage; lethargy
E	Vegetable oils and their products; nuts, seeds; present at low levels in other foods	Antioxidant to prevent plasma membrane damage; still under intense study	Possible anemia	Debatable; perhaps fatal in premature infants given intravenous infusion
K	Green vegetables; tea, meats	Aids in formation of certain proteins, especially those for blood clotting	Severe bleeding on injury: internal hemorrhage	Liver damage and anemia from high doses of the synthetic form menadione
Water soluble				
Thiamin (B-1)	Pork, legumes, peanuts, enriched or whole-grain products	Coenzyme used in energy metabolism	Beriberi (nerve changes, sometimes edema, heart failure)	?
Riboflavin (B-2)	Dairy products, meats, eggs, enriched grain products, green leafy vegetables	Coenzyme used in energy metabolism	Skin lesions	?

SAMPLE CHAPTER 3

can have many adverse effects (Table 7–2). An excess of vitamin D, for example, can cause hair loss; nausea; joint, bone, and muscle pain; and even diarrhea. Large doses taken during pregnancy can cause birth defects.

Vitamin excess is a condition largely encountered in the developed countries. Each year, approximately 4000 Americans are treated for vitamin supplement poisoning. To avoid problems from excess vitamins, nutritionists recommend eating a balanced diet that provides all of the vitamins the body needs, rather than taking vitamin pills, especially megadoses.

Dietary deficiencies of vitamins, like dietary ex-

TABLE 7–2 Important Information on Vitamins (continued)

VITAMIN	MAJOR DIETARY SOURCES	MAJOR FUNCTIONS	SIGNS OF SEVERE, PROLONGED DEFICIENCY	SIGNS OF EXTREME EXCESS
Niacin	Nuts, meats; provitamin tryptophan in most proteins	Coenzyme used in energy metabolism	Pellagra (which may be multiple vitamin deficiencies)	Flushing of face, neck, hands; liver damage
B-6	High protein foods in general, bananas, some vegetables	Coenzyme used in amino acid metabolism	Nervous and muscular disorders	Unstable gait, numb feet, poor hand coordination, abnormal brain function
Folacin	Green vegetables, orange juice, nuts, legumes, grain products	Coenzyme used in DNA and RNA metabolism; single carbon utilization	Megaloblastic anemia (large, immature red blood cells); gastrointestinal disturbances	Masks vitamin B-12 deficiency
B-12	Animal products	Coenzyme used in DNA and RNA metabolism; single carbon utilization	Megaloblastic anemia; pernicious anemia when due to inadequate intrinsic factor; nervous system damage	?
Pantothenic acid	Widely distributed in foods	Coenzyme used in energy metabolism	Fatigue, sleep disturbances, nausea, poor coordination	?
Biotin	Widely distributed in foods	Coenzyme used in energy metabolism	Dermatitis, depression, muscular pain	?
C	Fruits and vegetables, especially broccoli, cabbage, cantaloupe, cauliflower, citrus fruits, green pepper, strawberries	Maintains collagen; is an antioxidant; aids in detoxification; still under intense study	Scurvy (skin spots, bleeding gums, weakness); delayed wound healing; impaired immune response	Gastrointestinal upsets, confounds certain lab tests, poorer immune response

Source: From J. L. Christian and L. L. Greger, *Nutrition for Living*, 2d ed., copyright © 1988 by the Benjamin/Cummings Publishing Company. Used with permission.

cesses, can lead to problems. Vitamin deficiencies, for example, can reduce immunity, making people more susceptible to infectious disease. Most people afflicted by vitamin deficiencies are those who do not get enough to eat. One of every five people living in the nonindustrialized nations of the world goes to bed hungry; most of these people suffer from multiple deficiencies.[2] All told, about 10 million children under the age of 5 suffer from extreme malnutrition in the less-developed nations of the world. Another 90

[2]About 700–800 million people in the less-developed countries do not get enough to eat.

ther digested by enzymes. In the small intestine, amino acids, monosaccharides, and other small molecules produced by enzymatic digestion are absorbed into the bloodstream for distribution to body cells.

The Mouth: Physical Breakdown of Food

The mouth is a complex structure in which food is broken down mechanically and, to a much lesser degree, chemically. The jaws and teeth perform the mechanical breakdown. The sharp teeth in front slice and cut our food, while the flatter teeth toward the back of the mouth grind food into a pulpy mass. As the food is pulverized in the mouth, saliva is added by the **salivary glands**, three sets of exocrine glands located around the oral cavity (Figure 7–6). The release of saliva is triggered by the smell, feel, taste, and—sometimes—even the thought of food.

Saliva (1) liquifies the food, making it easier to swallow, (2) kills or neutralizes some bacteria via enzymes and antibodies it contains, (3) dissolves substances so they can be tasted, and (4) begins to break down starch molecules with the aid of the enzyme **amylase**. Saliva also cleanses the teeth, washing away bacteria and food particles. Since the release of saliva is greatly reduced when we sleep, bacteria tend to accumulate on the surface of the teeth. Here they break down microscopic food particles, producing some foul-smelling chemicals that give us "dragon breath" or "morning mouth."

The bacteria that live on the teeth secrete a sticky material called **plaque**. Plaque adheres to the surface of the teeth trapping bacteria. Entrapped in their own secretions, these bacteria release small amounts of a weak acid, which dissolves the hard outer coating of our teeth, the **enamel**. Small pits or **cavities** may form on the surface of the teeth and may deepen as the acids eat into the softer layer beneath the enamel. Brushing helps remove plaque and thus helps reduce the incidence of cavities. Most toothpastes also contain small amounts of fluoride, a chemical that hardens the enamel, reducing the incidence of cavities. Small amounts of fluoride are also added to domestic drinking water. Some recent research suggesting that fluoride may be carcinogenic has forced health officials to reexamine this practice .

Salivary flow during the day is much greater and tends to keep the teeth clean. A recent study showed that chewing gum also increases the release of saliva. Thus, by chewing sugarless gum also within 5 minutes of a meal, and for at least 15 minutes, you can

(continuing)

million under the age of 5 are moderately malnourished.

Deficiencies of vitamin A afflict over 100,000 children worldwide each year (Figure 7–4). If not corrected, vitamin A deficiency causes the eye to dry. Ulcers may form on the eyeball and can rupture, causing complete blindness. People suffering from vitamin deficiency typically complain of weakness and fatigue. Children with insufficient vitamin intake fail to grow.

Minerals. Humans require many minerals, such as sodium and iron, for normal body functions. These micronutrients are derived from the food we eat and the water we drink. Minerals are divided into two groups: the **major minerals** and the **trace minerals** (Table 7–3). Calcium and phosphorus, for example, are major minerals. They form part of the dense extracellular matrix of bone and are required in a much greater quantity than zinc or copper, two trace minerals that are components of some enzymes. Mineral deficiencies, like excesses, can result in many physiological problems (Table 7–3).

THE HUMAN DIGESTIVE SYSTEM

The food we eat is broken down by physical and chemical processes in the digestive system (Figure 7–5). In the mouth, for example, food is sliced, crushed, and torn by the teeth into smaller particles. In the stomach and intestines, these particles are fur-

TABLE 7–3   Important Information on Minerals

MINERAL	MAJOR DIETARY SOURCES	MAJOR FUNCTIONS	SIGNS OF SEVERE, PROLONGED DEFICIENCY	SIGNS OF EXTREME EXCESS
Major minerals				
Calcium	Milk, cheese, dark green vegetables, legumes	Bone and tooth formation; blood clotting; nerve transmission	Stunted growth; maybe bone loss	Depressed absorption of some other minerals
Phosphorus	Milk, cheese, meat, poultry, whole grains	Bone and tooth formation; acid-base balance; component of coenzymes	Weakness; demineralization of bone	Depressed absorption of some minerals
Magnesium	Whole grains, green leafy vegetables	Component of enzymes	Neurological disturbances	Neurological disturbances
Sodium	Salt, soy sauce, cured meats, pickles, canned soups, processed cheese	Body water balance; nerve function	Muscle cramps; reduced appetite	High blood pressure in genetically predisposed individuals
Potassium	Meats, milk, many fruits and vegetables, whole grains	Body water balance; nerve function	Muscular weakness; paralysis	Muscular weakness; cardiac arrest
Chloride	Salt, many processed foods (as for sodium)	Plays a role in acid-base balance; formation of gastric juice	Muscle cramps; reduced appetite; poor growth	Vomiting
Trace minerals				
Iron	Meats, eggs, legumes, whole grains, green leafy vegetables	Component of hemoglobin and enzymes	Iron deficiency anemia, weakness, impaired immune function	Acute: shock, death. Chronic: liver damage, cardiac failure
Iodine	Marine fish and shellfish; dairy products; iodized salt; some breads	Component of thyroid hormones	Goiter (enlarged thyroid)	Iodide goiter
Fluoride	Drinking water, tea, seafood	Maintenance of tooth (and maybe bone) structure	Higher frequency of tooth decay	Mottling of teeth; skeletal deformation

Source: Adapted from J. L. Christian and L. L. Greger, *Nutrition for Living*, 2d ed., copyright © 1988 by the Benjamin/Cummings Publishing Company. Used with permission.

also reduce the incidence of cavities. If you can't brush after every meal, chew sugarless gum.

After food is chewed it must be swallowed. The tongue plays a key role in swallowing by pushing food to the back of the oral cavity into the pharynx. The **pharynx** is a chamber that connects the oral cavity with the **esophagus**, a long muscular tube that leads to the stomach (Figure 7–5).

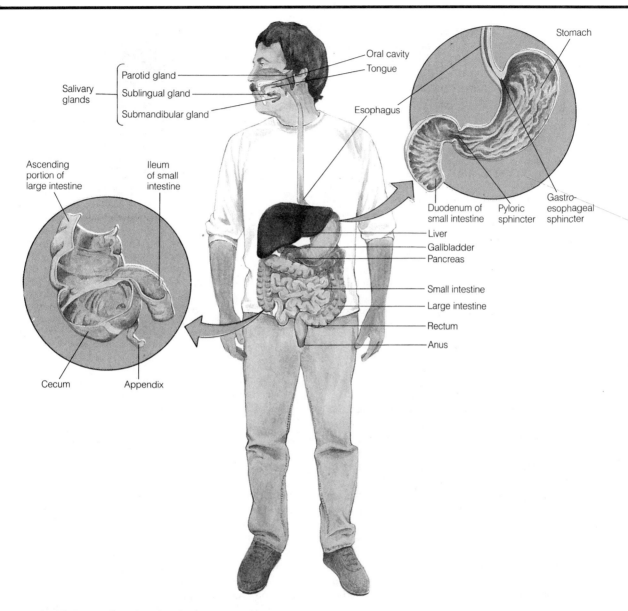

FIGURE 7–5   The Digestive System

The tongue, which also helps us form words, contains taste receptors, the **taste buds**, on its upper surface. Taste buds are stimulated by four basic flavors: sweet, sour, salty, and bitter (Figure 7–7). Various combinations of these (combined with odors we smell) give us the rich assortment of tastes (Chapter 13). Food propelled from the pharynx into the esophagus is prevented from entering the trachea, which

also opens into the pharynx, by the epiglottis. The **epiglottis** is a flap of tissue that acts like a trap door, closing off the trachea during swallowing.

Swallowing begins with a voluntary act—the tongue pushing food into the back of the oral cavity. Once food enters the pharynx, however, the process becomes automatic. Food stimulates receptors in the wall of the pharynx, which trigger the **swallowing**

reflex, an involuntary contraction of the muscles in the wall of the pharynx, which forces the food into the esophagus.

The Esophagus and Peristalsis

Involuntary contractions of the muscular wall of the esophagus propel the food to the stomach. The muscles of the esophagus contract above the swallowed food mass, squeezing it along (Figure 7–8a). This involuntary muscular action is called **peristalsis**. Peristalsis propels food (and waste) along the digestive tract. It is so powerful that you can swallow when hanging upside down.

Esophageal peristalsis sometimes proceeds in the opposite direction; this is known as **reverse peristalsis** or, more commonly, vomiting. Vomiting is a reflex action that occurs when irritants are present in the stomach. Vomiting is, therefore, a protective measure that allows the body to rid the stomach of bad food, viruses, or bacteria.

The Stomach: Liquification, Storage, and Release of Food

The stomach is an expandable, muscular organ that performs several key functions (Figure 7–9). First, the stomach stores and liquifies food. Second, it begins the chemical breakdown of some substances, and, third, it releases the highly liquified and partially digested food in timed pulses into the small intestine. The stomach, shown in Figures 7–5, lies on the left side of the abdominal cavity, partly under the protection of the rib cage.

Food enters the stomach from the esophagus. The opening to the stomach, however, is usually constricted to prevent stomach acid and food from percolating upward and irritating the esophagus, causing "heartburn." The opening to the stomach is closed off by the **gastroesophageal sphincter**, a functional valve produced by a slight thickening in the muscular wall of the stomach where the esophagus joins it.

As food enters the lower esophagus, the gastroesophageal sphincter opens to allow it to enter the stomach, then promptly closes, preventing food and acid from escaping (Figure 7–8b). Inside the stomach, food is liquified by acidic secretions of glands in the stomach wall, the **gastric glands**. The food is churned by peristalsis and converted into a liquid, called **chyme**.

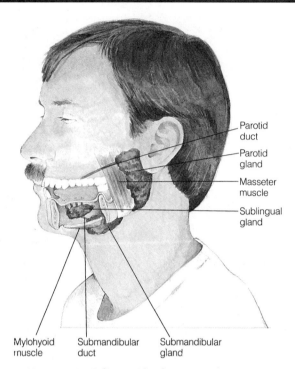

FIGURE 7–6   Salivary Glands   Three salivary glands (parotid, submandibular, and sublingual) are located in and around the oral cavity and empty into the mouth via small ducts.

The stomach holds 2 to 4 liters (2 quarts to 1 gallon) of chyme and releases it gradually into the small intestine, at a rate suitable for proper digestion and absorption. Glands in the wall of the stomach secrete hydrochloric acid (HCl) and a watery liquid that turns our meals into a paste. The churning action of the stomach's muscular walls breaks down large pieces of food. In some animals, such as dogs, the stomach has a considerable effect on food, allowing dogs to swallow their food with very little chewing. In humans, however, food must be chewed more thoroughly to ensure proper digestion.

Very little enzymatic digestion occurs in the stomach. Instead, the stomach's role is merely to prepare most food for enzymatic digestion that will occur in the small intestine. There are some exceptions, however. Protein, for example, is denatured by hydrochloric acid (Chapter 2). Denaturation, in turn, allows **pepsin**, an enzyme produced by the gastric glands, to begin breaking proteins into large peptide fragments.

CHAPTER 7   *Nutrition and Digestion*   175

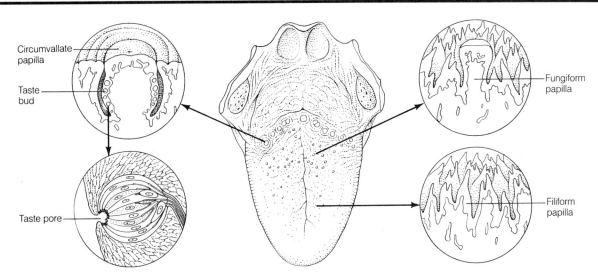

FIGURE 7–7 The Tongue and Taste Buds The tongue is a muscular organ that aids in swallowing and phonation (producing sounds). Its upper surface is dotted with protrusions called papilla. Three types are present: the fungiform, filiform, and circumvallate. Taste buds are located on the fungiform and circumvallate papillae shown in this figure. Taste buds have specialized cells that detect salt, bitter, sweet, and sour flavors. Foods dissolved in saliva enter the taste pore and stimulate these cells, which in turn trigger nerve impulses to the brain.

(continuing)

These fragments are further broken down in the small intestine, the next stop in the digestive process. Pepsin is secreted in an inactive form called **pepsinogen**, which is activated by HCl. Once some pepsin molecules are formed, they begin activating other pepsinogen molecules.

Lipids are also partially digested in the stomach with the aid of lipase, an enzyme produced by the salivary glands and transported to the stomach with the food.

Contrary to popular belief, the stomach does not absorb foodstuffs. Only a few substances, such as alcohol and aspirin, can actually penetrate the lining of the stomach and enter the bloodstream. Alcohol consumed on an empty stomach passes quickly through the stomach lining into the bloodstream, resulting in a rather immediate effect. The presence of food in the stomach, however, retards alcohol absorption, giving credence to the advice never to drink on an empty stomach.

Aspirin is also absorbed through the stomach lining. Excess aspirin can irritate the lining and cause bleeding. Large doses taken for pain over considerable periods may result in ulcers.

Hydrochloric acid creates an acidic environment in the stomach that is both useful and potentially harm-

SAMPLE CHAPTER 3

ful. Consider the benefits first. As noted above, HCl denatures protein, rendering it digestible. Moreover, HCl kills most bacteria, helping to protect the body. HCl also activates pepsinogen molecules. However, the dangerous mix of acid and proteolytic (protein-digesting) enzymes can also destroy the delicate stomach lining, forming sores or **ulcers**. Normally, the stomach lining is protected from destruction by an alkaline secretion called **mucus**, produced by some of the cells in the lining of the stomach. Mucus coats the stomach lining, protecting it from acid. The tissues beneath the epithelium are protected from acid leakage by the cells of the epithelium, which are tightly joined to one another, forming a leak-proof barrier.

Unfortunately, the stomach's protective mechanisms can break down. A number of factors, such as stress, coffee consumption, excess aspirin, and alcohol—or combinations of them—can increase acid levels in the stomach, overwhelming the mucous layer. Hydrochloric acid and pepsin come in contact with the epithelial cells and may digest parts of the wall of the stomach, forming painful ulcers. When detected early, most ulcers can be treated by reducing stress and changing one's diet—eating bland foods and reducing coffee, aspirin, and alcohol (Health Note 1–1). When ulcers are not detected early and when damage is severe, parts of the stomach may have to be removed surgically.

Chyme in the stomach is ejected into the small intestine by peristaltic muscle contractions. A peri-

staltic wave travels across the stomach every 20 seconds. When the wave of contraction reaches the far end of the stomach, the **pyloric sphincter** (a ring of smooth muscle at the juncture of the small intestine and stomach) opens, and chyme squirts into the small intestine.

The stomach contents are emptied in two to six hours, depending on the size of the meal and the type of food. Peristaltic contractions continue after the stomach is empty and are felt as hunger pangs.

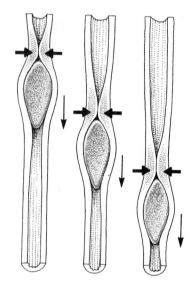

Ringlike peristaltic contraction sweeping down the esophagus

(a)

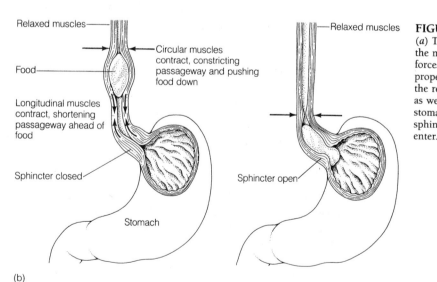

Relaxed muscles

Food

Circular muscles contract, constricting passageway and pushing food down

Longitudinal muscles contract, shortening passageway ahead of food

Sphincter closed

Stomach

(b)

Relaxed muscles

Sphincter open

FIGURE 7–8   Peristalsis
(*a*) The involuntary contraction of the muscular wall of the esophagus forces food to the stomach and propels chyme and waste throughout the remainder of the digestive tract as well. (*b*) When food reaches the stomach, the gastroesophageal sphincter opens, allowing food to enter.

FIGURE 7–9   The Stomach
The stomach lies in the abdominal cavity. In its wall are three layers of smooth muscle that help mix the food and force it into the small intestine where most digestion occurs. The gastroesophageal and pyloric sphincters control the inflow and outflow of food.

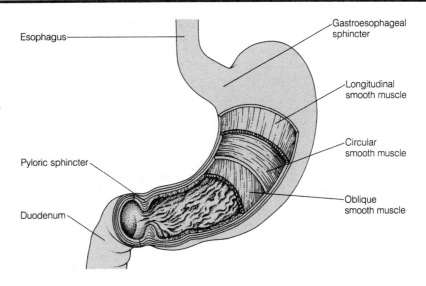

Esophagus

Gastroesophageal sphincter

Longitudinal smooth muscle

Circular smooth muscle

Oblique smooth muscle

Pyloric sphincter

Duodenum

Regulating the Stomach Function.   The stomach does not produce hydrochloric acid continuously. Continuous production would endanger the stomach lining. Instead, HCl is produced on demand. Its secretion is controlled by the endocrine and nervous systems (Chapters 12 and 15). The sight, smell, and taste of food activate centers of the brain, which, in turn, transmit nerve impulses to the stomach via the

vagus nerve. The vagus nerve terminates in the stomach wall and activates HCl production by cells in the gastric glands. Nerve impulses also stimulate the synthesis and release of a stomach hormone called gastrin. **Gastrin** increases the output of HCl. Amino acids and peptides in the stomach also activate acid production.

The Small Intestine and Associated Glands: Digestion and Absorption of Food

The small intestine is a coiled tube in the abdominal cavity about 6 meters (20 feet) long in adults (Figure 7–5). So named because of its small diameter, the small intestine digests macromolecules enzymatically, forming smaller molecules that are transported into the bloodstream and the lymphatic system. The lymphatic system, discussed in Chapter 8, is a network of vessels that carries extracellular fluid from the tissues of the body to the circulatory system. It also transports fats absorbed by the intestine into the bloodstream.

The Intestinal Epithelium.   In the small intestine, macromolecules in food are first broken into large fragments by enzymes. These enzymes are produced by the pancreas, described below, and released into the small intestine by a duct (Figure 7–10). The molecular fragments produced by enzyme digestion are further broken down by enzymes produced by the small intestine (Table 7–4). The intestine's enzymes

FIGURE 7–10   Organs of Digestion   The liver, gallbladder, and pancreas all play key roles in digestion and empty by the common bile duct into the small intestine in which digestion takes place.

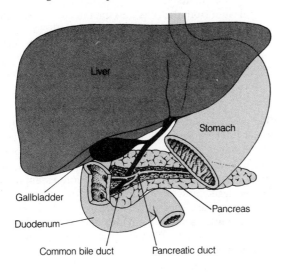

Liver

Stomach

Gallbladder

Pancreas

Duodenum

Common bile duct

Pancreatic duct

TABLE 7–4   Digestive Enzymes

SITE OF PRODUCTION	ENZYME	ACTION
Salivary glands	Amylase	Helps digest polysaccharides in the oral cavity
Stomach	Pepsin	Works in the stomach to break proteins into peptides
Pancreas	Trypsin	Cleaves peptide bonds of peptides and proteins
	Chymotrypsin	Same as trypsin
	Carboxypeptidase	Cleaves peptide bonds on carboxy end of peptides
	Amylase	Breaks starches into smaller units
	Phospholipase	Cleaves fatty acids from phosphoglycerides
	Lipase	Cleaves two fatty acids from triglycerides
	Ribonuclease	Breaks RNA into smaller nucleotide chains
	Deoxyribonuclease	Breaks DNA into smaller nucleotide chains
Epithelium of small intestine	Maltase	Breaks maltose into glucose subunits
	Sucrase	Breaks sucrose into glucose and fructose subunits
	Lactase	Breaks lactose in glucose and galactose subunits
	Aminopeptidase	Breaks down peptides

are embedded in the membranes of the cells lining the small intestine and are produced by the cells themselves. As a result, the final phase of digestion occurs just before the nutrient is absorbed into the cell.

Absorption in the Small Intestine.   Absorption is facilitated by three structural modifications of the small intestine. Figure 7–11b shows, for instance, that the lining of the small intestine is thrown into circular folds, which increase the overall surface area. The circular folds are comprised of many fingerlike projections called **villi** (Figures 7–11b and 7–11c). Like the circular folds, the villi also increase the surface area available for absorption. The intestinal surface area is further increased by **microvilli**, projections on the plasma membranes of the epithelial cells (Figure 7–11d). Each cell contains approximately 3000 microvilli. Two hundred million microvilli occupy a single square millimeter of intestinal lining. Thus, the surface area of the lining of the small intestine is 600 times greater than it would be without the circular folds, the villi, and the microvilli.

Although numerous mechanisms are involved in absorption, most molecules enter the intestinal epithelium by active transport, then move out of the intestinal cells and into the bloodstream or lymphatic

vessels by diffusion. Each villus of the small intestine has a rich supply of blood and lymph capillaries that carry off the nutrients (Figure 7–11b). Most of the nutrients diffuse into the capillaries, minute vessels of the circulatory system. Fatty acids and monoglycerides, however, are an exception. They first diffuse into the cells lining the villi where the triglycerides are reassembled. Triglycerides combine with cholesterol and phospholipids absorbed by the epithelial cells and are released from the cells into the interstitial fluid by exocytosis. In the extracellular fluid, the lipids form small globules. Blood capillaries, however, are relatively impermeable to fat globules. Most of the lipid globules, therefore, enter the more porous lymph capillaries.

The Liver.   Three organs work in concert with the small intestine, providing digestive secretions. They are the liver, the pancreas, and the intestinal glands. The liver is the largest organ in the body and one of the most versatile, performing many functions essential to homeostasis. Situated in the upper right quadrant of the abdominal cavity, under the protection of the rib cage, the liver is one of the body's main storage depots for glucose and fats (Figure 7–5). By storing glucose and fats and releasing them as they are needed,

(continuing)

the liver helps to ensure a constant supply of energy-rich molecules to body cells. The liver synthesizes some key blood proteins involved in clotting and stores iron and certain vitamins, releasing them as needed. The liver is an efficient detoxifier of poten-tially harmful chemicals, such as nicotine, barbiturates, and alcohol.

Last but not least, the liver plays an important role in the digestion of fats. The liver produces a fluid called **bile**, which contains water, ions, and chemicals, such as cholesterol, fatty acids, and bile salts. **Bile salts** are steroids that are produced by liver cells and are required for lipid digestion. Bile is transported to the **gallbladder**, a sac attached to the underside of the liver (Figure 7–5). The gallbladder removes water from the bile, thus concentrating the bile. Upon demand, bile is released into the small intestine through the common bile duct (Figure 7–10).

Bile salts are **emulsifying agents**—that is, chemical substances that break up fat globules into much smaller globules. This reduction in the size of the globules is essential for lipid digestion because the small intestine does not digest large globules efficiently.

Bile flow to the small intestine may be blocked by **gallstones**, deposits of cholesterol and other materials that form in the gallbladder. Gallstones may lodge in the ducts draining the organ, thus reducing—even completely blocking—the transport of bile to the small intestine. In the absence of bile salts, lipid digestion is greatly reduced. Because lipid digestion is reduced, fat globules remain in the undigested food mass, or feces. Fats are decomposed by bacteria in the large intestine, but not absorbed. The decomposition of these fats, therefore, gives the feces a foul odor. The higher percentage of fat also makes the feces quite buoyant and difficult to flush.

Approximately one of every ten American adults has gallstones, although many (30–50%) of these people exhibit no symptoms whatsoever. Gallstones occur more frequently in older individuals, and the incidence in the elderly is about one in every five. When they cause problems, gallstones are usually removed surgically. This procedure requires that the entire gallbladder be removed. Scientists are now testing a new drug that dissolves gallstones in many patients, thus eliminating the need for surgery.

The Pancreas.   The pancreas lies in the abdominal cavity under the stomach, nestled in a loop formed by the first portion of the small intestine, the **duodenum** (Figure 7–10). The pancreas is a dual-purpose organ: it produces enzymes needed to digest foodstuffs in the small intestine and also produces hormones that regulate blood glucose levels.

The digestive enzymes of the pancreas are produced in small glandular units and are carried away by ducts that converge to form the large pancreatic duct. The pancreatic duct joins with a duct from the gallbladder and drains into the duodenum. Each day approximately 1200–1500 milliliters (1.0 to 1.5 quarts) of pancreatic juice are produced and released into the small intestine. This liquid is composed of water, sodium bicarbonate, and several important digestive enzymes (Table 7–4).

Sodium bicarbonate in the pancreatic juice neutralizes acid in the chyme released by the stomach. This helps protect the small intestine from stomach acids and also creates conditions optimal for the function of the pancreatic digestive enzymes.

Pancreatic enzymes, listed in Table 7–4, break down lipids and macromolecules—protein, polysaccharides, and nucleic acids—into smaller molecules. Pancreatic **amylase**, for instance, digests starch molecules, forming smaller polysaccharide chains and the disaccharide maltose. Two other pancreatic enzymes, **chymotrypsin** and **trypsin**, break down proteins to form peptides. Pancreatic **lipase** removes some of the fatty acids from the glycerol molecule, forming monoglycerides, while **ribonuclease** and **deoxyribonuclease** break RNA and DNA into shorter nucleotide chains.

Like the stomach, the pancreas secretes its enzymes in an inactive form, helping protect the pancreas from self-destruction. **Trypsinogen**, for example, is the inactive form of the protein-digesting enzyme trypsin. Trypsinogen is activated by a substance on the epithelial lining of the small intestine. Trypsin, in turn, activates other enzymes.

The Large Intestine: Water Resorption

Undigested materials pass from the small intestine into the large intestine, so named because of its larger diameter (Figure 7–5). The large intestine is about 1.5 meters (5 feet) long and receives a mixture of water and undigested foods—fats, protein, and carbohydrate (mostly fiber)—from the small intestine. The large intestine supports a huge population of bacteria that feed on the unabsorbed nutrients. These bacteria synthesize several key vitamins: B-12, thiamine, riboflavin, and, most importantly, vitamin K, which is often deficient in the human diet. The large intestine absorbs vitamins produced by its bacteria, as well as sodium ions, potassium ions, and much (90%) of the water remaining in the feces.

The feces contain indigestible wastes and dead bacteria. Bacteria, in fact, account for about one-third of the dry weight of the feces.[3] The feces are propelled

---

[3]The feces are about 30% dead bacteria, 10–20% fat, 10–20% inorganic matter, 2–3% protein, and about 30% undigested roughage (cellulose).

by peristaltic contractions until they reach the rectum. When the rectum distends, it stimulates the defecation reflex. Fortunately, this reflex can be consciously overridden beginning early in life.

Controlling Digestion

Digestion is a complex and varied process that is controlled largely by nerves and hormones. Consider some key events. Digestion begins in the oral cavity and is largely under the control of the nervous system. As noted earlier, the sight, smell, taste, and sometimes even the thought of food stimulate the release of saliva. Chewing has a similar effect. Besides activating salivary production, these stimuli also cause the brain to send nerve impulses along the vagus nerve to the stomach, initiating the secretion of HCl and the hormone **gastrin**. Gastrin stimulates additional HCl secretion.

The concentration of HCl in the stomach is regulated by a negative feedback mechanism (Chapter 6). When the acid content rises too high, it inhibits gastrin secretion, thus shutting off acid production. Protein in the stomach tends to reduce the concentration of HCl by accepting free H^+. This reduces the acidity, which stimulates gastrin production, thus increasing acid secretion.

Chyme next enters the small intestine where its acids stimulate the release of another hormone, secretin. **Secretin** is produced by the cells of the duodenum and travels in the bloodstream to the pancreas where it stimulates the release of sodium bicarbonate. Sodium bicarbonate, in turn, is secreted into the small intestine where it neutralizes the acidic chyme and creates an environment optimal for pancreatic enzymes.

The release of pancreatic enzymes is triggered by another hormone, **cholecystokinin (CCK)**, produced by cells of the duodenum when chyme is present. CCK also stimulates the gallbladder to contract, releasing bile into the small intestine.

Recent evidence links abnormally low secretion of CCK to **bulimia**, an eating disorder characterized by recurrent binge eating, followed by vomiting. CCK has been found in the brain's hypothalamus with other hormones and may be involved in a range of behaviors, including bulimia. Approximately 4% of America's young adult women, and a far smaller fraction of men, are bulimic. Bulimia is thought to have both biological and psychological roots, but researchers have failed to identify a biochemical cause until

now. No single chemical is likely to control a complex behavior like appetite, but it appears that CCK plays an important role.

The small intestine produces one additional hormone, **gastric inhibitory peptide (GIP)**, in response to fatty acids and sugars in chyme. GIP inhibits acid production and peristalsis in the stomach, slowing down the rate at which chyme is released into the small intestine and providing additional time for digestion and absorption to occur.

ENVIRONMENT AND HEALTH: EATING RIGHT/LIVING RIGHT

In few places is the delicate balance between homeostasis and human health as evident as in human nutrition. Homeostasis requires an adequate supply of nutrients. Many studies suggest that a healthy, balanced diet can decrease the risk of cancer, heart disease, hypertension, and other diseases. All of these diseases may be caused by imbalance.

Consider a few examples. Magnesium is one of the major minerals, but is routinely ingested in insufficient amounts. New research suggests that such deficiencies may underlie a number of medical conditions including diabetes, high blood pressure, pregnancy problems, and cardiovascular disease.

Research shows that adding magnesium to the drinking water of rats with hypertension can eliminate high blood pressure. Studies in rabbits show that magnesium reduces lipid levels in the blood and also reduces plaque formation in blood vessels. Rabbits on a high-cholesterol, low-magnesium diet, for example, have 80 to 90% more atherosclerosis than rabbits on a high-cholesterol, high-magnesium diet.

Researchers have found that in humans magnesium deficiencies during pregnancy result in migraines, high blood pressure, miscarriages, stillbirths, and babies with low birth weight. Magnesium supplements greatly reduce the incidence of these problems. Research suggests that magnesium deficiency causes spasms in blood vessels of the placenta, reducing blood flow to the fetus.

Researchers believe that 80 to 90% of the American public may be magnesium deficient. One reason the American diet may be deficient in magnesium is that phosphates in many carbonated soft drinks bind magnesium in the intestine, preventing it from being absorbed into the blood. Magnesium deficiencies can be reversed by eating more green leafy vegetables, seafoods, and whole grain cereals. Mineral supplements could help as well, but they should be used with caution.

Zinc is a trace mineral that has also been implicated in a wide range of health problems. Rats fed diets severely deficient in zinc, for example, have more birth defects, are often stunted, and reach sexual maturation later than their counterparts fed normal diets. Concerned that less-severe zinc deficiencies may cause problems in humans, researchers followed 10 monkeys from birth through adolescence. One group was fed a diet low in zinc. The other received far more than they required. Monkeys fed the zinc-deficient diet showed several curious symptoms. Their immune function was suppressed 20 to 30%, making them more susceptible to disease. Significant learning impairments were also observed. The monkey studies substantiate studies in rodents and suggest concern for people in less-developed countries who often subsist on low-zinc diets consisting primarily of cereals.[4]

Over the years, numerous dietary recommendations have been issued to help Americans live healthier lives and reduce the risk of cancer and heart attack. Nutritionists recommend that we daily (1) consume fruit and vegetables, especially cabbage and greens, (2) consume high-fiber foods, such as whole wheat bread and celery, (3) and that we consume foods high in vitamins A and C. A healthy diet also minimizes the consumption of animal fat, red meat, and salt-cured, nitrate-cured, smoked or pickled foods including bacon and lunch meat.

Has the American public taken these recommendations to heart? The results of one recent study suggest that the answer is no. A survey of the eating habits of nearly 12,000 Americans conducted from 1976 to 1980 showed that the diets of both black and white Americans typically were deficient in the very foods that nutritionists recommended.[5] When asked to recall everything they had eaten in the previous 24-hour period, fewer than one in five people in the study reported eating any of these foods. In sharp contrast, many of the people surveyed had eaten red meat, bacon, and lunch meat.

---

[4]To determine if you are receiving an adequate supply of micronutrients, you can undergo a blood test or an analysis of your diet at a nutritional clinic. If there are problems, a trained nutritionist will be able to make recommendations to correct the problem.

[5]Critical thinking suggests caution in interpreting these results. Studies of the dietary habits of people in 1990 would be more informative.

A healthy diet results largely from habit and circumstance or environment. How does our environment affect our nutrition and health? In the hustle and bustle of modern society, many of us ignore proper nutrition, grabbing snack foods when we are hungry because we haven't the time to sit down to a nutritionally balanced meal. The fast-paced world we live in—that places a high premium on speed—often ignores the importance of eating right.

SUMMARY

1. Studies suggest that iron levels in the body may affect heat production in women, an example of the importance of diet to physiological processes.

A PRIMER ON HUMAN NUTRITION

2. Humans require two types of nutrients: macronutrients, substances needed in large quantity, and micronutrients, substances required in much lower quantities.
3. The four major macronutrients are water, carbohydrates, lipids, and proteins.
4. Water is in the liquids we drink and the foods we eat. Maintaining adequate water intake is important because water is involved in many chemical reactions in the body. Water helps maintain body temperature and a constant level of nutrients and wastes in body fluids.
5. Carbohydrates and lipids are major sources of cellular energy; 70 to 80% of all energy required by the body goes for basic functions.
6. Contrary to popular myth, protein does not supply much energy, except when lipid and carbohydrate intake is low or if protein intake exceeds daily requirements. Dietary protein is chiefly a source of amino acids for building proteins.
7. Amino acids produced by protein digestion can be used to build new protein or may be chemically modified to produce other amino acids. Amino acids that cannot be synthesized in the body and must be supplied in the food we eat are essential amino acids.
8. To ensure an adequate supply of all amino acids, individuals should eat complete proteins, such as milk or eggs, or combine protein sources.
9. Lipids provide energy during rest and aerobic activity. Lipids serve many other functions in the body, such as insulation.
10. Besides providing energy, carbohydrates serve other important functions. Dietary fiber, for example, increases the liquid content of the feces, reducing constipation, the incidence of diverticulitis, and the risk of colon cancer.

11. Micronutrients are needed in much smaller quantities and include two groups: vitamins and minerals.

12. Vitamins are a diverse group of organic compounds that act as enzyme cofactors. Vitamins are required in relatively small quantities.

13. Human vitamins fit into two categories: water soluble and fat soluble. The water-soluble vitamins include vitamin C and the B-complex vitamins. The fat-soluble vitamins include vitamins A, D, E, and K. Vitamin deficiencies and vitamin excesses can result in health problems.

14. Minerals fit into one of two groups: trace minerals, those required in very small quantity, and major minerals, those required in greater quantity. Deficiencies and excesses of both types of minerals can lead to serious health problems.

THE HUMAN DIGESTIVE SYSTEM

15. Food is chemically and physically broken down in the digestive system. Small molecules produced in this process are transported from the digestive system to the bloodstream or lymphatic system.

16. Food digestion begins in the mouth. The teeth mechanically break down the food. Saliva liquifies the food making it easier to swallow. Salivary amylase begins to digest starch molecules.

17. Food is pushed to the pharynx by the tongue where the food triggers the swallowing reflex. Peristaltic contractions propel the food down the esophagus to the stomach.

18. The stomach is an expandable organ that stores and liquifies the food. The churning action of the stomach, brought about by peristaltic contractions, mixes the food, turning it into a paste called chyme. The stomach releases food into the small intestine in timed pulses, ensuring efficient digestion and absorption. Very limited chemical digestion and absorption occur in the stomach.

19. The stomach produces hydrochloric acid, which denatures protein, allowing it to be acted on by enzymes. The stomach also produces a proteolytic enzyme called pepsin, which breaks proteins into peptides. The lining of the stomach is protected from acid by mucus. When the mucous protection fails, however, the lining may be eroded by acids, creating an ulcer.

20. The functions of the stomach are regulated by neural and hormonal mechanisms.

21. The small intestine is a long, coiled tubule in which most of the enzymatic digestion of food and absorption takes place. Enzymes for digestion come from the pancreas and the lining of the intestine itself.

22. The liver also plays an important role in digestion. It produces a liquid called bile that contains, among other chemicals, bile salts. Bile is stored in the gallbladder and released into the small intestine when food is present. Bile salts emulsify fats, breaking them into small globules that can be acted on by enzymes.

23. The pancreas produces sodium bicarbonate, which neutralizes the acid entering the small intestine with the chyme and also produces enzymes that act on macromolecules, breaking them into smaller ones.

24. Undigested food molecules pass from the small intestine into the large intestine, which carries the waste, or feces, to the outside of the body. The large intestine absorbs water, sodium, potassium, and vitamins produced by intestinal bacteria.

25. The digestive process is controlled by the nervous and endocrine systems.

26. Digestion begins in the mouth with enzymes released by the salivary glands. The release of saliva is stimulated by the sight, smell, taste, and sometimes even the thought of food. These stimuli also cause the brain to send nerve impulses to the gastric glands of the stomach, initiating the secretion of HCl and gastrin, a hormone that also stimulates HCl secretion.

27. Chyme entering the small intestine stimulates the release of two hormones, secretin and cholecystokinin. Secretin travels in the bloodstream to the pancreas where it stimulates the release of sodium bicarbonate. Cholecystokinin stimulates the release of pancreatic enzymes and also stimulates the gallbladder to contract, releasing bile into the small intestine.

ENVIRONMENT AND HEALTH: EATING RIGHT/LIVING RIGHT

28. Human health is dependent on good nutrition. Numerous studies suggest that a healthy, balanced diet can decrease the risk of cancer, heart disease, hypertension, and other diseases.

29. Nutritionists recommend the daily consumption of (a) fruit and vegetables, especially cabbage and greens, (b) high-fiber foods, such whole wheat bread and celery, and (c) foods high in vitamins A and C.

30. In addition, they recommend reducing consumption of animal fat, red meat, and salt-cured, nitrate-cured, smoked or pickled foods including bacon and lunch meat.

31. Studies suggest, however, that Americans have not taken these recommendations to heart. Many of us ignore proper nutrition, because we haven't the time to sit down to a nutritionally balanced meal. The fast-paced world we live in often ignores the importance of eating right.

EXERCISING YOUR CRITICAL THINKING SKILLS

Corn is a staple for 200 million people worldwide, including nearly half of the world's chronically malnourished people. Because corn is such an important source of calories and protein throughout the world, researchers have developed a new strain of corn called Quality-Protein Maize (QPM).

QPM has about the same amount of protein as common maize, but has twice the usable protein because its protein is more complete—that is, it supplies more of the essential amino acids. Normal maize has about 40% of the biological value of milk protein. QPM approaches that of milk, a common standard of nutritional excellence.

In countries where maize is a staple, QPM could double the efficiency of subsistence farming. A study by the National Research Council reports that QPM could allow families to combat malnutrition without outside help. QPM could prove helpful in Mexico, Central America, and Africa where hunger and starvation are common.

Using your critical thinking skills, examine this optimistic new finding. You might want to begin with the big picture. For example, will QPM be affordable to peasants in the Third World? Will it be more susceptible to insect pests than currently used native strains? Will it require costly pesticides? Will it require additional irrigation? Will it deplete the soil? How does it compare economically to other measures? What other questions can you think of that should be answered?

You may want to refer to an environmental science book (see Suggested Readings in Chapter 21) to find out more on world hunger. What other ways are there to solve the problem? How have efforts to improve crop yield worked in the past? Should QPM be supplemented by other strategies?

TEST OF TERMS

1. Water, carbohydrates, lipids, and proteins are all members of a class of nutrients called _____ .

2. The two main sources of energy in a well-balanced diet are _____ and _____ .

3. _____ exercise strives to maintain oxygen levels in muscles and relies primarily on _____ for energy.

4. Excess protein in the diet can be used to generate energy or be used to make _____ .

5. The amino acids the body cannot produce are called _____ amino acids. Proteins that supply all of these amino acids are said to be _____ .

6. Indigestible carbohydrates in fruits, vegetables, and grains are called _____ and are thought to reduce the incidence of _____ cancer.

7. _____ are a diverse group of organic compounds that act as cofactors for enzymes. They fit into two broad groups: _____ and _____ .

8. Minerals required in minute quantities such as zinc and copper are called _____ _____ .

9. The salivary glands produce two enzymes, _____ and _____ .

10. The taste receptors on the tongue are called _____ _____ .

11. The _____ connects the oral cavity with the esophagus.

12. The involuntary muscle contractions that propel food along the digestive tract are called _____ .

13. At the juncture of the esophagus and stomach is a ring of muscle called the _____ sphincter.

14. Food is converted to a liquified mass called _____ in the stomach.

15. The proteolytic enzyme, _____ , produced by the stomach, is released in an inactive form, _____ .

16. The ring of muscle at the junction of the stomach and small intestine that controls the passage of food into the small intestine is called the _____ sphincter.

17. The _____ produces bile, a fluid that is stored in the gallbladder and later released into the small intestine where its chief chemical component, _____ _____ emulsify fats.

18. The pancreas produces two major products: _____ and _____ .

19. Three major structural modifications increase the surface area for absorption in the small intestine; they are _____ _____ , _____ , and _____ .

20. Fats absorbed by the small intestine are carried away by _____ capillaries.

Answers to the Test of Terms are located in Appendix B.

TEST OF CONCEPTS

1. The body requires proper nutrient input to maintain homeostasis. Give an example and explain how the nutrient affects homeostasis.
2. You are an exercise physiologist in charge of a weight-control clinic. A client comes to you and asks your advice on a weight-loss program. Should he start lifting weights or join an aerobic class? Why?
3. Describe the conditions in which protein is used to provide cellular energy.
4. Using your knowledge of homeostasis and energy metabolism, describe the homeostatic control of blood glucose. Be sure to indicate the input, storage depots, and output.

5. If you were considering becoming a vegetarian, how would you be assured of getting all of the amino acids your body needs?
6. Describe how fiber may help reduce colon cancer.
7. What are vitamins and why are they needed in such small quantities?
8. A dietary deficiency of one vitamin can cause wide-ranging effects. Why?
9. What organs physically break food down and what organs participate in the chemical breakdown of food?
10. Describe the process of swallowing.

11. Describe the function of hydrochloric acid and pepsin in the stomach. How does the stomach protect itself from these substances?
12. How do ulcers form and how can they be treated?
13. Describe the endocrine and nervous system control of the stomach function.
14. The small intestine is the chief site of digestion. Where do the enzymes needed for this process come from, and how is the release of these enzymes stimulated? What other chemicals are needed for proper digestion?
15. Describe the functions of the large intestine.

SUGGESTED READINGS

Boskin, W., G. Graf, and V. Kreisworth. 1990. *Health dynamics: Attitudes and behaviors.* St. Paul, Minn.: West. Excellent information on health and nutrition.

Christian, J. L., and L. L. Greger. 1988. *Nutrition for living,* 2d ed. Menlo Park, Calif.: Benjamin/Cummings. Well-written and informative guide to nutrition with lots of practical advice and important biochemical information.

Guyton, A. C. 1986. *Textbook of medical physiology,* 7th ed. New York: Saunders. Excellent, in-depth coverage of digestion.

Long, P. 1989. Fat chance. *Hippocrates* 3(5): 38–47. This article helps you identify if you are overweight and discusses ways of losing weight.

McKenzie, A. 1989. A tangle of fibers. *Science News* 136(22): 344–45. Good discussion of the various types of dietary fiber.

Sizer, F. S., and E. N. Whitney. 1988. *Life choices: Health concepts and strategies.* St. Paul, Minn.: West. Contains excellent information on nutrition and health.

Vander, A., J. Sherman, and D. Luciano. 1985. *Human physiology: The mechanisms of body function.* 4th ed. New York: McGraw-Hill. General coverage of human physiology.

Whitney, E. N., E. M. N. Hamilton, and S. R. Rolfes. 1990. *Understanding nutrition,* 5th ed. St. Paul, Minn.: West. Superb coverage of nutrition for students interested in learning more.

SAMPLE CHAPTER 3

4 Sample Chapter

Managing Stress

SOURCE: Reprinted by permission of *Health Dynamics: Attitudes and Behaviors* by Warren Boskin, Gerald Graf and Virginia Kreisworth. Copyright 1990 by West Publishing Company. All rights reserved. All photographs and captions have been deleted.

CHAPTER 3

Managing Stress

What Do You Know?

Are the following statements true or false?

1. Stress is harmful and therefore should be avoided.
2. Chronic stress can lead to organic damage such as high blood pressure, kidney disease, and cancer.
3. The biggest source of interpersonal stress is one's family.
4. Anyone who undergoes many extreme changes in his or her life, such as the death of a close family member, divorce, loss of job, or flunking out of school will experience an increase in the frequency and severity of illness within the following two to three years.
5. When crisis has occurred, resulting in disequilibrium, it is necessary to have a realistic perception of the situation, adequate support, and adequate coping skills in order to restore balance.
6. Stress management is best approached holistically by simplifying and balancing positive health practices dealing with environmental, material, spiritual, and personal actions.
7. The best relaxation technique is meditation.
8. A social-support system consists of people who sustain us emotionally, give us tangible material support, and provide us with information and advice.
9. Although we know social support to be important for high-level human wellness, this fact hasn't really been proved empirically by research.
10. Having pets at home has been demonstrated to have positive health effects on elderly and homebound people.

58

▪ What Is Stress?

There's a bumper sticker that reads, "My worst day fishing is better than my best day working." We conjure up the image of someone out on a sunny day, drifting on a lake in a boat or sitting on the shore, without a care in the world. Our stereotyped image of that same person at work is of someone being hassled, trying to meet deadlines, and experiencing various other sorts of pressures.

Without a doubt, most of our waking and productive hours involve stress in one form or another; it can occur during work or play (including fishing). As we shall see, stress is not bad in and of itself, and a certain amount of it may be necessary for achieving a high quality of life. The optimal amount of stress may vary from person to person. Nevertheless, too much stress can be harmful, especially if steps are not taken to control the effects of inevitable stress.

A well-known researcher in the science of stress has been Dr. Hans Sclye. He has defined **stress** as "the rate of wear and tear within the body" as we respond to environmental stressors. The stressors may be the result of excessive stimuli or they may stem from stimulus deprivation, such as lack of physical contact.

Selye also defined stress as "the nonspecific response of the body to any demand made upon it." The key point to this definition is the fact that the body must adjust to any demand in an attempt to maintain a condition of **equilibrium.** This means that adaptation is the central purpose of the body's reaction to stress.

When stressors have a negative effect, such as causing stomach cramps or headaches, the effect is called **distress.** Not all stressors are harmful, however, and the term **eustress** has been coined to distinguish those stressors that are psychologically beneficial. An example of eustress is the elation that comes after an exhausting but satisfying performance in an athletic contest.

(continuing)

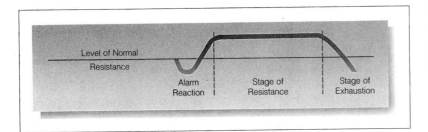

FIGURE 3–1 ■ **General Adaptation Syndrome**

SOURCE: Adapted from Hans Selye, *Stress Without Distress* (New York: S. B. Lippincott, 1974).

A person's reaction may be to coexist with the stressor or to directly combat the source of stress. One important factor is whether the person has learned to perceive stress as being personally threatening. Regardless of whether stressful events are pleasant or unpleasant, stress triggers the same general physiological reaction in the body. What may be more important is the *intensity* of its demands on the body's adaptive mechanisms.

Physiology of Stress

You are about to go on stage to perform in a play or concert. You are about to start an athletic competition—a ball game or a race. You are about to go out on a date with someone who you like but have only recently met. STRESS! Your heart starts pounding fast. Your palms and underarms become sweaty. You get a queasy feeling in the pit of your stomach. All of your body functions seem to be operating at double time. You probably recognize these symptoms as your body's response to the stressful situation.

Even though you tell yourself to keep calm, your body maintains its excited state. Why and how do these reactions occur? How does the brain and **neuroendocrine** system transform a psychological stress, such as taking an exam, into a physiological response? What is the nature of the response, and how does it effect bodily defenses and disease causation?

Selye has categorized the body's reactions to environmental stress into three phases, which he calls the *general adaptation syndrome* (GAS) (see Figure 3–1). In the first stage, there is a nonspecific, general *alarm reaction,* during which the **hypothalamus** portion of the brain is activated by the stressor. The hypothalamus, in turn, activates the **autonomic nervous system** and regulates the **pituitary gland,** which causes specific body defenses to be aroused. During this second phase of the GAS, called the *stage of resistance,* the hormone **epinephrine** is released, which helps the body either fight the stressor directly or take flight to avoid the stressor's harmful effects. If exposure to the same stressor is continued over a long period of time, the body will no longer be able to adjust or resist, and a *stage of exhaustion* will prevail. Adaptability is not infinite; we eventually succumb to the effects of the stressor, and our resistance breaks down. As you will see in the chapter dealing with AIDS, when the body's **immune system** is no longer able to cope with disease-causing organisms, death ensues.

Patterns of Stress

There are three basic patterns of stress response:

1. A stressor is present and is followed by adaptive change that returns the individual to a stress level no higher or lower than before (Figure 3–2a).

60

SECTION I ■ HEALTH AND THE MIND

FIGURE 3–2 ■ Short- and Long-Term Stress Responses

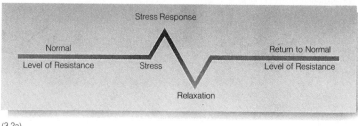

(3-2a)

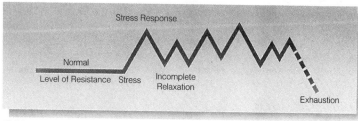

(3-2b)

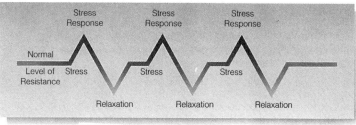

(3-2c)

■■■■ FAST FACTS ■

C hronic exposure to traffic jams tends to lead to higher baseline blood pressure, decreased frustration tolerance, an increase in aggressive driving behavior, and negative mood.

2. There is an increase in the level of stress but with no adaptive change strong enough to offset the stressful effects (Figure 3–2b).

3. Stress continues to escalate but it is accompanied by therapeutic actions aimed at maintaining normalcy (Figure 3–2c).

Selye discovered that chronic stress suppresses the immune system, thus diminishing the body's disease-fighting capabilities. In addition, continued chronic stress causes the body to produce excessive amounts of hormones, which, in turn, may lead to chronic diseases such as hardening of the arteries, high blood pressure, and arthritis.

■■ *PROBLEM SITUATION*   When it comes to making speeches in class, you always get anxious and experience thumping heartbeat and upset stomach beforehand. Although you recognize that it is beneficial to your maturing and learning process to encounter little stresses such as this, you'd like to control your body's physiological response to some degree. What steps can you take to diminish the immediate and direct effects of this stress, as well as the long-term stress reactions?

■ Sources Of Stress

Stressors can be found in all sorts of situations, forms, and environments. Table 3–1 identifies common sources of stress that bring tension and anxiety into your life. List a potential source of stress for yourself in each of these categories. Which areas seem to provide the most stress for you? What are your main sources of distress and eustress? How can you control the sources of distress and enhance eustress?

Stress can be either primary or secondary. A stimulus that results directly in a stress response is said to be a **primary stressor.** A **secondary stressor** occurs when, as a result of the initial stress response, further stress is created.

Assume, for example, that you and a friend have been looking forward to going to a concert, but as you get ready to leave the house, you discover that you have lost the tickets. You never do get into the concert. Instead you go to a local eatery and "pig out" on food and beer, a secondary stress response. If you create additional stress by feeling guilty for overindulging and hungover from excessive alcohol, further adaptive responses could be necessary.

Life Events and Change

A direct correlation exists between stressful life events and the occurrence of disease. Drs. Thomas Holmes and Richard Rahe, as well as others, have studied accumulated, stress-producing changes in people's lives. Their research confirms the notion that people with more stressful events in their lives have higher morbidity and mortality rates. One study by Holmes and Rahe found that 80 percent of those who had more than 300 Life Change Units (LCUs) on the Social Readjustment Rating Scale (see Self-Inventory 3.1) within the past year developed an illness within the next two years. This compared to a 37-percent chance of getting sick in the following two years for those who had less than 150 LCUs and a 51-percent risk of developing illness for those who scored between 150 and 300 LCUs. In addition, when those with over 300 LCUs did get sick, they were more likely to develop serious illnesses like cancer, heart

/ / / / FAST FACTS / /

About 14 percent of all occupational disease claims in 1988 were attributed to stress, compared to 5 percent in 1980.

/ / / / FAST FACTS / /

A 75-year old man who won $1,683 on a $2 bet at the racetrack was so stressed that he died of a heart attack as he stepped up to the window to cash in his winning ticket.

TABLE 3–1 ■ **Common Sources of Stress**

Classification	Explanation
1. *Intrapersonal conflict*	The turmoil within you that concerns which paths to take in life including goals, values, priorities, and decisions.
2. *Interpersonal relationships*	Stress resulting from interaction with others. Friends or peers are common sources of stress as you deal with the differences between you and learn to communicate and compromise.
3. *Family*	Although a major source of support, the family is also a source of stress because of the strength of the emotional ties among the people involved. Also, interaction among family members is more frequently of a judgmental nature.

(continued on page 62)

SECTION I ▪ HEALTH AND THE MIND

TABLE 3–1 ▪ Common Sources of Stress, continued

Classification	Explanation
4. *Work and school settings*	Involves work satisfaction and meeting standards expected of you.
5. *Money concerns*	Always with you, especially as college students, money problems are usually not a matter of having enough to survive (although it may seem like that at times) but how to prioritize how you spend your income.
6. *Global instability*	In the United States, we are more isolated from the type of regional war that occurs in many other parts of the world, but conflict in another part of the globe can have immediate, deleterious effects here. In addition, awareness of the destructive presence of nuclear arms can produce "passive" stress.
7. *Environmental abuse*	Can come in the form of pollution, crowding, crime, overstimulation (especially by the media), and ecological damage.
8. *Technology*	Advances such as the automobile, computer, and nuclear energy are stressful because they require adaptive change and speed up the pace of life. Most technological advances are associated with increased risk, such as the toxic waste and threat of radiation that accompany nuclear plants or the more than 50,000 accidental deaths per year in the United States involving automobiles.
9. *Change*	Any sort of change is a source of stress, although certain changes are clearly more stressful than others. The more changes present in your life and the faster these changes come about, the greater the stress you will encounter.
10. *Time pressure*	Time pressures can cause stress directly or increase the stress brought on by other factors. Many people are not instinctively effective at time-management skills.
11. *Spiritual issues*	Coming to terms with discovering meaning in your life or developing a code of ethical and moral behavior can be stressful, especially if it involves rejecting previously held beliefs. If no recognition is given to the spiritual dimension, it can affect how you cope with stress because of a lack of direction in your life.
12. *Health patterns*	Illness, injury, dietary imbalances, exposure to toxic substances, and the like are fairly obvious forms of stress. The physiological stress response is often more clearly seen in these instances than in situations involving social and psychological stress.

SELF-INVENTORY 3.1

The Social Readjustment Rating Scale

Life Event	Mean Value
1. Death of spouse	100
2. Divorce	73
3. Marital separation	65
4. Jail term	63
5. Death of close family member	63
6. Personal injury or illness	53
7. Marriage	50
8. Fired at work	47
9. Marital reconciliation	45
10. Retirement	45
11. Change in health of family member	44
12. Pregnancy	40
13. Sexual difficulties	39
14. Gain of new family member	39
15. Business readjustment	39
16. Change in financial state	38
17. Death of close friend	37
18. Change to different line of work	36
19. Change in number of arguments with spouse	35
20. Mortgage over $10,000	31
21. Foreclosure of mortgage or loan	30
22. Change in responsibilities at work	29
23. Son or daughter leaving home	29
24. Trouble with in-laws	29
25. Outstanding personal achievement	28
26. Spouse begin or stop work	26
27. Begin or end school	26
28. Change in living conditions	25
29. Revision of personal habits	24
30. Trouble with boss	23
31. Change in work hours or conditions	20
32. Change in residence	20
33. Change in schools	20
34. Change in recreation	19
35. Change in church activities	19
36. Change in social activities	18
37. Mortgage or loan less than $10,000	17
38. Change in sleeping habits	16
39. Change in number of family get-togethers	15
40. Change in eating habits	15
41. Vacation	13
42. Christmas	12
43. Minor violations of the law	11

Interpretation

Refer to the score range below to classify your life change score.

Score Range	Interpretation	Susceptibility
300+	Major life change	Major illness within year
250–299	Serious life change	Lowered resistance to diseases
200–249	Moderate life change	Depression
150–199	Mild life change	Colds, flus occasional depression
149–0	Very little life change	Good health

General Observations

1. Change in one's life is followed, about a year later, by associated health changes. Is this true of your life style?

2. Life changes tend to cluster significantly around health changes. Is this true in your case?

SOURCE: T. H. Holmes and R. H. Rahe, "The Social Readjustment Rating Scale," *Journal of Psychosomatic Research* 11 (1967): 213–218. Copyright 1967, Pergamon Press, Ltd.

SELF-INVENTORY 3.2 ◢◢◢◢◣◣◣◣

A Social Readjustment Rating Scale for College Students

Column A		Life-Change Event	Column B	Column C
_____	(1)	Entered college	50	_____
_____	(2)	Married	77	_____
_____	(3)	Trouble with your boss	38	_____
_____	(4)	Held a job while attending school	43	_____
_____	(5)	Experienced the death of a spouse	87	_____
_____	(6)	Major change in sleeping habits	34	_____
_____	(7)	Experienced the death of a close family member	77	_____
_____	(8)	Major change in eating habits	30	_____
_____	(9)	Change in or choice of major field of study	41	_____
_____	(10)	Revision of personal habits	45	_____
_____	(11)	Experienced the death of a close friend	68	_____
_____	(12)	Found guilty of minor violations of the law	22	_____
_____	(13)	Had an outstanding personal achievement	40	_____
_____	(14)	Experienced pregnancy, or fathered a pregnancy	68	_____
_____	(15)	Major change in health or behavior of family member	56	_____
_____	(16)	Had sexual difficulties	58	_____
_____	(17)	Had trouble with in-laws	42	_____
_____	(18)	Major change in number of family get togethers	26	_____
_____	(19)	Major change in financial state	53	_____
_____	(20)	Gained a new family member	50	_____
_____	(21)	Change in residence or living conditions	42	_____
_____	(22)	Major conflict or change in values	50	_____
_____	(23)	Major change in church activities	36	_____
_____	(24)	Marital reconciliation with your mate	58	_____
_____	(25)	Fired from work	62	_____
_____	(26)	Were divorced	76	_____
_____	(27)	Changed to a different line of work	50	_____
_____	(28)	Major change in number of arguments with spouse	50	_____

disease, and extreme depression than milder illnesses like common colds. A similar scale, based on the original Holmes and Rahe scale, was developed specifically for college students (see Self-Inventory 3.2).

The scores on these scales represent only a likelihood of an illness or injury occurring. There are too many other factors associated with individual susceptibility to make accurate predictions. Still, the results of these scales should make you consider whether or not to take overt steps to control the effects of high levels of stress in your life.

In a recent study, college students in Kentucky were asked which factors they thought were most stressful for them. Table 3–2 indicates the top 21 factors

Column A		Life-Change Event	Column B	Column C
_____	(29)	Major change in responsibilities at work	47	_____
_____	(30)	Had your spouse begin or cease work outside the home	41	_____
_____	(31)	Major change in working hours or conditions	42	_____
_____	(32)	Marital separation from mate	74	_____
_____	(33)	Major change in type and/or amount of recreation	37	_____
_____	(34)	Major change in use of drugs	52	_____
_____	(35)	Took on a mortgage or loan of less than $10,000	52	_____
_____	(36)	Major personal injury or illness	65	_____
_____	(37)	Major change in use of alcohol	46	_____
_____	(38)	Major change in social activities	43	_____
_____	(39)	Major change in amount of participation in school activities	38	_____
_____	(40)	Major change in amount of independence and responsibility	49	_____
_____	(41)	Took a trip or a vacation	33	_____
_____	(42)	Engaged to be married	54	_____
_____	(43)	Changed to a new school	50	_____
_____	(44)	Changed dating habits	41	_____
_____	(45)	Trouble with school administration	44	_____
_____	(46)	Broke or had broken a marital engagement or steady relationship	60	_____
_____	(47)	Major change in self-concept or self-awareness	57	_____
			TOTAL	_____

Directions for scoring: List the number of times each event has occurred to you within the past 12 months in Column A. Multiply that by the corresponding numerical value in Column B. Place that number in Column C. Total the scores in Column C.

Interpretation: High Risk 1450 + points
Medium Risk 890 points
Low Risk 347 − points

SOURCE: Martin B. Marx, Thomas F. Garrity, and Frank R. Bowers, "The Influence of Recent Life Experiences on the Health of College Freshmen," *Journal of Psychosomatic Research* 19 (1975): 97, Copyright 1975, Pergamon Press Ltd.

for men and women. Notice that most stressors relate to academics and relationships. Which factors seem to be most stressful for you? What other factors not on this list should make the top 21, in your opinion?

> ■ *PROBLEM SITUATION* During the past year and a half, you have accumulated an abundance of Life Change Units (see Self-Inventory 3.1 or 3.2) that put you into the high-risk category for experiencing illness or injury. What actions can you take that will ameliorate the distressing effects of the major life changes that you're going through?

66

SECTION I ■ HEALTH AND THE MIND

TABLE 3–2 ■ Perceived Intensity of Stress Factors for College Students

Rank	Males	Rank	Females
1.	Death of a parent	1.	Death of a parent
2.	Loss of intimate relationship	2.	Involved in pregnancy or abortion
3.	Final-exam week	3.	Final-exam week
4.	Breaking off a relationship	4.	Loss of a close friend
5.	Involved in pregnancy or abortion	5.	Breaking off a relationship
6.	Divorce or remarriage of parents	6.	Loss of intimate relationship
7.	Selecting or changing major	7.	Divorce or remarriage of parent
8.	Career opportunities after graduation	8.	Change in schools
9.	Change in schools	9.	Loss of close relative
10.	Loss of close friend	10.	Test anxiety
11.	Financial pressures	11.	Making plans for future
12.	Finding someone acceptable to date	12.	Oral presentations
13.	Putting off assignments or responsibilities	13.	Finding someone acceptable to date
14.	Making plans for future	14.	Academic workload
15.	Guilt for not doing better	15.	Financial pressure
16.	Oral presentations	16.	Deciding about or planning for marriage
17.	Loss of a close relative	17.	Putting off assignments or responsibilities
18.	Test anxiety	18.	Overweight or underweight
19.	Deciding about or planning for marriage	19.	Selecting or changing major
20.	Roommate adjustment	20.	Guilt for not doing better
21.	Concern about sexually transmitted diseases	21.	Career opportunities after graduation

SOURCE: Herman Bush, Merita Thompson, and Norman Van Tubergen, "Personal Assessment of Stress Factors for College Students," *Journal of School Health* 55(November 1985), 370–375.

////// FAST FACTS //

Approximately 15 percent of Vietnam veterans have been found to have combat-related stress disorders.

Managing Crises

When intense emotional stress becomes too great to handle, a crisis situation can arise. A **crisis** is any risky event or crucial time in life that cannot be managed with resources and actions that have worked in the past. It can lead to further anxiety that hampers one's ability to clearly think through solutions or that stymies independent action.

Figure 3–3 shows how crisis progresses from a condition of relative balance to a state of **disequilibrium.** The first step in dealing with this crisis, then, is to feel the need to restore the balance that has been disturbed. The satisfactory restoration of balance will depend on a number of factors, the first of which is our perception of the unbalancing event. If we are not aware of the source of the tension, it will be harder to handle. Can you see in Figure 3–4 the results

CHAPTER 3 ■ MANAGING STRESS   67

of Mary having incorrectly perceived the reason for failing an exam as personal failure rather than insufficient studying?

A second factor in overcoming a crisis is the availability of and access to an adequate support system consisting of friends, family members, and others involved in your life. It can include, for example, your good listener/friend or an empathetic counselor on campus.

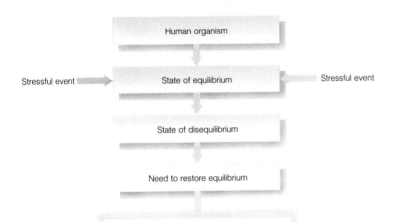

FIGURE 3–3 ■ **Paradigm: The Effect of Balancing Factors in a Stressful Event.**

SOURCE: Reproduced by permission from: Donna Aguilera and Janice Messick, *Crisis Intervention: Theory and Methodology* (St. Louis: C. V. Mosby, 1986).

*Balancing factors.

SECTION I ■ HEALTH AND THE MIND

The final factor in rebalancing emotional equilibrium is the adequacy of the set of personal coping mechanisms that you have developed. If your coping skills are not well developed, disequilibrium will continue. Once again, this is where a professionally trained counselor or therapist can help you. Thus, if you have a realistic perception of the stressful event or object, strong social support, and adequate coping skills, the problem can be resolved and balance restored.

FIGURE 3–4 ■ **Paradigm Applied to Case Study**

SOURCE: Reproduced by permission from: Donna Aguilera and Janice Messick, *Crisis Intervention: Theory and Methodology* (St. Louis: C. V. Mosby, 1986).

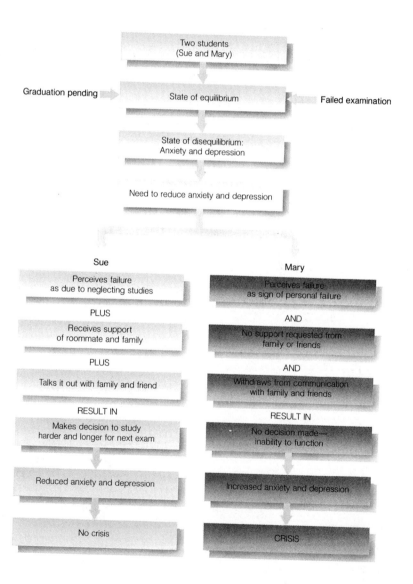

(continuing)

Anticipatory crisis may occur before many events and can be just as disabling as crisis produced by the event itself. Stress perceived as being great before an event takes place, such as prior to exams, can be beneficial, forcing you to gear up for the event, or can be harmful, mushrooming into a full-blown panic reaction. A certain amount of anticipation is good, but when stress interferes with the achievement of your goals, concrete action needs to be taken. For example, academic counselors and workshops are available on college campuses for students who suffer from math anxiety and who have formed mental blocks when it comes to understanding mathematical concepts.

> ■ *PROBLEM SITUATION* A good friend of yours is doing well in school academically but has encountered a critical financial situation because this person's parents have lost their family business and have declared bankruptcy. How could this potential crisis be dealt with satisfactorily? Using Figure 3–3, what are some factors that might prevent this from developing into a crisis for your friend, and what might cause it to escalate?

■ Manifestations Of Stress

Do you remember the ancient Greek myth of Achilles? His mother learned that if she dipped him in the River Styx when he was a baby, the water would make him invulnerable to injury or harm in battle. However, she held him by his heel, and therefore that part of his body wasn't covered by the water. Sure enough, later in his life, Achilles was shot in the heel in combat, which caused his demise. Hence, from this legend comes the term "Achilles heel," or weak spot. What is yours? When you succumb to the pressures of stress, where does it hit?

Why is it that when people are exposed to the same or similar psychological and pathological stressors, some remain healthy while others become sick? One approach to answering this question is to study the development of good health, called **salutogenesis,** an area that has been investigated extensively by the sociologist Aaron Antonovsky. Salutogenesis is an individual's ability to successfully cope with life's problems and the stressors encountered along the way.

Antonovsky found that people with a strong **sense of coherence** (knowing who they are in their environment and having a sense that they "fit") are less likely to succumb to stressors and therefore enjoy good health. He defines sense of coherence as:

. . . a global orientation that expresses the extent to which one has a pervasive, enduring though dynamic feeling of confidence that one's internal and external environments are predictable and that there is a high probability that things will work out as well as can reasonably be expected.

This definition emphasizes that a reasonable outcome is both *predictable* and *expected* for a person with a strong sense of coherence. The three core elements of one's sense of coherence are (1) making sense of the whole array of stimuli (stressors) that one is faced with, (2) having a realistic perception that the resources to manage daily problems are at one's command, and (3) seeing one's situation in the world as having meaning and purpose.

■ Managing Your Stress

We have seen what stress is and is not, and where stress usually comes from. We have also investigated how stress becomes manifest in the body and why people may differ in their reactions to it. Assuming that you have taken in all of this information, let's look at some things that you can do to promote eustress and diminish distress in your own life.

Coping Strategies

The basic, overriding principles of avoiding distress and promoting a long and healthful life can be traced at least as far back as the year 2697 B.C., which was when *The Yellow Emperor's Classic of Internal Medicine* (called the *Nei Ching* in Chinese) was put in written form. The *Nei Ching* says that to enjoy a full life, free from the harmful effects of stress, one should live in harmony with the natural way of things. It calls for moderation in drinking and eating plus a regular schedule of rising, working, playing, sleeping, and resting. The ancient Chinese gave excellent advice when they said that simplicity in living is the key to reducing stress and getting the most out of life.

This approach to stress management is very holistic in nature, because it fosters such positive practices as appropriate consumption of material goods, environmental awareness, concern for humanity in living and working, personal growth, and self-determinism. In practical everyday terms, it boils down to managing stress by engaging in good habits of exercise, rest, nutrition, social networking, and spiritual awareness and by experiencing positive stimulation and the achievement of aesthetic satisfaction.

Another key factor in stress management involves managing the limited amount of time that each of us has. There are only 60 minutes in an hour and 24 hours in a day. As a student, the chores you have to fit into that limited time frame include going to classes, studying and preparing for class, working, participating in extramural activities, family responsibilities, personal time for your hobbies, exercising, social affairs, and so on. Somehow you must either simplify your life when there is not enough time to do all that you must do or closely monitor and organize your time.

The first thing to understand about time management is that you really must manage yourself, because you are flexible and time is not—it just keeps moving along. If you've ever run a race and tried to "beat the clock," you're aware that the second hand never stops. Here are some suggestions that may help you manage your time, if that's a problem for you.

1. *Prioritize* what's truly important in your life. Don't overplan. If you are overscheduled, perhaps you can, for example, graduate from college a semester later without sacrificing anything really important.

2. You can't add more hours or minutes to your day, but you can *increase usable time*. Organize your schedule to make the most of what time you have. Identify and reduce "wasted" time, delegating certain activities to others in your social network instead of taking on too much by yourself. Schedule enough time for your high-priority activities. A problem that most of us have to some degree is procrastination—putting off today what may or may not wait until tomorrow. As far as academic procrastination is concerned, focus on avoiding or controlling distractions. For example, study in the library, where distractions are minimal.

3. You may want to *reduce the urgency* of time. Perhaps that task does not really have to be completed in the arbitrarily self-assigned time.

4. Another problem that affects optimal use of time is striving for perfection in the task that you're doing, thereby delaying its completion. It's okay to *give yourself permission to be imperfect*. You certainly don't want to do sloppy work, but recognize that most projects could be improved if only you began working on them sooner in order to spend more time on them.

5. Finally, be aware of procrastination that is caused by the fear of not being able to accomplish a task. If it seems overwhelming, *break the task down into smaller sub-tasks* to be done a piece at a time. If, however, the fear of failure stems from a lack of self-confidence in your ability to perform, you must *develop a positive attitude*. After all, you can't learn unless you try, and just because you fail at a task does not mean that you are not a good and capable person. With

GUIDELINES TO YOUR GOOD HEALTH

Positive thinking can be nurtured by taking these steps:

1. Psych yourself up for important events. Think over the upcoming situation and visualize it as being a successful experience.
2. Talk to yourself in a positive manner. It's like when Dorothy in the *Wizard of Oz* keeps telling herself, "I can. I can."
3. Be prepared. Develop a plan of action as well as contingency or alternate plans to use just in case circumstances change.
4. Label an upcoming event that might possibly cause undue tension a "positive learning experience." Look at exams, for example, as an opportunity to tell what you know, not as a test of what you don't know. What a feeling of power this can give you, if you're prepared.

SECTION I ■ HEALTH AND THE MIND

this attitude, it's easier to undertake a task with the anticipation that it will be a life-enhancing experience. As important as it may be to develop relaxation and stress-reducing techniques, having a positive mental attitude is equally vital.

On the negative side of the ledger, many people try to cope with stress through artificial, chemical means, which is rarely a satisfactory method in the long run. Unfortunately, the most widely prescribed drug in the United States is Valium (diazepam), a tranquilizer. Other popular, over-the-counter substances, usually contain nothing more than multiple vitamins. They have no proven stress-reducing properties.

FIGURE 3–5 ■ **Methods Of Meditation/Relaxation**

SOURCE: Courtesy of Arnold Shapiro, M.D., Student Health Services, San Francisco State University.

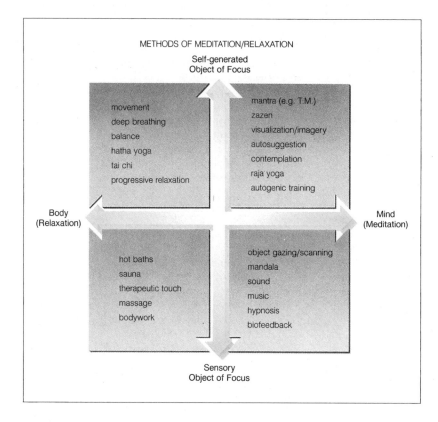

METHODS OF MEDITATION/RELAXATION

Self-generated
Object of Focus

movement
deep breathing
balance
hatha yoga
tai chi
progressive relaxation

mantra (e.g. T.M.)
zazen
visualization/imagery
autosuggestion
contemplation
raja yoga
autogenic training

Body
(Relaxation)

Mind
(Meditation)

hot baths
sauna
therapeutic touch
massage
bodywork

object gazing/scanning
mandala
sound
music
hypnosis
biofeedback

Sensory
Object of Focus

■■ *PROBLEM SITUATION*   Whenever you go through a stressful event, you seem to develop a headache, back ache, or a stiff neck. Knowing this pattern, what steps can you take that will help prevent or alleviate these bothersome, stress-related pains?

Relaxation Techniques

In Figure 3–2, we saw a graph of a long-term stress response showing elevated body activity that stayed at a high level without resolution. To alleviate this

GUIDELINES TO YOUR GOOD HEALTH

The following are basic conditions for eliciting a relaxation response using a meditative technique:

1. Find a *quiet place* where you will be free from extraneous noise, interruptions, or other distractions.
2. Get into a *comfortable position* (yet not so comfortable that you fall asleep). Sit or lie down, removing or loosening restrictive clothing and shoes.
3. A *passive attitude* is the next requirement for an optimal relaxation response. To help clear your mind, do some deep breathing, inhaling deeply and then emptying your mind as you slowly exhale. If you did nothing more than a few deep breathing exercises every hour or two during the day, you would be well ahead of the game of stress reduction.
4. Have a *mental focus* to dwell on. Closing your eyes will help you concentrate on this relaxing thought, image, or other mental device.
5. Allow for 15 to 30 minutes of *uninterrupted time*.

continued state of physiological readiness, we can perform various exercises aimed at activating the **parasympathetic nervous system,** which is that part of the nervous system responsible for taking in energy and initiating a relaxation response.

In Figure 3–5, the methods of relaxation are categorized as primarily involving the body (called relaxation activities) or the mind (called meditation exercises) and as having either a self-generated object of focus or a sensory focus. Which ones you choose to use depends on your personal preferences; there is no scientific evidence that one is better than the others.

Meditative skills consist of being quiet and paying attention. Some techniques encourage a free flow of ideas entering and leaving the mind, whereas others rely on either totally emptying the mind or concentrating on a single object.

The focus in a meditative exercise may be the body itself (as in concentrated deep rhythmic breathing), a repetitive sound (a word, phrase, or simple musical tune), or an imagined peaceful scenario. The focus may be a **mantra,** which is a word or phrase, often sanskrit, that is repeated over again in a melodic rhythm. The purpose of having an object of focus is to prevent the undisciplined "monkey mind" from flitting from subject to subject as various thoughts and stimuli enter the consciousness. As you become more experienced at meditating, it is easier for you to prolong and sustain concentration.

Besides concentrative meditation, there is a meditative form that involves "letting go" or "going with the flow" in such a way as to become more sensitive to your environment. To do this, first get into a comfortable, meditative position, sway back and forth as you "settle in," take some deep breaths, and let go a little each time you exhale. Sometimes intentionally relaxing a given part of the body for a while is helpful prior to "free" thinking. Thoughts are allowed to flow from one to the other without making an attempt to manipulate them. Distractions are allowed to be played out until attention can be gently brought back to the peaceful present. The aim of this sort of meditation is to lose self-consciousness and not to think in the perspective of "I." The self is forgotten,

SECTION I ▪ HEALTH AND THE MIND

and the world of NOW opens up. It is crucial to be in a quiet, serene place such as the shore, the woods, or a quiet place at home for this type of meditation.

Positive, creative imagery can have a suggestive effect that starts the mind moving toward a goal and weakens or overcomes negative images. By imagining where you want to be and visualizing how you will achieve that goal, you have gone a long way toward facilitating success. If you imagine failure, you are bound to fail; if you imagine success, you are more likely to succeed.

As with other relaxation techniques, visualization takes practice to work best. To practice creative imagery, first become "centered," or self-focused in the here and now, by getting relaxed as described previously. When you are fully relaxed, with your eyes closed and your breathing slow and steady, "breathe in energy and breathe out fatigue." Now begin to conjure up images in your mind, either of purely sensory sensations (for example, seeing blue skies, touching cottony clouds, smelling lemony fragrances, or hearing soft music) or of a desired scenario (for example, going out on the perfect date or spending 24 perfect hours). You can place yourself in an energy-enhancing environment and just allow good, peaceful thoughts to flow through your mind, imagining fantasies that are fulfilling and totally relaxing to you.

Physical exercise, preferably of the aerobic type (see Chapter 6), can also be a relaxation-evoking activity. A slow long-distance run, walk, swim, or bike ride can relieve stress and provide the added benefit of increasing physical fitness.

Keeping a Journal

Journaling is an excellent and powerful tool that can help you to understand and manage your stress, although it has the potential to be used in many areas of mental health. A personal journal is different from a diary in that the journal is more directive or tied to a theme or goal. It is kept in order to help you develop the self-directing and self-healing capacities in your life. The aim is to focus inward, encouraging spontaneity of thought and action by writing freely, followed by objective analysis. There is as much to gain from reading over and analyzing the journal as there is from actually keeping the journal. The following questions and answers will help you create a personal journal from which you can learn.

1. *What shall I write in?* Whatever you choose to write in, it will be a sort of companion of yours, so it should be easy to carry around and expandable.
2. *Where is the best place to write?* There is no single best place, but it is a good idea to write at a regularly scheduled time and in a place with minimum distractions, such as in your bedroom, the library, or even a quiet setting outdoors.
3. *How should I write?* It is important to write quickly and spontaneously with complete honesty and openness. This is your own personal journal; because you may not want to share it with another person, take some precautions to insure privacy. When you do make entries, they should focus primarily on the *positive*, although you'll want to examine all aspects of yourself.
4. *How often should I write in it?* This depends on what purpose your journal serves for you, but it should be on a regular basis. An intensive journal is done every day or so, whereas an occasional journal is written in on particular occasions.
5. *How shall I structure the journal and what shall I write about?* Journals have some degree of organization; they aren't merely free writing exercises. How you organize your journal is a highly individual and creative undertaking. First

decide what you want to learn from your journal, and then you will be able to choose the approach you'll take.

6. *What should I be looking for when I read it over?* In order to help examine your journal analytically, you might look for certain key-word indicators, such as labels used for people, where and how often the word "I" is used, or judgmentally laden words such as "never," "always," or "should." When reading over your journal, you may ask, "Do I still feel the same, or have I changed some of my views?" You might also write a summary statement of the journal as a means of becoming aware of your feelings, intuitions, senses, and intellect.

■ *PROBLEM SITUATION*   Your health education professor has assigned you to keep a personal journal of your total health status and health behaviors. It is an open-ended assignment, allowing you to create the journal to meet your own desires and inclinations. How would you structure the journal and what would you write about? What would your journal look like? When would you write in it and where? Would you share it with anyone else?

■ Social Well-Being And Stress

So far we considered what the individual alone can do to help control the effects of stress. Of equal importance in handling stress are the social aspects of wellness.

There isn't a person reading this book who hasn't been depressed by some event or bad news and needed to talk to someone about it. Perhaps you have needed to talk things over with someone because a difficult decision had to be made, such as what to major in at school or whether to drop a class or drop out of school altogether. Think back to a recent time when you felt particularly down in the dumps. Who did you call on for assistance or solace? When was the last time a friend, classmate, co-worker or relative needed some sort of help or support, and you were the one who provided it?

GUIDELINES TO YOUR GOOD HEALTH

Here are some suggested themes for personal journal entries:

■ Create *guided imageries* or fantasies centered on specific people, environments, or situations.
■ Write *unsent letters* to different people.
■ Create *dialogues* with various people, including public figures, personal acquaintances, or fictitious characters. You can even create dialogues with objects, events, or society in general.
■ Write *period logs* discussing particular times in your life, such as during high school or when you participated in a special activity or group.
■ Make *lists* of "things I love to do," "traits I like in friends," "people I'd like to spend time on a deserted island with," and so on.
■ Compose *portraits* of your ideal teacher, friend, doctor, parent, lover, clergyman, and so on.
■ Make *topical entries,* such as ones covered in this book, about mental health, spirituality, families, drugs, AIDS, parenting, physical fitness, and so on.

(continuing)

////// FAST FACTS //

I ndividuals who repress their feelings and who may be called "loners" are 16 times more likely to develop cancer than those who act out their emotions in an overt manner.

This give and take of assistance and support forms the very heart of what is considered to be social well-being. We depend on others to meet our physical-survival and mental health needs as well as for human and spiritual fulfillment. The need for love, in particular, is based on the human desire for connectedness with others. The ability to interact with people in a satisfactory way and to establish close interpersonal relationships is a sign of social wellness.

Two basic terms that will come up frequently are *social support* and *social network*. A **social support** is any person or persons who provide some sort of assistance in helping us meet basic needs. A social-support system may give *emotional support* by helping us maintain self-esteem and a positive self-concept; *feedback* about ourselves and our perceptions of others; *information and advice;* and *tangible support* in the form of money, time, or skills.

Social networks refer to specific relationships among people in a group that can be analyzed according to various properties of existing relationships. The questions that are usually examined are: how do the people in the network connect with one another as a whole, what is the nature of the relationships within the network, and what function does the network serve? Social networks may exist in a natural form and meet general needs, such as those involving family and friends, or they may be formal groups created intentionally to help meet the specific needs of their members, such as a support groups for cancer patients or for people who abuse alcohol or drugs.

Social Support and Health

It has been only within the last two decades or so that research has been conducted that points directly to social support as a factor in preventing disease, lessening its severity and improving rehabilitation. General susceptibility to disease increases as social ties lessen or disintegrate. Of course, there are other factors that may lower general resistance, but lack of a substantial social network is an important influence with many ramifications.

A landmark study linking disease to social networks was conducted in Alameda County, California, between 1965 and 1974. More than 7,000 people were included in the study, which found that both morbidity and mortality increased significantly among those who had few social ties as compared to those with strong social-support systems. This finding was consistent in all ethnic groups, sexes, and socioeconomic levels.

Another interesting study looked at two groups of nursing-home residents, each of whom was given a plant. The experimental group's members were told that the plant was theirs and that they had the responsibility to care for it, whereas the control group's members were told that the staff would take care of the plant just as the staff took care of the patients. Not only did people in the experimental group, who had the responsibility of caring for the plants, display better mental and physical health, but after a period of 18 months, they had a death rate that was half that of the control group's. Having a responsibility for the well-being of any organism provides a reason for living and maintaining good health. Similar studies have shown that elderly people who have pets such as dogs or cats are healthier, live longer, and recover from illnesses more quickly than senior citizens who are isolated and live alone.

How Social Supports Help

Exactly why social support promotes good health is not known at the present time, but two general explanations have been suggested. The first of these, called the *buffering* effect of social support, explains that when people are exposed to environmental stressors that can cause or contribute to illness, having strong social ties helps control the adverse effects of these stressors. The buffering effect of social support helps people to cope by allowing them to control their mood (for example, to avoid depression) and by enhancing normal functioning. The buffering effect also helps them to maintain feelings of self-esteem and a sense of mastery when exposed to adversity.

The second explanation of the positive effects of strong social ties on health and well-being is called the *direct* effect. The reasoning here is that an extensive support system may provide people with unconditional approval, which leads to general well-being that enables them to better cope with stress. The direct effect of social support may also prevent people from being exposed to certain environmentally harmful stressors, because they may follow good health practices recommended by members of their social groups. In a study done in Oregon that looked at the medical records of 2,600 adults during a period of seven years, it was found that having social ties, being trustful of others, and perceiving more control were all related to better health status. An interesting part of these findings was that people's belief that they have control over their lives is as important as whether they actually do have such self-control.

The following are some of the specific functions that social networks serve.

Esteem. Self-esteem is a basic need that all humans attempt to fulfill. When threats to our self-esteem arise, it becomes important to have someone around to talk to and to gain reassurance that we are accepted and valued.

Status. It is essential to have a strong sense of who we are in relation to our society, and our social network clarifies and strengthens our roles among family members and friends. Besides fulfilling the roles of parent, child, spouse, or boyfriend or girlfriend, we also belong to other community groups that provide a degree of status, showing us that we are valued within the larger community.

/ / / / FAST FACTS / /

A study of 110 men who were forcibly unemployed because of plant closures concluded that those men whose families and friends were highly supportive had fewer mental and physical health problems than those with fewer opportunities for social interactions.

Social Companionship. We live in a culture in which the majority of things we do outside our home and work are done with other people. On certain occasions we go to public events alone—and it is good to feel comfortable about being alone in public—but most people enjoy going to movies, sporting events, parties, and other forms of entertainment with someone else. Unfortunately, some people (such as elderly people who live alone and aren't very mobile) don't have natural companions with whom they can share these events. Companionship is desirable for its own sake, but it also leads to other forms of tangible and emotional support. Perhaps you can volunteer some of your time to provide temporary companionship to a person who is without a network of friends. Not only will it help that other person, but it will also make you feel good.

Information. Much of the information that we rely on to help us solve problems and make decisions comes in the form of advice and guidance. This information may not always be accurate, but because it comes from a source that we cherish as part of our social network, it is usually highly credible to us. Others within our social network often have insights into our problems and can be far more objective than we can be about ourselves.

Material Support. Let's face it, a great deal of our time during our waking moments is spent in the pursuit of material goods, because they are necessary for survival and they help satisfy other basic needs. If it weren't for social networking, it would be more difficult for us to acquire these goods and services. Tangible support may come in the form of money that is either given or loaned, time that is given to assist in a project, transportation, help in times of illness or distress, tutoring when we find it difficult to understand something, or any of a number of other offerings that lessen our burdens.

> ■ *PROBLEM SITUATION*   As a new student on campus with no established social-support system in town, you realize the need for friends and other sources of support to help you deal with the stresses associated with academic life, financial needs, and independent living. What are some of the steps you can take to *assess* your social-support needs concerning emotional support, tangible resources, companionship, information, or simply having someone to bounce ideas off? How can you go about meeting these needs?

In spite of the helpful aspects of social networks, there are some potentially negative aspects about them. For one thing, the group to which one belongs imposes demands on its members, and these may not always be in their best interests and might create conflict. Some groups may blame problems on scapegoats, thus reinforcing prejudices, or they may put down their own members from time to time. We know that abuse does occur within families and that it may be physical or psychological, including sexual abuse.

Even when those on whom we depend for social support mean well, they may do more harm than good. For example, they may simply pass along information to us that is incorrect. More insidious is the pressure put on us when group members give advice (such as parents give to children) and expect us to follow it without question. Resentment often occurs when we believe that others are trying to control us. By and large, however, social networks operate in a positive manner to help us meet our needs.

POSITIVE BEHAVIORS

I. *Place a check mark in front of each behavior that you now practice.*

_____ 1. I keep my life as simple as is practical. (SIMPLIFY)

_____ 2. When I get nervous before an event, I take the time to practice a relaxation response. (NERVOUS)

_____ 3. When stress starts building up, I always take overt steps to reduce the sources of stress or alleviate their detrimental effects. (STRESS REDUCTION)

_____ 4. When my life gets too hectic, I set up a daily time-management calendar for myself that isn't too ambitious but that allows me to accomplish all of my most important tasks. (TIME MANAGEMENT)

_____ 5. When I encounter an overwhelming primary stressor, I always take direct positive action rather than allowing it to cause secondary stress. (PRIMARY STRESS)

_____ 6. I am aware of the amount and seriousness of personal life changes I am undergoing, and I take steps whenever possible to prevent too many changes from occurring in a short time span. (LIFE CHANGES)

_____ 7. I have a wide array of activities that I rely on to help me cope with life's stressors. (COPING)

_____ 8. I supply emotional and material support for my friends, relatives, and others within my social network whenever I am able. (SUPPORT OTHERS)

_____ 9. I maintain a social network that is strong enough to meet my needs for health and happiness. (NETWORK)

II. *For each behavior that you DO NOT ENGAGE IN, write the KEY WORD(S) that is in the parentheses located at the end of the statement in the column below. Then put a check mark in the appropriate column to indicate whether you are going to keep or change that behavior.*

Behaviors I Don't Engage In   KEEP/CHANGE

_____ / _____
_____ / _____
_____ / _____
_____ / _____
_____ / _____
_____ / _____
_____ / _____
_____ / _____
_____ / _____

III. *For each of the preceding behaviors that you choose to KEEP, write a statement indicating why you are choosing to keep that behavior.*

I choose to keep behavior _____ because:
                              KEY WORD

For each of the preceding behaviors that you choose to CHANGE, write a statement indicating how you plan to implement that change.

I will change behavior _____ by:
                          KEY WORD

■■■■■■■■■■ *Now You Know*

1. FALSE. Stress is always present and can be beneficial as well as harmful.

2. TRUE. Excessive stress causes a weakening of the immune system and lowering of general resistance.

3. TRUE. Because we spend so much time growing up with our families and because emotional attachment is great, our families influence us in all ways, including being a source of stress.

4. FALSE. It is true that there is a correlation between life changes, stress, and illness, but not everyone is adversely effected.

5. TRUE. All three factors are necessary for resolution of the problem and restoration of equilibrium.

6. TRUE. Keeping our lives simple and harmonious is the best overall approach to stress control. This includes time management, positive self-perception, and regular relaxation exercises.

7. FALSE. There is no one best relaxation technique that suits everyone. For some it's meditation, but for others it may be jogging, swimming, painting, playing the piano or guitar, reading poetry, or listening to music.

8. TRUE. Social-support systems do these things and more, including giving us feedback about our ideas and actions, helping us maintain high self-esteem, and providing companionship.

9. FALSE. Many studies have shown a direct correlation between social support and health status.

10. TRUE. Not only are dogs, cats, fish, birds, and other pets beneficial to serving social needs, but even plants are valuable in giving people who live alone "someone to care for."

■ Summary

1. Stress has been defined by Dr. Hans Selye as "the rate of wear and tear within the body" as well as "the nonspecific response of the body to any demand made upon it."

2. Beneficial environmental stimuli lead to a state of *eustress,* whereas those stimuli that are damaging cause *distress*.

3. The body reacts to stressors in three stages—a general reaction stage, followed by a specific stage of resistance and, ultimately, exhaustion if the stress is too great. Selye calls this physiological pattern the General Adaptation Syndrome (GAS).

4. Stress my be short term or it may continue chronically over a period of time, in which case there are likely to be harmful effects on the body caused by excessive hormonal activity and imbalances.

5. Stress may occur directly from a primary stressor or as a result of a maladaptive response to the primary stressor, called secondary stress.

6. When too much change occurs in a person's life over too short a period of time, that individual has a significantly greater chance of becoming sick and also becomes less able to overcome illness.

7. It is important to recognize when situations have reached crisis proportions in our lives and to know how to go about reversing the imbalances created by these crises.

8. Exposure to the same forms and intensity of stress have different effects on different people. One possible explanation is that people have varying strengths of the sense of coherence (or the feeling of fitting into their environments). Those with a strong sense of coherence feel that they have better control of themselves.

9. Perhaps the best general approach to stress management is still to live simply and in harmony with the nature of things, maintaining balance and moderation, a philosophy that was advocated as long as 5,000 years ago in China.

10. Besides simplifying our lives, we can manage stress by better managing our time, doing regular relaxation exercises, and developing strong social supports.

11. One's social-support system consists of all people who provide help in meeting one's needs. A social network consists of our specific relationships among people in groups.

12. Having a substantial social network is an important factor in resistance to illness and recovery from disease.

13. A social-support system promotes good health by acting as a buffer against the harmful effects of stress and by increasing one's general resistance.

14. Social supports increase our bodies' general resistance by providing support for self-esteem, status, information gathering, companionship needs, and acquisition of material goods and services.

15. Although social networks are generally supportive and positive, they can also possess certain potentially negative qualities, such as when group members make demands that are too rigid or inappropriate.

16. How beneficial one's social network is depends on such factors as emotional closeness between members, the size and complexity of the network, the similarities of group members, and the frequency of interactions among members.

■ References

1. *A Guide to Managing Stress*. Daly City, Calif.: Krames Communications, 1985.

2. Antonovsky, Aaron. *Health, Stress, and Coping*. San Francisco: Jossey-Bass, 1979.

3. Barrera, Manuel Jr., Irwin N. Sandler, and Thomas B. Ramsay. "Preliminary Development of a Scale of Social Support: Studies of College Students." *American Journal of Community Psychology* 6(1981): 435–447.

4. Benson, Herbert. *The Mind/Body Effect*. New York: Simon and Schuster, 1979.

5. Berkman, Lisa, and Leonard Syme. "Social Networks, Host, Resistance and Mortality: A Nine-Year Follow-up Study of Alameda County Residents." *American Journal of Epidemiology* 109(1979): 186–204.

6. Bush, Herman S., Merita Thompson, and Norman Van Tubergen. "Personal Assessment of Stress Factors for College Students." *Journal of School Health* 55(1985): 370–375.

7. Curtis, John D., and Richard A. Detert. *How to Relax: A Holistic Approach to Stress Management*. Palo Alto, Calif.: Mayfield Publishing Company, 1981.

8. Dohrenwend, Barbara S., and Bruce Dohrenwend (eds.). *Stressful Life Events and Their Contexts*. New York: John Wiley and Sons, 1984.

9. Flynn, Patricia Anne Randolph. *Holistic Health*. Bowie, Md.: Robert J. Brady Company, 1980.

10. Friedman, Meyer, and Diane Ulmer. *Treating Type A Behavior—and Your Heart*. New York: Alfred A. Knopf, 1984.

11. Gordon, James S., Dennis T. Jaffee, and David E. Bresler. *Mind, Body and Health*. New York: Human Sciences Press, 1984.

12. Gottlieb, Benjamin H. (ed.) *Social Networks and Social Support*. Beverly Hills, Calif.: Sage Publications, 1981.

13. Gottlieb, Benjamin H. *Social Support Strategies*. Beverly Hills, Calif.: Sage Publications, 1983.

14. Greenberg, Jerrold S. *Comprehensive Stress Management*. Dubuque, Ia.: Wm. C. Brown, 1983.

15. Holmes, Thomas H., and Richard H. Rahe. "The Social Readjustment Rating Scale." *Journal of Psychosomatic Research* 11 (1967): 213–218.

16. Maguire, Lambert. *Understanding Social Networks*. Beverly Hills, Calif.: Sage Publications, 1983.

17. Minkler, Meredith. "The Social Component of Health." *Journal of Health Promotion* 1(1986): 33.

18. Milsum, John H. *Health, Stress and Illness*. New York: Praeger Publishers, 1984.

19. Pelletier, Kenneth R. *Mind as Healer, Mind as Slayer*. New York: Dell Books, 1977.

20. Schneiderman, Neil, and Jack T. Tapp. *Behavioral Medicine: A Biopsychosocial Approach*. Hillsdale, N.J.: Lawrence Erlbaum Associates, 1985.

21. Selye, Hans. *Stress Without Distress*. New York: J. B. Lippincott, 1974.

22. Selye, Hans. *The Stress of Life*. New York: McGraw-Hill, 1976.

23. Vieth, Ilza. *Huang Ti Nei Ching Su Wen: The Yellow Emperor's Classic of Internal Medicine*. Berkeley: University of California Press, 1966.

■ Suggested Readings

Cohen, Sheldon, and S. Leonard Syme (eds.). *Social Support and Health*. Orlando, Fla.: Academic Press, 1985.

Curtis, John D., and Richard A. Detert. *How to Relax: A Holistic Approach to Stress Management*. Palo Alto, Calif.: Mayfield Publishing Company, 1981.

Dohrenwend, Barbara S., and Bruce Dohrenwend (eds.). *Stressful Life Events and Their Contexts*. New York: John Wiley and Sons, 1984.

Gillespie, Peggy Roggenbuck, and Lynn Bechtel. *Less Stress in 30 Days: An Integrated Program for Relaxation*. New York: New American Library, 1986.

Girdano, Daniel A., and George S. Everly. *Controlling Stress and Tension: A Holistic Approach*. Englewood Cliffs, N.J.: Prentice-Hall, 1986.

Greenberg, Jerrold S. *Stress and Sexuality*. New York: AMS Press, 1987.

Rosch, Paul J., and Kenneth Pelletier. *Occupational Stress*. New York: AMS Press, 1988.

The Women's World: A Holistic Approach to Dealing with Stress. New York: AMS Press, 1987.

Glossary

A

abilities   power to do some special thing; skill

abstract   a brief statement of main ideas of an article, book, etc.; a summary

active listening   conscious control of the listening process through preplanned strategies

almanacs   annual publications which include calendars, weather forecasts, and other useful tabular information

analysis   a stage of critical thinking that requires an examination of information by breaking it into parts

antonym   a word that has the opposite meaning of another

appendices   additions at the end of a book or document; supplements

application   a stage of critical thinking that requires using information concerning the process, idea, and theory, etc. appropriately to accomplish what is required

aptitude test   an examination which predicts future performance in a given activity

aptitudes   natural tendencies or talents

assumption   an inference made with the use of given facts and global knowledge

atlas   a book of maps

auditory practice   repeating aloud information that you are trying to remember or discussing it with another student

author card   a catalog card filed under the author's last name which contains other bibliographical information

B

background knowledge   what you know about a topic

bar graph   a graphic in which bars indicate the frequency of data; shows quantitative comparisons; a histogram

behavior modification   a technique to change behavior by systematically rewarding desirable behavior and either ignoring or punishing undesirable behavior

bias   an opinion before there is a reason for it; prejudice

bibliography   a list of the books or articles consulted or referred to by an author in the preparation of a manuscript

burnout physical or mental exhaustion of a person's supply of energy, ambition, or ideas

C

call number a classification number assigned to library material to indicate its location in the library

card catalog an alphabetical listing with one or more cards for each item

cartographer one who draws maps or charts; a mapmaker

cause/effect in a communication, a stated or implied association between some outcome and the condition which brought it about

chapter maps provide verbal information in the context of a visual arrangement of ideas; show relationships among concepts and express an author's patterns of thought

charts information arranged by rows and columns; also called tables

chronology arrangement of data according to group features

chunks groups of information that are clustered together in order to remember through association

circle graph a graphic that shows how a whole unit is divided into parts

clipping file vertical file; source of print materials which have not been published in book form

closure the condition of being ended, finished, or concluded; the process by which incomplete figures, ideas, or situations tend to be completed mentally or perceived as complete

college catalog a book describing the services, curricula, courses, faculty, and other information pertaining to a post-secondary institution

comparison/contrast the organization of information for placing like or unlike ideas, situations, or characters together

comprehensive tests examinations that cover all materials presented in class over the course of an entire term

conclusions a decision, judgement, or opinion reached by reasoning or inferring

consistency reliability of information in both spoken and written forms

coping meeting or encountering success in overcoming problems or difficulties

cramming studying rapidly under pressure for an examination; usually done at the last minute instead of over time

creativity ultimate form of synthesis; taking all available information, creating hypotheses, drawing conclusions, and coming up with a new idea or product

credit hour the number of times a course meets in one week of a regular semester

critical thinking   thinking logically about information, people, and choices in order to make reasonable, informed decisions about learning, relationships, and life

cross-references   information which refers from one item, passage, or text to another

curricula   the total program of studies of a school

curve of forgetting   a line diagram which shows the relationship between recall of information without review and the amount of time since the material's presentation; also called the Ebbinghaus Curve

D

data base   collection of data arranged for ease of retrieval, especially by a computer

definition   a type of context clue in which punctuation marks that indicate that the meaning of an unknown word follows directly

denial   a coping mechanism that involves pretending that a problem doesn't exist or isn't important

derivations   the use of affixes to build new words from a root or base word, often with a change in the part of speech of the word

Dewey decimal system   library classification scheme which divides all knowledge into ten major groups by subject, each of which can be subdivided infinitely

diagram   plan, drawing, figure or combination thereof made to show clearly what a thing is or how it works

direct quote   showing a person's exact words

distractions   diversions which cause a turning away from the focus of attention.

distributed practice   a method of developing a skill by setting task or time limits (practicing a specified amount of time or information each day) rather than attempting to cram much practice into a small period of time; spaced study

disuse   release of information from memory that is seldom used

E

ellipsis   the omission of a word or phrase shown by a series of marks (...)

endnotes   a form of footnotes which occurs at the end of a book or document

(dictionary) entry   a term listed alphabetically, usually in boldface, in a dictionary

enumeration/sequence   placement of information in a systematic organizational pattern according to time or rank

ESL students   students whose native languages aren't English and who are enrolled in a program for learning English language skills (English as a Second Language)

essay   a brief paper expressing opinion about a single topic; theme

etymology   the study of the origins of words

evaluation   judgement, the highest level of thinking; requires being able to recall, translate, interpret, apply, analyze, and synthesize to judge and evaluate effectively

expert opinions   the judgement of one who has knowledge and skill in a particular subject about that subject

exploration   evaluation of oneself and one's career possibilities

external motivation   behavior directed toward satisfaction through anticipated rewards or punishment

F

fact   based on direct evidence, a statement of truth

fantasy   belief that one can have any career

feature analysis table   a table analyzing characteristics rather than amounts; a quality table

fiction   one of two types of writing; not based on fact or truth; written to entertain

flowchart   a drawing which shows the steps in a complicated process

footnotes   notes at the bottom of a page about something on the page

free elective   a course which is not specified in a degree program

full-time student   student carrying enough credit hours during a term to be considered as having a complete load of coursework

G

gazetteer   dictionary or index of geographical terms

general reference maps   maps which give general geographic information

government documents   library holdings consisting of material published by U.S. government agencies

grade point average (GPA)   the average of numerical values assigned to course grades

graphics   drawings or reproductions of drawings, maps, pictures, graphs, etc.

graphs   diagrams or charts in which various data is presented through differing lengths of bars (bar graphs), dots connected to form lines (line graphs), or pie-shaped wedges to form circles (pie or circle graphs); symbolic representations of information that show quantitative comparisons between two or more kinds of information

guide words   words that appear at the top of each page in a dictionary to aid in locating entries quickly

H

histogram a graphic in which bars indicate the frequency of data; shows quantitative comparisons; a bar graph

hypothesis an educated guess; an idea of what will happen next in a particular situation or of what the consequences of a given action will be

I

idea or concept map a graphic method of notetaking; a diagram, similar to a flowchart, which shows relationships between and among concepts

information matrices a table, picture, or diagram of information; a chart

interest inventory an informal checklist for exploring preferences for a given activity

interests a feeling of wanting to know, see, do, own, share in, or take part in

interference memory loss caused by the process of conflicting information

interlibrary loan a method by which one library borrows an item from the holdings of another library

internal motivation self-directed incentives for behavior

interpretation the ability to explain events through a knowledge of the connections that exist among ideas

intramural sports athletic events other than varsity competition involving members of the same school, college, or organization

introduction/summary placement of information for the purpose of initiating or ending a discussion of a topic

K

key a list of words or phrases giving an explanation of symbols and/or abbreviations used on a map; a legend

kinesthetic perception the drawings made from words or phrases that appeal to the senses; physical imagery; mnemonigraphs

L

lecture patterns the organizational pattern of a lecture (similar to text patterns)

legend a list of words or phrases giving an explanation of symbols and/or abbreviations used on a map

Library of Congress (LC) system a method of classifying publications using letters and numerals which allows for infinite expansion

line graphs a graphic used to show quantitative trends for one or more items over time

logical inference a conclusion that cannot be avoided; for example, if $a = b$ and $b = c$, then $a = c$

long-term goal   an objective which requires a lengthy time committment

long-term memory   permanent memory; last stage of memory processing

M

main entry card   the full catalog record of an item in the library's collection, often the author card

map   a two-dimensional graphic of a specific location

microfiche   a microfilm sheet containing rows of written or printed pages in reduced form

microfiche reader   a device which makes any microform large enough to be easily read

microforms   consist of microfiche, microfilm, ultrafiche; reduced forms of books, journals, articles, etc.

mnemonigraph   the drawings made from words or phrases that appeal to the senses; kinesthetic perception; physical imagery

N

need   something that is needed or desired

newspaper index   an index to selected daily/weekly published newspapers

non-comprehensive   examinations that do not cover all materials presented in class over the course of an entire term; examinations covering only a specific amount of material

non sequitur   a conclusion or statement that makes no sense; not supported by facts or preceding information

nonfiction   prose–based upon fact–written to explain, argue, or describe rather than to entertain

note-taking outline   outline made before reading a chapter as preview for the lecture

O

objective test   a type of test in which a student selects an answer from several choices provided by the instructor; included among these are multiple choice, true/false, matching and some fill-in-the-blank

opinion   a judgement or viewpoint

outlining   a formal or informal pattern of ideas

overlearning   overlapping study of information to reinforce initial learning

P

paraphrase   a summary; contains an unbiased version of what the author said.

parenthetical references   statements which help explain or qualify information

parody   copy of serious works or phrases through satire or burlesque

part-time student   student carrying less than the minimum number of credit hours to be considered full-time

peer pressure   a controlling mechanism that regulates group membership through conformity and loss of personal freedom

perception   reception of information that is understood in memory

periodical indicies   alphabetical listings, journals and magazines that list the authors, titles, and subjects of articles in periodicals.

perspective   point of view

pictorial graphs   graphics that use symbols to show quantitative amounts; symbol graphs

plagiarism   an idea, expression, plot, etc. taken from another and used as one's own

point of view   the position from which one looks at something

previewing   surveying to get the main idea about something that will be read later

primary source   original documents or first-person accounts of an event

prime study time   the time of day or night when a student is most mentally alert for learning and remembering information

procrastination   the act or habit of putting tasks off until later

projection   coping device in which the blame for a problem is placed on someone or something else

puns   use of words or phrases to suggest more than one meaning

Q

quality points   numerical value assigned to each letter grade from "A" to "F" when given as the final grade in a course; used to calculate grade point average

quality table   a table analyzing characteristics rather than amounts; a feature analysis table

R

rationalize   to cope by offering acceptable excuses are provided in place of the real one

ready reference   books held in reserve by a library for patrons to use only while they remain in the library

realistic period   career development stage consisting of exploration, crystallization, and specification

recall   the lowest level of understanding; requires little more than auditory or visual memory skills

reception   receiving information into short-term memory without understanding

recitation   silent, oral, or written repetition of information to increase recall

registration   the part of memory consisting of reception, perception, and selection; first stage of memory processing

relevance; relevancy   the state of being applicable, appropriate, pertinent, useful, etc.

report   a formal written presentation of facts

repression   coping device in which the cause of stress is blocked from memory

research paper   a lengthy, well documented written presentation

reserve books   books held in a special area of the library that can be checked out only for designated periods of time

rewards   recompense for something that you do or say

rough draft   an author's first attempt at writing a particular manuscript

S

scale of distance   a representation of size or space on maps; indicates the relationship between the distance of one place shown on a map and this distance in actuality

scan   reading quickly to find specific information; reading for specific answers

schedule   a written or printed statement of fixed times or appointments; a timetable

scope   range of application

secondary source   second-person accounts of an event

selection   a deliberate processing of information into memory or a deliberate disregard of it

self-talk   the dialogue inside your mind as you think to yourself about how to act or feel about a situation

semantic practice   writing or diagramming information that you are trying to remember

short-term goals   an objective which requires a brief time committment

short-term memory   immediate or brief memory; second stage of memory processing

skim   reading quickly to find main ideas

spaced study   a method of learning which requires setting task or time limits (practicing a specified amount of time or information each day) rather than attempting to cram much practice into a small period of time; distributed practice

special purpose maps   maps which highlight some specific natural or man-made feature; a thematic map

specification period   final career decision

stacks   shelves in the library for holding books and journals

stress   a physical or emotional factor that causes tension; anxiety

style manual   reference for the preparation of a manuscript

subject card   filed under the subject of the material, this card contains the full catalog record of an item in the library's collection

subject development   the organization of information for discussing a topic and its related details

subjective tests   type of exam in which students must provide an original written answer; included among these are essay and some fill-in-the-blank questions

summary   a condensed statement or paragraph that contains only the essential ideas of a longer statement, paragraph, or passage

symbol graphs   a graphic which uses symbols to show quantitative amounts; a pictorial graph

symbols   an idea or concept that stands for or suggests another idea or concept by means of association or relationship

synonym   a word which has a similar meaning to that of another word

synthesis   the combination of parts or elements into a whole

T

tables   a systematic listing of information in rows and columns

tentative period   one's realization that some careers are inappropriate goals while others are more appropriate goals

term papers   a lengthy, well documented written presentation

terms   specialized or technical vocabulary in a specific subject

test   an examination; a way of evaluating how well a student has mastered the material presented in class or in the textbook. These examinations may be comprehensive or non-comprehensive. There are two types of questions that may appear on a test, objective and subjective.

text labeling   helps you identify relationships and summarize information

text marking   finding important information and highlighting or underlining it

text structure   the way in which a written text is presented (outline, headings, sub-headings, etc.)

thematic maps   maps which highlight some specific natural or man-made feature; special purpose maps

theme   a brief paper expressing opinion about a single topic; essay

thesaurus   book of synonyms and sometimes antonyms

thesis statement   similar to a topic sentence, this sentence contains the main idea to be covered in a paper

time lines   a graphic outline of sequenced information; a chronology of important dates or events

time management   a system for scheduling commitments efficiently

title card   filed under the title of the material, this card contains the full catalog record of an item in the library's collection

transition words   terms that signal the identity and flow of a lecture's pattern

translation   the ability to convert information into your own words while retaining the essence of the idea

trends   changes in direction over time

U

unabridged dictionary   a dictionary whose number of entries have not been limited or reduced

V

values   that which is of worth/importance to an individual

verbatim information   information that you must remember word for word—exactly as it was written or said

vertical file   clipping file; source of print materials which have not been published in book form

visual practice   silently reading information that you are trying to remember

W

working bibliography   a list of the books or articles consulted or referred to by an author as the rough draft is written

working memory   part of memory where information is processed; limited in size; third stage of memory processing

Y

yearbooks   published yearly, this book contains a summary or review of facts

Index